INTERNATIONAL TAXATION OF PERMANENT ESTABLISHMENTS

Principles and Policy

The effects of the growth of multinational enterprises and globalization in the past fifty years have been profound, and many multinational enterprises, such as international banks, now operate around the world through branches known as permanent establishments. The business profits Article (Article 7) of the OECD model tax treaty attributes a multinational enterprise's business profits to a permanent establishment in a host country for tax purposes. Michael Kobetsky analyses the principles for allocating the profits of multinational enterprises to permanent establishments under this Article, explains the shortcomings of the current arm's length principle for attributing business profits to permanent establishments and considers the alternative method of formulary apportionment for allocating business profits.

MICHAEL KOBETSKY is an Associate Professor at the Melbourne Law School, University of Melbourne.

CAMBRIDGE TAX LAW SERIES

Tax law is a growing area of interest, as it is included as a subdivision in many areas of study and is a key consideration in business needs throughout the world. Books in the Cambridge Tax Law series expose and shed light on the theories underpinning taxation systems, so that the questions to be asked when addressing an issue become clear. Written by leading scholars and illustrated by case law and legislation, they form an important resource for information on tax law while avoiding the minutiae of day-to-day detail addressed by practitioner books.

The books will be of interest for those studying law, business, economics, accounting and finance courses in the UK, but also in mainland Europe, the USA and ex-Commonwealth countries with a similar taxation system to the UK.

Series Editor

Professor John Tiley, Queens' College, Director of the Centre for Tax Law.

Well known internationally in both academic and practitioner circles, Professor Tiley brings to the series his wealth of experience in tax law study, practice and writing. He was made a CBE in 2003 for services to tax law.

INTERNATIONAL TAXATION OF PERMANENT ESTABLISHMENTS

Principles and Policy

MICHAEL KOBETSKY

CAMBRIDGE
UNIVERSITY PRESS

CAMBRIDGE
UNIVERSITY PRESS

University Printing House, Cambridge CB2 8BS, United Kingdom

Cambridge University Press is part of the University of Cambridge.

It furthers the University's mission by disseminating knowledge in the pursuit of education, learning and research at the highest international levels of excellence.

www.cambridge.org
Information on this title: www.cambridge.org/9780521516327

© Michael Kobetsky 2011

This publication is in copyright. Subject to statutory exception and to the provisions of relevant collective licensing agreements, no reproduction of any part may take place without the written permission of Cambridge University Press.

First published 2011

A catalogue record for this publication is available from the British Library

Library of Congress Cataloguing in Publication data

Kobetsky, Michael.
International taxation of permanent establishments : principles and policy / Michael Kobetsky.
p.   cm. – (Cambridge tax law series)
ISBN 978-0-521-51632-7 (Hardback)
1. International business enterprises–Taxation–Law and legislation.   2. Branches (Business enterprises)–Taxation–Law and legislation.   3. Business enterprises, Foreign–Taxation–Law and legislation.   4. Double taxation–Treaties.   I. Title.   II. Series.
K4550.K634 2011
343.05′268–dc22
2011008593

ISBN 978-0-521-51632-7 Hardback

Cambridge University Press has no responsibility for the persistence or accuracy of URLs for external or third-party internet websites referred to in this publication, and does not guarantee that any content on such websites is, or will remain, accurate or appropriate.

CONTENTS

List of abbreviations   vi

1   Introduction   1

2   International taxation: policy and law   11

3   Some shortcomings of the tax treaty system   65

4   History of tax treaties and the permanent establishment concept   106

5   The role of the OECD Model Tax Treaty and Commentary   152

6   Defining the personality of permanent establishments under former Article 7 and the pre-2008 Commentary and the 2008 Commentary   179

7   Intra-bank loans under the pre-2008 Commentary and 1984 Report   238

8   Intra-bank interest under the 2008 Report   276

9   Business restructuring involving permanent establishments and the OECD transfer pricing methods   316

10   New Article 7 of the OECD Model and Commentary   351

11   Unitary taxation   393

12   Conclusion   430

Bibliography   436
Index   454

ABBREVIATIONS

BIAC	Business and Industry Advisory Committee (OECD)
OECD	Organisation for Economic Co-operation and Development
EU	European Union
UN	United Nations
UK	United Kingdom
US	United States

OECD Discussion Drafts

2001 Discussion Draft	OECD, *Discussion Draft on the Attribution of Profits to Permanent Establishments* (Parts I (General Considerations) & II (Banks)) (2001)
2003 Discussion Draft	OECD, *Discussion Draft on the Attribution of Profits to Permanent Establishments PES: Part II Banks* (2003)
2004 Discussion Draft	OECD, *Discussion Draft on the Attribution of Profits to Permanent Establishments: Part I General Considerations* (2004)

OECD Reports

2008 Report	OECD, *Discussion Draft on the Attribution of Profits to Permanent Establishments*
2010 Report	OECD, *Report on the Attribution of Profits to Permanent Establishments* (2010)

Model Tax Treaties

2008 OECD Model	OECD, *Model Tax Convention on Income and on Capital* (2008)
2010 OECD Model	OECD, *Model Tax Convention on Income and on Capital* (2010)
1992 Commentary	OECD, *Model Tax Convention on Income and on Capital* (1992)
2008 Commentary	The Commentary published in OECD, *Model Tax Convention on Income and on Capital* (2008).
Pre-2008 Commentary	Commentary on Article 7 last published in the OECD, *Model Tax Convention on Income and on Capital* (2005)
UN Model	UN, *United Nations Model Tax Convention Between Developed and Developing Countries* (2001)

Transfer Pricing Guidelines

1995 Transfer Pricing Guidelines	OECD, Transfer Pricing Guidelines for Multinational Enterprises and Tax Administrations (1995)
2009 Transfer Pricing Guidelines	OECD, Transfer Pricing Guidelines for Multinational Enterprises and Tax Administrations (2009)
2010 Transfer Pricing Guidelines	OECD, Transfer Pricing Guidelines for Multinational Enterprises and Tax Administrations (2010)

1

Introduction

1 Outline

The importance of bilateral tax treaties[1] has increased significantly over the last sixty years with the extensive integration of national economies and the growth in the number of enterprises operating internationally. The growth in the tax treaty network has been phenomenal and there are presently over 3,000 tax treaties in force. The primary objective of tax treaties is to support international trade and investment by, inter alia, reducing the risk to business of double taxation, resulting from the overlapping of two countries' jurisdictions to tax. Tax treaties deal with the problem of overlapping tax jurisdictions by allocating taxing rights over items of income or taxpayers between the contracting countries. Tax treaties do not create jurisdiction to tax; rather, they allocate taxing rights between the treaty countries to prevent double taxation.[2] International taxation comprises the interaction between the network of tax treaties and the domestic tax systems of countries. Most tax treaties are based on the Organisation for Economic Co-operation and Development (OECD) *Model Tax Convention on Income and Capital*[3] (OECD Model) and it has become the keystone of the international tax treaty system. Moreover, the United Nations (UN) Model is based on the OECD Model.[4]

A key feature of tax treaties is the allocation of business profits of international enterprises operating globally through permanent establishments under the business profits Article, Article 7 of the OECD Model. This provision became a broadly accepted treaty measure in

---

[1] In this book bilateral tax treaties are referred to as tax treaties.

[2] The Australian Commissioner of Taxation is of the view that Australia acquires additional tax jurisdiction under its treaties. As a result, transfer pricing adjustments in Australia are issued under both the domestic transfer pricing rules and Article 9 of Australia's treaties. This interpretation is controversial and has not been accepted by a court in Australia.

[3] The current version is the 2010 OECD Model.

[4] United Nations, *United Nations Model Tax Convention Between Developed and Developing Countries* (2001).

2   INTRODUCTION

the early part of the twentieth century when national economies were relatively independent and closed. Globalization has resulted in international enterprises and multinational enterprise groups operating across national borders as highly integrated businesses. International enterprises operate abroad through permanent establishments in host countries. On the other hand, multinational enterprise groups operate abroad through locally incorporated subsidiaries. International enterprises and multinational enterprise groups may use complex financial techniques and sophisticated tax planning arrangements to exploit the deficiencies in the tax treaty system. Former Article 7 has come under increasing pressure through globalization and there was no consensus interpretation of former Article 7 prior to the publication of the *Report on the Attribution of Profits to Permanent Establishments*[5] (2008 Report) and the adoption by the OECD of the 2008 OECD Model, which incorporated some of the measures from the 2008 Report in the Commentary on former Article 7. A new Article 7 was adopted by the OECD in the 2010 OECD Model which fully implements the principles in the 2008 Report.[6] At the same time, the OECD adopted the 2010 Report which is a revised version of the 2008 Report; the conclusions of the 2010 Report were amended to reflect the drafting and structure of new Article 7. Since 2001, the European Commission has been studying the implementation of formulary apportionment for EU enterprises.[7] The OECD Article 7 reforms and the EU's formulary apportionment proposals are essentially a debate over the relative merits of the arm's length principle as compared with unitary formulary apportionment for allocating the profits of enterprises which operate in more than one country.

The former Article 7[8] of the OECD Model and the new Article 7 are based on the arm's length principle. Under the arm's length principle a permanent establishment of an international enterprise is treated as a separate entity for the purposes of determining the profits that are attributable to the permanent establishment. Transfers of assets and funds between the head office of an international enterprise and its permanent establishment are treated as notional intra-entity transactions – which are called 'dealings' – between arm's length entities. The transfer prices for these notional intra-entity transactions must then conform to the transfer

---

[5] OECD, *Report on the Attribution of Profits to Permanent Establishments* (2008).
[6] 2010 OECD Model.
[7] Commission of the European Communities, *Towards an Internal Market without Tax Obstacles* (2001).
[8] 2008 OECD Model.

prices for comparable transactions between independent enterprises. The arm's length principle seeks to emulate open market transactions. The OECD initially acknowledged in 2001 that there is no consensus within member countries on the correct interpretation of former Article 7. This conclusion was confirmed by the International Fiscal Association in 2006.[9] This lack of a consensus interpretation and the inconsistent application of former Article 7 may result in either double taxation or under-taxation of the business profits of permanent establishments, and thereby makes former Article 7 ineffective in allocating business profits to permanent establishments.

The OECD rules for attributing business profits under former Article 7 to a permanent establishment, prior to 2008, were far less developed than the OECD's transfer pricing rules for associated enterprises of a multinational enterprise group under Article 9 of the OECD Model. In 1994, the OECD announced its intention to include permanent establishments within the scope of the Transfer Pricing Guidelines.[10] The 2008 Report and 2010 Report adapt the Transfer Pricing Guidelines for associated entities to attributing profits to permanent establishments. But this approach is flawed because it is based on a fundamental fiction as a matter of law, and, in reality, there cannot be transactions between parts of one enterprise. An alternative approach is being explored by the European Commission, which is considering comprehensive reforms to remedy the problems of a bilateral tax treaty system and the arm's length principle. The European Commission is looking at moving to unitary formulary apportionment, under which the profits of an international enterprise are allocated between European Union (EU) countries on the basis of an agreed formula. The European Commission's work on formulary apportionment for the EU was motivated in part by the challenges caused by transfer pricing and the arm's length principle in the EU. This proposal requires the implementation of an EU multilateral tax treaty for the taxation of companies. Clearly, reform of the methods of allocating profits to permanent establishments of international enterprises is a controversial issue.

The topic of this book is the allocation of business profits to permanent establishments of international enterprises under Article 7 of the OECD Model. The book studies the OECD principles for the

---

[9] International Fiscal Association (ed.), *The Attribution of Profits to Permanent Establishments* (2006).

[10] OECD, *Transfer Pricing Guidelines for Multinational Enterprises and Tax Administrations, Discussion Draft of Part I* (1994).

4 INTRODUCTION

allocation of business profits under the three versions of Article 7 and Commentary:

- the former Article 7 with the accompanying Commentary, called the pre-2008 Commentary in this book;[11]
- the former Article 7 with the accompanying 2008 Commentary,[12] reflecting the principles in the 2008 Report; and
- the new Article 7 and accompanying new Commentary were adopted by the OECD in the 2010 OECD Model,[13] reflecting the principles in the 2010 Report.[14]

As most tax treaties are based on former Article 7, it will take a considerable period of time before the use of new Article 7 is widespread as most treaties are only amended after ten years. But new Article 7 may not be widely adopted by OECD countries and non-OECD countries. This reflects differences within the OECD between Working Party No. 1, which is responsible for tax treaty issues, and Working Party No. 6, which is responsible for the taxation of multinational enterprises. Both Working Party No. 1 and Working Party No. 6 submit their conclusions to the OECD Committee on Fiscal Affairs for adoption as OECD principles. Working Party No. 6 developed the principles in the 2008 Report and the 2010 Report which are based on arm's length economics. The focus of Working Party No. 6 is transfer pricing and it has extended its area of responsibility from developing transfer pricing principles for multinational enterprise groups to applying these principles in attributing profits to permanent establishments of international enterprises. On the other hand, the members of Working Party No. 1 are usually treaty negotiators and they may not be convinced of the practical application of the arm's length principle to permanent establishments. As a consequence, there are doubts about whether treaty negotiators will adopt the new Article 7 when they negotiate new treaties and renegotiate treaties.[15]

---

[11] The pre-2008 Commentary was last published in the 2005 OECD Model.

[12] 2008 OECD Model. The former version of Article 7 and its Commentary have been reproduced in the 2010 OECD Model at pp. 154–73.

[13] 2010 OECD Model.

[14] OECD, *Report on the Attribution of Profits to Permanent Establishments* (2010).

[15] Five OECD countries recorded reservations on Article 7 in the 2010 OECD Model, reserving their right to use former Article 7. New Zealand reserved the right to use former Article 7 (taking into account its observations and reservations on former Article 7) because it does not agree with the approach reflected in Part I of the 2010 Report and therefore does not endorse the changes that were made to the Commentary on Article 7 in the 2008 OECD Model: 2010 OECD Model, p. 153, para. 95. Chile,

1 OUTLINE

5

Moreover, the UN has rejected adopting new Article 7 in the UN Model and this is likely to be influential with non-OECD countries.[16]

The book also studies the alternative of implementing a multilateral tax treaty using unitary formulary apportionment to allocate profits to permanent establishments. The key argument is that the arm's length principle, on which Article 7 is based, is inappropriate to use for allocating business profits to permanent establishments of international enterprises, particularly highly integrated international enterprises, such as international banks. The arm's length principle is asserted to be an ineffective measure for allocating business profits to permanent establishments because it does not reflect business reality. Moreover, international enterprises have a common profit motive. Conversely, the relationship between independent entities is governed by legally enforceable contracts. It is contended that there is no single economic basis for allocating profits within highly integrated international enterprises operating globally through permanent establishments. This book examines the alternative approach of unitary formulary apportionment under a multilateral tax treaty, which is contended to be a more effective method for allocating the profits of highly integrated international enterprises. A multilateral tax treaty would provide a global response rather than a bilateral response to a problem arising from the globalization of international business.

International banks are examined in this book as they operate in countries through branches, and branches of international banks are permanent establishments for tax treaty purposes. International banking was one of the first sectors to carry on business internationally through highly integrated branch operations, as they were quickly able to exploit the Internet and developments in communication and business information technologies. International banks are relatively mobile businesses with the flexibility to move out of countries in which after-tax profit targets are not being met. To operate abroad a bank does not need a great deal of investment in plant and equipment. The main entry requirements are prudential regulations specifying the amount of equity capital

---

Greece, Mexico and Turkey reserved the right to use former Article 7 and they do not endorse the changes made to the Commentary on Article 7 in the 2008 OECD Model: 2010 OECD Model, p. 153, para. 96.

[16] United Nations, *Report of Experts on International Tax Cooperation in Tax Matters* (2009), p. 9, para. 31. The following non-OECD countries have reserved the right to use former Article 7: Argentina; Brazil; India; Indonesia; Latvia; Malaysia; Romania; Serbia; South Africa; Thailand; and Hong Kong, China: 2010 OECD Model, p. 441, paras. 1–2.

6   INTRODUCTION

an international bank must have to support its business operations. Branches of international banks are an ideal type of permanent establishment to case study for establishing the flaws of using the arm's length principle to allocate business profits under the former Article 7.

2   Structure

The book compromises twelve chapters. Chapters 2 and 3 examine the structure and effectiveness of the international tax treaty system. It is argued in Chapter 2 that the rules for allocating taxing rights to countries under double tax treaties – based on source, residence and the arm's length principle[17] – have been eroded by globalization.[18] The chapter underscores the gap between the development of the international trade system and the development of the international tax treaty system. In the field of international trade, the response to globalization has been the creation of a multilateral trade treaty – the General Agreement on Tariffs and Trade (GATT) – supplemented in 1995 with the World Trade Organization Agreement, and the creation of a new supervisory body – the World Trade Organization (WTO). But in the international tax treaty system there have not been parallel developments.

Chapter 3 explores the deficiencies of the present international tax treaty system in taxing international enterprises operating abroad through permanent establishments and multinational enterprise groups operating abroad through locally incorporated subsidiaries. It considers flaws, such as the inflexibility of the tax treaty network, and identifies the treaty network as providing significant avoidance opportunities and tax planning opportunities for multinational enterprise groups through transfer pricing.[19] It examines empirical evidence on tax avoidance by international banks. The chapter argues that, as a result of developments in

---

[17] 'The old rules of the international tax game – separate-entity arm's length principle, permanent establishment, non-discrimination, source, residence, etc. – decreasingly serve to carve up the international tax base in a reasonable and sustainable way, whether in the EU or more generally.' Bird and Wilkie, 'Source- vs. residence-based taxation in the European Union' in Cnossen (ed.) *Taxing Capital Income in the European Union* (2000) 78–109, p. 90.

[18] Warren asserts that international developments, such as GATT, the WTO and corporate tax integration have rendered the existing tax treaty system obsolete. He also argues that there should be an examination of the relationship between the tax treaty system and the international trade system: Warren, 'Income Tax Discrimination Against International Commerce' (2001), p. 169; Ault, 'Corporate Integration, Tax Treaties and the Division of the International Tax Base: Principles and Practice' (1992), p. 566.

[19] Thuronyi, 'International Tax Cooperation and a Multilateral Treaty' (2001), p. 1641.

communication technology, international enterprises and multinational enterprise groups have become more integrated, and that therefore the allocation of profits using the arm's length principle is becoming more controversial and subject to more challenges.[20]

Chapter 4 provides a history of aspects of the tax work of the League of Nations, focusing on multilateral and bilateral model tax treaties developed by it. The chapter establishes that the League of Nations' preference was to have a multilateral tax treaty, but that the bilateral tax treaty model was proposed as a compromise measure that was acceptable to member countries. The chapter also surveys the development of the permanent establishment concept by the League of Nations.

Chapter 5 establishes the importance of the OECD Model and Commentary in the current tax treaty system. It illustrates the role of the Commentary in providing guidance to tax authorities and courts on the interpretation of Articles of the OECD Model. Chapter 5 claims that the OECD Commentary in force when a treaty is concluded may be used to assist in interpreting provisions of the treaty. It is contended that Commentaries adopted by the OECD subsequent to a tax treaty coming into force may be considered by a court in interpreting the treaty, but that they will have no weight as they were not in existence when the treaty was negotiated. In particular, the 2008 Commentary on Article 7, which reflects many of the sweeping reforms in the 2008 Report, should only be used to interpret the business profits Article of tax treaties concluded after 17 July 2008, the date on which the OECD adopted the 2008 OECD Model.[21] An exception to this assertion is that tax treaties which came into force before 2008 but were negotiated in anticipation of the 2008 Commentary may use the Commentary on former Article 7.[22]

The proposition that the arm's length principle is an ineffective measure for allocating business profits to permanent establishments is established in Chapters 6, 7 and 8. These chapters critically evaluate the OECD rules for attributing business profits to permanent establishments under the pre-2008 Commentary and the 2008 Commentary. Chapters 6 and 7 establish the flaws of using the arm's length principle

---

[20] Tanzi, *Taxation in an Integrating World* (1995), p. 139; Weiner, *Using the Experience in the US States to Evaluate Issues in Implementing Formula Apportionment at the International Level* (1999), p. 42.

[21] 2008 OECD Model.

[22] The US has claimed that its treaties with UK and Japan were negotiated in anticipation of the OECD, *Report on the Attribution of Profits to Permanent Establishments* (2006), which subsequently became the 2008 Report.

under Article 7 to allocate business profits to permanent establishments. Chapter 6 critically analyses the interpretation of Article 7 of the OECD Model and establishes that it is being interpreted inconsistently in member countries under the pre-2008 Commentary. It also considers the 2008 Commentary on Article 7 which reflects the 'authorized OECD approach' in the 2008 Report. Chapter 7 considers the OECD rules on the taxation of branches of international banks with a focus on the allocation of interest expenses within international banks under the pre-2008 Commentary. The OECD acknowledged the need for reform of this area because there is a lack of consistency in the interpretation of the business profits Articles by member countries.

Chapter 8 critically considers the 2008 Commentary which seeks to apply the Transfer Pricing Guidelines for associated entities to notional transactions between a branch and other branches or the head office of an international bank. This chapter asserts that the authorized OECD approach is flawed because the OECD's Transfer Pricing Guidelines for associated enterprises under Article 9 of the OECD Model cannot be adapted effectively to notional intra-bank transactions to attribute profits to branches of international banks. Article 9 of the OECD Model deals with adjusting the profits of an associated enterprise which arise from intra-group transactions that are not on arm's length terms. In the case of international banks operating through branches, there are no actual transactions that may be used for transfer pricing purposes, as intra-bank dealings are only notional transactions. Moreover, the measures in the 2008 Report are complex, impose significant compliance costs on international enterprises operating abroad through permanent establishments and tax authorities, and are based on a number of questionable assumptions. But support for the arm's length principle in the OECD is being challenged by the EU's unitary taxation reform proposals. Moreover, many EU countries are also OECD countries.

Chapter 9 examines the measures in the 2008 Report on business restructuring involving permanent establishments. While business restructuring is a vital activity for international enterprises to maintain their international competitiveness, business restructuring raises complex issues, particularly where it involves intangible assets. The chapter focuses on business restructures involving intangible property transferred to and from a permanent establishment under the authorized OECD approach. The chapter also considers the five transfer pricing methods – the three traditional transaction methods and the two transactional profit methods – which must be applied under the authorized OECD approach.

Under the former Transfer Pricing Guidelines, the transactional profits methods (the profit split method and the transactional net margin method) could only be used in so-called exceptional circumstances when the traditional transaction methods are inapplicable. The chapter claims that the transactional net margin method has for a significant time been the most commonly used method because the traditional transaction methods are usually inapplicable. In 2010, the OECD adopted the 2010 Transfer Pricing Guidelines which gave the transactional profit methods equal status with the traditional transaction methods; this reform reflected the significant time lag between practice and the Transfer Pricing Guidelines that had developed.[23]

Chapter 10 considers new Article 7 which fully implements the authorized OECD approach in the 2010 Report. New Article 7 is designed to provide the basis for the business profits Article of new tax treaties and renegotiated tax treaties. If new Article 7 is used in tax treaties it may provide for more consistency in the interpretation of the provision, but it is uncertain whether new Article 7 will be widely adopted by OECD countries and non-OECD countries. Moreover, it is likely to involve high compliance costs for international enterprises and administrative costs for tax authorities because of theoretical economic approach to the allocation of profits to permanent establishments which does not reflect business practice.

Chapter 11 considers the relative merits of implementing a multilateral tax treaty and focuses on the proposals being studied by the EU as key potential reforms. It is argued that the best method for allocating profits under a multilateral tax treaty would be a unitary method that reflects the integrated international operations of international enterprises. The arm's length principle cannot be applied effectively to allocate profits to permanent establishments because the dealings between a permanent establishment and the rest of an enterprise are fictional transactions. Permanent establishments do not operate as separate enterprises as they are parts of highly integrated businesses. Chapter 11 concludes by arguing that a unitary formulary apportionment method is a viable alternative to allocating the profits of international enterprises under a multilateral tax treaty.

This book is a critical analysis of the normative and practical aspects of the attribution of profits to permanent establishments. The debate over the arm's length principle and formulary apportionment has been

---

[23] 2010 Transfer Pricing Guidelines.

well documented in the literature. Until the announcement of the European Commission studies, formulary apportionment was the weakest line of argument in this international tax law debate. But the challenges to the international tax treaty system posed by globalization and developments in the EU have given new strength to formulary apportionment. However, the considerable degree of international cooperation required to negotiate a multilateral tax treaty and to develop a formula cannot be overstated. Even if unitary formulary apportionment and a multilateral tax treaty do not eventuate in the EU, formulary apportionment methods are likely to be accepted as conforming with an extended notion of the arm's length principle. This book is a contribution to the debate on the relative merits of the arm's length principle and formulary apportionment.

2

International taxation: policy and law

1 Introduction

The national income tax systems of developed countries and principles of tax jurisdiction were shaped in the early years of the twentieth century when their economies were relatively independent and closed. Before World War I income taxes were not used extensively in developed countries and most enterprises restricted operations to their domestic markets, with international trade and investment being limited and heavily regulated. Nevertheless, cross-border investment and commerce were growing, and, in response, countries entered into bilateral tax treaties (tax treaties) with other countries to overcome the double taxation arising from international trade and investment. The network of tax treaties expanded significantly following the development of a model tax treaty by the League of Nations in the 1920s, based on the principles, policies and concepts of the inter-war period. International taxation comprises national tax systems and a network of tax treaties.

While enterprises have globalized, and operate as integrated international businesses, tax authorities typically operate independently with some international cooperation measures, such as information exchange. Many international enterprises have acted deliberately to limit information they provide to tax authorities in the jurisdictions in which they operate, which may prevent tax authorities from having full knowledge about the operations of enterprises. Even though tax treaties contain exchange of information measures, these measures are still underused by tax authorities. Developments in international taxation have not reflected the significant changes in the international trade system that have occurred since the end of World War II. Globalization has created an integrated international economy, and the implications of this change are profound. International enterprises[1]

---

[1] The term international enterprises refers to enterprises operating abroad through permanent establishments and locally incorporated subsidiaries.

may engage in worldwide tax planning, but at times, the tax planning may amount to tax avoidance. This situation reflects the significant imbalance of power between international enterprises and national tax authorities.

This chapter begins with a definition of international taxation and whether there is an international tax system. The first major topic considered is international tax policy, including the concepts of capital export neutrality and capital import neutrality. Next, the concepts of jurisdiction to tax on the basis of the residency of a taxpayer and source of income are critically examined in the context of the two economic bases of taxation, the benefit principle and the ability to pay principle. The chapter also considers the concepts of tax planning, tax avoidance and tax evasion. The chapter defines the concepts of juridical double taxation and economic double taxation and the roles of tax treaties such as preventing double taxation. The effect of globalization on the tax treaty system is then examined. Finally, the tax treaty system is compared with the international trade system. This comparison identifies that developments in the international tax treaty system have not reflected the significant changes in the international trade system that have occurred since the end of World War II.

2 International taxation

International taxation may be broadly defined as the taxation of cross-border transactions and it has two main spheres of application. First, it deals with a country's taxation of persons (individuals and companies) who are residents of the country and who enter into cross-border transactions. This is referred to as the taxation of residents deriving foreign income (residence taxation). The basis for such taxation is that if a person is a resident of a particular country, the person has a nexus with that country, which provides the country with jurisdiction to tax the resident on worldwide income. Secondly, it deals with a country's taxation of persons who are not residents of the country and who enter into cross-border transactions involving that country. This is referred to as the taxation of non-residents deriving income that has a source within a country (source taxation). The basis for source taxation is that a resident from another country has derived income that has a nexus with the source country, which provides it with the jurisdiction to tax such income. Most countries assert jurisdiction to tax on the basis of source of income and residency of taxpayers.

At the international level, jurisdiction to tax on the basis of residence and source overlap and may result in double taxation which inhibits international trade and thereby distorts the efficient allocation of economic resources. Free international trade is premised on the notion that it will result in the efficient allocation of resources, thereby maximizing worldwide welfare. Consequently, the primary rationale for tax treaties is to prevent double taxation by allocating taxing rights over taxpayers and items of income between the contracting states. While tax treaties are reciprocal in application, this does not mean that one country may be making significantly larger revenue sacrifices than its treaty partner country because of differences in development and economic power. The key challenge in international taxation is determining the principles for an equitable allocation of revenue and expenses from cross-border transactions between treaty countries. However, because international enterprises may engage in international tax manipulation to avoid taxation, an objective of tax treaties is to counter tax avoidance primarily through the tax authorities of contracting states exchanging information. International taxation comprises the combined interaction of national tax systems and tax treaties.

There is ongoing debate as to whether the network of tax treaties and domestic tax systems form an international tax system. On one view, an international tax system exists and is premised on customary international tax law.[2] This is supported by the argument that tax treaties are part of international law, to which the normal principles of treaty interpretation in the Vienna Convention on the Law of Treaties applies.[3] It has also been claimed that there is an OECD international tax system, premised on the international principles and procedures for taxing international enterprises created by the OECD Committee on Fiscal Affairs.[4] This OECD regime, inter alia, reduces transaction costs of

---

[2] Avi-Yonah, 'International Tax as International Law' (2004), p. 500.

[3] McHugh J., of the High Court of Australia, Australia's highest court, in *Thiel* v. *Commissioner of Taxation* (1990) 171 CLR 338, concluded at p. 356 that tax treaties are to be interpreted under the rules recognized by international law which have been codified in the Vienna Convention on the Law of Treaties. The High Court was interpreting the Australia–Switzerland tax treaty. His Honour held that the Vienna Convention should be applied in the case even though Switzerland was not a signatory to the Convention as it reflects customary international law. Dawson J. at p. 349 used the Vienna Convention to interpret the Australia–Switzerland tax treaty. See Avi-Yonah, 'International Tax as International Law' (2004), pp. 491–2.

[4] Eden, 'Taxes, Transfer Pricing, and the Multinational Enterprise' in Rugman and Brewer (eds.), *Oxford Handbook of International Business* (2009) 591–619, p. 598.

14 INTERNATIONAL TAXATION: POLICY AND LAW

international capital and trade flows, and seeks to resolve tax disputes between international enterprises and tax authorities, and disputes between OECD countries. Nevertheless, Rosenbloom has questioned whether an international tax system truly exists as there is no formal multilateral document that embodies an international tax system.[5]

2.1 International tax policy

The essence of international taxation is the allocation of the profits and expenses of an international enterprise under a tax treaty between the contracting states. In a global economy, an individual government's international tax policy has the dual objectives of raising revenue and providing favourable conditions for business and investment.[6] A country's tax policies are influenced by the country's economic capacity, political environment, culture and history.[7] Allocating the profits of enterprises that operate across several jurisdictions is recognized as a considerable challenge and has been described in the following terms by Justice Brennan of the US Supreme Court:

> Allocating income among various taxing jurisdictions bears some resemblance, as we have emphasized throughout this opinion, to slicing a shadow. In the absence of a central coordinating authority, absolute consistency, even among taxing authorities whose basic approach to the task is quite similar, may just be too much to ask.[8]

International tax policy is complex and there are no definitive solutions, only compromises.[9]

2.2 Policy aims of international taxation

A country's domestic tax system has the main tax aim of raising revenue and protecting the domestic tax base. Nevertheless, this objective in a globalized world is tempered by the need for a country to have trade and investment policies that ensure that its economy remains internationally competitive. The key aim of a country's tax treaties is to

---

[5] Rosenbloom, 'The David R. Tillinghast Lecture' (2000), pp. 163–5.
[6] OECD, *Taxing Profits in a Global Economy, Domestic and International Issues* (1991), p. 13; United Nations, *World Investment Report 1993: Transnational Corporations and Integrated Production* (1993), p. 201.
[7] Graetz, 'The David R. Tillinghast Lecture' (2001), p. 279.
[8] *Container Corporation of America* v. *Franchise Tax Board* (1983) 463 US 159, p. 192.
[9] Arnold, 'Future Directions in International Tax Reform' (1988), p. 468.

2 INTERNATIONAL TAXATION

facilitate international trade and investment. The traditional policy goals of an ideal tax system are equity, neutrality and simplicity. In the international tax sphere, equity covers inter-nation equity and inter-taxpayer equity; neutrality is considered from the perspectives of capital export neutrality and capital import neutrality; and simplicity reflects the practical notion that a good tax system should have tax laws that can be interpreted and understood. These policy aims, while desirable, are conflicting, and a country must make trade-offs in deciding which policy aims to pursue over others. Realistically, simple international tax measures may be inequitable, and, conversely, equitable international tax measures might be complex and fail the desire for simplicity.

2.2.1 Raising revenue and protecting the tax base

Taxes play a crucial role in the functioning of modern society as governments are expected by their constituents to provide a broad range of programmes including, education, health services, social security, defence and public infrastructure. As US Supreme Court judge, Justice Oliver Wendell Holmes stated: 'Taxes are what we pay for civilized society',[10] and the former US President, Franklin D. Roosevelt, made a similar comment when he stated: 'Taxes, after all, are the dues we pay for the privileges of membership in an organized society.'[11] While sovereign countries have an obvious entitlement to raise revenue from cross-border transactions, the critical issue is what level and type of tax should be imposed on this tax base. The key aim of tax treaties is to promote international trade and investment between the treaty countries and to allocate income between them in a manner that is fair.

2.2.2 Trade and investment policy

It is important in a globalized international economy for a country to ensure that its tax system facilitates international trade and investment with other countries in order to encourage the efficient allocation of economic resources and development. Free trade is widely regarded as a very important policy aim for both developed countries and

---

[10] *Compania General de Tabacos Filipinas* v. *Collector of Internal Revenue* 275 US 87 (1927), p. 100.

[11] Campaign address, Worcester, Massachusetts, 21 October 1936, extracted in Parks and Parks (eds.), *Memorable Quotations of Franklin D. Roosevelt* (1965), para. 1:36

developing countries.[12] International trade allows trading countries to specialize in producing goods and providing services in which they have a comparative economic advantage.[13] The theory of comparative advantage is that a country should give priority to producing goods or providing services that it can produce or provide more efficiently than other countries. According to this theory, international trade between two or more countries will be of optimum benefit to each country if they export goods and services in which they have a comparative advantage. Moreover, international trade is, in almost all cases, mutually beneficial to both countries.[14] A common misconception is that international trade is not beneficial if there are material economic differences between trading countries, such as significant differences in productivity and wages.[15] Although countries benefit from international trade, some sectors in countries may be adversely affected by international trade, such as manufacturing industries in developed countries, which compete with imports from developing countries that have the advantage of lower labour costs.[16] The economic principle is that the efficient allocation of resources is maximized if the international market can operate freely without distortions. The undistorted location of economic activity and investment results in the welfare of countries being optimized.[17]

Despite the principle of comparative advantage, governments protect sectors of their domestic economy from competition by measures such as trade tariffs on imports, import quotas, subsidies for local producers, taxes and administrative requirements. Such measures are implemented for political or strategic reasons, to provide local producers with an advantage over foreign producers. For example, the US and EU provide protection to domestic food producers because of the strategic benefit of having a domestic food production sector in times of international conflict. Paul Samuelson, the Nobel Laureate economist, described the concept of comparative advantage as being the best example of an economic principle that is true, but which is difficult for many to understand.[18]

---

[12] For a discussion of the normative base of tax policy and trade policy see: McDaniel, 'Trade and Taxation' (2001).
[13] See Krugman and Obstfeld, *International Economics* (8th edn, 2009), Part 1, pp. 11–179.
[14] *Ibid.*, p. 4.   [15] *Ibid.*   [16] *Ibid.*
[17] Commission of the European Communities, *Company Taxation in the Internal Market* (2001), p. 56.
[18] Krugman and Obstfeld, *International Economics: Theory and Policy* (8th edn, 2009), p. 27.

2.2.3 Inter-nation equity

The policy of inter-nation equity[19] is the equitable sharing of the international tax revenue between two or more countries from cross-border transactions. Inter-nation equity is analysed using the principles of source country entitlement, non-discrimination and reciprocity.[20] The principle of 'source country entitlement' is that a source country has the prior right to tax income earned in its jurisdiction. The EU Commission claimed that the principle is justified on the basis of efficiency as it involves the redistribution of revenue to source countries, which are net importers of capital.[21] In these countries, the proportion of foreign-owned international enterprises is higher than in net capital-exporting countries. Moreover, source taxation is based on the benefit principle, as source taxation is the charge imposed on a non-resident for government services and public infrastructure. The non-discrimination principle is a treaty principle that the countries will not discriminate on the basis of nationality against non-resident taxpayers. This principle achieves horizontal equity, as taxpayers in similar economic circumstances should be treated in the same way by a country's tax laws irrespective of their nationality.

Reciprocity involves arrangements that result in similar effective tax burdens being imposed on investments by non-residents[22] and may provide a method for the fair allocation of profits between treaty countries.[23] This principle refers to the equality of withholding taxes imposed on interest, royalties and dividends by two tax treaty countries. A broader definition, known as effective reciprocity, requires 'the equality of effective tax burdens on foreign-owned investment between countries'.[24] For example, if two treaty countries have different rates

---

[19] The theory of inter-nation equity is attributed to Peggy Musgrave: R. A. Musgrave and P. B. Musgrave, *Public Finance in Theory and Practice* (4th edn, 1984), pp. 751–2; P. B. Musgrave, *United States Taxation of Foreign Investment Income* (1969), pp. 134, 153–4.

It has been argued that a similar, but less refined, theory was included in the 1923 report to the League of Nations: Kaufman, 'Fairness and the Taxation of International Income' (1998), pp. 197–9.

[20] Commission of the European Communities, *Company Taxation in the Internal Market* (2001), p. 69; Commission of the European Communities, *Report of the Committee of Independent Experts on Company Taxation* (1992), p. 37.

[21] Commission of the European Communities, *Company Taxation in the Internal Market* (2001).

[22] *Ibid.*

[23] Commission of the European Communities, *Report of the Committee of Independent Experts on Company Taxation* (1992), p. 38.

[24] *Ibid.*

18   INTERNATIONAL TAXATION: POLICY AND LAW

of company tax, reciprocity may be achieved by using different dividend withholding tax rates on dividends paid from one country to the other country. The country with the lower rate of company tax may be required to impose a higher rate of dividend withholding tax, and the dividends paid from the country with the higher rate of company tax may be exempt from taxation.

The main difficulty with inter-nation equity is that it does not provide a clear basis for sharing revenue between a source country and a residence country. A source country is entitled to tax income that originates within its borders, but this raises two issues. The first is how to allocate profits to the source country, and the second is the rate of tax that should be applied to profits allocated to a source country.[25] The division of profits within integrated international enterprises is a complex issue because there is no precise economic method for allocating profits from international transactions to any country.[26] Consequently, it is difficult to determine whether a particular allocation of revenues between a source country and a residence country is fair. The rate of tax that a source country may apply to income sourced within its borders but derived by non-residents is another complex issue. One approach suggested by Musgrave would be to have a set rate of tax for income derived by non-residents.[27] But there is no fixed uniform rate of tax for source income, and tax treaties will usually limit the rate of tax that a source country may impose on certain types of income such as dividends, interest and royalties.

2.2.4   Tax neutrality

The tax neutrality principle is that a tax system should not influence economic decisions on the basis that the allocation of scarce economic resources will be optimal if the market allocates the resources without distortions. Practically, it is impossible for a tax system to be neutral, as taxes influence economic decisions. The objective of tax neutrality in economies is to minimize the effect of taxes on business and investment decisions, as business and investment decisions should ideally be based on obtaining the best pre-tax rate of return. The provision of tax benefits to domestic producers to counter import competition encourages continued investment by these producers because they obtain

---

[25] P. B. Musgrave, 'Sovereignty, Entitlement, and Cooperation in International Taxation' (2001), pp. 1346–7.
[26] *Ibid.*, p. 1345.   [27] *Ibid.*, pp. 1345–6.

higher after-tax rates of return, despite their rates of return before tax being lower than those of their foreign competitors. The provision of tax benefits to domestic producers to make them internationally competitive results in reduced capital productivity, lower international output and lower living standards.[28] There are two types of tax neutrality – capital export neutrality and capital import neutrality. In the interests of understanding tax neutrality, it is helpful to consider separately the concepts of capital export neutrality and capital import neutrality.

2.2.4.1 Capital export neutrality

Under capital export neutrality, a country's resident taxpayers should be subject to tax at the same rate on their worldwide income. The aim of capital export neutrality is that a tax system should not affect a resident taxpayer's decision on whether to make an investment in the residence country or abroad. In this situation, capital should be invested in jurisdictions where it can generate the highest rate of return. Capital export neutrality is premised on the economic principle that if capital is invested where gross productivity is highest there will be an optimum allocation of capital resulting in worldwide welfare being maximized.[29] While capital export neutrality is based on worldwide welfare, it may not be the best policy for a particular country, as capital export neutrality does not deal with the allocation of income and resources between countries.[30]

---

[28] Commission of the European Communities, *Report of the Committee of Independent Experts on Company Taxation* (1992), p. 34.

[29] P. B. Musgrave, *United States Taxation of Foreign Investment Income* (1969), pp. 65–6.

[30] Musgrave noted that the worldwide welfare argument is based on equating worldwide welfare with total worldwide output, but it does not take into account the distribution of income and resources between countries. Musgrave contended that while international efficiency in the allocation of resources requires the use of a foreign tax credit system, US 'national efficiency' required that only a deduction be provided to US resident taxpayers for foreign taxes imposed on them: *ibid.*, pp. 134, 137. This approach is called national neutrality. A deduction for foreign taxes paid is less beneficial than a foreign tax credit, which is deducted directly from a taxpayer's tax liability. Musgrave contended that the US national income from domestic investment is gross income, but for income from foreign investment it should be net foreign income. In this situation, the foreign investment is beneficial to a US taxpayer after net foreign income equals or exceeds the gross return on the taxpayer's domestic investment before taxation in the US. Musgrave concluded that foreign investment continues to be profitable to US resident taxpayers after it has reached the point that it ceases to benefit US national income as taxpayers 'will invest abroad as long as the *net* return on foreign investment (after U.S. and foreign taxes) equals or exceeds the *net* return on domestic investment (after U.S. tax)' (p. 134). On the other hand, Graetz challenged Musgrave's argument that allowing a deduction for foreign income taxes would maximize the national welfare of a capital-exporting

The seminal economic analysis on capital export neutrality was published by Peggy Musgrave in 1963[31] and 1969.[32] One commentator argued that the theory of capital export neutrality has not been defended by analysis, as it has not been proven that a country's welfare is enhanced by the free flow of capital.[33] But in 2000, the US Department of Treasury concluded that the economic literature confirmed Musgrave's analysis,[34] and that both national and international economic welfare are maximized through capital export neutrality:

> With respect to the broader question of how to tax foreign investment to achieve economic policy goals, a careful review of the literature reveals that capital export neutrality is probably the best policy when the goal is to provide the greatest global economic output. Capital export neutrality requires structuring taxes so that they are neutral and do not cause investors to favor either domestic or foreign investment. Put another way, if taxes were structured based on capital export neutrality, investors would make their investment decisions as if there were no taxes. Similarly, with respect to national economic welfare, a careful review of the literature provides no convincing basis for rejecting the conclusions of the basic economic analysis that a country should tax income from outward foreign investment at a rate that is at least as high as the tax rate imposed on income from domestic investment.[35]

In summary, many economists consider that capital export neutrality is central to worldwide economic efficiency, as, ideally, a taxpayer's decision to invest will be based on the best pre-tax rate of return from an investment.[36]

---

country: Graetz, 'The David R. Tillinghast Lecture: Taxing International Income: Inadequate Principles, Outdated Concepts, and Unsatisfactory Policies' (2001), pp. 284–94. Graetz asserted that the US efficiency would not have been improved by only allowing a deduction for foreign taxes (p. 294).

   Shaviro asserts that although a country cannot focus on worldwide welfare and ignore its own national economic welfare, worldwide welfare analysis may encourage countries to cooperate with other countries resulting in all countries being better off: Shaviro, 'Why Worldwide Welfare as a Normative Standard in US Tax Policy?' (2007), p. 178.

[31] P. B. Richman [Musgrave], *Taxation of Foreign Investment Income* (1963), pp. 5–9.

[32] P. B. Musgrave, *United States Taxation of Foreign Investment Income* (1969), pp. 65–6, 74–5, 104–7.

[33] M. J. McIntyre, 'Guidelines for Taxing International Capital Flows' (1993), p. 320. McIntyre has further asserted that the case for capital export neutrality has not been established: M. J. McIntyre, 'The Design of Tax Rules for the North American Free Trade Alliance' (1994), pp. 777–8.

[34] US Department of the Treasury (Office of Tax Policy), *The Deferral of Income Earned Through US Controlled Foreign Corporations* (2000), pp. 23–36, 53.

[35] *Ibid.*, p. 23.   [36] Graetz, 'The David R. Tillinghast Lecture' (2001) 261, p. 270.

2 INTERNATIONAL TAXATION

Capital export neutrality is achieved by residence countries taxing foreign income derived by their resident taxpayers at the same rate as domestic income derived by resident taxpayers.[37] In theory, capital export neutrality could also be achieved by a pure resident country system in which only residence countries have an exclusive right to tax the worldwide income of their residents. But such a system is unlikely to be acceptable to source countries which are developing countries, because it would result in a loss of their tax base as they are net capital importers.

If source countries impose tax on income sourced within their countries, capital export neutrality requires that the residence country must provide relief for the foreign taxes imposed on resident taxpayers. This could be achieved if unlimited foreign tax credits were provided by a residence country for foreign taxes imposed on foreign income derived by resident taxpayers. In this situation, the total domestic tax and foreign tax imposed on foreign income is equal to the total domestic tax that would have been payable had the income been derived solely within the country of residence. But no country provides unlimited foreign tax credits because that would result in a loss of tax revenue in relation to domestic source income if foreign tax rates exceed domestic tax rates.[38] Consequently, residence countries limit foreign tax credits to the domestic tax rates applicable to foreign income derived by resident taxpayers. Countries may prescribe that any excess foreign tax credits for an income year must expire or allow excess foreign tax credits to be used in another income year. Capital export neutrality is not achieved if a resident taxpayer has excess foreign tax credits that cannot be used because it is subject to tax on foreign income at a rate in excess of the taxpayer's domestic tax rate.

---

[37] Commission of the European Communities, *Report of the Committee of Independent Experts on Company Taxation* (1992), p. 36.

[38] An unlimited foreign tax credit system would encourage source countries to set high tax rates. When the US initially implemented the foreign tax credit system for companies in 1918 it was unlimited: Revenue Act of 1918, Pub. L. 65-245, Ch. 18, s. 238(a), 40 Stat. 1057, 1080–1 (1919). In 1921, the foreign tax credit for companies was limited to the domestic tax rate on the foreign income: Revenue Act of 1921, Pub. L. 67-98, Ch. 136, s. 238(a), 227, 258 (1923). The amendment was enacted to prevent tax credits from countries with tax rates exceeding those in the US at the time reducing a US corporate resident taxpayer's liability on domestic source income. See Graetz, 'The David R. Tillinghast Lecture: Taxing International Income: Inadequate Principles, Outdated Concepts, and Unsatisfactory Policies' (2001) 54 *Tax Law Review* 261, pp. 261–2.

Countries may also quarantine foreign tax credits to protect revenue while international enterprises and multinational enterprise groups usually want to immediately use excess foreign tax credits to minimize their taxation liabilities. Quarantining prevents taxpayers with excess foreign tax credits from deriving passive income in low tax countries to use the excess foreign tax credits that might expire or be carried forward to a future income year. Some countries quarantine foreign tax credits derived from passive income and active income respectively,[39] or they may quarantine foreign tax credits on a country basis. While a limited foreign tax credit system may achieve capital export neutrality, it often results in high compliance costs for international enterprises because of the expenses of recording foreign income and foreign taxes imposed on it, and the associated currency conversion requirements. It is also costly for tax authorities to administer a foreign tax credit system and it requires active information exchange between treaty countries to minimize the scope for manipulation.[40]

2.2.4.2 Capital import neutrality

Capital import neutrality requires that if capital is invested in a country, the income should be subject to the same level of taxation, regardless of the investor's residency. Under this principle, the international movement of capital would tend to equalize the after-tax rate of return obtained by investors in various countries which is claimed to ensure an efficient allocation of savings between countries.[41] Capital import neutrality is achieved if source countries are given an exclusive right to tax income derived within their borders; this is called territorial taxation.[42] But it has been argued that capital import neutrality is not a tax principle, but a spending principle.[43] Achieving capital import neutrality requires that income derived by foreign investors in a source country is not taxed in their residence countries. In this situation, a country subjects income, which is sourced within its borders,

---

[39] Passive income includes income such as interest, royalties and dividends, which is highly mobile and may be derived in low tax countries. Active income includes business income.

[40] See section 2.5 'Worldwide taxation and territorial taxation' for a more detailed consideration of the compliance issues arising from foreign tax credit measures.

[41] Commission of the European Communities, *Report of the Committee of Independent Experts on Company Taxation* (1992), p. 35.

[42] This would be achieved by the residence country providing an exemption for foreign income derived by resident taxpayers.

[43] M. J. McIntyre, 'Guidelines for Taxing International Capital Flows' (1993), p. 321.

2 INTERNATIONAL TAXATION   23

to tax at the same rate, regardless of whether the income is derived by resident or non-resident taxpayers. It is also premised on income with a source in that country being easily identifiable. The principle is that all taxpayers, whether resident or non-resident, deriving income from a country should be taxed in the same way and consequently have the same after-tax rate of return. Consequently, business decisions to invest in a particular jurisdiction by resident taxpayers and foreign enterprises should be unaffected by tax considerations.

In theory, if the effective rate of tax on business and investment income were identical in all countries, it would be possible for capital export neutrality[44] and capital import neutrality to be achieved simultaneously.[45] But it is unrealistic that the effective rates of tax on business and investment would be identical around the world. Consequently, in practice, capital export neutrality and capital import neutrality are competing norms and each has consequences for international trade. Capital export neutrality supports residency taxation and capital import neutrality supports source country taxation.

2.3   Jurisdiction to impose taxes

There is general agreement among commentators that a sovereign country has almost unlimited fiscal jurisdiction.[46] Surrey argued in 1956 that the US jurisdiction to tax is not affected by international law and consequently US tax jurisdiction is a matter of national policy.[47] The contrary argument is that a country's fiscal power is marginally limited by rules of international law and domestic constitutional law,[48] such as restrictions on the taxation of diplomats, the rule against arbitrary extraterritorial taxation, and the rule preventing a government from

---

[44] On the basis that residence countries provide foreign tax credits for foreign taxes paid by resident taxpayers.

[45] Commission of the European Communities, *Report of the Committee of Independent Experts on Company Taxation* (1992), pp. 34–5.

[46] Knechtle, *Basic Problems in International Fiscal Law* (1979), p. 37; Sato and Bird, 'International Aspects of the Taxation of Corporations and Shareholders' (1975), pp. 395–6; Jackson and Davey, *Legal Problems of International Economic Relations* (2nd edn, 1986), p. 1107; Surrey, 'Current Issues in the Taxation of Corporate Foreign Investment' (1956), p. 817; Bird, *The Taxation of International Income Flows* (1987), p. 7.

[47] Surrey, *ibid.*, p. 817.

[48] Arnold, *Tax Discrimination Against Aliens, Non-Residents, and Foreign Activities* (1991), p. 7; Qureshi, 'The Freedom of a State to Legislate in Fiscal Matters under General International Law' (1987), p. 21; Jackson and Davey, *Legal Problems of International Economic Relations* (2nd edn, 1986), p. 1107.

operating in the territory of another government.[49] The rule against arbitrary extraterritorial taxation turns on a country's definition of residency but there are no international law limits on a country's definition of residency;[50] consequently, the rules on fiscal jurisdiction have not attained the status of customary international law.[51] More recently, some countries have acquired extraterritorial enforcement capacity through their tax treaties, which enables their tax debts to be collected by treaty partner tax authorities.[52]

A country's fiscal power is limited by its ability to enforce its powers as there is a distinction between a country's jurisdiction to tax and its power to enforce its jurisdiction to tax.[53] Inherent in the notion of fiscal jurisdiction is the power to impose a charge on individuals or companies that must be paid.[54] It is pointless for a country to impose a tax that it cannot enforce because being able to collect a tax is an essential feature of taxation.[55] As a country's fiscal jurisdiction is limited by international law, it has been asserted that some commentators have confused the issues of jurisdiction and enforcement.[56] In summary, a country's jurisdiction to tax is limited by international law, it is also limited by its ability to enforce its jurisdiction, and by its economic and political relations with other countries. Countries will usually limit their jurisdiction to tax by either bilateral or multilateral measures, such as tax treaties, or unilateral domestic law measures.

2.4   The concepts of residency and source

A country's tax jurisdiction is generally based on taxing its residents on their worldwide income, such as individuals and companies, and taxing non-residents on income sourced within its borders. Residence jurisdiction

---

[49] Jackson and Davey, *ibid.*, p. 1107.   [50] *Ibid.*

[51] Beveridge, *The Treatment and Taxation of Foreign Investment under International Law* (2000), pp. 76–7.

[52] See Article 27 of the 2010 OECD Model. This Article deals with treaty countries agreeing to provide assistance in the collection of taxes.

[53] Knechtle, *Basic Problems in International Fiscal Law* (1979), p. 37; Arnold, *Tax Discrimination Against Aliens, Non-Residents, and Foreign Activities* (1991), p. 7; Bird, *The Taxation of International Income Flows* (1987), p. 7; Beveridge, *The Treatment and Taxation of Foreign Investment under International Law* (2000), pp. 75–6; Skaar, *Permanent Establishment* (1991), p. 20.

[54] Brennan and Buchanan, *The Power to Tax* (1980), p. 8.

[55] Graetz, 'The David R. Tillinghast Lecture' (2001), pp. 312–13.

[56] Jeffery, *The Impact of State Sovereignty on Global Trade and International Taxation* (1999), p. 43.

2 INTERNATIONAL TAXATION

and source jurisdiction are the principal bases for the taxation of income in most jurisdictions. There are competing views on whether residence jurisdiction and source jurisdiction have achieved the status of customary law, but they may have achieved at least the status of being customary norms.[57] The economic basis of taxation is instructive in understanding the rationale for residency taxation and source taxation.

2.4.1 Economic basis of taxation

Economists use two main principles for determining how the tax burden should be allocated: the benefit principle and the ability to pay principle. Economists tend to base source taxation on the benefit principle,[58] and to base residence taxation on the ability to pay principle.[59] But source and residency are legal concepts that do not have a clear economic basis and this complicates their analysis.[60]

2.4.1.1 Benefit principle Under the benefit principle, a taxpayer in an equitable tax system should contribute taxes in accordance with the benefit the taxpayer receives from government programmes.[61] For tax policy purposes, the benefit principle suffers from two problems. The first problem is that the benefit principle is difficult to apply in practice because it is difficult to measure the benefit a taxpayer receives from government activity.[62] Measuring the benefit that taxpayers receive from certain government activities, such as defence, education, health and policing, would be arbitrary because of the differences between taxpayers. The second problem is that the benefit principle does not deal with a government role in redistributing income to lower income earners.[63] If a tax system is used to redistribute income, the benefit

---

[57] Kaufman, 'Fairness and the Taxation of International Income' (1998), p. 148.

[58] Musgrave asserts that source taxation is based on economic benefit: R. A. Musgrave and P. B. Musgrave, *Public Finance in Theory and Practice* (4th edn, 1984), pp. 1341–2.

[59] Kaufman, 'Fairness and the Taxation of International Income' (1998). Kaufman contends that source taxation is not based on benefit theory (p. 155) and that source countries have a legal right to tax income sourced within their borders under international law (p. 202).

[60] R. A. Musgrave and P. B. Musgrave, 'Inter-Nation Equity' in Bird and Head (eds.), *Modern Fiscal Issues* (1972) 63–85, p. 72.

[61] R. A. Musgrave and P. B. Musgrave, *Public Finance in Theory and Practice* (5th edn, 1989), p. 219.

[62] Slemrod, 'Introduction' in Slemrod (ed.) *Tax Progressivity and Income Inequality* (1994) 1–8, p. 2.

[63] *Ibid.*

26   INTERNATIONAL TAXATION: POLICY AND LAW

principle is inadequate because it seeks to assign tax burdens solely on the basis of the benefit a taxpayer receives from government activity. Consequently, for income redistribution purposes another principle is required to assign tax burdens.

2.4.1.2 Ability to pay principle The ability to pay principle, or economic interest principle, provides a basis for allocating tax burdens for redistributing income through transfer payments, such as social security benefits. Under this principle, residents of a jurisdiction benefit from government activities and should contribute taxes in accordance with their ability to pay, but there are several difficulties with this principle. It is difficult to define 'ability to pay' and yet progressive taxation is based on this principle because it is argued that a taxpayer's tax sacrifice increases proportionally as the taxpayer's income increases. A further difficulty is determining how the progressive rates of taxation should be set because the level of tax sacrifice for taxpayers cannot be accurately measured. As a result, the ability to pay principle is complex to apply in practice.

2.4.1.3 Economic allegiance The economic experts of the League of Nations were commissioned to develop the theoretical principles for international tax. The economic experts concluded in 1923 that the concept of economic interest was the basis for both residence taxation and source taxation:

> Taking the field of taxation as a whole, the reason why tax authorities waver between these two principles [residence and source] is that each may be considered as a part of the still broader principle of economic interest or *economic allegiance*, as against the original doctrine of political allegiance. A part of the total sum paid according to the ability of a person ought to reach the competing authorities according to his economic interest under each authority. The ideal solution is that the individual's whole faculty should be taxed, but that it should be taxed only once, and that the liability should be divided among the tax districts according to his relative interest in each. The individual has certain economic interests in the place of his permanent residence or domicile, as well as in the place or places where his property is situated or from which his income is derived.[64]

---

[64] Economic and Financial Commission, *Report on Double Taxation Submitted to the Financial Committee* (1923), p. 20.

2 INTERNATIONAL TAXATION

2.4.2 Residency jurisdiction

Residency jurisdiction is based on a connection between a taxpayer and a jurisdiction; this principle is alternatively called the political allegiance principle.[65] Residence jurisdiction is generally a global income tax concept because it is based on a taxpayer's ability to pay, by taking into account the taxpayer's worldwide income.[66] Moreover, in contrast to source taxation, it is a tax on a person and not a tax on the income itself. The scope of a country's residence jurisdiction depends on the tests used to determine if a taxpayer is a resident.[67]

Most countries have residency tests to determine which natural persons and companies have sufficient connection with them to be treated as residents for tax purposes. For companies, their residency should be based on the residency of their owners, the shareholders. But deciding the residency of a company's shareholders is complex, costly and impracticable. In the early part of the twentieth century when the tests of corporate residency were developed, shareholders of companies were usually resident in the same country as the company.[68] Thus, the residency of a company could be used as a convenient proxy test for determining the residence of its shareholders. But the increased mobility of capital and tax planning has resulted in a low correlation between corporate residence and the residence of individual shareholders of international companies.[69]

There are two main tests for a country to assert residence jurisdiction for companies. The first method is to examine a company's legal connection to a jurisdiction, through incorporation or registration under the jurisdiction's domestic law. The second test, for companies incorporated abroad, is the place of effective management test to determine if there is a commercial connection between a company and a jurisdiction. A company's place of effective management is the place where its key management and commercial decisions for the entire business operations of the company are made, which is usually

---

[65] Brean, 'Here or There? The Source and Residence Principles of International Taxation' in Bird and Mintz (eds.), *Taxation to 2000 and Beyond* (1992) 303–33, p. 308.

[66] Sato and Bird, 'International Aspects of the Taxation of Corporations and Shareholders' (1975), pp. 396–7.

[67] United Nations, *Draft Manual for the Negotiation of Bilateral Tax Treaties between Developed and Developing Countries* (2001), p. 2, para. 4.

[68] Arnold, Sasseville and Zolt, 'Summary of the Proceedings of an Invitational Seminar on Tax Treaties in the 21st Century' (2002), p. 79.

[69] *Ibid.*

the place where its board of directors meets.[70] While a company can have several places of management, the OECD considers that it can only have one place of effective management at a particular time.[71] This notion is expressed in some countries as the 'central management and control' of a company. In most countries, if either test is satisfied a company will be treated by a country as a resident of that country for tax purposes.

A country will usually have the power to impose taxes on resident companies, provided it is able to obtain reliable information on the income derived by them.[72] The residence principle, while appearing to be simple, may lead to problems when applied because countries use different tests of residency,[73] which can result in a company being treated as a resident of two countries simultaneously. Furthermore, as many companies have extensive international operations, to treat these companies as being resident in any one country is futile.[74]

The benefit rationale is expressed in two forms as the basis for taxing international enterprises.[75] First, international enterprises benefit from a jurisdiction's provision of legal, institutional and physical infrastructure. Company tax may be imposed as a tax on the use of a jurisdiction's resources by enterprises because it is not possible to impose benefit charges on enterprises.[76] Second, companies are given their legal form by the fiction of being treated as a separate personality with limited liability and perpetual life, which is another form of benefit provided by a country.[77] Bird claimed that neither of these benefit arguments justifies imposing special corporate income taxes on international companies.[78] Companies and other enterprises should pay for the benefits they receive from a company such as limited liability and perpetual life, but this does not provide the basis for imposing corporate income tax.[79] As a country can only provide the privileges of artificial legal personality, limited liability and perpetual life, it has a monopoly granting these benefits and could, in theory, charge monopoly fees for these benefits.[80] Nevertheless, a country's fees for these benefits of legal personality

---

[70] See 2010 OECD Model, pp. 88–9, para. 24.   [71] Ibid.

[72] United Nations, Draft Manual for the Negotiation of Bilateral Tax Treaties between Developed and Developing Countries, Report No. ST/ESA (2001), pp. 1–2, para. 3.

[73] Bird, The Taxation of International Income Flows (1987), p. 11.

[74] Williams, Trends in International Taxation (1991), p. 80, para. 413.

[75] Bird, 'Why Tax Corporations?' (2002), p. 196.

[76] Mintz, 'Globalization of the Corporate Income Tax' (1999), p. 392.   [77] Ibid.

[78] Bird, 'Why Tax Corporations?' (2002), pp. 196–7.   [79] Ibid.   [80] Ibid., pp. 196–7.

2 INTERNATIONAL TAXATION   29

should only reflect its costs in providing these benefits, such as process-ing fees and record-keeping fees.[81]

The residency of companies as an international tax principle is easily manipulated.[82] If one of the tests of residency is incorporation or registration, it is a simple process to incorporate a company in a jurisdiction with a favourable tax system. If another test of residency is the location of effective management, or central management and control, the effective management of an enterprise can also be based in a jurisdiction with a favourable tax system. International enterprises are able to locate their effective management in countries that provide tax advantages and maintain control of the enterprise from that location.[83] This would usually involve a company holding the meetings of its board of directors in a favourable tax country, and ensuring that the key management decisions of the entity were made at those meetings. Moreover, globalization through high speed and high quality communi-cation technology and information technology has created the capacity for companies to be controlled from almost any geographic location. If a company is incorporated or registered in a favourable tax country and its board of directors hold their meetings in that country making the key commercial decisions at those meetings, no other country is likely to be able to claim that the company is a resident taxpayer. At times, it may be difficult to objectively determine the residence of international com-panies under the effective management test. For example, a company's board of directors may hold video conference meetings in which the key management decisions are made, with the directors being located in several countries. In this situation, communication technology makes it very difficult to decide where the company is resident under the effective management test. Consequently, the residency principle is easily manipulated.

2.4.3 Source jurisdiction

The principle of 'source' in determining jurisdiction to tax is based on the economic connection an item of income has to a country[84] and it

---

[81] *Ibid.*, pp. 196–7.

[82] Arnold, Sasseville and Zolt, 'Summary of the Proceedings of an Invitational Seminar on Tax Treaties in the 21st Century' (2002), p. 79.

[83] Hufbauer, *US Taxation of International Income* (1992), p. 6.

[84] United Nations, *Draft Manual for the Negotiation of Bilateral Tax Treaties between Developed and Developing Countries* (2001), p. 1, para. 1; Ault, *Comparative Income Taxation* (1997), p. 431; Vann, 'International Aspects of Income Tax' in Thuronyi (ed.) *Tax Law Design and Drafting* (1998) 718–810, p. 734.

was initially developed by European countries with schedular tax systems.[85] The underlying rationale is that income should be treated as having its source in the jurisdiction in which it has a significant economic connection. But it is difficult to define the source principle in economics and law.[86] As taxation based on the source principle is imposed on an income flow, it is immaterial whether the recipients are resident taxpayers or non-resident taxpayers.[87] The ability to pay principle cannot be applied to source taxation because the source country is usually unable to measure a taxpayer's worldwide income over a period of time. Consequently, the source jurisdiction conflicts with the ability to pay principle.

Under the benefit principle, the rationale for source taxation is that non-residents receiving income from a source country have benefited from being able to derive income in that country, and accordingly they should be taxed in that country. Conversely, it has been asserted that source taxation is not based on benefit theory, but rather on the economic connection between the source country and the income derived within its borders.[88] The appropriate level of source country taxation that should be imposed on income is controversial. Some commentators argue that the benefits provided to resident taxpayers exceed the benefits provided to non-resident taxpayers; and consequently, source country taxes on non-residents should be significantly lower than taxes imposed on residents of the source country.[89] Other commentators argue that the benefits resident taxpayers receive from government operations are similar to those received by non-resident taxpayers and therefore source country taxes should be substantial.[90] The latter argument contends that source taxation is a justified charge for the use by non-resident taxpayers of a jurisdiction's physical, legal and economic infrastructure.[91]

---

[85] Sato and Bird, 'International Aspects of the Taxation of Corporations and Shareholders' (1975), p. 396.

[86] See Ault and Bradford, 'Taxing International Income' in Razin and Slemrod (eds.), *Taxation in the Global Economy* (1990) 11–46, p. 30; Bird, *The Taxation of International Income Flows* (1987), p. 11.

[87] Sato and Bird, 'International Aspects of the Taxation of Corporations and Shareholders' (1975), p. 396.

[88] Kaufman, 'Fairness and the Taxation of International Income' (1998), p. 202.

[89] Shay, Fleming and Peroni, 'The David R. Tillinghast Lecture' (2002), p. 90.

[90] *Ibid.*, pp. 90–1.

[91] *Ibid.*, p. 154; P. B. Richman [Musgrave], *Taxation of Foreign Investment Income* (1963), p. 26.

2 INTERNATIONAL TAXATION

A source country usually has the power to enforce its source jurisdiction as it has the power to tax income generated within its borders.[92] To enforce a tax, a jurisdiction needs both information and the ability to compel compliance.[93] It has been asserted that there is no justification for the source principle – the sole basis for this principle is that the source country is in the best position to enforce a tax on income made within its borders.[94]

Most countries have similar tests for source jurisdiction in order to be able to identify those non-residents over whom they should assert their taxing powers.[95] Jurisdictions generally use different methods for taxing passive income and active income. Passive investment income is usually taxed on a gross income basis using a withholding tax system, because a non-resident taxpayer usually has a limited connection with the source country. Many countries impose a withholding tax on interest, royalties and dividends derived by non-residents. The person paying income that is subject to withholding tax is usually required to withhold tax when such income is paid to a recipient outside the source country. Active income, such as the profits of a permanent establishment, is taxed on a net income basis. This approach to taxation for permanent establishments is appropriate because they generally have a significant and ongoing connection with their host countries.

2.4.4 Problems with the source principle

It is asserted that there is no objective economic method of allocating the profits and expenses in integrated international enterprises based on the location in which the profits and expenses are apparently made.[96] The transactions of an international enterprise are fungible and complex, consequently this makes it difficult for a tax authority to determine which profits were made within its borders.[97] Thus, the allocation of

---

[92] United Nations, *Draft Manual for the Negotiation of Bilateral Tax Treaties between Developed and Developing Countries* (2001), p. 1, para. 1.

[93] Shay, Fleming and Peroni, 'The David R. Tillinghast Lecture' (2002), p. 117.

[94] Green, 'The Future of Source-Based Taxation of the Income of Multinational Enterprises' (1993), pp. 31–2; Graetz, 'The David R. Tillinghast Lecture' (2001), pp. 312–13.

[95] Ault, *Comparative Income Taxation* (1997), p. 371.

[96] R. A. Musgrave and P. B. Musgrave, *Public Finance in Theory and Practice* (4th edn, 1984), p. 1345; C. E. McLure (ed.) *State Income Taxation of Multistate Corporations in the United States of America* (1974), p. 61, para. 2; Bird and Brean, 'The Interjurisdictional Allocation of Income and the Unitary Taxation Debate' (1986), p. 1383.

[97] Bird, 'Shaping a New International Tax Order' (1988), p. 294.

32   INTERNATIONAL TAXATION: POLICY AND LAW

profits on the basis of source within a highly integrated international enterprise is inherently arbitrary.[98]

The economic notion of income as the sum of consumption and change in net worth suggests that determining the source of income is inappropriate because it is attributable to an individual or an enterprise, not a geographical place.[99] The income of international enterprises comes from numerous transactions, and the claim that the income of these enterprises is able to be allocated to geographic sources is meaningless.[100] As income does not have a natural geographic location, the source of income for tax purposes is usually based on factors such as the location of the assets and the activities that generated the income.[101] The location of physical assets used to derive income is straightforward, but most of the income of international enterprises is derived from intangible assets, such as know-how, patents, copyright, and trademarks, which often have no single geographic location. Attributing a geographic location to intangible property is arbitrary.[102] An enterprise's profits are determined by calculating its income and subtracting expenses in accordance with tax and accounting rules. While the source principle is theoretically simple, it has practical limits as it is difficult to determine the source of income derived by an international enterprise.[103] Consequently, the source principle is an imprecise legal concept and there is no internationally accepted definition of source.[104]

Bird asserted that the source principle has not dominated international tax policy of governments for two reasons: first, it is difficult

---

[98] Brean, 'Here or There?' in Bird and Mintz (eds.), *Taxation to 2000 and Beyond* (1992) 303–33, p. 331.

[99] Graetz and O'Hear, 'The "Original Intent" of US International Taxation' (1997), p. 1032.

[100] Frenkel, Razin and Sadka (eds.), *International Taxation in an Integrated World* (1991), p. 3; C. E. McLure, 'Tax Assignment and Subnational Fiscal Autonomy' (2000), p. 633; Avi-Yonah, 'Globalization, Tax Competition, and the Fiscal Crisis of the Welfare State' (2000), p. 1647; Ault and Bradford, 'Taxing International Income' in Razin and Slemrod (eds.), *Taxation in the Global Economy* (1992) 11–46, pp. 30–1; Thuronyi, 'International Tax Cooperation and a Multilateral Treaty' (2001), p. 1661; M. J. McIntyre, 'The Design of Tax Rules for the North American Free Trade Alliance' (1994), pp. 775–6.

[101] United Nations, *Draft Manual for the Negotiation of Bilateral Tax Treaties between Developed and Developing Countries* (2001), p. 1, para. 2.

[102] Ault and Bradford, 'Taxing International Income' in Razin and Slemrod (eds.), *Taxation in the Global Economy* (1992) 11–46, p. 31.

[103] Sato and Bird, 'International Aspects of the Taxation of Corporations and Shareholders' (1975), p. 396.

[104] Shaviro, 'Why Worldwide Welfare as a Normative Standard in US Tax Policy?' (2007), p. 165.

to allocate an international enterprise's profits to a geographic source; and, second, it is difficult to then define the source principle in legislation.[105] He points out that the exercise of attributing source to income is meaningless:

> What is not nearly so well understood, however, is the unfortunate fact that as a rule there is, even in principle, no clear, objective economic basis on which to allocate revenues and costs to the particular units that comprise parts of a multijurisdictional enterprise. Almost by definition, the operation of multinational firms involve what economists call 'joint products' and 'nonmarketed intermediate goods', that is, activities involving costs which typically cannot be allocated with certainty to various branches and divisions, affiliates or subsidiaries of a firm . . .
>
> The allocation of profits within a multinational enterprise is thus inherently and unavoidably arbitrary since such businesses are, as a rule, inevitably 'unitary' in character. In addition, as noted above, the interjurisdictional allocation of costs and revenue must be expected to push against the constraints imposed on global profit maximization by national tax policies.[106]

Moreover, the source principle is being eroded by globalization as source is based on the physical foreign investment, such as mining, building or manufacturing.[107] The US Treasury Department noted the challenge of applying the source principle:

> The growth of new communications technologies and electronic commerce will likely require that principles of residence-based taxation assume even greater importance. In the world of cyberspace, it is often difficult, *if not impossible, to apply traditional source concepts to link an item of income with a specific geographical location.* Therefore, source based taxation could lose its rationale and be rendered obsolete by electronic commerce. By contrast, almost all taxpayers are resident somewhere. An individual is almost always a citizen or resident of a given country and, at least under US law, all corporations must be established under the laws of a given jurisdiction. However, a review of current residency definitions and taxation rules may be appropriate.[108] (emphasis added)

---

[105] Bird and Wilkie, 'Source- vs. residence-based taxation in the European Union' in Cnossen (ed.) *Taxing Capital Income in the European Union* (2000) 78–109, p. 81.

[106] Bird, 'The Interjurisdictional Allocation of Income' (1986), pp. 333–4.

[107] Bird and Wilkie, 'Source- vs. residence-based taxation in the European Union' in Cnossen (ed.) *Taxing Capital Income in the European Union* (2000) 78–109, pp. 93–4.

[108] US Department of the Treasury (Office of Tax Policy), *Selected Tax Policy Implications of Global Electronic Commerce* (1996), p. 23.

34   INTERNATIONAL TAXATION: POLICY AND LAW

In conclusion, most countries use a combination of source jurisdiction and residence jurisdiction, but globalization has highlighted the problems of the existing international tax principles. For integrated international enterprises, such as international banks, there are problems with trying to allocate profits and costs between countries using residence and source concepts. As a result, international enterprises are able to manipulate the source and residency rules of the countries in which they operate through tax planning.

2.5   Worldwide taxation and territorial taxation

Taxation of business income derived by international enterprises may be either worldwide (residence) taxation or territorial (source) taxation. The territorial taxation system limits the taxation of business income to source countries – international enterprises are exempted from taxation in their country of residence on foreign income they derive.[109] A pure territorial taxation system achieves the tax policy objective of capital import neutrality. Under the worldwide taxation system, the country of residence imposes taxation on a resident taxpayer's worldwide income and achieves the tax policy objective of capital export neutrality. The worldwide taxation system subjects resident taxpayers to tax on their foreign income at the same rate as domestic income, with a tax credit provided for foreign taxes imposed on their foreign income. Foreign tax credits are usually provided for the following source country taxes: withholding tax, underlying company tax paid by a subsidiary, and tax imposed on a permanent establishment. Such credits are limited to the rate of domestic tax imposed on foreign income. As foreign and domestic income is subject to identical taxation, taxpayers should, in theory, be indifferent as to whether they derive income from domestic or foreign operations. The rationale for worldwide taxation is that it should result in an efficient allocation of economic resources by resident taxpayers. Under worldwide taxation, a taxpayer should invest its capital, either domestically or abroad, where profits are highest. Worldwide taxation is regarded by economists as a tax on savings.[110] Residency jurisdiction relies on the principle of capital export neutrality as income derived by

---

[109] Territorial taxation may also be called the exemption method.
[110] Mullins, *Moving to Territoriality?* (2006), p. 5.

an international enterprise should be subject to the same level of tax regardless of whether it is derived domestically or abroad.

Territorial taxation is based on international enterprises or multinational enterprise groups being subject to tax on income only in the source jurisdiction. Under pure territorial taxation, resident taxpayers are exempt from tax in their country of residence on their foreign income. But pure territorial systems are not used by developed countries because of the risk of tax avoidance.[111] Under partial territorial taxation, a country exempts resident taxpayers on certain types of foreign income while continuing to subject non-qualifying foreign income to taxation. Territorial taxation may be implemented by a country through either its domestic law or tax treaties. Partial territorial taxation may be limited to foreign income derived in countries with which the residence country has a tax treaty, or source countries which impose tax on the income above a threshold minimum rate of tax. These two measures minimize the risk of tax avoidance as international enterprises may have an incentive to derive income in tax havens. Territorial taxation is premised on the principle of capital import neutrality, under which a taxpayer is only subject to tax in the source jurisdiction on foreign source income. Territorial taxation is viewed by economists as being a tax on investment.[112] The main benefit of capital import neutrality is that all business enterprises operating in a jurisdiction are subject to the same rate of taxation, irrespective of their residency. Consequently, resident and non-resident taxpayers are able to compete on the same basis in a jurisdiction. It has been suggested that a move to territorial taxation may result in tax competition and that the reduction in revenue is most likely to have a significant effect on developing countries.[113]

The worldwide taxation approach was once prevalent in developed countries, but by 2005, a pure worldwide approach was only used by less than half of the developed countries.[114] Developed countries usually use a partial territorial system which provides an exemption from taxation for active foreign business income. Consequently, most developed countries

---

[111] Pure territorial taxation is used by several countries in Central America, South America, Africa and East Asia: US Department of the Treasury (Office of Tax Policy), *The Deferral of Income Earned Through US Controlled Foreign Corporations* (2000), pp. ix–x.

[112] Mullins, *Moving to Territoriality?* (2006). [113] *Ibid.*, p. 24.

[114] US President's Advisory Panel on Federal Tax Reform, *Simple, Fair, and Pro-Growth* (2005), p. 103; Graetz and Oosterhuis, 'Structuring an Exemption System for Foreign Income of US Corporations' (2001), p. 771.

have a mixture of both worldwide taxation and partial territorial taxation. Developed countries usually provide resident taxpayers with an exemption for active foreign income derived in foreign countries with similar tax systems. A common minimum threshold requirement for exemption is that a resident taxpayer must have either a direct interest of at least 10 per cent in its foreign subsidiary entity (a non-portfolio interest), or carry on business in the foreign country through a permanent establishment.

The main advantage of territorial taxation is the respective compliance and administrative savings in the residence jurisdiction for taxpayers and tax authorities. The worldwide taxation of active foreign income derived in a country with a similar tax system usually results in no additional tax being imposed on the foreign income in the residence country.[115] But the costs of complying with a foreign tax credit system are significant for international enterprises, especially taking into account record-keeping requirements, timing differences and currency calculations.[115] On the other hand, developed countries usually impose worldwide taxation on passive income, such as interest, royalties and dividends, derived by taxpayers through controlled foreign companies. Controlled foreign company (CFC) measures prevent resident taxpayers deferring taxation on passive income derived abroad by their controlled foreign companies. The CFC measures attribute to the resident taxpayers on an accruals basis the passive income derived by their controlled foreign companies. CFC measures are necessary as passive income is highly mobile and may be located in lower-tax jurisdictions to exploit deferral opportunities. An example of worldwide taxation is the taxation

---

[115] In the US relatively little revenue is raised on foreign income derived by US resident corporations because of foreign tax credit offsets. According to the 2004 US Internal Revenue Service Statistical Tables for US Corporate Returns with a Foreign Tax Credit, the total net income subject to US tax of US corporations claiming a foreign tax credit was approximately US$533.2 billion. The US income tax on this income before tax credits was US$187.5 billion with US$56.6 billion being claimed as foreign tax credits against the US tax liability. The US income tax collected after credits (foreign tax credits, US possessions tax credit and general business credit) was US$118.9 billion.

[116] A US study published in 1995 found that costs of complying with US income tax laws were substantial and that 40 per cent of these costs related to foreign source income. Furthermore, the costs of compliance are very high when compared to the revenue raised from foreign source income. The study also noted that corporate tax advisers stated that at the time one of the most costly features of the US taxation of foreign source income was the foreign tax credit measures: Blumenthal and Slemrod, 'The Compliance Cost of Taxing Foreign-Source Income' (1995), pp. 51–2.

2 INTERNATIONAL TAXATION

of resident taxpayers, on an accruals basis, on passive income derived by their controlled foreign companies.

The US currently has a worldwide tax system for foreign income, but there has been extensive debate on the advantages of a move to partial territorial taxation.[117] Under US tax law, the foreign income of US taxpayers, companies and individuals is subject to tax in the US. Under the US foreign tax credit rules, taxpayers can only claim credit up to the domestic rate of tax on the foreign income. Any excess credits must be carried forward, or back, and used against other foreign income in the same quarantine category, usually called baskets. There are four US quarantine or basket categories,[118] but the foreign income of US companies is quarantined into two baskets.[119] This system is regarded as being complex with high costs of compliance imposed on US international enterprises.[120] The complexity and costs resulted in the 2005 US President's Advisory Panel on Federal Tax Reform recommending that the US move to a partial territorial system of taxation.[121] The recommendation was that the US should exempt corporate taxpayers deriving active foreign income from foreign subsidiary companies and that the dividends paid by the foreign companies to their US parent companies would be exempt from tax in the US. Foreign passive income derived by US taxpayers would be subject to US taxation upon derivation.

The main justifications for the proposal were to reduce complexity and to improve the competitiveness of US resident enterprises in foreign markets.[122] It has been suggested that a potential disadvantage

---

[117] See McDaniel, 'Territorial vs Worldwide Taxation' (2007); Mullins, *Moving to Territoriality?* (2006), pp. 9–15; Lokken, 'Territorial Taxation' (2006), pp. 770–1; Graetz and Oosterhuis, 'Structuring an Exemption System for Foreign Income of US Corporations' (2001); Graetz, 'The David R. Tillinghast Lecture' (2001).

[118] The four quarantine categories are: passive income, general limitation income, s. 901(j) income, and income resourced by treaty: Redmiles and Wenrich, 'A History of Controlled Foreign Corporations and the Foreign Tax Credit' (2007), p. 131.

[119] There were nine baskets prior to 1 January 2007: see Mullins, *Moving to Territoriality?* (2006), p. 9. The former US foreign tax credit rules were regarded as being very complex: US Department of the Treasury (Office of Tax Policy), *The Deferral of Income Earned Through US Controlled Foreign Corporations* (2000), p. 772.

[120] See Blumenthal and Slemrod, 'The Compliance Cost of Taxing Foreign-Source Income' (1995).

[121] US President's Advisory Panel on Federal Tax Reform, *Simple, Fair, and Pro-Growth* (2005), p. 105. In relation to the UK, see Griffith, Hines and Sorensen, 'International Capital Taxation' (2008), pp. 51–6, a chapter drafted for *Reforming the Tax System for the 21st Century: The Mirrlees Review.*

[122] *Ibid.*, pp. 104–5.

38   INTERNATIONAL TAXATION: POLICY AND LAW

of US territorial taxation is that it would encourage international enterprises to avoid taxation in the US and other higher-tax jurisdictions by shifting their operations to lower-tax jurisdictions. This could, in turn, lead to international tax competition which may have a significant impact on developing countries.[123] The recommendations of the 2005 US President's Advisory Panel were not implemented, but it is uncertain whether it would have succeeded in its objective of making US firms more competitive in carrying on business abroad through partial territorial taxation.[124]

2.6   International tax planning, tax avoidance and tax evasion

Tax planning or tax minimization is the use of legal forms that are effective in reducing or deferring a taxpayer's tax liability because they are entitled to arrange their affairs to minimize taxation, but this right is not unlimited. In practice, it can be difficult to distinguish between acceptable tax planning and tax avoidance. There are no internationally accepted definitions of the terms tax planning, tax avoidance and tax evasion.[125] Jurisdictions cannot allow some taxpayers to enter arrangements to avoid taxation, as public confidence in the integrity of a tax system is undermined if some taxpayers operating in the jurisdiction are able to significantly reduce or eliminate their tax liabilities, thus making taxation voluntary for these taxpayers.[126] Moreover, tax avoidance affects the criteria of both horizontal and vertical equity, and creates an incentive for other taxpayers to avoid taxation, leading to significant reductions in a tax system's voluntary compliance. The tax systems of all countries rely on high levels of voluntary compliance by taxpayers. One consequence of tax avoidance is that the tax burden falls disproportionately on those taxpayers who are unable to structure their affairs to avoid taxation, such as wage-earning employees, or taxpayers who do not wish to avoid taxation.

Defining 'tax avoidance' is difficult and the subject is controversial – its meaning has been closely examined by governments, courts, tax advisers, taxpayers and academics.[127] The notion of tax avoidance varies

---

[123] Mullins, *Moving to Territoriality?* (2006), p. 24.   [124] *Ibid.*, p. 23.

[125] Commission of the European Communities, *Report of the Committee of Independent Experts on Company Taxation* (1992), p. 138.

[126] United Nations, *International Co-operation in Tax Matters, Guidelines for International Co-operation Against the Evasion and Avoidance of Taxes* (1984), p. 11, para. 21.

[127] See Edgar, 'Designing and Implementing a Target-Effective General Anti-Avoidance Rule' in Duff and Erlichman (eds.), *Tax Avoidance in Canada after Canada Trustco and Mathew* (2007) 221–56, pp. 226–34 for a discussion of the following types of tax

between jurisdictions; the key feature of avoidance is manipulation of tax law that is legal but in conflict with the policy of the tax law. In other words, tax avoidance is the use of tax law in ways that were not foreseen or contemplated by a legislature. In the UK context, Lord Templeman of the UK House of Lords said that tax avoidance reduces the amount of tax paid by a taxpayer 'contrary to the intentions of Parliament'.[128] The key element of tax avoidance is that a taxpayer is not paying the amount of tax which the taxpayer should have paid on an objective interpretation of the tax law.[129] Arnold asserted that a purpose test provides a reasonable basis for distinguishing between tax avoidance and tax planning.[130] He argued that if the primary aim of a transaction is to achieve a business outcome, the transaction should be treated as acceptable tax planning. Tax avoidance must be considered in the context that taxpayers are only required to pay the minimum amount of tax intended in a jurisdiction under its tax laws. But it is difficult to determine, from a normative perspective, the amount of tax that a taxpayer should pay in a particular jurisdiction. In addition, in developed countries with complex tax laws it is, at times, difficult for tax authorities, taxpayers and courts to determine what a legislative body intended when it enacted its tax law.

International tax avoidance by the use of international transactions is undesirable, as it provides incentives for taxpayers to use resources to exploit domestic tax laws and tax treaties resulting in an inefficient allocation of economic resources. The mobility of capital in a globalized international economy provides taxpayers with opportunities to engage in tax arbitrage to exploit tax differences between countries.[131] For example, the technique of 'treaty shopping' provides taxpayers with the opportunity to exploit differences between tax treaties. In 2001, the UN noted the growth of international tax avoidance and evasion with increasing globalization:

> Various features of the globalized economy have enabled an increasing number of individuals and companies to resort to tax evasion or tax

avoidance: changes in real behaviour; transactional substitution; the creation of tax attributes; the transfer of tax attributes; and tax evasion.

[128] Shipwright (ed.), *Tax Avoidance and the Law* (1997), p. 1: source Hoffman, 'Tax Avoidance' (2005), p. 204.

[129] Hoffman, *ibid.*, p. 204.

[130] Arnold, 'The Canadian General Anti-Avoidance Rule' in Cooper (ed.), *Tax Avoidance and the Rule of Law* (1997), p. 228.

[131] For a discussion of tax arbitrage within the EU see: Commission of the European Communities, *Report of the Committee of Independent Experts on Company Taxation* (1992), pp. 39–40.

avoidance. These features include the ease and rapidity of communications, the progressive elimination of obstacles to the movement of persons and property, the expansion of international economic relations, the differences in national tax systems and hence in the tax burden from country to country, the growing sophistication and aggressiveness of taxpayers and their advisors in developing legal and illegal techniques for taking advantage of weaknesses in national tax systems.[132]

The underlying purpose of international tax avoidance is to use a legal form to exploit domestic tax laws and tax treaties to avoid taxation. Avoiding tax can result from either legitimate tax avoidance or illegitimate tax avoidance. Legitimate tax avoidance is the same as tax planning, which may be defined as the lawful way of minimizing a taxpayer's tax liability.[133] Taxpayers are entitled to engage in tax planning as the legislature, tax authorities and courts in a country have approved the use of certain tax minimization techniques. Taxpayers are entitled to use these approved techniques to reduce or avoid taxation. Illegitimate tax avoidance results when taxpayers use tax schemes which technically comply with tax law, but are found to be an abuse of the tax law because the principal purpose of the arrangement is to avoid taxes.[134] Often a key feature of illegitimate tax avoidance is that it complies with the tax law, but it is used in a manner that was unintended by a country's legislature.

The notions of tax avoidance and tax planning vary between countries and depend not only on the form of an arrangement, but also on the attitudes of a country's courts, government, legislature and public opinion.[135] Avoidance arrangements are characterized by artificiality and generally have no genuine business purpose.[136] Consequently, countries use specific and general anti-avoidance measures to counter tax avoidance. Specific international tax anti-avoidance measures include: transfer pricing rules, thin capitalization rules, and controlled foreign company rules. One shortcoming of specific anti-avoidance measures is that by providing taxpayers with a list of techniques that are proscribed in a jurisdiction, they thereby also provide taxpayers with the opportunity to design targeted tax avoidance schemes to avoid the jurisdiction's specific

---

[132] United Nations, *Draft Manual for the Negotiation of Bilateral Tax Treaties between Developed and Developing Countries* (2001), p. 26, para. 67.
[133] Commission of the European Communities, *Report of the Committee of Independent Experts on Company Taxation* (1992), p. 138.
[134] *Ibid.*   [135] OECD, *International Tax Avoidance and Evasion* (1987), Annex II, p. 16.
[136] *Ibid.*, p. 17.

anti-avoidance measures. Another shortcoming is that it is impossible to enact provisions to cover all potential avoidance techniques in a jurisdiction. On the other hand, general anti-avoidance provisions are usually used in some countries as a last line measure to counter arrangements that have been executed for the main purpose of tax avoidance. A general anti-avoidance rule allows for the substance approach to prevail over the form approach, to deny taxpayers tax benefits from illegitimate tax avoidance schemes. The general nature of the tests in a general anti-avoidance rule usually results in uncertainty on the distinction between legitimate tax planning and tax avoidance.

Tax evasion is defined as a criminal offence against a country's tax laws, such as a taxpayer's failure to disclose income, falsely claiming deductions or fabricating accounts.[137] Prosecution of a taxpayer for evasion may result in a criminal sanction being imposed on the taxpayer and advisers. By comparison, tax avoidance is more difficult to define as it is the use of techniques to reduce a taxpayer's tax liability, but it is behaviour that falls short of constituting a criminal offence. The UN has described tax avoidance as:

> Put very broadly, tax avoidance may be considered to occur when persons arrange their affairs in such a way as to take advantage of weaknesses or ambiguities in the law to reduce taxes, without actually breaking the law. Although tax avoidance may be regarded as immoral in some circumstances, the means employed are legal and not fraudulent.[138]

Depending on the existence of judicial or statutory anti-avoidance rules, tax avoidance may or may not be successful if a case is audited and litigated. However, to apply anti-avoidance rules, tax authorities typically must discover the relevant transactions in a tax audit, and then obtain and analyse the information necessary to apply their anti-avoidance rules. This may be difficult in a cross-border situation where information is located in several jurisdictions.[139] Moreover, tax authorities have limited resources and when their budgets are inadequate, they may respond by reducing their audit activities, which is likely to encourage avoidance activities. In addition the exchange of information between treaty countries may be limited.

---

[137] Vanistendael, 'Legal Framework for Taxation' in Thuronyi (ed.) *Tax Law Design and Drafting* (1996) 15–70, p. 44.

[138] United Nations, *Draft Manual for the Negotiation of Bilateral Tax Treaties between Developed and Developing Countries* (2001), p. 34, para. 74.

[139] *Ibid.*, pp. 27–8, paras. 70–1.

42 INTERNATIONAL TAXATION: POLICY AND LAW

At times, tax avoidance is disclosed only when an international enterprise becomes insolvent and is investigated. For example, the investigation of the Joint Committee on Taxation of the US Congress into the operations of Enron revealed that Enron had been avoiding taxation. But this discovery was made because Enron had gone bankrupt resulting in its business operations being investigated. The Joint Committee noted that:

> This Report's detailed analysis of Enron's structured transactions reveals a pattern of behaviour showing that Enron deliberately and aggressively engaged in transactions that had little or no business purpose in order to obtain favorable tax and accounting treatment. For Enron's leaders, financial statement income became paramount, and Enron announced to the world its target of $1 billion in net income for year 2000. As Enron's management realized that tax-motivated transactions could generate financial accounting benefits, Enron looked to its tax department to devise transactions that increased financial accounting income. In effect, the tax department was converted into an Enron business unit, complete with annual revenue targets. The tax department, in consultation with outside experts, then designed transactions to meet or approximate the technical requirements of tax provisions with the primary purpose of manufacturing financial statement income. The slogan 'Show Me the Money!' exemplified this effort. However, a bona fide business purpose, that is, a purpose other than to secure favorable tax and accounting treatment, was either lacking or tenuous in many of the transactions and clearly was not the impetus for the transactions.[140]

This report highlights the considerable tax avoidance efforts of a large international enterprise, and of particular concern was the use of Enron's tax department as a profit centre. Between 1995 and when Enron filed for bankruptcy in 2002, its tax benefits and accounting benefits were more than US$2 billion and Enron had paid approximately US$88 million in fees to its advisers and promoters.[141]

3 International tax law

International tax law is the body of domestic tax laws together with the collection of tax treaties applying to cross-border transactions. Taxation is a vital sovereign power, and taxes are imposed by countries relying on

---

[140] Joint Committee on Taxation, *Report of Investigations of Enron Corporation and Related Entities Regarding Federal Tax and Compensation Issues, and Policy Recommendations* (2003), p. 21.
[141] *Ibid.*, p. 9.

their domestic law. International taxation has two dimensions: the taxation of a country's taxpayers on income derived from foreign sources (out-bound transactions); and the taxation of non-residents on income derived within a country's borders (in-bound transactions). Countries apply their taxes on the basis of their residency jurisdiction and source jurisdiction, as an important part of a country's tax base is the income from cross-border transactions. But the overlap of the tax jurisdictions of two or more countries over taxpayers or items of income may result in double taxation. To prevent double taxation countries enter into tax treaties, which are the international aspect of these countries' tax laws. A tax treaty, in effect, modifies the domestic tax jurisdiction of the treaty countries to eliminate double taxation. Tax treaties play an important role in supporting international trade and investment and in allocating profits from international transactions which has resulted in developed countries having an extensive network of tax treaties with their main trading countries and neighbouring countries.

3.1 Domestic tax law

A country will impose tax on cross-border transactions under its domestic law, and set the primary tax liability on these transactions. The domestic tax rules contain the definitions of terms used in the tax law, specify what types of income or taxpayers are to be assessed, set the rates of tax, and specify the requirements a taxpayer must comply with. Domestic tax law can provide relief from double taxation for residents through either a foreign tax credits system or an exemption system. Domestic tax law may also provide exemptions from taxation on certain types of income for non-residents, such as an exemption from non-resident interest withholding tax. In theory, double taxation could be prevented by the coordinated use of full exemptions of income and capital gains from taxation, but, in practice, this degree of coordination is unlikely to be established through the exclusive use of domestic legislation.[142]

3.2 Tax treaties

Tax treaties are international agreements between countries and, although most of the agreements are bilateral, there are some significant regional multilateral tax treaties. Tax treaties allocate taxing rights over

[142] See Easson, 'Do We Still Need Tax Treaties?' (2000), p. 621.

44 INTERNATIONAL TAXATION: POLICY AND LAW

taxpayers and items of income between the treaty countries, thus modifying their respective jurisdiction to tax income and capital gains. Countries are willing to restrict their jurisdiction to tax by entering tax treaties because of the key policy objective of encouraging international trade and investment between the treaty countries,[143] and by 2008 there were approximately 3,000 tax treaties in operation.[144] A notional complete network of tax treaties would require around 16,000 bilateral treaties, but it is doubtful whether such a point would ever be reached, and the complexity of the network would be overwhelming.[145]

3.2.1 Economic and juridical double taxation

One of the key purposes of tax treaties is to prevent double taxation, which may be either juridical double taxation or economic double taxation, and to prevent tax avoidance. Economic double taxation occurs when two treaty countries tax the same item of income in the hands of two different persons. Transfer pricing adjustments of transactions between associated international enterprises may result in economic double taxation. For example, when associated enterprises engage in intra-group transactions they are required by the associated enterprise Article (Article 9 of the OECD Model and UN Model) to use transfer prices that comply with the arm's length principle. If a treaty country makes an adjustment to a transfer price used by an associated enterprise to increase its taxable income, economic double taxation will occur if the other treaty country does not make a corresponding adjustment to the associated enterprise in its jurisdiction. The concept of economic double taxation is less certain than juridical double taxation which has a precise meaning.[146]

Juridical double taxation occurs when two or more jurisdictions impose similar taxes on the same taxpayer on the same item of income or capital gains and for the same income period. The OECD notes that the harmful effects of juridical double taxation 'on the exchange of goods and services and movements of capital, technology and persons are so well known that it is scarcely necessary to stress the importance of removing

---

[143] See Sato and Bird, 'International Aspects of the Taxation of Corporations and Shareholders' (1975), p. 403; American Law Institute, *Federal Income Tax Project, International Aspects of United States Income Taxation II, Proposals on United States Income Tax Treaties* (1992), p. 1.

[144] 'OECD Model Tax Convention: Why It Works', *OECD Observer*, No. 260, October 2008.

[145] Easson, 'Do We Still Need Tax Treaties?' (2000), p. 620.

[146] 2010 OECD Model, p. 196, para. 41.

the obstacles that double taxation presents to the development of economic relations between countries'.[147] Juridical double taxation may arise in three situations.[148] In the first situation, two treaty countries may treat the same person as a resident (dual residency) and concurrently tax that person's worldwide income or capital. In the second situation, a person who is resident in one treaty country and derives foreign income or a capital gain in the other treaty country (source country) might be faced with both countries concurrently imposing tax on that income or capital gain. The third situation is where two countries concurrently subject a person to tax on income or capital gains and the person is not a resident in either country. For example, a taxpayer may be resident in country A and have a permanent establishment in country B which derives income from country C. In this situation, both country B and country C may concurrently treat the income as having a source in their countries and tax the income.

Juridical double taxation in the first two situations is resolved by tax treaties. In the first situation, Article 4 usually defines the term 'resident of a contracting state' to resolve the dual residency through tiebreaker tests which allocate sole residency to one of the treaty countries for the purposes of the treaty. In the second situation, the double taxation is resolved by allocating taxing rights between the source country and residence country. But tax treaties based on the OECD Model or UN Model are unable to apply in the third situation, as the person subject to juridical double taxation is resident in neither of the countries claiming source jurisdiction. A person may only claim the benefits of a tax treaty if the person is resident either in one or both treaty countries; Article 1 of the OECD Model and UN Model limits the operation of a tax treaty to persons who are either resident of one of the treaty countries, or both the treaty countries.

Tax treaties achieve the aim of countering tax avoidance through information exchange measures.[149] Without information exchange measures, international enterprises are able to avoid or evade taxation because tax authorities in the countries in which they operate will often have limited information on their operations.

Under a tax treaty, income is characterized by definition and the treaty then allocates the taxing rights over an item of income between the treaty countries. Tax treaties achieve the aim of preventing double taxation by allocating taxing rights through the use of two separate categories of rules.[150] First, a tax treaty will allocate taxing rights over

---

[147] *Ibid.*, p. 7, para. 1.   [148] *Ibid.*, p. 306, para. 3.
[149] *Ibid.*, Article 26, pp. 397–410.   [150] *Ibid.*, p. 11, para. 19.

certain types of income to the source country and the residence country. For certain types of income the residence country may have an exclusive taxing right which excludes the other country from taxing an item of income or capital gain and thereby avoiding double taxation. In relation to other items of income, the taxing rights are shared by the source country and the residence country. While both the source and residence countries have shared taxing rights, the tax treaty may limit the tax that the source country may impose. For example, the right to tax interest, royalties and dividends is usually shared by both the source country and the residence country. For interest, most treaties limit the source country's taxing right to 10 per cent of gross interest. Second, if a tax treaty allocates taxing rights to the source country, the residence country must provide relief to prevent double taxation.

Under a tax treaty a source country agrees to either relinquish its source country taxing rights or to limit its taxing rights over certain types of income. Treaties do not require a residence country to relinquish their taxing rights, but when a source country has a non-exclusive but unlimited right to tax, a residence country will, in effect, give up its taxing rights if its tax rate is the same or lower than the source country's tax rate. Thus, the taxing rights over income and capital under tax treaties may be divided into three separate categories:

- the source country and residence country share the taxing rights over income and capital, with the source country having unlimited but non-exclusive taxing rights;
- the source country and residence country share the taxing rights over income, with limits on the source country's taxing rights; and
- the residence country is given exclusive taxing rights over income and capital.

Tax treaties use two methods to prevent double taxation in the residence country, either the exemption method or the foreign tax credit method. Treaty countries usually negotiate to select which of these methods is used. Under the exemption method, the residence country exempts from taxation certain items of income derived in the source country. Under the credit method, the residence country determines a resident taxpayer's tax liability on its worldwide income, with the taxpayer receiving a tax credit for tax paid in the source country.[151]

---

[151] See Part 2.2.4.1 for a more detailed discussion of the foreign tax credit method.

3 INTERNATIONAL TAX LAW

Tax treaties usually include a mutual agreement procedure to resolve international tax disputes between the treaty countries. Under the mutual agreement procedure, the competent authorities of the treaty countries are authorized to resolve disputes on the interpretation or application of a tax treaty. A feature of this measure is that the competent authorities have the authority to communicate with each other without using the usual diplomatic channels of communicating between the countries. A taxpayer may make a request to a treaty country that the mutual agreement procedure be used to prevent double taxation. For example, the mutual agreement procedure is often used when a treaty country makes a transfer pricing adjustment to a resident entity and it seeks a consequential adjustment for an associated enterprise in the treaty partner country to prevent economic double taxation.[152] The mutual agreement procedure provision (Article 25) of the OECD Model provides for arbitration of unresolved issues.[153]

3.2.2 Tax treaties and domestic law

Tax treaties are negotiated agreements between countries, which are binding on the treaty countries. Tax treaties modify a country's jurisdiction to tax by allocating taxing rights over taxpayers or items of income between the treaty countries. Tax treaties take effect in the treaty countries and the treaty must prevail over domestic tax law in cases of inconsistency to give effect to allocating tax rights between the treaty countries, otherwise a treaty would be ineffective in altering the tax jurisdiction of the treaty countries. One of the key aims of tax treaties in preventing double taxation is to provide benefits to taxpayers of the treaty countries. The implementation of tax treaties and their status under the domestic law of the treaty countries depends on the constitutional law and the legal system of the contracting countries. International law focuses on the result of implementation but not the method through which implementation of a treaty takes place.[154]

There are two main doctrines on the relationship between international law and municipal law (domestic law), the monist doctrine and the dualist doctrine,[155] but neither doctrine adequately explains the theoretical basis of the relationship between international law and

---

[152] Article 25 of the 2010 OECD Model, pp. 354–96.   [153] *Ibid.*
[154] OECD, *Tax Treaty Overrides* (1989), para. 11.
[155] See Harris and Oliver, *International Commercial Tax* (2010), pp. 20–4.

48 INTERNATIONAL TAXATION: POLICY AND LAW

domestic law.[156] Under dualist theory, international law and domestic law are two separate legal orders. Under dualism, the source of domestic law is the state, but the source of international law is the collective will of individual states.[157] Accordingly, the subjects of domestic law were the natural persons and legal persons, such as companies, within a state, while the subjects of international law were the states themselves. This feature of dualism requires that international law be transformed or incorporated into domestic law, by either statute or common law (judge-made law), before it could affect the rights of natural persons and legal persons.[158] Under dualism, conflict between international law and domestic law was unlikely to arise and, consequently, it was unnecessary for one system to have priority in cases of conflict.[159] This theory relied on the naive belief that the transformation of international law into domestic law was limited to international law that was capable of being adapted without conflicting with domestic law.[160]

The monist doctrine treats international law and domestic law as being part of one system with international law prevailing. Under this theory, domestic law derived its binding force by way of delegation from international law.[161] There were competing interpretations under the monist doctrine on conflict between international law and domestic law. Extreme monists contended that all domestic law conflicted with international law and was void on the basis that domestic law derived its authority by way of delegation from international law.[162] Under moderate monist theory, international law and domestic law are treated as one legal system, with conflicting domestic law being treated as invalid in cases of conflict with international law. Under monist doctrine, a taxpayer may rely on a tax treaty once it is concluded, provided the treaty prevails over domestic law.

The status provided to a country's treaties depends on its constitution, legal systems and the way in which international law is implemented. A country's treaties may be given higher status than domestic law under its constitution, or the country may regard international law as being *lex specialis* giving priority to international law in cases of conflict.[163] But some countries give treaties the same status as domestic law – *lex posterior derogate legi priori* – resulting in conflicts being resolved through the last in time principle with the later law overriding the earlier law.

---

[156] Balkin, 'International Law and Domestic Law' in Blay, et al. (eds.), *Public International Law* (1997) 119–145, p. 119.
[157] *Ibid.* [158] *Ibid.* [159] *Ibid.*, p. 120. [160] *Ibid.*
[161] *Ibid.* [162] *Ibid.* [163] OECD, *Tax Treaty Overrides* (1989), para. 14.

3 INTERNATIONAL TAX LAW

The approach taken in OECD countries varies with France, the Netherlands and the US using the monist doctrine. Under Article 55 of the French Constitution of 1958, treaties that are ratified or accepted are treated from the time of publication as being superior to domestic law.[164] Article 94 of the Netherlands Constitution contains a similar principle. In France and the Netherlands, treaties are also given priority under domestic law in cases of conflict with both prior and posterior law.[165] The US under Article VI(2) of its Constitution gives treaties equal status with domestic law with the later-in-time principle applying in cases of conflict.

The UK and Australia use the dualist doctrine under which treaties become part of domestic law only by either transformation or incorporation into domestic law. The UK treaties are implemented through domestic legislation.[166] Australia enacts its tax treaties into domestic legislation with tax treaties and domestic income tax law being treated as one body of law,[167] with treaties having priority over domestic law in cases of conflict.[168] The Australian general anti-avoidance rule is excepted from the priority rule.[169]

3.2.3 The net benefits for countries under tax treaties

Tax treaty provisions are usually reciprocal and if the trade and investment flows between two countries are similar, the revenue one country loses as a source country it will pick up as a residence country. In this situation, the net benefit of a tax treaty between two developed countries of similar size would be the same for both countries. For example, under the business profits Article of a tax treaty a source country gives up its right to tax business profits sourced within its borders if the business profits are not derived through a permanent establishment in the source country. In this situation, the residence country is given exclusive taxing rights over business profits provided the permanent establishment threshold is not satisfied in the source country.

In theory, while the source country is losing a taxing right over income which is sourced within that country, it gains a reciprocal taxing right

---

[164] *Ibid.*, para. 15.   [165] *Ibid.*

[166] *Ibid.* See also Harris and Oliver, *International Commercial Tax* (2010), p. 21.

[167] Tax treaties are enacted schedules to the International Tax Agreements Act 1953 (Australia). Section 4(1) requires tax treaties and domestic income law to be treated as one body of law.

[168] Section 4(2) of the International Tax Agreements Act 1953 (Australia).

[169] Part IVA of the Income Tax Assessment Act 1936 (Australia).

50   INTERNATIONAL TAXATION: POLICY AND LAW

when its residents derive business profits in its treaty partner country. Although tax treaties are reciprocal, they will be of greater benefit to one country if there are significant differences in the economic power of the treaty countries. If trade and investment flows between treaty partner countries are dissimilar, which is likely to occur in tax treaties between developed and developing countries, the benefits from the operation of the tax treaty will be unequal. Nevertheless, a developing country may regard a tax treaty with a developed country as being important to their trade, investment and development, and may therefore be willing to give up some of its source country taxing rights under the treaty.

In certain cases, such as tax sparing, additional tax concessions may be provided under a tax treaty. Tax sparing is a tax treaty concession in which a non-resident is exempt from taxation in the source country, but is entitled to claim a foreign tax credit in its residence country under a legal fiction that the income was fully subject to tax in the source country. The economic result of tax sparing is to exempt the person from domestic tax on its foreign income derived from the source country under the tax treaty. Tax sparing is usually provided by a developed country to a developing country to encourage investment in the developing country by residents of the developed country. In the absence of tax sparing, developing country tax incentives may be ineffective in encouraging foreign investment if the other treaty country imposes worldwide taxation with foreign tax credit relief from double taxation. The net result of the developing country tax concession would be to increase the revenue of the residence country at the expense of the developing country.

3.3   The UN Model Tax Treaty and the OECD Model Tax Treaty

There are two key international tax treaty models, the *United Nations Model Tax Convention Between Developed and Developing Countries*[170] (UN Model) and the *OECD Model Tax Convention on Income and on Capital* (OECD Model).[171] These models, which are used by countries in negotiating tax treaties, has led to reduced diversity of tax treaties through the use of standard provisions.[172] The OECD has claimed that

---

[170] The latest version of the UN Model was published in 2001. United Nations, *United Nations Model Tax Convention Between Developed and Developing Countries* (2001).

[171] 2010 OECD Model.

[172] See Ross, 'International Tax Law: The Need for Constructive Change' in Stein (ed.) *Tax Policy in the Twenty-First Century* (1988) 87–100, p. 92.

there were close to 350 tax treaties between OECD countries and that by 2008 there were over 3,000 tax treaties worldwide, which are based on the OECD Model.[173] Under both models the basis for allocating profits within an international enterprise is the arm's length principle (also called separate accounting). The arm's length principle is intended to provide an equitable method for attributing the profits to permanent establishments of an international enterprise. Under the arm's length principle, the head office and permanent establishments of an international enterprise are treated as separate entities for the purpose of attributing the profits to the permanent establishments. In the case of an international corporate group, the arm's length principle in the *OECD Transfer Pricing Guidelines for Multinational Enterprises and Tax Administrations*[174] treats each corporation as an arm's length entity and the transfer prices are required to reflect arm's length prices.

The main purpose of the OECD Model is to provide OECD and non-OECD countries alike with a uniform basis for resolving the allocation of taxing rights with other jurisdictions, and to prevent tax avoidance. The emphasis of the OECD Model is residence jurisdiction as OECD countries are developed countries which are net exporters of capital. The current version of OECD Model was adopted in 2010. The UN Model favours the interests of developing countries by having fewer restrictions on source country taxation as developing countries are net importers of capital.[175] While the UN Model is a separate model, nevertheless significant parts of it are based on the OECD Model. The current version of the UN Model was adopted in 2001. Work has commenced on revising the UN Model and a new model is expected to be adopted by the UN in 2011. The UN Model is updated less frequently than the OECD Model. It has been asserted that the influence of the UN has declined in the taxation field because the OECD took over the role of coordinating the tax treaty system from the League of Nations.[176] In recent years, the UN has expanded its work on the UN Model and other international tax issues such as transfer pricing. The UN has a subcommittee on transfer pricing preparing a transfer pricing handbook for developing countries, with initial chapters expected to be adopted by the UN Tax Committee in 2011. Some developed

---

[173] 'OECD Model Tax Convention: Why It Works', *OECD Observer*, No. 260, October 2008.
[174] 2010 Transfer Pricing Guidelines.
[175] United Nations, *United Nations Model Tax Convention Between Developed and Developing Countries* (2001), p. xiv; Surrey, 'United Nations Group of Experts and the Guidelines for Tax Treaties Between Developed and Developing Countries' (1978), p. 10.
[176] See Avery Jones, 'The David R. Tillinghast Lecture' (1999), p. 2.

countries have their own model treaties, which are used as a basis for their negotiations, and these individual models may differ from the OECD Model and UN Model.[177] The US, because of its economic power, has exerted significant influence in the OECD on international tax matters and on the development of the international tax treaty system since World War II.[178] Evidence of this strong influence is the similarity between the revised versions of the US Model and OECD Model.[179]

4 Globalization

In the twentieth century, the process of international economic integration was coined 'globalization', and this integrated world a 'global village'.[180] Activities and transactions take place across national borders, leading to a weakened national sovereignty and the integration of national economies because of the integration of trade, finance and investment in the global market.[181]

4.1 Emergence of globalization

Globalization has been taking place 'intermittently for centuries'[182] and by the beginning of the twentieth century the main developed countries had achieved a high level of economic integration.[183] In the nineteenth century and early twentieth century, businesses derived incomes from business activities carried on in foreign jurisdictions.[184] Nevertheless, the process of global economic integration regressed between World War I and World War II because most developed countries imposed high tariff barriers designed to separate economies for political or economic reasons.[185] Although tariff barriers restricted trade in goods, financial

[177] See Ault, *Comparative Income Taxation* (1997), pp. 476–7.
[178] Bird, *The Taxation of International Income Flows* (1987), p. 7.
[179] Vann, 'A Model Tax Treaty for the Asian-Pacific Region? (Part I)' (1991), p. 102.
[180] 'Global village, a term popularized by M. McLuhan (1911–1980) for the world in the age of high technology and international communications, through which events throughout the world may be experienced simultaneously by everyone, so apparently "shrinking" world societies to the level of a single village or tribe; also in extended use', *Oxford Dictionary* (2nd edn, 1989).
[181] Olson, 'Globalization and the US International Tax Rules' (13 December 2002), para. 6.
[182] United Nations, *Draft Manual for the Negotiation of Bilateral Tax Treaties between Developed and Developing Countries* (2001), p. 4, para. 8.
[183] *Ibid.*   [184] *Ibid.*, p. 5, para. 12.
[185] Also, restrictions were forcefully implemented in the Cold War era by eastern European countries to limit the influence of western European countries and their ideologies.

markets were also restricted through regulation, which restricted the movement of capital, and allowed governments to fix currency exchange rates.

During World War II, the extensive destruction of economic capacity in many countries and the considerable resources directed to the war effort further stifled international trade and investment. Following World War II, pressure to remove trade barriers began to gather force and countries were encouraged to ease the barriers or to remove them completely. Many countries selectively reduced their barriers by entering into bilateral trade agreements to limit the barriers between themselves and a preferred trading partner. This trend was often supplemented with tax treaties. A significant advance in the spirit of cooperation in the process of easing trade barriers was made through the development of the General Agreement on Tariffs and Trade (GATT) in 1947. The GATT contained the rules for the international trade system and it led to the beginning of an unofficial de facto international organization, informally called the GATT.[186] The GATT rules were developed over several years. The last and largest GATT round of discussions was the settlement of the protracted Uruguay Round of the GATT in 1994, which was a significant milestone in the liberalization of world trade in goods and services. The Uruguay Round led to the creation of the World Trade Organization (WTO) in 1995. While the GATT was focused on trade in goods, the WTO and its agreements cover trade in services and trade in intellectual property, such as inventions, creations and designs.[187] In the finance sector, the liberalization process began in the 1970s, with countries allowing markets to set exchange rates and interest rates. By the 1980s, restrictions on cross-border transfers of capital were again reducing, but the remaining restrictions still exceeded those operating in the early part of the twentieth century.

Advances in information and communication technologies have complemented the easing of trade barriers to facilitate globalization with the result that it is now much easier to rapidly move information and funds across national borders. Technological progress has improved the quality and speed of telecommunications, and at the same time telecommunications costs have been declining rapidly. In particular, the advent of the Internet has accelerated this process allowing high quality instant communication. For example, in the banking sector the Internet allows customers to deal both with banks within their country

---

[186] World Trade Organization, *Understanding the WTO* (2010), p. 10.   [187] *Ibid.*

54   INTERNATIONAL TAXATION: POLICY AND LAW

of residence and with international banks located abroad. International credit cards and automatic teller machines allow bank customers to access funds within their country of residence and abroad with ease.

Globalization of the international economy provides the benefits of economic growth for all participating countries.[188] By the end of the twentieth century, the integration of national economies into a global economy had finally exceeded the levels of integration reached before World War I.[189] The operation of international organizations such as the UN, OECD, WTO, International Monetary Fund, World Bank, Asian Development Bank and Asian Development Bank Institute has accelerated the integration process. Countries have become interdependent because of the combined effects of several forces. Rapid advances in information and communication technologies, including the Internet, and the easing of trade barriers and restrictions on the movement of capital, have created the present degree of integration in the world economy.

4.2   Globalization of business, markets, and regulation

The emergence of highly integrated international production systems for goods and services is testing traditional notions and concepts. The classical concept of a company was developed in different conditions, but the concept has evolved, adapting to changes in economic, social and legal conditions.[190] The globalization of enterprises has profound consequences for public policy;[191] significantly, globalization creates pressure for global responses rather than uncoordinated national responses that must address the globalization of business enterprises, markets and regulation.[192]

The globalization of business develops as enterprises, having commenced operations in one jurisdiction, then expand their operations to other jurisdictions. International enterprises are enterprises that operate outside the country in which they are incorporated, through branches or subsidiaries. One reason why enterprises operate in other

---

[188] Trebilcock and Howse, *The Regulation of International Trade* (3rd edn, 2005), pp. xiii–xiiv.

[189] United Nations, *Draft Manual for the Negotiation of Bilateral Tax Treaties between Developed and Developing Countries* (2001), p. 4, para. 8.

[190] United Nations, *World Investment Report 1993: Transnational Corporations and Integrated Production* (1993), p. 181.

[191] *Ibid.*   [192] Braithwaite and Drahos, *Global Business Regulation* (2000), p. 8.

4 GLOBALIZATION   55

countries is to maximize total profit by exploiting their comparative economic advantages in each jurisdiction. The features of international enterprises are:

- highly integrated business operations;
- businesses operated on the basis of central control; and
- the ability to internalize costs and risks.[193]

Transactions between associated enterprises in a multinational enterprise group, or notional intra-enterprise transactions within an international enterprise, have expanded rapidly in recent years and account for a significant proportion of overall international trade.[194]

It is well accepted that some individual international enterprises have achieved levels of economic power that exceed the power of many individual countries.[195] The four largest international companies at 27 February 2009 were Exxon Mobil (US) with a share market valuation of US$335,540 million, PetroChina (China) with a share market value of US$270,560 million, Wal-Mart Stores (US) with a share market valuation of US$193,150 million, and China Mobile (Hong Kong and China) with a share market value of $175,850 million.[196] In 2009, the four most profitable companies were Royal Dutch Shell with an income of US$26,476 million, BP PLC with an income of US$21,666 million, Petroleo Brasileiro (Brazil) US$18,879 million, and Nestle S.A. with an income of US$18,038 million.[197] International banks also comprise a powerful sector and in 2009 the four largest public financial companies were the Royal Bank of Scotland (UK) with assets of US$3,490,800 million, Barclays (UK) with assets of US$2,947,840 million, Deutsche Bank (Germany) with assets of US$2,946,880 million, and BNP Paribas (France) with assets of US$2,888,730 million.[198] These international enterprises have significant economic power and they are able to influence governments and international organizations such as the UN and OECD. The consequence for countries is that although they remain politically sovereign, their economic power, including even that of the US, has been eroded by the economic power of international

---

[193] Li, 'Global Profit Split' (2002), p. 832.
[194] Tanzi, *Taxation in an Integrating World* (1995), p. 2.
[195] Nye, *The Paradox of American Power* (2002), p. 74.
[196] *Hoover's Handbook of World Business* (2009); *Hoover's Handbook of World Business* (2010), '*Forbes*' Largest Public Companies by Market Value', p. 7. The share market value was measured at 27 February 2009.
[197] *Ibid.*, 'The 100 Most Profitable Companies in Hoover's Handbook of World Business', p. 3.
[198] *Ibid.*, 'The World's 100 Largest Public Financial Companies', p. 14.

56   INTERNATIONAL TAXATION: POLICY AND LAW

enterprises.[199] The international economic importance and power of large international enterprises, such as banks and car manufacturers, was underscored in the global financial crisis, which commenced in 2008 when governments in developed countries felt compelled to provide financial support to these enterprises. The governments considered that the threat to their respective economies posed by these enterprises becoming insolvent outweighed the cost of using public funds to support these international enterprises. International enterprises, such as Citigroup,[200] were provided with financial support by the US government.[201]

Markets have been able to globalize through a reduction in market access barriers and significant advances in information and communications technologies.[202] As a result, transactions in some global markets are electronic transactions; for example, in a currency exchange market or a stock exchange, the buyers and sellers merely need a method of electronic communication and payment for transactions. The terms 'electronic commerce'[203] and 'electronic funds transfer' are now part of the lexicon of globalization. Using the Internet, buyers and sellers increasingly come from any country that has the necessary communication capacities and capabilities. In addition, globalization has also resulted in the international spread of some regulation norms,[204] such as international banking prudential standards which are set by the Bank of International Settlements and are enforced by the respective members' central banks.

5 Consequences of globalization for international tax policy

The principles underlying international taxation – residency, source and tax treaties – were developed in the early part of the twentieth century as

---

[199] Nye, *The Paradox of American Power* (2002), p. 74.
[200] Citigroup operates a worldwide banking business. In the US, the Citigroup operates through Citibank, Citi Markets & Banking, The Citi Private Bank, Smith Barney, Primerica, Diners Club, CitiFinancial, CitiMortgage, CitiCapital, and Citi Cards.
[201] The US government provided financial support to Citigroup under a complex support plan that involved US government providing backing to Citigroup for approximately US$306 billion in loans and to invest US$20 billion in Citigroup: Dash, Morgenson and Story, 'US Approves Plan to Let Citigroup Weather Losses'.
[202] Commission of the European Communities, *Company Taxation in the Internal Market*, Report No. SEC(2001)1681 (2001), p. 62.
[203] Defined as a wide array of commercial activities carried on through the use of computers, such as on-line trade, electronic funds transfers, trading of financial instruments: Doernberg and Hinnekins, *Electronic Commerce and International Taxation* (1999), p. 3.
[204] Braithwaite and Drahos, *Global Business Regulation* (2000), p. 8.

5 CONSEQUENCES OF GLOBALIZATION 57

the income tax systems of developed countries were being established.[205] Income taxes in many countries were implemented following the commencement of World War I to fund their war effort. At that time, trade was limited by high tariffs, the movement of goods was restricted, and movements of capital were limited. Consequently, most enterprises operated within the borders of their home economies. In most cases, profits of enterprises could be taxed by national tax authorities without competing claims by tax authorities of other countries.[206] The potential for double taxation in this environment was limited, and international tax considerations were of relatively minor importance. Still, tax treaties were developed in the 1920s and 1930s for the limited situations in which double taxation arose and this development was guided by the League of Nations.

Globalization has significantly altered the international economy and created new challenges for international tax policy. In particular, the OECD claimed that globalization limits the tax policy options available to countries.[207] When countries develop their tax policies they must be aware of the trade-off between raising adequate revenue and not harming their domestic economy by imposing tax rates that exceed those set by other countries in the region.[208] While globalization results in increased international competition between businesses, it may also lead to fiscal competition between states.[209] In 2002, the US Treasury notes the effect of globalization on US tax policy:

> The development of our international tax system began at a time when the global economy was very different from today... The globalization of the US economy puts ever more pressure on our international tax rules. When the rules first were developed, they affected relatively few taxpayers and relatively few transactions. Today, there is hardly a US-based company of any significant size that is not faced with applying the international tax rules to some aspect of its business . . .[210]

The US Treasury concluded that: 'A comprehensive re-examination of the US international tax rules is needed. It is appropriate to question the

---

[205] Tanzi, 'Globalization, Tax Competition and the Future of Tax Systems' (1996), p. 4.

[206] *Ibid.*

[207] Owens, 'Emerging Issues in Tax Reform: The Perspective of an International Bureaucrat' (1997), pp. 2035–6.

[208] See Frenkel, Razin and Sadka (eds.), *International Taxation in an Integrated World* (1991), p. 2.

[209] See Tanzi, *Taxation in an Integrating World* (1995), pp. 6–7.

[210] US Department of the Treasury, *Corporate Inversion Transactions: Tax Policy Implications* (2002), p. 28.

58 INTERNATIONAL TAXATION: POLICY AND LAW

fundamental assumptions underlying the current system.'[211] The US Treasury reiterated the need for reform of US international tax law in response to globalization: 'Viewed from the vantage point of an increasingly global marketplace, our tax rules appear outmoded, at best, and punitive of US economic interests, at worst.'[212]

Under globalization, international enterprises receive advice from international tax and accounting firms, financial services from international banks, and managerial and security advice from international firms.[213] These enterprises operate globally in an integrated and coordinated manner to exploit tax, investment and market opportunities. In comparison, national tax authorities do not operate at the same level. Tax authorities have not globalized to the same extent, they still operate independently, although there is a trend of some tax authorities engaging in international cooperation through tax treaties or international organizations such as the OECD and the UN.[214] The current international tax treaty system is based on national autonomy with limited cooperation between countries,[215] which may lead some countries to wrongly assume that they are competing with other tax authorities for their share of tax from international enterprises.[216] If tax authorities operate solely out of self-interest in seeking to tax international enterprises or associated enterprises in a multinational enterprise group, the gain may be temporary because it may hinder cooperation with other tax authorities. UNCTAD[217] has claimed that all jurisdictions would benefit if tax authorities pooled the information on the costs, prices and profits of international enterprises.[218] This may arise if a country overzealously applies its transfer pricing rules to the detriment of tax treaty partner countries. Consequently, some tax authorities are globalizing. The US Revenue Service Commissioner

---

[211] *Ibid.*, p. 29.

[212] Olson, 'Globalization and the US International Tax Rules' (2002), para. 2.

[213] Avery Jones, 'The David R. Tillinghast Lecture' (1999), p. 1; Williams, *Trends in International Taxation* (1991), pp. 80–1, para. 413.

[214] Avery Jones, *ibid.*, p. 1; see Ernst & Young, 'Tax Administration Goes Global: Complexity, Risks and Opportunities' (2007).

[215] Thuronyi, 'International Tax Cooperation and a Multilateral Treaty' (2001), p. 1646.

[216] United Nations, *World Investment Report 1993: Transnational Corporations and Integrated Production*, Report No. E93.II.A.14 (1993), p. 211.

[217] United Nations Conference on Trade and Development.

[218] United Nations, *World Investment Report 1993: Transnational Corporations and Integrated Production* (1993).

5 CONSEQUENCES OF GLOBALIZATION 59

underscored this trend of tax authorities seeking to improve cooperation to fight tax avoidance:

> Tax administration is being increasingly challenged by globalization, the mobility of capital, the immediacy and fluidity of information and knowledge transfer, and the access individuals and businesses have to sophisticated tax planning and, in some cases, tax avoidance advice and products. These developments pose a direct challenge to national tax administrations that act in isolation. In discussing these developments with FTA [Forum on Tax Administration, OECD] colleagues, I have been struck by FTA members' strong alignment in recognizing the need to address these challenges. There have been a number of steps in the last several years to increase international cooperation and improve our treaty relationships as well as the administration of the provisions of our tax treaties.[219]

The main form of tax coordination between countries is a tax treaty, which is generally effective in eliminating double taxation by allocating taxing rights between treaty countries. The network of tax treaties is supplemented with cooperative developments through the OECD and the UN, in which national tax authorities can discuss issues and develop consistent practices. These forums are significant because although tax treaties have exchange of information mechanisms, there is significant scope for improvement in this area. The OECD has acknowledged this flaw in the tax treaty system, and has responded by promoting the exchange of information between tax authorities as the best way of fighting non-compliance with the tax laws in an increasingly borderless world. The proposed measures include making better use of the bilateral exchange of information provisions in tax treaties with an overriding non-binding multilateral treaty.[220]

A key tax authority cooperation development was the creation in 2002 of the OECD Forum on Tax Administration. The tax authorities of over 34 countries participated in the OECD's 2009 Forum on Tax Administration, which issued the Paris Communiqué on improving tax cooperation between tax authorities:

> We are convinced that the financial and economic crisis offers new opportunities to improve the fairness of tax systems and tax compliance

---

[219] US Internal Revenue Service, 'Everson Chairs International Tax Forum, Emphasizes Enforcement' (1 August 2006).

[220] OECD, *Harmful Tax Competition, An Emerging Global Issue* (1998), Recommendation 8, p. 46. The Multilateral Convention for Mutual Assistance in Tax Matters was developed by the OECD and the Council of Europe.

60   INTERNATIONAL TAXATION: POLICY AND LAW

worldwide. To achieve this we will explore new ways of co-operating with each other. Today, we have committed to further increase our collective actions. These actions will not only contribute to the improvement of revenue yields but also increase fairness. We are also committed to intensify our dialogue with taxpayers and their advisers and are determined to ensure that tax compliance becomes part of the good corporate governance agenda.[221]

A significant exchange of information development was the formation in 2004 of the 'Joint International Tax Shelter Information Centre' (JITSIC) by the tax authorities of Australia, Canada, the US and the UK. The Japanese tax authority has subsequently joined JITSIC. The purpose of JITSIC is to provide assistance on the identification and understanding of tax avoidance schemes and to exchange information on tax avoidance schemes consistent with the provisions of bilateral tax conventions between the JITSIC countries. JITSIC has offices in Washington and London.

All countries tax domestic enterprises and international enterprises,[222] but international enterprises have the capacity to manipulate the tax rules of countries to avoid taxation. Globalization has increased the capacity of international enterprises to avoid taxation by exploiting the differences between tax systems and the tax concessions provided by some countries, which has resulted in some jurisdictions shifting their tax bases away from capital. In 1974, Shoup predicted that, while at that time there was no immediate crisis in the taxation of international enterprises, there was a threat of long-term deterioration of international taxation, which could lead to the erosion of the corporate tax base.[223] He concluded that the net effect of this deterioration would be a shifting of the tax base from capital to labour, and to regressive taxes such as sales tax and value added taxes. Subsequently, other commentators have claimed that as OECD countries have become more open economies, the taxes on capital have been falling while taxes on labour have risen.[224] The OECD revenue statistics support the claim that taxes on corporate income as a percentage of total taxation have fallen in some of the larger OECD countries.

---

[221] OECD, 'Fifth Meeting of the OECD Forum on Tax Administration', p. 2.

[222] Bird asserted that the arguments for taxing corporate profits are impressive and he sets out seven arguments found in the literature: see Bird, 'Why Tax Corporations?' (2002), pp. 198–9.

[223] Shoup (ed.) *Taxation of Multinational Corporations* (1974), p. 35, para. 105.

[224] Avi-Yonah, 'Globalization, Tax Competition, and the Fiscal Crisis of the Welfare State' (2000), p. 1577; McLure, 'International Aspects of Tax Policy for the 21st Century' (1990), pp. 167–70.

5 CONSEQUENCES OF GLOBALIZATION

Among OECD countries, between 1965 and 2008, the level of taxation has risen from 25.5 per cent of GDP in 1965 to 34.8 per cent in 2008 (unweighted averages), or by 9.3 percentage points.[225] The rise was continuous until 2000 when the tax burden fell back.[226] Although the level of taxes has been rising, the OECD claims that the tax mix or tax structures have remained stable during this period, with the main two sources of tax being tax on personal income and corporate income.[227] The level of corporate income tax revenue in OECD countries has increased by a modest margin between 1965 and 2007.[228] Nevertheless, in the US, Japan and Germany the taxation statistics support the claim that taxation of capital is falling, while in other OECD countries the corporate taxes share of total taxation has increased.[229] In the US, corporate taxes as a percentage of total taxation in 1965 were 16.4 per cent and fell to 10.9 per cent in 2007, falling to 7.1 per cent in 2008.[230] In the US during this period, taxes on personal income as a percentage of total taxation rose from 31.7 per cent in 1965 to 38.1 per cent in 2008, after peaking at 41.8 per cent in 2000.[231] In Japan, taxes on corporate income as a percentage of total taxation were 22.2 per cent in 1965, reaching 22.4 per cent in 1990, then falling to 16.8 per cent in 2007 and to 13.7 per cent in 2008.[232] In Japan during this period, taxes on personal income as a percentage of total taxation were 21.7 per cent in 1965, falling to 20.0 per cent in 2008.[233] In Germany, taxes on corporate income as a percentage of total taxation were 7.8 per cent in 1965 and fell to 2.8 per cent in 1995, rising to 6.1 per cent in 2007, then falling to 5.1 per cent in 2008.[234] In Germany during this period, taxes on personal

---

[225] OECD, *Revenue Statistics 1965–2009* (2010), p. 21.   [226] *Ibid.*   [227] *Ibid.*, p. 22.

[228] Taxes on corporate income as a percentage of total taxation in OECD countries have risen since 1965. In 1965, the unweighted average of taxes on corporate income as a percentage of total taxation was 8.8 per cent and went down to 8.0 per cent in 1985, then to 7.9 per cent in 1990 and 7.8 per cent in 1995. But it increased to 9.8 per cent in 2000, 10.2 per cent in 2005, 10.8 per cent in 2007, and 10.1 per cent in 2008. The decrease in 2008 was caused by the economic and financial crisis: *ibid.*, Table 13, p. 85. Between 1965 and 2008, taxes as a percentage of GDP rose in OECD countries. In 1965, the unweighted average tax as a percentage of GDP in OECD countries was 25.5 per cent which rose to 35.4 per cent in 2007, falling back in 2008 to 34.8 per cent: *ibid.*, Table 3, pp. 78–80.

[229] In Australia, the taxes on corporate income as a percentage of total taxation rose from 16.3 per cent in 1965 to 23.1 per cent in 2007 and falling to 21.7 per cent in 2008. The UK also followed this trend; corporate taxes as a percentage of total taxation were 4.4 per cent in 1965, rising to 9.4 per cent in 2007 and 10.0 per cent in 2008: *ibid.*, Table 13, p. 85.

[230] *Ibid.*   [231] *Ibid.*, Table 11, p. 84.   [232] *Ibid.*, Table 13, p. 85.

[233] *Ibid.*, Table 11, p. 84.   [234] *Ibid.*, Table 13, p. 85.

62   INTERNATIONAL TAXATION: POLICY AND LAW

income as a percentage of total taxation were 26.0 per cent in 1965, reaching 30.0 per cent in 1975 and returning to 26.0 per cent in 2008. Consequently, globalization has resulted in the contribution of taxes on corporate income to national revenue falling in several OECD countries.

Globalization has impaired the ability of individual countries to implement policies that vary significantly from those of other countries. The critical corporate tax reform issues are decided by the larger economies, such as the US or the EU, and other states appear to be forced to implement similar corporate tax measures.[235] The reduction in the company tax rate worldwide in the 1990s was an example of countries adjusting their domestic tax policies to conform to international trends.[236] This pressure to conform represents a loss of state sovereignty, and may be viewed as an undesirable consequence of globalization.[237] Yet, the pressures which limit the ability of a government to enforce its jurisdiction and lead to greater international conformity of policy may also result in greater international cooperation.[238] Conversely, if countries operate in a self-interested manner without regard for the consequences for other states, their ability to effectively tax international enterprises will be limited. For countries to be able to tax international enterprises effectively, a considerable degree of international cooperation will be required, and certainly a degree which exceeds the level of cooperation that exists today.

6   The effectiveness of international taxation

The achievements of the OECD, through its coordinating roles and the revisions of the OECD Model and Commentary, the Transfer Pricing Guidelines and information exchange measures, are significant. The OECD Model has been the impetus for relatively consistent tax treaties in OECD countries and non-OECD countries alike. While the OECD Model has guided the expansion of the tax treaty network, the OECD has also been

[235] Bird, 'Why Tax Corporations?' (2002), p. 203.
[236] Vann argues that the power of the US in the international tax field was demonstrated by the reforms made around the world in response to the US's 1986 tax reforms: Vann, 'A Model Tax Treaty for the Asian-Pacific Region? (Part I)' (1991), p. 111.
[237] In the context of the EU, there is debate on the extent to which national sovereignty is lost in specific policy areas. Radaelli's study suggested that for members of the EU some areas of taxation policy may be handed over to the EU: Radaelli, *The Politics of Corporate Taxation in the European Union* (1997), pp. 184–96.
[238] Graetz, 'The David R. Tillinghast Lecture' (2001), p. 279.

6 THE EFFECTIVENESS OF INTERNATIONAL TAXATION 63

able to coordinate the activities of tax authorities. The coherence within the international tax treaty system, based on consensus between countries, is a significant achievement[239] leading some commentators to argue that because of the work of the OECD, tax does not disrupt international trade, and business has a stable framework in which to operate.[240]

Despite the successes of the current international tax treaty system, significant flaws remain and there is considerable scope for improvement.[241] In the context of a globalized international economy, the tax treaty system is challenged in allocating the profits and expenses of branches of highly integrated international enterprises. The tax treaty system is a compromise arrangement that has evolved over time and is the result of the failure of countries to reach a general agreement on principles of international tax law.[242] Tax treaties, in the context of their history and current international tax rules, have been characterized as 'bolt-on' measures in damage limitation,[243] and criticized for not resolving all the problems that arise from the interaction of tax systems in a globalized economy.[244] By contrast, a multilateral tax treaty or regional multilateral tax treaties – sponsored by international organizations such the OECD and UN – would represent a general agreement on principles of international tax law.

The main area of criticism of the tax treaty system is that it has lagged behind the international trade field in developing broadly accepted rules. While multilateral rules and a general multilateral treaty are being progressively developed in international trade, the international tax treaty system still relies on a bilateral model developed by the League of Nations in the 1920s.[245] This lopsided comparative development is curious given that the mutual objective of the tax treaty system and the international trade system is to encourage international commerce for the efficient allocation of economic resources.[246] There are also normative

---

[239] Avi-Yonah, 'The Structure of International Taxation' (1996), p. 1304; Graetz and O'Hear, 'The "Original Intent" of US International Taxation' (1997), p. 1026.

[240] Spence, 'Globalization of Transnational Business' (1997), p. 144.

[241] Avi-Yonah, 'The Structure of International Taxation' (1996), p. 1304; Graetz, 'The David R. Tillinghast Lecture' (2001), p. 316.

[242] Tiley, *Revenue Law* (6th edn, 2008), p. 1233.

[243] Spence, 'Globalization of Transnational Business' (1997), p. 144.

[244] Tiley, *Revenue Law* (6th edn, 2008), pp. 1233–4.

[245] Warren, 'Income Tax Discrimination Against International Commerce' (2001), p. 147; Rigby, 'A Critique of Double Tax Treaties as a Jurisdictional Coordination Mechanism' (1991), pp. 303 and 310; Avery Jones, 'The David R. Tillinghast Lecture' (1999), p. 1.

[246] Rosenbloom notes that both international trade law and international tax law have developed considerable jurisprudence, but that each discipline takes limited notice of the other: Rosenbloom, 'What's Trade Got to Do with It?' (1994), p. 593.

64   INTERNATIONAL TAXATION: POLICY AND LAW

problems with the reliance of the tax treaty system on the arm's length principle because it does not reflect the realities of modern business. Indeed, the question arises as to whether the arm's length concept has ever truly reflected business reality.[247] The practice of treating the permanent establishments of an integrated international enterprise as separate entities for international tax purposes illustrates a fundamental divide between business reality and the theory underlying international tax law. Moreover, treating associated enterprises of a multinational enterprise group as separate enterprises for transfer pricing purposes suffers from the same flaws.

7 Conclusion

The international tax treaty system is a paradox; on the one hand, it has achieved considerable success, but on the other hand, it is not effective in taxing international enterprises. The achievements of the OECD and its predecessors, the League of Nations and the Organisation for European Economic Co-operation, in developing model tax treaties and guiding the development of the treaty network are significant. The tax treaty system is broadly supported by countries, and many modern treaties, apart from minor variations, are based on the OECD Model. But is an expanding network of more than 3,000 tax treaties appropriate for international taxation in a global economy?

The effect of the globalization process on international trade and international taxation has been considerable. There are significant differences between developments in international trade law and international taxation law. International trade has multilateral treaties, initially the GATT which was replaced by the WTO Agreement, and the WTO to administer the system. In contrast, the international taxation system has not developed the same degree of sophistication, and this lack of sophistication has restricted the ability of jurisdictions to effectively tax highly integrated international enterprises.

Tax treaties are a compromise measure for allocating income between jurisdictions, but tax treaties are still based on principles developed in the 1920s which have been eroded by globalization. While they overcome some problems, such as double taxation, they create other problems. The overriding effect of the globalization process to date has been to reveal flaws in the tax treaty system.

---

[247] Graetz, 'The David R. Tillinghast Lecture' (2001), p. 316.

3

Some shortcomings of the tax treaty system

1 Introduction

This chapter surveys two aspects of the current taxation of cross-border transactions: international tax avoidance, and problems in the operation of bilateral tax treaties. The chapter argues that there is a need for international tax reform in response to the globalization of international trade. The chapter focuses first on international tax avoidance, and outlines the ability of international enterprises[1] to avoid taxation through sophisticated tax planning techniques. A major form of international tax avoidance by international enterprises is transfer pricing manipulation by associated enterprises. Transfer pricing anti-avoidance measures, in tax treaties and domestic legislation, are based on the arm's length principle. The chapter considers transfer pricing manipulation and examines the difficulties of applying the arm's length principle to transactions between associated enterprises. While the appeal of the arm's length principle is that it is theoretically straightforward, it has proven very difficult to apply in practice.

The chapter considers some of the problems created by the current international tax measures. The main flaw with these measures is that they do not provide a framework for the coordinated and measured implementation of tax policies and practices developed through the multilateral negotiations of countries. The current international tax treaty system is focused on removing obstacles to international trade and investment by, inter alia, allocating taxing rights between two countries. As the network of tax treaties has expanded, it has proved to be unwieldy and exceptionally difficult to reform. Meanwhile, international enterprises operate integrated global businesses and are able

---

[1] The term 'international enterprise' in this chapter refers to an enterprise operating abroad through permanent establishments and locally incorporated subsidiaries.

66   SOME SHORTCOMINGS OF THE TAX TREATY SYSTEM

to exploit the current tax treaty system to avoid taxation. The chapter concludes with a brief consideration of the obstacles to international tax reform.

2   Tax avoidance

One of the major problems of the current tax treaty system is that globalization has provided international enterprises with significant tax planning and avoidance opportunities. International enterprises have the capacity and incentive to shift profits between jurisdictions to take advantage of the differences between national tax systems, such as company tax rates.[2] The economic incentive for international enterprises to avoid taxation is to maximize their after-tax profits, and they are usually indifferent as to the countries in which tax is paid.[3] International enterprises have an incentive to exploit tax benefits in jurisdictions, such as tax holidays, losses and dividend imputation systems. For example, an international enterprise may have an incentive to pay tax in its home jurisdiction if the home jurisdiction has a dividend imputation system.[4] This situation will arise if the majority of a corporation's shareholders reside in the corporation's home jurisdiction, and that jurisdiction's dividend imputation system provides tax credits to shareholders for tax paid by the corporation in that jurisdiction. If a corporation's shareholders demand dividends with maximum tax credits, there is an incentive to pay full company tax in the home jurisdiction. On the other hand, international enterprises resident in a country with a dividend imputation system will usually have an incentive to minimize their tax burdens in the source countries in which they operate because taxes paid outside their home jurisdictions usually cannot be applied for imputation purposes. The incentive to avoid taxation is also influenced by cultural, ethical and commercial issues.[5] Therefore, even though international enterprises have the capacity and

---

[2] US General Accounting Office, *IRS Could Better Protect US Tax Interests in Determining the Income of Multinational Corporations* (1981), Digest, p. i.

[3] See Vann, 'International Aspects of Income Tax' in Thuronyi (ed.) *Tax Law Design and Drafting* (1998) 718–810, pp. 779–80; Tanzi, 'The Impact of Economic Globalisation on Taxation' (1998), p. 340.

[4] Australia and New Zealand have imputation systems for corporate taxation.

[5] See Vann, 'International Aspects of Income Tax' in Thuronyi (ed.) *Tax Law Design and Drafting* (1998) 718–810, pp. 779–80.

2 TAX AVOIDANCE 67

incentive to avoid taxation, this does not automatically result in tax avoidance, but it is a revenue risk for countries.[6]

International enterprises may use tax planning to exploit the gaps and inconsistencies in the network of tax treaties and domestic tax laws. While some international enterprises may engage in tax avoidance they are unlikely to engage in evasion.[7] Nevertheless, international tax avoidance has been a persistent problem and it is likely to continue. In 1988, Arnold asserted that there had not been any multilateral responses to international tax avoidance and predicted that this may change over the next twenty-five years, but to date, this prediction seems optimistic.[8] Tanzi refers to 'fiscal termites' in asserting that international tax avoidance practices are undermining the foundations of the tax treaty system.[9] He describes the forces on the tax treaty system arising from globalization with compelling imagery:

> Like tectonic plates grinding against each other, the tax systems of different countries will develop arbitrage pressures created by different tax rates, by differences in the bases that are taxed, by different possibilities of avoidance and evasion, and so forth. These pressures will be strong in some areas and less strong in some others and will become more intense as the process of world integration proceeds. These pressures will be exploited by private economic operators to improve their economic welfare thus affecting tax revenue, economic efficiency, and the equity of the tax system. In some cases, they may also be exploited by some governments to gain tax revenue or other advantages at the expense of other governments.[10]

In a global economy capital is highly mobile and tax competition between jurisdictions for capital has inadvertently supported international tax avoidance.[11] Consequently, the more mobile an item of production is, the harder it is for a government to effectively tax that item.[12] As the OECD pointed out in 1991:

---

[6] US General Accounting Office, *IRS Could Better Protect US Tax Interests in Determining the Income of Multinational Corporations*, Report No. GGD-81-81 (1981), Digest, p. i.

[7] See Vann, 'International Aspects of Income Tax' in Thuronyi (ed.) *Tax Law Design and Drafting* (1998) 718–810, p. 780.

[8] Arnold, 'Future Directions in International Tax Reform' (1988), p. 468.

[9] Tanzi, 'The Nature and Effects of Globalization on International Tax Policy, Technological Developments, and the Work of Fiscal Termites' (2001), pp. 1261–5.

[10] Tanzi, *Taxation in an Integrating World* (1995), p. 6.

[11] See Thuronyi, 'International Tax Cooperation and a Multilateral Treaty' (2001), pp. 1646–7; Avi-Yonah, 'Globalization, Tax Competition, and the Fiscal Crisis of the Welfare State' (2000), p. 1675.

[12] Bird and Mintz, 'Introduction' in Bird and Mintz (eds.), *Taxation to 2000 and Beyond* (1992) 1–28, p. 8; Brean, 'Here or There?' in Bird and Mintz, *ibid.*, 303–33, p. 310.

68   SOME SHORTCOMINGS OF THE TAX TREATY SYSTEM

> Capital markets in OECD countries are increasingly integrated as Member countries have removed controls on international investment and foreign exchange regulations. At the same time, the proportion of international activities accounted for by large multinational enterprises has increased. One consequence of this gradual liberalisation and globalisation is that international capital flows may have become more sensitive to differences in the tax regimes between countries. Differences in the taxation of corporate profits may now be one of the few remaining political barriers to a better international allocation of capital.[13]

Hines contended that qualitative economic analysis supports the view that a jurisdiction's tax policies have significant influence on the activities of international enterprises.[14] The economic evidence indicates that a jurisdiction's tax policies have significant influence on foreign direct investment, corporate borrowing, transfer pricing, dividend payments and royalty payments.[15] Guttentag found that when he was a practitioner his clients were not interested in his advice on how to prevent double taxation – their sole focus was to avoid taxation.[16] In 2008, the US Government Accountability Office (GAO) concluded in a report that the location of the income of US multinational enterprise groups is influenced by the tax rates of the countries. The GAO found that:

> Reporting of the geographic sources of income is susceptible to manipulation for tax planning purposes and appears to be influenced by differences in tax rates across countries. Most of the countries studied with relatively low effective tax rates have income shares significantly larger than their shares of the business measures least likely to be affected by income shifting practices: physical assets, compensation, and employment. The opposite relationship holds for most of the high tax countries studied.[17]

---

[13] OECD, *Taxing Profits in a Global Economy, Domestic and International Issues* (1991), p. 12.

[14] Hines (ed.) *International Taxation and Multinational Activity* (2001), p. 1.   [15] *Ibid.*

[16] Mr Guttentag was a senior tax partner in the law firm of Arnold and Porter in Washington DC and Japan. He was also a former Deputy Assistant Secretary for International Tax Affairs, US Department of Treasury, and a former Chairman of the Committee on Fiscal Affairs of the OECD. Guttentag, 'Key Issues and Options in International Taxation' (2001), p. 550. See also Thuronyi, 'International Tax Cooperation and a Multilateral Treaty' (2001), p. 1647.

[17] US Government Accountability Office, *US Multinational Corporations: Effective Tax Rates Are Correlated with Where Income Is Reported* (2008).

2 TAX AVOIDANCE 69

2.1 Tax avoidance by international banks

A study of the taxation of international banks for 80 countries between 1988 and 1995 found empirical evidence that international banks engage in extensive profit shifting.[18] The research was based on comprehensive data covering 90 per cent of bank assets in most countries.[19] The study suggested that international banks have more opportunity than other international enterprises to avoid tax in high tax countries through transfer pricing manipulation.[20] International banks were found by the study to be able to shift profits in order to pay a lower amount of tax in several countries including the US.[21] The relatively light taxation of international banks might have resulted from jurisdictions seeking to retain or attract mobile international banks by providing them with tax concessions.[22] Moreover, measures to counter profit shifting by international banks, such as those in the US, were found by the study to be ineffective in preventing tax avoidance by international banks. The study concluded that while there is tax competition in the international banking sector in developed countries, countries are likely to gain from collective measures to improve the taxation of international banks.

2.2 Revenue consequences of tax avoidance

Tax avoidance by international enterprises makes it more difficult for countries to raise revenue from this sector of their economies. Although tax revenue in many countries is at historically high levels, it was claimed in 2001 that tax revenue in the 1990s had stopped growing in most countries and in some had started to decline.[23] The OECD claimed in 2010, that in the mid 1990s the tax component (called the average (unweighted) tax take) of gross domestic product (GDP) in OECD countries had stabilized, indicating that unweighted average tax level was peaking.[24] In 1995, taxes on income and profits as a percentage of GDP had reached at 11.9 per cent.[25] But, between 1995 and 2000, the OECD found that the tax-to-GDP ratio rose again, reaching 12.7 per cent of GDP in 2000. The statistics for 2002 to 2009 indicate that the average unweighted tax level in the OECD as a whole is

---

[18] Demirguc-Kunt and Huizinga, 'The Taxation of Domestic and Foreign Banking' (2001).
[19] *Ibid.*, p. 434.   [20] *Ibid.*, p. 430.   [21] *Ibid.*, p. 449.   [22] *Ibid.*
[23] Tanzi, 'The Nature and Effects of Globalization on International Tax Policy, Technological Developments, and the Work of Fiscal Termites' (2001), pp. 1261–3.
[24] OECD, *Revenue Statistics 1965–2009* (2010), p. 21.
[25] *Ibid.*, Table B, 'Taxes on income and profits as a percentage of GDP', p. 20.

70   SOME SHORTCOMINGS OF THE TAX TREATY SYSTEM

not rising and declined in 2008 and 2009.[26] Nevertheless, the OECD makes the qualification that OECD averages hide the different national tax levels.[27] Tax competition may impose 'market-induced limitations'[28] on a country's tax structure resulting in its tax base being shifted from capital to immobile factors of production, such as labour and land.[29] In 2000, it was predicted that the company income tax base will disappear within two decades because of tax competition, the failure to define company income properly, and the aim of governments to remove inefficient taxes on the global operations of international enterprises.[30] Therefore, in the absence of a coordinated response, the international tax base may shrink and force governments to rely on indirect taxes on immobile factors of production, which are easier to collect.[31]

3   Transfer pricing

Transfer pricing is the price at which a multinational enterprise group's[32] intra-group transactions take place and is a normal activity.[33] According to the OECD: 'Transfer prices are the prices at which an enterprise transfers physical goods and intangible property or provides services to associated enterprises.'[34] Associated enterprises are enterprises that satisfy the conditions in Article 9(1)(a) and (b) of the OECD Model. Under these tests, two enterprises are treated as being associated if one enterprise participates in the management, control or capital of the other enterprise (parent and subsidiary companies); or if the same persons participate in the management, control or capital of both enterprises (sister companies).[35] Transfer pricing has attracted the connotation of tax avoidance, but transfer pricing at large needs to be distinguished from transfer pricing manipulation.[36]

---

[26] *Ibid.*, p. 21.   [27] *Ibid.*, p. 22.

[28] McLure, 'Globalization, Tax Rules and National Sovereignty' (2001), p. 330.

[29] *Ibid.*, pp. 329–30; Stein (ed.) *Tax Policy in the Twenty-First Century* (1988); Tanzi, 'Forces That Shape Tax Policy' in Stein, *ibid.*, p. 277; Avi-Yonah, 'Globalization, Tax Competition, and the Fiscal Crisis of the Welfare State' (2000), p. 1576.

[30] Mintz and Chen, 'Will Corporate Income Tax Wither?' (2000), p. 45:11.

[31] *Ibid.* 45:1–16, p. 45:13; Guttentag, 'Key Issues and Options in International Taxation' (2001), p. 548.

[32] The term 'multinational enterprise group' refers to an enterprise operating abroad through locally incorporated subsidiaries.

[33] Eden, *Taxing Multinationals* (1998), p. 20.

[34] 2010 Transfer Pricing Guidelines, p. 19, para. 11.   [35] *Ibid.*

[36] Eden, *Taxing Multinationals* (1998), p. 20.

3 TRANSFER PRICING 71

Transfer pricing manipulation is the intentional setting of a transfer price for a transaction by one entity with an associated entity in another jurisdiction, for the purpose of reducing the aggregate tax burden of the multinational enterprise group.[37] Transfer pricing manipulation is a significant avoidance technique available to international enterprises and is consequently one of the major tax issues.[38] In 2008, the US Department of Treasury published a working paper on income shifting from transfer pricing which concluded that the empirical analysis generally supports concerns about transfer pricing manipulation by multinational enterprise groups to shift income under the current US transfer pricing rules.[39] The paper was based on theoretical and regression models and emphasized that some caution is required in interpreting the transfer pricing implications from the regression results. The scope for transfer pricing manipulation is significant because of the rapid increase in trade between associated enterprises of a multinational group (intra-group or intra-firm trade). Trade between associated international corporations reached 25 per cent of world trade in the 1980s[40] and it has continued to expand. The OECD noted in 2002 that while there is anecdotal material on this trend, there is a dearth of data on the growth of intra-firm trade.[41]

In 2005, the OECD claimed that the ratio of intra-firm trade to the total trade of countries publishing this data is 'quite high'.[42] Aggregate intra-firm trade data was only available for a few countries, including the US and Japan. In 1999, intra-firm trade comprised one third of goods exported from the US, and a third of US imports of goods and a quarter of Japanese imports of goods.[43] The United Nations Conference on Trade and Development (UNCTAD) estimated in 2009 that exports by associated enterprises account for one third of total world exports of

---

[37] *Ibid.*, pp. 20–1.

[38] Tanzi, 'The Nature and Effects of Globalization on International Tax Policy, Technological Developments, and the Work of Fiscal Termites' (2001), p. 1269; Avi-Yonah, 'The Rise and Fall of Arm's Length' (1995), p. 90.

[39] US Department of Treasury (Office of Tax Analysis), *Income Shifting from Transfer Pricing* (2008); see also US Department of the Treasury, *Report to Congress on Earning Stripping, Transfer Pricing and US Income Tax Treaties* (2007), p. 70.

[40] US General Accounting Office, *International Taxation: Problems Persist in Determining Tax Effects of Intercompany Prices* (1992), pp. 62–3.

[41] OECD, *OECD Economic Outlook*, Report No. 71 (2002), p. 70 and Table VI.2, p. 71.

[42] OECD, *Measuring Globalisation* (2005), p. 182.

[43] OECD, *OECD Economic Outlook*, Report No. 71 (2002), p. 163 and Table VI.1, p. 164.

72   SOME SHORTCOMINGS OF THE TAX TREATY SYSTEM

goods and services.[44] Between 2006 and 2009, the largest non-financial international enterprises, on average, accounted for 9 per cent of foreign asset sales, 16 per cent of sales and 11 per cent of employment for all international enterprises.[45] During the last fifteen years, the internationalization trend of the largest international enterprises has continued, with an increase in the proportion of these enterprises operating in the services sector.[46]

The OECD claimed that the increasing importance of foreign direct investment, in relation to world trade and production, is likely to continue, resulting in increased intra-firm trade.[47] Foreign direct investment peaked in 2007, after four years of consecutive growth, surpassing the previous peak of 2000.[48] In 2009, UNCTAD reported that global foreign direct investment was reduced by the global economic and financial crisis, falling from a historic high of US$1,979 billion in 2007 to US$1,697 billion in 2008, a decline of 14 per cent.[49] In 2009, there were approximately 82,000 international enterprises with 810,000 foreign affiliates (associated enterprises).[50] UNCTAD noted the high concentration levels in international enterprises, with the largest 100 international enterprises making a major contribution to the total international production in both developed and developing countries.[51]

Measures to counter transfer pricing manipulation consist of domestic transfer pricing rules and the associated enterprises Article in tax treaties. Transfer pricing measures are specific anti-avoidance rules. Transfer pricing rules prescribe that a price for a transaction between associated entities, or a notional transaction between a head office and a branch of an international enterprise, must be comparable to prices for similar transactions between independent entities, in accordance with the arm's length principle. If this requirement is not satisfied, a tax authority may make a transfer pricing adjustment. Under the arm's

---

[44] UNCTAD, *World Investment Report: Transnational Corporations, Agricultural Production and Development* (2009), p. 17.

[45] *Ibid.*

[46] *Ibid.* UNCTAD bases internationalization on its transnationality index, which is a composite of three ratios: foreign assets to total assets; foreign sales to total sales; foreign employment to total employment.

[47] OECD, *OECD Economic Outlook*, Report No. 71 (2002), p. 163.

[48] UNCTAD, *World Investment Report: Transnational Corporations, and the Infrastructure Challenge* (2008), p. 3.

[49] UNCTAD, *World Investment Report: Transnational Corporations, Agricultural Production and Development* (2009), p. xix.

[50] *Ibid.*, p. xx.   [51] *Ibid.*, p. 17.

length principle, the norm of the market-place is imposed on intra-enterprise or intra-group transactions.[52] But, the determination of arm's length transfer prices is not an exact method and a tax authority must use judgement in settling on an arm's length price from within a range of prices. Because of the growth in intra-firm trade, the arm's length principle is estimated to apply to significant proportions of cross-border trade.

Tax treaties based on the OECD and UN models are premised on the arm's length principle because Articles 7 and 9 of these models, respectively, treat each of the head office and permanent establishments (such as branches) of an international enterprise, and associated enterprises, as separate enterprises operating at arm's length. Under the arm's length principle the transfer prices for notional intra-entity transactions between the head office and a branch of an international enterprise, and transactions between associated enterprises, must reflect the prices that independent entities would have used for similar transactions. The OECD has paid significant attention to transfer pricing, centred on the arm's length principle, and in 1995 it published the Transfer Pricing Guidelines,[53] with the latest condensed edition being published in 2010.[54]

3.1 Arguments for using the arm's length principle

Under the arm's length principle, where an international entity operates abroad through permanent establishments, each permanent establishment is treated as a separate entity dealing at arm's length with the rest of the enterprise. Similarly, under the arm's length principle the associated entities in a multinational enterprise group are treated as separate entities dealing at arm's length with each other. Several rationales have been advanced as the basis for the use of the arm's length principle for transfer pricing. In an open market, companies considering a potential transaction are assumed to act rationally, and to evaluate alternative transactions to determine which is the most profitable type of transaction.[55] The aim of the arm's length principle is to emulate a market pricing system, which economists claim usually results in income being allocated to reflect the

---

[52] See Surrey, 'Reflections on the Allocation of Income and Expenses Among National Tax Jurisdictions' (1978), p. 414.

[53] 1995 Transfer Pricing Guidelines (loose-leaf).   [54] 2010 Transfer Pricing Guidelines.

[55] See Weiner, *Using the Experience in the US States to Evaluate Issues in Implementing Formula Apportionment at the International Level* (1999), pp. 2–3.

74 SOME SHORTCOMINGS OF THE TAX TREATY SYSTEM

economic contributions and competitive positions of the market partici-pants.[56] Under the arm's length principle, intra-entity or intra-group transactions are compared to transactions between unrelated entities to determine acceptable transfer prices. Thus, the market-place comprising independent entities is accepted as the mechanism for verifying whether transfer prices for intra-entity or intra-group transactions are acceptable for tax purposes.[57]

The rationale for the arm's length principle itself is that because the market governs most of the transactions in an economy, it is appropriate to treat intra-entity or intra-group transactions as equivalent to those between independent entities. Under the arm's length principle, the allocation of profit and expenses under intra-entity and intra-group transactions is tested and adjusted, if the transfer prices for the transactions deviate from the transfer prices for comparable arm's length transactions. The arm's length principle is argued to be acceptable to taxpayers and tax authorities because it uses the market-place as the norm, rather than allocating profits on the basis of a formula.[58] The US first incorporated the arm's length principle into its domestic tax law in 1936,[59] and promotes it as the accepted international norm. This view is not universal, however, with some describing the arm's length principle as having the status of customary international law,[60] and others claiming that it is not an international norm.[61]

A further argument in favour of using the arm's length principle is that it is geographically neutral because it treats profits from investments both in a residence jurisdiction and a source jurisdiction in the same manner.[62] But this claim of neutrality is conditional on consistent transfer pricing rules and consistent application of the arm's length principle, on which these rules are based, in the jurisdictions in which an international enterprise operates. In the absence of such consistency, international enterprises may be provided with an incentive to avoid taxation through transfer pricing manipulation or be subject to double taxation. The key argument in support of the arm's length principle is

---

[56] US Department of Treasury (Office of Tax Analysis), *Income Shifting from Transfer Pricing* (2008), p. 4.

[57] See Surrey, 'Reflections on the Allocation of Income and Expenses Among National Tax Jurisdictions' (1978), p. 414.

[58] US General Accounting Office, *International Taxation* (1992), p. 59.   [59] *Ibid.*

[60] See Thomas, 'Customary International Law and State Taxation of Corporate Income' (1996).

[61] See Langbein, 'The Unitary Method and the Myth of Arm's Length' (1986).

[62] *Ibid.*

3 TRANSFER PRICING   75

that if it is used by most jurisdictions, the risk of double taxation will be minimal.[63] Double taxation may still occur despite the use of the arm's length principle if one treaty country adjusts an associated enterprise's transfer prices but the other treaty country does not accept the adjusted transfer prices and refuses to make a corresponding adjustment to the associated enterprise resident in that country. The country being asked to make a corresponding adjustment may disagree on the transfer pricing method used, or the transfer prices selected, by the country which made the initial adjustment. There is a significant difference between describing the arm's length principle and establishing guidelines on the practical application of the principle.[64]

3.2 Problems with applying the arm's length principle to international enterprises

Several problems arise when applying the arm's length principle used in the Transfer Pricing Guidelines to the domestic laws of jurisdictions. The high level of integration of international enterprises, the intra-entity intangibles and services, and the use of sophisticated financing arrangements have eroded the normative basis for the arm's length principle, and made it more difficult to apply.[65] Thus, it is argued that the arm's length principle is flawed, and inadequate as a basis for allocating the profits of international enterprises. Prior to the globalization of the past fifty-five years, the arm's length principle may have been an appropriate method for allocating profits and expenses within an international enterprise when international trade was based on transactions involving tangible items.[66] When geographic and economic isolation prevailed, permanent establishments, such as branches, of an international enterprise and subsidiaries in a multinational enterprise group were autonomous, and consequently it may have been appropriate to treat branches and subsidiaries as separate enterprises. Moreover, there may have been generally comparable transactions between independent enterprises from which to derive comparative prices.

---

[63] US General Accounting Office, *International Taxation* (1992), p. 60.

[64] See Surrey, 'Reflections on the Allocation of Income and Expenses Among National Tax Jurisdictions' (1978), p. 419.

[65] See Vann, 'International Aspects of Income Tax' in Thuronyi (ed.) *Tax Law Design and Drafting* (1998) 718–810, p. 783.

[66] See Vann, 'A Model Tax Treaty for the Asian-Pacific Region? (Part I)' (1991), p. 105.

76 SOME SHORTCOMINGS OF THE TAX TREATY SYSTEM

But increasing globalization, sophisticated communication systems and advanced high speed information technologies allow an international enterprise to control the operations of its foreign branches, or a multinational enterprise group to control its subsidiaries from one or two locations worldwide. Trade between associated enterprises often involves intangible items as structural change in developed countries has resulted in significant growth in their service sectors. The nature of international trade on which the tax treaty system's principles are based has changed significantly,[67] which raises the issue of whether we should continue to apply the arm's length concept to globalized and integrated international enterprises and multinational enterprise groups. One of the foundations of the arm's length principle, comparative pricing, is rarely available, thus weakening the continued validity of the application of the principle and it is questionable whether significant resources should continue to be devoted to the administration of transfer pricing rules.[68] Therefore, the arm's length principle has significant limitations as a method for allocating the income of highly integrated international enterprises and multinational enterprise groups.

3.2.1 Administrative burden

Transfer pricing audits by tax authorities must be done on a case-by-case basis and are often complex and costly tasks for both tax authorities and the taxpayers, especially given the large volume of transactions that may potentially be examined.[69] The lack of comparable prices results in complexity because of the need for tax authorities to examine the facts and circumstances of each case to determine what they consider to be acceptable transfer prices.[70] Consequently, it is beyond the capacity of tax authorities to examine more than a limited number of transactions. Furthermore, it is likely to be impossible to find comparable transfer prices for highly integrated enterprises because of economies of scale and shared expenses.[71] Even if comparable transfer prices exist, the administrative burden on tax authorities in monitoring transfer prices to ensure compliance with transfer pricing rules is costly.[72]

---

[67] See Kingston, 'The David Tillinghast Lecture' (1998), p. 642.

[68] See Hamaekers, 'Arm's Length – How Long?' in Kirchhof, et al. (eds.), *International and Comparative Taxation* (2002) 29–52, p. 51.

[69] US General Accounting Office, *International Taxation* (1992), p. 60.   [70] *Ibid.*

[71] See McLure and Weiner, 'Deciding Whether the European Union Should Adopt Formula Apportionment of Company Income' in Cnossen (ed.) *Taxing Capital Income in the European Union* (2000) 243–92, p. 248.

[72] See *ibid.*, pp. 248–9.

3 TRANSFER PRICING

3.2.2   Intangible assets

Intangible assets may be divided into commercial intangibles, such as patents, copyright, licences and technical data, and marketing intangibles such as trademarks and branch names.[73] Enterprises owning unique intangible assets have a competitive advantage that allows them to make monopoly profits.[74] Determining the income from intangible assets is a major challenge under the arm's length principle, as intangible assets usually involve unique property, and, consequently, comparable prices will usually be unavailable.[75] Consequently, there is significant scope for transfer pricing disputes between international enterprises, or multinational enterprise groups, and tax authorities over intangible property.

In 2006, the largest US tax settlement was the transfer pricing settlement which centred on marketing intangibles created by GlaxoSmithKline (GSK US). GSK US settled its US transfer pricing dispute with the US Internal Revenue Service (IRS) for US$3.4 billion for the 1989 to 2005 tax years.[76] The dispute concerned the claim by the IRS that the transfer prices paid by GSK US to its UK parent, GlaxoSmithKline PLC (GSK UK), for pharmaceutical products were excessive. The transfer pricing dispute centred on a highly successful drug, Zantac, which treats peptic acid disease. The publicly available information on the GSK and IRS case is limited as the case was settled, nevertheless the following unsubstantiated comments have been published by commentators. It has been claimed that the IRS and GSK US failed to agree on the key facts in the case. In addition, it was claimed that GSK US asserted that it was a mere distributor for its group; and that the IRS argued that GSK was a fully integrated pharmaceutical company with operations which included research and development, manufacture and marketing of highly profitable drugs.[77] In addition, it was claimed the IRS claimed that as GSK US contributed to the trademarks and trade names of the GSK products it marketed in the US, it was the owner of these items of the marketing

---

[73] 2010 Transfer Pricing Guidelines, p. 192, para. 6.3.

[74] US General Accounting Office, *IRS Could Better Protect US Tax Interests in Determining the Income of Multinational Corporations* (1981), p. 33.

[75] US General Accounting Office, *International Taxation* (1992), p. 64; US Department of Treasury (Office of Tax Analysis), *Income Shifting from Transfer Pricing: Further Evidence from Tax Return Data* (2008), pp. 5–8.

[76] US Internal Revenue Service, 'IRS Accepts Settlement Offer in Largest Transfer Pricing Dispute' (11 September 2006).

[77] Ernst & Young, 'Global Transfer Pricing Update' (2006), p. 941.

78   SOME SHORTCOMINGS OF THE TAX TREATY SYSTEM

intangibles for the period 1989 to 2000.[78] Under the US transfer pricing rules at the time, it was claimed that GSK US may also have been treated as the owner of the underlying intellectual property for these pharmaceutical products, under the former 'developer-assister' rule.[79] GSK was confident of the strength of its arguments, but because of the size of the financial exposure and the resources being used in the case, it decided to settle the case to eliminate the cost and uncertainty of future transfer pricing litigation.[80] In 1999, GSK initiated the mutual agreement procedure under the UK–US tax treaty, but in 2004 the competent authorities were unable to reach agreement to settle the long-running dispute, after the then UK Inland Revenue supported GSK US's claim that no additional tax be paid to the IRS.[81] Under 'FIN 48',[82] GSK US would have been required to calculate and disclose reserves in its financial statements issued under US Generally Accepted Accounting Standards for the transfer pricing dispute. This may have influenced GSK to settle the dispute even though it was confident of its arguments.

3.2.3   Uncertainty

The lack of comparable arm's length prices creates uncertainty for multinational enterprise groups and international enterprises because they are potentially vulnerable to having their transfer prices adjusted by tax authorities.[83] Given the large volume of transactions entered into by international enterprises, such as international banks, even minor adjustments of transfer prices by tax authorities may result in large increases in their tax liabilities. These practical deficiencies in the arm's length principle have resulted in expensive litigation in which courts are required to determine if transfer pricing adjustments by tax authorities are justified.[84]

---

[78] Murray and Wilkie, 'GlaxoSmithKline Settles US Transfer Pricing Dispute for $3.4 Billion: What Lessons Can Be Learned?' (2007), p. 28.

[79] *Ibid.*

[80] GlaxoSmithKline (US), 'GSK Settles Transfer Pricing Dispute with IRS' (11 September 2006).

[81] Ernst & Young, 'Global Transfer Pricing Update' (2006), p. 941.

[82] The US Financial Accounting Standards Board issued interpretation 48 of the Financial Accounting Standard 109, 'Accounting for Uncertainty in Income Taxes', which is called FIN 48. FIN 48 requires companies subject to US Generally Accepted Accounting Principles to account for uncertain tax positions in their financial statements. FIN 48 applies to financial statements for fiscal years commencing after 15 December 2006.

[83] US General Accounting Office, *International Taxation: Problems Persist in Determining Tax Effects of Intercompany Prices* (1992), p. 61.

[84] *Ibid.*, pp. 47–8.

3.2.4 The arm's length principle does not reflect business reality

The arm's length principle results in uncertainty and administrative burdens because it does not reflect economic reality.[85] Associated companies in a multinational enterprise group do not treat each other as separate entities and do not use arm's length prices for their transfers in the absence of transfer pricing rules, but rather operate as a unitary and integrated business. Similarly, permanent establishments of an international enterprise do not treat each other as separate enterprises and are even more likely to operate as a unitary and integrated business because they are part of the same entity. The profits from notional transactions within an integrated international enterprise are so different from profits from actual transactions between independent entities that the arm's length principle provides no guidance in setting transfer prices.[86]

Hellerstein vividly characterizes this flaw in the arm's length principle by reflecting on *Alice in Wonderland*; the arm's length principle 'turns reality into fancy and then pretends it is in the real world'.[87] The arm's length principle ignores the interdependence and integration of a unitary international enterprise by treating it as a separate and independent entity. The arm's length principle ignores the integrated operations conducted by international enterprises, such as international banks, because it relies on comparative transactions between independent entities that have not integrated their operations.[88] This approach disregards the economic benefits that integrated international enterprises get from horizontal integration.[89]

In the case of international enterprises, their size and centralized control provide them with efficiencies and cost savings from their intra-entity, or intra-group transactions, which are unavailable to independent enterprises entering similar transactions. Moreover, international enterprises are likely to be more efficient than separate enterprises in raising equity capital, obtaining loans, obtaining discounts, advertising, and cost saving through economies of scale.[90] The defect in the arm's length principle is that it ignores the benefits of

---

[85] *Ibid.*, p. 61.   [86] *Ibid.*
[87] Hellerstein, 'Federal Income Taxation of Multinationals' (1993), p. 1136.
[88] See Newlon, 'Transfer Pricing and Income Shifting in Integrated Economies' in Cnossen (ed.) *Taxing Capital Income in the European Union* (2000) 214–42, p. 216.
[89] See Weissman, 'Unitary Taxation' (1983), pp. 50–6.
[90] US General Accounting Office, *International Taxation* (1992), p. 61.

80 SOME SHORTCOMINGS OF THE TAX TREATY SYSTEM

reduced costs and protected profits from intra-entity or intra-group transactions in integrated businesses. Moreover, the reduced costs and protected profits should be attributed to an entire enterprise, or entire group, and transfer pricing should not be used to allocate these advantages to separate parts of the enterprise or group.[91] Thus, transfer prices for an international enterprise operating through branches that incorporate these benefits of operating as a large and integrated business will not be the same as prices used by independent entities entering similar transactions.[92] An examination of the economic theory of the firm and the reasons for the existence of multinational enterprise groups and international enterprises illustrates the conflict between the arm's length principle and economic reality.

3.2.5 Theory of the firm and the reasons for the existence of international enterprises

Economists have developed a theory to explain the operation of firms, such as corporations, in an economy. In economic theory, firms are organizations that organize the production of goods and services.[93] In the absence of firms, production could be carried out through a series of arm's length transactions between individuals.[94] These transactions would require contracts between the independent producers, and the allocation of resources under such a system would reflect prices, but a significant part of these resources would be used in the process of making contracts.[95] The expenses of making contracts are called transaction costs, as resources are used in finding other persons with whom to contract, negotiating the contracts and having contracts finalized.[96] As transaction costs would be significant in an economy without firms, it is rational economic behaviour for individuals to create firms to organize these transactions provided the firms' costs of production are less than the costs of carrying out the transactions through the market of individuals.[97] Within a firm contracts between the various factors of production are eliminated and replaced with an administrative

[91] *Ibid.*, p. 62.   [92] *Ibid.*, pp. 61–2.

[93] United Nations, *World Investment Report 1993* (1993), p. 115; Coase, *The Firm, the Market and the Law* (1988), p. 115.

[94] United Nations, *ibid.* (1993); Coase, *ibid.*, p. 7; Coase, 'The Nature of the Firm: Influence' in Williamson and Winter (eds.), *The Nature of the Firm* (1991) 61–74, p. 65.

[95] Coase, 'The Nature of the Firm: Influence', *ibid.*, p. 65.

[96] Coase, *The Firm, the Market and the Law* (1988), p. 6.

[97] *Ibid.*, pp. 6–7; Coase, 'The Nature of the Firm: Influence' in Williamson and Winter (eds.), *The Nature of the Firm* (1991) 61–74, pp. 65–6.

3 TRANSFER PRICING 81

arrangement.[98] Usually, the administrative costs of organizing a transaction through a firm are less than the alternative of market transactions.[99] The theoretical limit to the expansion of a firm is the point at which its costs of organizing transactions are equal to the costs of carrying out the transactions through the market.[100] A firm will internalize the costs of production to the extent that it can achieve economies of scale in production and distribution and establish coordination economies.[101] UNCTAD noted, in 1993, that in many industries the expansion of internalized activities within international enterprises indicates that there are significant efficiency gains.[102]

A firm's functions in providing goods and services are called its value chain (or supply chain), and through the value chain the firm converts inputs into goods and services. Most firms begin by operating in their home market and then rely on their competitive advantages to enter markets abroad.[103] International enterprises create organizational structures and develop strategies to arrange the cross-border production of goods and services in locations around the world, and the level of intra-entity or intra-group integration.[104] UNCTAD claimed that there was a trend in many international enterprises across a broad range of industries to use structures and strategies with high levels of integration in their operations.[105] The integration included giving an associated enterprise control over a group-wide function or the sharing of group-wide functions between two or more enterprises.[106] A successful multinational enterprise group combines ownership, location and internalization advantages to maximize its market share and growth opportunities.[107] Integration of multinational enterprise groups provides them with the capacity to exploit integration economies, which are not available to domestic firms.[108]

The key to understanding the existence of international enterprises and multinational enterprise groups is that they are integrated or unitary businesses.[109] Significant levels of integration have been achieved through the development of high speed and high quality

---

[98] Coase, 'The Problem of Social Cost' (1960), pp. 16–17.   [99] Ibid.
[100] Coase, The Firm, the Market and the Law (1988), p. 7.
[101] United Nations, World Investment Report 1993 (1993), p. 115.   [102] Ibid.
[103] Ibid.   [104] Ibid., p. 117.   [105] Ibid.   [106] Ibid., pp. 117–18.
[107] Eden, Taxing Multinationals (1998), p. 135.
[108] Eden, 'Taxes, Transfer Pricing, and the Multinational Enterprise' in Rugman and Brewer (eds.), Oxford Handbook of International Business (2009) 591–619, p. 596.
[109] Eden, Taxing Multinationals (1998), p. 126.

communications systems and information systems.[110] Globalization has made it possible for international enterprises operating abroad through branches or an international group to have control centralized in one location. In addition, modern information and communications systems also provide increased horizontal communications across geographic and functional business lines.[111] This has resulted in many international enterprises providing services such as advisory, research and development, legal, accounting, financial management, and data processing from one or several regional centres for their international enterprises.[112]

International enterprises have common control, common goals and common resources, in which the units of the enterprise – parent company, subsidiaries or branches – are located in more than one country. Thus, many international enterprises are fully integrated businesses that plan and implement global strategies.[113] UNCTAD has asserted that integration of production by international enterprises and multinational enterprise groups creates challenges for policy-makers in adapting the methods for allocating the income and costs of these enterprises between jurisdictions for tax purposes, because integration makes it more difficult, for both these enterprises and tax authorities, to allocate income and costs among the jurisdictions in which they operate.[114] UNCTAD suggested, inter alia, that the use of unitary approaches for allocating income between jurisdictions be examined, as treating an international enterprise as a 'unitary enterprise may be more in tune with economic realities than those based on hypothetical market prices'.[115] But it noted that the use of unitary taxation is limited and that this reform requires broad government acceptance and an agreed formula.

Dunning and Lundan argue that the history of multinational enterprise groups was shaped by political, social and cultural events that influenced the ownership, organization and location of international production of their goods and services.[116] They claim that multinational enterprise groups integrated their operations until the late 1980s and then more recently chose to outsource some activities in which they do

---

[110] See United Nations, *World Investment Report 1993* (1993), pp. 125–6.
[111] *Ibid.*, p. 126.   [112] *Ibid.*, p. 206.
[113] See Eden, *Taxing Multinationals* (1998), p. 125; United Nations, *World Investment Report 1993* (1993), p. 211.
[114] United Nations, *World Investment Report 1993* (1993), pp. 210–11.   [115] *Ibid.*, p. 210.
[116] Dunning and Lundan, *Multinational Enterprises and the Global Economy* (2nd edn, 2008), p. 197.

3 TRANSFER PRICING
83

not have competitive advantages.[117] For most of the twentieth century multinational enterprise groups and international enterprises tended to expand the range of their value-adding activities and by the late 1980s firms had integrated their production and marketing functions. In multinational enterprise groups, there was limited or no outsourcing of operations and by the 1960s and 1970s they formed into large integrated conglomerations. But Dunning and Lundan argue in the last twenty years they began outsourcing many activities that were previously performed by the firms themselves. By the early 1990s, multinational enterprise groups began restructuring to specialize in the areas in which they had competitive advantages, such as unique firm-specific assets, in particular high value intangible assets, and capabilities that provide the firms with their market position and competitive edge.

Multinational enterprises and international enterprises examined their value chains to identify the functions in which they had no advantage over other firms. They then began deciding on which functions they would perform themselves and those which would be outsourced to independent firms.[118] While the initial functions that were outsourced were non-core activities such as payroll, billing and maintenance services, outsourcing has expanded to cover core activities. The core activities may involve producing goods or providing services. For example, many firms outsource call centre activities to independent firms in countries such as India and Ireland which have educated English-speaking workforces and relatively low cost labour. Consequently, modern multinational enterprise groups organize their cross-border operations through a network of contractual arrangements with independent enterprises and cooperative in-house relationships.

Treating integrated multinational enterprise groups, and permanent establishments of international enterprises, as independent entities under the arm's length principle, conflicts with the economic theory of the firm. If such enterprises were to enter arm's length transactions in the provision of goods and services, they would have no advantage over other enterprises which operate in the market by entering transactions with arm's length parties. This is the economic limit of a multinational enterprise group, or an international enterprise, under the theory of the firm, and, consequently, firms which are unable to produce goods and services at a cost that is less than the market are unlikely to survive.

---

[117] For what follows in this para. see: *ibid.*, p. 196.
[118] For what follows in this para. see: *ibid.*

84   SOME SHORTCOMINGS OF THE TAX TREATY SYSTEM

The flaw in the arm's length principle is that it ignores the normative nature of multinational enterprise groups and international enterprises as integrated businesses with common goals. Moreover, the intra-firm activities of these modern international firms reflect the fact that in these areas they have competitive advantages over other producers. Thus, this normative flaw tests the effectiveness of the arm's length principle being for allocating the profits of multinational enterprise groups or international enterprises between jurisdictions.[119]

3.3   Problems in applying transfer pricing rules: section 482 of the US Code: United States General Accounting Office Reports

As a result of the arm's length principle's normative flaw, tax authorities encounter difficulties in administering transfer pricing rules. Two studies by the US General Accounting Office of the US domestic transfer pricing rules reveal the difficulties encountered by the Internal Revenue Service (IRS) in administering the rules. There are significant parallels between the OECD's transfer pricing rules and the US transfer pricing rules, which are contained in section 482 of the US Internal Revenue Code of 1986 (section 482).[120]

3.3.1   The 1981 Report

In 1981, the US General Accounting Office studied the IRS's administration of the arm's length principle in determining transfer prices for transactions between associated corporations. The report of the study, *IRS Could Better Protect US Tax Interests in Determining the Income of Multinational Corporations*[121] (1981 Report), raised the following concerns about the use of the arm's length principle for determining transfer prices for transactions between associated corporations:

> Adjusting multinational intercorporate transactions for tax purposes under current section 482 regulations is administratively burdensome for both IRS and the corporate taxpayer. Moreover, the considerable amount of judgment necessary in most income adjustments recommended under the regulations creates uncertainty. In recent years, the

---

[119] Eden, *Taxing Multinationals* (1998), p. 125.

[120] The parallels between the OECD transfer pricing rules and section 482 are considered in more detail in Ch. 8.

[121] US General Accounting Office, *IRS Could Better Protect US Tax Interests in Determining the Income of Multinational Corporations* (1981).

regulations have been a source of dissatisfaction to all affected parties, including the courts.

In essence, section 482 enforcement is criticized because the theory on which it rests no longer corresponds to the realities of intercorporate transactions. In theory, a section 482 adjustment should be made when income reported for a multinational intercorporate transaction varies from the comparable uncontrolled price of a similar transaction between two unrelated businesses. The comparable uncontrolled price is the arm's length price for the transaction. In practice, however, IRS examiners have difficulty finding a comparable uncontrolled price for most transactions. Of the examinations we reviewed, only 3 per cent (12 of 403) of IRS' recommended adjustments between parents and foreign subsidiaries were based on comparable uncontrolled prices. The income adjusted through these arm's length prices amounted to only 3 per cent of the total income adjusted for section 482 issues.

The regulations provide some guidance for those instances where an arm's length price cannot be identified but, too frequently, the examiner must use considerable judgment in analyzing extensive data which often does not directly relate to the specific situation at hand. To the extent that the facts do not directly relate, the adjustment price becomes estimated.[122]

The 1981 Report cited a 1980 study in which multinational enterprise groups were surveyed on whether they operate as unitary businesses or as separate enterprises transacting at arm's length with each other. Not surprisingly, 59 per cent of the corporations surveyed responded that they operate as unitary businesses and not as separate enterprises.[123] The 1980 study concluded that the difficulties with section 482 stem from the arm's length principle's normative flaw.[124]

The US General Accounting Office suggested that the US Treasury should consider alternative apportionment methods:

> Tax experts and corporate taxpayers have suggested that Treasury reconsider the appropriateness of the arm's length standard in an economic world more complex than that which existed when the standard was adopted in 1934. For example, one alternative suggested is the use of formulas for apportioning income in certain situations. Apportionment formulas are presently used by the States, and some believe these formulas, when applicable, reflect market realities better than the arm's length standard.[125]

---

[122] *Ibid.*, p. 27.

[123] *Ibid.*, p. 45, citing Burns, 'How the IRS Applies the Intercompany Pricing Rules of Section 482' (1980).

[124] *Ibid.*   [125] *Ibid.*, p. 27.

86   SOME SHORTCOMINGS OF THE TAX TREATY SYSTEM

The US General Accounting Office concluded that:

> Making income adjustments using the arm's length standard has posed administrative burdens on both the IRS and corporate taxpayers. Because of the structure of the modern business world, IRS can seldom find an arm's length price on which to base its adjustments but must instead construct a price. As a result, corporate taxpayers cannot be certain how income on intercorporate transactions that cross national borders will be adjusted and the enforcement process is difficult and time-consuming for both the IRS and taxpayers . . .

> A major objection to the use of formula apportionment across national borders is that tax treaties between the US and other nations specify the arm's length standard for adjusting corporate income . . . However, we believe that as a world leader and international policy-setter, the US should not be hesitant to take the lead in searching for better ways to administer the tax consequences of intercorporate transactions that cross national boundaries.[126]

3.3.2   The 1992 Report

The report of the 1992 study by the US General Accounting Office, *International Taxation: Problems Persist in Determining Tax Effects of Intercompany Prices* (1992 Report), found that using the arm's length principle resulted in extensive administrative disputes.[127] The 1992 Report noted that transfer pricing manipulation is a significant revenue risk because international enterprises are integrated businesses, and for intra-entity or intra-group transactions, comparable prices are often unavailable.[128] The 1992 Report concluded that problems with the arm's length principle could be expected to continue[129] – a prediction in 1992 that was accurate.

The 1992 Report noted the following difficulties with the operation of the arm's length principle, although concluding that it was the best available method at the moment:

> The arm's length standard has been the US way of dealing with transfer pricing for decades and is considered to be the international norm as well. Using the standard as its foundation, Treasury has been working to resolve transfer pricing issues for years, to the point where it recently proposed new transfer pricing regulations. Nevertheless, arm's length pricing has created many problems, and difficulties will continue despite all the recent initiatives in the transfer pricing area.

---

[126] *Ibid.*, p. 53.
[127] US General Accounting Office, *International Taxation* (1992), pp. 35–55 and 56.
[128] *Ibid.*, p. 62.   [129] *Ibid.*, p. 56.

3 TRANSFER PRICING

There are many reasons why an early end to transfer pricing problems is not ensured. The large amount of globalization of trade and the resulting transfer pricing caseload, the transfer pricing problem's continuing factual nature, the uncertainty in how the controversy over intangibles will be resolved, and the hurdles to be overcome in the advance pricing agreement program all argue for the problem not going away soon . . .

Although we expect difficulties with arm's length pricing to continue, we can find no problem-free alternative that would dictate Treasury's abandoning its current course.[130]

The US General Accounting Office's conclusion is puzzling given the extensive academic criticisms of the arm's length principle. The proposals to introduce formulary apportionment in the EU may provide the impetus for the US to expand the arm's length principle to include other apportionment methods.[131] Although the US has reformed its transfer pricing rules, problems still persist. In 2002, the US Treasury acknowledged the difficulty of applying the arm's length standard to the outbound transfer of intangible assets.[132]

3.4 Problems for taxpayers in complying with transfer pricing rules

Not only do tax authorities find difficulties in administering transfer pricing rules, multinational enterprise groups and international enterprises encounter difficulties in complying with transfer pricing rules. Since 1995 the Ernst & Young international transfer pricing surveys have consistently found that multinational enterprise groups encounter difficulties in complying with transfer pricing rules. In 2007, Ernst & Young commissioned an independent firm to conduct a survey which involved interviews with 850 multinational enterprise groups from twenty-four countries.[133]

The 2007 survey findings were that:

- 40 per cent of the survey respondents identified transfer pricing as their most important tax issue;
- 74 per cent of parent company respondents and 81 per cent of subsidiary company respondents view transfer pricing as very important to them over the next two years;

---

[130] *Ibid.*, p. 93.   [131] The European Commission's proposals are considered in Ch. 10.
[132] US Department of the Treasury, 'Corporate Inversion Transactions' (2002), para. 8.3.
[133] Ernst & Young, *Precision under Pressure, Global Transfer Pricing Survey 2007–2008* (2007), p. 2.

88 SOME SHORTCOMINGS OF THE TAX TREATY SYSTEM

- 74 per cent of parent respondents will meet their expected increased need for transfer pricing resources by engaging external advisors; and
- 50 per cent of the respondents had transfer pricing audits since 2003, of which 27 per cent were audits of parent companies.[134]

The 2009 survey noted the following key transfer pricing trends:

- tax authorities are expanding their transfer pricing specialists;
- countries appear to be increasing audit activity, more transfer pricing penalties and increasing disputes with taxpayers; and
- significant differences exist between tax authorities and taxpayers in the practical application and enforcement of the arm's length principle.[135]

In particular, the economic and financial crisis in 2008 has created unforeseen transfer pricing challenges for international enterprises. Losses or significantly reduced margins have resulted in making the traditional approaches to transfer pricing difficult, if not impossible.[136] The survey concluded that maximizing operating performance and not minimizing tax was the most important issue affecting the transfer pricing policies of international enterprises.[137]

In contrast, the Transfer Pricing Guidelines have elsewhere been described as a major development in the harmonization of both transfer pricing rules and practices.[138] At the 2008 OECD conference, the OECD claimed that participants at its 2008 conference on the fiftieth anniversary of the OECD Model had voted overwhelmingly that the adoption of the Transfer Pricing Guidelines was the most important tax treaty development since the OECD Model was developed. One of the anticipated benefits of the 1995 revision of the OECD transfer pricing rules was simplification of the rules and procedures for tax authorities and international enterprises.[139] But the anticipated benefits for international enterprises were not achieved; survey participants have consistently listed transfer pricing as their main international tax issue.[140] Moreover, transfer pricing resulted in the biggest tax

---

[134] *Ibid.*

[135] Ernst & Young, *2009 Global Transfer Pricing Survey. Tax Authority Insights* (2009), p. 6.

[136] *Ibid.* [137] Ernst & Young, 'Transfer Pricing 1999 Global Survey' (1999), p. 1910.

[138] Avery Jones, 'The David R. Tillinghast Lecture' (1999), p. 7.

[139] Lodin, 'International Tax Issues in a Rapidly Changing World' (2001), p. 4.

[140] Ernst & Young, *Precision under Pressure, Global Transfer Pricing Survey 2007–2008* (2007), p. 2; O'Haver, 'Transfer Pricing' (2006), p. 407 (on the 2005–2006 Ernst & Young Global Transfer Pricing Survey); Ernst & Young, 'Transfer Pricing 1999 Global Survey' (1999), p. 1910.

3 TRANSFER PRICING

settlement in the US, and probably the world, with the 2006 Glaxo-SmithKline settlement of US$3.4 billion. Although it was expected that countries would implement transfer pricing rules based on the Transfer Pricing Guidelines leading to consistent rules, some countries have treated the Transfer Pricing Guidelines as merely a minimum standard that they may exceed.[141] These countries have enacted transfer pricing rules that are more onerous than the Transfer Pricing Guidelines in areas such as documentation.[142] Differing documentation requirements between countries significantly increase the costs for multinational enterprise groups of complying with transfer pricing rules in the various countries in which they operate. In summary, the Transfer Pricing Guidelines are a paradox as they are claimed to be the most significant OECD international tax measure, but transfer pricing is also the most significant tax concern for multinational enterprise groups.

3.5 The evolution of OECD transfer pricing methods

The arm's length principle in transfer pricing is not a static notion and the arm's length principle has been expanded over time.[143] The 2010 Transfer Pricing Guidelines set out the traditional transaction methods in Chapter II – the 'comparable uncontrolled price method', the 'resale price method' and 'cost plus method'.[144] Chapter III sets out the transactional profit methods – the 'profit split method' and the 'transactional net margin method' – used to estimate arm's length conditions when the traditional transaction methods cannot be applied.[145] These latter two methods are profit-based, and prior to 2010 could only be used as a last resort in situations in which the traditional transaction methods were inapplicable.[146] In 2010, the OECD adopted the 2010 Transfer Pricing Guidelines in which the first three chapters of the Transfer Pricing Guidelines were substantially revised. The key change was the removal of the requirement that the transactional profit methods have the status of last resort methods and they can only be used in exceptional circumstances. Nevertheless, for some time the transactional net margin had been the most used transfer pricing method because there are often inadequate comparable

---

[141] Lodin, 'International Tax Issues in a Rapidly Changing World' (2001), p. 4.
[142] *Ibid.*   [143] The OECD transfer pricing methods are considered in Ch. 9.
[144] 2010 Transfer Pricing Guidelines, pp. 63–76.   [145] *Ibid.*, pp. 77–105.
[146] 2009 Transfer Pricing Guidelines, p. 81, para. 3.50.

90   SOME SHORTCOMINGS OF THE TAX TREATY SYSTEM

transactions to apply the traditional transfer pricing methods.[147] The transactional profit methods are considered in Chapter 9.

Under the 2010 Transfer Pricing Guidelines the selected transfer pricing method should be 'the most appropriate method for a particular case'.[148] The tests for determining which transfer pricing method is the most appropriate for a particular case are:

- the relative strengths and weaknesses of the traditional transaction methods and the transactional profit methods;
- the appropriateness of the methods in light of a functional analysis of the controlled transaction, and whether uncontrolled transactions are available;
- the comparability between the controlled and uncontrolled transactions, including the adjustments required and whether the compatibility adjustments are reliable.[149]

Although the requirement that the transactional profits methods may only be used as a last resort has been removed, if both the traditional transaction methods and the transactional profits methods are equally reliable in a particular case, the traditional transaction methods have priority:

> Traditional transaction methods are regarded as the most direct means of establishing whether conditions in the commercial and financial relations between associated enterprises are arm's length. This is because any

---

[147] HM Revenue and Customs, United Kingdom 'UINTM463080 – Transfer Pricing: OECD and methodologies' www.hmrc.gov.uk/manuals/intmanual/INTM463080.htm; Mercader and Peña, 'Transfer Pricing and Latin American Integration' in Tanzi, Barreix and Villela (eds.) *Taxation and Latin American Integration* (2008), p. 271; Meenan, Dawid and Hulshorst, 'Is Europe One Market? A Transfer Pricing Economic Analysis of Pan-European Comparables Sets', Deloitte White Paper (2004), p. 1, reproduced in European Commission, *EU Joint Transfer Pricing Forum* (Brussels: 2004, Taxud/C1/LDH/WB); Reyneveld, Gommers and Lund, 'Pan-European Comparables Searches – Analysing the Search Criteria' (2007), p. 80; Przysuski and Lalapet, 'A Comprehensive Look at the Berry Ratio in Transfer Pricing' (2005), pp. 760–1; in relation to Advanced Pricing Agreements, Australian Taxation Office, *Advance Pricing Arrangement Program 2004–05 Update* (2005), p. 7; in relation to determining transfer prices for intra-group services, Hejazi, 'Should Depreciation Be Marked Up in a Transactional Net Margin Method Context for Service Providers?' (2008) *International Transfer Pricing Journal* 26, p. 27; in relation to India, Gajaria and Kale, 'Transfer Pricing in Emerging Markets – An Indian Perspective' (2006), p. 13.
[148] 2010 Transfer Pricing Guidelines, p. 59, para. 2.2.   [149] *Ibid.*, p. 59, para. 2.2.

3 TRANSFER PRICING

difference in the price of a controlled transaction from the price in a comparable uncontrolled transaction can normally be traced directly to the commercial and financial relations made or imposed between the enterprises, and the arm's length conditions can be established by directly substituting the price in the comparable uncontrolled transaction for the price of the controlled transaction. As a result, where, taking account of the criteria described at paragraph 2.2, a traditional transaction method and a transactional profit method can be applied in an equally reliable manner, the traditional transaction method is preferable to the transactional profit method. Moreover, where, taking account of the criteria described at paragraph 2.2, the comparable uncontrolled price method (CUP) and another transfer pricing method can be applied in an equally reliable manner, the CUP method is to be preferred. See paragraphs 2.13–2.20 for a discussion of the CUP method.[150]

The 2010 Transfer Pricing Guidelines acknowledge that the transactional profit methods are more reliable in certain circumstances:

[C]ases where each of the parties makes valuable and unique contributions in relation to the controlled transaction, or where the parties engage in highly integrated activities, may make a transactional profit split more appropriate than a one-sided method. As another example, where there is no or limited publicly available reliable gross margin information on third parties, traditional transaction methods might be difficult to apply in cases other than those where there are internal comparables, and a transactional profit method might be the most appropriate method in view of the availability of information.[151]

But the 2010 Transfer Pricing Guidelines include a proviso that the transactional profit methods cannot be used merely because it is difficult to find data on uncontrolled transactions or that data that has been obtained is incomplete.[152] The tests in paragraph 2.2 above (text preceding note 149) must be applied in determining whether the transactional profit methods are reliable in a particular case.

The OECD transactional profit methods are in effect formulary apportionment methods in treating associated companies as a unitary business. The transactional profit methods are acceptable under the arm's length principle if they produce the same results as situations in which entities are dealing with each other at arm's length. The 2010 Transfer Pricing Guidelines try, unconvincingly, to maintain the pretence that the transactional profit methods are not formulary apportionment methods:

---

[150] *Ibid.*, pp. 59–60, para. 2.3.   [151] *Ibid.*, p. 60, para. 2.4.   [152] *Ibid.*, p. 60, para. 2.5.

92   SOME SHORTCOMINGS OF THE TAX TREATY SYSTEM

> ... OECD member countries reiterate their support for the consensus on the use of the arm's length principle that has emerged over the years among member and non-member countries and agree that the theoretical alternative to the arm's length principle represented by global formulary apportionment should be rejected.[153]

Despite this pretence, the inclusion in the Transfer Pricing Guidelines in 1995 of the transactional profit methods represents a major achievement and a significant expansion of the arm's length principle. This OECD development was preceded in 1988 by a US Treasury Department and Internal Revenue Service White Paper, *A Study of Intercompany Pricing*,[154] on transfer pricing methods for intangibles. The White Paper led to the IRS issuing proposed regulations under section 482 in 1992 which accepted the use of the transactional profit methods.[155] The US development was described as a revolution in the US's approach to transfer pricing.[156] These reforms were described as representing the decline of the traditional arm's length principle due to the lack of comparable transactions and the acceptance of the transactional profit methods to approximate an arm's length result.[157]

It has been claimed by Mintz that for transfer pricing purposes the use of the transactional profit methods for non-arm's length transactions resembles a complicated form of formulary apportionment.[158] In particular, it has been argued that the profit split method is a formulary apportionment method.[159] And it has been asserted that the differences between the transactional profit methods and formulary apportionment are insignificant.[160] The transactional profit methods are usually more complex than formulary apportionment because they rely on the facts and circumstances of an international enterprise, rather than a uniform formula for all international enterprises.[161] Consequently, reform of the

---

[153] *Ibid.*, p. 41, para. 1.32.
[154] US Treasury Department and Internal Revenue Service White Paper, *A Study of Intercompany Pricing* (1988).
[155] INTL-0372-88; INTL-0401-88, 57 FR 3571. The 1992 proposed section 482 regulations were finalized in July 1994.
[156] Avi-Yonah, 'The Rise and Fall of Arm's Length' (1995), p. 135.   [157] *Ibid.*, p. 147.
[158] Mintz, 'Globalization of the Corporate Income Tax' (1999), pp. 402–4.
[159] Hellerstein, 'The Case for Formulary Apportionment' (2005).
[160] See Noren, 'The US National Interest in International Tax Policy' (2001), pp. 347–8; C. E. McLure 'US Federal Use of Formula Apportionment to Tax Income from Intangibles' (1997), p. 870; Hellerstein, 'The Case for Formulary Apportionment' (2005), p. 106.
[161] C. E. McLure 'US Federal Use of Formula Apportionment to Tax Income from Intangibles' (1997), p. 870.

3 TRANSFER PRICING

arm's length principle is the most likely line of international tax reform because a wholesale move to formulary apportionment would involve a major structural shift.

Eden questioned whether the OECD Transfer Pricing Guidelines and the inclusion of the transactional profit methods are modest repairs to the obsolete mechanisms of the 1970s, or an acceptance of the notion that multinational enterprises are unitary businesses which cannot be dissected into separate transactions with market equivalents.[162] Eden suggested that what is needed is an 'international tax transfer pricing regime for the twenty-first century, based on twenty-first-century multinationals'.[163]

3.5.1 Formulary apportionment

The main alternative to the arm's length principle is unitary taxation; the taxation of the worldwide income of a unitary business. Under unitary taxation, an international enterprise or a company group is treated as a unitary and integrated business. Unitary taxation uses formulary apportionment to allocate the net profit of an international enterprise to the jurisdictions in which it operates.[164] Although formulary apportionment has been advocated extensively in journal articles and books, it is viewed sceptically by some commentators and international organizations, including the OECD.[165] As the distinctions between formulary apportionment and the arm's length principle have been eroded since the implementation of the transactional profit methods, the better view is that the notions of arm's length principle and formulary apportionment are part of a continuum of methods – it is unclear where one method ends and the other begins.[166]

In theory, a formulary apportionment method based on factors that approximate the division of profits that would be imposed by the market-place would conform with the arm's length principle.[167] In this situation, the formulary apportionment method and the arm's length principle would have the same theoretical base, but they use different paths to reach the same goal – the division of profits that the

---

[162] Eden, *Taxing Multinationals* (1998), p. 652.   [163] *Ibid.*
[164] Formulary apportionment is considered in Ch. 11.
[165] Arnold and McDonnell, 'The Allocation of Income and Expenses Among Countries' (1993), p. 553.
[166] *Ibid.*, pp. 553–4.
[167] Surrey, 'Reflections on the Allocation of Income and Expenses Among National Tax Jurisdictions' (1978), pp. 417–18.

94 SOME SHORTCOMINGS OF THE TAX TREATY SYSTEM

market-place would produce.[168] In 1992, Langbein suggested a modified form of formulary apportionment which he asserted is consistent with the arm's length principle.[169] Under the proposal, there are two steps.[170] In the first step, each component of an international enterprise would be able to recoup its costs and a profit margin calculated as a return on tangible business assets used by the component. The profit margin would be a general rate of return reflecting the enterprise's overall profit levels. The application of the first step would result in unallocated profits being treated as residual profits. Residual profits would be allocated on the basis of a two-factor formula; the factors being assets and sales.[171] Langbein argues that this method is consistent with the arm's length principle, but overcomes the flaw in the arm's length principle of having to search for comparable prices.[172] In the second step, formulary apportionment is only applied to the residual profit made by an international enterprise. This proposal illustrates the potential for formulary apportionment techniques to be incorporated into the arm's length principle. Langbein's proposal is similar to the residual profit split method for transactions which involve services or high value intangible property.

4 Some problems arising from the bilateral operation of tax treaties

The effectiveness of the tax treaty system is severely limited because of its bilateral character. A tax treaty provides a basis for settling problems between two countries, but the network of tax treaties does not provide a comprehensive framework for a world tax system.[173] Tax treaties are negotiated between two countries to balance the competing interests of the contracting states, and the resulting consequences for the tax treaty system are usually incidental. For example, tax treaty negotiators may seek to obtain tax concessions for resident enterprises without considering the impact of the concessions on other jurisdictions.[174] Countries may also ensure that full relief from double taxation is not provided under their domestic laws as a bargaining leverage to be used in

---

[168] *Ibid.*, p. 418.
[169] Langbein, 'A Modified Fractional Apportionment Proposal for Transfer Pricing' (1992), p. 730.
[170] *Ibid.*, p. 720.   [171] *Ibid.*   [172] *Ibid.*, p. 730.
[173] Thuronyi, 'International Tax Cooperation and a Multilateral Treaty' (2001), p. 1653.
[174] *Ibid.*

4 PROBLEMS ARISING FROM BILATERAL OPERATION   95

negotiating tax treaties with other countries.[175] Furthermore, if one country provides full domestic relief from double taxation, other countries may lose the incentive to enter a tax treaty with that country and provide reciprocal relief.[176] Thus, the process of negotiating and renegotiating tax treaties significantly limits the amount of cooperation that can be achieved between jurisdictions under the current tax treaty system. Some of the problems caused by the bilateral operation of tax treaties are: treaty shopping; the difficulty of maintaining a treaty network; treaty override; maintaining consistent interpretations of treaty provisions; manipulation of tax treaties by international enterprises; the incomplete coverage of countries; and auditing international enterprises and associated enterprises.

4.1 Treaty shopping

The paradox of the tax treaty system is that tax treaties have become the vehicle for tax avoidance techniques – such as treaty shopping – even though one of the purposes of tax treaties is to counter tax avoidance. Treaty shopping occurs when a multinational enterprise group operates through a subsidiary incorporated in a foreign country specifically for the purpose of gaining access to the benefits of that country's tax treaties. Such treaty benefits would not be available to the multinational enterprise group if it operated in a more straightforward method by investing directly in the other country.[177] Most countries treat a company registered under their laws as a resident taxpayer. The rationale is that the country in which a company is incorporated provides the company with its legal form by the legal fiction of separate personality, with limited liability and perpetual life.[178] Therefore, the benefits of a country's tax treaties may be obtained by an enterprise in another jurisdiction using a subsidiary incorporated in that country.

---

[175] For example, the UK decided in 1950 not to provide full domestic relief from double taxation because to do so would affect its bargaining power in negotiating tax treaties: Williams, *Trends in International Taxation* (1991), pp. 114–16, para. 561.

[176] *Ibid.*

[177] OECD, *Double Taxation Conventions and the Use of Conduit Companies* (1986), para. 1.

[178] Legal form is a benefit provided by the laws of a country. Under the economic benefit principle this benefit entitles a country to treat companies registered under its law as resident enterprises and subject to that country's tax jurisdiction: Mintz, 'Globalization of the Corporate Income Tax' (1999), p. 392.

96   SOME SHORTCOMINGS OF THE TAX TREATY SYSTEM

The potential for abuse of tax treaties arises because of their bilateral nature and the differences between them.[179] Under the current tax treaty system, a country may provide particular benefits in some of its treaties because each treaty is negotiated separately, and this creates an incentive for multinational enterprise groups to engage in treaty shopping to avoid or minimize taxation. Bilateral tax treaties also provide the tax planning opportunity for enterprises to route income or gains to a particular jurisdiction by using a locally incorporated company. In 1987, the OECD issued a report dealing with treaty shopping, which contained measures to counter the practice.[180] There are two main treaty-shopping techniques; the direct conduit method and the stepping stone method.[181] Under the direct conduit method, a multinational enterprise group sets up a subsidiary in a country to gain access to a tax concession available to residents of that country under a tax treaty with another country. Under the stepping stone method, a multinational enterprise company makes payments, which are deductible in its home jurisdiction, to a conduit company in another jurisdiction in which the receipts are tax-free. The OECD report on conduit companies set out the techniques used in each method:

Direct conduits

A company resident of State A receives dividends, interest or royalties from State B. Under the tax treaty between States A and B, the company claims that it is fully or partially exempted from the withholding taxes of State B. The company is wholly owned by a resident of a third State not entitled to the benefit of the treaty between States A and B. It has been created with a view to taking advantage of this treaty's benefits and for this purpose the assets and rights giving rise to the dividends, interest, or royalties were transferred to it. The income is tax-exempt in State A, e.g. in the case of dividends, by virtue of a parent-subsidiary regime provided for under the domestic laws of State A, or in the convention between States A and B.

'Stepping stone' conduits

The situation is the same as in example 1. However, the company resident of State A is fully subject to tax in that country. It pays high interest,

---

[179] See Vann, 'International Aspects of Income Tax' in Thuronyi (ed.) *Tax Law Design and Drafting* (1998) 718–810, at p. 795.

[180] OECD, *Double Taxation Conventions and the Use of Conduit Companies* (1986), paras. 4–10.

[181] Van Weeghel, *The Improper Use of Tax Treaties* (1998), p. 120; Ginsberg, *International Tax Planning* (1994), pp. 6–8.

4 PROBLEMS ARISING FROM BILATERAL OPERATION 97

commissions, service fees and similar expenses to a second related 'conduit company' set up in State D. These payments are deductible in State A and tax-exempt in State D where the company enjoys a special tax regime.[182]

In both methods, the arrangement is premised on the conduit company not being subject to substantial taxation in the conduit country. If the conduit company is subject to tax in the conduit country, the advantage of treaty shopping is minimal. The tax benefit arises in the source country from the operation of a treaty.

The OECD views treaty shopping as an abuse of tax treaties and unsatisfactory:

(a) Treaty benefits negotiated between two States are economically extended to persons resident in a third State in a way unintended by the Contracting States; thus the principle of reciprocity is breached and the balance of sacrifices incurred in tax treaties by the contracting parties altered;

(b) Income flowing internationally may be exempted from taxation altogether or be subject to inadequate taxation in a way unintended by the Contracting States. This situation is unacceptable because the granting by a country of treaty benefits is based, except in specific circumstances, on the fact that the respective income is taxed in the other State or at least falls under the normal tax regime of that State.[183]

In 2002, the OECD Committee on Fiscal Affairs adopted the report *Restricting the Entitlement to Treaty Benefits* (the 2002 Report).[184] This report contains the Committee's response to recommendation 9 in the 1998 OECD report *Harmful Tax Competition: An Emerging Global Issue* (1998 Report) which recommended that work be undertaken on possible restrictions of entitlement to treaty benefits.[185] The 2002 Report recommendation that the Commentary on Article 1 be amended to suggest that treaty countries consider including specific anti-avoidance provisions in tax treaties to counter treaty shopping was implemented in the 2003 OECD Model update. Paragraph 9.6 of the 2010 Commentary on Article 1 states:

The potential application of general anti-abuse provisions does not mean that there is no need for the inclusion, in tax conventions, of specific provisions aimed at preventing particular forms of tax avoidance. Where

---

[182] OECD, *Double Taxation Conventions and the Use of Conduit Companies* (1986), para. 4.
[183] *Ibid.*, para. 7.   [184] OECD, *Restricting the Entitlement to Treaty Benefits* (2002).
[185] OECD, *Harmful Tax Competition: An Emerging Global Issue* (1998).

98   SOME SHORTCOMINGS OF THE TAX TREATY SYSTEM

specific avoidance techniques have been identified or where the use of such techniques is especially problematic, it will often be useful to add to the Convention provisions that focus directly on the relevant avoidance strategy. Also, this will be necessary where a State which adopts the view described in paragraph 9.2 above believes that its domestic law lacks the anti-avoidance rules or principles necessary to properly address such strategy.

The measures considered in the Commentary include using the concepts of place of effective management and permanent establishment and the subject-to-tax provisions, to reduce the treaty benefits obtained through the use of a conduit company. The look-through measure is designed to disallow treaty benefits to a company which is not owned directly or indirectly by residents of the country in which the company is resident (paragraphs 13–20 of the 2010 Commentary on Article 1). Another measure is the use of a subject-to-tax rule in a tax treaty (paragraphs 15 and 16 of the 2010 Commentary on Article 1) which denies treaty benefits in the source country if an item of income is not subject to tax in the residence country. Both of these measures require specific anti-avoidance provisions in tax treaties and this will take considerable time to implement. A shortcoming of specific anti-avoidance provisions is that they close a particular avenue of avoidance, but tax planning may disclose other avoidance techniques to obtain treaty benefits.

4.2 Maintaining a treaty network and treaty override

Tax treaties need to be reformed for a range of reasons: to keep pace with economic developments; to correct technical flaws in treaties; and to counter avoidance practices.[186] Moreover, tax treaties should be able to be amended on a timely basis to reflect changes in a country's tax policies and the policies of its tax treaty partners.[187] A significant problem for the current tax treaty system, making it inflexible and difficult to maintain, arises because changes to a country's tax treaties have to be renegotiated and approved by governments who are party to each respective treaty. Tax treaty renegotiations take considerable time and this makes it difficult for a country's tax treaties to keep pace with developments. The considerable lead-time required to implement tax treaty reforms is illustrated by the fact that the average age of OECD

[186] See Thuronyi, 'International Tax Cooperation and a Multilateral Treaty' (2001), p. 1660.
[187] *Ibid.*, p. 1661.

4 PROBLEMS ARISING FROM BILATERAL OPERATION 99

countries' tax treaties exceeds fourteen years.[188] Furthermore, as the tax treaty network expands it becomes increasingly inflexible because the time required to implement reform increases exponentially. If a tax treaty reform is required to counter avoidance, the treaties that are the last to be reformed might be used for tax avoidance via the treaty shopping process. The long lead-time required to implement tax treaty reform makes tax treaties vulnerable to manipulation. International tax advisers monitor tax treaty developments and seek out tax treaties that may be exploited because certain reforms have not been incorporated into them.

At times, a country may respond by overriding provisions in tax treaties with unilateral domestic legislation, resulting in the country breaching its international treaty obligations which have been codified in the Vienna Convention on the Law of Treaties of 23 May 1969 (Vienna Convention). Under Article 26 of the Vienna Convention, '[e]very treaty is binding on the parties to the treaty and must be performed by them in good faith'. This rule is called *pacta sunt servanda* which is a key principle of international law. Article 27 of the Vienna Convention expresses the principle of international law that a country should not override a treaty by enacting conflicting domestic legislation. The principles of the Vienna Convention are considered in detail in Chapter 5.

In relation to tax treaties, the OECD, in its *Tax Treaty Overrides* report, stated the following on the international law principle that treaties are binding and must be performed in good faith:

> In summary, it can be said that under international law treaties have to be observed by the parties as long as they are valid, and unless they have been formally denounced. Domestic legislation (whether subsequent to signature or otherwise) or other reasons in no way affect the continuing existence of that international obligation. All other parties to a treaty are entitled to insist on compliance by a party not performing its obligations.[189]

The OECD recommended that OECD countries 'avoid enacting legislation which is intended to have effects in clear contradiction to international treaty obligations'.[190] The effect of treaty override must be considered in the light of international law. Treaty override is likely to

---

[188] The average age is calculated from the date of signature, or the last protocol to the treaty, on the basis that this is the last time a change would have been made to a tax treaty: Sasseville, 'The Future of the Treaty Rules for Taxing Business Profits' (2000), pp. 5:10–11.

[189] OECD, *Tax Treaty Overrides* (1989), para. 12.   [190] *Ibid.*, para. 18.

100 SOME SHORTCOMINGS OF THE TAX TREATY SYSTEM

restrict the consensus between treaty countries. The *Tax Treaty Overrides* report made the following comments on the international law consequences of tax treaty override:

> Under a treaty the Contracting States mutually undertake the obligation to respect and apply the treaty provisions. This is the principle of '*pacta sunt servanda*'. Treaty override implies that a State by legislative action gives preference to domestic law over international law, and thus refuses to fulfil certain obligations arising out of the contractual nexus on grounds that the treaty obligations conflict with domestic law. When a treaty override occurs there is, therefore, a breach of the treaty. It should be noted that a breach of the treaty occurs when the overriding legislation is passed by the legislature and not only when it is applied to actual cases. Any breach of a treaty has an effect on the international relationships of the State concerned with other States, and the rights and obligations arising out of such action have to be determined under the rules of international law.[191]

In 2000, the Australian Parliament enacted domestic legislation to override its pre-1998 tax treaties in response to an adverse court decision.[192] The real property Article in several of Australia's pre-1998 tax treaties did not expressly apply to indirect ownership. The override extended Australia's taxing rights to indirect interests under the alienation of real property (immovable property) Article in its tax treaties.[193] The amendments were designed to unilaterally extend Australia's taxing rights to the indirect alienation of real property in which interposed entities are used. The aim of the amendments was to override the decision in *Federal Commissioner of Taxation* v. *Lamesa Holdings BV* (*Lamesa*) (1997).[194] The taxpayer in *Lamesa* successfully argued that the alienation of real property Article in the Australia–Netherlands tax treaty is limited to the direct alienation of real property.

A country's tax treaties limit its ability to implement tax policies or to counter tax avoidance by international enterprises. Governments implementing tax reform will seek to implement their changes swiftly to maintain revenue and give effect to their policies. If a country's tax reforms affect its tax treaties, the significant time required for the renegotiation process may result in governments implementing their reforms by unilaterally overriding their tax treaties, as shown in the

---

[191] *Ibid.*, para. 7.　　[192] See Kobetsky, 'The Aftermath of the *Lamesa* Case' (2005).

[193] Australia: Section 3A of the International Agreements Act 1953. The amending legislation was the Taxation Laws Amendment Act No. 4 (2000).

[194] 36 ATR 589; 97 ATC 4752.

4 PROBLEMS ARISING FROM BILATERAL OPERATION   101

Australian example above. This is a direct consequence of having a network of bilateral tax treaties that cannot be quickly amended.

4.3   Treaty interpretation

Tax treaties under the current tax treaty system are difficult to interpret because each treaty is in a separate instrument.[195] Courts interpreting tax treaties have limited precedents to apply, and generally will not apply precedents from other jurisdictions, leading to uncertainty.[196] Some uniformity in tax treaty interpretation has been provided by the OECD Model and Commentary, which is used by courts in several countries. It may be argued that the OECD Model has become a multilateral tax treaty and further, that the OECD Model may be reformed by amendments to the Commentary. The current tendency is to amend the Commentary and to rely then on the amended Commentary being applied to existing tax treaties. But it is pointless to amend the Commentary alone to reform tax treaties, unless there is a strong expectation that in OECD countries, tax authorities and courts will accept the amendments when they interpret tax treaties.[197]

4.4   Incomplete coverage of countries

The present network of tax treaties covers OECD countries, but a large number of countries, particularly developing countries, are left outside the system. The network of tax treaties in 2001 was estimated to be 1,700, covering only 15 per cent of countries.[198] Under the current tax treaty system, universal coverage of countries would be a challenging task because of the number of treaties required and the significant time it would take to negotiate and settle each treaty in the first instance.[199] Furthermore, each country's treaties would need to be updated from time to time and this would require further time to renegotiate. If all 183 International Monetary Fund countries were to be included in the tax treaty network, 15,653 tax treaties would be required.[200] The

---

[195] Treaty interpretation is considered in Ch. 5.

[196] See Loukota, 'Multilateral Tax Treaty Versus Bilateral Treaty Network' in *Multilateral Tax Treaties* (1998) 83–103, p. 90; Thuronyi, 'International Tax Cooperation and a Multilateral Treaty' (2001), pp. 1656–8.

[197] Avery Jones, 'The David R. Tillinghast Lecture' (1999), pp. 21–2.

[198] Thuronyi, 'International Tax Cooperation and a Multilateral Treaty' (2001), p. 1655.

[199] *Ibid.*, p. 1656.   [200] *Ibid.*, p. 1655.

disadvantage of the current tax treaty system is that there is only one direction in which to proceed – the creation of more tax treaties to extend international coverage.[201] As the tax treaty network continues to expand, it becomes more inflexible because the time and resources required to reform tax treaties increase exponentially. It is a paradox that, as the tax treaty network expands, its flaws become more significant,[202] leading to a conclusion that the creation of more tax treaties is not the best response to globalization.[203]

Most developed and developing countries accept that it is in their interests to enter into tax treaties.[204] The current treaty network covers developed countries satisfactorily, but the treaty network coverage in developing countries is limited. The UN has claimed that tax treaties contribute to the development of developing countries.[205] The main tax treaty benefits for these countries are to prevent double taxation and to remove possible tax obstacles to international technology transfers.[206] Other benefits of entering a tax treaty include: encouraging international investment; preventing discrimination between taxpayers in international trade; improved cooperation between tax authorities in administering their tax laws; and legal and fiscal certainty.[207] But many developing countries lack the resources, personnel and international influence to negotiate and finalize tax treaties with other countries, and in particular with developed countries. On the other hand, if they were to enter into a multilateral tax treaty they would be provided with the same range of benefits, but at a significantly reduced cost.[208] Thus, the benefits of the current tax treaty system are not available to smaller developing countries.

4.5   Auditing

Another problem of the current tax treaty system is that tax authorities administering a treaty may not have the information to audit an international enterprise if the enterprise operates in other countries. Although tax treaties have exchange of information provisions, this

[201] Avery Jones, 'The David R. Tillinghast Lecture' (1999), p. 3.
[202] Thuronyi, 'International Tax Cooperation and a Multilateral Treaty' (2001), p. 1660.
[203] Avery Jones, 'The David R. Tillinghast Lecture' (1999), p. 4.
[204] American Law Institute, *Federal Income Tax Project, International Aspects of United States Income Taxation II* (1992), p. 2.
[205] United Nations, *United Nations Model Tax Convention Between Developed and Developing Countries* (2001), para. 2, pp. vi–vii.
[206] *Ibid.*   [207] *Ibid.*
[208] See Thuronyi, 'International Tax Cooperation and a Multilateral Treaty' (2001), p. 1656.

4 PROBLEMS ARISING FROM BILATERAL OPERATION 103

measure has not been used to full effect by treaty partner countries. More recently, the OECD has sought to expand information exchange measures for the administration and enforcement of a country's tax law and its tax treaties. Exchange of information measures provides countries with the ability to exchange tax information with other countries, while respecting the sovereignty of other countries and the rights of taxpayers. The OECD instruments which provide for information exchange are: Article 26 of the OECD Model; the 'Agreement on Exchange of Information on Tax Matters' (developed jointly with non-OECD countries); and the 'Council of Europe and OECD Convention on Mutual Administrative Assistance in Tax Matters'. These instruments provide tax authorities with access to information from other tax authorities, together with strict confidentiality rules to prevent unauthorized disclosure of information. The OECD claims that it is working to improve legal access to information such as bank information for tax purposes and practical measures such as its *Manual on the Implementation of Exchange of Information Provisions for Tax Purposes*,[209] and the *Reference Guide on Sources of Information from Abroad*.[210] The OECD has made the following recommendations to improve the effectiveness of exchange of information: 'OECD Model Agreement for Simultaneous Tax Examinations'; 'Use of Tax Identification Numbers in an International Tax Context'; 'OECD Use of the Revised Standard Magnetic Format for Automatic Exchange of Information'; and 'OECD Model Memorandum of Understanding for Automatic Exchange of Information'. These OECD information exchange measures are considerable, but there is scope for improvement in the exchange of information between tax authorities.

Within a multinational enterprise group several million transactions may take place worldwide each day between associated enterprises. Consequently, it may be difficult for a tax authority to check all transactions between associated enterprises to prevent transfer pricing avoidance because the tax authority only has jurisdiction over part of the group's international business.[211] Associated enterprises are able to make their operations complex in order to limit potential audits by tax authorities.[212] In this situation, a tax authority may not be able to

---

[209] OECD, *Improving Access to Bank Information for Tax Purposes* (2000).

[210] OECD, *OECD Reference Guide on Sources of Information from Abroad* (2006).

[211] Eden, *Taxing Multinationals* (1998), pp. 21–3.

[212] The US Congress' Joint Committee of Taxation stated that Enron Corporation 'excelled at making complexity an ally': Joint Committee on Taxation, *Report of Investigations of*

effectively determine the tax liability of a permanent establishment of an international enterprise or a subsidiary of a multinational enterprise group. Thus, for some jurisdictions an enterprise itself may be the main source of information on its operations and, at times, this impairs the ability of a tax authority in the jurisdiction to get a complete picture of the enterprise's operations both in that jurisdiction and elsewhere.[213] The result is that it is difficult to enforce a tax on an international enterprise by its country of residence because part of its income is earned abroad and the tax authority in the residence country may not be able to verify the enterprise's foreign income.[214]

5 The need for international tax reform

An important issue is what stimulus is required to initiate international tax reform to prevent tax avoidance through means such as multilateral tax treaties using formulary apportionment allocation methods. The main impediment to multilateral tax reform is that jurisdictions perceive that they will lose sovereignty by having an international tax body taxing multinational enterprises.[215] Most significant international reforms are initiated by a crisis. Developments in the regulation of banking were initiated by the world debt crisis in the 1970s and 1980s.[216] One of the difficulties in achieving tax reform is that the interests of jurisdictions conflict philosophically with the interests of international enterprises. The aim of jurisdictions is to tax enterprises to fund government operations. On the other hand, the aim of multinational enterprise groups and international enterprises is often to minimize taxation payments. Hence, some enterprises are interested in maintaining the current tax treaty system which they exploit and manipulate to avoid taxation. By way of contrast, in the international trade field, countries and international enterprises have a common goal of achieving free trade, which has led to the creation of the GATT and the WTO.

Enron Corporation and Related Entities Regarding Federal Tax and Compensation Issues, and Policy Recommendations (2003), p. 23.

[213] Bird, 'The Interjurisdictional Allocation of Income' (1986), p. 339.

[214] Slemrod, 'Comments' in Tanzi, *Taxation in an Integrating World* (1995), p. 144.

[215] It has been argued that taxation is one area in which there has been a significant diminution of national sovereignty: Braithwaite and Drahos, *Global Business Regulation* (2000), p. 142.

[216] In the arena of environmental regulation, it has been suggested that the prospects for a carbon tax to encourage the reduction in carbon emissions into the atmosphere would improve if developed countries were to experience some hot summers: *ibid.*

6 Conclusion

In conclusion, the system of tax treaties was an effective measure for allocating taxing rights in the early part of the twentieth century, but this system is now reaching obsolescence and needs to be reformed. A key structural reform should be the implementation of a multilateral tax treaty system. This chapter examined some of the deficiencies of the tax treaty system. In the globalized international economy, international enterprises are able to exploit the deficiencies of the current tax treaty system to avoid tax. Tax is treated as an operating cost by many international enterprises, and to maximize their overall net profits they exploit the tax treaty system. Governments seek to counter this avoidance through the use of transfer pricing rules and other measures such as exchange of information. The main obstacles to tax authorities enforcing their rules are the lack of information and the significant resources that are required to scrutinize transfer prices. There is also a significant compliance cost for international enterprises that seek to comply with a country's transfer pricing rules.

But the problem with the transfer pricing rules is that they are founded on the arm's length principle that has a normative flaw – it does not reflect business reality. The arm's length principle, in treating an international enterprise, such as an international bank, as operating through an independent head office and independent branches, ignores the fact that an enterprise necessarily operates as an integrated unitary business. Moreover, the arm's length principle has limited application in determining the prices of integrated businesses that deal in intangible products such as financial services.

This chapter also considered some of the problems that arise from the bilateral nature of the tax treaty network and concludes that reform of the existing system is required to keep pace with the globalization of international enterprises. The current tax treaty network is difficult to reform in a timely and efficient manner. Moreover, as there is no international court to interpret tax treaties governments are able to interpret treaties inconsistently. The problem with the current system is that it can only expand with the implementation of more tax treaties, and as the system expands it gets more difficult and costly to reform.

4

History of tax treaties and the permanent establishment concept

1 Introduction

The current international tax treaty system still reflects the principles and structures developed in the 1920s by the League of Nations, despite the effects of globalization. These principles were developed in a world economy in which international trade was in tangible items and international communication was slow. During the inter-war period, the double taxation of cross-border income resulting from the overlap of source jurisdiction and residence jurisdiction led to calls for measures to prevent double taxation. The International Chamber of Commerce (ICC), on behalf of enterprises, articulated a pressing need for measures to prevent double taxation. In 1928, the League of Nations developed its first model tax treaty to prevent double taxation, and this was the foundation of the 2010 OECD Model, the UN Model[1] and of modern tax treaties. The League of Nations could not foresee the longevity of the principles and structure of its 1928 model tax convention, nor that the bilateral tax treaty system would become an extensive network. Its preference was for a multilateral tax treaty system with multiple bilateral tax treaties being a compromise intermediate measure.

This chapter surveys the history of the work of the League of Nations on international taxation and its dual focus of preventing double taxation and countering tax evasion. Despite the significant changes in international trade and commerce that have occurred since the 1920s, the main international tax issue is still the same – resolving the competing claims of a source country and a residence country to prevent double taxation, tax avoidance and tax evasion. The source country, where income is earned, and the residence country, where an international enterprise is based, both claim taxing rights over cross-border income.

[1] United Nations, *United Nations Model Tax Convention Between Developed and Developing Countries* (2001).

The principal aim of tax treaties is to resolve the competing and overlapping taxing rights of a source country and a residence country to prevent double taxation. But the allocation of source country and residence country taxing rights results in winners and losers. Usually developing countries prefer source country taxation as they are net importers of capital (capital-importing countries). On the other hand, developed countries prefer residence taxation as they are net exporters of capital (capital-exporting countries). The League of Nations attempted to strike a balance between these competing taxing rights. International enterprises and multinational enterprise groups, which are usually based in capital-exporting countries, and their national governments, have a common interest in preventing double taxation as it inhibits international trade and economic growth.

This chapter explores the meaning of the term 'double taxation' and the earliest instances of double taxation. In the Middle Ages there was municipal double taxation arising from an individual living in one municipality and owning land in another municipality. The origins of the permanent establishment concept in Prussian treaties is considered next, and then, in some detail, a survey of the evolution of double tax treaties, commencing with the first tax treaty followed by a review of the work of the League of Nations on preventing double taxation. This chapter examines the development of the League of Nations' model tax treaties, the permanent establishment concept, the proposals for a multinational tax treaty and measures to counter international tax evasion. It also traces the adoption of the arm's length principle by the League of Nations. Finally, the chapter considers the League of Nations' Mexico model and its London Model.

2 International juridical double taxation

International juridical double taxation is defined 'as the imposition of comparable taxes in two (or more) States on the same taxpayer in respect of the same subject matter and for identical periods'.[2] International juridical taxation is to be contrasted with economic double taxation, which is the taxation of the same item of income in the hands of different taxpayers.[3] One of the main aims of tax treaties is to prevent juridical and economic double taxation (double taxation) which is caused by the

---

[2] 2010 OECD Model, p. 7, para. 1.
[3] Juridical and economic double taxation are considered in Ch. 2, at 2.2.1.

overlapping tax jurisdiction of two or more countries. Tax treaties also seek to prevent economic double taxation of associated enterprises.

Overlapping tax jurisdiction arises from countries imposing taxes on the base of residence jurisdiction and source jurisdiction. In the absence of a tax treaty, two countries may assert the right to tax the same item of income in the hands of a taxpayer. If an enterprise derives income from abroad and the source country taxes that income, the taxpayer will receive the income in its residence jurisdiction, which may then impose tax on the resident's worldwide income. If no relief is provided by the residence country for the source country taxation, the enterprise will be subject to double taxation. Double taxation breaches the economic concept of horizontal equity as it results in an enterprise with cross-border income being subject to a significantly higher rate of taxation than resident enterprises with the same amount of income derived solely within the country of residence. In 1927 the League of Nations Technical Committee on Double Taxation made the following comments on double taxation:

> Double taxation, which affects mainly undertakings and persons who exercise their trade or profession in several countries, or derive their income from countries other than the one in which they reside, imposes on such taxpayers burdens which, in many cases, seem truly excessive, if not intolerable. It tends to paralyse their activity and to discourage initiative and thus constitutes a serious obstacle to the development of international relations and world production.
>
> At the same time, any excessive taxation, by its very burden, brings in its train tax evasion, the nature and grave consequences of which have been emphasised on earlier occasions; the suppression of double taxation is therefore closely connected with the measures for the systematic prevention or checking of such evasion.
>
> It is for this twofold purpose that efforts will have to be made to secure international co-operation, with a view to making it possible to put a stop to an evil which has become especially acute owing to the increase in the fiscal burdens consequent upon the war; the measures advocated by the experts could not fail to bring about a reduction in, and a better distribution of, such burdens.[4]

3 History of double taxation

The first recorded formal discussions at a state level on double taxation occurred in the Middle Ages with the introduction of new forms of tax

---

[4] Report Presented by the Committee of Technical Experts on Double Taxation and Tax Evasion, *Double Taxation and Tax Evasion* (1927), pp. 8–9.

in Italian and French towns.[5] The subject was considered by legal scholars and then by theologians who examined taxation and economic issues from the point of view of justice and morality.[6] Double taxation in the Middle Ages arose from the application of real property (also called immovable property) taxes.[7] Double tax problems usually arose in the Middle Ages when a person lived in one village and owned real property in another village. Some countries imposed taxes on real property located within the jurisdiction while other countries imposed taxes on all the property owned by a resident individual. Such double taxation existed for several centuries despite the recognition of the issue by legal scholars and theologians;[8] Seligman stated that with the decline of general property tax and the reduced importance of death taxes, the issue of double taxation attracted little attention in the eighteenth century and for most of the nineteenth century.[9] It was in the last third of the nineteenth century that the issue of double taxation again attracted attention.

Seligman argued that action to eliminate double taxation began in the last third of the nineteenth century, and he categorizes the history of this development into three forms. First, there were attempts to eliminate double taxation by the states of federal unions. In Germany, a federal law was enacted in 1870 and it was supplemented by further legislation in 1909. In Switzerland, the federal constitution of 1874 imposed an obligation on the cantons to enact laws that prevented inter-cantonal double taxation. This led to legislation which transferred responsibility for double taxation to the Swiss federal courts. Other national federations were Australia, Canada and the US. Second, efforts to prevent double taxation were made by quasi-independent members of an empire or imperial federation, such as the British Empire. Third, there were unilateral or bilateral measures to prevent double taxation by independent and sovereign states.[10] An example of a bilateral measure to prevent double taxation was the law enacted in 1819 by the Netherlands, which exempted foreign ships from paying a licence tax if the other country provided a reciprocal exemption for ships from the Netherlands.[11] The first bilateral tax treaty was between the Austro-Hungarian empire and Prussia in 1899.

---

[5] See Seligman, *Double Taxation and International Fiscal Cooperation* (1928), pp. 32–57.
[6] *Ibid.*, p. 32.   [7] *Ibid.*, p. 33.
[8] Davies, *Principles of International Double Tax Relief* (1985), p. 28.
[9] Seligman, *Double Taxation and International Fiscal Cooperation* (1928), p. 37.
[10] *Ibid.*   [11] Davies, *Principles of International Double Tax Relief* (1985), p. 28.

4 1845 to 1909: The emergence of the permanent establishment concept in the German Empire

The permanent establishment concept was developed in the middle of the nineteenth century in the German states to prevent double taxation among the Prussian municipalities.[12] At that time, municipalities in the eastern part of Prussia claimed that 'a trade with a fixed place of business'[13] should be taxed in the municipality in which it was located, even though the owner of the business lived in another municipality. Records on the early origins of the permanent establishment concept are limited, but it appears the term required a permanent location of a business in the region.[14]

The term permanent establishment was not used in German tax law until 1885,[15] and in 1891, the term permanent establishment was codified in Prussia. Under the codification, permanent establishments included business undertakings, branch operations and places for purchasing. The next major development of the permanent establishment concept was the enactment of the German Double Taxation Act of 1909 to prevent the double taxation of income within the German federation.[16] The definition of permanent establishment in the 1909 codification remained unchanged in Germany until it was amended in 1977. The current types of permanent establishment, such as the existence of a place of business and the permanence of the business, were included in the 1909 codification.[17]

5 1889 to World War I: Bilateral tax treaties and the permanent establishment concept

Industrialization and increasing international trade in the late nineteenth century and early twentieth century resulted in double taxation. The first treaty to prevent double taxation and to facilitate cross-border trade was the treaty between the Austro-Hungarian Empire and Prussia, which was signed on 21 June 1899. Under this treaty, business profits made by a permanent establishment were to be taxed in the country in which the permanent establishment was located. In the treaty, a permanent establishment was defined as a place of business in the host country, and the definition included several examples of permanent

---

[12] Skaar, *Permanent Establishment* (1991), p. 72.
[13] The German term was '*stehendes Gewerb*': *ibid.*   [14] *Ibid.*, p. 73.
[15] *Ibid.*, p. 75.   [16] *Ibid.*   [17] *Ibid.*

establishments. A common feature of the examples was that a fixed place of business will be a permanent establishment if it provides for the business activities of a foreign enterprise to be carried on in the host country. The definition of permanent establishment also included business operations carried on through an agent and a place of business maintained for purchasing.

6   World War I to 1946: The League of Nations

With world trade expanding through developments in manufacturing and transport, the issue of international double taxation was an expanding problem during the inter-war period. The consequences of double taxation were considerable because of the high tax rates at the time.[18] One of the leading double taxation researchers of this era, Seligman, claimed that the question of where a tax ought to be imposed involves a simple theoretical principle, but it creates difficult practical problems. Seligman put forward the proposition that taxation should be imposed on the basis of economic allegiance, modified at times by political allegiance. In developed countries at the time, economic interests were divided between the place of location, the place of domicile and the place of residence.[19] Another leading scholar at the time was Stamp, who claimed that the great dilemma for national tax authorities was the conflict between origin jurisdiction and residence jurisdiction.[20] Stamp stated that it is difficult for countries to choose between these two principles and that their concurrent application results in double taxation.[21]

There were increasing calls for measures to be implemented to prevent double taxation in the period between the World Wars. In 1919, immediately after World War I, the ICC was formed to represent international business interests. The ICC, at its 1920 Brussels Conference, requested the League of Nations to take measures to prevent double taxation which was an obstacle to financial reconstruction.[22]

---

[18] *Ibid.*, p. 77.   [19] Seligman, *Essays in Taxation* (10th edn, 1931), p. 119.
[20] Stamp, *The Fundamental Principles of Taxation* (1936), p. 130.   [21] *Ibid.*, p. 131.
[22] International Chamber of Commerce, Resolution No. 11 of the Constituent Congress in 1920 referred to in Report and Resolutions submitted by the Technical Experts to the Financial Committee, *Double Taxation and Tax Evasion* (1925), pp. 7–8.

6.1 The League of Nations – Committee of Experts (1923 Report)

In response to the request from the ICC, the League of Nations in 1921 appointed a committee of economists (Committee of Experts) to undertake a theoretical study of double taxation.[23] The Committee of Experts submitted its report in 1923.[24] The Committee focused on the economic consequences of double taxation and developed principles on the allocation of taxing rights between a source country and a residence country.[25] At that time, the most common type of double taxation was income from the investment of capital by an individual in a foreign country.[26] The Committee recommended that economic allegiance should be the basis on which individuals are taxed on cross-border income, and it defined the notion of economic allegiance and the ways in which it should be allocated between a source country and a residence country.[27]

The Committee of Experts established four bases of economic allegiance: the origin of wealth (the place of production of wealth); the location of wealth (the place of possession of wealth); the place of enforcement of rights to wealth; and residence or domicile (the place of consumption).[28] The production of wealth includes all the stages leading to the realization of wealth.[29] This covers all the stages leading to the acquisition of wealth and may be shared by both the source country and the residence country. The possession of wealth was the period in between the realization of profit and either its consumption or reinvestment. In this phase, there are a range of functions to establish title to profit and to preserve it which depend on the legal system in the country in which the profit is located.[30] The disposition of wealth occurs when profit is realized by an owner, who can either consume the profits or reinvest them.

The Committee concluded that the places of origin of wealth (source) and residence are the main bases of economic allegiance.[31] The Committee

---

[23] Economic and Financial Commission, *Report on Double Taxation Submitted to the Financial Committee* (1923), Introduction. The Committee of Experts were: Professor Bruins (Commercial University, Rotterdam); Professor Senator Einaudi (Turin University); Professor Seligman (Columbia University, New York); Sir Josiah Stamp, KBE (London University).

[24] *Ibid.*   [25] *Ibid.*, p. 40.

[26] Seligman, *Double Taxation and International Fiscal Cooperation* (1928), pp. 117–19.

[27] Economic and Financial Commission, *Report on Double Taxation Submitted to the Financial Committee* (1923), pp. 22–51.

[28] *Ibid.*, pp. 22–3.   [29] *Ibid.*, pp. 22–3.

[30] Seligman, *Double Taxation and International Fiscal Cooperation* (1928), p. 121.

[31] *Ibid.*, p. 25.

of Experts provided the theoretical evaluation for a country exerting its jurisdiction to tax on the basis of source or residence. Countries assert jurisdiction to tax on the basis of source or residence, or more usually, on a combination of both bases.[32]

The Committee settled on four alternative methods to prevent international double taxation:

1. The foreign tax credit method (called 'the method of deduction for income from abroad' by the Committee), under which the residence country provides a deduction from taxes imposed on resident taxpayers for foreign taxes paid by them on their income from abroad.
2. The exemption method, under which the source country[33] exempts non-residents from taxation on all income from sources within its borders.
3. The division method, under which the source country and residence country agree by convention to divide specific taxes so that the source country has a right to tax part of the income and the residence country has the right to tax the remainder of the income.
4. The classification method, under which the source country and residence country agree by convention to allocate taxing rights between them on specific types of income. The countries would agree that the source country would have exclusive taxing rights over certain types of income and that all other income derived by residents of the other country would be exempt from source country taxation.[34]

The Committee also surveyed cross-border taxation of income and concluded that source jurisdiction prevailed over residence jurisdiction, as most of the countries they surveyed were 'dominated by the desire to tax the foreigner'.[35] The Committee decided that in a situation of double taxation a country would be prepared to give up its residence jurisdiction rather than source jurisdiction.[36] Nevertheless, the Committee

---

[32] Bird, 'International Aspects of Integration' (1975), p. 303; Sato and Bird, 'International Aspects of the Taxation of Corporations and Shareholders' (1975), p. 396. Harris, *Corporate/Shareholder Income Taxation and Allocating Taxing Rights between Countries* (1996), p. 277.

[33] The source country was referred to as the country of origin in the Committee's report.

[34] Economic and Financial Commission, *Report on Double Taxation Submitted to the Financial Committee* (1923), pp. 41–2.

[35] *Ibid.*, p. 40.   [36] *Ibid.*

114   HISTORY OF TAX TREATIES

concluded that residence jurisdiction should be the preferred method for taxing cross-border income, with the treaty countries providing reciprocal exemptions from source jurisdiction for income derived by non-resident taxpayers.[37] The basis for this conclusion was that the non-residents could not be effectively taxed by source countries and that source taxation only has the potential to exclude or discourage investment by foreigners.[38] The Committee claimed that if the recommended approach was not acceptable to a country because it does not want to abandon its source jurisdiction, the country should negotiate tax treaties which preserve its source jurisdiction taxing rights.

6.1.1   The 1923 Report in context

The notion of taxing on the basis of economic allegiance was initially developed by Schanz in 1892.[39] He claimed that economic allegiance to a jurisdiction may be premised on consumption, investment or business activities. According to Schanz, allegiance of a person to a source country is more important than the person's allegiance to the residence country. He asserted that the residence country, to which a taxpayer is connected through consumption, is entitled to tax the taxpayer's foreign source income, but a source country is entitled to tax most of the income made within its borders. If a person has concurrent allegiance to a source country and a residence country, the allegiance to the former should prevail. Schanz claimed that the division of tax between a source country and a residence country should be 75 per cent to the source country and 25 per cent to the residence country. The Schanz approach was based on the benefit principle and he defended his approach on the basis that all taxes are based on this principle.[40] Vogel described Schanz's contribution to international tax as being both original and important, but concluded that Schanz's views were not influential.[41] The term economic allegiance was adopted by the Committee of Experts, but its conclusions[42] were the reverse of Schanz's views.[43] The Committee contended that the principle of economic allegiance was based on the

[37] *Ibid.*, p. 51.   [38] *Ibid.*, p. 42.
[39] Schanz, 'Zur Frage de Steuerpflicht' (Regarding Tax Liability), 9 II *Finanzarchiv* 1, 4 (1892): referred to in Vogel, 'Worldwide vs. Source Taxation of Income (Part I)' (1988), p. 219.
[40] *Ibid.*   [41] *Ibid.*, p. 220.
[42] Economic and Financial Commission, *Report on Double Taxation Submitted to the Financial Committee* (1923).
[43] Vogel, 'Worldwide vs. Source Taxation of Income (Part I)' (1988), p. 220.

6 WORLD WAR I TO 1946

concept of a taxpayer's ability to pay,[44] and it did not accept that economic allegiance was based on the benefit principle.[45]

Adams asserted that the theory of economic allegiance was developed as a theoretical guide and he considered it to be merely a generalized label.[46] While Adams agreed with the views that were associated with the theory of economic allegiance, he found the justifications to be practical but not scientific. He noted that the theory of economic allegiance varied between countries and resulted in most of the proponents of the theory asserting exaggerated jurisdiction of domicile taxing rights. Moreover, those advocating this approach tended to be from capital-exporting countries.[47]

The significance of the 1923 Report is itself a controversial issue as some commentators have argued that the 1923 Report was the theoretical base for the current tax treaties.[48] But others have contended that the significance of the 1923 Report has been overemphasized, and that the work of the ICC and the US legislation enacted in 1919[49] and 1921[50] was far more influential.[51] It has also been asserted that the 1923 Report was unconvincing and that its conclusions were not politically acceptable at the time, particularly for capital-importing countries.[52]

A major shortcoming of the 1923 Report was its failure to address the issue of apportionment of international business income.[53] Moreover,

[44] Economic and Financial Commission, *Report on Double Taxation Submitted to the Financial Committee* (1923), p. 21.

[45] Harris, *Corporate/Shareholder Income Taxation and Allocating Taxing Rights between Countries* (1996), p. 277.

[46] T. A. Adams, 'Interstate and International Double Taxation' in Magill (ed.) *Lectures on Taxation* (1932) 101–28, p. 126.

[47] *Ibid.*

[48] Ault, 'Corporate Integration, Tax Treaties and the Division of the International Tax Base' (1992), p. 567; Avi-Yonah, 'The Structure of International Taxation' (1996), p. 1305.

[49] Revenue Act of 1918, Ch. 18. §§ 222(a)(1), 238(a), 240(c), 40 Stat. 1057, 1073, 1080–2 (1919); Graetz and O'Hear, 'The "Original Intent" of US International Taxation' (1997), p. 1022. This Act provided unlimited foreign tax credits for individuals and companies. This meant that credits for foreign taxes could be used to reduce taxes on income sourced in the US if the rate of foreign taxes exceeded the rate of tax in the US.

[50] Revenue Act of 1921, Ch. 136, §§ 222(a)(5), 238(a), 42 1022 Stat. 227, 249, 258: *ibid.*, pp. 1022–3. This Act prevented US individuals and companies from using credits for foreign taxes to reduce their tax on US source income by limiting the foreign tax credits to US taxation on foreign source income.

[51] *Ibid.*, p. 1078; Harris, *Corporate/Shareholder Income Taxation and Allocating Taxing Rights between Countries* (1996), p. 301.

[52] Vogel, 'Worldwide vs. Source Taxation of Income (Part I)' (1988), p. 220.

[53] Graetz and O'Hear, 'The "Original Intent" of US International Taxation' (1997), pp. 1078–9.

116   HISTORY OF TAX TREATIES

the conclusions of the Committee favoured capital-exporting countries which benefit the most if residence jurisdiction is given priority and the Committee members were from capital-exporting countries.[54] Some have argued that the origin of the current bilateral tax treaty structure was the 1923 Report, but the first multilateral tax treaty signed in Rome in 1921 by Austria, Hungary, Italy, Poland, Yugoslavia and Romania also used the classification and assignment structure set out in the 1923 Report.[55] Moreover, this structure was recommended at the preceding 1923 Rome Resolutions of the ICC.[56]

The tax treaty policy work was transferred from the Committee of Experts to the Committee of Technical Experts (Technical Experts),[57] which comprised government officials from member countries.[58] It has been argued that the subsequent work by the Technical Experts was more important than the 1923 Report.[59] The Technical Experts described the 1923 Report as being a 'masterly report' which was of 'inestimable value' to the group and that it was essential for the Technical Experts to analyse the 1923 Report.[60] But the minutes of the meetings of the Technical Experts indicate that the 1923 Report was seldom considered, and the term 'economic allegiance' was not recorded in the minutes of the Technical Committee's 1927 meeting, in which there was controversy over allocation principles.[61] On the other hand, it has been claimed that the 'economic allegiance' principle articulated in the work of the League of Nations is the basis for most of the main rules on classification and assignment structure in modern tax treaties.[62] In summary, the contribution and influence of the 1923 Report was controversial.

While the 1923 Report considered the creation of a model tax treaty, the task of developing a model tax treaty was left to the Technical Experts. Although the Committee of Experts did not draft a model convention, the notion of a multilateral tax treaty was a controversial

---

[54] Seligman, *Double Taxation and International Fiscal Cooperation* (1928), p. 141.
[55] Graetz and O'Hear, 'The "Original Intent" of US International Taxation' (1997), pp. 1079–80.
[56] *Ibid.*, p. 1079.
[57] See section 6.2 below, 'The League of Nations – Technical Experts (1925 Report)'.
[58] *Ibid.*
[59] Graetz and O'Hear, 'The "Original Intent" of US International Taxation' (1997), p. 1078.
[60] Report and Resolutions submitted by the Technical Experts to the Financial Committee, *Double Taxation and Tax Evasion* (1925), p. 8.
[61] Graetz and O'Hear, 'The "Original Intent" of US International Taxation' (1997), p. 1079.
[62] Rosenbloom and Langbein, 'United States Tax Treaty Policy' (1981), p. 366.

6 WORLD WAR I TO 1946

issue in international taxation in 1922. The Committee of Experts' terms of reference challenged:

> Can any general principles be formulated as the basis for an international convention to remove the evil consequences of double taxation, or should conventions be made between particular countries, limited to their own immediate requirements? In the latter alternative, can such particular conventions be so framed as to be capable ultimately of being embodied in a general convention?[63]

6.2 The League of Nations – Technical Experts (1925 Report)

In 1922, the Secretary-General of the League of Nations established the Committee of Technical Experts to study the technical and administrative aspects of the issue of double taxation and tax evasion.[64] The Financial Committee of the League of Nations appointed government officials from seven European countries to the Committee.[65] The task of the Technical Experts was to develop a more equitable system for the allocation of income between nations and to prevent double taxation and tax evasion.[66] The Technical Experts emphasized that it was impartial and that its recommendations were made to reflect the interests of both member countries and non-member countries: 'the selected experts have attempted to carry out their task in an international spirit in conformity with the high purpose of the League'.[67] As the Technical Experts' report was not binding on member countries, officials were able to support recommendations which conflicted with their domestic legislation.[68] But it was argued that the main concern of the individual technical experts was to support policies which would be politically acceptable to their governments.[69] The Technical Experts submitted their report in 1925 (1925 Report).

The Technical Experts also considered the problem of tax evasion, but its main focus was double taxation.[70] The 1925 Report noted that some

---

[63] Economic and Financial Commission, *Report on Double Taxation Submitted to the Financial Committee* (1923), Introduction.

[64] Report and Resolutions submitted by the Technical Experts to the Financial Committee, *Double Taxation and Tax Evasion* (1925), p. 2.

[65] Belgium, Czechoslovakia, France, Great Britain, Italy, the Netherlands and Switzerland.

[66] Report and Resolutions submitted by the Technical Experts to the Financial Committee, *Double Taxation and Tax Evasion* (1925), p. 1.

[67] *Ibid.*, p. 5.   [68] *Ibid.*

[69] Seligman, *Double Taxation and International Fiscal Cooperation* (1928), p. 143.

[70] Report and Resolutions submitted by the Technical Experts to the Financial Committee, *Double Taxation and Tax Evasion* (1925), p. 27.

118 HISTORY OF TAX TREATIES

treaties of the day contained measures to prevent evasion and that tax evasion was a considerable problem at the time. The Technical Experts noted that:

> At the present time, there is a great deal of concealment of income, and there are taxable persons who pay no taxes at all. If the tax on all this income could be brought into the treasuries of the various States concerned, those States would find, as compared with the present position, a very important additional yield, which might not only enable them to indemnify themselves for the sacrifices necessitated by the abolition of multiple taxation, but also to reduce the rates of their taxes or to redeem their loans. We have clearly shown that public opinion in a number of countries is not yet ripe for the adoption of certain of the proposed measures. A change may, perhaps, take place when public opinion comes to realise clearly that the suppression of evasion may, and indeed must, contribute to lightening a burden of taxation on those honest citizens . . .[71]

The Technical Experts concluded that there was a need for an international commission to arbitrate in international taxation disputes.[72] The proposed commission would have the role of arbitrating between states on tax treaty disputes, but it would not have judicial powers and it would not be a court of appeal.[73] It is not surprising that the Technical Experts identified the need for an international tax commission to arbitrate in international tax disputes because it is best for treaty disputes to be arbitrated by an impartial entity whose members are international tax law experts. Moreover, countries are unlikely to agree to an international tax court with judicial power to decide disputes because of the fear that such a court would erode their national sovereignty.[74]

The Technical Experts supported the approach of the Committee of Experts in their 1923 Report that residence taxation should be the preferred method of international taxation. But it found that source taxation should be accepted for the imposition of impersonal taxes. The Technical Experts stated that its proposed division of taxing rights was

---

[71] *Ibid.*, p. 28.   [72] *Ibid.*   [73] *Ibid.*

[74] Countries are reluctant to provide jurisdiction to international courts. It took the UN fifty years to establish the International Criminal Court. In 1948 the UN recognized the need for an international criminal court and, at its fifty-second session, the General Assembly decided to convene the UN Diplomatic Conference of Plenipotentiaries on the Establishment of an International Criminal Court in Rome, Italy, from 15 June to 17 July 1998, 'to finalize and adopt a convention on the establishment of an international criminal court': www.un.org/icc/overview.htm. Finally, the Rome Statute of the International Criminal Court entered into force on 1 July 2002.

6 WORLD WAR I TO 1946

'made for purely practical purposes and no inference in regard to economic theory or doctrine should be drawn from this fact'.[75] The Technical Experts recommended that source taxation should be applied to:

- immovable property;
- agricultural undertakings; and
- industrial and commercial establishments.[76]

On the issue of commercial and industrial establishments, the Technical Experts recommended that if an enterprise has its head office in one country and carries on business in another country, each country should tax the part of the net income produced within its own territory.[77] The methods for carrying on business in a source country were through a branch, an authority, an establishment, a stable industrial or commercial organization, or a permanent representative. Thus, the Technical Experts recognized a source country's right to tax income made by a foreign enterprise within its borders.[78]

The Technical Experts recommended that the Financial Committee of the League of Nations consider establishing a conference of technical experts with broader terms of reference than the Technical Experts' terms of reference.[79] It also suggested that the number of officials from participating countries be increased. The Technical Experts recommended that the conference's terms of reference should be different from its terms of reference,[80] which implies that the Technical Experts considered that it had achieved its task and that the work on double taxation needed to progress to another level. The Technical Experts suggested that the proposed conference's terms of reference be based on the Technical Experts' resolutions with a view to preparing preliminary draft conventions.

The Technical Experts suggested that the proposed conference should be held after the draft conventions had been reviewed by the delegates and other opinions in the participating countries on the draft treaties had been obtained. The aim was to take the work of the League of Nations to the stage of settling a model tax treaty that would be accepted by the participating countries. It was intended that this consultation would result in settling a draft convention that was acceptable to member countries. The Technical Experts' suggestion for a conference

---

[75] Report and Resolutions submitted by the Technical Experts to the Financial Committee, *Double Taxation and Tax Evasion* (1925), p. 15.

[76] *Ibid.*, p. 31.   [77] *Ibid.*   [78] *Ibid.*, p. 15.

[79] *Ibid.*, pp. 29–30.   [80] *Ibid.*

120 HISTORY OF TAX TREATIES

on double taxation was accepted by the League of Nations, which led to the establishment of a Committee of Fiscal Experts to continue the work on double taxation and tax evasion. The Financial Committee of the League of Nations (Financial Committee) in its report dated June 1925 agreed with the broad approach taken in the resolutions of the Technical Experts.[81] The Financial Committee suggested that in future enquiries, consideration be given to 'the disadvantage of placing any obstacles in the way of the international circulation of capital, which is one of the conditions of public prosperity and world economic reconstruction'.[82]

The ICC and the League of Nations maintained close contact in studying the problem of double taxation.[83] In March 1923, the ICC informed the Financial Committee of the League of Nations of the resolutions settled at the ICC's London Congress. In particular, in April 1924 the ICC sent a delegation to the Technical Experts meeting to explain the resolutions adopted by the ICC in March 1924,[84] the main resolution being that the best method to avoid double taxation was to accept residence jurisdiction as the basis of tax on income.[85] The Technical Experts described the ICC resolution as a significant fact.[86] The ICC accepted that the application of this resolution could not be expected to exclude source taxation, but that countries imposing source taxation should be restricted to taxing only income that was derived within its territory. The ICC suggested that relief should be provided for source country taxation, but without indicating what method should be used.[87] The ICC advocated that countries should come to an agreement on the definition of residence for tax purposes and that countries should enter into bilateral tax treaties.[88]

6.3 League of Nations – Committee of Fiscal Experts (1927 Report)

The Committee on Double Taxation and Tax Evasion was instructed to prepare draft conventions based on the resolutions adopted by the Technical Experts in February 1925.[89] The Committee's report, which

---

[81] Referred to in the Report Presented by the Committee of Technical Experts on Double Taxation and Tax Evasion, *Double Taxation and Tax Evasion*, p. 5.

[82] *Ibid.*

[83] Report and Resolutions submitted by the Technical Experts to the Financial Committee, *Double Taxation and Tax Evasion* (1925), p. 8.

[84] *Ibid.*   [85] Quoted in *ibid.*, p. 8.   [86] *Ibid.*   [87] *Ibid.*   [88] *Ibid.*

[89] Report Presented by the Committee of Technical Experts on Double Taxation and Tax Evasion, *Double Taxation and Tax Evasion* (1927), Letter Addressed by the Chairman of the Committee of Technical Experts on Double Taxation and Tax Evasion to the Chairman of the Financial Committee.

6 WORLD WAR I TO 1946

contained four draft conventions,[90] was finalized in April 1927. The Committee confined itself to general rules because of the diversity of the legal systems of member countries and in order to find a model convention that was acceptable to both member countries and non-member countries. It was intended that countries would resolve issues of detail in negotiating bilateral tax treaties. Nevertheless, the Committee recognized the challenge of allocating taxing rights between a source country and a residence country: 'The Committee on Double Taxation and Tax Evasion is fully conscious that the work which it has just concluded is imperfect in that it does not provide solutions for all the difficulties which may arise in this very complex question.'[91]

An interesting feature of the 1927 report was the study on whether tax treaties should be a multilateral treaty signed by as many countries as possible or whether they should be merely bilateral tax treaties.[92] The Committee claimed that it would be preferable that the states conclude multilateral treaties or a single multilateral treaty.[93] However, the Committee considered that it was unable to justify this approach because, at the time, it would have been impossible to draft a multilateral convention. In particular, the differences between the tax systems of various countries would result in a multilateral treaty that could be drafted only in general terms and this was viewed by the Committee as being of no

---

[90] 'Draft Convention for the Prevention of Double Taxation', 'Draft Convention on Administrative Assistance in Matters of Taxation', 'Draft Convention on Administrative Assistance in Matters of Taxation', and 'Draft Convention on Judicial Assistance in the Collection of Taxes'.

[91] Report Presented by the Committee of Technical Experts on Double Taxation and Tax Evasion, *Double Taxation and Tax Evasion* (1927), Letter Addressed by the Chairman of the Committee of Technical Experts on Double Taxation and Tax Evasion to the Chairman of the Financial Committee.

[92] 'A question discussed at length by the Committee was whether the Conventions should be *collective*, that is, signed by as many States as possible, or whether they should be merely *bilateral.* It would certainly be desirable that the States should conclude collective conventions, or even a single convention embodying all others. Nevertheless, the Committee did not feel justified in recommending the adoption of this course. In the matter of double taxation in particular, the fiscal systems of the various countries are so fundamentally different that it seems at present practically impossible to draft a collective convention, unless it were worded in such general terms as to be of no practical value . . .

For this reason, the Committee preferred to draw up standard bilateral conventions. If these texts are to be used by Governments in concluding such conventions, a certain measure of uniformity will be introduced in international fiscal law and, at a later stage of the evolution of that law, a system of general conventions may be established which will make possible the unification and codification of the rules previously laid down.' *Ibid.*, p. 8.

[93] *Ibid.*

practical value.[94] On the issue of tax evasion, the Committee found that obtaining the agreement of all countries to a single convention would require prolonged and delicate negotiations.

The Committee concluded that as a practical compromise bilateral tax treaties should be implemented to meet the interests of taxpayers and those of the participating countries. Consequently, the Committee's preference was to draft a bilateral treaty to be used as a model treaty by countries.[95] The aim of the Committee was to achieve a degree of uniformity between tax treaties by implementing bilateral tax treaties based on the Committee's draft convention. Even though the Committee recommended the use of bilateral tax treaties, it was optimistic that in the future a multilateral treaty could be developed and implemented. Moreover, the Committee expected that in the future a system of general tax treaties might be created and that this might lead to the 'unification and codification of the rules previously laid down'.[96]

The Committee's draft bilateral treaty contained an Article providing for the taxation of business profits made by a permanent establishment. This was formal recognition in the draft bilateral treaty that a source country was entitled to tax business profits derived by non-resident persons through a permanent establishment. The terms of the draft business profits Article were:

> Income from any industrial, commercial or agricultural undertaking and from any other trades or professions shall be taxable in the State in which the persons controlling the undertaking or engaged in the trade or profession possess permanent establishments.

> The real centres of management, affiliated companies, branches, factories, agencies, warehouses, offices, depots, shall be regarded as permanent establishments. The fact that an undertaking has business dealings with a foreign country through a *bona fide* agent of independent status (broker, commission agent, etc.), shall not be held to mean that the undertaking in question has a permanent establishment in that country.

> Should the undertaking possess permanent establishments in both Contracting States, each of the two States shall tax the portion of the income produced in its territory.

[94] Report and Resolutions submitted by the Technical Experts to the Financial Committee, *Double Taxation and Tax Evasion* (1925).

[95] Report Presented by the Committee of Technical Experts on Double Taxation and Tax Evasion, *Double Taxation and Tax Evasion* (1927).

[96] *Ibid.*, p. 8.

6 WORLD WAR I TO 1946 123

> In the absence of accounts showing this income separately and in proper form, the competent administrations of the two Contracting States shall come to an arrangement as to the rules for apportionment.[97]

This definition of the term permanent establishment was very broad. The inclusion of associated companies in the definition illustrated the broad nature of the permanent establishment definition. The Commentary to the draft treaty states that the term 'undertakings' in the draft is to be interpreted in its widest sense and that the term includes all undertakings without making any distinction between natural persons and legal persons.[98] On the issue of an agent being a permanent establishment, the Commentary states that the exception for a bona fide agent means that the agent must be completely independent, from both an economic and legal perspective.[99] In addition, the Commentary notes that an independent agent's remuneration should not be below what is regarded as normal remuneration.

The Committee recommended that a standing committee be set up within the League of Nations to continue the work on achieving international cooperation in international taxation.[100] The Committee proposed that the members of the committee would be international tax experts and that the committee would meet once or twice a year to investigate international tax problems and report its conclusions. It would also work on the model bilateral tax treaty and perhaps a model multilateral tax treaty. The Council of the League of Nations requested that the Committee's report be distributed to member countries and non-member countries for comment and that a meeting of government experts be convened in 1928 to discuss the report.[101] This recommendation led to the establishment of a General Meeting of Government Experts on Double Taxation and Tax Evasion.

6.4 League of Nations – General Meeting of Government Experts on Double Taxation and Tax Evasion (1928 Report)

The task of the General Meeting of Government Experts on Double Taxation and Tax Evasion (General Meeting) was to study the model

---

[97] *Ibid.*, pp. 10–11.   [98] *Ibid.*, p. 15.   [99] *Ibid.*

[100] Report Presented by the Committee of Technical Experts on Double Taxation and Tax Evasion, *Double Taxation and Tax Evasion* (1927), p. 31.

[101] Report Presented by the General Meeting of Government Experts on Double Taxation and Tax Evasion, *Double Taxation and Tax Evasion* (1928), p. 5.

124   HISTORY OF TAX TREATIES

draft tax treaties finalized in 1927.[102] The General Meeting consisted
of representatives from twenty-seven countries.[103] The General Meeting
endorsed the principles adopted by the Committee of Experts and made
a resolution that the Committee's draft tax treaties form a basis for the
preparation of model tax treaties whose purpose was to prevent
double taxation and tax evasion.[104] In addition, the General Meeting
made certain changes to the text of the draft treaties as recommended by
the Committee of Experts in 1927. While the General Meeting attempted
to reach unanimous agreement on all essential points,[105] it was unable to
reach unanimous agreement on all the issues because 'of the diversity of
fiscal systems, the differences in national economic interests and the
divergent conceptions concerning both theory and practice'.[106] As
a compromise, the General Meeting left issues on which complete
agreement could not be reached to countries negotiating tax treaties in
the future. Nevertheless, the General Meeting went to great lengths to
reduce to a minimum the number and importance of issues on which
agreement could not be reached.[107]

The model tax treaties approved by the General Meeting were those
recommended by the Committee of Fiscal Experts with two major
amendments.[108] Apart from the amendments, the business profits Article
(Article 5) of the General Meeting's draft convention[109] was very similar
to the draft prepared by the Committee of Technical Experts.[110] The
first amendment was that associated enterprises were deleted from the
definition of a permanent establishment. The second amendment was
deleting any reference to the use of a taxpayer's separate accounts in
attributing profits to a permanent establishment.[111] The 1928 Report
directs in Draft Convention No. 1 that:

---

[102] *Ibid.*

[103] Austria, Belgium, Bulgaria, China, Czechoslovakia, Danzig, Denmark, Estonia, France,
Germany, Great Britain, Greece, Hungary, Irish Free State, Italy, Japan, Latvia, the
Netherlands, Norway, Poland, Romania, South Africa, Spain, Sweden, Switzerland,
United States, Union of Socialist Soviet Republics.

[104] Report Presented by the General Meeting of Government Experts on Double Taxation
and Tax Evasion, *Double Taxation and Tax Evasion* (1928).

[105] *Ibid.*, p. 6.   [106] *Ibid.*   [107] *Ibid.*

[108] Langbein, 'The Unitary Method and the Myth of Arm's Length' (1986), p. 631.

[109] Bilateral Conventions for the Prevention of Double Taxation in the Special Matters of
Direct Taxes: Skaar, *Permanent Establishment: Erosion of a Tax Treaty Principle* (1991),
pp. 7–9.

[110] Report Presented by the Committee of Technical Experts on Double Taxation and Tax
Evasion, *Double Taxation and Tax Evasion*, p. 8.

[111] Langbein, 'The Unitary Method and the Myth of Arm's Length' (1986), p. 631.

6 WORLD WAR I TO 1946

Should the undertaking possess permanent establishments in both Contracting States, each of the two States shall tax the portion of the income produced in its territory. The competent administrations of the two Contracting States shall come to an arrangement as to the basis for apportionment.[112]

In the Commentary on the business profits Article, the General Meeting discussed the methods of apportionment that could be used.

The competent administrations of the two Contracting States shall come to an arrangement as to the bases for apportionment.

These bases will vary essentially according to the undertakings concerned; in certain States account is taken, according to the nature of the undertakings, of the amount of capital involved, of the number of workers, the wages paid, receipts, etc. Similarly, in cases where the products of factories are sold abroad, a distinction is often made between 'manufacturing' and 'merchanting' profits, the latter being the difference between the price in the home market and the sale price abroad, less cost of transport. These criteria are, of course, merely given as indications.[113]

Consequently, Langbein claimed that the General Meeting's approach was not premised on separate accounting as the notion of separate accounting and the arm's length principle were not part of the League of Nations' model tax treaties in 1929.[114] In the context of this process, the fact that the business profits Article survived with a minor change was a significant achievement for source countries.

The business profits Article provides a source country with the right to tax the business profits made from a permanent establishment within its territory which is an exception to the principle established by the Committee of Experts that residence jurisdiction should prevail. It would be irresistible for a source country to allow an enterprise to carry on activities through a permanent establishment within its territory without taxing the permanent establishment on the profits attributable to it. The business profits Article is also a basis of taxation that is enforceable, as an enterprise with a permanent establishment in a host country will usually have assets in that jurisdiction. In the international economy of the early twentieth century, international trade was in tangible items. Consequently, to operate abroad international enterprises were required to have business operations in source countries, such as

---

[112] Report Presented by the General Meeting of Government Experts on Double Taxation and Tax Evasion, *Double Taxation and Tax Evasion* (1928), p. 8.

[113] *Ibid.*, p. 12.

[114] Langbein, 'The Unitary Method and the Myth of Arm's Length' (1986), p. 631.

business premises, offices, sales facilities, storage facilities and repair services. The assets of a permanent establishment in a country provide the host country's tax authority with the ability to enforce its tax law.

The General Meeting unanimously supported the Committee of Technical Experts' recommendation that a permanent committee be created as part of the League of Nations to study international tax issues.[115] The General Meeting proposed that the committee would deal with all questions connected to the study of fiscal problems and that the committee should examine 'rules for the apportionment of the profits or capital of undertakings operating in several countries'.[116] It was suggested that the proposed committee would be able to provide assistance to the Council of the League of Nations on taxation matters. Another function suggested for the proposed committee was to publish documents including an annual collection of tax treaties settled between countries, memoranda on existing systems of taxation, and an annual report.[117]

These publications were viewed as providing assistance to governments to settle tax treaties with the process evolving to the point where a uniform tax treaty could be settled as the basis for future tax treaties. The General Meeting thought that the 'annual collection of treaties' would provide assistance to governments concluding tax treaties if they had access to the texts of treaties already concluded. The proposed publications would enable governments to take advantage of the work being done abroad and to be aware of the tax treaty developments in other countries.[118] The General Meeting predicted that the publication of concluded tax treaties 'would have the further effect of strengthening the tendency towards uniformity in future Conventions'.[119] This illustrates that the aim of the various League of Nations' studies on double taxation was to settle on a model tax treaty that would be implemented by both member countries and non-member countries. It is indisputable that tax treaties would be effective in countering double taxation if there were a high degree of consistency in the settled tax treaties. But this objective was not achieved as many member countries did not closely follow the model tax treaty in their tax treaties.

The publication of 'memoranda on existing systems of taxation' was viewed by the General Meeting as being of assistance to governments

---

[115] Report Presented by the General Meeting of Government Experts on Double Taxation and Tax Evasion, *Double Taxation and Tax Evasion* (1928), p. 35.
[116] *Ibid.*, p. 35.   [117] *Ibid.*, pp. 35–6.   [118] *Ibid.*   [119] *Ibid.*, p. 35.

6 WORLD WAR I TO 1946

in the negotiation of tax treaties. For governments negotiating a tax treaty it is essential to have a detailed knowledge of the other country's domestic tax system. The General Meeting suggested that the tax authorities should survey their domestic tax systems and publish the survey to enable tax treaty negotiators to identify the similarities and differences between their tax systems. It was intended that the surveys would result in the negotiators being able to efficiently bring the two 'fiscal systems into harmony'.[120] This proposal had been first made in 1920 but was not able to be implemented because of the frequent changes to domestic tax systems that were made after World War I.[121] The General Meeting believed that, at the time, there was sufficient stability in domestic tax systems to enable the proposed surveys to be made, although in the 1920s, the difficulty of the task of surveying domestic tax systems was apparent. The General Meeting suggested that the proposed committee would publish an annual report on progress made during the year on preventing double taxation and on administrative assistance in the collection of taxes. The publication could be used to draw attention to the special characteristics of tax treaties concluded during the year. The recommendations of the General Meeting led to the creation of the League of Nations Fiscal Committee.

6.4.1 Thomas Adams: Multilateral tax treaty

Thomas Adams, an academic and respected US Treasury tax adviser in the 1920s, also was regarded as an influential figure in the development of the US system of international taxation.[122] Adams recognized the benefits of a multilateral tax treaty system over bilateral tax treaties and was optimistic on the prospect of having a multilateral tax treaty implemented.[123] Adams stated that: 'it is entirely practicable for the great nations of the world to get together and adopt a uniform multilateral treaty by which double taxation could be eliminated, except for these items of bond interest and dividends'.[124] Adams was unable to persuade the General Meeting to change its preference from a bilateral system to a multilateral system, despite his influence as a US Treasury

---

[120] *Ibid.*   [121] The Brussels Financial Conference.

[122] Adams held academic positions at the University of Wisconsin and Yale University. From 1917 to 1923 Adams was appointed as the Treasury's principal tax adviser by President Wilson. From 1923 until his death in 1933 Adams was the key spokesperson for the US on tax treaties: Graetz and O'Hear, 'The "Original Intent" of US International Taxation' (1997), 1027–30.

[123] *Ibid.*, pp. 1105–7.

[124] T. S. Adams, 'International and Interstate Aspects of Double Taxation' (1929), p. 196.

128 HISTORY OF TAX TREATIES

representative.[125] At the 1928 General Meeting no action was taken on Adams's proposal for a multilateral tax treaty system.[126]

In 1929, Adams predicted the disadvantages of a bilateral tax treaty system as being its complexity and the potential for manipulation through a large number of treaties in the bilateral tax treaty approach adopted by the League of Nations:

> Now, in the long run, whatever solutions are adopted by different pairs of nations, it is probable that Nation A in concluding a bilateral convention with Nation B will adopt some solution different from that which it might adopt in a similar treaty with Nation X. And if this piece-meal bargaining goes on for twenty years or more, as it is likely to go on, it may possibly result in a tangle of conflicting solutions applicable to the nationals of different countries, which will be highly complicated and highly mysterious, and about as bad as the situation that now exists. In short, there is in my mind, looking to the longer future, the strongest reason for the adoption on one uniform solution, if we could get it, or the settlement of this problem by a multilateral convention, in which a large group of nations would adopt the same solutions for the detailed problems which have to be settled.[127]

Adams was reputed to be practical and pragmatic[128] and he was able to foresee the benefits of a multilateral tax treaty long before the multilateral treaty was settled for international trade. Nevertheless, he was unable to convince the League of Nations of the benefits of implementing a multilateral tax treaty, even at a time before the bilateral tax treaty system had become entrenched.

6.5   League of Nations Fiscal Committee (1st Meeting, 1929)

The Fiscal Committee submitted its first report to the League of Nations Council in 1929.[129] The report dealt with a range of matters including an

---

[125] Graetz and O'Hear, 'The "Original Intent" of US International Taxation' (1997), p. 1105.

[126] T. S. Adams, 'International and Interstate Aspects of Double Taxation' (1929), p. 196.

[127] *Ibid.*, p. 195.

[128] A tribute written by Edwin Seligman described Adams's greatest qualities as his administrative and executive skills and his commonsense approach which enabled him to deal with the conflicting opinions on issues. He was a valued counsellor to statesmen. Referred to in Graetz and O'Hear, 'The "Original Intent" of US International Taxation' (1997), p. 1032.

[129] Fiscal Committee, *Report to the Council on the Work of the First Session of the Committee* (1929).

6 WORLD WAR I TO 1946

examination of recently concluded treaties. Of note is the consideration given to settling a multilateral tax treaty and developing rules for the apportionment of the profits of enterprises operating through permanent establishments. The report quoted the ICC's 1929 resolution at its Amsterdam Congress that work be undertaken to prepare a multilateral treaty on taxation.[130] The Fiscal Committee fully supported the ICC's proposal for a multilateral treaty:

> The Committee unanimously agreed that bilateral conventions only constitute a partial solution of the problem of double taxation. Though recognising that this solution appears at the present time in most cases to be the only possible one, the Committee felt that it should always be borne in mind that multilateral conventions would be better calculated to secure the desired unity of method and principle. It therefore thinks that an endeavour should be made to conclude such conventions as soon as agreement, even on a limited scale, seems to be possible.
>
> For instance, the Committee held that a multilateral convention for the avoidance of double taxation in the case of commercial and industrial enterprises having permanent establishments in several countries cannot be concluded until a precise definition of the terms 'permanent establishment' and 'autonomous agent' has been secured.
>
> The Committee hopes that the study it has undertaken in this connection will lead to a definition capable of general acceptance, and that, when this result has been achieved, steps may be taken to prepare a multilateral convention regulating the taxation of industrial and commercial enterprises which conduct business in more than one country.
>
> The Committee is also glad to note that the International Chamber of Commerce has instructed its national Committees to work to the same end. At its next session, the Committee proposes to examine such conclusions as these national Committees have reached.[131]

In response to the General Meeting's direction, the Fiscal Committee considered the issue of developing rules for allocating profits for businesses operating in several countries.[132] The Fiscal Committee concluded that to work on this matter it would require a detailed knowledge of the current practices in the various countries, and accordingly sent a questionnaire to member countries requesting detailed responses.[133] The

---

[130] 'The International Chamber of Commerce considers that it would be highly desirable for an international conference to be convened as soon as possible, consisting of: (a) Treasury officials, and (b) representative business men, appointed by the International Chamber of Commerce, for the purpose of unifying as far as possible the systems applied for the abolition of double taxation and preparing for a multilateral convention for the purpose.' Quoted in *ibid.*, p. 6.

[131] *Ibid.*, p. 6.   [132] *Ibid.*, pp. 4–5.   [133] *Ibid.*, p. 4.

Fiscal Committee also asked the ICC to cooperate with its inquiry and what 'in the opinion of the members of the Chamber, would be the best methods of apportionment'.[134]

6.6 League of Nations Fiscal Committee (2nd Meeting, 1930)

The Fiscal Committee, in its second meeting, reported on the issue of what is an autonomous agent in determining if an enterprise has a permanent establishment[135] and its progress on developing a multilateral tax treaty.[136] On the issue of a multilateral treaty the Fiscal Committee developed a proposal which it believed would be acceptable to a number of countries, if it were carefully drafted. The Fiscal Committee did not see a multilateral treaty as a panacea for double taxation, but that it would encourage a movement by countries to prevent double taxation by a uniform law.

> The adoption of a multilateral convention on the proposed lines would not wholly prevent double taxation among the contracting States even on the classes of income enumerated, but it would materially encourage the movement to reduce double taxation by uniform law – a method which in important respects is obviously superior to the method of reducing double taxation through the instrumentality of bilateral conventions.[137]

The Fiscal Committee appointed a subcommittee to draft a multilateral tax treaty to be submitted at the 1931 meeting of the Fiscal Committee. The Fiscal Committee directed that the proposed treaty was to be based on a number of listed proposals. The subcommittee was required to prepare a draft that would receive broad acceptance. One of the proposals was the version of the business profits Article developed by the Committee of Fiscal Experts in its 1927 Report.[138]

On the issue of determining the best method for apportioning profits to a permanent establishment, the Fiscal Committee noted that it received responses to its questionnaire from twenty countries.[139] It also acknowledged receiving a response from the ICC.[140] The Fiscal Committee acknowledged the complexity of the issue:

---

[134] Ibid., p. 5.
[135] Fiscal Committee, Report to the Council on the Work of the Second Session of the Committee (1930), p. 4.
[136] Ibid., p. 8.   [137] Ibid.   [138] Quoted above in section 6.3 above.
[139] Fiscal Committee, Report to the Council on the Work of the Second Session of the Committee (1930), p. 5.
[140] Ibid., p. 5.

The Committee held an exhaustive discussion, which revealed the complexity of the question and the numerous obstacles which face any attempted solution. Nevertheless, while fully realising the difficulty of the task, the Fiscal Committee is of opinion that the moment has come to deal with the real substance of the question, since, until this is settled, one of the principal causes of double taxation will continue to exist.[141]

The Fiscal Committee received a US$90,000 grant from the Rockefeller Foundation[142] to conduct its work on double taxation,[143] which it used to commission a study by a subcommittee of five members on apportioning income between a source and residence country.[144]

The Rockefeller Foundation's recommendations on the use of the grant suggested that the separate accounting and formulary apportionment methods should be considered as methods of apportioning profits of an international enterprise operating abroad through permanent establishments. The Rockefeller Foundation recommended that:

> This staff would, primarily, carry out research work in regard to the methods of allocating or apportioning profits made or distributed by undertakings operating in two or more countries.
>
> For that purpose the following subjects should be examined in detail:
>
> (a) The laws in force in the different countries; regulations, decrees, orders and decisions; administrative practice and procedure; working principles and methods of accounting; their effect upon international double taxation;
> (b) Methods – more particularly accounting methods – of ascertaining taxable profits which could be adopted by the fiscal administrations of the various countries and which would at the same time be equitable and reasonable from the point of view of the undertakings taxed, and would as far as possible prevent international double taxation, more particularly:
> (i) When the taxable profits are computed on the basis of separate accounts;

---

[141] *Ibid.*, p. 5.
[142] In 1913, the New York State Legislature passed legislation incorporating the Rockefeller Foundation. Its statement of purpose was: 'To promote the well-being of mankind throughout the world.' Following incorporation of the Rockefeller Foundation, John D. Rockefeller Sr made substantial donations to it.
[143] Fiscal Committee, *Report to the Council on the Work of the Second Session of the Committee* (1930), p. 7. The grant was obtained through the work of Professor Adams.
[144] *Ibid.*, p. 5.

132 HISTORY OF TAX TREATIES

(ii) When empirical methods are employed to obtain an approximate estimate of such profits;

(iii) When a system of fractional apportionment is employed.[145]

This suggests that at the time of making the grant the arm's length principle and formulary apportionment were both accepted methods of apportioning profits to a permanent establishment. Moreover, some have suggested that at that time the experts developing models were considering using formulary apportionment for allocating business profits to a permanent establishment.[146]

6.7 League of Nations Fiscal Committee (3rd Meeting, 1931)

At its third meeting, the Fiscal Committee unanimously accepted the subcommittee's draft multilateral tax treaty (Draft A). The Fiscal Committee made minor changes to Draft A and felt that it would be the basis for a multilateral tax treaty between countries for the prevention of double taxation.[147] It was acknowledged by the Fiscal Committee that Draft A would not be acceptable to several countries as it dealt with the positions of both residents and non-residents, with the aim of preventing double taxation for both categories of taxpayer for set classes of income. Accordingly, the Fiscal Committee predicted that Draft A would be rejected by some countries because it imposed rules on countries in respect of their own residents.[148] The Fiscal Committee considered that its alternative draft multilateral treaty dealing only with non-residents might be more readily accepted by countries (Draft B), but the consequent disadvantage of this approach was that it left some double taxation in place.[149] Nevertheless, the Fiscal Committee considered that Draft A was a comprehensive multilateral treaty that would prevent double taxation. It was noted by the Fiscal Committee that the draft treaty prepared in 1928 by the Committee of Government Experts also provided a basis for the development of a multilateral treaty for countries which require a distinction to be made between impersonal taxes and personal taxes.[150]

---

[145] *Ibid.*, p. 7.
[146] Langbein, 'The Unitary Method and the Myth of Arm's Length' (1986), pp. 632–3.
[147] Draft A, Appendix II, Fiscal Committee, *Report to the Council on the Work of the Third Session of the Committee* (1931), p. 3.
[148] *Ibid.*, p. 3.   [149] Draft B, Appendix III, *ibid.*, p. 3.   [150] *Ibid.*, pp. 3–4.

6 WORLD WAR I TO 1946　　　　　133

Although the Fiscal Committee was unable to reach a final decision on the proposal for two model multilateral tax treaties,[151] it concluded that it was necessary to examine 'whether there is any real possibility of an adequate number of accessions to either or both of these two types of convention'.[152] Even if only a limited number of countries were able to accept Draft A, the Fiscal Committee claimed that Draft B or the 1928 model treaty would be a positive step in avoiding double taxation.[153] Nevertheless, the Fiscal Committee optimistically hoped that some countries might sign both Draft A and Draft B simultaneously. The Fiscal Committee recommended that its report and appendices containing Draft A and Draft B be sent to members of the Fiscal Committee to find out if they would accept the drafts. If the prepared drafts were unacceptable to the countries represented on the Fiscal Committee, it also sought advice on whether the drafts would be acceptable if the models incorporated amendments suggested by them.[154]

It may be inferred from the Fiscal Committee's report that there was significant resistance within the Fiscal Committee to the proposals for a multilateral treaty. The member countries viewed a multilateral treaty as an infringement of their national sovereignty and they were therefore reluctant to enter into them. Even though the Fiscal Committee recognized the merits of a multilateral treaty, it was unable to persuade the individual Fiscal Committee members of the merits of this approach. The Fiscal Committee displayed optimism by pursuing a multilateral treaty despite the reluctance of Committee members to accept either of the proposed multilateral treaties.

6.7.1　The draft multilateral tax treaties

The Fiscal Committee report contained three draft multilateral treaties. Draft A dealt with the taxation of both residents and non-residents and it contained a series of exemptions to avoid double taxation.[155] On the other hand, the principle underlying Draft B was to protect the residents of each state from double taxation by exempting certain categories of income from source country taxation. Draft B was not comprehensive and certain categories of income were unaffected by it. Nevertheless, Draft B was viewed by the Fiscal Committee as being of potentially greater practical significance and wider scope. The Fiscal Committee members in support of this draft were of the view that countries

---

[151] *Ibid.*, p. 4.　　[152] *Ibid.*, p. 4.　　[153] *Ibid.*, p. 5.
[154] *Ibid.*　　[155] *Ibid.*, p. 4.

accepting this draft would be encouraged to provide relief to their residents for the categories of income not affected by the treaty because the treaty prevented source countries from taxing certain categories of income.[156] It was predicted that the residence countries would provide an exemption for income which was subject to source country taxation. A preliminary condition of Draft B was that there must be agreement on the categories of income that could be taxed at source before considering what relief from double taxation was to be provided by residence countries.[157]

6.8 The Carroll Report (1933)

Carroll reported to the Fiscal Committee on the apportionment of profits of enterprises operating in several countries after surveying tax law and practices of twenty-seven countries for both domestic enterprises and foreign enterprises. The Carroll Report summarized and compared the main features of different national laws. He attempted to identify a set of general rules used in a majority of countries in order to set a basis for an international agreement.

Carroll found that the two main apportionment methods were the arm's length principle and formulary apportionment.[158] Formulary apportionment was justified on the ground that in a unitary business 'it is impossible to determine accurately what part of the profit is attributable to each function or establishment of the business and consequently the profit can only be apportioned on some empirical basis – for example, an arbitrary apportionment formula'.[159] Moreover, an international enterprise that manufactures items from raw materials does not realize a profit until the goods have been sold. Carroll advocated that the League of Nations should adopt the arm's length principle as the superior method for attributing income to a permanent establishment:

> The adoption of separate accounting as the primary method of allocating income to the various countries in which an enterprise has permanent establishments is preferred by the great majority of Governments, and business enterprises represented in the International Chamber of Commerce, as well as by other authoritative groups. Broadly speaking, the objectives of the method of separate accounting are as follows:

---

[156] *Ibid.*   [157] *Ibid.*
[158] Carroll, *Taxation of Foreign and National Enterprises* (1933), p. 187, para. 664.
[159] *Ibid.*

(a) To maintain accounts for the establishment (or establishments considered as an accounting unit) in each jurisdiction which reflect the items of taxable income and related expense directly allocable thereto, and provide the essential data for apportioning items of joint income and expenses (e.g., pertaining to the joint activities of two establishments) which cannot be directly allocated;

(b) To preclude taxing the establishment in so far as possible on unrealised profits;

(c) To fulfil these objectives by the use of data pertaining directly to the establishment which can be verified in the country of the branch establishment with the minimum use of data pertaining to the enterprise as a whole.[160]

Carroll favoured the arm's length principle as it was the method being used in the US and UK for international taxation, both of which he claimed had the most experience in the taxation of cross-border income and that their accountants were of the highest professional standing.[161] He also claimed that these accounting firms had developed accounting systems to monitor the complex structures of multinational enterprises, but he noted that even with the arm's length principle disputes may arise over what is a fair transfer price.[162]

It has been claimed that the Carroll Report recommended the use of separate accounting to attribute profits to a permanent establishment at the expense of the formulary apportionment method.[163] In addition, the promulgation in 1934 of US transfer pricing regulations prescribed, for the first time, the arm's length principle for determining the 'true net income' of associated enterprises.[164] While a link between these developments has not been established, it is nevertheless striking that these developments were contemporaneous.[165] Moreover, it is expected that at the time the US would have significantly influenced the policies of the League of Nations. Thus, it has been suggested that Carroll's role was to ensure that the arm's length principle was the accepted League of Nations method for the allocation of profits for permanent establishments rather than formulary apportionment.[166]

---

[160] *Ibid.*, p. 189, para. 671.   [161] *Ibid.*, p. 47, para. 128.   [162] *Ibid.*, p. 47, para. 129.

[163] Langbein, 'The Unitary Method and the Myth of Arm's Length' (1986), pp. 631–2.

[164] Hellerstein, 'Federal Income Taxation of Multinationals' (1993), p. 1133.

[165] Langbein, 'The Unitary Method and the Myth of Arm's Length' (1986), p. 633.

[166] *Ibid.*, p. 638.

6.9 League of Nations Fiscal Committee (4th Meeting, 1933)

The Fiscal Committee considered the results of the Carroll inquiry on the apportionment of income from enterprises operating in several countries.[167] The Fiscal Committee also considered a draft multilateral treaty on the allocation of profits of international enterprises prepared by its subcommittee.[168] This draft treaty was restricted to double taxation of industrial and commercial enterprises and was prepared by the subcommittee at its meeting in March 1933, at the invitation of the American Section of the ICC. The subcommittee indicated that its recommendations could be implemented either in treaties or in a country's domestic legislation. The Fiscal Committee accepted the draft multilateral convention and the accompanying commentary, and annexed them to its report.[169] A key feature of the draft treaty was that it was the first model tax treaty to adopt the arm's length principle in the allocation of business profits between a source country and a residence country rather than have specific rules for different types of enterprises.[170] The Fiscal Committee considered that the arm's length principle was flexible and adaptable to various types of industries, but it acknowledged that an exception was required for bank enterprises. By 1933, the arm's length principle had been established as the better method of apportionment.

The Fiscal Committee accepted the text drafted by the General Committee in 1928 and focused its attention on the allocation of profits of international enterprises operating through permanent establishments in host countries, which was an issue that was left unresolved in 1928. The Fiscal Committee concluded that a permanent establishment should be treated in the same manner as independent enterprises operating under similar or identical circumstances, with a permanent establishment's taxable income being based on its financial accounts.[171] It was assumed that a permanent establishment's accounts accurately reflected the profit allocation within an international enterprise, but the draft treaty did not address the differences between the accounting methods

---

[167] Fiscal Committee, *Report to the Council on the Fourth Session of the Committee* (1933), p. 2.

[168] *Ibid.*

[169] Fiscal Committee, *Report to the Council on the Fourth Session of the Committee* (1933), pp. 2–3.

[170] Rosenbloom and Langbein, 'United States Tax Treaty Policy' (1981), p. 367.

[171] Fiscal Committee, *Report to the Council on the Fourth Session of the Committee* (1933), pp. 2–3.

6 WORLD WAR I TO 1946   137

then used by international enterprises.[172] As this model was based on the arm's length principle, it was premised on the accounts of an international enterprise being a reliable basis for allocating profits within the enterprise. But this approach contained the potential for international tax avoidance by altering the allocation of profits within an international enterprise through techniques such as transfer pricing.

The Fiscal Committee concluded that its draft treaty represented the 'first result of important studies and of a long and exhaustive preparatory work',[173] and that the draft was a significant development in the prevention of double taxation of international enterprises. The Fiscal Committee noted the aim of the ICC to encourage the use of tax treaties to prevent double taxation and concluded that: 'In view of its limited scope, and of the international restriction of its provisions to the fundamental rules, this draft by itself might, in the Committee's opinion, form the basis of a multilateral Convention.'[174] The Fiscal Committee recommended that the multilateral draft tax treaty be provided to member countries for comment. It also invited member countries to suggest amendments to the draft multilateral treaty and to indicate if they were willing to enter into negotiations to establish a multilateral tax treaty.

The Fiscal Committee predicted that if several member countries were to sign the treaty, considerable progress could be made in the prevention of double taxation. Furthermore, the Fiscal Committee considered that if member countries were not willing to enter a multilateral treaty they might be willing to use the multilateral draft as a model for their bilateral tax treaties. This suggests that the Fiscal Committee was optimistic that while the draft multilateral treaty may initially have been used by member countries for the negotiation of bilateral treaties, this might set a base from which member countries could enter into a future multilateral treaty. If countries were opposed to entering multilateral treaties, encouraging those countries to use the multilateral draft provisions in their bilateral tax treaties would make it easier for them to subsequently enter a multilateral treaty.

6.10   League of Nations Fiscal Committee (5th Meeting, 1935)

At the 1935 meeting, the Fiscal Committee reported on the responses to the multilateral draft concluded in 1933. Following its consultation with member countries on its multilateral tax treaty proposal, the Fiscal

---

[172] *Ibid.*   [173] *Ibid.*, p. 2.   [174] *Ibid.*

Committee decided to convert the draft multilateral tax treaty into a bilateral treaty. This change of direction was a compromise measure, as the Fiscal Committee considered that greater progress could be achieved through the conclusion of bilateral treaties, despite a number of member countries indicating that they were willing to enter a multilateral treaty.[175] The Fiscal Committee found that most member countries considered that bilateral tax treaties were more appropriate, even though they accepted the principles in the 1933 draft multilateral treaty.[176] Moreover, the Fiscal Committee viewed a bilateral treaty system as being effective in preventing double taxation and it drafted a model bilateral tax treaty to be used in negotiations between member countries, with an expectation that the finalized tax treaties would reflect the provisions of the model treaty. The Fiscal Committee claimed that it 'is strongly of opinion that this procedure is likely in the end to lead to more satisfactory results and to have a wider and more lasting effect than the convocation of an international conference with a view to concluding a multilateral convention, even though it may at first attract less general attention and interest'.[177] The Fiscal Committee did not specify the reasons for the reluctance of member countries to enter a multilateral treaty, but it may be inferred that countries were concerned about losing their tax sovereignty.

The Fiscal Committee found that by 1935, 140 bilateral double tax treaties had been concluded and of these, 60 had been concluded since 1929.[178] The Fiscal Committee concluded that the statistics reflected the influence of the League of Nations and the practical scope of the studies undertaken by it.[179] On the issue of the allocation of profits, the Fiscal Committee decided that a subcommittee should prepare a draft with the key terms to be used in treaties and, in particular, on the allocation of business income. The view was that the proposed definitions may provide norms for countries to use in drafting their treaties.[180]

6.11 League of Nations Fiscal Committee (6th Meeting, 1936)

In 1936, the Fiscal Committee turned its attention to fiscal evasion as it recognized that the League of Nations, while it concentrated on measures to prevent double taxation, had neglected international tax

---

[175] *Ibid.*, p. 3.   [176] *Ibid.*, pp. 3–4.
[177] Fiscal Committee, *Report to the Council on the Fifth Session of the Committee* (1935), p. 4.
[178] *Ibid.*   [179] *Ibid.*   [180] *Ibid.*

6 WORLD WAR I TO 1946

evasion.[181] Nevertheless, the Committee considered that the priority given to the prevention of double taxation was appropriate because the existence of double taxation motivated taxpayers to avoid taxation. The Fiscal Committee concluded that the main form of tax evasion, at the time, involved income from mobile capital (called moveable capital by the Fiscal Committee), such as interest and dividends (passive income), and that this form of evasion was increasing at that time.[182] The Fiscal Committee accepted that measures to counter this form of evasion could be developed, but that they had to be implemented by member countries. Otherwise, unilateral measures by some countries to counter tax evasion could easily be avoided by the transfer of the capital to another country in which income from capital was either untaxed or lightly taxed.

The Fiscal Committee recommended that countries should implement exchange of information measures under a general agreement to prevent the evasion of capital taxation. The key measure was that in the contracting states, persons or companies who made payments on movable capital to non-residents must report these payments to their tax authorities. The reports on income from moveable capital were to be provided to the tax authority in the country in which the recipient of income from moveable capital was resident.[183] Under this proposal tax authorities would collect and provide information on cross-border interest and dividends, originating within their borders, to other tax authorities to assist them in taxing the recipients of the interest and dividends. The Fiscal Committee considered that this measure would be ineffective if only a limited number of member countries accepted this recommendation. The Committee referred to the observations of the Group of Technical Experts in 1925 on the need for a multilateral treaty to prevent evasion:

> Unlike double taxation, in connection with which any problems arising between two States can be settled appropriately by means of bilateral conventions, the question of tax evasion can only be solved in a satisfactory manner if the international agreements on this matter are adhered to by most of the States and if they are concluded simultaneously. Otherwise, the interests of the minority of States, which would alone have signed the conventions, might be seriously prejudiced.[184]

---

[181] Fiscal Committee, *Report to the Council on the Fifth Session of the Committee* (1935), p. 2.
[182] *Ibid.*   [183] *Ibid.*, p. 3.
[184] *Ibid.*, p. 4 quoting the Report and Resolutions submitted by the Technical Experts to the Financial Committee, *Double Taxation and Tax Evasion* (1925), p. 34.

140 HISTORY OF TAX TREATIES

The Fiscal Committee recommended that the League of Nations Council evaluate the prospects of reaching a general agreement at one meeting. But if only a small number of countries entered into the agreement, the Fiscal Committee considered that the agreement would be counterproductive.[185]

6.12 League of Nations Fiscal Committee (7th Meeting, 1937)

The response of member countries to the proposed multilateral anti-avoidance agreement was that it would be difficult for countries to modify their domestic legislation to demand information from resident individuals and enterprises for the benefit of foreign countries.[186] But this approach was short-sighted as it ignored the fact that a collective effort is required to counter evasion and that the measures were reciprocal. The proposed scheme attempted to provide participating countries with complete details of the passive income of their residents from foreign sources. The Fiscal Committee commented on the self-interested nature of the countries' responses:

> To these arguments it is easy to answer that the prevention of tax evasion benefits all States, and that States which to-day have no interest in such benefits may to-morrow be in a position when they would be glad of them. It may also be pointed out – as the Fiscal Committee has done more than once – that tax evasion does not merely mean depriving States of their legitimate resources, but also exerts an influence on movements of capital. It reduces, therefore, not only the revenue of States, but also the supply of capital. The Fiscal Committee cannot, however, shut its eyes to the fact that the force of these arguments is apparent only in times of financial stringency. The Committee fears that there is no chance at present of inducing States to alter their point of view or of persuading revenue authorities to change their methods in such a way as to render them compatible with international control.
>
> Does that mean that the upshot of the consultation of States referred to is the conclusion that tax evasion in the case of moveable capital cannot at present be suppressed, and that nothing can be done to prevent it until public opinion on the subject has developed further under pressure of necessity? That certainly was not the attitude adopted by the Assembly of the League when it requested the Fiscal Committee to continue its labours, and did so in terms which would appear to recommend, not

---

[185] Fiscal Committee, *Report to the Council on the Fifth Session of the Committee* (1935), p. 5.

[186] Fiscal Committee, *Report to the Council on the Seventh Session of the Committee* (1937), p. 2.

an enquiry into measures with immediate effect, but rather a progressive approach to better conditions. It is along the latter lines that the Fiscal Committee has proceeded.[187]

The Fiscal Committee was disappointed with the member countries' lack of cooperation in countering tax evasion. As a compromise measure, the Fiscal Committee sought to identify other methods to encourage revenue authorities of member countries to exchange tax information. The member countries which responded to the Fiscal Committee on this issue were unable to accept that the mutual benefits in collecting information on passive income outweighed the costs of the proposal.

6.13   League of Nations Fiscal Committee (8th Meeting, 1938)

In 1938, the Fiscal Committee continued to pursue measures to counter evasion and found that member countries used a variety of methods to prevent evasion. The Fiscal Committee's view was that the methods used by countries 'were for the most part the result of a slow adaptation of the laws and regulations to the circumstances'.[188] The diversity of approaches prevented the Fiscal Committee from being able to set out a general measure that could be used in all countries. As a result, the Fiscal Committee concluded that exchange of information through bilateral tax treaties was the best option as member countries have the ability to obtain information which may be of value to their treaty partners. This measure was largely ineffective in countering the evasion and avoidance of income from mobile capital and the issue was not considered again by the League of Nations.

The League of Nations was unable to implement comprehensive measures to counter fiscal evasion in relation to passive income. The ability of investors to pass on withholding taxes allowed this avenue of evasion to flourish in the post-war period. For example, the ability of investors to pass on interest withholding taxes increased the cost of borrowing in debtor countries, which resulted in many countries providing exemptions from interest withholding tax for non-resident lenders to reduce the cost of borrowing. The piecemeal responses by member countries to counter the evasion of tax by those earning passive income were unsuccessful. Today we have reached the point that some

---

[187] *Ibid.*

[188] Fiscal Committee, *Report to the Council on the Work of the Eighth Session of the Committee* (1938), p. 2.

governments now accept that income from mobile capital should be lightly taxed in order to avoid the fear of the 'flight of capital', if a government were to apply its ordinary tax rules to such income. Tax evasion by some taxpayers narrows a country's tax base and, accordingly, increases the taxation of other taxpayers. It may be argued that the measures proposed by the Fiscal Committee would have been ineffective, but the failure of member countries to take coordinated action may be viewed, no matter how unreasonably, as being tacit acceptance by the member countries that income from capital should either be exempted from taxation or subject to concessional tax rates.

6.14   League of Nations Fiscal Committee (9th Meeting, 1939)

The 1939 Meeting was the last meeting of the Fiscal Committee before World War II. At the meeting, the Fiscal Committee turned its attention to domestic tax measures rather than measures to prevent double taxation.[189] It considered the effect of economic fluctuations on tax receipts of governments and suggested practical recommendations for the structure of a country's tax system and the temporary measures available to national governments at the various stages of the economic cycle. The Fiscal Committee suggested that the 1928 model bilateral treaty be revised by the General Meeting of Government Experts to reflect the changes in the drafting of treaties that had taken place since 1928 and to include the recommendations of the Fiscal Committee made since 1928.[190]

6.15   League of Nations Fiscal Committee (10th Meeting, 1945) – The London Model

The League of Nations 1928 model tax treaty was redrafted by the Mexico conference and was again amended at the London conference. The revision of the 1928 draft treaty was undertaken by a subcommittee which met at The Hague in April 1940 and the work was carried on at two conferences held in Mexico City in June 1940 and July 1943 (Mexico Model). The London conference of the Fiscal Committee in 1945 concluded that the Mexico Model was an improvement, but the Fiscal

---

[189] Fiscal Committee, *Report to the Council on the Work of the Ninth Session of the Committee* (1939).

[190] Fiscal Committee, *Report on the Work of the Tenth Session of the Committee* (1946), pp. 6–7.

6 WORLD WAR I TO 1946   143

Committee noted that the composition of the participants at the two conferences differed.[191] At the Mexico conferences, there were participants from capital-importing countries and the conferences resolved to amend the treaty to allow source countries to tax income from capital. The participants at the London conference were predominantly from capital-exporting countries, and this conference altered the draft to restrict the ability of source countries to tax interest, dividends, royalties, annuities and pensions.[192]

In 1946, at the request of the Fiscal Committee, its Secretariat produced one Commentary on both the Mexico Model and the London Model.[193] The Commentary was only a working paper to study the Mexico Model and London Model, it was not a statement of the views of the Fiscal Committee. It was intended, at that time, that the Mexico Model and the London Model would be reviewed by a group of tax administrations and experts from capital-importing and capital-exporting countries and from developed and developing countries when the UN took over the work of the League of Nations on international taxation.[194] But this intention was not fulfilled at that time.

6.15.1 A comparison of the Mexico Model and the London Model

On the issue of the attribution of business profits,[195] the Commentary notes that the threshold tests in the models were different. The Mexico Model had a low threshold requirement for source country taxation; if a foreign enterprise carried on business activities in a source country, the business profits from that activity were subject to tax in the source country, with an exception provided for isolated or occasional transactions.[196] The London Model threshold for source country taxation on business income was that an international enterprise must have a permanent establishment in the source country. The lower threshold for

---

[191] *Ibid.*, pp. 7–8.   [192] *Ibid.*, p. 8.

[193] Fiscal Committee, *London and Mexico Model Tax Conventions: Commentary and Text* (1946).

[194] Fiscal Committee, *Report on the Work of the Tenth Session of the Committee* (1946), p. 8.

[195] Under the Mexico Model and the London Model 'income from any industrial, commercial or agricultural enterprise and from any other gainful occupation' is governed by Article IV of the Model Convention and Articles IV to VIII of the Protocol. The League of Nations noted that such income is mainly represented by 'business profits' and consequently it used this term for the purpose of brevity: Fiscal Committee, *London and Mexico Model Tax Conventions: Commentary and Text* (1946), p. 13.

[196] *Ibid.*, pp. 13–14.

the application of the business profits Article in the Mexico Model was argued to prevent source countries from losing revenue from business activity in a source country, which was not carried out through a permanent establishment. This approach was also seen to discourage tax avoidance because some international enterprises may otherwise avoid taxation by carrying on a business in a source country without maintaining a permanent establishment in that country. In addition, some enterprises may conceal the existence of a permanent establishment to avoid taxation in a source country.[197]

The Fiscal Committee in London reviewed the Mexico Model and decided that the permanent establishment concept defined by the Fiscal Committee in its earlier work was contained in nearly all existing tax treaties dealing with business income.[198] It also concluded that the permanent establishment concept could not be used for anti-avoidance purposes because under the model treaty the total tax liability of an international enterprise was claimed to be the same, regardless of the attribution of the business profits between the residence country and the source country in which the business was carried on. Further, the issue of an international enterprise concealing a permanent establishment from a tax authority in a host country was an administrative matter for the host country tax authority. Finally, it was argued that 'past experience was said to show that it is extremely difficult to tax foreign enterprises efficiently and equitably when they do not possess a permanent establishment in a country'.[199]

The Commentary on the threshold tests for the application of the business profits Article illustrates the tension between source countries and residence countries. Source countries will seek to cast the permanent establishment threshold tests as broadly as possible to be able to tax profits arising from foreign enterprises carrying on business within their borders. Source countries, which are capital-importing countries, were in effect giving up a disproportionate part of their taxing rights when the threshold tests for taxing business profits are set at a relatively high level. Consequently, carrying on business without a permanent establishment was viewed by the source countries in Mexico City as satisfying the economic allegiance requirement, thus entitling source countries to tax business profits attributable to transactions in those countries.

On the other hand, the capital-exporting countries, as residence countries, sought to impose a higher threshold requirement to limit

---

[197] *Ibid.*   [198] *Ibid.*, p. 14.   [199] *Ibid.*

6 WORLD WAR I TO 1946

the taxing rights of source countries. The countries in which international enterprises were resident, such as in Europe, the UK and the US, based the business profits Article on the existence of a permanent establishment. The approach in the Mexico Model was seen as an aberration from the earlier League of Nations models, which used a permanent establishment threshold test for taxing business profits. This may, of course, merely reflect the fact that it was only at the Mexico City meetings that source countries were able to assert their views. However, the existence of a permanent establishment in a source country does have the advantage of enabling that country to enforce its taxing rights as it is likely that the permanent establishment will have assets and accounting records. A permanent establishment's accounting records allow a national tax authority to verify the business profits attributed to a permanent establishment.

The term 'permanent establishment' was defined in Article V of the London Model as having a fixed place of business in the host country where that place of business contributed to the enterprise's income.[200] The two requirements in the definition were cumulative and therefore if an enterprise had a fixed place of business, but it did not contribute to the profits of the enterprise, the permanent establishment was not subject to taxation in the source country under the business profits Article.

The London conference emphasized that these requirements were cumulative in claiming that the following permanent establishments did not directly contribute to business profits: research laboratories, experimental plants, information bureaux, storehouses, purchasing offices, advertising displays and showrooms where goods were not sold.[201] The Fiscal Committee claimed that to apply income tax on notional profits of these establishments would result in arbitrary or extraterritorial taxation.[202] Consequently, the Fiscal Committee decided to refrain from allocating profits to such permanent establishments, even though they contributed indirectly to the business profits of their international enterprises.

The London Model and the Mexico Model further developed the distinction between a permanent establishment and an independent agent. If an enterprise transacts in another country through an independent agent, such as a broker or commission agent, it is not liable to

---

[200] *Ibid.*   [201] *Ibid.*, p. 15.   [202] *Ibid.*

146 HISTORY OF TAX TREATIES

taxation in that country (Article V(3)). An agent will not be treated as being an independent agent if:

- the agent habitually uses the name of an enterprise as an authorized agent and enters contracts on behalf of the enterprise,
- the agent is an employee on salary and enters transactions on the enterprise's behalf on a regular basis, or
- the agent holds goods, belonging to an enterprise, on a regular basis, for the purpose of sale.[203]

On the issue of establishing whether an agent was independent, Article V(5) directs that if the office and business expenses of an agent were paid for by an enterprise, this relationship will be treated as a contract of employment for the purposes of the Article. In this situation, the enterprise will be treated as having a permanent establishment. This measure sought to reduce the scope for avoidance by enterprises purporting that its agents in a source country were independent agents.[204]

It was noted in the Commentary that the following criteria may be used to determine if an international enterprise has a permanent establishment:

- the power of an agent to bind the enterprise;
- the existence of a contract of employment with an agent;
- whether the enterprise maintains a stock of goods under the control of the agent; or
- whether the enterprise pays the agent's rental and office expenses.

These criteria are independent, and if an enterprise satisfies any one of them, it is treated as having a permanent establishment, provided the condition which is satisfied 'corresponds to a permanent state of things or an habitual practice'.[205] The Commentary claimed that subsidiaries cannot be permanent establishments of their parent companies because subsidiaries are independent entities and should be taxed independently. It was also claimed that there were mechanisms to counter profit shifting between associated entities.[206]

On the issue of allocating profits to a permanent establishment, the income attributed to a permanent establishment must be income that is the direct result of its activities. Under the arm's length principle, which

---

[203] Fiscal Committee, *London and Mexico Model Tax Conventions: Commentary and Text* (1946), p. 16.
[204] *Ibid.*   [205] *Ibid.*   [206] *Ibid.*, p. 17.

relied on separate accounting, the income attributable to a permanent establishment must be the income it would have made if it were an independent enterprise carrying on the same business in the host country. This method of profit allocation relies on the separate character of accounts of a permanent establishment, which should reflect arm's length transactions. The Commentary justified the use of the arm's length principle on the following grounds:

> The use of the method of separate accounting as the fundamental procedure for the determination of profits attributable to each country in which an enterprise has an establishment is intended to serve four purposes: first, by treating a branch establishment not as part of an enterprise but as a self-contained unit and thus generally avoiding reference to results or data outside the country concerned, it gives the taxation of branch establishments a strictly territorial scope not extending beyond the boundaries of the countries concerned; secondly, the method helps to enforce the principle of equality of treatment of foreigners by placing, in principle, branches of foreign enterprises on the same footing as similar establishments of domestic enterprises as regards the computation of receipts and expenses, which, once they have been allocated or apportioned by separate accounting, are to be treated in accordance with the tax laws of the country to which they have been attributed; thirdly, the use of separate accounting as a basis for the assessment of income tax conforms to the usual practice among concerns engaged in international business of keeping separate accounts for each of their establishments; finally, separate accounting serves the revenue interests of the country concerned, since, when it is properly applied and supervised, it prevents the concealment of profits or their diversion from one country to another.[207]

The Commentary also discussed the adjustment of a permanent establishment's accounts if they do not conform to the arm's length principle. In this situation, a tax authority would make an initial adjustment of the accounts of the permanent establishment to comply with the arm's length principle, which would require a corresponding adjustment in other jurisdictions, to prevent double taxation arising from the initial adjustment. The Commentary claimed that the method of separate accounting is based on the records being complete and accurate, and being available to the tax authority in the permanent establishment's host country. If these requirements were not met, the Commentary asserted that a permanent establishment's assessment will be based on presumptions. The Commentary noted that an adjustment

---

[207] *Ibid.*, pp. 18–19.

would be required if there is a dispute between a tax authority and the international enterprise, and the accounts were either not produced or the accounts were deficient. The Commentary claimed that in this situation the 'profits of the establishment involved may be determined by applying a certain percentage to its gross receipts'.[208] The percentage should be based on the profits of similar enterprises operating in the host country.

If these remedies were not applicable because a meaningful comparison cannot be made with other enterprises, Article VI of the draft treaty provided for the use of limited formulary apportionment (called fractional apportionment in the Report) as an alternative method of attributing profits to a permanent establishment.[209] This requires the calculation of the profit of a permanent establishment as a proportion of the profits of an international enterprise based on its balance sheet and profit and loss accounts. Under limited formulary apportionment, only the profits derived by the international establishment from transactions involving the permanent establishment may be used. Unlimited formulary apportionment – under which a permanent establishment's profits were based on the international enterprise's worldwide profits – was rejected by the Commentary as an acceptable method for attributing profits to permanent establishments.

The following factors may be used to determine the proportion of an international enterprise's profits which were to be attributed to a permanent establishment under limited formulary apportionment: plant and equipment; circulating capital; payrolls; cost of production; physical output; and turnover.[210] The Commentary noted that the weighting of the factors will depend on the type of enterprise that it involved. However, the formulary apportionment method used should be selected to ensure that the results approximate, as closely as possible, those which would be reflected under the arm's length principle.[211] The Commentary also claimed that even though limited formulary apportionment was the third available method, this 'does not mean that the partial use of fractional apportionment is excluded when, as is generally desirable, branch establishments are taxed according to the method of separate accounting'.[212]

---

[208] *Ibid.*, p. 19.   [209] *Ibid.*, p. 20.   [210] *Ibid.*

[211] Fiscal Committee, *Report to the Council on the Fifth Session of the Committee* (1935), pp. 20–1.

[212] Fiscal Committee, *London and Mexico Model Tax Conventions: Commentary and Text* (1946), p. 21.

Article VI of the Protocol to the draft conventions provided that for banking and financial enterprises, interest cannot be levied on the equity capital allocated to a branch.[213] This rule applied even though such an international enterprise provides equity capital funding to a branch in the form of a loan. On the other hand, if the funds provided to a branch of a banking and financial enterprise were not equity capital, the branch was entitled to a deduction for notional interest on the notional intra-entity loan made to the branch by its head office or other foreign branches, and the notional lender was required to treat the notional interest as income.[214]

6.15.2   Evolution of tax treaties

The Fiscal Committee noted that, since the 1920s, sixty general tax treaties had been concluded and that around 250 special agreements on a range of international tax matters had been signed. In addition, treaties of friendship and establishment, commercial treaties and other international instruments had clauses dealing with taxation.[215] The Fiscal Committee identified two areas for further study. It suggested a study be undertaken on a comprehensive set of rules for determining and allocating the business income of international enterprises carrying on business in more than one country. The Fiscal Committee also suggested a study be made on the taxation of interest and dividends as differences persisted between the capital-importing countries and capital-exporting countries in this area. It suggested that the differences could be 'reconciled in the negotiation of tax treaties if studies were undertaken of the various legal, administrative and economic aspects of this problem'.[216]

The proposal to reconcile the differences between capital-importing countries and capital-exporting countries was ambitious. These two categories of countries in negotiating treaties were competing for their respective allocations of income. As capital is mobile, attempts by source countries to tax interest and dividends were likely to be fruitless because investors will shift their investments to countries providing either lower taxes or exemptions for passive income. In addition, capital-exporting countries were unlikely to concede to source countries the right to tax passive income because the balance of power, at the time, was with the developed capital-exporting countries such as the US and the UK.

---

[213] *Ibid.*   [214] *Ibid.*

[215] Fiscal Committee, *Report on the Work of the Tenth Session of the Committee* (1946), p. 10.

[216] *Ibid.*

150 HISTORY OF TAX TREATIES

Capital-importing countries negotiating treaties with developed capital-exporting countries were often required to concede source country taxation on interest and dividends as a trade-off for concluding tax treaties with more powerful countries. The capital-importing countries sought tax treaties with capital-exporting countries in order to increase trade and investment in the capital-importing countries, and in turn, their economic development.

In conclusion, the advances made by the League of Nations in international taxation were significant and the main initiative of the League of Nations was its use of the 'classification and assignment' structure for its model tax treaty.[217] This structure is reflected in current tax treaties, the OECD Model and the UN Model. The classification and assignment method was chosen as a compromise to reflect the differences between capital-importing countries and capital-exporting countries.[218]

7 Conclusion

The work of the League of Nations, and its 1928 tax model, are reflected in the OECD Model and UN Model and the current tax treaties. The work of the League of Nations reflects debates that remain current, on the competing taxing rights of source countries and residence countries. While it is unquestionable that double taxation affects international trade, economic growth and maximization of worldwide welfare, striking a balance between source countries and residence countries in tax treaties is challenging. Tax treaties provide reciprocal taxing rights, but trade and income flows between treaty countries may not be equal, particularly in the case of trade between a capital-importing country and a capital-exporting country. Consequently, the allocation of taxing rights under tax treaties creates winners and losers. The League of Nations recognized this imbalance in its work on the allocation of taxing rights.

Despite the achievements of the League of Nations, it was unable to gain acceptance of its proposal for a multilateral tax treaty or a general agreement on information exchange to counter tax evasion. The League of Nations initially preferred a multilateral tax treaty to the alternative of bilateral tax treaties as the studies undertaken by various working groups in the League of Nations recognized the advantages of having a

---

[217] Rosenbloom and Langbein, 'United States Tax Treaty Policy: An Overview' (1981), p. 366.
[218] *Ibid.*

multilateral tax treaty. A multilateral tax treaty was also advocated by the ICC in 1929, and in 1930 the first draft multilateral tax treaty was presented to the League of Nations Fiscal Committee. While a multilateral treaty on trade was established through the General Agreement on Trade and Tariffs in 1947, a broad-ranging multilateral tax treaty on tax was not achieved. The League of Nations attempted to limit fiscal evasion in 1936 through a general agreement on information exchange. Concurrent with the emergence of double taxation was international tax avoidance and evasion, and some taxpayers may have been motivated to prevent potential double taxation through avoidance. Despite the efforts of the League of Nations, it was unable to implement a general agreement on information exchange. In 1937, the Fiscal Committee of the League of Nations found that member countries were unwilling to enter a general agreement and this allowed tax evasion on interest and dividends at the time to flourish unchecked. Another achievement of the League of Nations was the development of the permanent establishment concept. The League of Nations developed the permanent establishment threshold tests which are reflected in the OECD Model and UN Model.

5

The role of the OECD Model Tax Treaty and Commentary

1 Introduction

The foundation of the tax treaty system is the extensive network of tax treaties that has evolved since the work of the League of Nations in the 1920s. The OECD assumed a lead role in guiding the tax treaty system following the disbandment of the League of Nations and its replacement by the UN. The OECD's main vehicle for guiding the tax treaty system norms is the OECD Model and Commentary, together with reports on specific topics. The tax treaties of OECD countries are based on the OECD Model which is the centrepiece of the tax treaty system. As countries vigorously protect their sovereignty and jurisdiction to tax, the implementation of the OECD Model and Commentary in the tax treaties of both OECD and non-OECD countries is a considerable achievement.

This chapter considers the importance of the OECD Model and Commentary in the tax treaty system. OECD countries are expected to base their treaties on the OECD Model, thus the OECD Model and Commentary provides the context in which tax treaties are negotiated by OECD countries. The chapter argues that OECD countries are required to use the Commentary as an extrinsic aid in interpreting their tax treaties and it is also used by non-OECD countries in the interpretation of tax treaties. In Chapter 6 the meaning of former Article 7 of the OECD Model is examined in light of the pre-2008 Commentary and the 2008 Commentary. Chapter 7 studies the issue of deductions for interest on intra-bank loans under former Article 7 by reference to the pre-2008 Commentary.

This chapter also studies the proposals of the League of Nations, the Organisation for European Economic Co-operation (OEEC) and the former OECD proposals for a multilateral tax treaty and that the use of a bilateral model was a compromise measure. Each of these organizations considered a multilateral tax treaty to be the best approach, but they were not confident that it would be widely accepted initially. Instead, they considered that the implementation of a multilateral tax treaty should be gradual. The use of the OECD Model as a basis for bilateral tax treaties was intended to provide uniform principles, but it has not resulted in consistent rules being developed within OECD countries and non-OECD countries.

This chapter begins by considering the role of the OECD Model. It then reviews the history of the OECD Model and the status of the bilateral model as a pragmatic alternative. It examines the OECD's earlier preference for a multilateral tax treaty and notes that this was also the preference of both the League of Nations and the OEEC. The chapter establishes the role of the OECD Model and Commentary and its extensive influence on the tax treaty system. Finally, the chapter examines the role of the Commentary in the interpretation of tax treaties.

2   The OECD Model

2.1   The role of the OECD Model

The aim of the OECD Model is 'to clarify, standardise and confirm the fiscal situation of taxpayers who are engaged in commercial, industrial, financial or any other activities in other countries through the application by all countries of common solutions to identical cases of double taxation'.[1] The OECD Model seeks to provide a uniform method for the resolution of most frequently occurring problems arising in international juridical double taxation.[2] OECD countries are obliged to conform with the OECD Model and Commentary:

> As recommended by the Council of the OECD, member countries, when concluding or revising bilateral conventions, should conform to this Model Convention as interpreted by the Commentaries thereon and having regard to the reservations contained therein and their tax authorities should follow these Commentaries, as modified from time to time and subject to their observations thereon, when applying and interpreting the provisions of their bilateral tax conventions that are based on the Model Convention.[3]

Although the OECD Model and Commentary is not binding on OECD countries, many tax treaties entered into by OECD countries conform with the OECD Model, including those with countries which are non-OECD

---

[1] 2010 OECD Model, p. 7, para. 2.   [2] *Ibid.*, p. 7, para. 3.   [3] *Ibid.*

countries.[4] Tax authorities of OECD countries are expected to apply the Commentary in interpreting tax treaty provisions, subject to any reservations and observations recorded in the Commentary. Moreover, the OECD Model and Commentary may be used by courts in OECD countries when interpreting a tax treaty.

2.2 History of the OECD Model

The OECD Model has its origins in the work of the League of Nations in the 1920s and 1930s, as the advances made by the League of Nations in international taxation at that time were significant.[5] The League of Nations developed its first bilateral model treaty in 1928[6] and its final two models were the Mexico Model Convention in 1943 and, later, the London Model Convention in 1946.[7] While these models influenced tax treaties that were negotiated or renegotiated around that time, neither the London nor Mexico Models were broadly accepted. Moreover, these models had several gaps and there were considerable differences between them.[8] It has been asserted that the main contribution of the League of Nations was the use of the 'classification and assignment' structure as the structure for its model tax treaty.[9] This same structure is used in current tax treaties, and in the OECD Model and UN Model. Responsibility for carrying on the work of the League of Nations on bilateral tax models was initially assumed by the OEEC, which subsequently became the OECD.

2.2.1 Organisation for European Economic Co-operation Fiscal Committee

The OEEC adopted its first recommendation on double taxation on 25 February 1955.[10] At that time, seventy bilateral tax treaties had been signed between developed countries. As a result of the increasing economic integration of OEEC countries in the post-war period, the problem of double taxation became a pressing issue. Some of the OEEC countries had a handful of tax treaties with other OEEC countries, while

---

[4] United Nations, *United Nations Model Tax Convention Between Developed and Developing Countries* (2001), p. xiv, para. 19.

[5] Vogel, 'Double Tax Treaties and their Interpretation' (1986), p. 11.

[6] Report Presented by the General Meeting of Government Experts on Double Taxation and Tax Evasion, *Double Taxation and Tax Evasion* (1928).

[7] Fiscal Committee, *London and Mexico Model Tax Conventions* (1946).

[8] 2010 OECD Model, p. 7, para. 4.

[9] Rosenbloom and Langbein, 'United States Tax Treaty Policy' (1981), p. 366.

[10] 2010 OECD Model, p. 7, para. 4.

2 THE OECD MODEL

some OEEC countries had no tax treaties.[11] At the same time, the Council of the OEEC recognized that measures to prevent double taxation were required, and it recommended that the network of tax treaties be extended to cover all OEEC countries.[12] Moreover, it was clear even at that time that harmonization of tax treaties was desirable.[13]

The Fiscal Committee of the OEEC (OEEC Fiscal Committee), set up in 1956, was instructed in 1958 by the OEEC to submit a draft Convention for the avoidance of double taxation with respect to taxes on income and capital. It was also required to produce concrete proposals for the implementation of the Convention. The OEEC Fiscal Committee prepared four reports between 1958 and 1961 which were published under the title *The Elimination of Double Taxation*.[14] In the 1958 report, the OEEC Fiscal Committee stated that its aim was to implement a multilateral tax treaty,[15] and it proposed to establish a model bilateral tax treaty which would be acceptable to OEEC countries.[16] The OEEC Fiscal Committee proposed to replace the model bilateral tax treaty with a multilateral tax treaty, but the OEEC recognized that it was impossible to predict how long this ultimate aim would take to implement.[17] The OEEC Fiscal Committee's objectives of initially developing a model bilateral tax treaty and finally establishing a multilateral tax treaty were restated in its third report in 1960.[18]

The OEEC Fiscal Committee noted that the International Chamber of Commerce (ICC), at its Congress in Tokyo in 1955, adopted a resolution suggesting that the OEEC examine the possibility of concluding a multilateral tax treaty between OEEC countries.[19] The OEEC was influenced by the views of the ICC that the implementation of a multilateral tax treaty would result in uniform principles and practices.[20] Implicit in the views of both the OEEC and the ICC was the recognition that a bilateral network of tax treaties would not result in uniform principles and practices.

The OEEC Fiscal Committee concluded that the process of implementing a multilateral tax treaty should be gradual. To create a base for a multilateral tax treaty, the OEEC Fiscal Committee suggested that as

---

[11] *Ibid.*, pp. 7–8, para. 5.   [12] *Ibid.*   [13] *Ibid.*

[14] OEEC, *The Elimination of Double Taxation* (1958); OEEC, *The Elimination of Double Taxation, Second Report of the Fiscal Committee* (1959); OEEC, *The Elimination of Double Taxation, Third Report of the Fiscal Committee* (1960); OEEC, *The Elimination of Double Taxation, Fourth Report of the Fiscal Committee* (1961).

[15] OEEC, *The Elimination of Double Taxation* (1958), p. 16, para. 14.

[16] *Ibid.*   [17] *Ibid.*

[18] OEEC, *The Elimination of Double Taxation, Third Report of the Fiscal Committee* (1960).

[19] OEEC, *The Elimination of Double Taxation* (1958), p. 16, para. 15.   [20] *Ibid.*

specific provisions were settled by it, they should be incorporated into the existing tax treaties, thereby encouraging more uniform tax treaties.[21] If a degree of uniformity were established within the existing treaty network, this would facilitate the implementation of a multilateral tax treaty among OEEC countries.[22] The OEEC's 1958 report also highlighted the lack of uniformity in the rules of the tax treaties between OEEC countries,[23] and noted that identical provisions in tax treaties between OEEC countries were being interpreted inconsistently by them.[24]

2.2.2 OECD Draft Double Tax Convention (1963)

In 1961 the OEEC was transformed into the OECD, which confirmed the OEEC Fiscal Committee's mandate. In 1963 the Fiscal Committee of the OECD (Fiscal Committee) submitted its final report titled *Draft Double Tax Convention on Income and Capital* (1963 Draft Convention).[25] The Fiscal Committee of the OECD retained the OEEC's objective of implementing a multilateral tax treaty:

> The Draft Convention could also be the basis for multilateral Conventions among certain groups of countries, until it proves possible, after further studies, to conclude a multilateral Convention among all Member countries of the OECD. In the conclusions of the report, the Fiscal Committee submits to the Council concrete proposals as to the recommendations which it suggests should be made to Member countries in order that the Draft Convention may be the medium through which a substantial advance can be made forthwith towards the co-ordination of bilateral Conventions and the abolition of double taxation.[26]

The aims of the Fiscal Committee in preparing the 1963 Draft Convention were to establish a draft convention that could be used to resolve double taxation problems between OECD countries and that the proposed draft be acceptable to OECD countries.[27] The Fiscal Committee considered that the 1963 Draft Convention could be easily interpreted and applied even though OECD countries have different domestic tax laws and economic interests.[28] It also asserted that the 1963 Draft Convention provided the means of resolving on a uniform basis the most common problems of double taxation.[29] When it presented its report the Fiscal Committee foresaw that the 1963 Draft Convention would need to be revised following further study. A revised draft convention could reflect:

---

[21] *Ibid.*, p. 17, para. 19. [22] *Ibid.* [23] *Ibid.*, p. 11, para. 6.
[24] *Ibid.* [25] OECD, *Draft Double Taxation Convention on Income and Capital* (1963).
[26] *Ibid.*, p. 7, para. 2. [27] *Ibid.*, p. 10, para. 6. [28] *Ibid.* [29] *Ibid.*

2 THE OECD MODEL

157

- experiences gained in negotiating and applying bilateral tax treaties;
- changes in individual countries' tax systems;
- increases in international fiscal relations;
- the development of new sectors of business activity; and
- the emergence of complex business organizations at an international level.[30]

2.2.3 The OECD Model since 1977

The Fiscal Committee revised the 1963 Draft Convention and accompanying Commentary, resulting in the publication of the 1977 OECD Model to reflect the changes in economic conditions at that time. The pressure for reform was the development of new technologies and developments in international transactions, and the ability of international enterprises and multinational enterprise groups to be able to manipulate the tax treaty system through sophisticated tax avoidance arrangements. In the 1980s, globalization processes and the liberalization of international trade placed further pressures on the 1977 OECD Model. The Committee on Fiscal Affairs and Working Party No. 1 studied a range of issues relating to the 1977 Model OECD resulting in several reports, which recommended amendments to the OECD Model and Commentary.[31]

In 1991, it was recognized that the revision of the OECD Model and Commentary should be a more dynamic process.[32] Consequently, the Committee on Fiscal Affairs developed the concept of an ambulatory model tax treaty, to be revised by periodic updates and amendments, rather than issuing less frequent consolidated revisions of the OECD Model and Commentary.[33] Moreover, in recognition of the influence of the OECD Model beyond OECD countries, the OECD decided to invite other international organizations, non-OECD countries and interested parties to participate in the process of revising the OECD Model.[34] The Committee on Fiscal Affairs believed that the involvement of these parties in the revision of the OECD Model would assist the Committee 'in its continuing task of updating the Model Convention to conform with the evolution of tax rules and principles'.[35]

This more dynamic reform process led to the publication in 1992 of the OECD Model and Commentary in a loose-leaf form to facilitate the OECD amending the model more frequently in response to developments.[36]

---

[30] 2010 OECD Model, p. 8, para. 7.   [31] *Ibid.*, p. 8, para. 8.   [32] *Ibid.*, p. 9, para. 9.
[33] *Ibid.*   [34] *Ibid.*, p. 9, para. 10.   [35] *Ibid.*   [36] *Ibid.*, p. 9, para. 11.

158   OECD MODEL TAX TREATY AND COMMENTARY

The 1992 version of the OECD Model and Commentary included many of the OECD recommendations made since 1977; although it was not a complete revision of the model, it was the first product of the new reform process.[37] Since the publication of the 1992 OECD Model,[38] updates were published in 1994, 1995, 1997, 2000, 2003, 2005, 2008 and 2010. Revisions to the OECD Model are published in a condensed version and an electronic version. The latest condensed version was published in 2010 and the latest electronic version was issued in 2008.[39]

In its 1992 Commentary, the OECD abandoned the aim of implementing one multilateral tax treaty because it had recognized the potential for groups of countries to form regional multilateral tax treaties adapted from the OECD Model. The OECD stated that:

> The Nordic Convention on Income and Capital entered into by Denmark, Finland, Iceland, Norway and Sweden, which was concluded in 1983 and replaced in 1987, 1989 and 1996, provides a practical example of such a multilateral convention between a group of member countries and follows closely the provisions of the Model Convention.
>
> Also relevant is the Convention on Mutual Administrative Assistance in Tax Matters, which was drawn up within the Council of Europe on the basis of a first draft prepared by the Committee on Fiscal Affairs. This Convention entered into force on 1 April 1995.
>
> Despite these two conventions, there are no reasons to believe that the conclusion of a multilateral tax convention involving all member countries could now be considered practicable. The Committee therefore considers that bilateral conventions are still a more appropriate way to ensure the elimination of double taxation at the international level.[40]

Despite this statement, the OECD has not encouraged OECD countries to form regional multilateral tax treaties, nor has it studied the issue. This lack of action suggests that the implementation of regional multilateral tax treaties has been a low priority for the OECD. The issue of regional multilateral tax treaties has become topical again since the EU announced it is studying proposals to develop a multilateral tax system for the taxation of corporate profits in the EU.[41] The framework for a potential EU multilateral tax treaty is within the OECD's guidelines. But the EU is proposing to use formulary apportionment allocation methods rather than the arm's length method. As the EU countries are

---

[37] *Ibid.*   [38] 1992 OECD Model (loose-leaf).   [39] 2010 OECD Model.

[40] *Ibid.*, p. 16, paras. 38–40. Adopted in 1992.

[41] Commission of the European Communities, *Company Taxation in the Internal Market* (2001).

2 THE OECD MODEL

a major, influential group within the OECD, the direction the EU takes could affect the OECD Model and Commentary.[42]

2.3   Influence of the OECD Model

Since its publication in 1963, the OECD Model has influenced the negotiation, application and interpretation of tax treaties in OECD countries and non-OECD countries.[43] The OECD Model is used as the basis for the *UN Model Double Taxation Convention Between Developed and Developing Countries*[44] which reproduces significant parts of the provisions of the OECD Model and Commentary.[45] Since 1996, the OECD has allowed non-OECD countries to participate in its annual discussions on the revision of the OECD Model and Commentary.[46] In recognition of the influence of the OECD Model in non-OECD countries, the OECD separately publishes[47] their views, expressly identifying those parts of the OECD Model and Commentary with which the non-OECD countries disagree. A comparative analysis reveals that most bilateral tax treaties follow the OECD Model, even down to the Article number, and that variations in tax treaties are generally minor.[48] The OECD has become the main international organization shaping the development of the tax treaty system,[49] and the OECD Model is the keystone of the tax treaty system with its influence extending well beyond OECD countries. The OECD Model has even been described as having reached the status of a multilateral instrument.[50] The OECD Model and Commentary are used by both OECD countries and many non-OECD countries. Thus, the OECD Model and Commentary underpin the tax treaty system involving OECD countries and many non-OECD countries.

[42] This issue is considered in Ch. 11.   [43] 2010 OECD Model, p. 9, para. 10.

[44] United Nations, *United Nations Model Tax Convention Between Developed and Developing Countries* (2001).

[45] 2010 OECD Model, p. 10, para. 14.   [46] *Ibid.*, p. 9, para. 10.

[47] The 2010 OECD Model reflects the views of the following countries: Albania, Argentina, Armenia, Belarus, Brazil, Bulgaria, Croatia, Democratic Republic of the Congo, Estonia, Gabon, Hong Kong (China), India, Indonesia, Israel, Ivory Coast, Kazakhstan, Latvia, Lithuania, Malaysia, Morocco, People's Republic of China, Philippines, Romania, Russia, Serbia, South Africa, Thailand, Tunisia, Ukraine, United Arab Emirates, Vietnam: 2010 OECD Model, pp. 427–63.

[48] American Law Institute, *Federal Income Tax Project, International Aspects of United States Income Taxation II* (1992), p. 3; Avery Jones, 'The David R. Tillinghast Lecture' (1999), pp. 1–2.

[49] Avery Jones, *ibid.*, p. 2.

[50] American Law Institute, *Federal Income Tax Project, International Aspects of United States Income Taxation II* (1992), p. 3.

160 OECD MODEL TAX TREATY AND COMMENTARY

3 Tax treaty interpretation

3.1 Vienna Convention on the Law of Treaties

The rules on international treaty interpretation have been codified in the Vienna Convention on the Law of Treaties[51] (Vienna Convention). Under Article 26 of the Vienna Convention '[e]very treaty is binding on the parties to the treaty and must be performed by them in good faith'. This rule – *pacta sunt servanda* – is a fundamental principle of international law. The importance of this principle is that it 'applies throughout international relations; but it has a particular importance in the law of treaties and is indeed reiterated in article 27 [now Article 31] in the context of the interpretation of treaties'.[52] One purpose of Article 26 is to require countries to 'abstain from acts calculated to frustrate the object and purpose of the treaty'.[53] While it is implicit in the *pacta sunt servanda* principle that a country should not attempt to frustrate a treaty, the drafters of the Vienna Convention chose to put this issue beyond doubt by expressly including a requirement that countries abstain from acts intended to frustrate the operation of a treaty.[54] Article 18 provides that a state 'is obliged to refrain from acts which would defeat the object and purpose of a treaty' when the state has signed the treaty which is subject to ratification, acceptance or approval, or the state has agreed to be bound by the treaty pending its entry into force. The Vienna Convention deals with a potential aspect of this problem by providing in Article 27 that a 'party may not invoke the provisions of its internal law as justification for its failure to perform a treaty'.[55] Article 27 expresses the rule of international law that a country should observe its treaties and not override a treaty by enacting conflicting domestic legislation. If a country concludes that one of its tax treaties needs to be amended, Articles 26 and 27 require the country to observe the treaty.

---

[51] Vienna, 23 May 1969.

[52] United Nations, *United Nations Conference on the Law of Treaties, First and Second Sessions, Official Records* (1971), p. 31.

[53] *Ibid.*   [54] *Ibid.*

[55] Article 27 is expressed as being without prejudice to Article 46. Article 46 provides:

'A State may not invoke the fact that its consent to be bound by a treaty has been expressed in violation of a provision of its internal law regarding competence to conclude treaties as invalidating its consent unless that violation was manifest and concerned a rule of its internal law of fundamental importance.

A violation is manifest if it would be objectively evident to any State conducting itself in the matter in accordance with normal practice and in good faith.'

3 TAX TREATY INTERPRETATION 161

In this situation the country may request that the other country agree to an amendment to the treaty. If the other country is not willing to agree to the proposed amendment, then the country seeking the amendment may either leave the existing treaty in place or decide to terminate the treaty. In relation to tax treaties, the OECD has made the following statement on the international law requirement that treaties are binding and must be performed in good faith.[56]

Article 31 of the Vienna Convention requires that treaties be interpreted in good faith, in accordance with the ordinary meaning to be given to the terms of the treaty, and in the light of its objects and purpose.[57] Article 31 requires that the literal terms of a treaty be interpreted in the context of its purpose. In interpreting a treaty a court should determine the relative importance of the text of the treaty in light of its context and purpose. Under Article 31(2) the context for treaty interpretation purposes includes, in addition to the text of a treaty, its preamble and annexes, any agreement relating to the treaty which was made by the parties in connection with the conclusion of the treaty (Article 31(2)(a)) and any instrument made by the parties in connection with the conclusion of the treaty (Article 31(2)(b)). Article 31(3) of the Vienna Convention provides that, in

---

[56] OECD, *Tax Treaty Overrides* (1989), para. 12.

[57] 'Article 31: General rule of interpretation

1. A treaty shall be interpreted in good faith in accordance with the ordinary meaning to be given to the terms of the treaty in their context and in the light of its object and purpose.
2. The context for the purpose of the interpretation of a treaty shall comprise, in addition to the text, including its preamble and annexes:
   (a) Any agreement relating to the treaty which was made between all the parties in connexion with the conclusion of the treaty;
   (b) Any instrument which was made by one or more parties in connexion with the conclusion of the treaty and accepted by the other parties as an instrument related to the treaty.
3. There shall be taken into account, together with the context:
   (a) Any subsequent agreement between the parties regarding the interpretation of the treaty or the application of its provisions;
   (b) Any subsequent practice in the application of the treaty which establishes the agreement of the parties regarding its interpretation;
   (c) Any relevant rules of international law applicable in the relations between the parties.
4. A special meaning shall be given to a term if it is established that the parties so intended.'

interpreting a treaty, subsequent agreements between the parties regarding the interpretation of the treaty or the application of provisions may be taken into account. Article 31 appears to give additional weight to the factor of context in treaty interpretation. Article 32 allows the use of supplementary material in certain circumstances. Supplementary material may be used if the interpretation of a treaty using the principles of Article 31 results in a meaning that is ambiguous or leads to a result that is unreasonable or absurd. Nevertheless, supplementary material is made available to a tribunal which can then decide in light of that material, even if it states that it was not used as the meaning of the terms was clear. Under Article 31 recourse may also be had to supplementary material to confirm the meaning of a term, and the OECD Model and Commentary are often used by courts in OECD countries as supplementary material when interpreting tax treaties.

3.2   OECD Model and Commentary

The OECD contends that the extensive influence of the OECD Model has resulted in the use of the Commentary by many countries as the basis for interpreting tax treaties:

> [T]he worldwide recognition of the provisions of the Model Convention and their incorporation into a majority of bilateral conventions have helped make the Commentaries on the provisions of the Model Convention a widely-accepted guide to the interpretation and application of the provisions of existing bilateral conventions. This has facilitated the interpretation and the enforcement of these bilateral conventions along common lines. As the network of tax conventions continues to expand, the importance of such a generally accepted guide becomes all the greater.[58]

Nevertheless, the role of the Commentary in the interpretation of tax treaties is a controversial issue. The OECD's directions on the role of the Commentary in the interpretation of tax treaties merit examination, and the views of the US, Canadian and Australian courts on the use of the OECD Model and Commentary in the interpretation of tax treaties provide evidence of the nature of this role.

---

[58] 2010 OECD Model, p. 10, para. 15.

The OECD Model gives the following directions on the role of the Commentary:

> As the Commentaries have been drafted and agreed upon by the experts appointed to the Committee on Fiscal Affairs by the Governments of Member countries, they are of special importance in the development of international fiscal law. Although the Commentaries are not designed to be annexed in any manner to the conventions signed by Member countries, which unlike the Model are legally binding international instruments, they can nevertheless be of great assistance in the application and interpretation of the conventions and, in particular, in the settlement of any disputes.[59]

Controversy about whether the Commentary should be considered in the interpretation of a country's tax treaties arises from these OECD directions. The directions imply that the Commentary is not a legally binding instrument; however, this implication is qualified by the encouragement of the OECD that the Commentary can be of significant assistance in the interpretation of tax treaties. It is curious that the Commentary does not assert in less qualified terms that it is the official interpretation of the OECD Model and that OECD countries are expected to rely on this interpretation in negotiating tax treaties, unless they have recorded reservations and observations in the OECD Model. It is also curious that the Commentary does not require OECD countries to enact legislation requiring their courts to consider the Commentary when interpreting tax treaties between OECD countries.[60] Moreover, the OECD Model itself makes no reference to the Commentary and its role in the interpretation of the model. It is a paradox that the Commentary is treated by the OECD as not binding on OECD countries, but it is regularly being updated. This has resulted in general uncertainty about the role of the Commentary in the interpretation of provisions of tax treaties. Nevertheless, while Commentaries may be used in interpreting treaty provisions it is emphasized that they are not binding.[61]

As the OECD Commentary is not binding on OECD countries, they cannot use Article 30(3)(a) of the Vienna Convention to claim that a version of the OECD Commentary published subsequent to the

---

[59] Ibid., p. 14, para. 29.
[60] Avery Jones, 'The David R. Tillinghast Lecture' (1999), p. 19.
[61] See Hill, 'The Interpretation of Double Taxation Agreements – the Australian Experience' (2003), p. 325. Hill, a former distinguished judge of the Federal Court of Australia, claimed that he treats Commentaries as having the same status as an opinion of a textbook author.

conclusion of a tax treaty should be used to interpret the provisions of a previously concluded treaty. Article 30(3)(a) of the Vienna Convention provides that: 'There shall be taken into account, together with the context: (a) any subsequent agreement between the parties regarding the interpretation of the treaty or the application of its provisions.' This provision requires the subsequent agreement to be binding on the treaty countries.

Commentators are divided on the role of the OECD Commentaries in the interpretation of tax treaty provisions. Article 31(1) of the Vienna Convention focuses on a literal interpretation of treaty provisions in the context of their purpose, which precludes using Commentaries in the interpretation of tax treaties. It is unlikely that a court will treat a Commentary as part of the context of a tax treaty.[62] Moreover, Article 31(3) of the Vienna Convention is equally inapplicable to Commentaries as they are not formal agreements in connection with a tax treaty. The OECD Model expressly states that the Commentaries are not legally binding on OECD countries.[63] There are also challenges in using a Commentary under Article 32 which authorizes the use of supplementary material to confirm a meaning under Article 31, or when an interpretation under Article 31 results in an ambiguous or obscure meaning (Article 32(a)) or leads to a result that is manifestly absurd or unreasonable (Article 32(b)). Nevertheless, the Australian High Court has authorized the use of Commentaries in interpreting Australia's tax treaties under Article 32.[64]

Although there are formal restrictions on the use of Commentaries in tax treaty interpretation, Commentaries are widely used by tax advisers, tax authorities and courts. But the weight to be accorded to Commentaries by tax authorities and courts is the key issue. In addition, although Commentaries are widely used in interpreting tax treaties by tax advisers and tax authorities, Commentaries are at times contradictory. Some of the contradictions in Commentaries may reflect the compromises reached between countries in settling the Commentaries. The membership of the OECD working parties that draft the Commentaries is broad and at times there are differences of opinion which may be reflected in the Commentary. As stated above, while Article 32 authorizes the use of a Commentary to confirm an interpretation under Article 31, it would

---

[62] See Ault, 'The Role of the OECD Commentaries in the Interpretation of Tax Treaties' in Alpert and van Raad (eds.), *Essays on International Taxation* (1993) 61–8, p. 63.

[63] 2010 OECD Model, p. 14, para. 29.   [64] See below section 3.2.3 'Australia'.

be difficult to argue that a Commentary could be used under this provision if the ordinary meaning of a treaty provision was clear but the Commentary has a different interpretation of the provision.[65]

Ault contends that the combined use of Article 31(4) and Article 32 provides a basis for the use of Commentaries in interpreting tax treaty provision.[66] Article 31(4) provides that: 'A special meaning shall be given to a term if it is established that the parties so intended.' Ault claims that Article 31(4) authorizes the use of Commentaries to indicate the intention of treaty negotiators to use a treaty provision in particular way, even though there is no ambiguity under the other provisions of Article 31. This reflects the reality that when tax treaties are negotiated between OECD countries, the OECD Model and Commentary may be regarded as background material when the treaties were negotiated, subject to the reservations and observations made by the OECD countries. As non-OECD countries participate in OECD meetings and have their views on the OECD Model and Commentary recorded,[67] treaties involving non-OECD countries may also use the OECD Model and Commentary as background material.[68] Consequently, if a treaty provision reflects an OECD Model provision, it may be assumed that the treaty negotiators adopted the Commentary in force at the time of the treaty negotiations on the provision.

Ault argues that the Commentary is a 'default' setting for tax treaties that are based on the OECD Model on the presumption that for OECD countries, the Commentary reflects the intention of OECD countries, but the presumption is rebuttable because OECD countries concluding tax treaties are able to deviate from the OECD Model.[69] If a country has a general objection to an Article of the OECD Model or the views expressed in the Commentary, it should have an observation recorded in the Commentary to alter its own default position for its tax treaties. Under Ault's approach the Commentary becomes an ancillary document which may be considered in the interpretation of a country's tax treaties. If this approach is accepted by courts it becomes critical for a country to ensure that its recorded observations and reservations are consistent

---

[65] Ault, 'The Role of the OECD Commentaries in the Interpretation of Tax Treaties' in Alpert and van Raad (eds.), *Essays on International Taxation* (1993) 61–8, p. 65.

[66] *Ibid.*   [67] 2010 OECD Model, pp. 429–63.

[68] This would include treaties involving two non-OECD countries or an OECD country and a non-OECD country.

[69] Ault, 'The Role of the OECD Commentaries in the Interpretation of Tax Treaties' in Alpert and van Raad (eds.), *Essays on International Taxation* (1993) 61–8.

166   OECD MODEL TAX TREATY AND COMMENTARY

with its tax treaties. On the other hand, Vogel argued that in the interpretation of tax treaties between OECD countries, the Commentary can only be used with significant reservations.[70] He stated that the presumption that the Commentary either defines the ordinary meanings of treaty terms used in a tax treaty, or that the treaty negotiators and the parliament or executive government implementing a treaty intended to adopt the 'special meaning' in the Commentary on treaty provisions, has been undermined by the OECD's practice of changing the OECD Model and Commentary at relatively short intervals.[71]

To put the role of the Commentary beyond doubt, countries negotiating a tax treaty may direct that the Commentary be used in interpreting the treaty by incorporating a provision directing that the treaty is to be interpreted in accordance with the Commentary.[72] This direction may be restricted to the Commentary in force when the particular treaty was negotiated, or the countries may take an ambulatory approach and direct that the treaty is to be interpreted in accordance with the prevailing version of the Commentary. The ambulatory approach is usually used in international organizations in which the interpretation of the organization's constitution can be based on the practice of OECD states in dealing with the constitution: *Legal Consequences for States of the Continued Presence of South Africa in Namibia (South West Africa) notwithstanding Security Council Resolution 276 (1970), Advisory Opinion, ICJ Reports 1971*, p. 47.[73] If a tax treaty contained such directions, irrespective of whether the countries are OECD countries or non-OECD countries, the tax authorities and courts of the contracting countries would have to consider the Commentary when interpreting the particular treaty. Despite the certainty this approach provides on the use of the Commentary in interpreting treaty provisions, it is rarely used in tax treaties.[74] Nevertheless, to provide certainty on the use of the Commentary, it remains open for countries negotiating a tax treaty to include a provision directing that the treaty has to be interpreted in accordance with the Commentary.

---

[70] Vogel, 'The Influence of the OECD Commentaries on Treaty Interpretation' (2000), p. 616.

[71] *Ibid.*   [72] Avery Jones, 'The David R. Tillinghast Lecture' (1999), pp. 19–20.

[73] See also on treaties in general *Gabčíkovo-Nagymaros Project (Hungary/Slovakia)*, Judgment, ICJ Reports 1997, p. 7.

[74] Avery Jones mentions that this technique was used in the Memorandum of Understanding to the US–Austrian tax treaty: Avery Jones, 'The David R. Tillinghast Lecture' (1999), p. 19.

While it is generally accepted that the Commentary may be used to interpret the provisions of tax treaties based on the OECD Model, there is some debate about which version of the Commentary should be used. Under the 'static' approach, the interpretation of a tax treaty would be based on the Commentary as it stood at the time the treaty was negotiated. This issue is significant because it is easier for the OECD to alter the Commentary on a provision than altering the provision itself. For example, the OECD published the 2008 Report and amended the Commentary on former Article 7 in the 2008 OECD Model, but new Article 7, fully implementing the 2008 Report and 2010 Report, was finalized two years later in the 2010 OECD Model. Vogel claims that the static approach may only be used and that a change in a Commentary may not be used to interpret tax treaties concluded before the Commentary was published.[75] A change in a Commentary after a tax treaty was concluded cannot change the meaning of a provision of the treaty.[76] It may be argued that a subsequent Commentary may be considered by a court but that no weight could be given to the subsequent Commentary, especially if it includes a new interpretation of treaty provision, such as the 2008 Commentary on former Article 7.

Tax treaties are usually enacted by the parliaments or the executive governments of the treaty countries and become a binding agreement. The most compelling argument in favour of the static interpretation is that the Commentary in force at the time a treaty was negotiated may be treated as being adopted by the parliaments or governments enacting a tax treaty and thus part of the context of a treaty for the purposes of Article 31 of the Vienna Convention, if the treaty provisions reflect the OECD Model.[77] Consequently, there is no basis for claiming that change to the Commentary by the OECD Committee on Fiscal Affairs – a committee of the OECD – can prevail over a tax treaty enacted by a parliament or executive government which is based on the OECD Model and Commentary in force at the time the treaty was negotiated. The only exception is if a parliament or government enacts a treaty in anticipation of a forthcoming Commentary or a draft Commentary on a provision.

Under the 'ambulatory' approach, a version of the Commentary published after the particular treaty was negotiated may be used to assist

---

[75] Vogel, 'The Influence of the OECD Commentaries on Treaty Interpretation' (2000), pp. 614–15.

[76] *Ibid.*

[77] See Wattel and Marres, 'The Legal Status of the OECD Commentary' (2003), p. 224.

168 OECD MODEL TAX TREATY AND COMMENTARY

the interpretation. The OECD contends that the ambulatory approach should be used and that tax treaties should be interpreted in the spirit of revised OECD Commentaries:[78]

> Needless to say, amendments to the Articles of the Model Convention and changes to the Commentaries that are a direct result of these amendments are not relevant to the interpretation or application of previously concluded conventions where the provisions of those conventions are different in substance from the amended Articles. However, other changes or additions to the Commentaries are normally applicable to the interpretation and application of conventions concluded before their adoption, because they reflect the consensus of the OECD Member countries as to the proper interpretation of existing provisions and their application to specific situations.[79]

The application of the static and ambulatory approaches in three OECD countries, US, Canada and Australia, is illustrated in the following leading tax treaty cases.

3.2.1 The US

The role of the Commentary in the US was considered by Turner J of the Court of Federal Claims in *National Westminster Bank PLC* v. *US* (NatWest I).[80] The taxpayer argued that US domestic law on the taxation of branches of foreign banks was inconsistent with Article 7 of the US–UK tax treaty, which was concluded in 1980 (1980 US–UK treaty).[81] The Court of Federal Claims found that the 1980 US–UK treaty was based on the OECD Model and Commentary in force at the time the treaty was concluded, and commented on their use in interpreting treaties:

> The initial explanatory material of the OECD Document and the Commentaries in Annex II thereof are important and helpful in determining the probable mutual understanding of countries which used the Document as the basis for a tax treaty. This was intended by the drafters of the OECD Document. Thus, explanatory material in the OECD Document is appropriate for use in divining probable intent of countries adopting treaties based thereon . . .

---

[78] 2010 OECD Model, pp. 15–16, paras. 33–6. [79] *Ibid.*, p. 15, para. 35.

[80] 44 Fed. Cl. 120 (1999).

[81] Convention Between the Government of the United States of America and the Government of the United Kingdom of Great Britain and Northern Ireland for the Avoidance of Double Taxation and the Prevention of Fiscal Evasion with Respect to Taxes on Income and Capital Gains (entered into force in April 1980) 31 UST 5668 TIAS No. 9682.

3 TAX TREATY INTERPRETATION 169

The Commentaries on the Articles of the Draft Convention, OECD Document, Annex II, are presumed to have been in the minds of the negotiators when they drafted the Treaty; consequently, they are persuasive in resolving disputed interpretations.[82]

The static approach was used in this case; the court concluded that it must only consider the version of the Commentary in force at the time the 1980 US–UK treaty was negotiated. This prevented the court from considering OECD material on the taxation of branches of international banks published after the 1980 US–UK treaty was negotiated. On appeal in *National Westminster Bank PLC* v. *US* (2008),[83] Lourie, Schall and Gajarsa JJ of the US Court of Appeals for the Federal Circuit, affirmed the judgment of Turner J.

In *National Westminster Bank PLC* v. *United States*[84] (NatWest II), the government argued that an OECD report[85] and two OECD discussion drafts (Discussion Draft I[86] and Discussion Draft II[87]) published after the 1980 US–UK treaty was concluded, supported the government's arguments. Firestone J of the US Court of Federal Claims rejected the claim that these OECD publications supported the government's arguments.[88] Firestone J rejected the claim that Discussion Draft I published in 2001 could be used to interpret the 1980 US–UK treaty:

> [T]he 2001 Discussion Draft is ultimately irrelevant to this litigation. First, there can be no doubt that the 2001 Discussion Draft *could not and does not reflect the understandings of the Treaty partners in 1975*. Subsequent statements made many years later do not reflect intent at the time of ratification. Moreover, the 2001 Discussion Draft expressly acknowledges that the proposals contained in the Discussion Draft may not reflect 'the original intent or historical practice and interpretation of Article 7.' 2001 Discussion Draft at P 6. Indeed, the Drafters state that 'it may be that clarifying amendments, either to this Article or its Commentary, would be necessary to validate the proposed interpretation.' 2001 Discussion Draft at P 49. Thus, by its terms, the 2001 Discussion Draft states that additional negotiations will likely be necessary to finalize the Model Treaty.

[82] 44 Fed. Cl. 120 (1999), p. 125.   [83] 512 F.3d 1347 (2008), pp. 1349, 1362.
[84] 58 Fed. Cl. 491 (2003); 2003 U.S. Claims LEXIS 332; 2004-1 U.S. Tax Cas. (CCH) P50, 150; 92 A.F.T.R.2d. (RIA) 7013.
[85] OECD, *Transfer Pricing and Multinational Enterprises (Three Taxation Issues)* (1984).
[86] OECD, *Discussion Draft on the Attribution of Profits to Permanent Establishments* (2001).
[87] *Ibid.*; OECD, *Discussion Draft on the Attribution of Profits to Permanent Establishments: Part II (Banks)* (2003).
[88] 58 Fed. Cl. 491 (2003), p. 499.

170 OECD MODEL TAX TREATY AND COMMENTARY

> ... the 2001 Discussion Draft is of no assistance to the court in interpreting the proper scope of the 1975 Treaty. It simply offers no insights into the 'genuine shared expectations of the contracting parties . . .'. Maximov, 299 F.2d at 568.[89] (emphasis added)

Firestone J also rejected the use of the 2003 Discussion Draft:

> In sum, while the 2003 Discussion Draft shows the continued thinking of the OECD on attributing capital to branches and its post-1995 evolving views on arm's length principles, the 2003 Discussion Draft does not reflect the understanding of the 1975 Treaty partners, and is, thus, ultimately irrelevant to the court's conclusion.[90]

On appeal in *National Westminster Bank PLC* v. *US* (2008),[91] the Federal Court of Appeals for the Federal Circuit affirmed the judgment of Firestone J.

The static use of the OECD Commentary is supported by the US Treasury's announcement in 2007 that it would not apply the 'authorized OECD approach' for attributing profits to permanent establishments to its existing treaties with the exception of two treaties.[92] The authorized OECD approach was published in the OECD Commentary in 2008. The US has incorporated the authorized OECD approach in the 2001 US–UK treaty and the 2003 US–Japan treaty as this was expressly contemplated in the negotiation of these treaties.[93]

3.2.2 Canada

In Canada, the courts have established that the Commentary may be used to interpret its tax treaties, but there is some doubt on which version of the Commentary should be used, as Canadian courts have used both the static and ambulatory approaches. It has been claimed that Canadian courts interpreting tax treaties appear to place equal importance on the text of the treaties and on their object and purpose.[94]

The Supreme Court of Canada in *Crown Forest Industries Ltd* v. *R*[95] (*Crown Forest*) stated:

---

[89] *Ibid.*, pp. 501–2.   [90] *Ibid.*, p. 503.   [91] 512 F.3d 1347 (2008), pp. 1349, 1362.

[92] 'Treasury Releases Statement on PE Attribution of Profits' (7 June 2007), 2007 *Tax Notes Today* 112–53.

[93] *Ibid.*

[94] Ward, 'Tax Treaties: An Eroding Set of Rules' in Report of the Proceedings of the Fifty-First Tax Conference (1999) 41:1–21, p. 41:2.

[95] (1995) 125 DLR (4th) 485.

3 TAX TREATY INTERPRETATION 171

> In interpreting a treaty, the paramount goal is to find the meaning of the words in question. This process involves looking to the language used and the intentions of the parties.[96]

The Court also stated that:

> Reviewing the intentions of the drafters of a taxation convention is a very important element in delineating the scope of the application of that treaty.[97]

The Court asserted that:

> Clearly the purpose of the Convention has significant relevance to how its provisions are to be interpreted. I agree with the intervener Government of the United States' submission that, in ascertaining these goals and intentions, a court may refer to extrinsic materials which form part of the legal context (these include accepted model conventions and official commentaries thereon) without the need first to find an ambiguity before turning to such materials.[98]

On the issue of the OECD Model, the Court made the following comments:

> Of high persuasive value in terms of defining the parameters of the *Canada–United States Income Tax Convention (1980)* is the Organisation for Economic Co-operation and Development (O.E.C.D.), Committee on Fiscal Affairs, *Model Double Taxation Convention on Income and on Capital* . . . As noted by the Court of Appeal, it served as the basis for the *Canada–United States Income Tax Convention (1980)* and also has worldwide recognition as a basic document of reference in the negotiation, application and interpretation of multilateral or bilateral tax conventions.[99]

While it is accepted that the Commentary will be considered by Canadian courts in the interpretation of Canada's tax treaties, the question arises as to which version of the Commentary should be used.

In 1995, the Supreme Court of Canada in *Crown Forest* did not comment on this issue but used the 1977 version of the Commentary.[100] The 1992 version of the OECD Model and Commentary was in force at the time the case was heard, but the taxation years in issue were 1987, 1988 and 1989. The Supreme Court's approach suggests that the OECD Model and Commentary in force at the time a treaty was negotiated should be used for the purpose of treaty interpretation;[101] and it might

---

[96] *Ibid.*, p. 493, para. 22.   [97] *Ibid.*, p. 499, para. 43.   [98] *Ibid.*, p. 499, para. 44.
[99] *Ibid.*, p. 503, para. 55.   [100] *Ibid.*
[101] Li and Sandler, 'The Relationship between Domestic Anti-Avoidance Legislation and Tax Treaties' (1997), p. 911.

be argued that it would have been unfair for the Supreme Court to use the 1992 version of the OECD Model and Commentary because it was not in force during the taxation years in question. However, the Supreme Court did not expressly restrict its consideration to the OECD Model and Commentary in force at the time a particular tax treaty was negotiated. This leaves scope for a court to consider either the version of the OECD Model and Commentary which was in force at the time a case is heard or the version which was in force during the taxation year under consideration. Under the first alternative, a litigant in a case involving the interpretation of a tax treaty would need to assert that the court should use the version of the OECD Model and Commentary in force at the time of hearing even though that version was not published at the time the tax events under consideration took place. Under the second alternative, the taxpayer and the Canadian tax authority would have had access to the version of the OECD Model in force at the time the taxation events occurred. This latter argument is consistent with the approach of the Canadian Federal Court of Appeal in using the 1977 version of the OECD Model and Commentary when considering a tax treaty concluded in 1942.

In *Cudd Pressure Control Inc.* v. *R*,[102] the Canadian Federal Court of Appeal examined whether a deduction was available to a permanent establishment under the Canada–US Reciprocal Tax Convention (1942). McDonald JA considered reports of the League of Nations Fiscal Committee, published in the 1930s and 1940s, on its model tax treaty and the 1977 OECD Model and Commentary as extrinsic material on the intention of the drafters of the tax treaty. In relation to the OECD Model and Commentary McDonald JA said:

> The relevant commentaries on the OECD Convention were drafted after the 1942 Convention and therefore their relevance becomes somewhat suspect. In particular, they cannot be used to determine the intent of the drafters of the 1942 Convention. However, although the wording and arrangement of the provisions are significantly different in the two conventions, the 1942 Convention follows the same general principles as the OECD model. The OECD Commentaries, therefore, can provide some assistance in discerning the 'legal context' surrounding double taxation conventions at international law, and in particular in ascertaining when it is appropriate to allow a deduction for a notional expense.[103]

[102] 98 DTC 6630, leave to appeal refused (1999), *Cudd Pressure Control Inc* v. *Minister of National Revenue* 242 NR 400 (note) (SCC).
[103] *Ibid.*, para. 28.

The 1985 taxation year was under consideration in this case, and at that time, the 1977 version of the OECD Model and Commentary was in force. Ward asserted that Canadian courts are inclined to rely on the Commentary that existed when the treaty under consideration was made.[104] Nevertheless, Ward argues that as the Canadian tax authority follows the recommendations of the OECD, in which Canada participates, the authority's interpretation of Canada's existing tax treaties should change as the Commentary is amended.[105]

In June 1999 Canadian banking law was amended to allow international banks to operate in Canada through branches.[106] Prior to June 1999 international banks could only operate in Canada through subsidiary banks incorporated in Canada. The issue of which version of the Commentary a court should use in interpreting Canada's tax treaties in relation to the taxation of branches of international banks may be controversial because Canada's tax treaties, apart from those settled since 1999, were concluded without consideration of the taxation of Canadian branches of international banks. Consequently, using the version of the OECD Model in force at the time a particular tax treaty was concluded, to interpret a provision of the treaty, may not be appropriate. In 2000, the Canadian Federal Government released new rules for the taxation of branches of international banks for public comment. At the time the proposals were being developed, the Canadian Federal Government had the opportunity to record its observations in the Commentary; however, it has not recorded a reservation or observation on the business profits Article in the Commentary.

In *MIL (Investments) SA* v. *R*,[107] the government in the Tax Court of Canada raised, as an alternative argument, in a treaty shopping case, that the taxpayer was not entitled to the benefits of the Canada–Luxembourg tax treaty, which was concluded in 1989, as there is an inherent anti-abuse principle in tax treaties. The government claimed that the 2003 OECD Commentary, published after the Canada–Luxembourg tax treaty was concluded, supported its argument. In addition, the government asserted that the *Cudd Pressure* case supported the use, for interpretation purposes, of an OECD Commentary published after a treaty was concluded.

---

[104] Ward, 'Tax Treaties: An Eroding Set of Rules' in Report of the Proceedings of the Fifty-First Tax Conference (1999) 41:1–21, p. 41:4.

[105] *Ibid.*, p. 41:5.

[106] (Canada) Bill C-67, An Act to Amend the Bank Act, 1st Session, 36th Parliament 1999 (assented to 17 June 1999, S.C. 1999 c. 28).

[107] 2006 CarswellNat 2558; 2006 TCC 460; 2006 D.T.C. 3307 (End); [2006] 5 C.T.C. 2552.

174 OECD MODEL TAX TREATY AND COMMENTARY

Bell TCJ rejected the government's arguments on the use of an OECD Commentary published after a treaty was concluded:

> The Respondent presented the 2003 revisions to the OECD commentary as support for the existence of an inherent anti-abuse rule in tax treaties. Article 31(1)(c) of the Vienna Convention states 'there shall be taken into account, together with the context, any relevant rules of international law applicable in the relations between the parties.' I interpret that to mean that one can only consult the OECD commentary in existence at the time the Treaty was negotiated without reference to subsequent revisions.[108]

In *Prevost Car Incorporated* v. *R*,[109] in the Federal Court of Canada, the issue of using OECD Commentaries was considered to interpret tax treaties prior to the conclusion of a tax treaty. The taxpayer appealed a Tax Court of Canada judgment by Rip ACJ, in which the judge referred to the OECD the 1986 *Conduit Companies Report*[110] and the 2003 OECD Commentary in a case interpreting the Canada–Netherlands tax treaty, which was completed in 1986. The 1977 OECD Commentary was in force at the time the treaty was negotiated. While the judge made references to the 2003 Commentary, the judge did not apply it in making his decision.[111] The judge's references to the 2003 Commentary could be interpreted to be mere background material which had no weight in the judgment. Nevertheless, the Federal Court endorsed the use of the 2003 Commentary and *Conduit Companies Report* to the previously concluded Canada–Netherlands tax treaty. The court concluded:

> [W]ith respect to later commentaries, when they represent a fair interpretation of the words of the Model Convention and do not conflict with Commentaries in existence at the time a specific treaty was entered and when, of course, neither treaty partner has registered an objection to the new Commentaries. For example, in the introduction to the Income and Capital Model Convention and Commentary (2003), the OECD invites its members to interpret their bilateral treaties in accordance with the Commentaries 'as modified from time to time' (par. 3) and 'in the spirit of the revised Commentaries' (par. 33). The Introduction goes on, at par. 35, to note that changes to the Commentaries are not relevant 'where the provisions . . . are different in substance from the amended Articles' and,

---

[108] CarsewellNat 2558, para. 86.
[109] 2009 CarswellNat 480; 2009 FCA 57; 2009 D.T.C. 5053 (Eng.); [2009] 3 C.T.C. 160; 387 N.R. 161; 2009 D.T.C. 5053.
[110] OECD, *Double Taxation Conventions and the Use of Conduit Companies* (1986).
[111] See Kandev and Wiener, 'Some Thoughts on the Use of Later OECD Commentaries After Prevost Car' (2009), p. 671.

3 TAX TREATY INTERPRETATION   175

> at par. 36, that 'many amendments are intended to simply clarify, not
> change, the meaning of the Articles or the Commentaries'.
>
> I therefore reach the conclusion, that for the purposes of interpreting
> the Tax Treaty, the OECD Conduit Companies Report (in 1986) as well as
> the OECD 2003 Amendments to the 1977 Commentary are a helpful
> complement to the earlier Commentaries, insofar as they are eliciting,
> rather than contradicting, views previously expressed. Needless to say, the
> Commentaries apply to both the English text of the Model Convention
> ('beneficial owner') and to the French text ('bénéficiaire effectif').[112]

The Federal Court endorsed the use of a Commentary published after a
treaty was concluded, but the endorsement is qualified as the Court
failed to provide guidance on such use of a Commentary. Moreover, the
Court did not specify what weight should be given to Commentaries
published after a treaty was concluded.[113]

Canadian courts interpreting a tax treaty will consider the OECD
Model and Commentary, but there is some uncertainty as to which
version would be used as both the static and ambulatory approaches
have been used. But when an ambulatory approach has been used, little
weight has been given to a Commentary published after a treaty was
completed. It is asserted that the best approach is to use the version of
the OECD Commentary in force when a treaty was completed for
interpreting the treaty.[114]

3.2.3 Australia

Australia is a party to the Vienna Convention, which applies to the
interpretation of Australia's tax treaties. In *Thiel* v. *Federal Commissioner
of Taxation*,[115] the High Court of Australia (Australia's highest court)
held that the Vienna Convention applies to tax treaties between Australia
and a tax treaty partner which is not a party to the Vienna Convention
because it reflects customary international law. Australia joined the
OECD in 1971 and in *Thiel* the High Court confirmed that the OECD
Model and the accompanying Commentary (Commentary) may used as
supplementary means of interpretation under Article 32 of the Vienna
Convention in the interpretation of Australia's tax treaties.[116] McHugh J
of the High Court concluded that, if a term of a tax treaty is ambiguous,

---

[112] 2009 CarswellNat 480, paras. 11–12.

[113] Kandev and Wiener, 'Some Thoughts on the Use of Later OECD Commentaries After
Prevost Car' (2009).

[114] See Lang and Brugger, 'The Role of the OECD Commentary in Tax Treaty Interpretation' (2008), pp. 106–8.

[115] (1990) 171 CLR 338.   [116] *Ibid.*, pp. 349–50.

176 OECD MODEL TAX TREATY AND COMMENTARY

a court should consider '"supplementary means of interpretation" in interpreting the Agreement'.[117] The judge found that the 'supplementary means of interpretation' in the case were the use of the 1977 OECD Model and accompanying Commentary. Mason CJ, Brennan and Gaudron JJ of the High Court concurred with the reasoning of McHugh J.[118] Dawson J found that the OECD Model and Commentary in force when a treaty is being negotiated: 'form the basis for the conclusion of bilateral double taxation agreements of the kind in question and, as with treaties in *pari materia*, provide a guide to the current usage of terms by the parties. They are, therefore, a supplementary means of interpretation to which recourse may be had under Article 32 of the *Vienna Convention*'.[119] The High Court concluded that the OECD Model and Commentary may be used in Australia as supplementary material under the Vienna Convention.

In conclusion, the status of the Commentary appears to be uncertain. The OECD asserts in the Commentary that it is obligatory for OECD countries to use it in interpreting their tax treaties, but the OECD Model does not mention the Commentary or its role in the interpretation of tax treaties. Nevertheless, the Commentary is used by US courts, Canadian courts and Australian courts in the interpretation of their tax treaties. Although the Commentary may be used by courts in these countries in interpreting tax treaties, there is some uncertainty as to which version of the Commentary should be used. The OECD contends that the ambulatory approach should be used, but courts in OECD countries, such as the US, Canada and Australia, have used the static approach.

Despite the unequivocal guidance of the High Court on the use of the OECD Model and Commentary, in *Lamesa Holdings* v. *Federal Commissioner of Taxation*,[120] the trial judge of the Federal Court of Australia, sitting alone, after referring to *Thiel*'s case, concluded that the 1977 Commentary was relevant in interpreting the Australia–Netherlands tax treaty which was concluded in 1976.[121] The judge relied on expert evidence that the 1977 OECD Model and Commentary had been published before the conclusion of the Australia–Netherlands treaty in 1976.[122] The judge also claimed that: 'the relevant paragraphs from the 1977 OECD Model are the same or substantially the same as the corresponding paragraphs of the 1963 OECD Model'.[123] The judge appeared to

---

[117] *Ibid.*, p. 357. [118] *Ibid.*, p. 344. [119] *Ibid.*, p. 350. [120] (1997) 35 ATR 239.
[121] *Ibid.*, p. 247. See also Lang and Brugger, 'The Role of the OECD Commentary in Tax Treaty Interpretation' (2008), p. 107.
[122] (1997) 35 ATR 239. [123] *Ibid.*

conclude that although the 1963 Commentary was the official Commentary to be used in interpreting the treaty, it had been unofficially displaced by the 1977 Commentary on the basis that it was published before the treaty was finalized. Nevertheless, if the applicable parts of the 1963 Commentary and 1997 Commentary were 'substantially the same', the use of the latter Commentary had no influence on the judgment. On appeal, the Full Federal Court of Australia in *Federal Commissioner of Taxation* v. *Lamesa Holdings BV*,[124] in a joint judgment, did not consider Einfeld J's use of the 1977 Commentary, but instead the court confined its comments on treaty interpretation to the principles established in *Thiel*'s case. The Full Federal Court judgment only refers to the High Court's comments on the use of the OECD Model and Commentary in *Thiel*'s case.

4 Conclusion

The pivotal importance of the OECD Model in the tax treaty system is in evidence through its use by OECD countries and non-OECD countries alike. Most tax treaties are based on the OECD Model, and the Commentary is also widely used in the interpretation of tax treaties. Tax authorities in OECD countries are obliged to use the Commentary in the interpretation of treaty provisions, subject to their country's reservations on an Article of the OECD Model and observations on the Commentary. Tax authorities in non-OECD countries are also likely to use the Commentary, particularly those countries which participate in the OECD's discussions on the OECD Model and Commentary. Moreover, courts are likely to use the Commentary as an interpretative guide when examining tax treaty provisions. This chapter established that US, Canadian and Australian courts have relied on the Commentary in deciding cases. Under the Vienna Convention only the OECD Commentary in force when a tax treaty was concluded, the static approach, should be used for interpreting a tax treaty. While Commentaries published after a tax treaty was completed may be considered by courts in some countries, such Commentaries should be given no weight. In particular, if a subsequent Commentary reflects a new interpretation of a treaty provision, such as the 2008 Commentary on former Article 7, the subsequent Commentary should not be used to interpret treaties which came into force before the Commentary was published. The static approach is premised on

---

[124] 36 ATR 589.

the principle that if a treaty provision is based on the OECD Model, the Commentary in force when the treaty was negotiated was treated by the parliaments enacting the treaty as part of the context of the treaty and thus adopted by the two parliaments.

Now, Chapter 6 examines the meaning of the terms of former Article 7 and the guidance provided in the pre-2008 Commentary and 2008 Commentary on the interpretation of former Article 7. Chapter 7 studies the deductibility of intra-bank interest under former Article 7 in the light of the pre-2008 OECD Commentary and a specific OECD report dealing with the topic. Chapter 8 considers the deductibility of intra-bank interest under the 2008 Commentary and the 2008 Report.

Finally, the League of Nations was the genesis of the one time aim for a multilateral tax treaty, which had been the first preference of the OECD. The compromise measure of a bilateral tax treaty model has been the focus of OECD developments. But in the future, EU enterprises operating in the EU may be taxed under a multilateral EU tax treaty, as the EU is considering using formulary apportionment rather than the arm's length principle for allocating profits under the proposal. This issue is addressed in Chapter 11.

6

Defining the personality of permanent establishments under former Article 7 and the pre-2008 Commentary and the 2008 Commentary

1 Introduction

Former Article 7 establishes a long-standing treaty principle for allocating the business profits of an international enterprise operating through permanent establishments.[1] The rationale underlying former Article 7 is that when an enterprise operates in a host country through a permanent establishment, the enterprise is participating in the economic life of that country. Consequently, former Article 7 allocates to a host country taxing rights over business profits attributable to a permanent establishment in the host country. Former Article 7 is based on the arm's length principle and purports to treat a permanent establishment as a separate entity for the purpose of allocating profits and expenses to it.

Prior to the publication of the 2008 Commentary on former Article 7 there was no OECD consensus interpretation of the provision, despite the revision of the Commentary in 1994. This led to the OECD issuing a series of discussion drafts on former Article 7 resulting in the publication in July 2008 of the 'authorized OECD approach' on interpreting former Article 7 – the consensus interpretation – in the 2008 Report. In order to quickly adopt the 2008 Report, the OECD used a two-step implementation procedure, which has created uncertainty. In the first step, in 2008 the OECD amended the Commentary on former Article 7 (2008 Commentary) which implemented the parts of the 'authorized OECD approach' in the 2008 Report that do not conflict with the pre-existing version of the Commentary (pre-2008 Commentary).[2] This approach

---

[1] The text of Article 7 of 2008 OECD Model is almost identical to its original form in the 1963 version of the 1963 OECD Model, *Draft Double Taxation Convention on Income and Capital* (1963). See Abeele, 'The Coordination of Tax Policy: The EU Experience' (2000) 1:1–9.

[2] The pre-2008 Commentary is the Commentary on Article 7 which was published in the 2005 OECD Model.

180 DEFINING PERSONALITY OF PERMANENT ESTABLISHMENTS

implies that the 2008 Commentary may be used to interpret the business profits Article of tax treaties concluded before July 2008. It is bold for the OECD to claim that the 'authorized OECD approach', which is a new interpretation, can be immediately applied to tax treaties finalized before July 2008 on the unconvincing claim that the authorized OECD approach in the 2008 Commentary does not conflict with the pre-2008 Commentary.[3] The authorized OECD approach is a new interpretation of former Article 7 which was established after several years of discussions by OECD countries.

Under international law, the OECD Commentary in force at the time a treaty is negotiated may be used as an extrinsic aid in the interpretation of a tax treaty. Although the OECD Commentary in force at the time treaties are negotiated should be used in the interpretation of these treaties, some OECD countries and non-OECD countries may apply the 2008 Commentary to treaties negotiated before July 2008. The OECD encourages countries to apply the current Commentary to tax treaties concluded before the publication of the Commentary.[4] It is asserted that it is inappropriate to use the 2008 Commentary, which incorporates extensive changes, to tax treaties concluded before July 2008, especially when the OECD acknowledges that prior to the publication of the 2008 Report there was no consensus interpretation of former Article 7.[5] In 2007 the US announced that it will not apply the authorized OECD approach to its existing treaties.[6] In the second step, the OECD has adopted a new Article 7 and Commentary in the 2010 OECD Model.[7] The OECD rejected the alternative approach of implementing the 2008 Report exclusively through the adoption of a new Article 7 and Commentary.

This chapter deals with both the pre-2008 Commentary and the 2008 Commentary. As the average time for a treaty to be renegotiated is

---

[3] 2008 Report, p. 8, para. 8.

[4] 2008 OECD Model, pp. 14–15, paras. 35–36.1; 2010 OECD Model, pp. 15–16, paras. 35–36.1. The Commentary on former Article 7 in the 2008 OECD Model has been reproduced in the 2010 OECD Model.

[5] The 2008 Commentary may be used to interpret tax treaties concluded before 17 July 2008, if the treaties were negotiated in anticipation of using the 'authorized OECD approach' in the 2008 Report.

[6] 'Treasury Releases Statement on PE Attribution of Profits' (7 June 2007), 2007 *Tax Notes Today* 112–53. The exceptions to the prospective application of the 2008 Commentary were the US–Japan treaty and the US–UK treaty as these treaties were negotiated in anticipation of the authorized OECD approach.

[7] 2010 OECD Model.

fourteen years, the pre-2008 Commentary will be the appropriate version of the Commentary to be used in interpreting the business profits Article of tax treaties for many years. Moreover, OECD and non-OECD countries will continue to use former Article 7. This chapter examines the attribution of profits to permanent establishments under former Article 7 of the OECD Model and the pre-2008 Commentary and the 2008 Commentary.[8] The analysis reveals former Article 7 to be unclear and ambiguous, and the pre-2008 Commentary on former Article 7 to be inadequate and inconsistent. The ambiguities in its drafting have resulted in former Article 7 being inconsistently interpreted within OECD countries. The critical flaw in former Article 7 is its normative base – the arm's length principle – which is inappropriate for allocating profits to permanent establishments of highly integrated enterprises. An international enterprise and its permanent establishments are part of a unitary business with a common profit-making goal. Permanent establishments do not operate as separate entities, but as part of an integrated business. The interaction between an international enterprise's permanent establishments is governed by common control, whereas transactions between independent entities are governed by their contracts, representing competing interests.

Under former Article 7 a permanent establishment is treated as a separate entity for certain purposes, but as part of a larger single entity for other purposes. The concurrent reliance on the separate entity and single entity approaches directly affects the allocation of business profits between the residence jurisdiction of an international enterprise and the host jurisdiction of its permanent establishments. Not surprisingly, this concurrent reliance on the competing approaches of separate and single entity in former Article 7 and the pre-2008 Commentary has resulted in the failure by OECD countries to establish a consensus interpretation. The consequence of former Article 7 being inconsistently interpreted is the possible double taxation or under-taxation of permanent establishments.

The chapter first examines the attribution of business profits to permanent establishments under former Article 7. Former Article 7 allocates to the host country of a permanent establishment of an international enterprise the right to tax the permanent establishment's business profits. The chapter demonstrates the use of the separate entity and single entity methods in the interpretation of former Article 7 in

---

[8] New Article 7 and Commentary are considered in Ch. 10.

182   DEFINING PERSONALITY OF PERMANENT ESTABLISHMENTS

the pre-2008 Commentary. The chapter highlights the conflicting interpretations of the term 'profits of an enterprise' in former Article 7(1), resulting from the practice in some OECD countries of using the separate entity method and in others of using the single entity method. It then considers the purported use of the functional separate entity approach under the 2008 Commentary. The chapter examines the separate entity method used in former Article 7(2) and the interaction between former Articles 7(1) and (2) in allocating profits to permanent establishments. The chapter also examines the 2008 amendments to the Commentary on this provision. It then considers former Article 7(3) and the extent to which it prescribes a single entity approach for the allocation of expenses to permanent establishments under the pre-2008 and 2008 Commentaries. The chapter concludes with an examination of the interaction between former Articles 7(2) and (3) under these Commentaries.

2   Background: the definition of a permanent establishment

The purpose of the concept of a permanent establishment under tax treaties is to determine if source country has taxing rights over business profits derived by an enterprise which is resident in the other country. A source country (host country) has taxing rights over profits derived by a non-resident enterprise if it has a permanent establishment in the host country, but the taxing right is limited to profits which are attributable to the permanent establishment. The term 'permanent establishment' is defined in Article 5 of the OECD Model by a series of threshold tests.[9] The first test in Article 5(1) is that a permanent

---

[9] Article 5 of the OECD Model provides:

'1. For the purposes of this Convention, the term "permanent establishment" means a fixed place of business through which the business of an enterprise is wholly or partly carried on.
2. The term "permanent establishment" includes especially:
   (a) a place of management;
   (b) a branch;
   (c) an office;
   (d) a factory;
   (e) a workshop, and
   (f) a mine, an oil or gas well, a quarry or any other place of extraction of natural resources.
3. A building site or construction or installation project constitutes a permanent establishment only if it lasts more than twelve months.

2 THE DEFINITION OF A PERMANENT ESTABLISHMENT 183

establishment is a fixed place of business through which the business of an enterprise is carried on. The OECD Commentary describes the Article 5(1) test:

> Paragraph 1 gives a general definition of the term 'permanent establishment' which brings out its essential characteristics of a permanent establishment in the sense of the Convention, i.e. a distinct 'situs', a 'fixed place of business'. The paragraph defines the term 'permanent establishment' as a fixed place of business, through which the business of an enterprise is wholly or partly carried on. This definition, therefore, contains the following conditions:
>
> - the existence of a 'place of business', i.e. a facility such as premises or, in certain instances, machinery or equipment;

4. Notwithstanding the preceding provisions of this Article, the term "permanent establishment" shall be deemed not to include:
   (a) the use of facilities solely for the purpose of storage, display or delivery of goods or merchandise belonging to the enterprise;
   (b) the maintenance of a stock of goods or merchandise belonging to the enterprise solely for the purpose of storage, display or delivery;
   (c) the maintenance of a stock of goods or merchandise belonging to the enterprise solely for the purpose of processing by another enterprise;
   (d) the maintenance of a fixed place of business solely for the purpose of purchasing goods or merchandise or of collecting information, for the enterprise;
   (e) the maintenance of a fixed place of business solely for the purpose of carrying on, for the enterprise, any other activity of a preparatory or auxiliary character;
   (f) the maintenance of a fixed place of business solely for any combination of activities mentioned in subparagraphs (a) to (e), provided that the overall activity of the fixed place of business resulting from this combination is of a preparatory or auxiliary character.
5. Notwithstanding the provisions of paragraphs 1 and 2, where a person – other than an agent of an independent status to whom paragraph 6 applies – is acting on behalf of an enterprise and has, and habitually exercises, in a Contracting State an authority to conclude contracts in the name of the enterprise, that enterprise shall be deemed to have a permanent establishment in that State in respect of any activities which that person undertakes for the enterprise, unless the activities of such person are limited to those mentioned in paragraph 4 which, if exercised through a fixed place of business, would not make this fixed place of business a permanent establishment under the provisions of that paragraph.
6. An enterprise shall not be deemed to have a permanent establishment in a Contracting State merely because it carries on business in that State through a broker, general commission agent or any other agent of an independent status, provided that such persons are acting in the ordinary course of their business.
7. The fact that a company which is a resident of a Contracting State controls or is controlled by a company which is a resident of the other Contracting State, or which carries on business in that other State (whether through a permanent establishment or otherwise), shall not of itself constitute either company a permanent establishment of the other.'

184 DEFINING PERSONALITY OF PERMANENT ESTABLISHMENTS

- this place of business must be 'fixed', i.e. it must be established at a distinct place with a certain degree of permanence;
- the carrying on of the business of the enterprise through this fixed place of business. This means usually that persons who, in one way or another, are dependent on the enterprise (personnel) conduct the business of the enterprise in the State in which the fixed place is situated.[10]

Under Article 5, a branch of an international enterprise, such as an international bank, located in a host country will be a permanent establishment for tax treaty purposes because the branch is a fixed place of business and the international enterprise's business is carried on through the fixed place of business. In addition, Article 5(2)(b) states that an example of a permanent establishment is a branch of an international enterprise.

3 The meaning of former Article 7

Former Article 7(1) of the OECD Model provides a method for allocating business profits of international enterprises operating in host countries through permanent establishments.[11] Under the OECD Model, a source country's taxing rights over business profits of an international

---

[10] 2010 OECD Model, p. 92, para. 1.
[11] Former Article 7 of the 2008 OECD Model provides:

'1. The profits of an enterprise of a Contracting State shall be taxable only in that State unless the enterprise carries on business in the other Contracting State through a permanent establishment situated therein. If the enterprise carries on business as aforesaid, the profits of the enterprise may be taxed in the other State but only so much of them as is attributable to that permanent establishment.

2. Subject to the provisions of paragraph 3, where an enterprise of a Contracting State carries on business in the other Contracting State through a permanent establishment situated therein, there shall in each Contracting State be attributed to that permanent establishment the profits which it might be expected to make if it were a distinct and separate enterprise engaged in the same or similar activities under the same or similar conditions and dealing wholly independently with the enterprise of which it is a permanent establishment.

3. In determining the profits of a permanent establishment, there shall be allowed as deductions expenses which are incurred for the purposes of the permanent establishment, including executive and general administrative expenses so incurred, whether in the State in which the permanent establishment is situated or elsewhere.

4. Insofar as it has been customary in a Contracting State to determine the profits to be attributed to a permanent establishment on the basis of an apportionment of the total profits of the enterprise to its various parts, nothing in paragraph 2 shall preclude that Contracting State from determining the profits to be taxed by such an apportionment

3 THE MEANING OF FORMER ARTICLE 7

enterprise under former Article 7(1) are dependent on the existence of a permanent establishment within its borders. Under former Article 7, an international enterprise operating in another country through a permanent establishment is subject to tax in the host country to the extent that business profits are attributable to the permanent establishment. Former Article 7(2) directs that the profits attributable to a permanent establishment are the profits that it would have made, if it were a separate and distinct enterprise engaged in the same or similar activities. The legal fiction of treating a permanent establishment as a separate and independent entity is based on the arm's length principle. Former Article 7(4) provides an exception to the separate entity approach used in former Article 7(2), but the situations in which this exception may be used are very limited. Former Article 7(4) may be applied only if the use of formulary apportionment is customary in a country, subject also to the proviso that the result conforms with the arm's length principle. Former Article 7 contains three specific rules for the calculation of profits and expenses attributable to a permanent establishment. Former Article 7(3) states that expenses incurred by an international enterprise for the permanent establishment are deductible in determining the profits of the permanent establishment. Former Article 7(5) asserts that profits may not be attributed to a permanent establishment for the purchasing of goods on behalf of other parts of the enterprise and former Article 7(6) prescribes that the method used to attribute profits to a permanent establishment must be the same in each income year unless there is a justifiable reason for changing methods.

The Commentary claims that 'Articles 7 and 9 are not particularly detailed and were not strikingly novel or particularly detailed when they were adopted by the OECD.'[12] Nevertheless, the meaning of the terms used in former Article 7 is ambiguous and the interaction between the

> as may be customary; the method of apportionment adopted shall, however, be such that the result shall be in accordance with the principles contained in this Article.
>
> 5. No profits shall be attributed to a permanent establishment by reason of the mere purchase by that permanent establishment of goods or merchandise for the enterprise.
>
> 6. For the purposes of the preceding paragraphs, the profits to be attributed to the permanent establishment shall be determined by the same method year by year unless there is good and sufficient reason to the contrary.
>
> 7. Where profits include items of income which are dealt with separately in other Articles of this Convention, then the provisions of those Articles shall not be affected by the provisions of this Article.'

[12] 2008 OECD Model, p. 113, para. 2.

186 DEFINING PERSONALITY OF PERMANENT ESTABLISHMENTS

paragraphs of former Article 7 is unclear and controversial. For example, there is an argument that the meaning of the separate entity principle in former Article 7(2), under the pre-2008 Commentary, is ambiguous and that its interaction with former Articles 7(1) and (3) is unclear.[13] The scope of the separate entity fiction in attributing profits to a permanent establishment has led to heated debate.[14] The pre-2008 Commentary on former Article 7 compounded the problem by failing to provide a consensus interpretation of the provision. Moreover, the directives in the pre-2008 Commentary have been criticized as being inconsistent with its very terms.[15] The revision of the Commentary in 1994 provided some guidance on when an enterprise could charge a profit margin on notional intra-entity transactions with a permanent establishment. However, the 1994 revisions were of a minor nature and were not enough to develop a consensus interpretation within the OECD resulting in OECD countries using various conflicting interpretations of former Article 7. The OECD asserts that the 'authorized OECD approach' of the 2008 Report is now a consensus interpretation of former Article 7.

3.1 Inconsistent interpretations of former Article 7 by OECD countries in the pre-2008 Commentary

The main objectives of a tax treaty are to prevent double taxation or under-taxation, and to counter tax avoidance. A tax treaty is likely to be effective in allocating revenue and expenses between the treaty countries if the terms of the tax treaty are clear, unambiguous and interpreted consistently. The methods used in tax treaties for allocating profits to permanent establishments must be applied consistently and symmetrically within the tax treaty network. The methods should be based on sound theory, reflect economic reality, be simple, and minimize the accompanying compliance and administrative costs. Although tax treaties apply reciprocally, the allocation of profits under former Article 7 under a tax treaty will be imbalanced if there are significant economic differences between the countries. Countries enter into tax treaties with

---

[13] Arnold and Darmo, 'Summary of Proceedings of an Invitational Seminar on the Attribution of Profits to Permanent Establishments' (2001), p. 528.

[14] Vogel, *Klaus Vogel on Double Tax Conventions* (3rd edn, 1997), pp. 427–8, referring to the debate on the scope of the separate entity fiction in the Netherlands and Germany.

[15] Arnold and Darmo, 'Summary of Proceedings of an Invitational Seminar on the Attribution of Profits to Permanent Establishments' (2001), p. 529; Ward, 'Attribution of Income to Permanent Establishments' (2000), p. 564.

3 THE MEANING OF FORMER ARTICLE 7   187

more developed countries because they consider the economic benefits gained from the treaties exceed the cost of losing taxing rights over business profits sourced in their countries by non-resident enterprises without a permanent establishment. Nevertheless, the critical requirement in interpreting tax treaties is that their provisions be interpreted consistently. If treaty provisions are interpreted inconsistently as between jurisdictions, international enterprises will use planning techniques to exploit the different interpretations. A consensus interpretation of a treaty provision by the OECD countries, which is applied consistently, will minimize the potential of double taxation or under-taxation and tax avoidance, even if the interpretation is not based on an objective theoretical foundation.

It is routinely asserted that there is no objective economic method for allocating revenue and costs within an international enterprise because of the integrated nature of their business operations.[16] The revenue and costs of an international enterprise come from a number of sources, so any attribution of geographic location to profits is artificial.[17] Any mechanism that seeks to allocate the revenue and costs of an international enterprise to a country in which it operates will be arbitrary because the flows of funds of an international enterprise do not have geographic indicia, they are merely the profits and costs of the enterprise.[18] Not surprisingly, international enterprises seek to maximize their profits and minimize their tax obligations. International enterprises are able to engage in tax arbitrage by exploiting the differences between the tax systems in the countries in which they operate. Consequently, any method for the allocation of revenue and expenses under a treaty's business profits Article, and thereby to the countries in which the enterprise carries on business through permanent establishments, is inherently arbitrary.[19] Although any method is likely to make certain

---

[16] P. B. Musgrave, 'Sovereignty, Entitlement, and Cooperation in International Taxation' (2001), p. 1345; C. E. McLure (ed.) *State Income Taxation of Multistate Corporations in the United States of America* (1974), p. 61, para. 2; Bird and Brean, 'The Interjurisdictional Allocation of Income and the Unitary Taxation Debate' (1986), p. 1383.

[17] Ault and Bradford, 'Taxing International Income' in Razin and Slemrod (eds.), *Taxation in the Global Economy* (1990) 11–46, p. 29.

[18] It has been argued that the allocation method should be evaluated in terms of the principle of inter-nation equity and that the allocation method should be able to minimize avoidance opportunities: Edgar and Holland, 'Source Taxation and the OECD Project on the Attribution of Profits to Permanent Establishments' (2005), p. 532.

[19] Brean, 'Here or There?' in Bird and Mintz (eds.), *Taxation to 2000 and Beyond* (1992) 303–33, p. 331.

188   DEFINING PERSONALITY OF PERMANENT ESTABLISHMENTS

jurisdictions winners and others losers, it would be effective in allocating profits if it were simple and applied uniformly by jurisdictions. A consensus interpretation and practical application of former Article 7 would minimize the risk of tax distortions in the form of double taxation or under-taxation of permanent establishments.

Since 1963, the OECD has asserted in the Commentary that former Article 7 is consistently interpreted by OECD countries. The Commentary on former Article 7 provides:

> The question of what criteria should be used in attributing profits to a permanent establishment, and of how to allocate profits from transactions between enterprises under common control, has had to be dealt with in a large number of double tax conventions and it is fair to say that the solutions adopted have generally conformed to a standard pattern. It is generally recognised that the essential principles on which this standard pattern is based are well founded, and it has been thought sufficient to restate them with some slight amendments and modifications primarily aimed at producing greater clarity.[20]

But in 2001, the OECD acknowledged that there was a lack of consensus by OECD countries on the interpretation of former Article 7 and that the need for reform had become a pressing issue.[21] In the *Report on the Attribution of Profits to Permanent Establishments* the OECD stated:

> To date, there has been considerable variation in the domestic laws of OECD member countries regarding the taxation of PEs. In addition, there has previously been no consensus amongst the OECD member countries as to the correct interpretation of Article 7. This lack of a common interpretation and consistent application of Article 7 can lead to double, or less than single, taxation. The development of global trading of financial products and electronic commerce has helped to focus attention on the need to establish a broad consensus regarding the interpretation and practical application of Article 7.[22]

The continued use of inconsistent interpretations of former Article 7 by OECD countries has meant that the provision is ineffective for attributing profits to a permanent establishment. The branch reports to the 2006 International Fiscal Association Congress compellingly confirm the

---

[20] OECD, *Model Tax Convention on Income and on Capital* (2005), pp. 113–14, para. 2. This statement has been in the OECD Model since 1963 (OECD, *Draft Double Taxation Convention on Income and Capital* (1963)).

[21] 2001 *Discussion Draft on the Attribution of Profits to Permanent Establishments* (2001 Discussion Draft) Introduction, pp. 6–7, para. 3.

[22] OECD, *Report on the Attribution of Profits to Permanent Establishments* (2008), para. 2.

3 THE MEANING OF FORMER ARTICLE 7

differing interpretations of former Article 7.[23] A uniform interpretation of treaty provisions is required to ensure the efficient and equitable application of tax treaties.[24] Inconsistent interpretations of former Article 7 are likely to result in double taxation or under-taxation, which is at odds with the role of tax treaties. While the OECD provides detailed Transfer Pricing Guidelines[25] for associated enterprises under Article 9, by contrast, the rules on the attribution of profits to a permanent establishment prior to 2008 were limited and inconsistent. In 2008, the OECD published a consensus interpretation of former Article 7 in the 2008 Report and the 2008 Commentary. The OECD claimed that it had established its 'authorized OECD approach' in the 2008 Report, which had been previously issued as discussion drafts.

3.1.1 OECD Discussion Drafts on the attribution of profits to permanent establishments

The OECD issued the 2001 Discussion Draft in which it sought to establish a consensus interpretation of the attribution of profits to permanent establishments under former Article 7. Part I of the 2001 Discussion Draft set out the proposed principles for the attribution of profits and expenses to permanent establishments, and Part II applied the proposals to branches of international banks. The aim of the OECD's proposed reforms was to adapt the OECD's transfer pricing rules for associated entities to permanent establishments. The OECD chose international bank branches on which to test its proposed reforms because international banks usually operate globally through branches. In 2003, the OECD reissued Part II of the 2001 Discussion Draft on the taxation of branches of international banks and issued Part III on global trading of financial instruments (2003 Discussion Draft).[26] In 2004, the OECD reissued Part I of the 2001 Discussion Draft (2004 Discussion Draft) for public comment.[27] In 2005, the OECD issued Part IV (Insurance)[28] and

---

[23] Baker and Collier, 'General Report' in *Cahiers de droit fiscal international* (2006), p. 34.

[24] Vogel, 'Double Tax Treaties and their Interpretation' (1986), p. 85.

[25] First published in OECD, *Transfer Pricing Guidelines for Multinational Enterprises and Tax Administrations* (loose-leaf) (1995).

[26] OECD, *Discussion Draft on the Attribution of Profits to Permanent Establishments* (PEs): *Part II (Banks) and Part III (Global Trading of Financial Instruments)* (2003).

[27] OECD, *Discussion Draft on the Attribution of Profits to Permanent Establishments: Part I (General Considerations)* (2004).

[28] *Discussion Draft on the Attribution of Profits to Permanent Establishments: Part IV (Insurance)* (2005).

190 DEFINING PERSONALITY OF PERMANENT ESTABLISHMENTS

a revised Part IV was released in August 2007. The OECD reform proposals in the 2003 Discussion Draft and 2004 Discussion Draft were controversial.[29]

In January 2005, the OECD announced that the Committee on Fiscal Affairs (Committee) had reviewed the process for work on the proposals and that Parts I to III were not finalized and would retain the status of OECD discussion drafts. This change in approach was prompted by comments from the business sector in 2004. In 2005, the OECD claimed that while industry generally endorsed the principles underlying the OECD proposals, there were significant concerns about certain issues. The OECD proposed that further work would be done to refine and finalize the proposed measures, and that at the same time the Commentary on former Article 7 would be revised.

3.1.2   OECD, Report on the Attribution of Profits to Permanent Establishments

In December 2006, the OECD Fiscal Committee published its *Report on the Attribution of Profits to Permanent Establishments*[30] (Parts I–III) and in 2007, issued proposed amendments to the Articles of the OECD Model and Commentary for public comment. The final report, the 2008 Report (Parts I–IV), was issued on 17 July 2008 and provides the views of the Committee on the attribution of profits to a permanent establishment. The 2008 Report noted that:

> It replaces all previous drafts of the various Parts, which should no longer be considered to reflect the views of the Committee. There is a broad consensus among OECD countries that the conclusions reflected in this Report represent a better approach to attributing profits to permanent establishments than has previously been available. The Committee recognises, however, that there are differences between some of these conclusions and the practices and historical interpretation of Article 7 (as it has read since its last amendment in 1977) that were reflected in the Commentary on Article 7 as it read before the adoption of this Report (*i.e.* as most recently published as part of the 2005 OECD Model Tax Convention).[31]

The Committee decided on a two-stage implementation of the 2008 Report. Under the first stage the Commentary on former Article 7 was

---

[29] See Ch. 8; Kobetsky, 'Attribution of Profits to Branches of International Banks: The OECD Discussion Drafts' (2005); Edgar and Holland, 'Source Taxation and the OECD Project on the Attribution of Profits to Permanent Establishments' (2005).

[30] OECD, *Report on the Attribution of Profits to Permanent Establishments* (2006).

[31] 2008 Report, p. 8, para. 7.

3 THE MEANING OF FORMER ARTICLE 7   191

amended in 2008 to reflect the conclusions in the 2008 Report that are considered to be consistent with the existing version of former Article 7 and the pre-2008 Commentary. The second stage implemented the remaining conclusions in the 2008 Report, in new Article 7 and accompanying Commentary adopted in the 2010 OECD Model.[32] The 2008 Report was republished as the 2010 Report to reflect the provisions of new Article 7.[33] This two-step implementation resulted in the publication of the 2008 Commentary on former Article 7.

3.2   The 2008 Commentary on former Article 7

It was asserted by the Committee that many of the conclusions in the 2008 Report are not in conflict with the pre-2008 Commentary on former Article 7. Consequently, the Committee decided that the Commentary on former Article 7 could be amended in 2008:

> In addition, however, the Committee considers that many of the conclusions reflected in this Report do not conflict with the Commentary on Article 7 as that Commentary read before the adoption of this Report. Therefore, in order to provide improved certainty for the interpretation of existing treaties based on the current text of Article 7, the Committee decided to revise the Commentary on the current version of Article 7 to take into account the conclusions of this Report that do not conflict with the previous Commentary. A revised Commentary on the current text of Article 7 was prepared for the 2008 update to the OECD Model Tax Convention. The Report should therefore be read in that context, taking care, when interpreting bilateral treaties that include the current text of Article 7 (as it appears in the Appendix), to use only the parts of the Report that do not conflict with the Article 7 Commentary as so revised.[34]

It is bold to assert on the one hand that there was no consensus on the interpretation of former Article 7 prior to 2008 and to then establish a consensus and claim that it is consistent with the pre-2008 Commentary. It is curious to move from a situation in which the OECD asserts that prior to the finalization of the 2008 Report there was no consensus among OECD countries, but from 2008 certain conclusions can be implemented which are consistent with former Article 7 and the pre-2008

---

[32] 2010 OECD Model.
[33] OECD, *Report on the Attribution of Profits to Permanent Establishments* (2010).
[34] *Ibid.*

192 DEFINING PERSONALITY OF PERMANENT ESTABLISHMENTS

Commentary. It is impossible to retrospectively claim that conclusions finalized in the 2008 Report were in some way implied and generally accepted conclusions in relation to former Article 7.

The suggested application of the 2008 Commentary to tax treaties finalized before July 2008 also conflicts with the guidance provided in the Commentary itself. The Commentary claims that some amendments to Commentary merely express the consensus opinion of OECD countries:

> However, other changes or additions to the Commentaries are normally applicable to the interpretation and application of conventions concluded before their adoption, because they reflect the consensus of the OECD Member countries as to the proper interpretation of existing provisions and their application to specific situations.
>
> Whilst the Committee considers that changes to the Commentaries should be relevant in interpreting and applying conventions concluded before the adoption of these changes, it disagrees with any form of *a contrario* interpretation that would necessarily infer from a change to an Article of the Model Convention or to the Commentaries that the previous wording resulted in consequences different from those of the modified wording. Many amendments are intended to simply clarify, not change, the meaning of the Articles or the Commentaries, and such *a contrario* interpretations would clearly be wrong in those cases.
>
> Tax authorities in Member countries follow the general principles enunciated in the preceding four paragraphs. Accordingly, the Committee on Fiscal Affairs considers that taxpayers may also find it useful to consult later versions of the Commentaries in interpreting earlier treaties.[35]

This guidance in the Commentary is limited to amendments to the Commentary that reflect an existing and established consensus opinion. The 2008 Commentary – being a new and negotiated interpretation of former Article 7 – should be restricted to tax treaties concluded after July 2008 because prior to July 2008 the OECD accepted that there was no consensus interpretation of former Article 7 in OECD countries. Even if the 2008 Commentary were to be considered by a court interpreting former Article 7 in a treaty concluded before July 2008, it is expected that it would be given very little, if any, weight.

The split implementation process used by the OECD has created uncertainty as to which parts of the 2008 Report were implemented in the 2008 Commentary. The OECD rejected the comments (from the business sector on the exposure draft of the 2008 Commentary) that the

---

[35] 2008 OECD Model, pp. 16–17, paras. 35–36.1; 2010 OECD Model, pp. 15–16, paras. 35–36.1.

3 THE MEANING OF FORMER ARTICLE 7   193

2008 Report should be implemented in one step to prevent this uncertainty. Further, the commentators pointed out that it was uncertain which measures from the 2008 Report were being implemented in the draft 2008 Commentary, but the Commentary was not amended to remedy these concerns.[36]

3.3   New Article 7 and Commentary

The Committee concluded that the former version of Article 7 needed to be amended to incorporate the consensus established in the 2008 Report. This is consistent with the OECD's statement first made in 2001 that its reform process should not be restricted by either original intent or historical practice. Its aim is to establish a method for attributing profits to permanent establishments under the business profits Article in the context of the contemporary operations of international enterprises.[37]

> From the Committee's perspective, the best way to provide tax administrations and taxpayers with maximum certainty as to how profits should be attributed to permanent establishments is to redraft Article 7 in a way that will remove the potential for different interpretations based on these practices and the Commentary. The conclusions reflected in this Report will therefore be reflected in a new version of Article 7, and a new Commentary on that Article, to be used in the negotiation of future treaties and of amendments to existing treaties.[38]

In summary, we have two Commentaries on former Article 7, the pre-2008 Commentary and the 2008 Commentary, which may be used for interpreting Article 7 of tax treaties based on the OECD Model Convention. But there may be confusion and uncertainty on which version of the Commentary should be used in interpreting the business profits Article of tax treaties negotiated prior to 17 July 2008, the day on which the OECD adopted the 2008 Model.[39] Moreover, there is the potential for double taxation to arise should two treaty countries use different

---

[36] See BIAC (Business Industry Advisory Committee to the OECD), *Comments on OECD Revised Commentary on Article 7 of the OECD Model Tax Convention* (2007), pp. 5–6; BIAC, *Comments on the OECD Public Discussion Draft: Draft Comments of the 2008 Update to the OECD Model Convention* (31 May 2008), p. 6.

[37] OECD, *Discussion Draft on the Attribution of Profits to Permanent Establishments*, p. 7, para. 6 and restated at 2008 Report, p. 7, para. 3.

[38] 2008 Report, p. 8, para. 8.

[39] BIAC, *Comments on the OECD Revised Commentary on Article 7 of the OECD Model Tax Convention* (2007), pp. 3–4.

versions of the Commentary to interpret Article 7 of a tax treaty. This is a potential problem the OECD created through the two-step implementation of the 2008 Report.

3.4 Pre-2008 Commentary: applying separate and single entity methods

The concurrent use of the separate entity method and single entity method in allocating profits and expenses to permanent establishments in the pre-2008 Commentary led to divergent interpretations of former Article 7 in OECD countries. There was controversy about the scope of the separate entity fiction in former Article 7(2) in the pre-2008 Commentary. The arm's length principle allocates profits to a permanent establishment by treating it as a separate legal entity transacting at arm's length with the rest of the enterprise – the separate entity method.[40] Under the separate entity method intra-entity transfers are treated as arm's length transactions, by attributing to the transferring part of an enterprise the profit it would have made if it were transacting with an independent enterprise. For the purposes of profit attribution under former Article 7(2) a permanent establishment should be treated in the same way as a subsidiary.[41] But a permanent establishment is one part of a whole enterprise with a unitary profit motive and common control.[42] For highly integrated international enterprises, such as banks, the use of the separate entity fiction creates challenges from both normative and practical perspectives.

Transfers of assets and funds to and from a permanent establishment are not transactions to which the arm's length principle may be applied as they are merely intra-entity transfers. Moreover, problems with the application of former Article 7 occur in industries that are dominated by integrated international enterprises because comparative prices will

---

[40] The separate entity approach for the taxation of permanent establishments was accepted by the League of Nations Fiscal Committee in 1933: Fiscal Committee, *Report to the Council on the Fourth Session of the Committee* (1933), p. 2, para. 2. The Fiscal Committee accepted the views of Mitchell B. Carroll, who conducted a study on its behalf of allocation methods used in twenty-seven countries. The report states: 'for tax purposes, permanent establishments must be treated in the same manner as independent enterprises operating under the same or similar conditions, with the corollary that the taxable income of such establishments is to be assessed on the basis of their separate accounts.'

[41] Vogel, *Klaus Vogel on Double Tax Conventions* (3rd edn, 1997), p. 428, para. 64. Vogel uses the term absolute (hypothetical) independence.

[42] See Li, 'Global Profit Split' (2002), pp. 832–4.

rarely be available.[43] Some commentators have argued that the arm's length principle is an inappropriate method of allocating profits and expenses to branches of unitary international businesses because the principle conflicts with the very reason that international enterprises come into existence.[44]

There is significant controversy over the extent to which a permanent establishment should be treated as a separate entity.[45] While former Article 7 treats a permanent establishment as a separate and independent enterprise for most purposes, in certain situations it treats a permanent establishment as part of the one enterprise – the single entity method.[46] The single entity method does not treat a permanent establishment as a subdivision of an international enterprise for certain purposes.[47] The reason for using the single entity approach is that it reflects the business reality that a permanent establishment is part of a unitary business enterprise, and this fact cannot be completely ignored when allocating profits within the enterprise.[48] Under the single entity approach, in determining the expenses to be attributed to a permanent establishment, other parts of the enterprise are not allowed to make a profit on notional intra-entity transactions with the permanent establishment, thereby preventing tax avoidance. The single entity method attributes expenses to a permanent establishment at their historical cost, which means they must be traced back to transactions between the international enterprise and separate enterprises.

The use of both the separate entity and single entity approaches in the pre-2008 Commentary complicated the interpretation of former Article 7 and created uncertainty. This issue was studied by the International Fiscal Association at its 1986 Congress, which concluded that applying former Article 7 was troublesome.[49] The OECD acknowledged the following concerns prior to its 1994 revision of the Commentary:

---

[43] In 1981 the US General Accounting Office concluded that one of the difficulties with the arm's length method was finding comparable transactions: US General Accounting Office, *IRS Could Better Protect US Tax Interests in Determining the Income of Multi-national Corporations* (1981), pp. i, v, 3; Hamaekers, 'Arm's Length – How Long?' in Kirchhof, et al. (eds.), *International and Comparative Taxation* (2002) 29–52, p. 51.

[44] See Ch. 3 for a discussion of the theory of the firm.

[45] Vogel, *Klaus Vogel on Double Tax Conventions* (3rd edn, 1997), p. 428, para. 63.

[46] Professor Vogel used the term restricted independence for this approach: *ibid.*, p. 428, para. 64.

[47] *Ibid.*   [48] *Ibid.*

[49] OECD, *Model Tax Convention: Attribution of Income to Permanent Establishments* (1994), para. 1.

> Nevertheless, the fact remains that this duality of approach leads to uncertainty which may in itself lead to results incompatible with the underlying principles of double taxation agreements (the avoidance of economic double taxation and a fair allocation of taxation rights between countries) where the outward transfer country taxes a given transfer of goods or services on the basis of a price which includes a profit while the inward transferring country takes into account only the residual accounting value or historic cost price (similar problems may arise where the situation is reversed).
>
> The problem is more acute where the country of residence of the enterprise gives relief for the tax levied by the host country of the permanent establishment by exempting those profits from tax. In this situation, the computation of the exempted profits and the computation of the profits as taxed by the host country may be inconsistent, which may lead to either economic double taxation or to under taxation.[50]

But the 1994 revision of the Commentary did not resolve the problems arising from the use of the separate entity and single entity approaches in former Article 7.

In summary, former Article 7 is based on the arm's length principle in treating a permanent establishment as a separate entity. But there is controversy over the extent to which a permanent establishment may be treated as a separate entity for the purposes of allocating income and expenses to it. This controversy reflects the theoretical flaw in the arm's length principle of seeking to separate one part from an inseparable whole. The concurrent and inconsistent use of the separate entity and single entity approaches leads to deficiencies in former Articles 7(1), (2) and (3).

3.5 Interpretation of former Article 7(1): determining the profits of an enterprise under the pre-2008 Commentary

The pre-2008 Commentary on former Article 7(1) deals with two tax treaty principles. The first principle is that an enterprise of one country will not be taxed in another country unless it carries on business in the other country (host country) through a permanent establishment.[51] Conversely, if an enterprise of a residence country derives business profits from a host country, but does not have a permanent establishment in that country, the residence country has exclusive rights to tax the business profits. If an enterprise does not have a permanent establishment the pre-2008 Commentary claims that the enterprise 'should not properly

---

[50] Ibid., para. 2.   [51] 2008 OECD Model, p. 119, para. 9.

3 THE MEANING OF FORMER ARTICLE 7

be regarded as participating in the economic life of that other State to such an extent that it comes within the jurisdiction of that other State's taxing rights'.[52] In this situation, the profits derived by the international enterprise may have a source in the host country, but under the tax treaty the host country gives up its taxing right, allowing the residence country to have an exclusive taxing right over the business profits of the enterprise. On the other hand, if a non-resident enterprise has a permanent establishment in a host country, it passes the economic participation threshold and is subject to tax in the host country. Thus, the permanent establishment threshold is used to determine whether the residence country or host country has the right to tax business profits derived by an international enterprise from the host country.

The second principle is that a host country in which a permanent establishment is located is only entitled to tax profits that are attributable to the permanent establishment. The pre-2008 Commentary rejects[53] the force of attraction principle.[54] The rejection is defended on the grounds of simplicity and reducing both tax compliance and administration costs. It was also claimed that the principle reflects the way in which business is carried on. But modern business is highly complex, and integrated international enterprises do not treat their permanent establishments as notional separate enterprises.

The pre-2008 Commentary includes an example to illustrate that only profits attributable to a permanent establishment may be taxed by the host country under former Article 7. For example, if an enterprise carries on a manufacturing business in a host country in which it also sells goods through independent agents, the pre-2008 Commentary claims that the enterprise may have valid business reasons for operating in this manner. In this situation, the host country can only attribute manufacturing

---

[52] *Ibid.*

[53] 2008 OECD Model, pp. 119–20, para. 10; 2005 OECD Model, pp. 115–16, paras. 5–10.

[54] Under the force of attraction principle, once an international enterprise has a permanent establishment in a country, that country has the right to tax certain profits the enterprise makes from that country, irrespective of whether the transactions were conducted through the permanent establishment. There are two versions of the force of attraction principle. Under the restricted force of attraction principle, if an international enterprise has a permanent establishment in a country, profits from direct transactions made by the head office of the enterprise in that country will be attributed to the permanent establishment, to the extent that the transactions are similar to those made by the permanent establishment. Under the unrestricted force of attraction principle, if an international enterprise has a permanent establishment in a country, all the profits made by an enterprise from that country will be attributed to its permanent establishment: Burgers (ed.) *The Taxation of Permanent Establishments* (1994) (loose-leaf), p. 13.

profits to the permanent establishment. The business profits the enterprise derives through its independent agents, which fail the permanent establishment threshold in Article 5, are not attributable to the permanent establishment and should only be subject to tax in the residence country. The OECD contends that if the host country attributed this income to the permanent establishment it would be contrary to the second principle of former Article 7(1) that a host country may only tax profits which are attributable to the permanent establishment, and it claims that the host country would be interfering with ordinary business operations.

An important issue in the interpretation of former Article 7 is the meaning of the term 'profits of an enterprise'. The OECD acknowledged that the pre-2008 Commentary on former Article 7 'provides little in the way of guidance on how to interpret the term "profits of an enterprise", beyond confirming that, "the right to tax does not extend to profits that the enterprise may derive from that State otherwise than through the permanent establishment"'.[55] This directive prevents host countries from using the force of attraction principle in calculating the profits of a permanent establishment: 'However, the question arises as to whether the term "profits of an enterprise" is a further limitation on the taxing rights of the host country.'[56]

The lack of guidance in the pre-2008 Commentary on the meaning of the term 'profits of an enterprise' resulted in OECD countries developing inconsistent and conflicting interpretations. Two primary means of interpreting the term 'profits of an enterprise' were developed in OECD countries: the 'relevant business activity' approach; and the 'functional separate entity' approach. A comparative study of these two interpretations illustrates their differences and the potential they create for double taxation or under-taxation. These two approaches reflect the use of either the separate entity method or the single entity method. The relevant business activity approach is based on the single entity method, while the functional separate entity approach is, as the name suggests, premised on the separate entity method.

3.5.1   The 'relevant business activity' approach

Under the 'relevant business activity' approach the term 'profits of an enterprise' is interpreted as referring only to the profits of a business activity in which the permanent establishment participated.[57] Under this approach, former Article 7(1) restricts the profits that may be attributed

---

[55]   2008 Report, p. 23, para. 60.   [56]   *Ibid.*   [57]   2008 Report, p. 23, para. 61.

to a permanent establishment under former Article 7(2): 'the attributed profits could not exceed the profits that the whole enterprise earns from the relevant business activity'.[58] The term 'relevant business activity' is not used in either former Article 7 or the pre-2008 Commentary; the OECD asserts that it 'emerges from country practices on interpreting what is meant by the phrase 'profits of the enterprise' in Article 7(1).[59] This method may also be called the single enterprise approach.[60] The profits of the entire enterprise are those which it makes from transactions with independent parties and transactions with related enterprises. Consequently, the profits made from related party transactions may have to be adjusted under the transfer pricing rules if they do not conform with the arm's length principle.

According to the relevant business activity approach, the 'profits of an enterprise' are the sum of profits and losses made from its business activities, and the profits of an enterprise attributable to a permanent establishment under former Article 7(1) are the profits made from the 'relevant business activity' carried on by the permanent establishment.[61] The profits attributed to a permanent establishment under this method are affected by all parts of the enterprise which engage in the particular business activity. If another part of the enterprise carries on a particular business activity and incurs a loss, the loss will reduce the profits available for attribution to a permanent establishment because the loss reduces the enterprise's overall profit from the 'relevant business activity'.[62]

The 'relevant business activity' approach has been inconsistently applied by the OECD countries, creating further complexity and increasing the potential for double taxation or under-taxation.[63] The definition of 'relevant business activity' affects the profits available to be attributed to a permanent establishment. The more broadly that relevant business activity is defined, the greater the influence of other parts of an enterprise on the profits to be attributed to a particular permanent establishment. If 'relevant business activity' is widely defined, the notional independence of a permanent establishment is restricted, reflecting the single entity approach. This approach reflects business reality because a permanent establishment operates as an integrated part of a business with a common profit motive. For example, assume that an international

---

[58] *Ibid.*, p. 23, para. 62.   [59] *Ibid.*, p. 23, para. 61.
[60] Baker and Collier, 'General Report' in *Cahiers de droit fiscal international* (2006), p. 30.
[61] 2008 Report, p. 23, para. 63.   [62] *Ibid.*   [63] 2008 Report, pp. 23–4. para. 64.

enterprise creates and sells computer software, and it incurs an overall loss in the sale of a particular type of software because of the costs incurred to fix flaws in the software. Assume further that the enterprise uses its permanent establishments to distribute the software to customers. If the relevant business activity of the enterprise is broadly defined as all the business activities for the software product line (the development and sale of software), profits cannot be attributed to the permanent establishments. But if the permanent establishments were separate entities, profits would be attributed to them for their distribution activities irrespective of the enterprise's loss on the sale of the software. In reality, a permanent establishment is part of an international enterprise with a common profit motive.

On the other hand, if the 'relevant business activity' of an enterprise is defined narrowly, by reference to function instead of product line, there is less scope for other parts of the enterprise to participate in that function.[64] The narrow definition restricts the instances in which the profit limitation applies to a permanent establishment. Under the narrow definition, it would be possible to attribute profits to a permanent establishment even if an enterprise incurs an overall loss from a particular business activity. The narrow definition of relevant business activity is more sympathetic with the separate entity method because a separate enterprise would only perform activities for a fee. But this approach conflicts with the business reality that a permanent establishment is an integrated part of an international enterprise.

Defining 'relevant business activity' becomes more complex if a permanent establishment and the other parts of the enterprise are engaged in similar activities.[65] If an enterprise has two permanent establishments which perform distribution functions, this raises the issue of whether each country should consider only the distribution function in that country and ignore the distribution function carried on by the other permanent establishment in the other country.[66] In the usual case, an enterprise's permanent establishments will perform the same functions. For example, an international bank in its residence country may operate as both a retail bank and a wholesale bank, but its branches around the world may only operate in wholesale banking. Host countries are reluctant to limit the profit attributed to a permanent establishment on the basis of activities carried on in another country by a different part of the enterprise.[67] In addition, it may be

---

[64] 2008 Report, p. 24, para. 65.   [65] *Ibid.*   [66] *Ibid.*   [67] *Ibid.*

3 THE MEANING OF FORMER ARTICLE 7   201

difficult for the host country of a permanent establishment to verify the activities of other permanent establishments of the same enterprise.

The use of the relevant business activity approach is controversial. Some commentators have argued that the terms of former Article 7(1) do not support the definitions of relevant business activity used by the OECD countries.[68] They argue that in the expression '[t]he profits of an enterprise of a Contracting State' in Article 7(1), the term 'enterprise of a Contracting State' as defined in Article 3(1)(d) means an enterprise carried on by a resident of a contracting state.[69] Further, under Article 3(1)(c), the term 'enterprise' applies to the carrying on of any business. Under this construction, the term enterprise in former Article 7(1) refers to business activity and not to the entity carrying on the business.[70] The alternative argument is that the term 'enterprise' used in the two sentences of former Article 7(1) refers to the entity rather than the business activity.[71] Thus, the meaning of 'enterprise' in former Article 7(1) is ambiguous and confusing.

On the issue of the time period over which the 'relevant business activity' is determined, several methods were used by the OECD countries, which increased the potential for inconsistent interpretations of former Article 7.[72] Some OECD countries evaluate the 'relevant business activity' over a period exceeding an income year. If a 'relevant business activity' of an international enterprise resulted in a loss for an income year but was profitable over a number of years, some OECD countries attribute a profit to a permanent establishment for the loss year. Another variation is that a host country bases its taxing rights on a rebuttable presumption that the 'relevant business activity' would make adequate profits over several years. Under this approach, a host country may determine that there are profits of an enterprise to attribute to a permanent establishment, although the profits were realized at different times by different parts of the enterprise.[73]

Several other variations of the relevant business activity approach were used by the OECD countries. Some OECD countries apply the method to gross profits attributable to permanent establishments, while other countries apply the limitation separately to income and expenses.[74] But these two methods were unlikely to result in the profit of a permanent establishment being limited as they do not consider expenses incurred by other parts of an international enterprise.[75]

---

[68] Arnold and Darmo, 'Summary of Proceedings of an Invitational Seminar on the Attribution of Profits to Permanent Establishments' (2001), p. 538.
[69] *Ibid.*   [70] *Ibid.*, pp. 538–9.   [71] *Ibid.*   [72] 2008 Report, p. 24, para. 67.
[73] *Ibid.*   [74] *Ibid.*, p. 24, para. 68.   [75] *Ibid.*

202   DEFINING PERSONALITY OF PERMANENT ESTABLISHMENTS

In summary, certain OECD countries used the relevant business activity approach to define 'profits of an enterprise' in former Article 7(1). There are several problems with this. First, the meaning of 'relevant business activity' was uncertain and debatable. Second, the relevant business activity approach is inconsistently applied by the countries using this method. Third, there are differences within the countries using this approach on the time period to be applied; some countries apply the relevant business activity method on the basis of an income year, while other countries treat the income period as being longer than one year. Thus, within the group of countries using the relevant business activity method there was no consensus on the definition of the term, the application of the method or the time period over which it is to be applied. The inconsistent application of this method is likely to result in either double taxation or under-taxation. But the potential for inconsistent attributions of profits increased significantly if, in relation to a treaty between two OECD countries, one country used the relevant business activity approach and the other used the functional separate entity approach.

3.5.2   The 'functional separate entity' approach

The second method used by the OECD countries to interpret the term 'profits of an enterprise' is the 'functional separate entity' approach. This method does not restrict the profits attributed to a permanent establishment on the basis of profits made by the entire enterprise or of a particular business activity carried on by the permanent establishment.[76] This approach relies on the separate entity method:

> Under this approach, paragraph 1 of Article 7 is interpreted as not affecting the determination of the quantum of the profits that are to be attributed to the permanent establishment, other than providing specific confirmation that, 'the right to tax [of the host country] does not extend to profits that the enterprise may derive from that State otherwise than through the permanent establishment', i.e. there is no 'force of attraction' resulting from the existence of a permanent establishment (see paragraph 13 above). The profits to be attributed to the permanent establishment are the profits that the permanent establishment would have earned at arm's length as if it were a 'distinct and separate' enterprise performing the same or similar functions under the same or similar conditions, determined by applying the arm's length principle under Article 7(2).[77]

---

[76] 2008 Report, p. 15, para. 69.   [77] *Ibid.*

3 THE MEANING OF FORMER ARTICLE 7

Furthermore, the OECD claims that the separate entity method reflects the terms of former Article 7(2) as it states that the profits attributed to a permanent establishment are those that 'it might be expected to make if it were a distinct and separate enterprise . . . dealing wholly independently with the enterprise of which it is part'.[78]

For both approaches, an important issue in interpreting the term 'profits of an enterprise' is whether profits can be attributed to a permanent establishment by a host country.[79] Paragraph 15 of the pre-2008 Commentary on former Article 7 provides: 'Many States consider that there is a realisation of a taxable profit when an asset, whether or not trading stock, forming part of the business property of a permanent establishment situated within their territory is transferred to a permanent establishment or the head office of the same enterprise situated in another State.'[80] Under the functional separate entity approach, profits are attributed to a permanent establishment regardless of whether the enterprise as a whole is making a profit from the notional transaction. If a permanent establishment performs an activity for an enterprise it must be remunerated for the activity as if it were an independent entity. An independent entity would not perform services for another enterprise without reward. The functional separate entity method requires that if a permanent establishment perform functions it must be remunerated for the functions performed, even though the international enterprise as a whole has not made a profit from the particular business activity. In contrast, the 'relevant business activity' method would attribute profits to a permanent establishment only when the enterprise as a whole has realized profits from the relevant business activity.

A key difference between the 'relevant business activity' and 'functional separate entity' approaches is the method used to compute the profits attributed to a permanent establishment.[81] The functional separate entity approach uses as its starting point the notional intra-entity transactions of a permanent establishment, but the relevant business activity approach uses as its base the dealings of the whole enterprise in connection with the particular business activity. It is indisputable that there is a significant risk of double taxation or under-taxation if the host

---

[78] *Ibid.*   [79] 2008 Report, p. 25, para. 70.

[80] 2005 OECD Model, p. 119, para. 15, quoted in the 2008 Report, p. 25, para. 70. Para. 15 was amended and it is now para. 21, p. 124, of the 2008 OECD Model; 2010 OECD Model, pp. 160–1, para. 21.

[81] 2008 Report, p. 25, para. 71.

204 DEFINING PERSONALITY OF PERMANENT ESTABLISHMENTS

and residence countries use different methods for determining the profits attributable to permanent establishments. Although the OECD contends that if under the 'relevant business activity approach' the 'profits of the enterprise' attributable 'are at least equal to the quantum of profits computed under the "functional separate entity" approach, there should, in theory, be no difference to the profits attributed to the permanent establishment under either approach'.[82] This contention is premised on the claim that under former Article 7(2) the arm's length principle should be applied, in theory, in the same way under these two competing approaches. However, in practice, if a host country and residence country use different methods for interpreting the phrase 'profits of an enterprise' there is a high probability of double taxation or under-taxation.[83]

3.5.3 Other deficiencies in the interpretation of former Article 7(1)

The term 'profits' is not defined in the OECD Model or the pre-2008 Commentary for the purposes of former Article 7.[84] The Commentary notes that while 'profits' has not been defined, it should be interpreted as having a broad meaning that includes 'all income derived in carrying on an enterprise'[35] because this interpretation reflects the use of the term in the domestic tax laws of most OECD countries. But there is the potential for a host country and residence country to apply a different definition of profit. To eliminate double taxation under Article 23 of the OECD Model, a residence country must determine the profits of an enterprise under its domestic law.[86] The result may be that the profits determined under the domestic law of the host and residence countries differ. Clearly, profit is another treaty term on which a consensus interpretation has not developed. In its discussion on the use of domestic law to interpret the meaning of 'profits', the OECD did not refer to the general restriction in Article 3(2) of the OECD Model that domestic law of a treaty country cannot be used to define terms that are undefined if the context requires otherwise.

[82] *Ibid.*   [83] *Ibid.*

[84] Other terms not defined in Article 7 are 'business' and 'enterprise'. Under Article 3(2) of the 2008 OECD Model, terms which are not defined have their meaning determined under the domestic laws of the contracting state. The exception is where the context in which a term is used in a treaty requires the application of a different meaning.

[85] 2005 OECD Model, p. 129, para. 32.

[86] 2004 Discussion Draft, p. 16, para. 46; 2001 Discussion Draft, p. 13, para. 37. This para. was not included in the 2008 Report.

3 THE MEANING OF FORMER ARTICLE 7 205

3.6 2008 Report: former Article 7(1), the functional separate entity approach

The 2008 Report acknowledged that the OECD countries were using both the relevant business activity approach and functional separate entity approach.[87] The significance of this practice is critical because the most important requirement of a tax treaty provision is that it is applied consistently and symmetrically by the contracting countries. Consistent and symmetrical interpretation of former Article 7(1) minimizes the risk of tax distortions. The 2008 Report noted that the lack of a consensus interpretation of former Article 7(1) is unsatisfactory, as it is likely to result in either double taxation or under-taxation.[88] Since 2001 the OECD has sought to establish the functional separate entity approach as the consensus interpretation by the OECD countries.[89]

In the 2008 Report the OECD adopted the functional separate entity approach as the consensus method for interpreting former Article 7(1):

> After considering the expected merits of both approaches, the OECD member countries have decided, on balance, to adopt the 'functionally separate entity' approach as the authorised OECD approach or the preferred interpretation of paragraph 1 of Article 7. In addition, there was wide support for the 'functionally separate entity' approach from the public comments and the consultation.
>
> Accordingly, the authorised OECD approach is that the profits to be attributed to a PE are the profits that the PE would have earned at arm's length if it were a legally distinct and separate enterprise performing the same or similar functions under the same or similar conditions, determined by applying the arm's length principle under Article 7(2). The phrase 'profits of an enterprise' in Article 7(1) should not be interpreted as affecting the determination of the quantum of the profits that are to be attributed to the PE, other than providing specific confirmation that 'the right to tax does not extend to profits that the enterprise may derive from that State otherwise than through the permanent establishment' (*i.e.* there should be no 'force of attraction principle').[90]

The 2008 Report asserted that the functional separate entity approach has several advantages over the relevant business activity approach. The functional separate entity approach does not limit the profits attributable to a permanent establishment using the arm's length principle in

---

[87] 2008 Report, p. 26, para. 72.   [88] *Ibid.*

[89] 2008 Report, pp. 23–7, paras. 59–79; 2004 Discussion Draft, pp. 11–12, paras. 22–9; 2001 Discussion Draft, pp. 11–12, paras. 25–31.

[90] 2008 Report, p. 27, paras. 78–9.

206 DEFINING PERSONALITY OF PERMANENT ESTABLISHMENTS

former Article 7(2).[91] It was also claimed that the functional separate entity approach is easier to administer as it is unnecessary for host countries to determine an enterprise's worldwide profits arising from a relevant business activity, unless a profit split method is used.[92] In addition, the functional separate entity approach does not require host countries to review annual assessments for a permanent establishment, after the prescribed review period has ended, to determine the relative performance of a relevant business activity of an international enterprise.[93] Moreover, it is claimed that the functional separate entity method reflects the analysis that would be done if a permanent establishment were a distinct and separate enterprise.[94] Finally, it was claimed that the functional separate entity approach results in a profit attribution to a permanent establishment for a business activity that is neutral.

The 2008 Report indicates that the OECD gained support for the functional separate entity method with most of the OECD countries previously using the relevant business activity approach. Although these countries asserted that they consider the relevant business activity approach is supported by the terms of former Article 7(1), they agreed to change to the functional separate entity approach if it were adopted in the Commentary.[95] These countries indicated that the advantage of switching is that the functional separate entity approach is consistent with the terms of both former Article 7(2) and the associated enterprises Article (Article 9). Consequently, it appears that most of the countries that use the relevant business activity approach are willing to change to the functional separate entity approach. Nevertheless, some countries may continue to use the relevant business activity approach.

Another issue is the timing when these countries change to the functional separate entity method, as distortions will be minimized if the timing of the change is on a consistent basis. The change may be implemented immediately if OECD countries either amend their domestic law to implement the functional separate entity approach or apply the 2008 Commentary to tax treaties negotiated before July 2008. But the better approach for these countries is to adopt the functional separate entity approach only when they implement new tax treaties reflecting the 2008 Commentary. When the Commentary is

---

[91] *Ibid.*, para. 74. [92] *Ibid.*, para. 75. [93] *Ibid.* [94] *Ibid.* pp. 26–7, para. 75.
[95] *Ibid.*, p. 26, para. 73.

3 THE MEANING OF FORMER ARTICLE 7 207

used to implement a major change, such as expressly adopting the functional separate entity method, it should only be implemented on a prospective basis by countries that formerly used the relevant business activity approach.

3.7 2008 Commentary on former Article 7(1)

The 2008 Commentary reflects the functional separate enterprise approach – the authorized OECD approach – but it makes no reference to the term functional separate entity. The main difference between the relevant business activity approach and the functional separate entity approach is that profits may be attributed to a permanent establishment under the functional separate entity approach even though the international enterprise itself has made a loss. The 2008 Commentary expressly supports this feature of the functional separate entity approach:[96] '[T]he directive of paragraph 2 may result in profits being attributed to a permanent establishment even though the enterprise as a whole has never made profits; conversely, that directive may result in no profits being attributed to a permanent establishment even though the enterprise as a whole has made profits.'[97] This interpretation of former Article 7(1) gives a host country the right to tax the profits of an enterprise resident in a treaty country if they are attributable to a permanent establishment located in the host country, and the 2008 Commentary claims that former Article 7(2) determines the meaning of the phrase 'profits attributable to a permanent establishment'. Consequently, profits may be attributed to a permanent establishment, irrespective of whether the enterprise itself has derived profits from the business activities carried on by a permanent establishment.

The Commentary states that this interpretation of former Article 7(1) is justified as the provision must be interpreted in the context of former Article 7(2), which deals with the profits which can be attributed to a permanent establishment. But former Article 7(1) is not expressly subject to former Article 7(2), whereas former Article 7(2) is expressly subject to former Article 7(3). The drafters of the provision chose not to make former Article 7(1) expressly subject to former Article 7(2), which may diminish the claim that former Article 7(1) must be subordinated to former Article 7(2) to support the functional separate entity interpretation.

---

[96] 2008 OECD Model, p. 120, paras. 11–12; 2010 OECD Model, p. 158, paras. 11–12.
[97] 2008 OECD Model, p. 120, para. 11: 2010 OECD Model, p. 158, para. 11.

208 DEFINING PERSONALITY OF PERMANENT ESTABLISHMENTS

The Commentary was amended to state that the force of attraction approach has been rejected by the OECD and that it is now a generally accepted principle in tax treaties.[98] This amendment is not a policy change, but rather a redrafting of the rejection of the force of attraction concept in the pre-2008 Commentary. The OECD has gone to considerable lengths to reject the force of attraction principle. Under the force of attraction principle, a host country in which a permanent establishment is located subjects to full taxation all income derived in the host country by the enterprise, despite the income not being derived by the permanent establishment. The 2008 Commentary prescribes that a host country should only attribute profits to a permanent establishment that were derived by it. Other income derived by an international enterprise in the host country, such as other business income, interest, royalties and dividends, that are not attributable to the permanent establishment, should be taxed under other Articles of a tax treaty.

The Commentary was amended to deal with the issue of double taxation. The 2008 Commentary states that a residence country of an international enterprise carrying on business in a host country through a permanent establishment will want former Article 7(2) to be properly applied by the host country to prevent double taxation.[99] As the directive in this provision has mutual application, the residence country is obliged under Article 25 (mutual agreement Article) to provide for relief of double taxation of profits which are properly attributed to the permanent establishment. If a host country seeks to attribute profits to a permanent establishment solely on the basis of force of attraction, double taxation will occur. If the profits are business profits or royalties which are not connected with the permanent establishment in the host country, the residence country has an exclusive taxing right under former Article 7(2). If the profits are dividends or interest that are not attributable to the permanent establishment, the host country and residence country will have shared taxing rights.

4 Former Article 7(2): pre-2008 Commentary and the separate entity approach

Former Article 7(2) contains the main directive on attributing profits to a permanent establishment.[100] This provision applies the arm's length

---

[98] 2008 OECD Model, pp. 119–20, para. 10; 2010 OECD Model, pp. 157–8, para. 10.

[99] 2008 OECD Model, p. 121, para. 12; 2010 OECD Model, p. 158, para. 12.

[100] 2008 OECD Model, p. 121, para. 14; 2010 OECD Model, pp. 158–9, para. 14; 2005 OECD Model, p. 117, para. 11.

4 FORMER ARTICLE 7(2)

principle to determine the profits attributable to a permanent establishment. It states that the profits to be attributed to a permanent establishment are those which it would have made if it were dealing with an entirely separate entity under conditions and prices prevailing in the ordinary market. The pre-2008 Commentary states that under former Article 7(2), the trading accounts of a permanent establishment will be used by a tax authority in determining the profits attributable to the permanent establishment.[101] The justification for relying on a permanent establishment's accounts is the presumption that a properly managed business will want to assess the profit being made through the permanent establishment. The accounts of a permanent establishment are treated as the starting point for any process of adjustment:

> It should perhaps be emphasized that the directive contained in paragraph 2 is no justification for tax administrations to construct hypothetical profit figures in vacuo; it is always necessary to start with the real facts of the situation as they appear from the business records of the permanent establishment and to adjust as may be shown to be necessary the profit figures which those facts produce.[102]

But the 2008 Commentary was amended to add that a permanent establishment's 'records and documentation must satisfy certain requirements in order to be considered to reflect the real facts of the situation'.[103]

This conclusion in the 2008 Commentary and pre-2008 Commentary raises the issue of how much reliance may be placed on a permanent establishment's accounts when they record notional intra-entity transactions.[104] The notional transactions may be between the head office of an enterprise and a permanent establishment. Alternatively, the notional transactions may be between two permanent establishments of an enterprise. Such transactions are only notional transactions that are not legally binding agreements because an enterprise cannot enter into a transaction with itself. The notional transactions are merely transfers of assets and funds within an enterprise.

Article 7(2) is ambiguous and difficult to apply:[105] the rules are not clear on the manner in which assets and liabilities are to be allocated to a

---

[101] 2008 OECD Model, p. 121, para. 16; 2010 OECD Model, p. 159, para. 16; 2005 OECD Model, p. 117, para. 12.

[102] *Ibid.*   [103] *Ibid.*

[104] 2008 OECD Model, pp. 123–4, para. 19; 2010 OECD Model, p. 160, para. 19; 2005 OECD Model, pp. 117–18, para. 12.1.

[105] Burgers (ed.) *The Taxation of Permanent Establishments* (1994), pp. 16–17.

210 DEFINING PERSONALITY OF PERMANENT ESTABLISHMENTS

permanent establishment, and there is uncertainty on the circumstances in which a deduction for interest on intra-entity loans is allowed.[106] The pre-2008 Commentary provides the following guidance on the situations in which an enterprise's accounts may be relied upon by a tax authority:

> [T]o the extent that the trading accounts of the head office and the permanent establishments are both prepared symmetrically on the basis of such agreements and that those agreements reflect the functions performed by the different parts of the enterprise, these trading accounts could be accepted by tax authorities. In that respect, accounts could not be regarded as prepared symmetrically unless the values of transactions or the methods of attributing profits or expenses in the books of the permanent establishment corresponded exactly to the values or methods of attribution in the books of the head office in terms of the national currency or functional currency in which the enterprise recorded its transactions. However, where trading accounts are based on internal agreements that reflect purely artificial arrangements instead of the real economic functions of the different parts of the enterprise, these agreements should simply be ignored and the accounts corrected accordingly.[107]

According to paragraph 14 of the pre-2008 Commentary, the profits attributed to a permanent establishment should be based on the accounts of that permanent establishment to the extent the accounts represent the real facts of the situation.[108] But the pre-2008 Commentary does not provide guidance on how to identify the real facts, resulting in uncertainty for both taxpayers and tax authorities over what the real facts are. It is difficult for a tax authority to know when it needs to scrutinize a permanent establishment's accounts to assess whether they represent the real facts. There is a corresponding difficulty for taxpayers in knowing that they have relied on the real facts in their accounts and returns. The pre-2008 Commentary states that even if a permanent establishment provides detailed accounts on the profits arising from its activities, a tax authority may still need to amend the accounts in accordance with the arm's length principle.[109] This action would be necessary to prevent an international enterprise from shifting profits from a permanent establishment to another part of the enterprise.

The separate entity method was applied in the following two US cases. In *North West Life Assurance Company of Canada* v. *Commissioner of*

---

[106] *Ibid.*   [107] 2005 OECD Model, pp. 117–18, para. 12.1.
[108] 2005 OECD Model, pp. 118–19, para. 14.   [109] 2005 OECD Model, p. 118, para. 13.

4 FORMER ARTICLE 7(2)

Internal Revenue,[110] one issue was the extent to which a US branch of a Canadian corporation should be treated as a separate entity. The taxpayer contended that Article VII (business profits Article) of the US–Canada tax treaty required a separate entity approach to be applied to its US branch. The taxpayer argued that Article VII conflicted with US domestic legislation and that it prevailed over US legislation to the extent of the inconsistency. The US Tax Court held that Article VII required a separate entity interpretation, and it pointed out the difficulty in interpreting Article VII:

> In sum, we are confronted with a situation in which the language of article VII, paragraph (2) is at best murky, and the interpretations of both parties have advantages and disadvantages. We are impressed that the Canadian Convention may give an economic advantage to Canadian insurance companies operating through a permanent establishment in the United States. Nevertheless, our view is that the petitioner's interpretation of article VII, paragraph (2) best carries out the intent of the United States and Canada as set forth in the Canadian Convention and satisfies the purpose of Article VII of the Canadian Convention – to attribute income to a permanent establishment based on its real facts, and, accordingly, we so hold.[111]

The National Westminster Bank PLC (NatWest) case involved the interpretation of the business profits Article (Article 7) of the 1980 US–UK tax treaty.[112] The central issue in the litigation was whether Article 7 conflicted with Treasury Regulation § 1.882-5 (1980), which provides a formula to determine the interest deductions of a US branch of a foreign enterprise. NatWest argued that Article 7 was in conflict with Treasury Regulation § 1.882-5 (1980) and that Article 7 prevailed. Consequently, Treasury Regulation § 1.882-5 (1980) could not be used to reduce NatWest's US branch's interest deductions. The US Court of Appeals for the Federal Circuit (Court of Appeals) in *National Westminster* v. *United States*[113] (2008) (NatWest (2008)) held that Article 7 conflicted with Treasury Regulation § 1.882-5 (1980) and affirmed the preceding decisions by the trial courts in favour of NatWest.

In *National Westminster Bank PLC* v. *United States*[114] (NatWest I) the US Federal Claims Court applied the separate entity method under

[110] (1996) 107 TC 363.   [111] *Ibid.*, p. 398.
[112] This US–UK treaty was signed in 1975, but did not become operative until 1980.
[113] 512 F.3d 1347 (2008); 2008 U.S. App. LEXIS 811; 2008-1 U.S. Tax Cas. (CCH) P50, 140; 101 A.F.T.R.2d (RIA) 490.
[114] 44 Fed. Cl. 120 (1999); 1999 U.S. Claims LEXIS 154; 99-2 Tax Cas. (CCH) P50 p. 654; 84 A.F.T.R.2d (RIA) 5086.

212 DEFINING PERSONALITY OF PERMANENT ESTABLISHMENTS

Article 7 of the 1980 US–UK treaty and found that interest on notional intra-bank loans was deductible.[115] The taxpayer (NatWest), an international bank resident in the UK, carried on wholesale banking operations in the US through six branch locations (the US branch). The US branch was supported by the bank's worldwide equity capital, and it obtained funds from its head office or NatWest branches abroad. In relation to the notional loans between the head office and the US branch, interest was charged as if the branch were a separate entity. The US branch claimed a deduction for the interest on its notional intra-bank loans from its head office or the foreign branches. The US government disallowed the deduction, arguing that the US branch's interest deduction had to be determined under the US domestic law on the taxation of branches (US Treasury Regulation § 1.882-5(1980)).

Turner J of the US Federal Claims Court held that Treasury Regulation § 1.882-5 conflicted with Article 7 of the 1980 US–UK treaty. Both parties accepted that the taxpayer's US branch should be treated as a separate entity, but the US IRS contended that in calculating the business profits attributable to the US permanent establishment, it could not claim a deduction for interest on notional intra-bank loans. On appeal, the US Court of Appeals, in NatWest (2008), affirmed the judgment of Turner J in NatWest I.[116] The basis of the decision was that Article 7 of the 1980 US–UK treaty was based on the separate enterprise principle and consequently Treasury Regulation § 1.882-5 was inconsistent with the 1980 US–UK treaty.[117]

The decision in NatWest I was that Treasury Regulation § 1.882-5 could not be used to determine the interest deduction of the NatWest US branch. The issue in *National Westminster Bank PLC* v. *United States*[118] (NatWest II) was the methods used to determine a foreign bank branch's interest deduction under Article 7 of the 1980 US–UK treaty. Firestone J of the US Federal Claims Court held that the 1980 US–UK treaty required the government to use the properly maintained accounts of NatWest's US branch to determine the business profits attributable to it under Article 7. Firestone J rejected the government's argument that it could treat part of a branch's funding as notional equity capital. The judge also rejected the government's contention that the OECD's statements in its 1984 report, entitled *Transfer Pricing and Multinational*

---

[115] The NatWest judgments are also considered in Chs. 5 and 7.
[116] 512 F.3d 1347 (2008), p. 1349.   [117] *Ibid.*, p. 1359.
[118] 58 Fed. Cl. 491 (2003); 2003 U.S. Claims LEXIS 332; 2004-1 U.S. Tax Cas. (CCH) P50, 150; 92 A.F.T.R.2d. (RIA) 7013.

4 FORMER ARTICLE 7(2)

Enterprises (Three Taxation Issues) (1984 Report),[119] the 2001 and 2003 Discussion Drafts supported the government's position.[120] Firestone J concluded that a foreign bank branch's profits must be based on the branch's books, and they may only be adjusted if they do not correctly reflect intra-bank loans, or where the branch's intra-bank interest expense exceeds arm's length rates.[121]

The US Court of Appeals, in *National Westminster Bank PLC v. US* (2008),[122] affirmed the judgment of Firestone J in NatWest II. The court was influenced by a UK Counsel's opinion that the 1980 US–UK treaty does not provide authority for imputing equity capital to a foreign bank branch.[123] On the basis of this opinion the court concluded that when the 1980 US–UK treaty was negotiated there was no understanding by either country that the separate enterprise principle was authority for the imputation of equity capital to US branches of financial institutions.

In *National Westminster Bank PLC v. United States*[124] (NatWest III), one of the issues was whether NatWest's six US branch offices should be treated as a single permanent establishment or as six permanent establishments. The government argued that each of NatWest's six US branch offices should be treated as a separate entity under the 1980 US–UK treaty. NatWest maintained separate books and accounting records for each of its US branch offices. NatWest contended that the 1980 US–UK treaty and the OECD Commentary refer to whether a taxpayer has a permanent establishment in the host country. Consequently, it argued that the books and accounting records for its six US branch offices should be aggregated for the purpose of allocating business profits to the bank's US branch. Firestone J of the US Federal Claims Court held that NatWest had one US permanent establishment under the 1980 US–UK treaty and that it was appropriate to aggregate the records of the six branches. Firestone J made the following comments in finding that it was unprecedented to treat each of the branch offices as separate permanent establishments in either the US or the UK:

> The fact that NatWest operated separate banking operations in New York, San Francisco and Chicago does not mean that it operated several permanent establishments. The court agrees that under the Treaty the host country may tax profits if the foreign corporation operates an

---

[119] OECD, *Transfer Pricing and Multinational Enterprises (Three Taxation Issues)* (1984).
[120] 58 Fed. Cl. 491 (2003), p. 499.   [121] *Ibid.*, p. 505.
[122] 512 F.3d 1347 (2008), pp. 1349, 1362.   [123] *Ibid.*, p. 1362.
[124] 69 Fed. Cl. 128; 2005 U.S. Claims LEXIS 386; 2006-1 U.S. Tax Cas. (CCH) P50, 107; 97 A.F.T.R.2d (RIA) 369.

214 DEFINING PERSONALITY OF PERMANENT ESTABLISHMENTS

enterprise in the host country. Under Article 5(1) of the Treaty, 'permanent establishment' is defined to mean 'a fixed place of business through which the business of an enterprise is wholly or partly carried on' in the host country . . . There is no precedent for treating six branch offices as six separate permanent establishments in either the United States or in the United Kingdom . . .

Moreover, it is not disputed that the United States always treated the six branch offices as a single establishment for tax purposes. The government has not identified a single instance where any other foreign bank with more than one branch office has been treated as having more than one permanent establishment in the US. For all of these reasons, the court agrees with NatWest that as a matter of law NatWest operated a single permanent establishment in the United States and thus NatWest may account for the capital and interest paid on capital contributions on an aggregated basis.[125]

In NatWest III the US government argued that NatWest's US branch should have equity capital necessary to support a separate entity. The government contended that the US branch had inadequate equity capital and that part of its intra-bank loans should be treated as notional equity capital. Consequently, the interest on notional equity capital should be non-deductible for the branch. Firestone J held that the US branch should not be treated as having notional equity capital.[126] In rejecting the government's argument Firestone J reached the following conclusions on the issue of notional equity capital:

Contrary to the government experts' assertions, the Treaty and the [United Kingdom's Inland Revenue Banking] Manual are not designed to ensure that banks conducting business in a host country maintain a level of capital adequate to cover economic risk. Rather, they are designed to ensure that the branches properly account for income. The regulatory and economic grounds for requiring banks to maintain capital at adequate levels are not at issue in this tax case.[127]

. . .

Thus, the government's contention that NatWest was required to maintain 'economic capital' is rejected. NatWest was not obligated to identify an amount to be treated as allotted capital to account for the economic risk posed by the activities conducted by the US branch. NatWest's failure to account for 'economic capital' does not preclude summary judgment for NatWest.[128]

---

[125] *Ibid.*, 2005 U.S. Claims Lexis 386, pp. 41–3.   [126] *Ibid.*, p. 38.   [127] *Ibid.*, p. 48.
[128] *Ibid.*, pp. 50–1.

Following NatWest I, the 1980 US–UK treaty was replaced by a new treaty signed in 2001, which entered into force in 2003. The treaty negotiators wanted to ensure that Article 7 of the 2001 treaty applied the separate entity approach expressed in the 2001 OECD Discussion Draft. Article 7(2) of the 2001 treaty includes the following sentence: 'For this purpose, the business profits to be attributed to the permanent establishment shall include only the profits derived from the assets used, risks assumed and activities performed by the permanent establishment.' The exchange of notes on the application of Article 7 of the 2001 US–UK tax treaty includes a directive that Article 7 is to be interpreted in light of the Transfer Pricing Guidelines.[129] This directive is based on the 2001 Discussion Draft, and the approach was in anticipation of its being adopted by the OECD. It has been suggested that implementing a new attribution method in a vital tax treaty is unprecedented.[130] It is puzzling that the treaty negotiators adopted an approach that was merely under discussion by OECD countries. The dilemma is compounded because Part II of the 2001 Discussion Draft on the attribution of business profits to international banks has since been modified.

4.1 Symmetrical accounts for notional intra-entity transactions

The requirement in former Article 7(2), that the profits attributed to a permanent establishment be calculated in each contracting state on a symmetrical basis, must be satisfied in order for the permanent establishment to claim a deduction for a notional intra-entity transaction. A significant concern for jurisdictions in recognizing notional intra-entity transactions is the potential for tax avoidance by international enterprises. One method by which international enterprises may avoid tax in higher-tax

---

[129] In relation to Article 7, the exchange of notes to the 2001 US–UK tax treaty states: '[I]t is understood that the OECD Transfer Pricing Guidelines will apply, by analogy, for the purposes of determining the profits attributable to a permanent establishment. Accordingly, any of the methods described therein – including profits methods – may be used to determine the income of a permanent establishment so long as those methods are applied in accordance with the Guidelines. In particular, in determining the amount of attributable profits, the permanent establishment shall be treated as having the same amount of capital that it would need to support its activities if it were a distinct and separate enterprise engaged in the same or similar activities. With respect to financial institutions other than insurance companies, a Contracting State may determine the amount of capital to be attributed to a permanent establishment by allocating the institution's total equity between its various offices on the basis of the proportion of the financial institution's risk-weighted assets attributable to each of them.'

[130] Sheppard, 'NatWest Revisited in the New British Treaty' (2001), p. 1507.

216   DEFINING PERSONALITY OF PERMANENT ESTABLISHMENTS

jurisdictions is to attribute the expenses on notional intra-entity transactions to permanent establishments in higher-tax countries, while not declaring the corresponding amounts as income in the counterparts of the enterprise. Consequently, tax authorities will usually require substantiation that the amounts claimed as deductions for notional intra-entity transactions under former Article 7 are declared as income in the other parts of the enterprise. Thus, for notional intra-entity transactions, the account entries of a permanent establishment must be symmetrical with the account entries of its transaction counterpart in the enterprise.

The deductibility of notional intra-entity rent was considered by the Canadian Federal Court of Appeal in *Cudd Pressure Control Inc* v. *The Queen*.[131] The taxpayer was contracted by a gas well control company for an underground blow in an exploratory gas well being drilled by Mobil. The taxpayer was a US corporation which created a permanent establishment in Canada by providing snubbing services to Mobil for an eight-month period. Snubbing services are the use of complex hydraulic equipment, called snubbing units, to work on oil or gas wells in order to remove drill pipe casings from the wells. The taxpayer used two snubbing units to provide the services; the snubbing units were unique and were owned by the taxpayer. This snubbing service operation satisfied the definition of permanent establishment in the US–Canada tax treaty. The US head office of Cudd Pressure Control Inc. provided the snubbing units used in Canada and claimed that its Canadian permanent establishment was entitled to a deduction for the notional rent for the use of the snubbing equipment. But a transfer of funds for the notional rent for leasing the equipment was not recorded in the Canadian permanent establishment's financial accounts. Moreover, a corresponding receipt of funds was not recorded in the US head office of the taxpayer. Consequently, the accounts of the taxpayer's head office and permanent establishment did not record a symmetrical movement of funds. The court held that the notional rent was not deductible under Article VII of the US–Canada tax treaty. One of the grounds of the decision was the obvious tax avoidance consequence of the head office's failure to record the notional rent as income. McDonald JA stated:

> While no actual money had to exchange hands between the appellant, Cudd Pressure Control Inc., and its parent, RPC (indeed, the point is that the expense is notional), it nevertheless must be included as income in the parent corporation's return so that, if necessary, it can be subject to tax.

---

[131] [1999] 1 CTC 1.

Including the amount of notional rent in the parent corporation's return also accords with the separate accounts principle. Under this method, profits and expenses must be reflected in the separate accounts of the permanent establishment and the parent corporation: see Carroll, Draft Convention, *supra*. The appellant can not derive the benefit of having its profits drastically reduced and then not have the amount included as income in the parent corporation's records. If this were not the case, then the payment of rent would never be subjected to tax.[132]

The *Cudd Pressure* case raised the problems of applying the separate entity fiction in the permanent establishment context to a taxpayer with an international snubbing unit monopoly. The trial judge in this case[133] made a finding of fact that the taxpayers' Canadian permanent establishment, if it were a notional separate entity, would have purchased rather than rented the snubbing units. This finding was based on the taxpayer having a monopoly and that it had never before rented out snubbing units in the ordinary course of its business. In addition, the trial judge concluded that the taxpayer won the contract with Mobil because of its snubbing unit monopoly. On this issue, McDonald JA of the Federal Court of Appeal agreed with the findings of the trial judge:

> I am also of the view that the facts do not establish that in the normal course of business the snubbing equipment would have been rented to the appellant's permanent establishment in Canada. Indeed, it is more likely that the head office would have been contacted directly to take on this contract given that it is the only one to have had equipment of this kind during the relevant period. An independent company in the position of the permanent establishment would not have entered into this type of relationship unless it had the necessary equipment to perform its duties under the contract. In this case, the appellant did not have the necessary equipment and would likely have declined the contract.[134]

The issue of whether the Canadian permanent establishment would have leased or purchased the snubbing units underscores the difficulties created by the separate entity fiction. Once a permanent establishment is treated as a separate entity there is significant uncertainty in determining under this fiction what would have happened if the permanent establishment were actually a separate entity. Rosenbloom illustrated the inherent uncertainty created by legal fictions in transfer pricing with

---

[132] *Ibid.*, para. 38.   [133] [1995] 2 C.T.C. 2382 (T.C.C.).
[134] *Cudd Pressure Control Inc.* v. *The Queen* [1999] 1 CTC 1, para. 17.

the question: 'If I had a brother would he like cheese?'[135] Once a legal fiction is used, considerable uncertainty is created for taxpayers and their advisers and tax authorities in determining the extent of the fiction.

4.2 Reliance on an international enterprise's accounts

Article 7 relies on the trading accounts of international enterprises to record their notional intra-entity transactions.[136] But to what extent can an international enterprise's accounts be relied upon by tax authorities to reflect its notional intra-entity transactions based on the real facts? Vogel argued that the risk of profit shifting caused by relying on an international enterprise's accounts is overstated.[137] He suggested that tax authorities have methods to control artificial valuations, such as comparing the recorded prices with those used by arm's length parties. Vogel asserted that it cannot be assumed that enterprises with foreign subsidiaries or foreign branches are prepared to commit fraud in recording intra-group transactions. In addition, an international enterprise cannot be properly managed if its accounting records do not correctly reflect transactions.

The income and costs of various parts of an enterprise are essential information from which its management can evaluate the enterprise's efficiency and effectiveness. Vogel concluded that the management of an enterprise would not risk losing valuable information on its performance for a tax benefit, although he qualified his arguments for an enterprise with a limited number of product lines. He found that separate accounting, controlled by an effective tax authority, is a reliable method for determining the profits of a branch or subsidiary and for allocating them between two countries.[138]

In contrast, Bird and Brean argued that an international enterprise's accounts may not be relied upon to objectively reflect the profits and costs allocated to branches because an enterprise is a unitary business with a common profit objective.[139] International enterprises employ global tax planning techniques to minimize their global tax liability

---

[135] Professor David Rosenbloom (New York University School of Law), International Fiscal Association, Transfer Pricing Seminar at the University of Melbourne Faculty of Law, August 2005.
[136] 2005 OECD Model, pp. 117–18, para. 12.1; 2008 OECD Model, pp. 123–4, para. 19; 2010 OECD Model, p. 160, para. 19.
[137] Vogel, 'Worldwide vs. Source Taxation of Income (Part III)' (1988), pp. 319–20.
[138] Ibid.
[139] Bird and Brean, 'The Interjurisdictional Allocation of Income and the Unitary Taxation Debate' (1986), pp. 1383–4.

through tax arbitrage. An international enterprise's accounts will reflect profits and expenses allocated to a branch which achieve the enterprise's tax arbitrage objectives. Bird and Brean asserted that, in either economics or accounting, there is no single objective method for allocating profits and expenses within an international enterprise.[140] In international tax, international enterprises have full control and access to their tax and accounting records. Apart from situations in which there are effective tax treaty information exchange measures, international enterprises are usually the only source of information for national tax authorities. In allocating profits and expenses between the head office and branches of an international enterprise, a tax authority cannot rely on the compliance and goodwill of the enterprise.[141] Thus, the separate accounting approach is ineffective for attributing profits and costs in an international enterprise.

The reliance of the arm's length principle on the accounts of international enterprises provides considerable opportunities for international tax avoidance through a range of techniques, including transfer pricing and restructuring. The literature on transfer pricing indicates the risk of relying on the accounts of multinational enterprises, because it is unlikely that the accounts will reflect transactions equivalent to those between independent parties. Intra-firm transactions have the potential to be influenced by the tax minimization strategies of international enterprises.[142] The unavoidable conclusion is that there is a strong risk that an international enterprise's accounts may be manipulated through transfer pricing to shift a branch's profits to a lower-tax jurisdiction or a jurisdiction with other tax benefits such as a dividend imputation system.

4.3 Pre-2008 Commentary: the two approaches used in former Articles 7(1) and (2)

Under the pre-2008 Commentary, the interaction between former Articles 7(1) and (2) is controversial; there are three broad interpretations.[143] The first is that former Articles 7(1) and (2) are consistent: former Article 7(1) should be interpreted in the light of former Article 7(2), with the

---

[140] *Ibid.*, p. 1383.
[141] Bird, 'The Interjurisdictional Allocation of Income' (1986), p. 333.
[142] Clausing, 'The Impact of Transfer Pricing on Intrafirm Trade' in Hines (ed.) *International Taxation and Multinational Activity* (2001) 173–94, p. 191.
[143] Arnold and Darmo, 'Summary of Proceedings of an Invitational Seminar on the Attribution of Profits to Permanent Establishments' (2001), pp. 539–40.

latter being treated as stating the underlying principles. The second interpretation is that former Articles 7(1) and (2) are inconsistent, and the inconsistencies may be resolved by treating former Article 7(2) as prevailing over former Article 7(1) because former Article 7(2) is a more specific provision. The third interpretation is that former Article 7(1) is a substantive provision on attributing profits to permanent establishments, and that it may not be given a subordinate role. These potential constructions on the interaction between former Articles 7(1) and (2) indicate a significant degree of ambiguity.

It has been argued that these inconsistencies reflect the use of the separate entity and single entity approaches, to calculate the profits of a permanent establishment, in former Article 7:

- the accounts-based approach (accounts approach) that tends to be used by civil law countries, which use an exemption method to prevent double taxation; or
- the allocation method (allocation approach) that tends to be used by common law countries, which use a credit method to prevent double taxation.[144]

Under the accounts approach used in civil law countries, transfers of goods and services between a head office and a permanent establishment of an international enterprise are treated as transactions. Civil law countries usually calculate the taxable income of a permanent establishment from its financial accounts. This is the separate entity approach which allows for profit margins to be made on notional intra-entity transactions. For example, if a branch of an international enterprise manufactures goods and they are sold to its head office, under the separate entity method the branch is treated as receiving market value consideration. If the branch also sells the goods to independent customers, this approach allows the branch to make its usual profit margin on the intra-entity transaction.[145]

Under the allocation approach used by common law countries, only transactions with independent enterprises are considered. Common law countries usually do not rely on a permanent establishment's financial

---

[144] Arnold, Sasseville and Zolt, 'Summary of Proceedings of an Invitational Seminar on the Taxation of Business Profits Under Tax Treaties' (2003), p. 197, referring to R. J. Vann's paper. Vann, 'Reflections on Business Profits and the Arm's Length Principle' in Arnold, et al. (eds.), *The Taxation of Business Profits under Tax Treaties* (2003) 133–69, pp. 158–9.

[145] Vann, *ibid.*, p. 159.

4 FORMER ARTICLE 7(2)

accounts; rather, they prescribe rules in their domestic law on the attribution of profits to permanent establishments. This approach is based on the notion of worldwide taxation of an international enterprise as a whole, instead of determining the profits of the head office and its permanent establishments. This is the single entity approach which prevents a profit margin from being imposed on intra-entity transactions. The profits and expenses from transactions with other enterprises are allocated to either the enterprise's head office or its permanent establishments.[146]

It has been suggested that both methods are acceptable if the result conforms with the arm's length principle.[147] It is also asserted that the Commentary on former Article 7 is a mixture of the two methods; former Article 7(1) supports the allocation approach while former Article 7(2) uses the accounts approach. Even though both methods may be justified as conforming with the arm's length principle,[148] uncertainty and confusion arise from their concurrent use because of the interaction between former Articles 7(1) and (2).

4.4   2008 Commentary on former Article 7(2)

The Commentary states that former Article 7(2) is based on the arm's length principle which should be applied by both the host country and residence country. But the profits attributable to a permanent establishment by the host country may differ from the profits recognized by the residence country because of differences between the domestic laws of the two treaty countries. The differences between the taxable income in each country may be caused by differences in timing, recognition and depreciation rates, and restrictions on the deduction of expenses. Consequently, the profits attributed to a permanent establishment by a host country may differ from the profits on which the residence country is required to provide relief under Articles 23 A or 23 B.[149]

The main change in the 2008 Commentary on former Article 7(2) is when the profits attributed to a permanent establishment may be altered by the host country. A permanent establishment's profits may be altered if they are less than the profits that would have been derived under the legal fiction of the permanent establishment as a separate

---

[146] *Ibid.*, pp. 159–60.   [147] *Ibid.*, p. 161.

[148] Arnold, Sasseville and Zolt, 'Summary of Proceedings of an Invitational Seminar on the Taxation of Business Profits Under Tax Treaties' (2003), p. 197.

[149] 2008 OECD Model, p. 121, para. 15; 2010 OECD Model, p. 159, para. 15.

enterprise. Under this fiction, a permanent establishment is treated as entering into intra-entity transactions (called dealings) with the head office or other permanent establishments of the enterprise.[150] The Commentary then incorporates part of the 2008 Report – sections D-1 and D-2 of Part I – into the Commentary on the two-step procedure to describe how the separate entity legal fiction is to be applied to permanent establishments. The approach set out in this part of the 2008 Report provides the principles for attributing profits to permanent establishments. The 2008 Report adapted the Transfer Pricing Guidelines to the attribution of profits to permanent establishments.

The first step indentifies the activities carried on through a permanent establishment using the functional and factual analysis set out in the Transfer Pricing Guidelines. This step identifies a permanent establishment's 'economically significant activities and responsibilities'.[151] A permanent establishment's activities are examined in the context of the activities and responsibilities of the entire international enterprise. A significant part of this step is looking at the notional transactions, called dealings, between the permanent establishment and the other parts of the international enterprise.

The second step is a comparative exercise in which the rewards attributable to the activities and responsibilities of a permanent establishment are determined by applying by analogy the principles established in the Transfer Pricing Guidelines. The criteria used in this comparative exercise are the functions performed by a permanent establishment, the assets used by it, and the risk assumed by the permanent establishment. Steps 1 and 2 are considered in Chapters 8 and 9.

5 Former Article 7(3): the single entity approach in the pre-2008 Commentary

The pre-2008 Commentary states that former Article 7(3) clarifies the general directive laid down in former Article 7(2).[152] But the role of former Article 7(3) is confusing and contentious.[153] Former Article 7(3) expressly provides that in calculating the profits of a permanent establishment, allowance is to be made for the expenses incurred for the

---

[150] 2008 OECD Model, p. 122, para. 17; 2010 OECD Model, p. 159, para. 17.
[151] 2008 OECD Model, p. 123, para. 18; 2010 OECD Model, pp. 159–60, para. 18.
[152] 2005 OECD Model, p. 121, para. 16; 2008 OECD Model, pp. 125–6, para. 27; 2010 OECD Model, p. 162, para. 27.
[153] Ward, 'Attribution of Income to Permanent Establishments' (2000), p. 563.

purposes of the permanent establishment. The Commentary states that some expenses will need to be estimated. The general administrative expenses incurred by the head office of an enterprise may be estimated on the basis of the ratio of a permanent establishment's turnover to that of the entire enterprise.[154] However, this approach for general administrative expenses is an exception to the general rule set out in the Commentary that the amount of expenses, to be taken as incurred for the purposes of a permanent establishment, should be the actual amount so incurred.[155] Thus, former Article 7(3) appears to use the single entity approach, and consequently, intra-entity expenses may only be attributed to a permanent establishment at cost. In other words, a permanent establishment is only allowed to reimburse another part of an enterprise, at cost, for expenses incurred for the purposes of the permanent establishment.

The use of the single entity approach in former Article 7(3) raises both a normative difficulty and a practical difficulty. There is a normative inconsistency in treating a permanent establishment as a separate entity for some purposes but not others. Perhaps surprisingly, the Commentary expressly denies this normative difficulty:

> In fact, whilst the application of paragraph 3 may raise some practical difficulties, especially in relation to the separate enterprise and arm's length principles underlying paragraph 2, there is no difference of principle between the two paragraphs. Paragraph 3 indicates that in determining the profits of a permanent establishment certain expenses must be allowed as deductions whilst paragraph 2 provides that the profits determined in accordance with the rule contained in paragraph 3 relating to the deduction of expenses must be those that a separate and distinct enterprise engaged in the same or similar activities under the same or similar conditions would have made. Thus, whilst paragraph 3 provides a rule applicable for the determination of the profits of the permanent establishment, paragraph 2 requires that the profits so determined correspond to the profits that a separate and independent enterprise would have made.[156]

According to the Commentary former Articles 7(2) and (3) both conform with the arm's length principle in concurrently applying the separate entity and single entity approaches. The approach taken in the

---

[154] 2005 OECD Model, p. 121, para. 16; 2008 OECD Model, pp. 125–6, para. 27; 2010 OECD Model, p. 162, para. 27.

[155] *Ibid.*

[156] 2005 OECD Model, p. 121, para. 16; 2008 OECD Model, p. 126, para. 29; 2010 OECD Model, pp. 161–2, para. 29.

224 DEFINING PERSONALITY OF PERMANENT ESTABLISHMENTS

Commentary on former Article 7(3) gives rise to the practical difficulty of deciding when a profit margin may be charged by one part of an international enterprise on a notional intra-entity transaction with a permanent establishment. The Commentary provides the following guidance on applying the separate entity and single entity approaches:

> Whilst in general independent enterprises in their dealings with each other will seek to realise a profit and, when transferring property or providing services to each other, will charge such prices as the open market would bear, nevertheless, there are also circumstances where it cannot be considered that a particular property or service would have been obtainable from an independent enterprise or when independent enterprises may agree to share between them the costs of some activity which is pursued in common for their mutual benefit. In these particular circumstances it may be appropriate to treat any relevant costs incurred by the enterprise as an expense incurred for the permanent establishment.[157]

This statement in the pre-2008 Commentary fails to provide a convincing rationale for the concurrent use of the separate and single entity approaches. It states that a profit margin may not be imposed on intra-entity expenses attributed to a permanent establishment, if the goods or services could not be provided by an independent entity. Given the expansion of service providers in developed economies, independent contractors provide a broad range of administrative functions. For example, an international enterprise could use contractors for a variety of administrative services such as personnel, information technology, electronic communications and mail. Even management functions can be provided by contractors and there is a wealth of evidence in the public domain that management consulting has been a growth area in the past fifteen years. Thus, it would be exceptional to identify a service that could not be provided by an independent entity.

The statement in the pre-2008 Commentary – that separate and independent entities may agree to share costs in certain circumstances – relies on the single entity approach and appears to be difficult to apply. But this approach acknowledges that international enterprises operate as unitary enterprises and not as collections of separate entities. Nevertheless, applying this statement is problematic, as independent enterprises are likely to share costs only in exceptional circumstances. The Commentary states that a profit margin may be imposed on a permanent

---

[157] 2005 OECD Model, p. 122, para. 17.1; 2008 OECD Model, pp. 126–7, para. 31; 2010 OECD Model, p. 163, para. 31.

5 ARTICLE 7(3)

establishment's notional intra-entity transactions if those transactions are typical of the business carried on by the enterprise. The Commentary describes the test in the following terms:

> The question must be whether the internal transfer of property and services, be it temporary or final, is of the same kind as those which the enterprise, in the normal course of its business, would have charged to a third party at an arm's length price, i.e. by normally including in the sale price an appropriate profit.[158]

The Commentary then sets out specific categories of expenses on which it considers that a profit margin may not be imposed for notional intra-entity transactions, and it contains statements on the deductibility of interest on intra-entity loans.

5.1 Intra-entity dealings in goods and intangible property

The pre-2008 Commentary advocates that for intra-entity dealings in goods for resale, the separate entity principle should be applied, with the head office or permanent establishment of an international enterprise supplying the goods making a profit margin on the supply.[159] This principle applies irrespective of whether the goods are raw materials, semi-finished goods or finished goods. The Commentary indicates that there are exceptions to this rule, but this qualification is contradictory as the only example provided deals with goods not provided for resale. The example deals with goods that are provided by one part of an enterprise to other parts for temporary use in business operations. In this case the Commentary directs that the parts of the international enterprise using such goods should share the actual costs of the goods.

For intangible property, the transfer pricing rules for enterprises of the same group cannot be used for the intra-dealings of an international enterprise.[160] These principles deal with issues such as the payment of royalties for the use of intangible property, or cost sharing arrangements to create or develop intangible property. The first problem with intangible property is determining which part of the enterprise owns it, and to then claim that under the separate enterprise principle the rest of the enterprise

---

[158] *Ibid.*
[159] 2005 OECD Model, pp. 122–3, para. 17.3; 2008 OECD Model, p. 127, para. 33; 2010 OECD Model, pp. 163–4, para. 33.
[160] 2005 OECD Model, p. 123, para. 17.4; 2008 OECD Model, pp. 127–8, para. 34; 2010 OECD Model, p. 164, para. 34.

226 DEFINING PERSONALITY OF PERMANENT ESTABLISHMENTS

will be charged royalties if they use the intangible property. Moreover, it is difficult to treat one part of the enterprise, such as the head office, as owning the intangible property.

The OECD uses the single entity principle for intangible property to reflect the legal and economic reality that an international enterprise is a single entity: 'Since there is only one legal entity it is not possible to allocate legal ownership to any particular part of the enterprise and in practical terms it will often be difficult to allocate the costs of creation exclusively to one part of the enterprise.'[161] Consequently, the OECD has chosen to use a proxy method of attributing the cost of creating intangible property to the parts of an enterprise that use it. But there is no definition of what is use of intangible property. The costs that may be allocated under this method are the costs of creating the intangible property, and any costs that are incurred after the creation of the intangible property. The Commentary proscribes any mark-up for profit or royalties for the intra-entity use of intangible property. The Commentary also directs tax authorities that adverse costs resulting from research and development may be allocated to the parts of an enterprise. The Commentary is remarkably brief on this topic and no further guidance is provided on this matter, even though intangible property is often the most valuable asset of an international enterprise. In summary, one part of an international enterprise cannot claim to own intangible property and charge the other parts of the enterprise a royalty for using it.

5.2 Intra-entity dealings in services

For services, the OECD uses the separate enterprise principle in directing that a profit margin may be charged for intra-entity services if the business of an international enterprise includes providing services to external customers.[162] In this situation, the international enterprise should have standard charges for particular services. The OECD indicates that these charges should be used when intra-entity services are provided. The Commentary provides an exception to this principle if the main business of a permanent establishment is to provide intra-entity services, but such services are not provided to external customers.[163]

---

[161] *Ibid.*

[162] 2005 OECD Model, p. 123, para. 17.5; 2008 OECD Model, p. 128, para. 35; 2010 OECD Model, p. 164, para. 35.

[163] 2005 OECD Model, p. 123, para. 17.6; 2008 OECD Model, p. 128, para. 36; 2010 OECD Model, p. 164, para. 36.

If these services provide benefits to the enterprise and the cost of the services is a significant expense of the enterprise, the host country may require that the permanent establishment makes a profit margin for the provision of services. The OECD indicates that a host country should not use 'schematic solutions', but should use the value of these services based on the facts and circumstances of the situation. The Commentary does not provide guidance on how to determine the value of services. Moreover, a host country may have difficulty in testing the value of services in this situation if there are no external comparable prices for the services.

The OECD requires that, under the single enterprise principle, the general management activities of an international enterprise may only be attributed to other parts of the enterprise at cost.[164] These costs may only be attributed to a permanent establishment if the costs were incurred for the benefit of the permanent establishment. Many intra-entity services will be treated as part of the general management function of an international enterprise, such as training and administrative software. For example, the head office of an international enterprise may provide training to the employees of its permanent establishments, which benefits the whole enterprise. In this situation, the cost of providing the training should be treated as a general administrative service.

The Commentary requires that if a head office provides general management services, under the single enterprise principle, these expenses may only be attributed at cost.[165] The OECD rejects the proposition that part of the profits of an international enterprise should be allocated to good management. General management expenses, such as the board of directors' expenses, may only be allocated to the other parts of the enterprise at actual cost. To illustrate the point, the OECD uses the example of an international enterprise with a head office which is only used for directors' meetings and legal formalities, with all its business being carried on through a permanent establishment. As the head office is providing general management services through the board of directors, then it may be contended that part of the profits should be attributed to the head office. But the OECD claims that in this situation, on the basis of practical considerations 'it is thought that it would not be right to go further by deducting and taking into account some notional figure for

---

[164] 2005 OECD Model, pp. 123–4, para. 17.7, 2008 OECD Model, p. 128, para. 37; 2010 OECD Model, pp. 164–5, para. 37.

[165] 2005 OECD Model, pp. 123–4, para. 17; 2008 OECD Model, p. 128, para. 37; 2010 OECD Model, pp. 164–5, para. 37.

228 DEFINING PERSONALITY OF PERMANENT ESTABLISHMENTS

"profits of management".[166] In determining the profits of the permanent establishment, an expense cannot be attributed to the permanent establishment for a notional amount for profits of management.

But the OECD acknowledges that in certain countries, it is customary to allocate part of the profits to the head office of an international enterprise to reflect the profit attributable to good management. The flexibility of interpreting former Article 7(3) is revealed in the OECD's statement that this customary approach is possible under the provision. Nevertheless, a host country is not required under former Article 7(3) to provide a corresponding deduction to a permanent establishment to reflect the profits of management attributable to the head office. Although the application of treaty provisions is reciprocal, residence countries in which international enterprises are based have an incentive to take the separate entity approach to attribute profits to good management. On the other hand, host countries are likely to use the single enterprise approach and only provide a deduction for management services at cost. The lack of a consensus interpretation on the attribution of general management expenses means that double taxation is likely. If the residence country treats part of an enterprise's profits as being attributable to good management, and the host country only provides a deduction for the actual costs of management, the combined taxable profits of the enterprise will be excessive, resulting in double taxation. The Commentary suggests that to prevent double taxation, the residence country should alter its approach and conform to the approach taken by the host country of not attributing profits to good management.[167] The inference is that the better approach is to only allocate general management expenses at cost to avoid double taxation.

5.3 Intra-entity loans in non-bank enterprises

The OECD examined the issue of the deductibility of interest on intra-entity loans in *Transfer Pricing and Multinational Enterprises – Three Taxation Issues* (1984 Report).[168] The Commentary and the 1984 Report reflect the OECD's views on the deductibility of interest on intra-entity loans. On the issue of whether a permanent establishment may deduct its interest expense on intra-entity loans, the OECD says that special

---

[166] *Ibid.*

[167] 2005 OECD Model, p. 126, para. 23; 2008 OECD Model, p. 129, para. 40; 2010 OECD Model, p. 165, para. 40.

[168] OECD, *Transfer Pricing and Multinational Enterprises (Three Taxation Issues)* (1984).

considerations apply. According to the pre-2008 Commentary, it must be determined whether an arm's length rate of interest, incorporating a profit margin, should be charged on intra-entity loans.[169] Under the separate entity method, an enterprise is allowed to include a profit margin on intra-entity loans. Under the single entity method, an enterprise may only attribute the cost of the loan to a branch. The OECD distinguishes between intra-entity loans in banking enterprises and those in non-bank enterprises. Intra-bank loans are recognized using the separate entity method,[170] but for non-bank enterprises, intra-entity loans are not recognized under the single entity method. The OECD's position is that, for funds borrowed by a non-bank international enterprise for use in a permanent establishment, interest must be attributed to the permanent establishment at cost under former Article 7(3).

The OECD was concerned with recognizing intra-entity interest as intra-entity loans may be used for tax avoidance:

> [F]rom the economic standpoint internal debts and receivables may prove to be non-existent, since if an enterprise is solely or predominantly equity-funded it ought not to be allowed to deduct interest charges that it has manifestly not had to pay. While, admittedly, symmetrical charges and returns will not distort the enterprise's overall profits, partial results may well be arbitrarily changed.[171]

The policy reason for not recognizing intra-entity loans appears to be the desire to prevent transfer pricing manipulation. The origin of this potential for tax avoidance was noted in Carroll's survey of national tax systems in the 1930s.[172] Carroll found that some countries allowed a permanent establishment to deduct the proportionate amount of the international enterprise's overall interest expenses – the apportionment of interest expenses within an international enterprise.[173] In contrast, some countries did not allow a deduction for the proportionate part of the interest on an international enterprise's general indebtedness.[174] This proscription appears to be based on the potential for an international

---

[169] 2005 OECD Model, p. 124, para. 18.
[170] See Kobetsky, 'Intra-Bank Loans: Determining a Branch's Business Profits under Article 7 of the OECD Model' (2005).
[171] 2005 OECD Model, p. 124, para. 18; 2008 OECD Model, pp. 129–30, para. 41; 2010 OECD Model, pp. 165–6, para. 41.
[172] Van Raad, 'Deemed Expenses of a Permanent Establishment under Article 7 of the OECD Model' in Lindencrona, et al. (eds.), *International Studies in Taxation* (1999) 285–95, p. 291.
[173] Carroll, *Taxation of Foreign and National Enterprises* (1933), p. 101.
[174] Ibid., pp. 102–3.

enterprise to use the interest expenses on intra-entity loans to shift profits away from certain permanent establishments. Thus, intra-entity loans were viewed as a means of shifting profits from permanent establishments in higher-tax countries.

The direct and indirect apportionment of interest expenses within an enterprise is no longer used in the OECD Model because it was not applied in a uniform manner.[175] There were two main difficulties with the direct and indirect apportionment approach. First, there are practical problems in attempting to indirectly apportion an enterprise's total interest charges. Second, the direct apportionment of interest charges may not reflect the cost of financing for a permanent establishment because an enterprise is able to control where loans are booked. If an international enterprise controls where a loan is booked, the OECD claims that adjustments were required to reflect economic reality. The direct and indirect apportionment of interest expenses has the advantages of simplicity and low compliance costs, provided there is a consensus interpretation in treaty countries.

The OECD's second concern with recognizing intra-entity interest, is that intra-entity transactions are notional because only one true entity is involved: '[F]rom the legal standpoint, the transfer of capital against payment of interest and an undertaking to repay in full at the due date is really a formal act incompatible with the true nature of a permanent establishment'.[176] The reason offered in the 1984 Report for disallowing a profit margin to be charged by a non-bank enterprise on intra-entity loans is that the loans are 'merely movements of funds within an enterprise'.[177]

For non-bank enterprises, the OECD's approach in the pre-2008 Commentary is that intra-entity loans should not be recognized because they are artificial and they therefore should be ignored in calculating the profits of a permanent establishment. In this situation, the OECD uses the single entity method under which loan funds provided to a permanent establishment must be provided at cost. In the case of non-bank enterprises, intra-entity interest can be recognized only if it reflects the interest paid to an independent lender.[178] This requires a permanent establishment of a non-bank international enterprise to trace its interest expenses

---

[175] 2005 OECD Model, p. 124, para. 18.2; 2008 OECD Model, p. 130, para. 44; 2010 OECD Model, p. 166, para. 44.
[176] 2005 OECD Model, p. 124, para. 18; 2008 OECD Model, pp. 129–30, para. 41; 2010 OECD Model, pp. 165–6, para. 41.
[177] 1984 Report, p. 56, para. 45.   [178] Ibid., p. 57, para. 49.

to external lenders if it wishes to deduct interest on intra-entity loans from the profits attributed to it. As money is fungible, in a highly integrated international enterprise, it would be exceptional for the enterprise to be able to trace loan funds provided to a permanent establishment back to the original lender. The approach taken in relation to non-bank enterprises on this issue imposes significant compliance costs on them to maintain detailed records of the debt capital allocated to permanent establishments.

In summary, the OECD concluded that the majority of countries decided that the best approach is 'to look for a practical solution that would take into account a capital structure appropriate to both the organization and functions performed'.[179] Consequently, the OECD concluded in the pre-2008 Commentary that the prohibition on deducting interest on intra-entity loans should continue to apply. Thus, non-bank enterprises must attribute expenses for loans only at cost, using the single entity approach. The use of this approach places a significant compliance burden on non-bank enterprises because they are required to trace interest on intra-entity loans back to the original source. This is usually a pointless exercise since money is fungible. Intra-bank loans are the only exception to the rule proscribing a deduction for interest on intra-entity loans.

5.4 The interaction between former Articles 7(2) and 7(3) under the pre-2008 Commentary

The meaning of former Articles 7(2) and (3) is uncertain. The ambiguity arises from the terms of former Article 7 and the concurrent use of the single entity and separate entity methods. The consequence is the provisions are applied inconsistently to notional intra-entity transactions when allocating expenses. According to former Article 7(2) the profits to be attributed to a permanent establishment are the profits it would be expected to make if it were an independent and separate entity. Under this provision, any notional transactions between a permanent establishment and other parts of the same enterprise should be treated as dealings between arm's length parties. Former Article 7(2) applies the legal fiction of a separate entity to determine the profits and expenses of a permanent establishment, but former Article 7(2) is subject to former Article 7(3), which deals exclusively with expenses.

---

[179] 2005 OECD Model, pp. 124–5, para. 18.3; 2008 OECD Model, p. 130, para. 45; 2010 OECD Model, p. 166, para. 45.

Article 7(3) provides that in determining the profits of a permanent establishment, the expenses incurred for the purposes of the permanent establishment will be allowed as deductions. A permanent establishment may deduct executive and general administrative expenses, and these expenses may be incurred in the host country, or elsewhere. Under former Article 7(2) it is clear that a permanent establishment is entitled to claim a deduction for expenses incurred in deriving income, but there is some doubt about the precise role of former Article 7(3). Vann argued that the purpose of former Article 7(3) is to override the domestic law on the taxation of permanent establishments in common law countries, in order to ensure that permanent establishments may deduct interest expenses incurred outside the host country.[180] He asserted that, under the allocation approach used in common law countries, domestic rules at times prevented expenses incurred in another country from being attributed to a permanent establishment. Vann also argued that these domestic rules often do not allow apportioning an expense incurred for a permanent establishment and other parts of the enterprise. When one part of an enterprise incurs an expense for another part of the enterprise, some of the expense is attributable to the profits of a permanent establishment and some of the expense relates to the profits made by the enterprise in another jurisdiction. Restrictions on claiming a deduction for expenses incurred abroad are usually imposed to prevent tax avoidance as it is exceptionally difficult for a tax authority to verify expenses incurred in another jurisdiction. Vann concluded that the purpose of former Article 7(3) is to override these domestic restrictions on attributing expenses to a permanent establishment in order to ensure that these apportionable expenses can be deducted.

There are two potential interpretations of former Article 7(3). The first is that former Article 7(3) is superfluous because former Article 7(2) provides for expenses to be attributed to a permanent establishment. Under this construction, it may be argued that former Article 7(3) merely puts beyond doubt that expenses which are only partly, rather than solely, incurred for a permanent establishment, may be deducted by the permanent establishment. The reference in former Article 7(3) to executive and administrative expenses supports the construction that the provision has only a minor clarification role. This construction is supported by Vann's assertion that, in common law countries, former

---

[180] Vann, 'Reflections on Business Profits and the Arm's Length Principle' in Arnold, et al. (eds.), *The Taxation of Business Profits Under Tax Treaties* (2003) 133–69, pp. 159–61.

Article 7(3) is intended to override domestic laws proscribing deductions for expenses incurred for a permanent establishment in another jurisdiction or for apportionable expenses. The pre-2008 Commentary, however, makes no reference to such a construction of former Article 7(3).

Under an alternative construction, former Article 7(2) is subject to Article 7(3), which requires that intra-entity expenses may only be attributed to a permanent establishment at cost. Under this construction, former Article 7(3) imposes the single entity approach and limits intra-entity expenses to cost prices, preventing a permanent establishment from being charged a profit margin on these expenses.[181] The pre-2008 Commentary on former Article 7(3) supports this construction which limits the application of the principle in former Article 7(2) – that a permanent establishment is entitled to deductions for expenses as if it were a separate entity – to a limited range of expenses. Unfortunately, the uncertainty about the interaction of former Articles 7(2) and 7(3) results in inconsistent interpretations, which may result in double taxation or under-taxation of a permanent establishment. The ambiguities in the terms of former Articles 7(2) and 7(3) should have been resolved by amending these provisions, rather than using the Commentary to clarify this ambiguity. These ambiguities create the potential for conflict between international enterprises and tax authorities.

5.5 Former Article 7(2) under the 2008 Commentary

The focus of the amendments to the Commentary on former Article 7(2) was intra-entity loans. The 2008 Commentary maintains the existing principle that a head office cannot charge interest on notional intra-entity loans.[182] As with the pre-2008 Commentary, if a head office borrows funds to finance the operations of a permanent establishment, the head office may pass on its interest expense to the permanent establishment, without imposing a profit margin in accordance with the single enterprise principle.[183] The issue is to determine the permanent establishment's deductible interest expense on intra-entity borrowings. The challenge is in determining a permanent establishment's total working capital and then dissecting it into equity capital and debt capital. The head office of

---

[181] 2005 OECD Model, p. 121, para. 16; 2008 OECD Model, pp. 125–6, para. 27; 2010 OECD Model, p. 162, para. 27.
[182] 2008 OECD Model, p. 130, para. 42; 2010 OECD Model, p. 166, para. 42.
[183] 2008 OECD Model, p. 130, para. 43; 2010 OECD Model, p. 166, para. 43; 2005 OECD Model, p. 124, para. 18.1.

an international enterprise cannot impose an interest charge on the equity capital, called the 'free capital', provided to the permanent establishments.[184] Once the permanent establishment's working capital and equity capital are determined, the difference between these amounts is its debt capital. If its entire debt capital was obtained through its head office, then the interest expense imposed on the head office may be passed on, at cost, to the permanent establishment. If a permanent establishment has borrowed funds from an independent lender, the interest expense will be a deductible expense, provided the funds were used by it in carrying on business in the host country.

The 2008 Commentary expressly requires a permanent establishment's equity capital to support its functions, assets and risks. The pre-2008 Commentary was silent on this point, enabling the OECD to claim that the changes to the Commentary are consistent with the pre-2008 Commentary. According to the arm's length principle, a permanent establishment as a notional separate enterprise is required to hold equity capital to support its business activities, the assets it economically owns, and the risks it assumes. While it is possible to assess the business activities of a permanent establishment, it is more challenging to determine the economic owner of assets, especially intangible assets. In addition, business risk cannot be isolated to a permanent establishment as it can be for a subsidiary which is a separate enterprise with independent personality. A subsidiary company is able to own assets and assume risks that are usually isolated to the enterprise; consequently the transfer pricing principles of requiring equity capital to support these items reflects ordinary legal principles. In practice, however, a multinational group of companies is operated as a single enterprise with common control and a common profit motive. But applying the transfer pricing principles to permanent establishments is a legal fiction that does not reflect company law, property law, or the way in which modern international enterprises operate.

While the OECD requires permanent establishments to have notional equity capital, it was unable to establish a single 'authorized OECD approach' to determine a permanent establishment's equity capital.[185] Instead, the 2008 Commentary states that there are several acceptable methods for determining equity capital, which are set out in the 2008 Report.[186] The 2008 Commentary acknowledges that each approach

---

[184] 2008 OECD Model, p. 130, para. 45; 2010 OECD Model, p. 166, para. 45.
[185] 2008 OECD Model, p. 131, para. 46; 2010 OECD Model, p. 166, para. 46.
[186] 2008 Report, pp. 39–53, Part I. section D-2(v)(b).

has its strengths and weaknesses and that there is no single amount of arm's length equity capital. The OECD's inability to establish a consensus method raises the risk of double taxation or under-taxation. It is curious that the OECD claims that a permanent establishment must have equity capital, but it cannot establish a single and uniform method for dealing with the issue. Host countries will usually seek to attribute higher amounts of equity capital to permanent establishments as it will increase their profitability. On the other hand, residence countries may seek to limit the equity capital allocated to permanent establishments as it decreases their profitability.

The 2008 Commentary sets out a so-called practical procedure to deal with the double taxation problems resulting from the concurrent use of the two different OECD accepted methods for determining a permanent establishment's equity capital by treaty partner countries.[187] A permanent establishment's interest deduction in its host country for the purpose of double taxation relief will be determined under this procedure if two conditions are met. First, the different capital attributions must result from a conflict between the domestic law of the host country and residence country. Second, there must be agreement between the treaty partners that:

- the host country has used an 'authorized OECD approach' to attribute equity capital to the permanent establishment; and
- the approach produces a result consistent with the arm's length principle.

This resolution process appears to be cumbersome and onerous as both treaty countries must agree on the matters in the second step. If the treaty countries fail to agree on these issues an international enterprise is likely to suffer unrelieved double taxation. In this situation the double taxation may be resolved as:

> OECD member countries consider that they are able to achieve that result either under their domestic law, through the interpretation of Articles 7 and 23 or under the mutual agreement procedure of Article 25 and, in particular, the possibility offered by that Article to resolve any issues concerning the application or interpretation of their tax treaties.[188]

The drafting of paragraph 48 of the 2008 Commentary is unclear and difficult to understand. The 2008 Commentary takes an approach on

---

[187] 2008 OECD Model, p. 131, para. 48; 2010 OECD Model, p. 167, para. 48.
[188] Ibid.

this highly contentious issue that creates uncertainty for international enterprises and tax authorities. Whenever a permanent establishment seeks a deduction for interest based on external funding obtained through another part of the enterprise, double taxation may arise. In most cases no one method will have accounting precision and be accepted by all countries, but a compromise method has the advantage of consistency to avoid double taxation. The tension within the OECD arises as OECD countries are either capital-exporting or capital-importing countries. Although tax treaties are reciprocal, countries are likely to use a method that gives them the best net result.

The Commentary was amended to specify that former Article 7(3) only deals with expenses that may be attributed to a permanent establishment for the purpose of determining the profits that are attributable to a permanent establishment.[189] But after expenses are attributed to a permanent establishment under this provision, the domestic law determines whether the expenses are deductible in determining a permanent establishment's taxable income in the host country. The host country's domestic law must comply with Article 24 which deals with non-discrimination. This provision prevents a country from using domestic law that discriminates against international enterprises resident in a home country.

6 Conclusion

Former Article 7 of the OECD Model is a significant provision because it allocates taxing rights over an international enterprise's business profits between a residence country and a host country. Under former Article 7, if an international enterprise has a permanent establishment in a host country, the host country has the right to tax the profits attributable to the permanent establishment. But, even though the history of former Article 7 dates back to the 1920s, its precise meaning and the interaction between the paragraphs of former Article 7 are uncertain and controversial. The ambiguities in former Article 7 are reflected in the pre-2008 Commentary, which fails to provide clear guidance on its interpretation. The net result of the uncertainties in former Article 7 is that it is not uniformly interpreted by the OECD countries, resulting in uncertainty for taxpayers and tax authorities alike.

---

[189] 2008 OECD Model, p. 126, para. 30; 2010 OECD Model, p. 163, para. 30.

6 CONCLUSION

The flaws in former Article 7 are the result of applying the arm's length principle to highly integrated international enterprises that operate as unitary businesses. There is no objective economic or accounting measure, using the arm's length principle, for allocating profits and expenses within an international enterprise operating through permanent establishments. International enterprises are by their nature unitary businesses with a common profit-maximizing purpose. Thus, the arm's length principle is inappropriate as a means of allocating profits to a permanent establishment that is part of a highly integrated international enterprise. The arm's length principle has a normative flaw in that it does not reflect operational or economic reality for international enterprises. This normative flaw leads to inconsistent interpretations of former Article 7. As former Article 7 concurrently applies the separate entity approach and the single entity approaches, this is likely to lead to double taxation or under-taxation.

7

Intra-bank loans under the pre-2008 Commentary and 1984 Report

1 Introduction

Globalization has led to international banks operating through foreign branches, significantly expanding the scope and scale of operations of such banks. Since the 1990s, most developed countries allow international banks to operate through branches rather than requiring them to establish locally incorporated subsidiaries. But it is a challenging task for an international bank to attribute business profits to its branches for tax treaty purposes. A key factor in determining the business profits of a branch of an international bank is the deductibility of interest on intra-bank loans, which are a major source of funds for branches of international banks. Former Article 7 (Article 7 of the 2005 OECD Model and Commentary (pre-2008 Commentary)) and pre-2008 Commentary contain principles on the deductibility of interest on intra-bank loans. In 1984 the OECD published *Transfer Pricing and Multinational Enterprise (Three Taxation Issues)*[1] (1984 Report) which deals, inter alia, with the allocation of business profits[2] on intra-bank loans to branches of international banks. Together, the views expressed in the pre-2008 Commentary on former Article 7[3] and the 1984 Report represent the OECD principles on the allocation of business profits on intra-bank loans to branches for most treaties completed before July 2008.

The OECD has recognized the need to revise the international tax principles for determining the business profits of branches of international banks and other permanent establishments under former Article 7. In 2001, the OECD released a *Discussion Draft on the Attribution of Profits to Permanent Establishments*[4] (2001 Discussion Draft)

---

[1] OECD, *Transfer Pricing and Multinational Enterprises (Three Taxation Issues)* (1984).
[2] The term profits used in this Article includes expenses.
[3] 2005 OECD Model.
[4] OECD, *Discussion Draft on the Attribution of Profits to Permanent Establishments* (2001).

containing proposals for attributing profits to a permanent establishment under former Article 7 of the OECD Model. The objective of the proposals was to establish a consensus interpretation of former Article 7. The 2001 Discussion Draft contained two parts, Part I setting out the proposed measures and Part II applying them to branches of international banks. In 2003 the OECD released a revised Part II of the Discussion Draft[5] (2003 Discussion Draft).[6] The proposals in Part II of the 2003 Discussion Draft were designed to replace the 1984 Report. A feature of the proposals is to treat a branch of an international bank as a distinct and separate bank. In 2008, the OECD published the 2008 Report and the 2008 OECD Model with a revised Commentary on former Article 7 (2008 Commentary). The 2008 Commentary incorporated part of the 2008 Report. Part II of the 2008 Report (Special Considerations for Applying the Authorized OECD Approach to Permanent Establishments of Banks) replaces the 1984 Report and was incorporated in the 2008 Commentary. But the 1984 Report may be used for the numerous tax treaties which were concluded before 22 July 2008. Although some countries may seek to apply the 2008 Commentary to treaties concluded before 22 July 2008, other countries may not take that approach, as the changes to the 2008 Commentary were significant and it would be inappropriate to apply these changes to treaties concluded before 22 July 2008. As some tax treaties concluded before 22 July 2008 were negotiated in anticipation of the 2008 Report, it may be appropriate to use Part II of the 2008 Report in applying former Article 7 and the 2008 Commentary to branches of international banks.[7]

This chapter critically examines the OECD principles in the pre-2008 Commentary on former Article 7 and the 1984 Report on the deductibility of interest under intra-bank loans. The chapter suggests that these OECD rules are flawed in theory and in practice. The arm's length principle, on which the rules rely, is ineffective for allocating profits within international banks because treating branches of international banks as separate entities ignores economic reality. A branch of an international bank is part of a highly integrated business, and it is unrealistic to treat a branch as a separate entity. A significant deficiency

---

[5] OECD, *Discussion Draft on the Attribution of Profits to Permanent Establishments: Part II (Banks)* (2003).
[6] In 2004 the OECD issued a revised Part I (General) of the Discussion Draft (2004 Discussion Draft).
[7] For example, the 2001 US–UK treaty and the 2003 US–Japan treaty: 'Treasury Releases Statement on PE Attribution of Profits' (7 June 2007).

of the rules is the failure within the OECD to develop a consensus on the interpretation and application of former Article 7 of the OECD Model to branches of international banks because of the dissent by two major OECD countries, the US and Japan. The dissent by the former is significant in particular because most international banks have branches in the US. The conflicting interpretations stem from the use by the majority of the OECD countries of the separate entity approach, while the minority countries, the US and Japan, used the single entity approach in attributing profits to bank branches. Despite the significant differences between the majority and minority countries, they both assert that their approach conforms with the arm's length principle.

The chapter first examines the problem of allocating profits on intra-bank loans to branches in accordance with the arm's length principle. This is followed by a consideration of three key issues in resolving the main question of whether interest on intra-bank loans is deductible. The first issue is whether the interest expense on intra-bank loans is recognized for tax purposes, and the second issue is whether an international bank can impose a profit margin on notional intra-bank loans. The third issue relates to determining the equity capital of a branch to ensure that interest is not charged on it.

2 The problem of allocating profits to branches of international banks

In the 1984 Report the OECD highlighted the problem of allocating profits on notional intra-bank transactions to a branch which is part of a highly integrated international bank:

> [T]he transactions between the various parts of an international banking organisation are so frequent and so complex that the problem of deciding to which particular part of the organisation any particular element of the total profit should be related for tax purposes often becomes one of considerable difficulty.[8]

International banks operating through branches can be expected to organize their business operations to maximize their total after-tax profits. This aim may be achieved by international banks allocating their expenses to branches in lower-tax countries and their revenues to branches in lower-tax countries through transfer pricing manipulation. Transfer pricing manipulation allows an international bank to engage in

---

[8] 1984 Report, p. 51, para. 32.

cross-border arbitrage to manipulate the differences between the tax rules of two or more countries with the objective of tax avoidance. International banks may structure notional intra-bank transactions to exploit the differences or inconsistencies in tax rules to either substantially reduce or eliminate taxation. International banks, as part of their tax minimization aims, may also allocate profits to certain branches to ensure that tax benefits, such as losses which can be carried forward, are used. Some international banks may use transfer pricing to prevent the double taxation arising from the inconsistent interpretation of treaty provisions by the contracting countries. Thus, in dealing with the problem of allocating profits and expenses between the jurisdictions in which an international bank operates, the tax authorities in those jurisdictions cannot rely on the bank's cooperation and voluntary compliance with their respective rules.[9]

The methods used in tax treaties for allocating profits within international banks must be established by clear and objective rules that are applied consistently and symmetrically within the tax treaty network. The methods should be based on sound theory, reflect economic reality, be simple, and minimize the accompanying compliance and administrative costs. The critical requirement in interpreting tax treaties is that their provisions be interpreted consistently. If treaty provisions are interpreted inconsistently as between jurisdictions, international banks will use transfer pricing to exploit the different interpretations. A consensus interpretation of a treaty provision by the OECD countries which is applied consistently by treaty countries, even if the interpretation is not based on a sound theoretical foundation, will minimize the potential for double taxation or under-taxation. While such a method may make certain jurisdictions winners and others losers, it would be an effective profit allocation method if it were simple and uniformly applied by jurisdictions.

The OECD principles in the pre-2008 Commentary for attributing profits to bank branches are based on the arm's length principle, but the principle is difficult to apply to notional intra-bank transactions. The main advantage of the arm's length principle is that it is the accepted international norm. If the arm's length norm is consistently interpreted and applied by treaty countries, double taxation and under-taxation should be minimized. In theory, application of the arm's length principle

---

[9] Bird and Brean, 'The Interjurisdictional Allocation of Income and the Unitary Taxation Debate' (1986), p. 1383.

should be neutral in allocating profits to branches of international banks, but the arm's length principle is not uniformly applied by the OECD countries. For example, when attributing interest expenses to branches of international banks some countries under former Article 7 of the pre-2008 Commentary use the separate entity method, while other countries apply the single entity method. The inconsistent interpretation of former Article 7 by the OECD countries creates the potential for double taxation or under-taxation.

The notion of precision suggested by the arm's length principle is a fallacy, as arm's length pricing usually comprises a wide range of prices. Moreover, the arm's length principle is an arbitrary method for allocating profits and costs in the joint business and marketing processes of international banks operating through branches because the banks function as integrated businesses.[10] Applying the arm's length principle in the allocation of profits attempts to separate the inseparable because it ignores the internationalization benefits banks gain from vertical and horizontal integration.[11] A key problem in applying the arm's length principle to allocating profits within international banks is that it focuses on notional transactions which are merely transfers of funds within a bank. Thus, the arm's length principle ignores the economic reality of the way in which international banks operate.

The 1984 Report considered the problems of applying the arm's length principle to intra-bank loans under former Article 7 of the OECD Model. The OECD stated in the 2001 Discussion Draft and the 2003 Discussion Draft that the starting point for analysis of this issue is the 1984 Report,[12] which provided principles for interest on intra-bank loans involving branches of international banks, and on the equity capital attributable to them.[13] The 1984 Report was published to supplement the 1979 Report entitled *Transfer Pricing and Multinational Enterprises*[14] (1979 OECD Report) because it did not deal with intra-bank loans. Although the 1984 Report provided the principles on the deductibility of intra-bank interest for branches of international banks under tax

---

[10] Bird, 'The Interjurisdictional Allocation of Income' (1986), p. 333.
[11] Eden, *Taxing Multinationals* (1998), p. 565.
[12] OECD, *Discussion Draft on the Attribution of Profits to Permanent Establishments* (2001), p. 42, Part II, para. 1; OECD, *Discussion Draft on the Attribution of Profits to Permanent Establishments: Part II (Banks)* (2003), p. 42, Part II, para. 3.
[13] 1984 Report, p. 55, para. 40. The 1984 Report also deals with the effect of transfers of business from one part of an enterprise to another, and the application of interest withholding taxes to notional interest on intra-bank loans.
[14] OECD, *Transfer Pricing and Multinational Enterprises* (1979).

treaties, there is a dearth of analytical material on the 1984 Report.[15] The 1979 Report was superseded by the 1995 OECD publication of the Transfer Pricing Guidelines.[16] In the 1994 draft version of the Transfer Pricing Guidelines, the OECD claimed that the proposed Transfer Pricing Guidelines would amalgamate the 1979 Report and the 1984 Report.[17] Moreover, the OECD announced its intention to include the attribution of profits of permanent establishments under the arm's length principle in the Transfer Pricing Guidelines at a later date, but this was not done.[18] The curious outcome was that the 1984 Report remained current until the 2008 Commentary was published in July 2008, but the report which the 1984 Report was designed to supplement had been replaced in 1995. This reflects the difficulties the OECD encountered in establishing a consensus interpretation of former Article 7 of the OECD Model prior to the publication of the 2008 Report and 2008 OECD Model.

3 The deductibility of notional interest paid on intra-bank loans: the special considerations

A significant factor in determining the business profits of a branch of an international bank is the treatment of interest on intra-bank loans. The following statement in the pre-2008 Commentary that accepts the principles in the 1984 Report on the deductibility of interest on intra-bank loans effectively incorporates that part of the 1984 Report into the pre-2008 Commentary. On the question of whether the interest paid by branches on intra-bank loans should be deductible, the pre-2008 Commentary on former Article 7 stated that special considerations apply to notional payments of interest within an international bank:

> It is, however, recognised that special considerations apply to payments of interest made by different parts of a financial enterprise (e.g. a bank) to each other on advances etc. (as distinct from capital allotted to them), in view of the fact that making and receiving advances is closely related to the ordinary business of such enterprises. This problem, as well as other problems relating to the transfer of financial assets, are considered in the report on multinational banking enterprises included in the OECD 1984

---

[15] The 1984 Report was studied in Burgers, *Taxation and Supervision of Bank Branches* (1992), Ch. 19.
[16] 1995 Transfer Pricing Guidelines (loose-leaf), p. 16.
[17] OECD, *Transfer Pricing Guidelines for Multinational Enterprises and Tax Administrations, Discussion Draft of Part I* (1994), p. 5.
[18] *Ibid.*, p. 16, para. 16.

publication entitled *Transfer Pricing and Multinational Enterprises – Three Taxation Studies*. This Commentary does not depart from the positions expressed in the report on this topic.[19]

But the pre-2008 Commentary and the 1984 Report provide limited direction on the application of former Article 7 to branches of international banks. The 1984 Report contains a brief outline of former Article 7, but it does not provide details on the scope of this provision in allocating business profits to branches of international banks.[20] The pre-2008 Commentary on former Article 7 directs that 'real facts' should be the starting point for allocating profits to branches of international banks, but does not provide further detail on what the real facts might be. The 1984 Report failed to provide guidance on how to identify the 'real facts' for branches of international banks.[21] This failure to specify clear rules, including those for identifying the real facts for a branch, results in tax authorities using a case-by-case approach which is inherently arbitrary and inconsistent.[22]

In the 1984 Report the OECD countries failed to establish a consensus interpretation on the treatment of interest on intra-bank loans; this has resulted in uncertainty and created the potential for double taxation or under-taxation. A majority of the OECD countries applied the separate entity principle and these countries conclude that, under former Article 7(3) of the OECD Model, interest on intra-bank loans, including a profit margin, should be recognized for tax purposes. This approach allows international banks a margin for profit on intra-bank loans. In contrast, a minority of the OECD countries – the US and Japan – applied the single entity method; they asserted that loan funds allocated to a branch by another part of the international bank must be provided at cost. Under the minority approach, the profit margin imposed by an international bank on interest on loan funds allocated to a branch is not recognized for tax purposes. This approach reflects economic reality that a branch and the rest of the bank are parts of a unitary enterprise. The shortcoming of this approach is that it allocates the entire profit on funds raised by one branch and lent to a customer by another branch, to the branch lending the funds to the customer. Thus, the main difference between the majority and minority approaches is the recognition of profit margins on intra-bank loans.

---

[19] 2005 OECD Model, p. 125, para. 19.
[20] Burgers, *Taxation and Supervision of Bank Branches* (1992), p. 454. [21] *Ibid.*, p. 455.
[22] Wickham and Kerester, 'Tax Policy Forum' (1992), p. 405.

3 THE DEDUCTIBILITY OF NOTIONAL INTEREST 245

3.1 The majority view: the separate entity approach

The majority view was that intra-bank loans are recognized for tax purposes in order to determine the arm's length profits of a branch. The 1984 Report stated the majority view:

> It is, in the view of the majority of OECD Member countries, necessary to take account of intra-bank payments of interest in ascertaining the arm's-length profits of a branch of a bank, in order to ensure that the taxation of the profits of the foreign bank branch is consistent, in principle, with the taxation of the operating profit of branches of other enterprises (see, however, paragraph 52 [minority approach]).[23]

The OECD asserted that the special considerations for recognizing intra-bank loans are twofold. The first reason is that former Article 7 requires the profits of a branch of an enterprise to be ascertained as if the branch were an independent and separate enterprise in its dealings with the other parts of the enterprise. An essential part of carrying on a banking business is to receive interest from, and pay interest to, customers. Consequently, the majority contended that under former Article 7 intra-bank interest payments are taken into account in determining the profits allocated to a branch of an international bank. This approach was confirmed by the amendment to the Commentary in 1994, which stated that, for an intra-entity transaction to be recognized, it must be of the same kind as transactions which were entered into in the normal course of carrying on business.[24]

The second reason for taking intra-bank interest into account relates to the very nature of the banking business. An essential feature of banking is the borrowing of funds from independent lenders in order to derive a profit margin by making loans to customers. Consequently, the 1984 Report asserted that:

> In the case of banks, however, since it is the main business of a bank to borrow money outside the enterprise for the purpose of lending it outside the enterprise there is every reason to suppose that by far the greater part of money lent by [the] head office to a branch and vice versa and money lent by one branch to another will in fact have been borrowed at some stage from an independent third party and will be lent eventually to independent third parties. Thus, the interest taken into account can be regarded as representing real outgoings or receipts of the enterprise as a whole and from the pragmatic point of view, to take account in this context of all intra-bank interest payments (except those directly related

---

[23] 1984 Report, p. 57, para. 47.   [24] 2005 OECD Model, p. 122, para. 17.1.

to the provision of capital . . .) produces a result consistent with that spelled out in the Commentary on Article 7 in the case of enterprises not carrying on the business of borrowing and lending money. These are the 'special circumstances' related to banking activities . . .[25]

These two reasons, although purported by the OECD to explain the 'special circumstances' of banks, do not explain their special circumstances.[26] In the above quote, the OECD merely applied the rule in former Article 7(3) that a branch is entitled to claim deductions for expenses incurred by an enterprise with independent enterprises, on behalf of the branch. The assumption in the 1984 Report is that, in the case of a bank branch, any interest expenses attributable to a branch reflect the interest actually paid to independent lenders by the bank.[27] But this assumption is flawed because international banks, in order to minimize the business profits that may be allocated to certain branches, will usually assert, especially in higher-tax countries, that their branches are funded exclusively with debt capital. For example, in the UK prior to 2003, UK branches of international banks were allowed to assert, and did assert, that they had little or no equity capital. This allowed UK bank branches to be treated as borrowing every pound lent to a customer.[28] To counter this form of avoidance, the UK introduced measures in 2003 requiring permanent establishments to have equity capital. Thus, the presumption that interest expenses attributable to a branch represent real outgoings to independent lenders is unfounded. Moreover, this presumption is artificial because, in a highly integrated international bank, it would be impossible to trace borrowing expenses in order to ascertain if intra-entity loans reflect interest paid to external lenders.

In the 2001 Discussion Draft, the OECD acknowledged its failure to identify what special considerations should apply to international banks:

> However, currently there is not a general consensus as to what special considerations should apply to financial enterprises. Some Member countries directly take into account internal interest payments at arm's-length prices. Others will only apportion a fraction of the actual interest paid by the enterprise as a whole.[29]

---

[25] 1984 Report, p. 57, para. 49.
[26] Burgers, *Taxation and Supervision of Bank Branches* (1992), p. 456. [27] Ibid.
[28] UK Inland Revenue, Budget 2002, REV BN 25, 'Taxation of UK Branches of Foreign Companies', 17 April 2002.
[29] 2001 Discussion Draft, p. 31, para. 130.

The statement in the 1984 Report that intra-bank interest reflects the interest paid by an international bank to independent lenders suggests that an international bank is not entitled to make a profit on intra-entity loans.[30] Despite the implication that intra-bank interest must represent only the external cost of funds provided to a branch, the majority approach is that it is appropriate for an international bank to recognize arm's length profits on intra-bank loans.[31] The rationale for allowing an international bank to make a profit on intra-bank loans is to ensure that the profit on loans with customers is properly allocated within the bank to reflect the roles of the various parts of the bank in the process of making the profit. If a branch were able to deduct only the external interest cost on intra-bank loans, this would result in the entire profit on the loans with customers being allocated to the branch. In this situation, no profit would be allocated to the other parts of the bank which raised the funds that were provided to the branch to lend to customers. Unsurprisingly, an independent bank would not lend funds at cost in normal circumstances. Thus, the profit on intra-bank loans must be shared between those parts of the bank which obtained the funds and the branch which lent the funds to a customer. But recognizing that branches of international banks are part of a highly integrated business, and given the scale and complexity of transactions and the fungibility of funds, there is no method of allocating profits to branches which objectively reflects economic activity.

One example in the 1984 Report illustrates that the notional interest paid by a branch of an international bank to its head office allows the head office to make a profit on the transaction if the transaction reflects arm's length rates. The 1984 Report contended that, if a branch's intra-bank loans are treated as being at arm's length rates, the head office will usually be able to make a profit on the transaction. The 1984 Report claimed that:

> The deduction of interest expense calculated by reference to the arm's-length rate of interest for such a loan as if the branch and the head office were independent enterprises would, of itself, produce a figure of profit or loss attributable on the arm's-length basis to the branch, leaving to the head office, where appropriate, its own arm's-length element of the total profit or loss.[32]

This direction is supplemented with an example to further illustrate the point. In the example, if the branch of an international bank borrows

---

[30] 1984 Report, p. 57, para. 49.   [31] Ibid., p. 57, para. 50.   [32] Ibid.

from arm's length sources at a rate of 10 per cent and lends the funds to its head office at an arm's length rate of 11 per cent, the branch is operating as if it were an independent entity. If the head office lends the funds to an independent borrower at a 12 per cent rate of interest, the net profit of the bank as a whole is 2 per cent, less other expenses. In this situation, a 1 per cent profit margin is properly attributed to the branch in accordance with the arm's length principle. The illustration also clearly allows the branch of an international bank to make an arm's length profit on intra-bank loans. There would be a symmetrical result if the original borrower was the head office and the funds were lent to its branch. Thus, the majority of OECD countries recognize the interest paid on intra-bank loans, provided the interest rate is an arm's length rate of interest. Intrinsic to this rationale is the question: what is an arm's length rate of interest?

3.2 The meaning of arm's length rate of interest

The majority view advocates that arm's length interest rates be used for notional intra-bank loans in order to ensure that the profit allocation on such loans corresponds to the role played by each part of the bank in any given notional loan. The arm's length principle is used to ensure that the interest on intra-bank transactions reflects the market rates of interest by comparing them to the interest rates applying between unrelated banks. But is this an effective method of allocating profits on intra-bank loans within an international bank? The deficiency of the arm's length principle is that in practice it is a complex task, whether for international banks or tax authorities, to scrutinize the interest on intra-bank loans to ensure that the interest on these loans conforms with arm's length rates.[33] The need to examine the interest on intra-bank loans leads to significant compliance costs because of the vast range of intra-bank loans. It is also costly for tax authorities to examine the interest rates to determine if they reflect the arm's length rates generally charged in a market.[34] Moreover, there is no single arm's length interest rate, but rather a range of rates reflecting a variety of transactions between independent entities.[35] The net result is enforcement action that is often unpredictable and based on guesswork.[36]

---

[33] US General Accounting Office, *International Taxation* (1992), pp. 60–1.
[34] US General Accounting Office, *IRS Could Better Protect US Tax Interests in Determining the Income of Multinational Corporations* (1981), pp. 36–40.
[35] Ibid., p. ii. [36] Ibid., p. 43.

The 1984 Report stipulated guidelines on arm's length interest rates for subsidiaries and branches.[37] The appropriate arm's length rate of interest for a loan between associated banking enterprises was described as 'the rate that would be charged in similar circumstances in a transaction between unrelated parties'.[38] The interest rates for inter-bank financial markets provide comparative rates to determine if the interest rates on intra-bank loans reflect transactions between independent banks. Inter-bank deposit rates, such as LIBOR,[39] are published each business day. The 1984 Report noted that the interest rate on an inter-bank loan may differ from the published daily rate, and the OECD accepts that the rates may deviate significantly:

> It should be recognised, however, that the effective rate applied in any individual transaction may diverge somewhat from the rate quoted publicly. Euro-currency rates may vary sharply during a day, as money market rates may do generally in all countries.[40]

This conclusion by the OECD reflects business reality, as publicly quoted interest rates are averages which are drawn from all the rates used between the upper and lower extremes of the range. Thus, the relevant arm's length measure to be applied to test the interest on intra-bank loans is not a single rate, but rather a range of rates that may vary significantly from the published daily rates. The range of rates that will meet the arm's length requirement creates the potential for double taxation and provides scope for transfer pricing manipulation by international banks.

The potential for double taxation arises because two countries may apply different arm's length rates to an intra-bank transaction. For example, if a branch in country A of an international bank lends funds to its head office in country B at a non-arm's length rate of interest, the countries are entitled to adjust the notional interest rate. Country A may assert that the appropriate rate for the transaction is LIBOR plus 25 basis points, but country B may decide that the appropriate rate is LIBOR less 5 basis points. If it can be assumed that both rates reflect arm's length rates in the market, this means that the branch in country A is treated as

---

[37] 1984 Report, p. 64, para. 72.   [38] *Ibid.*, pp. 52–3, para. 35.
[39] LIBOR means London Inter-Bank Offer Rate and is the rate of interest at which banks borrow funds from other banks, in marketable size, in the London inter-bank market. It is an average of rates submitted by banks for transactions that broadly reflect transactions in the inter-bank deposit market.
[40] 1984 Report, p. 53, para. 36.

receiving LIBOR plus 25 basis points, but the head office in country B is allowed a deduction for only LIBOR less 5 basis points. Thus, while both countries have applied arm's length rates to the same loan, their failure to agree on a single rate results in double taxation as there is an over-attribution of profits to the branch in country A. A survey of transfer pricing reported that many taxpayers contend that transfer pricing adjustments often result in double taxation.[41]

The variations in interest rates used in the published daily rates provide international banks with a limited ability to engage in transfer pricing manipulation, as long as they do not exceed the range of rates used in an established inter-bank financial market.[42] Given the volume of funds flowing into and out of branches of international banks, a minor change in the interest rate on intra-bank loans can have significant consequences for the profit allocation within a bank. For example, if a bank lends funds to a branch at the lower end of the range, the bank is shifting profits to the branch. If a bank lends funds to a branch at the upper end of the range, the bank is able to minimize the profit allocated to the branch. A major problem with determining arm's length interest rates is finding comparative rates because, for many transactions, comparative rates are unavailable.[43] While comparative interest rates are available for short-term loans, such rates are more difficult to find for long-term loans. Using long-term intra-bank loans is another means by which a bank can move profits into or out of a particular branch. Attempts to find comparative rates often involve significant compliance costs for taxpayers and administrative costs for tax authorities.[44] This can lead to tax authority officials constructing a price that is a mere estimate.[45]

Because of the large number of notional intra-bank loans, a tax authority has great difficulty in identifying questionable loans.[46] As intra-bank loans can be altered or terminated by an international bank without documentation, only limited information on them is available to a tax authority, thus making the tax authority's enforcement task

---

[41] Ernst & Young, 'Transfer Pricing 1999 Global Survey: Practices, Perceptions, and Trends for 2000 and Beyond' (1999), p. 1910. In the survey, of those reporting transfer pricing adjustments, 42 per cent claimed that the adjustments resulted in double taxation.
[42] Langbein, 'The Unitary Method and the Myth of Arm's Length' (1986), p. 658.
[43] Avi-Yonah, 'The Structure of International Taxation' (1996), pp. 1342–3; Eden, *Taxing Multinationals* (1998), p. 566.
[44] US General Accounting Office, *IRS Could Better Protect US Tax Interests in Determining the Income of Multinational Corporations* (1981), p. v.
[45] Ibid. [46] Ibid., p. 36.

exceptionally difficult. In conclusion, intra-bank loans are fictional. An international bank may set interest rates on intra-bank loans which comply with the arm's length principle, but provide the bank with scope to shift profits from branches in higher-tax countries to branches in lower-tax countries. If an international bank uses non-arm's length rates on intra-bank loans to shift profits, the administrative task for a tax authority to identify and adjust the rates is difficult, complex and costly.

In summary, the majority of the OECD countries contend that, in the case of intra-bank loans, a bank is expected to charge arm's length interest rates using the separate entity approach of treating each branch as a separate business. The arm's length interest charge on intra-bank loans should, according to the arm's length principle, reflect the cost of the funds and a profit margin for the notional lender. If the notional lender is a branch, it will be assessable on its share of the profits. If the notional lender is the head office, the branch is entitled to claim a deduction for the interest on its intra-bank loans. The underlying principle is that, if arm's length interest rates are charged, the profits on loans by international banks to customers will be properly and separately allocated to each branch and head office. But the arm's length principle does not reflect economic reality in the allocation of profits within an international bank.[47] An international bank does not function as a collection of separate entities operating at arm's length because in a globalized economy an international bank is a highly integrated business under unitary control.[48] Advanced information and communications technologies allow the management of an international bank to stay abreast of major issues in all parts of the bank. A branch of an international bank is not a separate and autonomous profit centre. Moreover, an arm's length interest rate is not a single rate but represents a range of rates; within this range, an international bank can set interest rates to shift profits to branches in lower-tax countries and minimize the profits allocated to branches in higher-tax countries. A further disincentive to use the arm's length principle is that it is based on a transactional approach involving high compliance and administrative costs.

---

[47] US General Accounting Office, *International Taxation: Problems Persist in Determining Tax Effects of Intercompany Prices* (1992), pp. 61–2.
[48] US General Accounting Office, *IRS Could Better Protect US Tax Interests in Determining the Income of Multinational Corporations* (1981), p. 45.

3.3 Dissenting view of the US and Japan: the single entity approach

The US and Japan, in the minority, were of the view that the majority approach, in relying on the notion of separate entity, went too far and did not reflect paragraph 17 of the pre-2008 Commentary on former Article 7.[49] They asserted that paragraph 17 does not indicate which operative rule should flow from the 'special considerations'. Further, in 'the view of Japan and the United States there is no basis for requiring that intra-bank interest should be taken into account'.[50] The US and Japan concluded that paragraph 19 of the pre-2008 Commentary merely permits, but does not require, intra-bank interest payments to be taken into account.[51] The US and Japan argued that their approach also conforms to the arm's length principle. The 1984 Report mentioned that both the US and Japan 'provide for a deduction for interest paid when the profits of a branch of a foreign bank are being computed for tax purposes'.[52] The view of the US and Japan in the 1984 Report differs from the view of the other OECD countries on the issue of what payments form the basis for calculating a deduction.

The dissent of the US and Japan in the 1984 Report impeded the development of a consensus interpretation on the deductibility of interest on intra-bank loans. These countries use the single entity approach in asserting that intra-bank loans do not have to be recognized under former Article 7. Under the single entity approach, only the cost of funds provided by an international bank to its branch can be deducted by the branch which prevents the part of a bank that raises funds which a branch then lends to customers from being rewarded for its role. The statement that paragraph 17 of the pre-2008 Commentary permits, but does not require, intra-bank interest to be recognized for tax purposes creates uncertainty on when intra-bank interest is recognized. The minority approach is that the recognition of intra-bank interest is discretionary, creating significant uncertainty for both taxpayers and tax authorities. In conclusion, the majority and minority approaches illustrate the competing approaches that are purported to conform with the arm's length principle. The different approaches stem from the difficulties of applying the arm's length principle in practice to

---

[49] 1984 Report, p. 58, para. 52. [50] *Ibid.*
[51] Para. 19 of the Commentary on Article 7 in 2005 was para. 17 of the Commentary on Article 7 in the 1997 OECD Model which was the model in force in 1984.
[52] *Ibid.*

allocate the profits on intra-bank loans, and may result in double taxation or under-taxation.

3.4 Application of former Article 7 in the US: the National Westminster Bank case

The US has not consistently advocated the single entity approach as expressed in the 1984 Report for notional intra-entity transactions. The switch in views was illustrated in the case of *National Westminster Bank PLC v. United States*,[53] (NatWest I).[54] The US Federal Claims Court in NatWest I applied the separate entity method under Article 7 of the 1980 US–UK tax treaty (1980 US–UK treaty) and concluded that interest on notional intra-bank loans was deductible.[55] This approach is at odds with the views of the US expressed in the 1984 Report, but the 1984 Report was not considered as an interpretive aid in NatWest I. It appears that, until the late 1970s, the US Treasury asserted that Articles 7(2) and (3) applied the separate entity approach and this permitted notional intra-entity transactions to be recognized for tax purposes. The extraneous OECD material used as an interpretive aid in NatWest I was the 1963 OECD Model and Commentary,[56] which was the version applicable at the time the 1980 US–UK treaty was concluded; a new US–UK treaty entered into force on 31 March 2003. NatWest I nevertheless provides case law on the deductibility of interest on intra-bank loans under Article 7 of the terminated 1980 US–UK treaty. It also illustrates that the US had changed its interpretation of former Article 7 in the 1984 Report from a separate entity approach to the single entity approach.

The taxpayer in NatWest I was National Westminster Bank (NatWest), an international bank engaged in a range of banking, financial and related activities throughout the world. NatWest conducted its banking business in the US through a branch supported by NatWest's worldwide capital. The US branch obtained its funds from its head office in the UK or from other branches of NatWest. Regarding intra-bank loans obtained by the US branch from its head office, notional interest was charged as if

---

[53] 44 Fed. Cl. 120 (1999); 1999 U.S. Claims LEXIS 154; 99-2 Tax Cas. (CCH) P50, 654; 84 A.F.T.R.2d (RIA) 5086.
[54] The NatWest judgments are also considered in Chs. 5 and 6.
[55] Convention Between the Government of the United States of America and the Government of the United Kingdom of Great Britain and Northern Ireland for the Avoidance of Double Taxation and the Prevention of Fiscal Evasion with Respect to Taxes on Income and Capital Gains (entered into force in April 1980) 31 UST 5668 TIAS No. 9682.
[56] 1963 Draft OECD Convention.

the US branch were a separate entity. The US branch's accounts recorded the interest it paid to the other parts of the bank on intra-bank loans and the interest it received from the other parts of the bank. The US branch claimed a deduction for interest on intra-bank loans. On audit, the US Internal Revenue Service disallowed part of the interest expense for notional intra-bank loans, and contended that the branch's interest deduction had to be determined under US Treasury Regulation § 1.882-5 (1980).

NatWest argued successfully that the application of Treasury Regulation § 1.882-5 conflicts with the separate entity requirement in Article 7 of the 1980 US–UK treaty. Both parties agreed that a branch must be treated for tax purposes as if it were a separate entity, but they disagreed on whether, in calculating the profits attributable to the US branch, they should include the interest paid on notional intra-bank loans. Turner J characterized Treasury Regulation § 1.882-5 as applying a formulary method for interest allocation:

> In practical terms, the precise, narrow issue for resolution at this juncture in the proceedings is whether, in the determination of the interest expense deduction for the US Branch, the interest expense reflected in its books of account – with appropriate adjustments, if necessary, to reflect imputation of adequate capital and arm's-length, market interest rates in intra-corporate 'borrowing' transactions – may be used in calculating plaintiff's US tax liability, or whether, with respect to interest expense, the defendant may require use of a formulary approach, such as that in *Treas. Reg* § *1.882-5*, which disregards intra-corporate 'lending' transactions reflected in the books of account.[57]

Turner J examined Article 7 of the 1980 US–UK treaty in light of Article 7 of the 1963 OECD Model.[58] The judge concluded that the Commentary and the Articles of the OECD Model applicable in 1975 (when the 1980 US–UK treaty was negotiated) are presumed to have been in the minds of the negotiators when they drafted the treaty; consequently, the 1963 OECD Model and Commentary are persuasive in resolving disputed interpretations.[59] The judge made the following conclusions on Article 7 of the 1980 US–UK treaty:

> The face of Article 7, then, would appear to provide in the context of this case that, to determine [the] taxable income of the US Branch, the US Branch is to be regarded as an independent, separate entity dealing at

---

[57] 44 Fed. Cl. 120 (1999), p. 123. [58] 1963 Draft OECD Convention.
[59] 44 Fed. Cl. 120 (1999), p. 125.

arm's length with other units of NatWest as if they were wholly unrelated, except that the US Branch may deduct, in addition to its 'own' expenses, a reasonable allocation of home office expense. Words such as 'distinct' and 'separate' and the phrase 'dealing *wholly* independently' (emphasis added) would appear to permit no other interpretation.

Contemporaneous commentaries and reports generally support this interpretation.[60]

The US approach expressed in the 1984 Report is a single entity approach to intra-bank loans for purposes of former Article 7(3). But the US Treasury report on Article 7(3) of the 1980 US–UK treaty clearly supported the separate entity approach.[61] The judge concluded, on the basis of the US Treasury report, that Article 7(3) supported the separate entity approach:

With respect to paragraph 3 of Article 7, the Treasury report said: 'Expenses, wherever incurred, which are reasonably connected with profits attributable to the permanent establishment, . . . will be allowed as deductions in determining the business profits of the permanent establishment.'

The Report of the Senate Committee on Foreign Relations, dated April 25, 1978, concerning its consideration and favorable recommendation of the Treaty, in explanation of Article 7 stated:

'The profits of a permanent establishment are to be determined on an arm's-length basis. Thus, there is to be attributed to it the... commercial profits which would reasonably be expected to have been derived by it *if it were an independent entity* engaged in the same or similar activities under the same or similar conditions and *dealing at arm's-length with the resident of which it is a permanent establishment*.'[62] (emphasis added)

The judge concluded that, on the basis of former Article 7 of the 1963 OECD Model and Commentary, Article 7 of the 1980 US–UK treaty prescribed the use of the separate entity method and that this requirement conflicted with Treasury Regulation § 1.882-5. Consequently, Article 7 prevailed over Treasury Regulation § 1.882-5 and allowed NatWest to claim a deduction for intra-bank interest.[63] On the issue of the separate entity method, Turner J stated:

---

[60] *Ibid.*, p. 124.
[61] Treasury Department Technical Explanation of the United States and United Kingdom Income Tax Treaty, March 9, 1977: cited in 44 Fed. Cl. 120 (1999), p. 124.
[62] 44 Fed. Cl. 120 (1999), p. 124.
[63] The parties agreed that in the case of inconsistency between Article 7 of the 1980 US–UK tax and Treasury Regulation § 1.882-5, the tax treaty prevails: *Ibid.*, p. 122.

> We find that rather than treating the US branch of foreign enterprises as separate entities, the regulation plainly treats each US branch as a unit of a worldwide enterprise and, thus, is inconsistent with the 'separate entity' provision of Article 7(2) of the Treaty.
>
> Stated broadly, Treas. Reg. § 1.882-5 is inconsistent with Article 7 of the Treaty for two reasons. First, the regulation, in the computation of the interest expense deduction, disregards all interbranch transactions, even for banking operations (although a portion of a US branch's interbranch borrowing will typically be restored in step three of the deduction calculation). Second, the regulation computes liabilities (in step two), and from that figure the ultimate interest deduction (in step three), on the basis of worldwide assets and worldwide liabilities of the entire foreign enterprise, rather than determining the interest deduction on the basis of the separate, independent operations of the US branch.
>
> ...
>
> In sum, insofar as the US branch of a banking corporation is concerned, Treas. Reg. § 1.882-5 is fundamentally incompatible with paragraphs 2 and 3 of Article 7 of the Treaty.[64]

On appeal, the US Court of Appeals, in NatWest (2008), affirmed the judgment of the Turner J in NatWest I.[65] The basis of the decision was that Article 7 of the 1980 US–UK treaty was based on the separate enterprise principle and that NatWest's US branch was entitled to deductions for intra-bank interest expenses.[66] The court concluded that Treasury Regulation § 1.882-5 was inconsistent with the 1980 US–UK treaty.

After the ruling in NatWest I that Treasury Regulation § 1.882-5 may not be used by the US government to calculate the interest deduction of NatWest's US branch, the issue in *National Westminster Bank PLC* v. *United States*[67] (NatWest II) was how to calculate a branch's deductible interest under Article 7 of the 1980 US–UK treaty. Firestone J held that the 1980 US–UK treaty required the government to use the properly maintained accounts of NatWest's US branch to determine its business profits under Article 7. Firestone J rejected the US government's contention that it could treat part of the branch's funding as notional equity capital. The judge stated that amounts could be treated as notional capital only if they were allotted to the branch. The judge rejected the US government's argument that the OECD's statements in the 1984 Report, the 2001 Discussion Draft and the 2003 Discussion Draft

---

[64] *Ibid.*, pp. 130–1.   [65] 512 F.3d 1347 (2008), p. 1349.   [66] *Ibid.*, p. 1359.
[67] 58 Fed. Cl. 491 (2003); 2003 U.S. Claims LEXIS 332; 2004-1 U.S. Tax Cas. (CCH) P50,105; 92 A.F.T.R.2d (RIA) 7013.

supported the government's position.[68] Freestone J found that, even though the 1984 Report was concluded after the 1980 US–UK treaty was ratified, it did not allow the government to attribute equity capital to a branch of an international bank:

> Thus, the 1984 Report does not suggest that the taxing authority can attribute a hypothetical amount of equity capital to the branch based on the amount of capital a separately-incorporated bank of the same size might hold. The 1984 Report states that the amount of equity capital attributed to a branch should equal the amount of equity capital it 'in fact' receives from the head office. Thus, the 1984 Report recognizes that the taxing authorities may review the books of the branch and disallow a deduction for interest on the amount of 'working capital' the branch receives . . . This does not, however, give the government the right to attribute to the branch equity capital infusions that it did not 'in fact' receive, as measured by the amount of equity capital a domestic bank of similar size might be expected to hold.[69]

In summary, the NatWest I case illustrates the US judicial interpretation that Article 7 of the 1980 US–UK treaty required the use of the separate entity approach. The court found that this interpretation was supported by the US Treasury report and the 1963 OECD Model and Commentary. Subsequently, the US interpretation set out in the 1984 Report was that former Article 7 required a single entity approach to interest on intra-bank loans. The court in NatWest I did not consider the 1984 Report because it did not form part of the 1963 Commentary. Nevertheless, the case highlights the conflict between the judicial interpretation and the views the US expressed in the 1984 Report. The US, in renegotiating its treaty with the UK, reverted to the separate entity approach. The exchange of notes on the application of Article 7 of the 2003 US–UK treaty includes a direction that Article 7 is to be interpreted in light of the Transfer Pricing Guidelines, which reflects the 2001 Discussion Draft.[70]

---

[68] Ibid., p. 499.   [69] Ibid., p. 501.

[70] The 2003 US–UK tax treaty *Exchanges of Notes*, in relation to Article 7 states that: 'it is understood that the OECD Transfer Pricing Guidelines will apply, by analogy, for the purposes of determining the profits attributable to a permanent establishment. Accordingly, any of the methods described therein – including profits methods – may be used to determine the income of a permanent establishment so long as those methods are applied in accordance with the Guidelines. In particular, in determining the amount of attributable profits, the permanent establishment shall be treated as having the same amount of capital that it would need to support its activities if it were a distinct and separate enterprise engaged in the same or similar activities. With respect to financial institutions other than insurance companies, a Contracting State may determine the

3.5 *The substantiation requirement: tracing intra-bank loans*

The next issue considered is the compliance requirements for determining the appropriate interest rate on intra-bank loans. The majority of the OECD countries accepts that intra-bank payments of interest should be considered in determining the business profits of a branch of an international bank.[71] One of the main deficiencies of the arm's length principle is the onerous and costly compliance requirements for taxpayers, and the administration requirements for tax authorities are also costly.[72] The arm's length principle directs that charges for intra-bank transactions conform with the kinds of charges for transactions between independent entities. The OECD claims that, in theory, this requires a branch to trace borrowed funds back to their source. But the OECD acknowledged that tracing funds might be difficult because of the complex nature of a branch's transactions; a branch might borrow funds from a diverse range of depositors and make loans out of a fungible pool of funds to borrowers. Imposing a tracing of funds requirement on intra-bank loans involves two deficiencies.

The most significant deficiency of this requirement is that money is fungible. Once funds are deposited with a branch of an international bank, they are merged with the other funds held by the bank. When the branch transfers funds to another branch, it is impossible to trace the funds back to their original source. Tracing funds in an international bank is as meaningless as attempting to trace the flow of water into a pond to a stream of water flowing out of the pond. Only in exceptional circumstances is it possible to trace the flow of funds in an international bank. For example, if a branch of an international bank has a customer seeking a US$100 million loan, the branch might seek the funds from its head office. Assuming that the head office has a customer seeking to make a deposit of the same amount, at the same time and for the same (loan) period, the international bank might seek to the pair the deposit and the loan. Such a coincidence of deposited funds and a loan, however, is likely to be rare, and the funds for the loan are typically supplied out of a general pool of deposits within the bank. The tracing of funds within an international bank is meaningless because of the fungibility of money.

---

amount of capital to be attributed to a permanent establishment by allocating the institution's total equity between its various offices on the basis of the proportion of the financial institution's risk-weighted assets attributable to each of them.'

[71] 1984 Report, pp. 58–9, para. 53.
[72] See Avi-Yonah, 'The Rise and Fall of Arm's Length: A Study in the Evolution of US International Taxation' (1995), p. 150.

The other deficiency of a tracing of funds requirement is that it does not reflect the business practices of international banks. In making loans, a branch or head office of an international bank will not consider the sources of funding, but rather the bank's overall cost of funds and funding profile (loan periods, currencies and associated hedges). International banks have separate groups responsible for obtaining funds from customers and making loans to them. The parts of a bank obtaining deposits from customers will seek to obtain funds at the lowest cost. The parts of a bank making loans to customers will seek to obtain the highest return on the funds. International banks will usually seek to balance their borrowing and lending books each day to ensure that they have adequate funds to operate and that they meet their prudential requirements. When an international bank has an imbalance, it will seek to remedy the situation. If an international bank has a surplus of funds, it will usually seek to lend the money out at discount rates. On the other hand, if an international bank has inadequate funds from which to make loans to its customers, the bank will usually seek to raise funds immediately, and it may be necessary to pay a premium for the funds. Thus, in an international bank the tracing of funds serves no business purpose, does not reflect business reality and involves significant compliance costs.

The difficulty of tracing debt capital within an international bank was recognized by the OECD, and simplification measures may be used to overcome the burdens and costs of a tracing requirement.[73] The OECD's acceptance of simplification measures illustrates the practical difficulty of applying the transactional approach to intra-bank loans, which is required by the arm's length principle. While the need for simplification is accepted, the 1984 Report also mentioned the need to look at the amount of interest paid on individual transactions. There appear to have been differences within the OECD majority on the trade-off between simplification and the requirement to look at individual transactions. Even in 1984, when the 1984 Report was being finalized, the tracing requirement would have been excessive, but today, given the current size and range of transactions in international banks, a tracing requirement is impossible. Such a requirement would result in excessive compliance costs for international banks; the administrative costs for a tax authority scrutinizing transactions would also be prohibitive. On the issue of tracing, the 1984 Report concluded:

[73] 1984 Report, pp. 58–59, para. 53.

> Thus, it may be convenient to look at groups or categories of transaction rather than at each separate transaction individually, and to use rates of interest perhaps derived from averages of rates paid in comparable market situations to unrelated parties. Though the difficulties cannot be ignored and the need for such expedients may be accepted, the majority of OECD Member countries are convinced that it does not follow that it is, in principle, permissible to ignore the actual payments of interest by the branch.[74]

It is not clear from this statement which payments of interest by a branch must be traced.[75] One construction is that it refers to all interest payments by a branch, and another is that it refers to interest payments by a branch to independent lenders. A third construction is that it might refer to notional interest payments on intra-bank loans. As the statement appears in the context of a discussion on tracing, the second construction appears to be the best. Nevertheless, the notion of requiring a branch to trace interest payments to independent lenders would be excessive and of questionable value. While a bank will rightly be concerned with its cost of funds, currency and loan profile, identifying the actual sources of its funds is meaningless.

Again, the OECD was unable to form a consensus interpretation on this issue. While the US and Japan take the view that the OECD Model does not allow for intra-bank interest payments to be included in determining the business profits of a bank branch, these countries allow a deduction for interest based on a strict tracing of funds.[76] The US and Japan require that the funds lent by an international bank to borrowers be traced within the bank back to their original depositors, the rationale being to prevent tax avoidance opportunities for international banks. As argued above, the tracing requirement is impossible given the large number of deposit and loan transactions of international banks.

Despite Japan's theoretical adherence to a strict tracing approach, it accepted that a strict application of this method was impossible.[77] To overcome this problem, a branch of an international bank in Japan is allowed to estimate the cost of funds it has used. According to the 1984 Report:

> The interest cost is measured by the amount incurred to the third party provider of the funds only when the source of the funds can be traced and is demonstrable by documentation. Usually, however, such tracing of funds to specific sources is impossible and the interest cost reasonably

---

[74] *Ibid.* [75] Burgers, *Taxation and Supervision of Bank Branches* (1992), p. 459.
[76] 1984 Report, p. 59, para. 54. [77] *Ibid.*, p. 59, para. 55.

3 THE DEDUCTIBILITY OF NOTIONAL INTEREST 261

estimated by the Japanese branch is accepted so long as this estimated cost reflects the prevailing arm's-length rate of interest. Here, so long as the interest rate used corresponds broadly to that paid in the open market for similar kinds of loan, the Japanese approach may often not differ very significantly from that of the other OECD Member countries.[78]

The approach taken by Japan in theory allows a branch to deduct only the actual cost of funds it acquires from its head office; the approach does not allow an international bank to make a profit on intra-bank loans, thus applying the single entity approach in interpreting former Article 7. This approach allows a branch of an international bank to deduct intra-bank interest expenses at arm's length rates. The references in the 1984 Report to arm's length interest rates do not distinguish between arm's length borrowing rates and arm's length lending rates. The difference between these rates is the profit an international bank would make on inter-bank loans. The use by a branch of arm's length lending rates on intra-bank loans allows the head office of an international bank to make a profit on the loan. Conversely, if a branch is required to apply an arm's length borrowing rate, its head office will be unable to make a profit on intra-bank loans. As Japan used the single entity approach in the 1984 Report, it is presumed that the interest rate to be used is the arm's length borrowing rate. But the comment that the results under Japan's approach will be similar to the results under the majority separate entity approach suggests that the arm's length lending rate should be used.

The US, the other country in the minority, used an approach different from the tracing requirement. Under US law, one of the acceptable methods is a branch book/dollar pool method, which relied on the original cost of funds to an international bank.[79] This approach assumed that if an international bank obtains funds from depositors outside the US and lends the funds through its US branch to its US customers, the branch's cost of funds will be the interest paid to the overseas depositors. On this basis, an international bank's cost of borrowing is the average cost of all borrowings. In the 1984 Report, the OECD concluded that the method of the US and Japan produces results similar to the specific payments method adopted by the majority of the OECD countries.[80] The 1984 Report contended:

> To sum up, although very different, both the Japanese method and the United States tracing method described above may well, in many cases,

[78] *Ibid.*   [79] *Ibid.*, p. 59, para. 56.   [80] *Ibid.*

produce results which are the same or very close to those which would be produced by using the specific payments approach adopted by the other OECD Member countries.[81]

The failure of the minority to compromise its tax policies and develop a consensus interpretation underscores the disappointingly limited level of cooperation among the OECD countries at that time. While the minority dissent was based on a stated strict adherence to the single entity principle, the 1984 Report claimed that the results produced by the majority and minority approaches are similar. Nevertheless, significant benefits would have been gained if the OECD countries had agreed on a genuine consensus interpretation and applied consistent policies and practices, as a consensus interpretation minimizes the risk of double taxation or under-taxation. Clearly, a dissent by powerful OECD countries is far more significant than a dissent by countries whose economies are smaller. The size of the financial markets in the US and Japan means that a dissent by these two countries created the potential for significant distortions through double taxation or under-taxation.

3.6 The US fungibility approach

The US allowed international banks to use an alternative method, the separate currency pool method, to determine the cost of intra-bank funds (the fungible method).[82] The US is the only country that used this method, but given its dominant economic influence, the US is able to unilaterally develop rules and have them reflected in OECD reports. The approach is based on the principle that money is fungible. Under the fungible method, the funds borrowed by one part of an international bank are regarded as contributing to the lending capacity of the entire bank. The fungible method ignores the actual movement of funds within an international bank and allows a branch to deduct a rate of interest on intra-bank loans based on the average rate of interest paid by the whole bank to its depositors. This method has the advantage of moving away from examining individual transactions and, instead, using a global approach based on an international bank's actual cost of funds. The fungible method recognizes that international banks are integrated enterprises and that examining individual transactions is time-consuming and costly. It also highlights the difficulty and artificiality of treating the various parts of an international bank as separate entities as occurs

[81] Ibid., p. 59, para. 57.   [82] Ibid., pp. 59–60, para. 58.

3 THE DEDUCTIBILITY OF NOTIONAL INTEREST   263

under the arm's length principle. The 1984 Report statement acknowledged that the fundamental flaw in the arm's length principle is that it seeks to separate the inseparable:

> A justification for fungibility methods would be that the banking industry is pre-eminently one in which the affairs of branches are very much interwoven with those of the head office and other parts of the enterprise. Normally, as has already been indicated, creditors subject money advanced to a bank to the risk of the bank's entire activities and look to the general credit of the bank for repayment. Thus, a bank's receipts and payments of interest may be regarded as all flowing into and out of one common pool. From this viewpoint, money which is taken out of the pool at one point is thus not identifiable as money which came into the pool at that or any other point; all that can be said is that the inflow at any one point helps to make the outflow at that or another point possible. When money is borrowed by the bank for a specific purpose this is still the case since such borrowing generally frees other funds for other purposes. On this basis, it is inappropriate to seek to calculate a balance of inflow and outflow at each point of access to the pool by reference to a precisely calculated locally related outflow to the rest of the pool or inflow from it. The activity of the whole enterprise contributes so much, it is argued, to the profit or loss derived by each part of the enterprise that, though it may not be possible to quantify the contribution precisely, it must be acknowledged in the attribution of profit or loss to any particular permanent establishment of the enterprise. It would be going too far to do this by simply attributing to the permanent establishment a share of the total profit or loss of the whole enterprise, and in any case, if such an attempt were made, there would remain the question of what basis should be used for that attribution and all the other problems of the whole enterprise approach (Article 7, paragraph 4 of the OECD Model Convention). But it would be appropriate, it is argued, to regard the interest expenses of the whole enterprise as incurred for the common purposes of the enterprise and thus as properly attributable to each part on some average basis ... No account would be taken of any payments of interest by the branch to any other part of the bank or vice versa. Nor, in general, would any deduction be allowed in computing the branch's profits for the actual interest paid by the branch. On the other hand, there would be set, against the branch's receipts from third parties, a share of the average interest paid by the bank as a whole.[83]

The OECD noted that the fungible method has problems and is likely to produce results which are inconsistent with the arm's length principle.[84] If a branch's business differs from the business carried on by the rest of the bank, the branch's liabilities may not be properly represented as a

[83] Ibid., p. 60, para. 59.   [84] Ibid., pp. 60–1, para. 60.

proportion of the liabilities of the whole bank. The 1984 Report mentioned that money may not be wholly fungible because of exchange controls and the differences that arise from the strengths and weaknesses of particular currencies. This argument is of limited relevance in a global economy. International exchange controls are now very limited and, through financial derivatives, loans in one currency may easily be converted into another currency. Thus, in a globalized economy, money may be regarded as being fully fungible. Moreover, the fungible method recognizes the futility of examining individual transactions in an international bank.

In 1984, the US moved to a modified version of the fungible method (modified method).[85] The 1984 Report discussed this method to identify the method used in the US at the time the 1984 Report was published. Under the modified method, the average rate of interest for each currency is calculated separately, and the payment of intra-bank interest by a branch is ignored. The main advantage of the modified method, over the fungible method, is the simplicity of using the global interest expense of an international bank rather than tracing numerous individual transactions. The modified method also has the administrative advantage for tax authorities of not requiring a comparison of the interest rates on loans made by a branch with the arm's length interest rate standards, such as LIBOR. In the 1984 Report, the OECD accepted that the task of determining the average rates of interest for an international bank may be complex for both banks and tax authorities.[86] But international banks monitor the cost of funds to ensure profitability; thus, if the fungible method is used, the compliance costs of banks are minimized because they already maintain records on their cost of funds. According to the 1984 Report, the failure to recognize intra-bank loans prevents branches of international banks from being rewarded for the funds they raise for use in the other parts of the bank. But the 1984 Report noted that if the fungible method used in the US produces results which deviate from the arm's length principle, an international bank would be tempted to exploit the differences to avoid tax by shifting profits to lower-tax countries.[87]

In summary, the main deficiency of the modified fungibility approach is that, within the OECD, it was only used in the US. But the advantage of the fungibility approach is that it reflects business reality that an international bank operates as a unitary business. Moreover, it is simple and involves lower compliance costs than the tracing required by the

[85] *Ibid.*, p. 61, para. 61.   [86] *Ibid.*, p. 61, para. 62.   [87] *Ibid.*, p. 61, para. 63.

majority method. Nevertheless, the fungible method was rejected by the majority of the OECD countries as being inconsistent with Articles 7(2) and (3) of the OECD Model. Consequently, the OECD countries, apart from the US, denied a branch of an international bank a deduction for interest expenses based on the whole bank's average cost of funds. They do, however, allow international banks to make a profit margin on intra-bank loans, provided the rate of interest conforms with an arm's length rate of interest. The main shortcoming of the majority approach was its reliance on a transactional method. The majority and minority approaches to intra-bank loans highlight the significant policy differences that exist between the OECD countries. In a global economy, with highly integrated international banks, the use of a transactional approach to allocate profits and expenses on intra-bank loans is exceptionally difficult.

4 Determining the equity capital of branches of international banks

One of the reasons asserted by the OECD in the 1984 Report for recognizing intra-bank loans was that these funds reflected an international bank's debt capital.[88] In theory, this would prevent a branch of an international bank from claiming a deduction for the equity capital provided to it by its head office. Measures are required under the arm's length principle to ensure that a branch of an international bank is charged interest only on intra-bank loans that reflect funds deposited with the international bank by customers. To ensure that a branch is charged interest on debt capital only, part of the branch's working capital must be treated as equity capital. A branch's profitability is affected by its equity capital funding because equity capital funds are cost-free. International banks will usually assert that their branches in higher-tax countries are funded by debt capital to maximize the bank's interest deductions and thus minimize the profits allocated to the branches.[89] This enables an international bank to exploit tax arbitrage by shifting profits to its branches in lower-tax countries.

[88] *Ibid.*, p. 57, para. 49.
[89] In the UK prior to 1 January 2003 a UK branch of a foreign enterprise could operate with little or no equity capital. From 1 January 2003 a UK branch of an international enterprise will be treated as having the amount of equity capital that it would require if it were a separate corporation operating in the UK: Inland Revenue, Budget 2002, REV BN 25, 'Taxation of UK Branches of Foreign Companies', 17 April 2002.

The task of objectively determining a particular branch's equity capital is significant since money is fungible and both equity capital and debt capital may be moved between different parts of an international bank with ease. In fact, this very flexibility in transferring capital is the main reason that international banks operate through branches. It is virtually impossible to develop a method that objectively determines a branch's equity capital because it is a fictional exercise. While a bank's equity capital on a global basis may be determined for prudential purposes, it is a fiction to attribute equity capital to individual branches. In the case of subsidiaries, they are usually required for reporting purposes to record their equity capital because they have a separate legal personality. But a branch of an international bank is an inseparable part of the bank. The pre-2008 Commentary on former Article 7 notes that the OECD was unable to develop a consensus within the OECD countries on the attribution of equity capital to branches of international banks:

> [The 1984 Report] also addresses the issue of the attribution of capital to the permanent establishment of a bank in situations where actual assets were transferred to such a branch and in situations where they were not. Difficulties in practice continue to arise from the differing views of Member countries on these questions and the present Commentary can only emphasise the desirability of agreement on mutually consistent methods of dealing with these problems.[90]

4.1 Branches with allotted equity capital

The starting point for determining an international bank's equity capital is the prudential banking regulations. The bank regulations in several countries require branches of international banks to maintain equity capital and to record it in their balance sheets.[91] The 1984 Report stated: 'Regulations of this kind will frequently form the basis of taxation but will not necessarily do so.'[92] This comment suggests that the prudential banking regulations will be the starting point for determining the equity capital of a branch, but that a tax authority may determine that a particular branch has a different amount of equity capital. Tax authorities following such an arbitrary approach may create inconsistencies and uncertainty; international banks want clear and unambiguous rules for determining the equity capital of a branch.

---

[90] 2005 OECD Model, p. 125, para. 20.   [91] Ibid., pp. 65–6, para. 76.   [92] Ibid.

4 DETERMINING THE EQUITY CAPITAL OF BRANCHES   267

The 1984 Report mentioned that, irrespective of banking regulations, an international bank may make allotments of equity capital to its branches in order to ensure that the branches have allotted equity capital.[93] The allotted equity capital will usually be covered by the assets held by the branch, as if it were the owner. The kinds of assets referred to in the 1984 Report are real estate, bonds, debentures and cash funds. The income derived from allotted equity capital should be attributed to a branch under the general principles in former Article 7 of the OECD Model. Conversely, the 1984 Report asserted that, in certain cases, 'the capital allotted to a branch is not covered by assets held by the branch itself as if it were the owner'.[94] The 1984 Report then contended that if the head office of an international bank transfers funds or other assets to a branch as equity capital in the form of a loan, the rhetorical 'question arises as to whether the interest or other consideration paid for the loan is deductible from the branch's profit'.[95] It is no surprise that in the 1984 Report the OECD concluded that the interest paid by a branch on equity capital should be ignored in determining the branch's business profits under former Article 7.[96] This conclusion requires no justification because it reflects the accepted business norm that an enterprise cannot charge the other parts of the enterprise for the use of its equity capital. Nevertheless, the 1984 Report cited the following reasons for not allowing a branch a deduction for interest on allotted equity capital:

> The passage quoted from page 76[97] of the Commentary on the Model Convention precludes the deductibility of interest on capital allotted by [the] head office, and it can clearly be seen that, insofar as such capital is used for the purposes of the capital infrastructure of the enterprise as such, rather than for trading purposes of the branch, then the payment of interest on it to [the] head office is no different from interest paid by a branch of a non-banking concern to its head office. It may also be argued that it would be inappropriate for the branch to pay interest since this kind of capital is akin to the capital which entitles the bank's shareholders to a share in the profit.[98]

But the OECD deviates from the business norm by directing that a branch may be charged interest on the bank's equity capital in certain situations. According to the 1984 Report, if an international bank's

---

[93] Ibid.   [94] 1984 Report, p. 66, para. 77.   [95] Ibid.
[96] Ibid., pp. 66–8, paras. 77–83.
[97] Para. 17 of the Commentary on Article 7 of the 1977 OECD Model was changed; it became para. 19 of the Commentary on Article 7 of the 1992 OECD Model.
[98] 1984 Report, p. 66, para. 77.

equity capital is provided to a branch in a form that is not allotted equity capital, the branch may be entitled to a deduction for an advance under the arm's length principle:

> On the other hand, where the head office of a bank makes an advance to a branch in some form other than allotted capital, there does not seem, by reference to the arm's-length principle, to be any case for refusing a deduction in respect of interest paid to the head office even though the source of the advance happens to be capital funds. An independent bank would not refrain from requiring another independent bank to pay interest merely because the source of the advance made was a capital one. Such advances would therefore be treated appropriately as advances on exactly the same basis as if their source had been borrowing from third parties and an arm's-length rate of interest normally therefore would appropriately be allowed in computing the profit of the branch.[99]

Application of the approach set out above is restricted to situations in which a branch of an international bank has allotted equity capital in its balance sheet.[100] This approach is premised on a branch being required, by its host country's prudential banking regulations or general commercial rules, to have equity capital 'and these balance sheet statements are followed for tax purposes'.[101] In some countries, branches of international banks should be allowed to declare equity capital in excess of the minimum requirements. The 1984 Report stated that this approach should be taken if domestic banks in those countries are allowed any of the following options: to declare equity capital which exceeds the normal prudential requirements; to 'step up' declared amounts; or to increase their equity capital on account of undistributed profits.

If a country allows a domestic bank to increase its equity capital and this practice is recognized for tax purposes, similar declarations by branches of international banks should, according to the 1984 Report, be recognized for tax purposes.

International banks have an incentive to allocate excessive amounts of equity capital to branches located in lower-tax countries to increase the profitability of these branches and thereby minimize overall taxation. Thus, only lower-tax countries are likely to encounter either domestic banks or branches of international banks asserting that their equity capital levels exceed the minimum prudential banking requirements. An exception to this practice may arise if a branch in a higher-tax country wants to use a tax benefit. For example, if a branch has incurred

---

[99] Ibid.   [100] Ibid., p. 66, para. 78.   [101] Ibid.

4 DETERMINING THE EQUITY CAPITAL OF BRANCHES 269

tax losses, its host jurisdiction may allow the losses to be carried forward and deducted against future income. The international bank may allocate additional equity capital to the branch to increase the branch's profitability in order to ensure that the benefit of carry-forward losses is used as soon as possible.

No tax authority is likely to discourage bank branches in its jurisdiction from arguing that their equity capital exceeds the minimum requirements imposed by prudential regulations because additional equity capital increases the business profits attributable to the branches, which in turn usually means higher-tax collections. While allocating excessive amounts of equity capital to branches in lower-tax countries will decrease the profits allocated to branches in other countries, it is virtually impossible for a single tax authority having jurisdiction over one branch of an international bank to determine the bank's overall equity capital. The tax authority in the host country will have access to only a limited amount of information, and neither the international bank nor other tax authorities are likely to cooperate in supplying further information under the exchange of information Article, unless there is a formal request for such information. The bank will protect its information with the aim of securing its maximum total profits; the other tax authorities will wish to ensure that the tax collections in their own jurisdictions are not reduced.

The 1984 Report also dealt with the situation in which a bank branch's equity capital is claimed to exceed, on a proportionate basis, the equity capital of the international bank as a whole.[102] For example, this situation arises if a branch claims that its equity capital is 6 per cent of its total funds, while the equity capital of the bank as a whole is 4 per cent. For the reasons stated above, this situation is likely to arise only in lower-tax jurisdictions. The 1984 Report acknowledged this point: 'It will seldom be possible to decide with certainty whether this is the case, since the methods and criteria used in drawing up balance sheets vary from one country to another.'[103] The 1984 Report contended that, in some cases, a branch's equity capital may be partly financed out of borrowings made by the head office. The interest expense incurred by the international bank would then be treated in the same manner as borrowings used as equity capital for a foreign subsidiary. The 1984 Report concluded that a notional interest expense charged by an international bank to a branch or subsidiary would not be deductible from

---

[102] Ibid.   [103] Ibid., pp. 66–7, para. 79.

the branch's or the subsidiary's profits. The 1984 Report cited the following exception to this rule:

> It may, however, happen that in appropriate circumstances a deduction for interest paid by the head office falls to be allowed against the branch profits for other reasons, e.g. because it is incurred for the purposes of the permanent establishment and thus falls within Article 7(3) of the Model Convention. In that case it would be appropriately charged by the head office to the branch.[104]

This exception is significant, as it provides international banks with the means to arrange their operations to maximize the interest deductions of their branches in higher-tax countries. An international bank could be expected to assert that its branches in higher-tax countries are funded by loans raised by the head office on behalf of its branches in order to ensure that the branches can maximize their deductions for interest. It is likely that this exception has been exploited by international banks, even despite the compliance costs involved in establishing that funds were borrowed for use by a branch.

4.2 Branches without allotted equity capital: determining notional equity capital

In some jurisdictions, the banking rules do not require branches to have allotted equity capital, but the tax rules may impose minimum equity capital requirements on branches.[105] In such cases, the issue of non-discrimination set out in Article 24(4) of the OECD Model would be raised.[106] Under the non-discrimination principle, the tax treatment of a permanent establishment in its host country should not be less favourable than the tax treatment of enterprises of that state carrying on the same activities. The OECD accepts that if a country does not require domestic banks to show allotted equity capital, a branch of an international bank cannot be required to show equity capital. Moreover, it is possible

---

[104] Ibid.   [105] Ibid., p. 67, para. 80. The discussion in this para. is based on para. 80.
[106] Article 24(4) of the 2010 OECD Model: 'Except where the provisions of para. 1 of Article 9, para. 6 of Article 11, or para. 4 of Article 12, apply, interest, royalties and other disbursements paid by an enterprise of a Contracting State to a resident of the other Contracting State shall, for the purpose of determining the taxable profits of such enterprise, be deductible under the same conditions as if they had been paid to a resident of the first-mentioned State. Similarly, any debts of an enterprise of a Contracting State to a resident of the other Contracting State shall, for the purpose of determining the taxable capital of such enterprise, be deductible under the same conditions as if they had been contracted to a resident of the first-mentioned State.'

4 DETERMINING THE EQUITY CAPITAL OF BRANCHES 271

for a tax authority to treat part of an interest payment by a branch to its head office as remuneration for the use of equity capital, even though the amount is not shown as equity capital in the branch's books. As a practical matter, the OECD's statement is of limited relevance because most OECD countries require international banks to hold equity capital for prudential reasons. Furthermore, most OECD countries are members of the Bank of International Settlements, which sets guidelines on prudential standards.

The rule that a branch of an international bank may not claim a deduction for the interest paid on equity capital is difficult to apply to branches in practice because the equity capital of a bank branch cannot be determined with precision. To deal with this situation, the OECD directs that a formula may be used to estimate the intra-bank interest charged on equity capital.[107] The formula is a substitute for the notional interest charged on a branch's equity capital and is a weighted average of the rates charged by the head office on loans to its branches. Items offsetting or self-balancing are ignored in this formula. An alternative approach is to treat the interest on capital as a form of thin capitalization, applying a country's domestic rules as far as practicable.[108] Both of these methods conform with formulary apportionment by moving away from an analysis of transactions and using a branch's consolidated records to determine its equity capital. As the arm's length principle is difficult to apply in practice, the OECD accepts the use of approximation methods. While approximations are justifiable as conforming with the arm's length principle, they are in essence formulary apportionments because they are based on a bank's global operations.

The OECD acknowledged that both the formula and the thin capitalization approach have shortcomings, but the use of any method is arbitrary since international banks operate as unitary businesses.[109] As money is fungible and banks can move funds around the world with ease, any method of determining a branch's equity capital is arbitrary. The advantages of the formulary methods are certainty, simplicity and lower compliance costs. The OECD suggested that 'it would be desirable to ensure that other methods could be used if they produced results more acceptable to both taxpayers and tax authorities'.[110] On the other hand, the thin capitalization approach may go too far in treating a branch in the same way as a resident company. The 1984 Report stated:

---

[107] 1984 Report, p. 67, para. 81.   [108] Ibid., p. 67, para. 82.
[109] Ibid., p. 67, paras. 81 and 82.   [110] Ibid., p. 67, para. 81.

Although paragraph 2 of Article 7 of the OECD Model Convention says that 'the profits attributed to a branch shall be those which it might be expected to make if it were a distinct and separate enterprise' it goes on to say that the enterprises should be regarded as 'engaged in the same or similar conditions'.[111]

On this basis, it may be argued that the equity capital attributed to a branch as if it were a distinct and separate enterprise is the equity capital that it actually uses, rather than an amount prescribed by the thin capitalization rules or rules for resident banks. The OECD concludes by saying that the treatment depends to a large extent on the particular facts of each case.

The OECD direction that this issue be resolved on a case-by-case basis creates uncertainty for international banks and tax authorities and is likely to lead to disputes. The OECD failed to establish clear rules for banks and tax authorities to apply in determining a branch's equity capital. The inability to set clear rules is a consequence of the normative flaw in the arm's length principle, which treats a branch as a separate entity when this treatment does not reflect business reality.[112] The allocation of equity capital to a branch seeks to separate the inseparable. The working capital of a branch of an international bank cannot be dissected with any precision because, in a globalized economy, a branch is an inseparable part of the bank. Determining a branch's equity capital on a case-by-case basis involves high compliance and administrative costs. As argued above, the aim of most international banks is to allocate their debt capital to their branches in higher-tax countries to make the cost of head office funds deductible expenses for the branches.[113] For their part, most countries will endeavour to allocate, for tax purposes, an 'appropriate' proportion of an international bank's equity capital to branches located within their borders which decreases a branch's deduction for interest and accordingly increases its profits (or decrease its losses).

A simplified formulary method that uses the financial records of a branch of an international bank will generally be the most effective method of determining the branch's equity capital. The 1984 Report concluded:

---

[111] Ibid., p. 67, para. 82.
[112] US General Accounting Office, *International Taxation: Problems Persist in Determining Tax Effects of Intercompany Prices* (1992), pp. 61–2.
[113] This issue was considered in section 4.1, 'Branches with allotted equity capital'.

4 DETERMINING THE EQUITY CAPITAL OF BRANCHES

It seems to be generally accepted, however, that where some part of the working capital of the branch of a bank is treated as derived from equity sources and a deduction consequently denied for interest thereon, the proportion of such capital to total assets is to be expected to be comparatively small and to be of much the same order as the proportion for the bank as whole. Some countries may find it convenient to use a fixed percentage of the bank's total worldwide capital, although this procedure, because it must to a certain extent be arbitrary, carries the risk of producing distorted results and may need to be accompanied by provisions enabling the branch to substitute another amount if it can show good cause for doing so.[114]

The acceptance of a fixed percentage of a branch's funding as equity capital is a recognition of the difficulties in attempting to allocate the equity capital of an international bank between the head office and its branches around the world. But the 1984 Report did not suggest that a comparison be made between the equity capital of a branch and the equity capital of a domestic bank operating in the same market. This supports the argument that the usual arm's length measure of comparing a branch's equity capital with the equity capital of a domestic bank would be pointless.[115] The nature of international banking makes it meaningless to use domestic banks as comparable entities because of the differences between domestic and international banks. Conversely, the UK, in enacting a requirement that permanent establishments, including bank branches, maintain the equity capital they would need to have if they were a separate entity, argued that this requirement conforms with the 1984 Report.[116] The UK requirement is that a bank branch must maintain the equity capital that a domestic (UK) bank would have to hold for prudential purposes. The normative flaw in this approach is that it treats a branch as a separate entity when the branch is merely an integrated part of an international bank.

In theory, the proportion of debt capital and equity capital in a branch of an international bank should be the same as for the entire bank. But the tax authorities in most countries will not be in a position to determine the equity capital of the entire international bank, and the

---

[114] 1984 Report, pp. 67–8, para. 83.
[115] Burgers, *Taxation and Supervision of Bank Branches* (1992), p. 465.
[116] 'The legislation incorporates into UK domestic legislation the relevant principles in the Commentary on the Business Profits Article of the OECD Model Tax Convention and in the OECD publication "Transfer Pricing and Multinational Enterprises: Three Taxation Issues"': 'Draft Guidance on Capital Attribution to Banks' (UK Inland Revenue, 2002), p. 9, para. 6.1.

bank itself is unlikely to be helpful. This underscores the difficulty of treating a branch as a separate entity under the arm's length principle. Unlike a subsidiary, a branch of an international bank is an inseparable part of a highly integrated enterprise. The flaws in the arm's length principle require the use of formulary methods to estimate amounts such as a branch's equity capital. Thus, as calculating an international bank's ratio of equity capital to debt capital is beyond the ability of a particular tax authority, a fixed percentage is used as a proxy method. The percentage prescribed is an approximation of the equity capital of an international bank. The statement that the approach should be subject to amendment if the branch can show good cause may lead to the exception being the rule in higher-tax jurisdictions if branches successfully claim that their actual equity capital levels are lower than those when a fixed percentage is used.

5 Conclusion

The OECD rules in the pre-2008 Commentary on former Article 7 and the 1984 Report on the taxation of banks are flawed in theory and in practice. Branches are inseparable parts of an international bank, and treating them as separate entities is a serious theoretical weakness. Moreover, the arm's length principle has significant practical limitations when applied to intra-bank loans. As a consequence of this theoretical flaw and of the practical difficulties with former Article 7, the OECD has failed to develop a consensus interpretation and application of former Article 7 to the taxation of notional intra-bank loans. The inconsistent interpretation of former Article 7 by the OECD countries leads to uncertainty for banks and tax authorities, and creates the risk of double taxation or under-taxation. The main flaw in the OECD countries in the pre-2008 Commentary and the 1984 Report is their failure to provide a consensus interpretation of former Articles 7(2) and (3).

The dissents by the US and Japan undermined the strength of the majority approach. In particular, the dissent by the US was significant because most international banks operate in the US and its influence in the financial sector is significant. The failure to develop a consensus interpretation of former Article 7 on the deductibility of interest on intra-bank loans arises from the inconsistent use of the separate entity and single entity methods by the OECD countries. The inconsistent use of these methods reflects the practical difficulties in applying the arm's length principle to branches of international banks. In allocating interest on intra-bank loans under the pre-2008 Commentary, the majority countries used the separate entity approach and the minority countries the single entity approach. Prior to the 2008 Report and 2008 OECD Model and Commentary, the OECD was unable to develop a consensus interpretation of former Article 7 that was interpreted and applied consistently by treaty countries. While a formulary apportionment method is the better method for allocating profits within an integrated international bank, the separate entity method is the next best option, although it is difficult to apply in practice.

The pre-2008 Commentary and the 1984 Report were the OECD principles on the deductibility of interest on intra-bank loans until July 2008, but the scope of the rules was limited and the rules have been dated and theoretically flawed for some time. The international banking industry has been a major component in the globalization process, but the pre-2008 Commentary did not reflect this significant development. In particular, the developments in information and communications technologies have enabled international banks operating globally through branches to function as highly integrated businesses. Thus, it is inappropriate to treat a branch of an international bank as a notional separate entity when it is really one part of a unitary bank operating for a common profit purpose. The globalization of international banking is testing the arm's length principle; the OECD in the 1984 Report and pre-2008 Report was unable to establish effective rules for using the arm's length principle for attributing profits to branches of international banks. Reforms moving away from the arm's length principle to global formulary apportionment methods are needed; such methods would be more appropriate for allocating profits of highly integrated international banks operating through branches in a global economy.

8

Intra-bank interest under the 2008 Report

1 Introduction

This chapter critically considers measures in the 2008 Report on the application of former Article 7. This chapter shows the OECD's approach to be theoretically flawed, complex and costly to apply to branches of international banks and other international enterprises because they are not separate entities engaging in arm's length transactions with associated enterprises. The interpretation of the arm's length principle advocated in the 2008 Report – called the 'authorized OECD approach' – is based on legal fictions and does not reflect business practice. In addition, the OECD's approach may not result in a consensus interpretation of former Article 7 by the OECD countries. Although the OECD has established the authorized OECD approach, it may not be consistently implemented by OECD countries because each country will be acting in its own self-interest. A lack of consensus will inevitably result in double taxation or under-taxation, and disputes with taxpayers. One major issue on which the OECD was unable to establish a single authorized OECD approach was on the method for allocating equity capital[1] to branches of international banks. As a compromise measure, several authorized approaches may be used, but this will lead to double taxation or under-taxation if an international bank's residence country and the host country, in which it has a permanent establishment, use different methods for allocating equity capital to bank branches; resolving the double taxation disputes will be costly and time consuming.

The chapter begins with the allocation of business profits to permanent establishments under former Article 7 of the OECD Model and the adjustment of profits for transactions between associated enterprises under Article 9 as set out in the Transfer Pricing Guidelines. Next the chapter examines the authorized OECD approach for the allocation of business profits to permanent establishments. It then illustrates that the

---

[1] The term 'free' capital is used in the 2008 Report.

authorized OECD approach is based on the arm's length principle under Article 9 for associated enterprises and that these rules are different to the rules developed under former Article 7 for permanent establishments. The chapter traces the origins of the OECD's transfer pricing rules to the domestic US transfer pricing rules for associated enterprises. The chapter then considers the treatment of a permanent establishment as a functionally separate enterprise under the authorized OECD approach. The chapter examines the measures under the first step of the authorized OECD approach for the allocation of equity capital to bank branches, and the chapter then critically reviews the difficulty of allocating equity capital to bank branches. Finally, the chapter focuses on some of the flaws of the first step of the authorized OECD approach.

2 Background

An important part of the OECD Model is the allocation of business profits of international enterprises operating globally through permanent establishments under former Article 7. Enterprises also operate globally by incorporating subsidiaries in foreign countries (multinational enterprise groups). Article 9 of the OECD Model and the Transfer Pricing Guidelines deal with adjustments to transfer prices for transactions between associated enterprises. This section outlines former Article 7 and the Transfer Pricing Guidelines.

Former Article 7 deals with the method for allocating the business profits of international enterprises operating in host countries through permanent establishments. Under former Article 7, an international enterprise operating in a host country through a permanent establishment is subject to tax in the host country, to the extent that business profits are attributable to the permanent establishment. Former Article 7(2) directs that the profits attributable to a permanent establishment are the profits it would have made if it were a separate and distinct enterprise engaged in the same or similar activities. The legal fiction of treating a permanent establishment as a separate and independent entity is based on the arm's length principle.

Article 9 of the OECD Model deals with adjusting the profits of an enterprise from transactions with associated enterprises. The Transfer Pricing Guidelines set out the methodologies that may be used to adjust profits between associated enterprises when they are not transacting on arm's length terms. These guidelines prescribe that a price for a transaction between associated entities must be comparable to prices for similar transactions between independent entities, in accordance with the arm's length principle. If this requirement is not satisfied, a tax authority may make a transfer pricing adjustment. Under the arm's length principle, the norm of the market-place is imposed on intra-group transactions.[2] But the determination of arm's length transfer prices is not an exact method and a tax authority must use judgment in settling on an arm's length price from within a range of prices.[3] Because of the growth in intra-group trade, the arm's length principle is estimated to apply to a significant amount of cross-border trade.[4]

The OECD Model is premised on the arm's length principle because Articles 7 and 9, respectively, treat each of the head office and branches of an international enterprise, and associated enterprises, as separate entities operating at arm's length. Under the arm's length principle the transfer prices for notional transactions between the head office and a branch of an international enterprise, and transactions between associated enterprises, must reflect the prices that independent entities would have used for similar transactions. The OECD has given significant attention to transfer pricing, centred on the arm's length principle, and in 1995 it issued the Transfer Pricing Guidelines.

3 The authorized OECD approach

The 2008 Report established the 'authorized OECD approach' for interpreting former Article 7 – the consensus interpretation of former Article 7 amongst OECD countries minimizes the risk of tax distortions of double taxation or under-taxation of permanent establishments.[5] In the OECD discussion drafts,[6] the OECD developed a working hypothesis for attributing profits to a permanent establishment under former Article 7 applying the criteria of simplicity, administerability and sound tax policy.[7] The OECD's working hypothesis examined 'how far the

---

[2] Surrey, 'Reflections on the Allocation of Income and Expenses Among National Tax Jurisdictions' (1978), p. 414.
[3] Ibid., pp. 429–30.
[4] Intra-firm trade is considered in Ch. 3, section 3 Transfer Pricing.
[5] OECD, *Discussion Draft on the Attribution of Profits to Permanent Establishments* (2004), p. 10, para. 3.
[6] OECD, *Discussion Draft on the Attribution of Profits to Permanent Establishments* (2001); OECD, *Discussion Draft on the Attribution of Profits to Permanent Establishments* (2004).
[7] Ibid.

approach of treating a PE as a hypothetical distinct and separate enterprise can be taken and how the guidance in the [Transfer Pricing] Guidelines could be applied, by analogy, to attribute profits to a PE in accordance with the arm's length principle of Article 7'.[8] The general rules on the application of the working hypothesis to permanent establishments was issued in Part I of the 2001 Discussion Draft and reissued in the 2004 Discussion Draft. To test the working hypothesis, it was applied to the banking sector and the results were issued as Part II of the 2001 Discussion Draft and it was reissued in the 2003 Discussion Draft. The reforms proposed by the OECD were significant and were not restricted to the current terms of former Article 7:

> The development of the authorised OECD approach has not been constrained by either the original intent or by the historical practice and interpretation of Article 7. Instead, the focus has been on formulating the most preferable approach to attributing profits to a PE under Article 7 given modern-day multinational operations and trade. Once finalised, the conclusions of Parts I–III will be implemented through the Commentary on Article 7. This will require consideration as to whether a particular conclusion is adequately authorised under the existing language of the Commentary on Article 7.[9]

The aim of the working hypothesis was to adapt the Transfer Pricing Guidelines for the purpose of attributing profits and expenses to permanent establishments.[10] The testing was also used to identify modifications required because of the differences between a separate entity and a permanent establishment.

The OECD's aim to adapt the transfer pricing rules contained in the Transfer Pricing Guidelines to permanent establishments dates from 1994 when it announced its intention to deal with the application of the arm's length principle to permanent establishments in an update to the Transfer Pricing Guidelines.[11] The Transfer Pricing Guidelines were issued in final form in 1995, but permanent establishments were excluded from its scope. The reforms in the 2008 Report are controversial and the business sector in OECD countries has expressed the following concerns on the draft version of the Commentary:

---

[8] OECD, *Discussion Draft on the Attribution of Profits to Permanent Establishments* (2004), p. 4, para. 3.
[9] *Ibid.*, p. 7, para. 4.   [10] *Ibid.*, p. 7, para. 5.
[11] OECD, *Transfer Pricing Guidelines for Multinational Enterprises and Tax Administrations, Discussion Draft of Part I* (1994), p. 5, para. 13.

- the uncertainty of legal effect of the proposed 2008 Commentary;
- that many issues in the proposed 2008 Commentary have not been resolved, but the issues are expressed as being fully developed;
- the proposed 2008 Commentary contains unjustified administrative burdens and implementation issues.[12]

The delay between the issue of the 2001 Discussion Draft and the publication of the 2008 Report suggests that there were significant differences of opinion in OECD countries on the interpretation and application of former Article 7; OECD countries are zealously seeking to protect their taxing rights over permanent establishments and are unwilling to compromise their positions. In contrast, the OECD developed a consensus interpretation of the transfer pricing rules for associated enterprises in 1995.

3.1 The reasons for using the OECD's transfer pricing rules for permanent establishments

The authorized OECD approach is based on former Article 7(2) which uses the separate entity approach for the allocation of profits and expenses to permanent establishments. The 2008 Report claims that former Article 7(2) 'can be considered the statement of the arm's length principle in the context of permanent establishments'.[13] The Commentary on former Article 7 notes that the language in former Article 7(2) 'corresponds to the "arm's length principle" discussed in the Commentary on Article 9'.[14] This premise is used by the OECD for applying the Transfer Pricing Guidelines to permanent establishments by analogy. The OECD states that the Transfer Pricing Guidelines are a detailed analysis on the application of the arm's length principle under Article 9 of the OECD Model in the context of a multinational group[15] and that the Transfer Pricing Guidelines are more modern than the last amendments to the pre-2008 Commentary on Article 7.[16] Thus, the OECD claims that the authorized OECD approach for former Article 7(2) applies the arm's length principle expressed in the Transfer Pricing Guidelines.

In other words, as both Articles 7 and 9 are based on the arm's length principle, the transfer pricing rules for Article 9 may be adapted to

---

[12] BIAC, *BIAC Comments on OECD Revised Commentary on Article 7 of the OECD Model Tax Convention* (2007), p. 1.
[13] 2008 Report, p. 27, para. 81.   [14] *Ibid.*
[15] *Ibid.*, p. 11, para. 5.   [16] *Ibid.*

3 THE AUTHORIZED OECD APPROACH

former Article 7. But the authorized OECD approach ignores the fact that the rules developed under the arm's length principle for permanent establishments are different to the Transfer Pricing Guidelines developed for associated enterprises. A review of the history of the OECD transfer pricing rules for associated enterprises under Article 9 illustrates this proposition. Rather, separate rules are required for permanent establishments and associated enterprises because of their fundamental differences. The rules developed under Article 9 of the OECD Model and the Transfer Pricing Guidelines were not designed to apply to permanent establishments and should not be so applied.

3.2 The history of OECD's transfer pricing rules under Article 9

The OECD arm's length principle for associated enterprises reflects transfer pricing developments in the US under s. 482 of the *US Internal Revenue Code of 1986* (section 482 of the US Revenue Code) for associated enterprises.[17] As the US was developing its transfer pricing rules in the 1960s, based on the arm's length principle, the US sought to have them accepted internationally through the OECD. Basing the OECD's interpretation of Article 9 of the OECD Model on regulations made under section 482 of the US Revenue Code would eliminate the risk of conflict between section 482 regulations and Article 9 for the US in its own tax treaties. The influence of the US in the preparation of the OECD's *Report on Transfer Pricing and Multinational Enterprises* (1979 Report) appears to be significant, but there are no publications on this issue. Moreover, there are no public documents on whether the OECD examined whether the 1979 OECD Report was consistent with the arm's length principle developed by the League of Nations for former Article 7.[18] The US influence in the preparation of the 1995 Transfer Pricing Guidelines, however, is reflected in publications.[19] The transfer pricing rules were developed for associated entities and were not used for permanent establishments. The authorized OECD approach was the final step in bringing permanent establishments within the scope of the Transfer Pricing Guidelines. But this development is questionable given that section 482 of the US Revenue Code only applies to transactions

---

[17] Vann, 'Reflections on Business Profits and the Arm's Length Principle' in Arnold, et al. (eds.), *The Taxation of Business Profits Under Tax Treaties* (2003) 133–69, pp. 135–6.
[18] *Ibid.*, p. 136.
[19] OECD, *Tax Aspects of Transfer Pricing Within Multinational Enterprises: The United States Proposed Regulations* (1993).

between associated entities and has never been applied to permanent establishments in the US.

3.2.1 The 1979 OECD transfer pricing report

In 1965, US Secretary Surrey suggested that the transfer pricing methods used in section 482 of the US Revenue Code for associated enterprises be used by the OECD as the starting point for its study on the allocation of profits between associated enterprises.[20] At that time, some fifty-four years after the League of Nations had first commenced its work on the allocation of profits to associated enterprises, there was no international consensus on the arm's length principle.[21] In 1968 the US administration issued regulations (1968 Regulations) that introduced four transfer pricing methodologies for associated enterprises under section 482 of the US Revenue Code:

1. comparative uncontrolled price method;
2. cost plus method;
3. retail price method; and
4. a residual method arising from a provision that if the other methods cannot be applied, another appropriate method can be used.

After implementing the 1968 Regulations the US sought to have its transfer pricing rules accepted internationally through the OECD.

It is recognized that the OECD adopted the section 482 approach to transfer pricing in its 1979 Report, but the working papers and records of discussions within the OECD are not publicly available.[22] Significant evidence to this effect is that the US requested the OECD to commence work on developing transfer pricing rules for associated enterprises. Secretary Surrey reported that the US had encouraged the OECD Fiscal Committee to establish a working party on transfer pricing in 1965.[23] In 1976 the OECD Council directed the Fiscal Committee to prepare a report on transfer pricing for recommendation to OECD countries, which led to the publication of the 1979 Report. The objectives of the 1979 Report were stated as follows:

> The main objectives of the report are to set out as far as possible the considerations to be taken into account and to describe, where possible,

---

[20] 'Secretary Surrey Reports on Developments in Treasury's Foreign Tax Program' (1966), p. 56, referred to in Langbein, 'The Unitary Method and the Myth of Arm's Length' (1986), p. 647.
[21] Langbein, *ibid.*, pp. 647–8.   [22] *Ibid.*, pp. 648–9.   [23] *Ibid.*, p. 648.

generally agreed practices in determining transfer prices for tax purposes. It is hoped that, by doing so, the report will not only help tax officials to approach more effectively the problems presented to them by the transfer prices of multinational enterprises but will also help the enterprises themselves by indicating ways in which mutually satisfactory solutions may be found to those tax problems. The basic point of reference in all the various chapters of this report is the arm's length price.[24]

Section 482 of the US Revenue Code provided the OECD with a well-developed transfer pricing precedent. The 1979 Report sets out the methods to be used by the OECD countries in applying the arm's length principle to transactions between associated entities. The methods were very similar to those already developed for section 482.[25] Thus, the 1968 Regulations formed the basis for the 1979 Report. This report did not form part of the Commentary on Article 9, but was a separate report on the interpretation and application of Article 9 of the OECD Model. The OECD did not explain how the 1979 Report reflects the original intention of the League of Nations.[26] The OECD asserted that the 1979 Report was part of its construction of a set of internationally accepted rules on the methods used in OECD countries to tax profits from international transactions.[27] Moreover, the OECD claimed that: 'The principles set out in the 1979 Report have been widely followed by Member countries, including the United States, and are strongly endorsed by the business community and tax practitioners.'[28]

The OECD's interpretation of the arm's length principle for branches under former Article 7 has always been different to the interpretation used for associated enterprises under Article 9. The 1992 revision of the Commentary on Article 9 made the following reference to the 1979 Report:

> The Committee has also studied the transfer pricing of goods, technology, trade marks and services between associated enterprises and the methodologies which may be applied for determining correct prices where transfers have been made on other than arm's length terms. Its conclusions, which are set out in the report entitled 'Transfer Pricing and

---

[24] OECD, *Transfer Pricing and Multinational Enterprises* (1979), pp. 9–10, para. 5.
[25] 1. comparable uncontrolled price method; 2. cost plus method; 3. resale price method; and 4. other reasonable methods which produce an acceptable figure.
[26] Vann, 'Reflections on Business Profits and the Arm's Length Principle' in Arnold, et al. (eds.), *The Taxation of Business Profits Under Tax Treaties* (2003) 133–69, p. 136.
[27] OECD, *Tax Aspects of Transfer Pricing Within Multinational Enterprises: The United States Proposed Regulations* (1993), p. viii, paras. 5–7.
[28] Ibid., p. viii, para. 7.

Multinational Enterprises', represent internationally agreed principles and provide valid guidelines for the application of the arm's length principle which underlies Article 9.[29]

Clearly, the 1992 Commentary on Article 9 directly endorses the use of transfer pricing rules for associated enterprises. Significantly, the 1992 Commentary on former Article 7 made no reference to the 1979 Report.

3.2.2 Transfer Pricing Guidelines

The nexus between the Transfer Pricing Guidelines for associated enterprises and developments in the US under section 482 is disclosed in publications. The US Tax Reform Act of 1986 amended section 482 to require that consideration for intangible property transferred in a transaction between associated companies is commensurate with the income attributable to intangible property. The US Conference Committee report recommended that the US Internal Revenue Service conduct a comprehensive study and consider whether the 1968 Regulations should be modified. In response, the Internal Revenue Service and the Treasury Department issued a White Paper in 1988, *A Study of Intercompany Pricing*.[30] The Internal Revenue Service issued draft regulations under section 482 in 1992 (1992 Regulations).[31] Commentators have criticized several aspects of the 1992 Regulations, and the OECD issued a report on the differences between the section 482 regulations and the methods used in other OECD countries.[32] The purpose of the report was to provide the US with the collective views of the OECD countries on the proposed regulations.[33] In 1994, the OECD issued its Draft Transfer Pricing Guidelines, which reflect the measures in the 1992 Regulations.[34] The Draft Transfer Pricing Guidelines and the final version of the section 482 regulations were both issued in June 1994.[35] The final version of the Transfer Pricing Guidelines issued in 1995 reflected the regulations under section 482, and was limited to associated entities, despite the OECD's intention that the guidelines should also apply to permanent

---

[29] 1992 OECD Model (loose-leaf), p. C(9)-2, para. 3.
[30] (Notice 88-123, 1988-2 C.B. 458).   [31] (INTL-0372-88; INTL-0401-88, 57 FR 3571).
[32] OECD, *Tax Aspects of Transfer Pricing Within Multinational Enterprises: The United States Proposed Regulations* (1993).
[33] 1992 OECD Model, p. vii, para. 3.
[34] OECD, *Transfer Pricing Guidelines for Multinational Enterprises and Tax Administrations, Discussion Draft of Part I* (1994).
[35] Vann, 'Reflections on Business Profits and the Arm's Length Principle' in Arnold, et al. (eds.), *The Taxation of Business Profits Under Tax Treaties* (2003) 133–69, p. 137.

establishments.[36] Thus, the notion of the arm's length principle contained in the OECD's Transfer Pricing Guidelines reflects the regulations under section 482 of the US Revenue Code developed for associated entities.

The current version of the Commentary on Article 9 again expressly refers to the Transfer Pricing Guidelines and makes the following statement on their status and role:

> The Committee has spent considerable time and effort (and continues to do so) examining the conditions for the application of this Article, its consequences and the various methodologies which may be applied to adjust profits where transactions have been entered into on other than arm's length terms. Its conclusions are set out in the report entitled *Transfer Pricing Guidelines for Multinational Enterprises and Tax Administrations*, which is periodically updated to reflect the progress of the work of the Committee in this area. That report represents internationally agreed principles and provides guidelines for the application of the arm's length principle of which the Article is the authoritative statement.[37]

In comparison, the pre-2008 Commentary on former Article 7 made no reference to the Transfer Pricing Guidelines.

In summary, the Transfer Pricing Guidelines were developed to apply to transactions between associated enterprises and were asserted to conform with the arm's length principle. These rules reflect the regulations made under section 482 of the US Revenue Code which deal exclusively with associated enterprises; section 482 does not apply to permanent establishments in the US. The authorized OECD approach seeks to adapt the Transfer Pricing Guidelines to permanent establishments.

4 A permanent establishment as a functional separate enterprise

The 2008 Report treats a permanent establishment as a 'functional separate enterprise' for the purposes of former Article 7(1):[38]

> Accordingly, the authorised OECD approach is that the profits to be attributed to a PE are the profits that the PE would have earned at arm's length if it were a legally distinct and separate enterprise performing the same or similar functions under the same or similar conditions, determined by applying the arm's length principle under Article 7(2). The phrase 'profits of an enterprise' in Article 7(1) should not be interpreted as affecting the determination of the quantum of the profits that are to be

---

[36] OECD, *Transfer Pricing Guidelines for Multinational Enterprises and Tax Administrations* (loose-leaf) (1995).
[37] 2010 OECD Model, p. 181, para. 1.   [38] 2008 Report, p. 12, para. 28.

attributed to the PE, other than providing specific confirmation that 'the right to tax does not extend to profits that the enterprise may derive from that State otherwise than through the permanent establishment' (*i.e.* there should be no 'force of attraction principle').[39]

The term 'profits of an enterprise' in former Article 7(1) is interpreted, under the authorized OECD approach, to mean the profits a permanent establishment would have made if it were a separate entity. Under the authorized OECD approach, profits may be attributed to a permanent establishment for its activities even though the enterprise has made an overall loss. The denial of the force of attraction approach under the current interpretation of former Article 7 is maintained by the authorized OECD approach. If the profits derived in a host country by an international enterprise are unconnected to the enterprise's permanent establishment in that country, such profits cannot be attributed to the permanent establishment.

The major flaw in the 'functional separate entity' approach is that it does not reflect business reality and results in an arbitrary allocation of profits within an international enterprise operating through branches.[40] A US House Report explained that the problem of treating associated enterprises as if they were independent entities conflicts with business reality:

> A fundamental problem is the fact that the relationship between related parties is different from that of unrelated parties. Observers have noted that multinational companies operate as an economic unit, and not 'as if' they were unrelated to their foreign subsidiaries. In addition, a parent corporation that transfers potentially valuable property to its subsidiary is not faced with the same risks as if it were dealing with an unrelated party. Its equity interest assures it of the ability ultimately to obtain the benefit of future anticipated or unanticipated profits, without regard to the price its sets.[41]

Treating a permanent establishment as a separate entity conflicts with the business reality that a permanent establishment is part of a unitary international enterprise.[42] International enterprises exist because their operating costs are lower than those of independent entities through

---

[39] *Ibid.*, p. 27, para. 79.
[40] Institute of International Bankers, 'Comments on the OECD Discussion Draft on the Attribution of Profits to Permanent Establishments' (2001), p. 483. Comments on the 2001 Discussion Draft.
[41] The House Report on House Bill 3838 House of Representatives Report No. 426, 99th Congress. Quoted in Avi-Yonah, 'The Rise and Fall of Arm's Length' (1995), p. 130.
[42] Bird and Wilkie, 'Source- vs. Residence-Based Taxation in the European Union' in Cnossen (ed.) *Taxing Capital Income in the European Union* (2000) 78–109, p. 91.

internalizing costs and risks,[43] and through economies of scale.[44] The relationship between a branch and its head office and other branches is based on common control and a common profit motive. The board and senior managers control an international enterprise and make decisions on how branches will operate to maximize overall profits. Branches of an international enterprise do not operate in practice as separate entities; they are parts of a unitary business. In contrast, the relationship between independent entities transacting at arm's length reflects their contracts.[45] Typically, a contract governs the relationship between two independent parties to a transaction.

A flaw in the arm's length principle is that it seeks to allocate a geographic location to profits of an international enterprise under existing international tax concepts.[46] The profits of an international enterprise come from a number of sources and any attribution of geographic location to profits is artificial and arbitrary.[47] An international enterprise is, other things being equal, indifferent to the locations in which it operates provided that the enterprise is maximizing its profit potential. Moreover, the transfers of funds and assets between different parts of an enterprise are not formal business transactions and they might not be fully documented. Conversely, in the case of associated companies, the Transfer Pricing Guidelines may be applied to transactions between separate legal entities because these transactions are recognized by law. Therefore, treating a branch as a separate entity under the arm's length principle does not reflect the business reality that international enterprises operating through branches are highly integrated unitary businesses.

5 The first step of the authorized OECD approach

The interpretation of former Article 7(2) under the authorized OECD approach requires a two-step process.[48] The first step is a functional analysis to treat a permanent establishment and the rest of the enterprise

---

[43] Li, 'Global Profit Split' (2002), p. 834.
[44] McLure, 'Replacing Separate Entity Accounting and the Arm's Length Principle with Formulary Apportionment' (2002), pp. 586–7.
[45] Lebowitz, 'Transfer Pricing and the End of International Taxation' (1999), p. 1203.
[46] Bird and Wilkie, 'Source- vs. Residence-Based Taxation in the European Union' in Cnossen (ed.) *Taxing Capital Income in the European Union* (2000) 78–109, p. 93.
[47] Ault and Bradford, 'Taxing International Income' in Razin and Slemrod (eds.), *Taxation in the Global Economy* (1990) 11–46, p. 31.
[48] 2008 Report, p. 28, para. 85.

as if they were associated enterprises. Each notional enterprise is treated as undertaking activities using assets and assuming risks. This step is not based on transactions recognized under the general law, but on economic fictions. The second step is to determine the arm's length profits of the notional separate entity using the adapted transfer pricing methods in the Transfer Pricing Guidelines. This chapter focuses on the first step of the authorized OECD approach to illustrate the difficulties in applying the arm's length principle to permanent establishments. Transfers of assets and funds to and from a branch by the other parts of the enterprise are treated as notional transactions for transfer pricing purposes.

The first step is based on the requirement in former Article 7(2) which states that a permanent establishment must be treated as a separate enterprise 'engaged in the same or similar activities under the same or similar conditions'.[49] 'The approach of the [Transfer Pricing] Guidelines in linking the earning of profit to the performance of "functions" would appear to be capable of being applied in the permanent establishment context by equating "functions" to "activities".'[50] The first step of the authorized OECD approach is to apply the functional and factual analysis to a permanent establishment to determine the functions of the notional distinct and separate entity based on its activities.[51] The role of the functional and factual analysis is to:

- attribute to the permanent establishment the rights and obligations arising out of transactions between the international enterprise and separate and independent entities;
- determine the functions of the permanent establishment as a separate enterprise and the economic characteristics relating to the performance of those functions;
- attribute risk to the various parts of the international enterprise based on identifying the significant people functions connected to the risks;
- attribute economic ownership of assets among the various parts of the international enterprise, based on identifying the significant people functions connected to attributing economic ownership;
- recognize and determine the nature of notional transactions, called dealings, between the permanent establishment and other parts of the international enterprise; and

---

[49] Article 7(2) quoted from the 2008 Report, p. 27, para. 80.
[50] Ibid., p. 28, para. 86.   [51] Ibid., p. 29, para. 88.

• attribute equity capital to the permanent establishment on the basis of assets and risks attributed to the permanent establishment.[52]

5.1 Functional analysis

The OECD claims that the functional analysis requirements in the Transfer Pricing Guidelines are capable of being applied directly to a permanent establishment to determine the 'activities' of the permanent establishment as a notional separate entity.[53] The first step of the authorized OECD approach prescribes a functional and factual analysis of the economic characteristics of a permanent establishment to create a legal fiction that the permanent establishment is 'engaged in "comparable" activities under "comparable" conditions'.[54] Under the second step, the permanent establishment's notional intra-entity transactions, called dealings, are compared to the transactions of independent enterprises with 'the same or similar economic characteristics'.[55] But the OECD states that the principles in the Transfer Pricing Guidelines on comparability must be applied by analogy to permanent establishments because the Transfer Pricing Guidelines are based on a comparison of transactions between associated enterprises and similar transactions between independent enterprises.[56]

To this purpose, the functional analysis requires a determination of which activities and responsibilities of an enterprise are associated with a particular permanent establishment and the extent of this association. The functional analysis assumes that, in most cases, the activities performed by a permanent establishment will be carried on exclusively within the host country's jurisdiction.[57] Under the functional analysis all the activities performed by, or on behalf of, a permanent establishment must be taken into account, including any activities performed by other parts of the enterprise outside the jurisdiction of the host country. The issues examined under a functional analysis are: attributing functions to a branch; attributing a credit rating to a branch; and attributing equity capital to a branch.[58]

The 2008 Report states that, in the banking sector, the activities that lead to the creation of a loan (financial asset) involve the following functions: sales and marketing; sales and trading; trading and treasury;

---

[52] Ibid. [53] Ibid., p. 30, para. 90. [54] Ibid. [55] Ibid.
[56] Ibid. [57] Ibid., p. 30, para. 94. [58] Ibid., p. 31, para. 96.

and sales and support.[59] After a financial asset has been created, an international bank would perform the following functions during the life of the asset: loan support; monitoring and managing the risks associated with the loan; treasury; and sales and trading (securitization).[60] The key entrepreneurial risk-taking functions will be the creation and management of a loan. The 2008 Report states that these functions in relation to loans are usually performed by people.[61] The OECD contends that a functional analysis should be able to determine which of the functions are carried out by a bank branch by examining whether the people performing these functions are located within the branch. In addition to analysing the functions performed by a branch, the functional analysis requires an examination of the assets used and the risks assumed by the branch. The 2008 Report states that on the issue of allocating assets to bank branches, the general rules for permanent establishments are adequate without modification.[62] On the issue of risks, the 2008 Report claims that the key entrepreneurial risk-taking functions create the greatest risks, such as credit risk, operational risk and market risk.[63]

The authorized OECD's functional analysis is an arbitrary and complex exercise. The complexity arises from the need to examine in detail every transaction to determine profit and expense allocations.[64] A functional analysis of a loan made by an international bank in order to attribute rewards to the various functions conflicts with business reality.[65] While an international bank makes a loan for profit-making purposes, it is indifferent to allocating the loan to a geographic region or dissecting the functions performed. From a theoretical perspective the creation and maintenance of a loan to a customer would involve the above steps. But an international bank would never fragment its operations along these lines, nor would it make notional allocation of profits and expenses on the basis of a functional analysis.

The work required by an international bank in documenting and justifying the methods and the prices used for a large number of transactions would be a major burden for both the bank and a tax authority.[66] Any allocation of profits and expenses to reflect these

---

[59] Ibid., p. 76, para. 7. [60] Ibid., p. 77, para. 8. [61] Ibid., pp. 90–1, para. 65.
[62] Ibid., p. 92, para. 70. [63] Ibid.
[64] US General Accounting Office, IRS Could Better Protect US Tax Interests in Determining the Income of Multinational Corporations (1981), 36.
[65] Sheppard, 'NatWest Revisited in the New British Treaty' (2001), p. 1499.
[66] US General Accounting Office, International Taxation: Problems Persist in Determining Tax Effects of Intercompany Prices (1992), pp. 60–1.

functions would be a purely arbitrary and fictional exercise. International banks would have to undertake this exercise to allocate assets to branches solely for tax purposes because the authorized OECD approach does not rely on records that a bank would otherwise be expected to keep. To make a functional analysis and to then allocate profits and expenses on this basis, an international bank would have to employ a large team of economists for this sole purpose. The authorized OECD approach is likely to result in significant compliance costs for banks. In addition, the ability of a tax authority to scrutinize the attribution of assets to a branch would be limited because of the time needed to accomplish the exercise.

5.2 Assets used

The purpose of the functional analysis requires consideration to be given to the assets used, and the risks assumed, by a permanent establishment. The OECD acknowledges that this aspect of the functional analysis is difficult:

> Determining ownership of the assets used by a PE can present problems not found in separate enterprises where legal agreements can be relied upon to determine ownership. In a PE context the assets owned by the enterprise belong, legally, to the enterprise of which the PE is part. It is therefore necessary to introduce the notion of 'economic ownership' in order to attribute economic ownership of assets to a PE under the first step of the authorised approach. In determining the characteristics of the PE for taxation purposes, it is the economic (rather than legal) conditions that are most important because they are likely to have a greater effect on the economic relationships between the various parts of the single legal entity. Economic ownership of an asset is determined by a functional and factual analysis and in particular rests upon performance of the significant people functions relevant to ownership of the asset . . .[67]

From a legal perspective, the assets of an enterprise operating internationally through permanent establishments are owned by the enterprise as a whole. Property law principles in common law countries have been developed through an extensive body of case law, but under the authorized OECD approach, legal ownership principles are replaced by economic ownership guidelines which are by nature imprecise. Under former Article 7(2) the facts and circumstances of a permanent establishment are examined to decide which assets (tangible and intangible assets) are economically owned by a permanent establishment or are used by it

[67] 2008 Report, pp. 32–3, para. 101.

in performing its functions.[68] The first step of the authorized OECD approach requires an analysis of, first, whether a permanent establishment is using assets of the enterprise in carrying on its business, and second, on what conditions the assets are being used.[69] Assets may be used by a permanent establishment as either a sole owner or a joint owner, such as a licensee or member of a cost contribution arrangement.

Under the functional analysis, an international bank must examine the assets used and risks involved in creating and subsequently managing a loan.[70] In the banking sector, financial assets such as loans, cash and reserves, are used to earn interest income or interest equivalents. Infrastructure assets used by a bank branch, such as business premises, computer systems and software, will also have to be examined under a functional analysis.[71] The 2008 Report claims that on the issue of equity capital, the functional analysis to be used for the banking sector is the same as that used for non-bank enterprises.[72] The following rationale is provided for reaching this conclusion:

> Capital is relevant to the performance of traditional banking business because in the course of a traditional banking business, banks assume risk, for example, by lending money to third parties some of whom may not repay the full amount of the loan. In order to assume risk, a bank needs 'capital', *i.e.* the ability to absorb any losses due to the realisation of assumed risks. This is because capital, in this context, refers to funds placed at the bank's disposal by investors who are prepared to accept some higher level of risk in respect of their investment in exchange for an economic return which is expected to be significantly higher than the risk-free rate. For example, a bank's equity holders (like those of any business) stand to lose their entire investment if the bank becomes insolvent, but also are able to share in the after-tax profits of the bank. Retained profits also form part of capital in this sense because until distributed to equity holders as dividends they remain available to absorb losses.[73]

The OECD states that banks should take into account the following issues in undertaking a functional analysis of assets and risks:

> However, given that capital is essential in order to enable banks to assume the risks arising from their traditional banking business, the functional and factual analysis would need to pay particular attention to an examination of the issues related to capital adequacy and attribution of capital.

---

[68] *Ibid.*   [69] *Ibid.*   [70] *Ibid.*, p. 78, para. 14.   [71] *Ibid.*, p. 79, para. 15.
[72] *Ibid.*, pp. 81–2, para. 28.   [73] *Ibid.*, p. 81, para. 24.

Finally, and as a separate matter, the analysis would also consider the funding arrangements of the bank's financial assets.[74]

The principle that an enterprise needs equity capital to reflect the level of risk assumed by an enterprise is sound. Prudent managers of an enterprise will manage the equity capital and risk levels for the enterprise as a whole, but they are unlikely to be concerned about the exact location, at any point in time, of the equity capital or the risk assumed by the enterprise. The principle assumes that a functional analysis of an enterprise can be used to determine the business profits of the enterprise's permanent establishments. But the reason international enterprises undertake international operations through permanent establishments is to maximize the flexibility in their operations and in the allocation of debt and equity capital. An enterprise would operate through a subsidiary structure if it wanted a direct correlation between the equity capital and risks assumed by its operations abroad. The emphasis on assumption of risk within an enterprise is that this will lead to a rigorous method of allocating equity capital to a permanent establishment. But the emphasis on risk does not reflect general law or business reality. Within an enterprise, the assumption of risk can only be measured in theory, because in law the enterprise as a whole is liable for risk being managed by either the head office or a permanent establishment. The functional analysis requires international enterprises to operate a separate set of accounts which is both time-consuming and costly.

A tax authority checking the accounts of a permanent establishment to ensure compliance with the authorized OECD approach would be pressed to determine whether transactions do not conform with the arm's length principle. If corporate auditors are unable at times to detect suspect accounts that have eventually led to the collapse of a publicly listed company, tax authority auditors would be even less likely to be able to detect suspect transactions. Examples of high profile corporate collapses indicate the ability of corporate taxpayers to manipulate accounts to deceive their external auditors. In December 2001 Enron Corporation (Enron), once one of the world's largest electricity and natural gas traders, filed for Chapter 11 bankruptcy protection in the United States.[75] This collapse, in turn, led to the collapse in 2002 of the company's auditor, the international accounting firm Arthur

---

[74] Ibid., pp. 81–2, para. 28.
[75] *Washington Post*, Timeline of Enron's Collapse, 25 February 2002.

Andersen LLP. Arthur Andersen saw Enron's books each year for sixteen years and the auditors were unable to find and report on suspect accounts. In Australia, a similar sequence of events took place with the collapse of HIH, a publicly listed insurance company. The independent auditors, again Arthur Andersen, were unable to detect that there were insufficient reserves to cover the risks HIH was assuming. The overstatement of reserves was made to allow HIH to declare larger profit levels, which meant that the value of HIH's shares was maintained, and led to more tax being paid by HIH than the real, lower profit levels warranted. A Royal Commission of inquiry was established in Australia to investigate the collapse of HIH.[76] These cases highlight the challenge for a tax auditor in detecting accounts which do not conform with the arm's length principle.

5.3 Functional analysis of risks assumed by an international bank branch

The business of banking involves the assumption of risk from customers. When a bank makes a loan to a customer it assumes several types of risk: credit risk, interest rate risk, and foreign exchange risk.[77] A critical factor to be considered in a functional analysis is an international bank's credit rating because this directly affects the rates at which the bank can borrow and, in turn, its profit potential. Interest rates have two components. The first component is the interest rate the lender can demand in the market from a bank with a high credit rating (e.g. a bank with an AAA rating). The second component is the additional interest a lender can demand to reflect the risk that a bank may become insolvent and be unable to pay the interest and principal in accordance with agreed terms; this is called the risk premium (e.g. a bank with a BB rating). If a bank has a high credit rating, the interest rate it pays investors will not include risk premiums. A lender who wants to receive a higher interest rate will have to lend to a bank with a lower credit rating but risk losing funds if the bank becomes insolvent.

Bank credit ratings are set by independent rating agencies. These agencies predict a bank's chance of being unable to repay the interest and principal components of funds lent to it and so help lenders set the

---

[76] In June 2001, the Prime Minister of Australia announced a Royal Commission inquiry into the reasons for the collapse of the HIH Insurance group of companies: www.hihroyalcom.gov.au/About/index.asp.
[77] 2008 Report, pp. 78–9, para. 18.

rate of interest they should demand when lending to banks. The factors that a credit rating authority may take into account are a bank's equity capital, reputation and profit history. The 2008 Report mentions that a credit rating is usually assigned to a whole bank on the basis that the bank's equity capital is available to meet the bank's liabilities.[78] This reflects the legal principle that an international bank is a legal person, and of its equity capital being available to meet any of the bank's liabilities regardless of where the liabilities originate. On the other hand, the authorized OECD approach operates on the basis that an international bank's operations can be dissected to allocate profits and expenses in a logical and rigorous manner within the bank.

5.4 Risks assumed

From a legal perspective, an enterprise operating internationally through permanent establishments bears all the risks for the enterprise. If an enterprise operates abroad through subsidiaries, generally the risks assumed by each entity are restricted to that entity under the concept of limited liability. However, a holding company may waive its entitlement to limited liability by providing guarantees to entities dealing with its subsidiaries. The attribution of risk within an international enterprise is a difficult task because there is an absence of a contract between a permanent establishment and the enterprise of which it is part. The attribution of risk to a permanent establishment 'will have to be highly fact-specific'.[79] 'Following, by analogy, paragraph 1.28 of the [Transfer Pricing] Guidelines, the division of risks and responsibilities within the enterprise will have to be, "deduced from their conduct and the economic principles that govern relationships between independent enterprises".[80] This process may include studying the internal practices of an enterprise and comparing them with what independent enterprises would do in similar circumstances, and may also include an examination of any internal information purporting to detail the attribution of risk within the enterprise.

The 2008 Report concludes that when attributing profits to a non-bank permanent establishment, risks must be considered if these risks were assumed by the international enterprise because of the significant people functions performed by the permanent establishment.[81] It would be expected that a permanent establishment's accounts would reflect its assumption

---

[78] Ibid., p. 82, para. 31.   [79] Ibid., p. 31, para. 98.
[80] Ibid.   [81] Ibid., pp. 31–2, para. 99.

of risks and that it would bear the fiscal consequences flowing from these risks. On the other hand, risks cannot be considered when attributing profits to a permanent establishment, if the risks assumed by an international enterprise are not connected with significant people functions performed by the permanent establishment. A separate question is whether the initial assumption of risk by a permanent establishment has been altered by a dealing transferring the risk to another part of the enterprise. Risk will be considered to be transferred to another part of an enterprise by a dealing if there is documentation supporting the dealing, provided the other part of the enterprise performs the significant people function of managing the risk. A part of the enterprise will only be considered to have taken over risks if it is managing the risks because 'risk cannot be separated from function under the authorised OECD approach'.[82] For banks, the key entrepreneurial risk-taking functions are the acceptance and management risks for loans, which are considered below at 6.1.

6 Attributing equity capital to a bank branch

Determining the equity capital of an international bank is a controversial aspect of the first step of the authorized OECD approach in the 2008 Report. The OECD was unable to develop a single consensus method for allocating equity capital to branches of international banks. The authorized OECD approach seeks to allocate equity capital within a highly integrated international bank to its branches, with the residual amount of equity capital being allocated to the bank's head office. As money is fungible, it is difficult to determine with precision where equity capital is allocated within an international bank. Moreover, any method of determining where equity capital is used within an international bank is flawed because of the degree of integration within these enterprises. An international bank requires equity capital to meet prudential requirements for the bank as a whole in its home jurisdiction, but it does not have to allocate equity capital to branches. An international bank has to be able to satisfy the central bank in its residence country that its equity capital is adequate according to international prudential standards. A functional analysis of a branch's assets and associated risk under the authorized OECD approach cannot provide the basis for the allocation of equity capital allocation to the branch. The rules for the allocation of

---

[82] Ibid.

6 ATTRIBUTING EQUITY CAPITAL TO A BANK BRANCH   297

equity capital under the authorized OECD approach are complex, resulting in significant compliance costs for international banks.

International banks are subject to prudential supervision by the regulatory authorities in their residence countries. The regulatory authorities supervise their countries' international banks to ensure they have appropriate equity capital for their international business operations (capital adequacy); such prudential supervision is necessary to ensure the stability of the international banking sector. The Basel Committee on Banking Supervision (Basel Committee) publishes supervisory regulations on the capital adequacy of active international banks.[83] In 2006 the Basel Committee published the *International Convergence of Capital Measurement and Capital Standards: A Revised Framework (Comprehensive Version)*,[84] which is known as the Basel II Capital Framework. In this chapter a reference to the Basel II is a reference to the 2006 Comprehensive Version. Basel II is based on three pillars: minimum equity capital requirements; supervisory review; and market discipline. Under Basel II, regulators and banks are able to select from a range of methods for determining the equity capital requirements for credit risk.[85] It also provides regulators with a limited degree of national discretion in applying the methods to reflect the different conditions of national markets.

The equity capital of a bank is classified into tiers on the basis of permanency of the funding. Tier 1 capital has the highest level of permanency and the main form of capital is shareholder's funds and retained earnings; these funds enable banks to absorb losses and are permanently available for this purpose.[86] Moreover, banks have full

---

[83] The Basel Committee on Banking Supervision (the Basel Committee) formulates broad supervisory prudential standards and guidelines for international banks. It recommends statements of best practice and it expects that national authorities will implement its recommendations through arrangements which are best suited to their national systems. The Committee encourages convergence towards common approaches and common standards without seeking to harmonize the supervisory techniques of member countries. The Basel Committee does not have any supranational supervisory authority and its conclusions do not have the force of law. The member countries are: Australia, Belgium, Brazil, Canada, China, France, Germany, India, Italy, Japan, Korea, Luxembourg, the Netherlands, Russia, Spain, Sweden, Switzerland, UK and US. Bank of International Settlements, 'History of the Basel Committee and its Membership' (April 2009) www.bis.org/bcbs/history.pdf.

[84] Basel Committee on Banking Supervision, *International Convergence of Capital Measurement and Capital Standards: A Revised Framework, Comprehensive Version* (2006).

[85] Ibid., p. 2, para. 7

[86] Basel Committee on Banking Supervision, 'Instruments Eligible for Inclusion in Tier 1 Capital' (October 1998).

control over these amounts allowing them to conserve resources when they are under stress. Tier 1 capital also includes perpetual non-cumulative preference shares and minority interests in the equity of subsidiaries. Tier 2 capital comprises: asset revaluation reserves; subordinated term debt; general loan-loss reserves; hybrid capital instruments; and undisclosed reserves which have passed through the profit and loss account provided they have been accepted by the bank's supervisory authority.[87] An international bank's capital adequacy requirements are determined by dividing the bank's capital base by its total risk-weighted assets; the result is the bank's capital ratio. The risk weighting of the assets takes into account credit risk, market risk and operational risk. An international bank is required to have a minimum capital level equivalent to at least 8 per cent total qualifying capital total risk-weighted assets.[88] The minimum Tier 1 capital is 4 per cent of total risk-weighted assets of the bank.

If an international bank is supervised by the banking regulators in its residence country in accordance with Basel II, its branches will not usually have minimum capital requirements imposed on the branch by the host countries' banking regulators. But Basel II does not require equity capital to be allocated to the branches or head office of an international bank; rather, the requirements are imposed on an enterprise basis. In theory, an international bank's branch operations could be funded exclusively from debt but, if the international bank were to use subsidiary banks in those countries, each subsidiary would have to satisfy the banking requirements in their residence countries including the minimum capital requirements. This would require each subsidiary to have equity capital in each country to satisfy the banking regulation requirements in each jurisdiction. Thus Basel II does not provide a model on which equity capital can be attributed to individual branches of an international bank for tax purposes.

6.1 The allocation of equity capital to international bank branches under the 2008 Report

The 2008 Report notes that the Revised Framework does not require branches to have equity capital, which means that branches could be treated as only being funded by debt.[89] Prudential standards require an

---

[87] Basel Committee on Banking Supervision, *International Convergence of Capital Measurement and Capital Standards, Comprehensive Version* (2006), pp. 14–16 and 244–7.
[88] *Ibid.* p. 2, para. 5.   [89] 2008 Report, p. 95, paras. 87–8.

international bank to maintain minimum equity capital only for the entire bank. Nevertheless, the 2008 Report claims that for tax purposes:

> an arm's length attribution of 'free' capital to the permanent establishment may have to be made to ensure an arm's length attribution of taxable profit to the permanent establishment, even though no 'free' capital has actually been allocated to the permanent establishment for regulatory or other purposes.[90]

In the first step, assets of a bank are attributed to the branches which are treated as the economic owners of the assets in accordance with a functional and factual analysis of the branches' operations. In a traditional banking business, the key entrepreneurial risk-taking functions for wholesale commercial lending are: the sales and trading function involving the initial assumption of risk; and the risk management function for the ongoing management of risk.[91] The financial assets of a bank will initially be attributed to the branches in which the assets were created – the sales and trading function. If a branch alone performed the sales and trading function leading to the creation of a financial asset, the asset will be attributed to that branch.[92] The 2008 Report states that a branch's books are a practical starting point for determining if a branch is the economic owner of assets, provided the branch performs the key entrepreneurial risk-taking functions for the assets.[93] The attribution of assets within an international bank becomes more complex if more than one branch was involved in creating a financial asset.[94] In this situation, the notional transactions between the branches will have to be taken into account under the second step of the authorized OECD approach.

The authorized OECD approach requires assets to be attributed to a branch on the basis of the key entrepreneurial risk-taking functions and the significant people functions.[95] Significant people functions that may be associated with creating financial assets include functions which are connected with non-financial assets, such as marketing intangibles and trade intangibles (information technology systems).[96] This approach requires all functions to receive arm's length consideration. Requiring an international bank to identify and record all the activities involved in the creation of financial assets is complex and imposes high compliance costs on international banks. Moreover, a tax authority would have significant difficulty in scrutinizing all the activities of an international

---

[90] *Ibid.*, p. 95, para. 89.   [91] *Ibid.*, p. 91, para. 68.   [92] *Ibid.*, p. 93, para. 74.
[93] *Ibid.*, p. 92, para. 72.   [94] *Ibid.*, p. 93, para. 74.
[95] *Ibid.*, pp. 90–1, para. 65.   [96] *Ibid.*, pp. 90–1, para. 65.

bank in creating a financial asset in a branch. For example, if a customer borrowing funds from an international bank were significantly influenced by its reputation, an attribution should be made for marketing intangibles. Taking marketing intangibles into account further complicates the process of attributing financial assets to branches of international banks.

After an international bank's assets are attributed within the bank, the next step under the authorized OECD approach is to attribute the equity capital to a branch to support the risks that are attributed to the branch.[97] The authorized OECD approach claims that attributing equity capital to a branch to support its risks complies with the arm's length principle because independent enterprises would require additional equity capital to support riskier financial assets.[98] The OECD acknowledges that measuring risk of a branch of an international bank is a difficult exercise and that any method used must be flexible.[99] As already mentioned, the OECD was unable to establish a single consensus method for attributing equity capital to a branch of an international bank. Instead, the 2008 Report authorizes the use of three methods:

(i) the capital allocation approaches;
(ii) the thin capitalization approaches; or
(iii) the 'quasi-thin capitalization/regulatory minimal capital approach', the safe-harbour approach.[100]

The capital allocation approaches involves an international bank's equity capital being allocated to a branch to reflect the financial assets and risks attributed to it. The thin capitalization approaches involve an international bank's equity capital being attributed to a branch to reflect the amount of equity capital that an independent banking enterprise would be required to have if it were carrying on the same or similar activities under the same or similar conditions in the host country of the branch. The quasi-thin capitalization/regulatory minimal capital approach requires that the branch of an international bank must have at least the minimum amount of equity capital that it would be required to have for regulatory purposes in the host country. This method is not only a compromise method because it is very difficult to allocate equity capital to branches of an international bank on a consistent basis and with

---

[97] Ibid., pp. 95–6, para. 90.   [98] Ibid.
[99] Ibid., p. 96, para. 91.   [100] Ibid., pp. 97–8, para. 98.

precision, but it is arbitrary.[101] Although the above three methods are different, they are not based on the book value of assets, they 'require risks to be measured'.[102]

The 2008 Report concluded that the Basel Accord is a proxy for the arm's length principle:

> [T]he 'standardised' approaches of risk-weighting assets under the latest version of the Basel Accord seem to be a reasonable proxy for measuring risks under the arm's length principle and have the advantage of providing an internationally accepted and reasonably consistent way of measuring risk. Recent regulatory developments to maintain and improve the reliability of the standardised (credit risk) approach relative to the 1988 Basel Accord have the potential to provide an even more accurate method of measuring credit risk and so provide a more reliable proxy for the arm's length principle.[103]

But the Basel Accord is an inappropriate proxy, because it is a prudential measure applied on a consolidated basis and cannot be adapted for tax purposes. The Basel Accord is concerned with an international bank meeting prudential requirements for only its global operations; the prudential requirements do not deal with intra-bank allocation of equity capital. Moreover, this aspect of the authorized OECD approach places excessive emphasis on a theoretical principle at the expense of compliance costs.[104] The banking industry has indicated that the allocation of risk-weighted assets to branches of international banks is not a simple exercise.[105] As the trend in international banking is towards central booking of transactions, the allocation of equity capital to branches is arbitrary.[106]

---

[101] British Bankers' Association, London Investment Banking Association and the Foreign Banks and Securities Houses Association, 'Public Comments Received on the Discussion Draft of the Attribution of Profits to Permanent Establishments – Part II (Special Considerations for Applying the Working Hypothesis to Permanent Establishments of Bank)' (2001), paras. 26–7.
[102] 2008 Report, pp. 95–6, para. 90.   [103] Ibid., p. 97, para. 95.
[104] KPMG, *OECD Discussion Draft on the Attribution of Profits to Permanent Establishments, Representations of KPMG's Worldwide Banking Tax Practice* (2001), para. 19. Commenting on the *2001 Discussion Draft*.
[105] Comments Received from a Joint Working Group Representing: The British Bankers Association, The London Investment Banking Association; The Association of Foreign Banks, OECD Revised Discussion Draft on the Attribution of Profits to Permanent Establishments – Part II (Banks), p. 2, para. 9.
[106] *Ibid.*

6.2 Use of the Basel Accord for tax purposes

The 2008 Report claims that the Basel Accord[107] may be used to measure risks attributed to a permanent establishment because the Basel Accord requires a bank's assets to be allocated with a credit risk weighting.[108] In January 1996, the Basel Accord was amended to include market risks to improve the accuracy of the risk-weighting system.[109] In addition, Basel II provides for operational risk to be assessed. The 2008 Report states that as the Basel II is an international standard for measuring risk, the international standard may increase the prospect of host countries and residence countries agreeing on risk weightings, thus reducing the risk of double taxation.[110] Nevertheless, the OECD accepts that the Basel Accord may be inconsistently interpreted and applied by host countries and residence countries. The banking industry claims that national banking regulators are entitled to use discretion when they apply the Basel II regulatory requirements, which results in differences in the way the requirements are applied in different countries.[111] After a branch has risk-weighted assets attributed to it, the next step is to determine the amount of the bank's equity capital that has to be allocated to the branch to cover its notional risk under the arm's length principle.[112]

It is not surprising that the OECD was unable to develop a consensus on the equity capital measures for bank branches:

> The consultation process has shown that there is an international consensus amongst governments and business on the principle that a bank PE, just like any other type of PE, should have sufficient capital to support the functions it undertakes, the assets it uses and the risks it assumes. However, the consultation process has also shown that it will not be possible to develop a single internationally accepted approach for making that attribution of capital, including 'free' capital. As can be seen

---

[107] Bank of International Settlements, International Convergence of Capital Measurement and Capital Standards, Basel Committee on Banking Supervision (July 1988).
[108] 2008 Report, p. 96, para. 92.
[109] Bank of International Settlements, *Consultative Paper Issued by the Basel Committee on Banking Supervision*, Basel Committee Publications No. 50 (1999), 'A New Capital Adequacy Framework'.
[110] Ibid., p. 96, para. 92.
[111] British Bankers' Association London Investment Banking Association and the Foreign Banks and Securities Houses Association, 'Public Comments Received on the Discussion Draft of the Attribution of Profits to Permanent Establishments – Part II (Special Considerations for Applying the Working Hypothesis to Permanent Establishments of Bank)' (2001), para. 31.
[112] 2008 Report, pp. 97–8, para. 98.

from the discussions above, there is no single approach which is capable of dealing with all circumstances.[113]

The OECD was unable to develop a consensus approach because the allocation of equity capital to a branch is an arbitrary exercise. Any attempt to allocate equity capital to a bank branch is arbitrary for two reasons: first, funds are fungible; and second, a bank branch is an integrated part of an international bank.

The BIAC and the banking sector have claimed that the failure to establish a single consensus method for allocating equity capital to branches of international banks poses grave risks of double taxation for international banks.[114] The BIAC also asserted that this part of the authorized OECD approach is a regression from the version of Part II of the 2001 Discussion Draft; it claimed that the Bank of International Settlements' risk-weighted assets ratio method was the most appropriate approach for attributing equity capital to a branch in accordance with the arm's length principle.[115]

6.3 The shortcomings of the authorized OECD approach in attributing equity capital to branches

The method advocated by the authorized OECD approach for allocating equity capital to branches is extremely complicated and would impose significant compliance costs on taxpayers and administrative burdens on tax authorities. The allocation of equity capital and debt to branches of international banks under the authorized OECD approach is an artificial and arbitrary exercise. It is illusory for the 2008 Report to assert that the Basel II regulatory requirements provide a method for allocating equity capital to branches of an international bank. International prudential standards are imposed at an enterprise level and do not deal with the allocation of equity capital within an international bank. Moreover, international banks operating through branches have the flexibility to allocate their equity capital and debt within their branches to exploit business opportunities. It has been asserted that the arm's length principle is an appropriate measure to attributing equity capital to branches of international banks.[116]

[113] 2008 Report, p. 103, para. 124.
[114] BIAC, *Comments on the 2001 Discussion Draft* (2001), p. 2.
[115] 2001 Discussion Draft, p. 59, para. 87.
[116] KPMG, *OECD Discussion Draft on the Attribution of Profits to Permanent Establishments* (2001), para. 23.

6.3.1 The off-balance sheet exposures of an international bank

The 1988 Basel Accord set minimum capital levels for international banks incorporating both balance sheet exposures and off-balance sheet exposures.[117] As the aim of the Basel Accord is to ensure the soundness and stability of the international banking system, the capital adequacy rules take into account all potential claims against an international bank. Balance sheet items include bank financial assets such as loans made to customers, and other liquid investments such as shares and government securities. Off-balance sheet items for an international bank include derivatives such as swaps, guarantees of subsidiaries and letters of credit. The Basel Accord sets the minimum capital requirements so that an international bank can support both its balance sheet and off-balance sheet exposures.

Under ordinary accounting principles, the sum of the equity capital and debt of an international bank equals the sum of its balance sheet assets. This means that an international bank's equity capital and debt are invested in its assets.[118] Although an international bank is required to maintain equity capital to support its off-balance sheet exposures, it therefore cannot invest funds in off-balance sheet items because they are unfunded positions.[119] This means that there is no correlation between the equity capital of an international bank and its off-balance sheet exposures. Thus, while an international bank will be required to maintain equity capital to support off-balance sheet exposures, its working capital can only be allocated among balance sheet items.[120] Taking off-balance sheet items into account in the process of allocating equity capital can lead to distorted results which can potentially be exploited by an international bank.[121]

---

[117] Bank of International Settlements, *A New Capital Adequacy Framework* (1999), p. 8.
[118] Institute of International Bankers, 'Comments on the OECD Discussion Draft on the Attribution of Profits to Permanent Establishments' (2001), p. 482.
[119] *Ibid.*, p. 492. The Institute states that an off-balance sheet item may be funded if the exposure is marked-to-market for financial or regulatory purposes.
[120] *Ibid.*, p. 493.
[121] *Ibid.*, pp. 493–5. The Institute of International Bankers article considers the allocation of capital to branches in a range of situations and concluded that the results are inconsistent and leave significant scope for manipulation, and thus provide tax avoidance opportunities.

6.3.2 The Basel II standards as a proxy for the arm's length principle under the authorized OECD approach

Apart from the conceptual difficulties of allocating equity capital to branches on a risk-weighted basis, the 2008 Report concluded that the Basel II ratio provides a valid proxy for the arm's length principle.[122] The proposal to adopt the Basel II for the purposes of former Article 7 of the OECD Model is contentious and fraught with difficulties. From a theoretical perspective there would appear to be merit in examining whether the Basel II, as an international prudential standard, could be adapted to allocate equity capital for the purposes of former Article 7 of the OECD Model. The Basel II is an international standard that is applied at the entity level by the regulatory authorities in the residence country of the international bank. The objective of Basel II is to 'strengthen the soundness and stability of the international banking system while maintaining sufficient consistency that capital adequacy regulation will not be a significant source of competitive inequality among internationally active banks'.[123]

The equity capital requirements are set for the bank to cover the risk levels of its assets, and it is immaterial in which parts of the bank the assets are located. Basel II is inappropriate to use as a proxy for equity capital under the arm's length principle because it is designed to ensure capital adequacy. The consequence of ineffective capital adequacy requirements is that an international bank might not have adequate equity capital and this would place the bank at risk of collapse. If the same requirements are used for the purposes of determining the equity capital of a branch, the branch's tax liability in its host country would be directly affected by the Basel II capital adequacy requirements.

While Basel II has improved the capital adequacy requirements, the banking industry predicted that Basel II would not be a rigorous measure of risk.[124] The compelling evidence supporting this argument was the 2008–09 global economic and financial crisis – the most severe economic crisis since the Great Depression – in which the excessive risk-taking of US and other international banks was exposed. The near collapse in 2008–09 of the international banking system vividly exposed Basel II as imperfect and in need of reform. One of the factors

---

[122] 2008 Report, p. 97, para. 95.
[123] Basel Committee on Banking Supervision, *International Convergence of Capital Measurement and Capital Standards* (2006), p. 2, para. 4.
[124] Institute of International Bankers, 'Comments on the OECD Discussion Draft on the Attribution of Profits to Permanent Establishments' (2001), p. 492.

contributing to the severity of the economic and financial crisis was the excessive on- and off-balance sheet leverage of some banks.[125] In addition, there was an erosion of the capital base of many banks and they were holding inadequate liquid assets. Banks sought higher returns but without adequately assessing the risks they were assuming and failing to exercise appropriate due diligence. Other factors that made the international financial system vulnerable were poor underwriting standards, inadequate risk management and increasingly complex financial products.[126] These developments resulted in many banks being unable to cover the systemic trading and credit losses they had incurred during the crisis, resulting in a loss of confidence in the solvency and liquidity of many banks.[127] The crisis in the banking sector spread through the financial economy and then to the rest of the economy, resulting in a severe credit crisis. This led to the public sector providing the banking sector in many countries with an unprecedented injection of liquidity, capital support and guarantees at the expense of taxpayers. Accordingly, the failure of Basel II underscores the significant challenge in adapting proven imperfect international banking supervisory measures to attribute equity capital to branches of international banks.

Apart from the difficulties of adapting a banking supervisory measure for tax purposes, there will always be a significant information gap between a branch of an international bank and the host country tax authority. Determining the risk levels of an international bank and the equity capital necessary to support these risks requires detailed knowledge of the national banking regulations, sophisticated understanding of risk modelling and knowledge of the positions the bank is taking. This task has been made more difficult by the size of international banks and their use of innovative systems for information processing and financial technology for measuring and controlling risks. The US Federal Reserve has claimed that these systems have made it very difficult for regulatory authorities to examine a bank's financial position.[128] In addition, these systems allow banks to arbitrage between the risk measures used by the regulators and the real risk levels of the bank.[129]

---

[125] Basel Committee on Banking Supervision, *Consultative Document* (2009), pp. 1–2, para. 4.
[126] G20 'Declaration Summit on Financial Markets and the World Economy' (15 November 2008), para. 3.
[127] Basel Committee on Banking Supervision, *Consultative Document* (2009).
[128] Board of Governors of the Federal Reserve System, *Using Subordinated Debt as an Instrument of Market Discipline* (1999), pp. 1–2.
[129] Ibid.

6 ATTRIBUTING EQUITY CAPITAL TO A BANK BRANCH   307

As a consequence, the bank's executives will always have an information advantage over the regulatory authority.[130] But it has also been contended that the management of international banks fail to fully understand the risks of innovative financial instruments.[131] The international banking sector did not fully understand the financial instruments that they were trading. In particular, a Bank of England official noted that the documentation required to understand the elements of a particular financial product exceeded 1 billion pages.[132] While financial instruments were designed to limit risk, due to their complexity and widespread use they created more risk.[133] Not only are the regulatory authorities suffering an information disadvantage, but the tax authorities will be at an even more significant disadvantage.

The Basel Committee on Banking Supervision's capital adequacy requirements have taken considerable time to be reformed since they were implemented in 1988. Given the significant developments in international banking since 1988 the strikingly slow progress in the Basel prudential principles suggests that the reform process in the Basel Committee is unable to keep pace with developments. The Basel Committee issued its consultative paper for reforms in 1999, and in 2004 announced that the reforms had been accepted.[134] National regulatory authorities began implementing Basel II in 2008, but it will take several years to be fully implemented. In 2009, the G20 Communiqué urged member countries to progressively adopt the Basel II capital framework.[135] This illustrates the significant time required to reform the capital adequacy rules. Moreover, given the rapid pace of developments in international banking and finance, regulatory responses by the Basel Committee and regulatory authorities will always lag behind these developments.[136]

---

[130] Bebchuck and Spamann, *Regulating Bankers' Pay* (2009), p. 35.
[131] Hu, 'Misunderstood Derivatives: The Causes of Informational Failure and the Promise of Regulatory Incrementalism' (1993), p. 1462.
[132] Haldane, 'Rethinking the Financial Network' (2009), p. 17. Haldane is a Bank of England official commenting on collateralized debt obligations.
[133] *Ibid.*
[134] The Basel Committee announced in 2004 that the new framework, called Basel II, will be available for implementation in member jurisdictions at the end of 2006. The full title of Basel II: *International Convergence of Capital Measurement and Capital Standards: A Revised Framework*. 'G10 central bank governors and heads of supervision endorse the publication of the revised capital framework', June 2004.
[135] G20, 'Declaration on Strengthening the Financial System', London (2 April 2009).
[136] Wood, *Governing Global Banking, The Basel Committee and the Politics of Financial Globalisation* (2005), p. 66.

As Basel II was only implemented in 2008, its role in the 2008–09 economic and financial crisis was limited, but this underscores the significant lag between implementing banking supervisory reforms and the speed of financial innovation. Nevertheless, the Basel Committee has acknowledged that Basel II needs to be modified because of the flaws exposed by the 2008–09 economic and financial crisis.[137] The Basel Committee failed its key goal of maintaining the soundness and stability of the international banking system during the 2008–09 financial crisis, in which collapse of the international banking system was averted only by national governments providing finance to their banks.[138] The proposed reforms are designed to reduce the risk and severity of financial crises by establishing a 'more robust supervisory and regulatory framework for the banking sector'.[139] The proposed areas of reform include:

- better coverage of banks' risk exposures;
- more and higher quality capital to cover these exposures;
- countercyclical capital buffers that are expanded in good times and used in economic crises;
- introducing a non-risk based measure to supplement Basel II and to assist in limiting leverage in the banking system;
- higher liquidity buffers; and
- stronger risk management and governance standards.[140]

In 2009, the Bank for International Settlements issued a consultative document on proposals to improve global capital and liquidity regulations, called Basel III. Basel III reforms are a response to improve the banking sector's ability to deal with financial and economic stress.[141] This aim was endorsed by the G20 leaders and the Financial Stability Board. In 2010, the G20 Communiqué announced that that G20 members were committed to reaching an agreement on stronger capital and liquidity standards as a key reform and endorsed the work of the Basel Committee on Banking Supervision.[142] In December 2010, the Basel Committee issued the Basel III rules text on global regulatory

---

[137] Basel Committee on Banking Supervision, 'Initiatives in response to the crisis by the Basel Committee', Press Release, 30 March 2009.
[138] The US government provided banks with funding of US$88 billion to US banks in 2008.
[139] Basel Committee on Banking Supervision, 'Initiatives in response to the crisis by the Basel Committee', Press Release, 30 March 2009.
[140] Ibid.   [141] Ibid.
[142] G20, Communiqué, 'Meeting of Finance Ministers and Central Bank Governors' (5 June 2010).

standards on bank capital adequacy and liquidity adopted by the Governors and Heads of Supervision, and endorsed by the G20 Leaders at their November 2010 Seoul summit.[143] The aim of Basel III was described as being to maintain financial stability and to encourage sustainable economic growth.[144]

Therefore, it may be inappropriate to base tax rules on the Basel II's capital adequacy requirements because they are complex, imprecise and lag behind developments in international banking.

6.4 A simplified method for estimating the equity capital of a bank branch

It is arbitrary to determine the equity capital of a branch because a branch is a highly integrated part of a unitary international bank. The current trend in international banking is towards central booking. Many banks book transactions either in one jurisdiction or in a small number of jurisdictions. As a branch is not a separate entity its equity capital and debt levels are not fixed. Moreover, one of the reasons that international banks operate globally is the flexibility this provides in their allocation of equity capital and debt funding between their branches and head offices. Thus, any method for allocating equity capital to a branch of an international bank is arbitrary. A better approach would be to treat a branch as having a fixed amount of equity capital. This is the approach advocated in the OECD's 1984 Report on branch banking.[145] Under this approach a branch would determine its deduction for interest under the domestic law in the host country and then a fixed portion of this amount would be disallowed. The advantage of this method is that it is simple and easy to administer. The figure could be set at 5 per cent, such as already applies in Canada.[146]

Canada's income tax law treats 5 per cent of a foreign bank branch's liabilities as being funded from equity capital. Section 20.2 of the Income Tax Act[147] deals with the interest deductions available to a branch of an

---

[143] Bank for International Settlements, 'Basel III rules text and results of the quantitative impact study issued by the Basel Committee', Press Release, 16 December 2010.
[144] Ibid.
[145] OECD, *Transfer Pricing and Multinational Enterprises (Three Taxation Issues)* (1984), p. 67, para. 82.
[146] The Canadian rules are considered in Kobetsky, 'The Tax Treaty Implications of the Foreign Bank Branch Tax Measures' (2002). The US measures are in US Treasury Regulation 1.882-5.
[147] Income Tax Act, R.S.C. 1985, c. 1 (5th Supp.).

international bank in determining the Canadian business income of an authorized foreign bank. A foreign bank branch is entitled to claim deductions for interest in respect of three types of liabilities:

- interest expenses incurred by the branch for loan funds from independent lenders;
- interest expenses notionally incurred by the branch for funds obtained through intra-bank loans; and
- interest expenses for a residual amount called the 'top up'.

Section 20.2 limits the amount a foreign bank branch may deduct for its interest expenses. As this provision treats a branch as having a notional amount of 5 per cent, section 20.2 restricts a branch's deductions to liabilities that are less than 95 per cent of its asset base. The 95 per cent limit applies separately to each of the above three categories of liability. If a foreign bank branch has not exceeded this limit for the first two categories, it may claim a deduction under the third category for the difference between the percentage of total liabilities under the first two categories and the 95 per cent limit. Section 20.2 treats a foreign bank branch as having an equity capital of 5 per cent irrespective of the equity capital of the entire bank. International banks operating through branches are able to move their equity capital and debt between branches with relative ease. One of the advantages of this method is that international banks do not have to spend time and money determining a branch's equity capital. The formula is based on a branch's deductions and may be scrutinized by a tax authority in host countries.

The advantage of a simplified method is that it provides certainty for international banks. If this method were to be adopted, the main issue for the OECD countries to consider would be setting the fixed percentage of notional equity capital through negotiation. If a higher rate of notional equity capital is set, the countries in which foreign bank branches are located will benefit as the branches' business profits will be relatively higher in those jurisdictions. If a lower rate of equity capital is set, the profits of foreign bank branches will be relatively lower in the host jurisdictions. The main advantage of a simplified approach is that it could be applied symmetrically between treaty countries and accordingly is less likely to result in double taxation.

Some of the US tax treaties provide the US branches of foreign banks with the option of using either the treaty approach or domestic approach for determining the equity capital of the branches. Treasury Regulation § 1.882-5 contains the rules for determining the interest expense deductions for foreign banks. Treasury Regulation § 1.882-5(a)(2) when enacted stated that the 'provisions of this section provide the exclusive rules for determining the interest expense attributable to the business profits of a permanent establishment under a U.S. income tax treaty'. The regulation was amended to reflect US tax treaties which allow the contracting parties to treat a permanent establishment:

> as having the same amount of capital that it would need to support its activities if it were a distinct and separate enterprise engaged in the same or similar activities. With respect to financial institutions other than insurance companies, a Contracting State may determine the amount of capital to be attributed to a permanent establishment by allocating the institution's total equity between its various offices on the basis of the proportion of the financial institution's risk-weighted assets attributable to each of them.[148]

US branches of foreign banks have the option of using either the treaty or Treasury Regulation § 1.882-5 to calculate the branch's interest expense. The treaty method risk weights the branch's assets and includes other differences from Treasury Regulation § 1.882-5. But the US Treasury and US Internal Revenue Service are of the view that Treasury Regulation § 1.882-5 has significant advantages over the treaty method as it results in a sufficient allocation of equity capital to a permanent establishment and has the advantage of simplicity.[149]

In summary, it is exceptionally difficult to allocate equity capital to a branch of an international bank because it requires the bank or a tax authority to separate the inseparable. International banks operate as highly integrated unitary businesses, and, as money is fungible, any method of allocating equity capital is arbitrary. Economic theory is unable to provide an objective measure to allocate equity capital within an international bank. This led to the 2001 Discussion Draft using the Basel supervisory principles for allocating equity capital to a branch of an international bank. In response to criticism, the authorized OECD approach uses Basel II or two other broad methods for allocating equity capital to branches, but the OECD failed to develop a single consensus method for allocating the equity capital to branches of international banks. A better approach would be to use a single simplified method that treats branches of international banks as having a fixed amount of equity

---

[148] Exchange of Letters constituting an Agreement Setting Out Various Understandings and Interpretations as they apply to the Conventions between Canada and the United States of America with Respect to Taxes on Income and on Capital, 1980, 2007 Protocol.

[149] Internal Revenue Bulletin No. 2005-32, 8 August 2005, p. 264.

capital for taxation purposes as it limits the risk of double tax or undertaxation. The US currently provides US branches of foreign banks from certain countries with the option of using such a method which has the benefits of simplicity and reduced compliance requirements.

7 The problems with the authorized OECD approach

The first step of the authorized OECD approach is based on the Transfer Pricing Guidelines developed for testing transfer pricing on transactions between associated enterprises. The objective of the arm's length principle in Article 9, on which the Transfer Pricing Guidelines are based, is to ensure that transfer prices reflect comparable transactions between unrelated entities. The fundamental flaw in the authorized OECD approach is that a permanent establishment is not a separate entity under the general law, and consequently a permanent establishment cannot enter transactions with other parts of the enterprise.[150] The Transfer Pricing Guidelines are based on the general law, but in the case of permanent establishments, the measures are applied to a fictional entity and equally fictional transactions.

Under the authorized OECD approach, a permanent establishment is only treated as a separate entity for a limited range of purposes. The OECD Model does not treat a permanent establishment as a separate entity for the purposes of other Articles. Article 10 does not allow a dividend withholding tax to be imposed on permanent establishments. Article 11 does not allow an interest withholding tax to be imposed on notional intra-bank interest paid by branches of international banks. On the issue of risk allocation within an international enterprise, as a permanent establishment is an inseparable part of a legal entity, any allocation of risks within an enterprise is purely fictional. The enterprise as a whole has to bear any risk associated with its business activities, as under the general law risk cannot be isolated in a particular part of an enterprise. In the case of subsidiaries, risks may be restricted to the subsidiaries, provided the parent company did not provide guarantees. For example, if a subsidiary enters into transactions without hedging and becomes insolvent, in the absence of parent guarantees the subsidiary will be liquidated, but the rest of the group will remain unaffected.

---

[150] Sheppard, 'NatWest Revisited in the New British Treaty' (2001), p. 1501.

7 PROBLEMS WITH THE AUTHORIZED OECD APPROACH 313

Under the general law, a subsidiary is able to own assets, but a permanent establishment cannot separately own property. Moreover, in the case of intangible assets such as funds and intellectual property, the assets may be moved around within an international enterprise with ease. To assert that certain assets must be identified with permanent establishments in particular geographic locations is purely fictional and does not reflect business practice. Finally, a subsidiary is able to enter transactions with related parties which are recognized under the general law. But a permanent establishment cannot enter a transaction with other parts of its enterprise. In the case of real transactions there are records which may be scrutinized for tax purposes, but in the case of permanent establishments, intra-entity transactions are fictional and might not be fully recorded.[151] Branch accounts cannot be equated with the financial records of a subsidiary because a subsidiary's financial statements record transactions that are recognized by law and enforceable, even though they are transactions between associated enterprises. A critical difference between a permanent establishment and a subsidiary is that a subsidiary has an independent capital structure. A permanent establishment is not a separate entity, and thus mobile equity capital allocated to it may be transferred with ease to another part of the enterprise. A branch's accounts are not the same as a subsidiary's financial statements because the branch's accounts in the case of intra-entity transactions reflect notional and not real transactions.[152]

There are significant concerns about the practical application of the authorized OECD approach; its shortcomings reflect the flaws in the arm's length principle. The main concern with the authorized OECD approach is significant administrative burdens will be placed on taxpayers. First, they will have to make a functional analysis and, second, they will have to test their dealings to determine if they meet the threshold requirements to be recognized for tax purposes. If an international enterprise makes errors in applying the authorized OECD approach, it faces the risk of tax adjustments and penalties. While the authorized OECD approach is justified as being based on economics, its approach is inconsistent with the business and economic realities of a permanent establishment.[153] The authorized OECD approach imposes significant

---

[151] Arnold and Darmo, 'Summary of Proceedings of an Invitational Seminar on the Attribution of Profits to Permanent Establishments' (2001), p. 540.
[152] Ibid., p. 541.
[153] Institute of International Bankers, 'Comments on the OECD Discussion Draft on the Attribution of Profits to Permanent Establishments' (2001), p. 483.

compliance burdens on international enterprises of undertaking functional and comparative analyses of their operations.[154]

Another flaw in the authorized OECD approach is its reliance on a permanent establishment's records of intra-enterprise dealings. It is not possible to determine accurately the source of the income within these enterprises because of the economic integration of international enterprises.[155] The reasons for this are twofold. First, an international enterprise's accounts are not designed to attribute its income to the various countries in which it operates. Second, international enterprises are generally highly integrated and the activities performed in one part of an enterprise may have economic consequences for other parts of the enterprise that cannot be quantified.[156] Moreover, the arm's length principle is difficult to apply to intangibles because of the lack of arm's length prices and the difficulty of assigning these assets to the particular jurisdictions in which an enterprise operates.[157]

8 Conclusion

The OECD's objective of applying the Transfer Pricing Guidelines to permanent establishments is justified as conforming to the arm's length principle. But it is inappropriate to apply a concept developed for associated enterprises to a permanent establishment that is part of an integrated international enterprise. This chapter has highlighted some of the shortcomings of the authorized OECD approach. While this approach is premised on the arm's length principle, it deviates from this principle, without acknowledging the deviation, for reasons of simplicity or administrative ease. The main shortcoming of this approach is that international banking enterprises will have to maintain a separate set of records to satisfy the requirements in the authorized OECD approach; the compliance costs will be significant. Moreover, the complexity of the authorized OECD approach is also likely to result in significant costs for tax authorities scrutinizing the records of a permanent establishment.

The main flaw in the authorized OECD approach is the proposal to apply the Transfer Pricing Guidelines by analogy to permanent establishments. In the case of associated enterprises, the entities are separate entities and actual transactions between them can be scrutinized. But

---

[154] *Ibid.*
[155] McLure, 'Tax Assignment and Subnational Fiscal Autonomy' (2000), p. 633.
[156] *Ibid.*   [157] *Ibid.*, p. 634.

in the case of international banks, their transactions with the rest of their enterprises are only notional because only one entity is involved. Moreover, treating a branch of an international bank as a separate enterprise conflicts with the intrinsic integrated operation of international enterprises.

One of the main problems with the 2008 Report was its failure to develop a single method for determining the equity capital of branches of international banks. The three broad methods in the 2008 Report for determining equity capital are predicted by the banking industry to result in double taxation or under-taxation. The allocation of equity capital to branches is the Achilles heel of the authorized OECD approach. The allocation of equity capital to branches of international banks is problematic because branches are integrated parts of unitary banking businesses. A better approach is to treat branches as having a fixed amount of equity capital, which is the approach taken in Canadian and US domestic tax law. This method has the advantage of simplicity and it provides a platform on which consensus between the OECD countries could be established. This measure disallows a fixed portion of a branch's interest deduction as a proxy for its equity capital. For the OECD to achieve its goal of preventing under-taxation or double taxation it is vital that the OECD and non-OECD countries act in concert to implement the authorized OECD approach in a consistent manner.

9

Business restructuring involving permanent establishments and the OECD transfer pricing methods

1 Introduction

The key features of international enterprises and multinational enterprise groups are that they carry on business operations in several countries and they conduct cross-border transactions;[1] their size and centralized control provide them with efficiencies and cost savings from their intra-entity or intra-group transactions respectively, which are unavailable to independent enterprises carrying on similar business operations. Their reason for engaging in business restructuring is usually to either maintain or improve their competitive position; these enterprises engage in business restructuring to maximize synergies and economies of scale, to streamline the management of business lines and to improve the efficiency of global operations.[2] Business restructuring is defined by the OECD as the cross-border transfer by an enterprise of functions, assets and risks.[3]

A permanent establishment is treated as a separate and independent enterprise under the authorized OECD approach[4] for attributing profits to the permanent establishment under the 2008 Commentary on former Article 7(2)[5] and new Article 7(2). Permanent establishments may be involved in the business restructuring of an international enterprise if assets, functions and risks are transferred to, or from, a permanent establishment. The authorized OECD approach requires such transfers to be recognized for the purposes of Article 7. Business restructuring of international enterprises operating abroad through permanent

---

[1] Dunning and Lundan, *Multinational Enterprises and the Global Economy* (2nd edn, 2008), p. 6.
[2] OECD, *Transfer Pricing Aspects of Business Restructurings: Discussion Draft for Public Comment* (2009), p. 7, para. 4.
[3] *Ibid.*, p. 6, para. 2.   [4] 2008 Report, pp. 12–13, paras. 12–14.
[5] 2008 OECD Model, pp. 121–2, paras. 12–17; 2010 OECD Model, pp. 158–9, paras. 12–17.

establishments inevitably leads to changes in the allocation of business profits to the permanent establishments involved in the restructuring. Under former Article 7 the change in the allocation of profits must be consistent with the arm's length principle, but applying the arm's length principle to permanent establishments raises complex issues. Under the authorized OECD approach in the 2008 Report, a two-step process is used to attribute profits to a permanent establishment. The first step involves a functional analysis which in the case of business restructuring involving a permanent establishment requires examining whether assets, functions and risks have been transferred to, or from, a permanent establishment. Such transfers will qualify as notional intra-entity transactions. Under the second step, a transfer price must be determined for the transaction using the transfer pricing methods.

Transfers of intangible property under the authorized OECD approach involving permanent establishments and business restructuring are particularly challenging. The difficulties stem from attempting to apply the arm's length principle to notional intra-entity transactions within highly integrated international enterprises which are unlikely to be engaged in by independent parties. First, there is the difficulty of identifying whether intangible property has been transferred to, or from, a permanent establishment. Second, establishing transfer prices for intangible property is very difficult and inevitably arbitrary.

This chapter examines business restructuring involving notional intra-entity transfers of assets by a permanent establishment under the 2008 Commentary on former Article 7(2)[6] and the 2008 Report. It also examines the intra-entity transfers of intangible property under new Article 7. The chapter also considers the transfer pricing methods in the Transfer Pricing Guidelines which are used in applying the second step of the authorized OECD approach. The chapter explains the transfer pricing methods, and concludes with an examination of why the transactional net margin method is a widely used transfer pricing method and justifies the OECD's 2010 reform removing the former requirement that the transactional profit methods are only a method of last resort.

2 Background

The OECD's views on business restructuring involving the attribution of profits to permanent establishments are set out in the 2008 Report and

[6] *Ibid.*

2010 Report. The OECD has been studying business restructuring involving multinational enterprise groups, and in 2005 the OECD established a Joint Working Group (JWG) on Business Restructuring. The JWG was a group of treaty and transfer pricing experts that was created as a subsidiary body of Working Party No. 1 and Working Party No. 6 to work on the OECD's business restructuring and transfer pricing project. The JWG studied the treaty and transfer pricing aspect of business restructuring. In 2007, the OECD referred the work on the transfer pricing aspects of business restructuring in relation to Articles 7 and 9 of the OECD Model to the newly created Working Party No. 6 (WP6) Special Sessions on Business Restructuring. The work on the permanent establishment threshold issues under Article 5 of the OECD Model was referred to Working Party No. 1. In 2009, the OECD issued a discussion paper on business restructuring under Article 9, the associated enterprises Article of the OECD Model (Discussion Draft).[7] In the 2010 Transfer Pricing Guidelines, Chapter IX deals with business restructuring (the internal reallocation of functions, assets and risks) between associated parties under Article 9 of the OECD Model; it does not deal with the attribution of profits to permanent establishments resulting from intra-entity business restructuring.[8]

The OECD has found that since the mid-1990s business restructurings have included:

- converting fully fledged distributors into limited-risk distributors or commissionaires for a related party that might operate as a principal;
- converting fully fledged manufacturers into contract manufacturers or toll manufacturers for a related party that might operate as a principal; and
- transfers of intangible property rights to a central entity (IP company) within a multinational enterprise group.[9]

3 Authorized OECD approach on former Article 7(2)

The 2008 Commentary on former Article 7(2) requires profits to be attributed to a permanent establishment as if it were a separate and

---

[7] OECD, *Transfer Pricing Aspects of Business Restructurings: Discussion Draft for Public Comment* (2009).
[8] 2010 Transfer Pricing Guidelines, p. 237, para. 9.7.   [9] *Ibid.*, pp. 235–6, para. 9.2.

independent enterprise dealing with other parts of an international enterprise.[10] The OECD 2008 Commentary on former Article 7 directs that:

> Sections D-2 and D-3 of Part I of the Report *Attribution of Profits to Permanent Establishments* describe the two-step approach through which this should be done. This approach will allow the calculation of the profits attributable to all the activities carried on through the permanent establishment, including transactions with other independent enterprises, transactions with associated enterprises and dealings (e.g. the *internal transfer of capital or property* or the internal provision of services – see for instance paragraphs 31 and 32) with other parts of the enterprise (under the second step referred to above) . . . [emphasis added].[11]

The Commentary then deals with the realization of a profit when a permanent establishment transfers an asset to other parts of the enterprise:

> There may be a realisation of a taxable profit when an asset, whether or not trading stock, forming part of the business property of a permanent establishment situated within a State's territory is transferred to a permanent establishment or the head office of the same enterprise situated in another State. Article 7 allows the former State to tax profits deemed to arise in connection with such a transfer. Such profits may be determined as indicated below. In cases where such transfer takes place, whether or not it is a permanent one, the question arises as to when taxable profits are realised. In practice, where such property has a substantial market value and is likely to appear on the balance sheet of the importing permanent establishment or other part of the enterprise after the taxation year during that in which the transfer occurred, the realisation of the taxable profits will not, so far as the enterprise as a whole is concerned, necessarily take place in the taxation year of the transfer under consideration. However, the mere fact that the property leaves the purview of a tax jurisdiction may trigger the taxation of the accrued gains attributable to that property as the concept of realisation depends on each country's domestic law.[12]

But the 2008 Commentary on former Article 7(3) restricts this principle to assets other than intangible assets.

> In the case of intangible rights, the rules concerning the relations between enterprises of the same group (e.g. payment of royalties or cost sharing arrangements) cannot be applied in respect of the relations between parts

---

[10] 2008 OECD Model, p. 122, para. 17; 2010 OECD Model, p. 159, para. 17.
[11] *Ibid.*
[12] 2008 OECD Model, p. 124, para. 21; 2010 OECD Model, pp. 160–1, para. 21.

of the same enterprise. Indeed, it may be extremely difficult to allocate 'ownership' of the intangible right solely to one part of the enterprise and to argue that this part of the enterprise should receive royalties from the other parts as if it were an independent enterprise. Since there is only one legal entity it is not possible to allocate legal ownership to any particular part of the enterprise and in practical terms it will often be difficult to allocate the costs of creation exclusively to one part of the enterprise. It may therefore be preferable for the costs of creation of intangible rights to be regarded as attributable to all parts of the enterprise which will make use of them and as incurred on behalf of the various parts of the enterprise to which they are relevant accordingly. In such circumstances it would be appropriate to allocate between the various parts of the enterprise the actual costs of the creation or acquisition of such intangible rights, as well as the costs subsequently incurred with respect to these intangible rights, without any mark-up for profit or royalty. In so doing, tax authorities must be aware of the fact that the possible adverse consequences deriving from any research and development activity (e.g. the responsibility related to the products and damages to the environment) shall also be allocated to the various parts of the enterprise, therefore giving rise, where appropriate, to a compensatory charge.[13]

Consequently, if a permanent establishment is treated as the economic owner of intangible property under the authorized OECD approach in the 2008 Report, a gain derived by a permanent establishment transferring intangible property to another part of the enterprise cannot be recognized under former Article 7 and the 2008 Commentary. Such gains are recognized under new Article 7.

The first step of the authorized OECD approach treats a permanent establishment as a distinct and separate enterprise engaged in similar activities under similar conditions determined by a functional and factual analysis. Under this analysis, assets, risks and equity capital are attributed to the permanent establishment, in addition to income and expenses resulting from intra-entity transactions and transactions with independent entities. Former Article 7(2) requires the profits attributed to a permanent establishment to be based on a hypothetical distinct and separate enterprise 'dealing wholly independently with the enterprise of which it is a permanent establishment'.[14] In treating a permanent establishment as a separate entity under former Article 7(2), notional intra-entity transactions (called dealings) must be recognized to

---

[13] 2008 OECD Model, pp. 127–8, para. 34. 2010 OECD Model, p. 164, para. 34.
[14] 2008 OECD Model, p. 26.

3 AUTHORIZED OECD APPROACH ON FORMER ARTICLE 7(2) 321

attribute profits to the permanent establishment under the second step of the authorized OECD approach.[15]

Under the authorized OECD approach, the profits attributed to a permanent establishment from intra-entity transactions that qualify as dealings must be the same as the transactions between independent enterprises. The authorized OECD approach requires that 'internal dealings are postulated *solely* for the purposes of attributing the appropriate amount of profit' to a permanent establishment.[16] The OECD transfer pricing methods are based on comparing controlled transactions between associated enterprises with comparable uncontrolled transactions between independent enterprises. Consequently, the authorized OECD approach requires the transfer pricing methods to be adapted for a permanent establishment's intra-entity transactions.

3.1 Recognizing intra-entity transactions: first step of the authorized OECD approach

The authorized OECD approach creates a legal fiction of recognizing intra-entity transactions which are not otherwise recognized.[17] First, a permanent establishment is not a separate entity as it is not legally separate from the rest of the enterprise of which it is part; and second, transactions require that at least two independent entities are transacting. The 2008 Report claims that intra-entity transactions require greater scrutiny than transactions between associated enterprises, including greater scrutiny of documentation recording intra-entity transactions.[18] Consequently, the greater scrutiny requires that a threshold must be passed before an intra-entity transaction is recognized as a notional transaction for the purposes of former Article 7(2). The Transfer Pricing Guidelines prescribe that certain transactions between associated enterprises which are legal transactions may not be recognized for tax purposes if 'they do not take place under the normal commercial conditions that would apply between independent enterprises'.[19] As intra-entity transactions are a legal fiction, the 2008 Report notes that

---

[15] 2008 Report, p. 53, para. 207.   [16] *Ibid.*, p. 53, para. 208.
[17] *Ibid.*, p. 54, para. 210.   [18] *Ibid.*
[19] *Ibid.*, p. 54, para. 211. The Transfer Pricing Guidelines set out the circumstances in which transactions between associated enterprises are not recognized or would be altered to reflect normal commercial transactions between independent enterprises: 2009 Transfer Pricing Guidelines, pp. 38–9, paras. 1.37–1.38.

they 'are perhaps more susceptible to being disregarded or restructured than transactions between associated enterprises'.[20]

The 2008 Report directs that the starting point for evaluating intra-entity transactions is the accounting records and internal documentation.[21] The authorized OECD approach claims that intra-entity transactions will be recognized for the purposes of attributing profit to a permanent establishment, provided they reflect real and identifiable events, such as the physical transfer of stock in trade, the provision of services, use of an intangible asset, a change in the use of a capital asset, or the transfer of a financial asset. A functional and factual analysis of a permanent establishment is used to determine whether intra-entity transactions have occurred and whether they are economically significant. An intra-entity transaction will be recognized as a dealing under the functional and factual analysis if it satisfies these tests, irrespective of the enterprise's accounting records or other documentation.[22] Recognized intra-entity transactions must reflect economically significant transfers of risks, responsibilities and benefits.[23]

If intra-entity transactions are recognized as dealings they are treated as transactions between associated enterprises, and paragraphs 1.28 and 1.29 of the Transfer Pricing Guidelines can be applied in the permanent establishment context by analogy.[24] Paragraph 1.28 states that the terms of a contract between associated enterprises may be inferred from the communications between the parties. The 2008 Report claims that in applying this guideline by analogy, the contractual terms of an intra-entity transaction are the accounting records and contemporaneous internal documentation claiming to transfer risks, responsibilities and benefits which involve a permanent establishment. In addition, paragraph 1.26 of the Transfer Pricing Guidelines states that it must be determined whether a purported transfer of risk reflects the economic substance of an associated party transaction. Paragraph 1.27 notes that 'an additional factor to consider in examining the economic substance of a purported risk allocation is the consequence of such an allocation in arm's length transactions. In arm's length dealings it generally makes sense for parties to be allocated a greater share of risks over which they have relatively more control.'[25]

The 2008 Report directs that accounting records and contemporaneous documentation are useful starting points for the purposes of

---

[20] 2008 Report, p. 54, para. 211. [21] Ibid., p. 54. para. 212. [22] Ibid.
[23] Ibid., p. 54, para. 213. [24] Ibid., pp. 54–5, para. 214. [25] Ibid.

recognizing intra-entity transactions, if the documentation reflects a transfer of economically significant risks, responsibilities and assets. Consequently, international enterprises are encouraged to prepare such documentation to minimize the risk of disputes. Moreover, under the 2008 Report, tax authorities will recognize such documentation despite its lack of legal effect if the following three conditions are satisfied:

- the documentation is consistent with the economic substance of the activities taking place within the enterprise as revealed by the functional and factual analysis;
- the arrangements documented in relation to the dealing, viewed in their entirety, do not differ from those which would have been adopted by comparable independent enterprises behaving in a commercially rational manner or, if they do so differ, the structure as presented in the taxpayer's documentation does not practically impede the tax administration from determining an appropriate transfer price; and
- the dealing presented in the taxpayer's documentation does not violate the principles of the authorized OECD approach by, for example, purporting to transfer risks in a way that segregates them from functions.[26]

The 2008 Report states that if the above threshold test is satisfied, the authorized OECD approach applies by analogy the principles in paragraphs 1.26 to 1.29 and 1.36 to 1.41 of the Transfer Pricing Guidelines.[27] The principles are applied to the intra-entity transactions between a permanent establishment and the other parts of the international enterprise. Intra-entity transactions must initially be based on the purported transactions using the transfer pricing methods applied by the international enterprise, provided they comply with the methods in the Transfer Pricing Guidelines. Tax authorities are required to apply the guidance in paragraph 1.36 of the Transfer Pricing Guidelines when attributing profits to a permanent establishment and should not disregard intra-entity transactions or substitute other dealings for them. But a tax authority may disregard intra-entity transactions under paragraph 1.37 of the Transfer Pricing Guidelines in the following two situations. First, if the economic substance of a transaction differs from its form, a tax authority may re-characterize a transaction to reflect its economic substance.[28] The Transfer Pricing Guidelines state that:

---

[26] Ibid., p. 55, para. 216.   [27] Ibid., p. 55, para. 217.
[28] 2009 Transfer Pricing Guidelines, pp. 38–9, para. 137.

The second circumstance arises where, while the form and substance of the transaction are the same, the arrangements made in relation to the transaction, viewed in their totality, differ from those which would have been adopted by independent enterprises behaving in a commercially rational manner and the actual structure practically impedes the tax administration from determining an appropriate transfer price.[29]

In the second circumstance, a tax authority may re-characterize the transaction so that it reflects the terms that independent enterprises would have used.

3.2 Second step: determining the profits of the hypothesized distinct and separate enterprise based on a comparability analysis

The authorized OECD approach requires a permanent establishment's intra-entity dealing to be compared to transactions between independent entities. The comparison is made by following the comparability analysis in the Transfer Pricing Guidelines. The comparability analysis requires that either:

- the differences between a dealing and comparable transactions between independent enterprises do not materially affect the measure used to attribute profits to the permanent establishment; or
- that reasonably accurate adjustments can remove the material effects of any differences.[30]

The authorized OECD approach requires that the traditional transaction transfer pricing methods in the Transfer Pricing Guidelines should be applied to intra-entity dealings.

3.3 Applying the second step of the authorized OECD approach

3.3.1 Change in the use of a tangible asset

If an international enterprise carries on operations abroad through permanent establishments, the enterprise is the legal owner of its tangible assets; but former Article 7 requires its tangible assets to be allocated to its permanent establishments at the time of their acquisition if the permanent establishments are the economic owners of the assets. In addition, when assets are transferred by a permanent establishment to another part of an international enterprise the change in economic

---

[29] Ibid.   [30] 2008 Report, p. 56, para. 218.

ownership of the assets must be recognized as a dealing for the purposes of former Article 7. The 2008 Report states that there is a broad consensus in OECD countries to attribute the economic ownership within an international enterprise of a tangible asset to the country in which the asset is being used, unless the circumstances require a different approach.[31] Consequently, if an asset is moved from a permanent establishment to another part of an international enterprise, this usually results in a change in the economic ownership of the asset. In such a situation, the transfer of an asset by a permanent establishment would be a 'real and identifiable event' which is a recognized internal dealing.[32] The example provided in the 2008 Report is a transfer of manufacturing equipment from the head office of an international enterprise to a permanent establishment. If the equipment is used by the permanent establishment in its business operations, the change in the place of use of the asset results in an intra-entity dealing that is recognized under the authorized OECD approach.

The next issue is to account for the transfer of an asset to a permanent establishment in the process of attributing profits to it. In this situation there would be no contract as the dealing is merely an intra-entity transfer. The 2008 Report directs that the principles in paragraphs 1.28 to 1.29 of the Transfer Pricing Guidelines should be applied by analogy to a dealing and that the terms of the dealing are implied from the accounting records, the conduct of the permanent establishment, and contemporaneous internal documentation on the transfer of risks, responsibilities and benefits to the permanent establishment.[33] The fair market value of an asset transferred to a permanent establishment would be used for depreciation purposes in the host country.

The factual analysis may indicate that a permanent establishment and other parts of the international enterprise have created an agreement comparable to a cost contribution agreement type activity in which the tangible asset is used by different parts of the enterprise on a serial basis.[34] Applying the principles in Chapter VIII of the Transfer Pricing Guidelines by analogy, there may not be a need to recognize any change in the value of the tangible asset at the time of transfer of the asset, provided the asset is transferred within the enterprise in a manner which complies with the intended serial use of the asset under the cost contribution type agreement.

---

[31] Ibid., pp. 58–9, para. 229.   [32] Ibid., p. 54, para. 212.
[33] Ibid., p. 59, para. 230.   [34] Ibid., p. 59, para. 232.

On the other hand, if the use of an asset does not comply with the cost contribution type agreement, the change in value of the asset would need to be recognized.[35] The examples provided in the 2008 Report were that the asset may be used in an activity which is not part of the cost contribution agreement, the part of the enterprise using the asset may have ceased to be a participant in the cost contribution type agreement, or a part of the enterprise may have commenced using the asset and become a new participant in the cost contribution type agreement.

A notional lease of an asset will occur if a permanent establishment is the economic owner of an asset that has been transferred to another part of the enterprise, and the functional and factual analysis indicates that the situation is similar to a lease.[36] In this situation, the profit attributed to the permanent establishment would be an arm's length charge for the right to use the asset under a comparable lease or licence between independent parties. Because the permanent establishment is treated as the economic owner of the asset, a profit or loss would not be attributed to the permanent establishment when the asset is transferred.

3.3.2 Change in use of an intangible asset: New Article 7

3.3.2.1 Effect on the profits attributed to a permanent establishment

As stated above, the principles in the 2008 Report on intra-entity transfers of intangible property by a permanent establishment cannot be recognized under the 2008 Commentary. This part of the 2008 Report was implemented under the new Article 7. If a functional and factual analysis of a permanent establishment indicates that it has created an intangible asset or has incurred extraordinary marketing expenses for an intangible asset, the permanent establishment would be entitled to a return that is comparable to that of an independent enterprise performing a similar activity.[37] Where a permanent establishment is treated as either the sole or joint economic owner of an intangible asset, the principles in Chapter VI of the Transfer Pricing Guidelines on special considerations for intangible property should be followed by analogy in attributing profits to the permanent establishment. The principles in Chapter VII on services should be applied by analogy if a permanent establishment has provided services in the development of intangible property. Moreover, there must be an examination of the conditions under which a permanent establishment provides services connected

---

[35] *Ibid.*, p. 59, para. 233.   [36] *Ibid.*, p. 59, para. 234.   [37] *Ibid.*, p. 60, para. 235.

with creating intangible property and whether the permanent establishment is a sole or joint economic owner of the property.[38]

A permanent establishment that only performs the functions of a contract researcher, under paragraph 7.41 of the Transfer Pricing Guidelines, is entitled to a return that is consistent with the returns earned by independent enterprises performing similar functions and will not be the owner of any intangible property that is created.[39] On the other hand, a permanent establishment and other parts of the enterprise may be participating in a comparable cost contribution type arrangement – an arrangement which reflects a cost contribution arrangement between associated enterprises. In this situation, the permanent establishment and the other participants will jointly contribute to the development of the intangible property and share in any return from it. For cost contribution type arrangements, the principles in Chapter VIII of the Transfer Pricing Guidelines should be applied by analogy.

The Transfer Pricing Guidelines describe a cost contribution arrangement between associated enterprises as:

> A CCA [cost contribution arrangement] is a framework agreed among business enterprises to share the costs and risks of developing, producing or obtaining assets, services, or rights, and to determine the nature and extent of the interests of each participant in those assets, services, or rights. A CCA is a contractual arrangement rather than necessarily a distinct juridical entity or permanent establishment of all the participants. In a CCA, each participant's proportionate share of the overall contributions to the arrangement will be consistent with the participant's proportionate share of the overall expected benefits to be received under the arrangement, bearing in mind that transfer pricing is not an exact science. Further, each participant in a CCA would be entitled to exploit its interest in the CCA separately as an effective owner thereof and not as a licensee, and so without paying a royalty or other consideration to any party for that interest. Conversely, any other party would be required to provide a participant proper consideration (*e.g.* a royalty), for exploiting some or all of that participant's interest.[40]

A permanent establishment that is either the sole or joint owner of intangible property must, under the authorized OECD approach, receive an arm's length return if the property is used by other parts of the international enterprises.[41] A permanent establishment may receive a royalty from other parts of the international enterprise for the use of intangible

---

[38] *Ibid.*, p. 60, para. 236.   [39] *Ibid.*
[40] 2009 Transfer Pricing Guidelines, p. 180, para. 83.   [41] 2008 Report, p. 60, para. 238.

property. Alternatively, a royalty may be embedded into a separate payment that covers a range of matters. In this situation it may be necessary for the permanent establishment to determine that it has recognized the expenses incurred in the creation, development or maintenance of the intangible asset.[42]

Under the authorized OECD approach the term royalty refers to the arm's length consideration for the use of intangible property if the owner were an independent enterprise.[43] Independent enterprises owing intangible property may include a notional royalty in the price of goods they sell to customers, or they may use the residual profit split method to share the overall profit with the owner of the intangible property. If a permanent establishment entered into similar arrangements with other parts of an international enterprise, it would be required to identify a separate notional royalty amount.[44] The 2008 Report expressly states that identifying a notional royalty payment is considered only for the purpose of attributing profits to a permanent establishment and that the issue of withholding taxes is outside the scope of the report.

The 2008 Report claims that under the authorized OECD approach the objective is to ensure that a permanent establishment owning intangible property receives an arm's length rate of return for its use, but a specific internal royalty does not need to be identified. A return from intangible property may be implicitly attributed to a permanent establishment with a specific royalty under a profit method.[45] Under the transactional profit split method a return for use of intangible property may be an explicit factor or the return may be implicitly included in other factors. In this situation the permanent establishment has received consideration for the use of its intangible property.

On the issue of equity capital, if a permanent establishment is the owner of intangible property it will be required to have equity capital to support the risks connected with the development of the intangible property.[46] While it is difficult to determine precisely the risks of developing intangible property, if the risks are significant they must be determined under the authorized OECD approach. On the other hand, a permanent establishment that is a contract researcher would not require limited amounts of equity capital as it would receive progressive payments for its research by the other parts of the international enterprise.

---

[42] Ibid., p. 60, para. 237.   [43] Ibid., p. 60, para. 238.   [44] Ibid.
[45] Ibid., pp. 60–1, para. 239.   [46] Ibid., p. 61, para. 240.

3.3.2.2 Internal dealings and the use of intangible property
Intangible property owned exclusively by the head office of an international enterprise may be provided to a permanent establishment for use in its business operations, which may occur when a permanent establishment enters into new business areas. In this situation, under the authorized OECD approach, a functional and factual analysis may indicate that an intra-entity dealing has occurred.[47] The profit to be attributed to the dealing is required to reflect comparable transactions between independent parties. Under the authorized OECD approach, a change in use of an intangible asset may result in either a permanent establishment acquiring a non-exclusive right to use the asset or a beneficial interest in the asset.[48] The value of the interest that a permanent establishment acquires in an intangible property intra-entity dealing would be based on comparable transactions between independent entities.[49] The 2008 Report states that a permanent establishment may be treated as acquiring intangible property at fair market value and the permanent establishment may, depending on the host country's rules, be able to base its depreciation deductions on this value. A functional and factual analysis may indicate that a permanent establishment has a right to use intangible property as a licensee under a notional licence agreement. If the licence agreement reflects agreements between independent parties, the permanent establishment may be able to claim a deduction for a notional royalty payment.[50]

If an international enterprise enters into a licensing agreement with an independent party to use an intangible asset, the right to use the asset would be an asset. The economic owner of this asset is the part of the international enterprise performing the significant people functions connected with the right to use the intangible property.[51] Thus, if a permanent establishment is the economic owner of the licence, it may enter into an intra-entity dealing with another part of the enterprise in which it may be transferring the economic ownership or providing the right to use the intangible property. The terms and type of the intra-entity dealing depend on a functional and factual analysis. Determining the economic owner of intangible property in a highly integrated international enterprise is a challenging task as the authorized OECD approach requires the enterprise to analyse its business operations in an artificial manner. Moreover, it will be costly for an international

---

[47] Ibid., p. 61, para. 241.   [48] Ibid., p. 61, para. 242.   [49] Ibid., p. 61, para. 243.
[50] Ibid., pp. 61–2, para. 244.   [51] Ibid., p. 62, para. 245.

enterprise to undertake a functional and factual analysis purely for the purposes of its notional intra-entity dealings with permanent establishments involving intangible property.

3.3.2.3 Cost contribution arrangements
A permanent establishment may enter into a cost contribution type arrangement with its head office and other permanent establishments. In this situation the permanent establishment and other parts of the international enterprise would be the economic participants in a notional intra-entity cost contribution arrangement (CCA) and their intra-entity dealings would reflect similar arrangements between associated enterprises in a CCA.[52] The 2008 Report directs that the principles in Chapter VIII of the Transfer Pricing Guidelines setting out the requirements for a CCA must be applied by analogy to permanent establishments participating in a notional intra-entity CCA. The 2008 Report notes that if a permanent establishment claims to be a participant in an intra-entity CCA, its host country will expect supporting material, such as documentation. The documentation requirements would reflect those necessary to establish that a CCA between associated enterprises exists under the principles in Chapter VIII of the Transfer Pricing Guidelines.[53] A functional and factual analysis is also required to establish the business activities of the participants to the notional CCA and their economic relationships under the purported arrangement. The functional and factual analysis should disclose the entitlements and requirements imposed on participants to the notional CCA.

A permanent establishment in a host country claiming to be a participant to an intra-entity CCA must be able to prove to that country's tax authority that its contribution to the arrangement is 'consistent with what an independent enterprise would have agreed to contribute under comparable circumstances given the benefits it reasonably expects to receive from the arrangement'.[54] A permanent establishment purporting to participate in an intra-entity CCA is required to have comprehensive documents reflecting the intentions and economic relationships of the participants. Moreover, the documents proving the intention to establish an intra-entity CCA must be contemporaneous.[55] The 2008 Report indicates that a permanent establishment cannot retrospectively claim

---

[52] Ibid., p. 62, para. 247.   [53] Ibid., p. 62, para. 248.
[54] Transfer Pricing Guidelines, para. 8.8, quoted in the 2008 Report, p. 63, para. 249.
[55] 2008 Report, p. 63, para. 250.

that an intra-entity CCA exists when there is no contemporary proof to support the claim, such as documentary evidence.

CCAs have caused significant challenges for taxpayers and tax authorities, which further reveal the weakness in the arm's length principle. CCAs involving intangible property are problematic as it may be uncertain which items of intangible property are involved and it is very difficult to price the cost of buying into (buy-ins) or selling out (buy-outs) of a CCA. The experience in the US reveals the problems in pricing CCAs, particularly buy-ins.[56] The problem of dealing with buy-ins is determining the nature, scope and value of the intangible property rights transferred under a cost sharing arrangement.[57] Other issues are the form, structure and timing of buy-in payments by a new entrant to a cost sharing arrangement. The experience in the US is that there were disputes with taxpayers using cost sharing arrangements in which intangible property was subject to a buy-in, and there were also difficulties in valuing the intangible property.[58]

The most challenging part of CCAs is valuing the intangible property. CCAs usually involve two types of intangible property.[59] First, it may be intangible property that has not yet been created but is envisioned intangible property for a CCA; in this case, the parties to the CCA expect to exploit the envisioned as property after it is developed. Second, it may be existing intangible property which contributes to the development of the envisioned intangible property, but the intangible property which cannot currently be exploited. This may be called 'in process' intangible property and it is extremely difficult to value.[60] The existing intangible property may be provided by one or more of the parties to the CCA. The complexity of CCAs and in particular the valuation problems have created the potential in the US for profit shifting. In 2007, the US Department of the Treasury found undervaluations of CCAs resulted in international income shifting from non-arm's length transfer pricing.[61] The US Internal Revenue Service (IRS) has had many transfer pricing disputes with taxpayers over CCAs involving significant sums. Moreover, these disputes were costly to both the US IRS and taxpayers. These disputes have involved the valuation of intangible property, determining which intangible property is the subject of a buy-in, and

---

[56] US Department of Treasury (Office of Tax Analysis), *Income Shifting from Transfer Pricing: Further Evidence from Tax Return Data* (2008).
[57] US Department of the Treasury, *Report to Congress on Earning Stripping, Transfer Pricing and US Income Tax Treaties* (2007), p. 48.
[58] Ibid.   [59] Ibid.   [60] Ibid., pp. 48–9.   [61] Ibid., p. 49.

the nature of deemed transfers.[62] These challenges could be expected to occur in cost contribution type arrangements involving an international enterprise and its permanent establishments.

4 Transfer pricing methods

The authorized OECD approach requires that the transactional transfer pricing methods in the Transfer Pricing Guidelines should be applied to intra-entity dealings. The Transfer Pricing Guidelines set out five transfer pricing methods to determine whether a transfer price for a controlled transaction is an arm's length price. There are three traditional transaction profit methods and two transactional profit methods. The traditional transaction methods compare controlled transfer prices to prices in uncontrolled transactions to determine if controlled transfer prices are at arm's length while the transactional profit methods focus on net profits from controlled transactions. In practice, the traditional transaction methods are difficult to apply because of the lack of comparative transactions resulting in the transactional profit methods being more commonly used.

4.1 Comparative uncontrolled price method

The best method of determining whether a price charged for property or services is arm's length is to compare controlled transactions to uncontrolled transactions. The comparative uncontrolled price (CUP) method 'compares the price charged for property or services transferred in a controlled transaction to the price charged for property or services transferred in a comparable uncontrolled transaction in comparable circumstances'.[63] If comparable uncontrolled transactions can be identified, a CUP may be extracted from which to test transfer prices used by associated enterprises in controlled transactions to ensure that the transfer prices comply with the arm's length principle. If there is a significant difference between transfer prices used by associated enterprises and the potential CUPs that have been identified, the CUPs may need to replace the transfer prices that were used by the associated enterprises. The CUP method is the most direct way of determining arm's length prices.

---

[62] *Ibid.*
[63] 2009 Transfer Pricing Guidelines, pp. 52–3, para. 2.6; 2010 Transfer Pricing Guidelines, p. 159, p. 63, para. 2.13.

For a CUP to be reliable, property or services provided and the circumstances of their provision must be identical to the property or services and circumstances in transactions between associated enterprises. A CUP will be reliable if differences between the controlled and uncontrolled transactions would not affect the prices in the open market. If there are any differences, adjustments will be required to make the CUP a reliable comparator. If numerous adjustments are required to a CUP this method may not be reliable as an indicator of arm's length prices. The factors that need to be considered to ensure the reliability of a CUP are the relative differences in:

- the characteristics of the products or services being compared;[64]
- the contractual terms of controlled and uncontrolled transactions;[65] and
- markets in which the associated enterprises and independent entities operate.[66]

The CUP works best for commodities for which there is a world market price, such as coal, oil and wheat. But even in relation to commodities it may be difficult at times to find a reliable CUP. In practice it is very difficult to find a CUP for products that are not commodities.

4.2 Resale price method

The resale price method (RPM) is used to establish a transfer price if an entity (the reseller) purchases products from associated enterprises in

---

[64] 2009 Transfer Pricing Guidelines, p. 32, para. 1.19; 2010 Transfer Pricing Guidelines, p. 44, para. 139. The Transfer Pricing Guidelines set out the following characteristics of tangible property, intangible property or services which may be considered in determining the comparability of controlled and uncontrolled transactions. In the case of tangible property the characteristics are: the features of the property, the quality of the property, the property's reliability, the availability of the property, and the volume of sales. For intangible property they are, whether the intangible property is being sold or licensed, the type of intangible property, the duration of the arrangement, and the benefits predicted to arise from the use of the property. In relation to services, the nature and extent of the services are examined.

[65] The terms of a contract, which may be express or implied, deal with the allocation of entitlements, risks and obligations between the contracting parties: 2009 Transfer Pricing Guidelines, p. 35, paras. 1.28–1.29; 2010 Transfer Pricing Guidelines, pp. 47–8, paras. 152–4.

[66] The factors to be considered include the geographic market, the type of market, the size of the market, the degree of competition in the market, the availability of substitute goods and services, and the supply and demand levels in the particular market: 2009 Transfer Pricing Guidelines, pp. 35–6, para. 1.30; 2010 Transfer Pricing Guidelines, pp. 48–9, paras. 155–8.

controlled transactions and then resells the products to independent buyers. In this situation, the RPM determines a transfer price for a product by starting with the price paid by an independent buyer for the product and then deducting an appropriate gross profit margin for the functions performed by the reseller. The resulting price is the appropriate transfer price for the product. The gross profit margin used in the RPM is the margin an independent reseller would seek in order to cover its operating expenses and provide an appropriate return for the functions performed, assets used, and risks assumed by the reseller. If a reseller acquires property under both controlled and uncontrolled transactions, the gross profit margin for the controlled transactions may be calculated by reference to the reseller's gross profit margin derived from the uncontrolled transactions. In this situation an internal comparator is used to determine the appropriate gross profit margin. For associated enterprises that only acquire products through controlled transactions, the gross profit margins derived by independent entities selling similar products in uncontrolled transactions may be used to determine comparable gross profit margins. As with the CUP method, adjustments are required for any differences between controlled and uncontrolled transactions. The advantage of the RPM over the CUP method is that fewer adjustments are required to reflect product differences because minor differences in products are less likely to materially affect the reseller's gross profit margins.

4.3 Cost plus method

The cost plus method (CPM) determines an arm's length price by adding an appropriate gross profit margin to an associated enterprise's costs of producing products or providing services. The gross profit margin should reflect the functions performed by an entity and should include a return for capital used and risks accepted by the entity. The gross profit margin for a controlled transaction is calculated by reference to the gross profit margins made in comparative uncontrolled transactions. Ideally the comparative transactions should be the same or very similar to the controlled transactions. If an associated enterprise engages in both controlled and uncontrolled transactions for the supply of the same products or services, the uncontrolled transactions may provide a comparative gross profit margin.

The comparison under the CPM should reflect the functions performed, risks involved and contractual terms. While the products being compared under the CPM need not be similar, there are limitations to the product differences. If there is a significant difference between the products being produced by controlled and uncontrolled transactions, the product differences may reflect different functions being performed by the suppliers and would make these transactions unreliable comparators. When applying the CPM comparable accounting methods should be used. If there are differences between the accounting methods used for the controlled and uncontrolled transactions, the data will need to be adjusted to ensure the same costs and the same methods of measuring the costs are being used. The gross profit margins for controlled and uncontrolled transactions have to be measured consistently to ensure that the uncontrolled comparator being used is a reliable indicator of arm's length prices.

The factors that may be used to determine if comparative gross profit margins are reliable are:

- complexity of manufacturing or assembly;
- engineering of production and process;
- procurement, purchasing and inventory control;
- testing;
- selling, general and administrative expenses;
- foreign currency risk; and
- contractual terms, such as warranties, volume of sales, trade credit and transportation costs.[67]

The OECD suggests that CPM is most appropriate where semi-finished products are sold between related parties, where associated parties have joint facility agreements, long-term buy-and-supply arrangements are in place, or where the controlled transaction is the provision of services.[68]

4.3.1 Contract manufacturing and toll manufacturing

The CPM is also used for contract manufacturing and toll manufacturing. In manufacturing there are principal manufacturers, contract manufacturers and toll manufacturers. A principal manufacturer carries on a business of manufacturing goods and may subcontract some of its manufacturing work to contract and toll manufacturers. The principal manufacturer will own its product lines and will usually hold some intangible property which may include valuable trademarks and patents.

---

[67] United Nations, *Transfer Pricing* (2001), p. 16.
[68] 2009 Transfer Pricing Guidelines, p. 60, para. 2.32; 2010 Transfer Pricing Guidelines, pp. 70–1, para. 239.

Contract manufacturers provide manufacturing services to principal manufacturers, and own the raw materials that are used in manufacturing and the finished products before sale to a principal manufacturer. The contract manufacturer does not develop product lines and performs manufacturing functions for principal manufacturers. Contract manufacturers do not have to bear market risk because they have an assured return for the work they are performing. Contract manufacturers may hold some know-how on the manufacturing process and procedures in acquiring raw materials for the manufacturing process. Toll manufacturers perform a manufacturing service for principal manufacturers. Toll manufacturers are provided with the raw materials to be used in the manufacturing and they do not own the products produced prior to delivery to a principal manufacturer. Toll manufacturers, like contract manufacturers, do not have market risk. Toll manufacturers receive a lower return than contract manufacturers as they are only service providers. Contract and toll manufacturers are usually rewarded on a per unit of production or a fee for service basis.

The CPM can only rarely be used for principal manufacturers as their profit margin will vary depending on the goods they produce. The gross profit margins will vary for each good produced and if there is a well-recognized trademark, the gross profit margins may be significant. In practice, it is usually difficult to find comparable product lines for principal manufacturers where significant trademarks exist, thereby preventing the CPM from being applied.

The CPM does have some problems in application, including the calculation of the costs of a supplier. While a business must at a very minimum be able to derive profits that cover its costs, the costs may not be determinative of appropriate gross profit margins for certain entities. Moreover, the OECD notes that in certain cases there may be no link between a business's costs and the market price for the products or services it produces.[69] Adjustments under the CPM need to be made to ensure that comparable costs are being compared. For example, if a supplier in a controlled transaction is operating from leased premises, the costs cannot be compared with a supplier in uncontrolled transactions operating from premises which it owns.

It is important that under the CPM comparable costs are being used in relation to the functions performed and risks being assumed by the

---

[69] 2009 Transfer Pricing Guidelines, p. 61, para. 2.36; 2010 Transfer Pricing Guidelines, p. 72, para. 243.

parties. Expenses may be classified as operating expenses and non-operating expenses including financing expenses. The OECD suggests that the following factors be considered:

- If a supplier's expenses reflect a functional difference which has not been taken into account in applying this method, an adjustment to the cost plus mark-up may be required.
- If a supplier's expenses reflect additional functions that are distinct from the activities tested by the method, additional compensation for these functions may be required.
- If differences in the costs of the parties being compared reflect efficiency or inefficiency, then adjustments to the gross profit margins being compared may not be required.[70]

4.4 The transactional profit methods

The OECD claims that the CUP method, RPM and CPM are the most direct means of determining transfer prices, but in practice it is unusual to find reliable comparable transactions.[71] The OECD argues the profit-split method and the transactional net margin method are the only profit methods that satisfy the arm's length principle requirement. Prior to the adoption of the 2010 Transfer Pricing Guidelines the OECD directed that multinational enterprise groups could use the transactional profit methods only in exceptional circumstances where there was no comparable data available or it is unreliable,[72] but in practice, the transactional net margin method has been the most commonly applied transfer pricing method.[73] The key feature of the transactional profit

---

[70] 2009 Transfer Pricing Guidelines, p. 62, para. 2.38; 2010 Transfer Pricing Guidelines, pp. 72–3, para. 2.45.
[71] See Przysuski, Lalapet and Swaneveld, 'Transfer Pricing Method Selection in the United States and Canada' (2004) 5 *Corporate Business Taxation Monthly* 7, p. 12.
[72] 2009 Transfer Pricing Guidelines, pp. 67–8, para. 3.2.
[73] HM Revenue and Customs, United Kingdom (UINTM463080) – 'Transfer Pricing: OECD and Methodologies', www.hmrc.gov.uk/manuals/intmanual/INTM463080.htm; Mercader and Peña, 'Transfer Pricing and Latin American Integration' in Tanzi, Barreix and Villela (eds.) *Taxation and Latin American Integration* (2008), p. 271; Meenan, Dawid and Hulshorst, 'Is Europe One Market? A Transfer Pricing Economic Analysis of Pan-European Comparables Sets' (2004), p. 1: reproduced in European Commission, *EU Joint Transfer Pricing Forum* (2004, Taxud/C1/LDH/WB); Reyneveld, Gommers and Lund, 'Pan-European Comparables Searches – Analysing the Search Criteria' (2007), p. 80; Przysuski and Lalapet, 'A Comprehensive Look at the Berry Ratio in Transfer Pricing' (2005), pp. 760–1; in relation to Advanced Pricing Agreements, Australian Taxation Office, *Advance Pricing Arrangement Program 2004–05 Update* (2005), p. 7; in

methods is that the profits from controlled transactions are allocated to an associated enterprise instead of checking the actual transfer prices used in each controlled transaction between associated enterprises.

4.5 The transactional profit split method

If transactions are between highly integrated associated enterprises it may be impossible to evaluate each transaction separately for transfer pricing purposes. The OECD asserts that in this situation independent entities would set up a partnership and agree on a profit split for the business operation. The transactional profit split method (TPSM) identifies the profit from controlled transactions between associated enterprises that are to be allocated between them. This profit is then split between the associated enterprises on an economic basis. The profit allocated under this method is in theory required to reflect the profit allocation that unrelated entities would have used for performing similar functions. There are several approaches that may be used for estimating the allocation of profits based on either actual profits or expected profits. The Transfer Pricing Guidelines set out two methods that may be used: the contribution analysis, or the residual analysis.[74] Under a contribution analysis, the OECD suggests that the profits from controlled transactions should be allocated on the basis of a 'reasonable approximation of the division of profits that independent enterprises would have expected to realize from engaging in comparable transactions'.[75] But in the absence of comparable data, the profits should be allocated on the basis of the relative value of the functions performed by each associated enterprise. The contribution analysis should be supplemented with external market data to indicate how independent entities would have allocated the profits in similar circumstances.

Under the residual analysis, the profits from controlled transactions are allocated in two steps. This analysis may be used if an international enterprise has profits flowing from high value intangible property, such as internationally recognized trademarks, which cannot be readily

---

relation to determining transfer prices for intra-group services, Hejazi, 'Should Depreciation Be Marked Up in a Transactional Net Margin Method Context for Service Providers?' (2008), p. 27; in relation to India, Gajaria and Kale, 'Transfer Pricing in Emerging Markets – An Indian Perspective' (2006), p. 13.

[74] 2009 Transfer Pricing Guidelines, p. 71, para. 3.15; 2010 Transfer Pricing Guidelines, p. 96, para. 2.118

[75] 2010 Transfer Pricing Guidelines, pp. 96–7, para. 2.119.

allocated to one of the associated enterprises. Under the first step, each associated enterprise is allocated 'sufficient profit to provide it with a basic return appropriate for the type of transactions in which it is engaged'.[76] The associated enterprises are rewarded for the functions they perform, the tangible assets used and the risks accepted by each of the associated enterprises. The basic profit allocation would be determined by reference to the profits derived by independent entities from similar transactions. External market data is used to make the allocation under the first step. The OECD suggests that the split should be on a basis that reflects the division of profits that would have been anticipated in an arm's length agreement.[77] Under the second step, any residual profit or loss is allocated between the associated enterprises 'on an analysis of the facts and circumstances that might indicate how this residual would have been divided between independent enterprises'.[78] Factors considered in the application of this step are the relative contributions of the parties to the creation of the intangible property and their relative bargaining positions. It should be emphasized that the allocation of profits flowing from valuable intangible property, under a residual analysis between associated enterprises, is in most cases very difficult.

The main strength of the TPSM is that its application does not depend on finding comparable uncontrolled transactions. This enables the method to be used in situations where there are no comparable uncontrolled transactions readily available. The profit allocation under the TPSM reflects the functions performed by the associated enterprises. The OECD argues that under the TPSM, if comparable data is available, it may be used in the profit split analysis to determine the profit allocation independent parties would have used in comparable circumstances.[79] Comparable data may also be used for deciding the relative value of the contributions of each associated entity to the controlled transactions.[80] Consequently, one of the benefits of the TPSM is the flexibility it provides, and it is asserted by the OECD to conform to the arm's length principle because it reflects the profit allocations that unrelated entities would have used.

Another major advantage of the TPSM is that the profits allocated between the associated enterprises will be balanced as the relative contributions of both entities are being evaluated. This method is particularly useful in analysing the relative contributions of intangible

---

[76] *Ibid.*, p. 29.   [77] *Ibid.*, p. 93, para. 2.108.   [78] *Ibid.*, p. 97, para. 2.121.
[79] *Ibid.*, p. 94, para. 2.110.   [80] *Ibid.*

property used in the controlled transactions. A risk with the other transfer pricing methods is that they are one-sided and the profits allocated under them may be excessive as the relative contribution of the other associated enterprise is not being considered. A further advantage of this method is that it can be applied to allocate profits that arise from economies of scale or the efficiencies that associated enterprises may be able to exploit in controlled transactions.

The TPSM has several shortcomings. The external data required for valuing the functions performed by the associated enterprises will not be as closely connected to those functions as with the traditional transaction methods. This results in the allocation of profits under the functional analysis being arbitrary. But this is a difficulty that arises from trying to allocate profits from highly integrated business operations being carried on by the associated enterprises. Another shortcoming of the TPSM is that an associated enterprise may not have access to the amount of profits derived from controlled transactions by its associated enterprise in another jurisdiction. Even if the information of both associated enterprises is available, common accounting approaches in both jurisdictions would have to be used to ensure that the profits from the controlled transactions are being measured on a consistent basis.

4.6 *Transactional net margin method*

A commonly used transfer pricing method is the transactional net margin method (TNMM).[81] The TNMM tests an associated enterprise's net profits from controlled transactions relative to an appropriate base, such as sales, assets or costs. The TNMM has similarities with the CPM or the RPM except that it measures net profits rather than gross profits. One problem with the CPM and RPM is that they rely on gross profit margins, but gross profit figures are often not available to taxpayers or tax authorities. On the other hand, net profit margins for comparison purposes are more commonly available. The TNMM must be applied in a similar manner to the CPM or RPM for it to be reliable. If an associated enterprise engages in both controlled and uncontrolled

---

[81] The TNMM is often applied in practice because the traditional transaction methods cannot be applied as comparable data is unavailable or is unreliable. BIAC 'Response to OECD's Invitation to Comment on Transactional Profit Methods' (2006), p. 2. An advantage of the TNMM is greater public availability of comparable data on net profit levels: pp. 2 and 17. BIAC supported the proposal to remove the requirement that the transactional profit methods only be used as a measure of last resort, p. 1.

transactions, provided these transactions are comparable, the net margin it derives from the controlled transaction should reflect the net margins derived from the uncontrolled transactions. But associated enterprises will often only engage in controlled transactions and therefore it is necessary to determine for comparison purposes the net profit margin that an independent enterprise would have derived from comparable uncontrolled transactions.[82] As with the previously mentioned transfer pricing methods, the TNMM requires a functional analysis to be undertaken. The functional analysis is required to determine whether the uncontrolled transactions are sufficiently comparable for them to be used as a guide. It is also important to only use profit comparisons derived from uncontrolled international transactions.

There are several measurements that may be used in applying the TNMM. The appropriate ratio depends on the circumstances of the controlled transactions that are being examined. The aim of the TNMM is to determine an associated enterprise's net profit from its core business activities. The following ratios may be of use under the TNMM:

- The ratio of net profit before tax to sales. This ratio provides an indication of an enterprise's profitability. The net profit is net operating profit with non-operating income and costs excluded.
- The ratio of net profit before interest and tax to sales (NBIT). This profit measure is called earnings before interest and tax. A feature of NBIT is that the funding of the enterprises (whether by debt or equity) is excluded from the comparison of operating profit from core business.
- The Berry ratio[83] of gross profit to operating expenses provides a test of net profitability. A ratio of 1:1 is a break-even point under this ratio.
- The ratio of net profit before tax to shareholders' funds. This ratio provides a measure of the return to shareholders on capital and retained earnings.
- The ratio of earnings before interest and tax to assets provides a return on assets.

---

[82] 2009 Transfer Pricing Guidelines, pp. 74–5, para. 3.26; 2010 Transfer Pricing Guidelines, p. 93, para. 2.108.
[83] The Berry ratio was named after C. Berry, an economist, who first developed the formula as an adviser in a US transfer pricing case, *E. I. du Pont de Nemours and Company* v. *United States* (1979) 608 F.2d 445.

- The ratio of net profit before tax to the number of employees, or the ratio of sales to the number of employees, may be used to test the relative efficiency of a business.[84]

The above profit ratios may be distorted by factors such as business financing, business strategies and business efficiency.

There are several advantages in using the TNMM. The main advantage of the method is that net profit margins are less likely to be affected by transactional functional differences than the traditional transaction methods. Differences between functions performed in controlled and uncontrolled transactions should be reflected in operating expenses. Another advantage of the TNMM is that data is not required from an associated enterprise in a foreign jurisdiction. Furthermore, under the TNMM it is usually not necessary for the accounting records of the participants in a particular business operation to be stated on a common basis, nor is it necessary to allocate costs for all participants.[85] The main disadvantage of the TNMM is that an associated enterprise's net profit margin from controlled transactions may be affected by factors that do not have an effect on price or gross margins. In this situation a reliable determination of arm's length net margins is problematic.

4.7 The rise of the TNMM

The TNMM has become one of the most commonly used transfer pricing methods despite its being classified as a method of last resort under the Transfer Pricing Guidelines prior to 2010. The OECD has recognized this development with its 2010 amendment of the Transfer Pricing Guidelines which introduced a best method rule. Under a best method rule, the transactional profit methods have equal status with the traditional transaction methods in determining transfer pricing for intra-group and intra-entity trade. The main advantage of the TNMM is that it recognizes the difficulty of testing particular transactions and instead moves to test the net profit derived by an entity from intra-group trade. The traditional transaction methods operate at the transaction level which is impractical due to the extensive range of transactions that may occur between associated enterprises. The transactional profit

---

[84] Australian Taxation Office, Taxation Ruling TR 97/20 'Income tax: arm's length transfer pricing methodologies for international dealings', para. 3.81.
[85] 2009 Transfer Pricing Guidelines, p. 75, para. 3.28; 2010 Transfer Pricing Guidelines, p. 79, para. 263.

methods have an advantage over the traditional transaction methods in that they do not depend on close comparables and they do not test individual transactions. While the OECD does not express a preference for either of the transactional profit methods, the main disadvantage of the TPSM is that it requires tax information from another jurisdiction which may not be readily available. The TNMM is a one-sided analysis, which provides a tax authority with the benefit of being able to apply the TNMM on the basis of information available within its jurisdiction. In situations where intangibles are shared between associated enterprises the TPSM is considered to be the best method, but this method has the obstacle of requiring access to tax information from another jurisdiction. Nevertheless, if intangibles are not shared by associated enterprises the TNMM is likely to be the most appropriate transfer pricing method.

4.8 Best method rule

The traditional transaction methods had the status prior to 2010 of being the main methods that should be applied in determining an international enterprise's transfer prices. Despite the transactional profit methods having the status of methods of last resort prior to 2010, in practice the exception has become the norm due to the lack of comparables required by the traditional transaction methods. The 2009 Transfer Pricing Guidelines stated that the transactional profit methods could only be used:

> ... in those exceptional cases in which the complexities of real life business put practical difficulties in the way of the application of the traditional transaction methods and provided all the safeguards set out in this Chapter [III] are observed, the application of the transactional profit methods (profit split and transactional net margin method) may provide an approximation of transfer pricing in a manner consistent with the arm's length principle. However, the transactional profit methods may not be applied automatically simply because there is difficulty in obtaining data. The same factors that led to the conclusion that it was not possible to reliably apply a traditional transaction method must be reconsidered when evaluating the reliability of a transactional profit method.[86]

While the adoption of the transactional profit methods in the Transfer Pricing Guidelines was a significant achievement in 1995, this development was qualified by giving the traditional transaction methods

---

[86] 2009 Transfer Pricing Guidelines, pp. 67–8 para. 3.2.

priority of application over the transactional profit methods. It is likely that the hierarchy of methods was used during member country discussions as a bargaining measure to attain consensus within OECD member countries on adopting the transactional profit methods. Broad international consensus on transfer pricing methodologies is a critical requirement of an effective international transfer pricing system. But for some time prior to 2010 the TNMM had been a commonly used transfer pricing method and as a result the Transfer Pricing Guidelines prior to 2010 conflicted with international practice. Belatedly, the OECD has recognized this flaw, and in 2006 it issued an Invitation to Comment on Transactional Profit Methods (Invitation Paper). The Invitation Paper was initiated by Working Party No. 6 of the OECD Committee on Fiscal Affairs (WP6) which concluded that the application of the transactional profit methods should be examined with a view to amending the Transfer Pricing Guidelines. The issues considered in the Invitation Paper included the status of the transactional profit methods as last resort methods, the use of the transactional profit methods in conjunction with a traditional transaction method or a sanity check to test the plausibility of the outcome of a traditional transaction method, the application of the TNMM standard of comparability and the application of the TNMM determination of the net margin.

In January 2008, the OECD published a discussion draft (2008 Discussion Draft) on the transactional profit methods[87] in which WP6 reached a tentative conclusion that the Transfer Pricing Guidelines should be amended to no longer treat the transactional profit methods as methods of last resort.[88] This was implemented in the 2010 OECD Transfer Pricing Guidelines:

> Parts II and III of this chapter respectively describe 'traditional transaction methods' and 'transactional profit methods' that can be used to establish whether the conditions imposed in the commercial or financial relations between associated enterprises are consistent with the arm's length principle. Traditional transaction methods are the comparable uncontrolled price method or CUP method, the resale price method, and the cost plus method. Transactional profit methods are the transactional net margin method and the transactional profit split method.
>
> The selection of a transfer pricing method always aims at finding the most appropriate method for a particular case. For this purpose, the selection process should take account of the respective strengths and

---

[87] OECD, *Transactional Profit Methods: Discussion Draft for Public Comment* (2008).
[88] Ibid., p. 6, paras. 5–6.

weaknesses of the OECD recognised methods; the appropriateness of the method considered in view of the nature of the controlled transaction, determined in particular through a functional analysis; the availability of reliable information (in particular on uncontrolled comparables) needed to apply the selected method and/or other methods; and the degree of comparability between controlled and uncontrolled transactions, including the reliability of comparability adjustments that may be needed to eliminate material differences between them. No one method is suitable in every possible situation, nor is it necessary to prove that a particular method is not suitable under the circumstances.[89]

But the OECD maintained its preference for the traditional transaction methods if the traditional transaction methods and transactional profit methods may be applied.[90]

It is asserted that the 2010 reform of using the most appropriate method was long overdue and essential for the Transfer Pricing Guidelines to reflect transfer pricing practice.[91] Although the OECD still gives priority to traditional transactions methods if both the traditional transaction methods and transactional profits methods may be equally applied, this situation is unlikely to occur as the traditional transaction methods are usually inapplicable. It is surprising that the gap between the principles in the Transfer Pricing Guidelines and practice was allowed to develop and perhaps reflects the limited resources available within the OECD to monitor and reform the Transfer Pricing Guidelines and the difficulty in reaching agreement on reforms. After reform proposals are prepared it is a significant task to attain a consensus agreement within OECD countries. Nevertheless, given the increasing importance of transfer pricing in international trade, it is expected that Transfer Pricing Guidelines should be reformed on a regular basis to reflect practice and thereby minimize the costs for taxpayers of complying with the transfer pricing rules, and minimize the costs for tax authorities of administering transfer pricing rules.

The 2010 OECD reform, to adopt a best method rule, is to be commended. Under a best method rule, all the transfer pricing methods would have equal status and the best method in particular circumstances

---

[89] 2010 Transfer Pricing Guidelines, p. 59, paras. 2.1–2.2.
[90] *Ibid.*, pp. 50–60, para. 2.3.
[91] The BIAC states that the transactional profit methods are frequently used by taxpayers: BIAC, 'Response to OECD's Invitation to Comment on Transactional Profit Methods' (2006), p. 2.

should be used. The US domestic transfer pricing rules use a best method principle.[92] While the US transfer pricing methods are similar to the OECD methods[93] they differed from the former Transfer Pricing Guidelines in prescribing a best method rule. The US best method rule states that: 'The arm's length result of a controlled transaction must be determined under the method that, under the facts and circumstances, provides the most reliable measure of an arm's length result.'[94]

The 2010 Transfer Pricing Guidelines adopt a best method rule, but the reform maintains a preference for the traditional transaction methods. The reason the transactional profit methods are used is because the traditional transaction methods usually cannot be used due to the lack of comparable transactions and the lack of data on gross profit margins. The expansion over time of cross-border intra-group trade, particularly in intangible items, will continue to result in fewer available comparable transactions apart from those involving commodities.[95] Nevertheless, maintaining the preference for the traditional transaction methods is merely rhetoric if the transactional profit methods have equal status with the traditional transaction transfer pricing methods.

4.9 The erosion of the traditional transaction methods

Even with the adoption by the OECD in 2010 of a best method rule, there might still be some areas of dispute in selecting a transfer pricing method. In theory, it should be possible for an international enterprise to determine that reliable comparable transactions are unavailable and to apply the TNMM as the best method. But an international enterprise may encounter disputes with a tax authority which applies a traditional transaction method and argues that the particular method used is the best method in the facts and circumstances of a particular situation. The

---

[92] Section 482 of the Internal Revenue Code (US).
[93] Section 482 of the Internal Revenue Code uses a method called the Comparable Profits Method (CPM) which is similar to the TNMM. The CPM uses profit level indicators to determine an arm's length result. There is some debate about the differences between these methods, but the structure of these methods is the same: Li, 'Slicing the Digital Pie with a Traditional Knife' (2001), pp. 785–6. Culbertson has contended that the methodology of the CPM and the TNMM are the same: Culbertson, 'A Rose by Any Other Name: Smelling the Flowers at the OECD's (Last) Resort' (1995), p. 382.
[94] Regulation 1.482-1(c) of the Income Tax Regulations (US).
[95] See Eden, *Taxing Multinationals* (1998), pp. 592–3.

factors that determine which is the best method will be the available data and the assumptions that are being made.[96] As transfer pricing is an art and not a science there is always scope for significant differences of opinion to develop.

Despite the well-recognized lack of comparable transactions the OECD boldly asserts that:

> The arm's length principle has also been found to work effectively in the vast majority of cases. For example, there are many cases involving the purchase and sale of commodities and the lending of money where an arm's length price may readily be found in a comparable transaction undertaken by comparable independent enterprises under comparable circumstances.[97]

The OECD retained this statement in the 2010 Transfer Pricing Guidelines, but Rosenbloom asserts that this statement is amusing to individuals working on a sophisticated transfer pricing matter as it is based on an exceptional situation.[98] The main reason for the decline in the use of the traditional transaction methods is the lack of reliable comparable transfer prices. As stated above, under globalization multinational enterprise groups and international enterprises operate as highly integrated businesses. Due to the dominance of these enterprises in international trade, few comparable arm's length transactions actually occur. The OECD acknowledges the difficulty in applying the arm's length principle to intra-group trade within international enterprises with its statement that:

> Nevertheless, there are some significant cases in which the arm's length principle is difficult and complicated to apply, for example, in MNE groups dealing in the integrated production of highly specialised goods, in unique intangibles, and/or in the provision of specialised services.[99]

> A practical difficulty in applying the arm's length principle is that associated enterprises may engage in transactions that independent enterprises would not undertake ... Where independent enterprises seldom undertake transactions of the type entered into by associated enterprises, the arm's length principle is difficult to apply because there is little or

---

[96] United Nations, *Transfer Pricing* (2001), p. 13.
[97] 2009 Transfer Pricing Guidelines, pp. 27–8, para. 1.8; 2010 Transfer Pricing Guidelines, p. 34, para. 1.9.
[98] Rosenbloom, 'Angels on a Pin: Arm's Length in the World' (2005), p. 525.
[99] 2009 Transfer Pricing Guidelines, pp. 27–8, para. 1.8; 2010 Transfer Pricing Guidelines, p. 34, para. 1.9.

no direct evidence of what conditions would have been established by independent enterprises.[100]

In this statement the OECD acknowledges the theoretical flaw in the arm's length principle, yet it is nevertheless advocated as the method for determining transfer prices. The arm's length principle ignores the fact that international enterprises operate as a single integrated business with the motive of maximizing the business's overall profits. The globalization of international enterprises with high speed and high quality information and communications systems has eroded the bedrock of the arm's length principle. The consequence for international enterprises is that they are forced to incur high costs to comply with transfer pricing rules based on a fiction. In addition, tax authorities are also required to incur high administrative costs in scrutinizing transfer pricing methods used by taxpayers.

The comparative analysis of transactions required by the Transfer Pricing Guidelines is often difficult to apply because comparable transactions do not exist. The comparison test requires 'a comparison of the conditions in a controlled transaction with the conditions in transactions between independent enterprises'.[101] For international enterprises carrying on businesses for which there are no comparable independent business operations, the traditional transaction methods are impossible to apply. In addition, the traditional transaction methods require individual transactions to be examined, but some international enterprises are so highly integrated that it has been argued that it is difficult to identify a transaction in the first place.[102]

The main advantage of the TNMM is that it is relatively easy to apply.[103] The TNMM does not require a high level of comparability and it can be applied using publicly available operating data from financial statements published by entities listed on stock exchanges. Under the TNMM, the main area for dispute is establishing which profit indicator is the most appropriate profit method. The OECD's Business and Industry Advisory Committee (BIAC) pointed out that the main advantage of the TNMM is due to the publicly available data and that

---

[100] 2009 Transfer Pricing Guidelines, pp. 27–8, para 1.110; 2010 Transfer Pricing Guidelines, p. 34, para. 1.9.
[101] 2009 Transfer Pricing Guidelines, p. 30, para. 1.15; 2010 Transfer Pricing Guidelines, p. 41, para. 1.33.
[102] Li, 'Slicing the Digital Pie with a Traditional Knife' (2001), p. 798.
[103] Horst, 'The Comparable Profits Method' (1993), p. 1443.

under self-assessment associated enterprises can only use this data in undertaking their transfer pricing analysis.[104]

5 Conclusion

Business restructuring is a normal and ongoing aspect of enterprises in maintaining or improving their international competitiveness. Under the authorized OECD approach of the 2008 Report and the 2008 Commentary on former Article 7, transfers of assets, functions or risks either to, or from, a permanent establishment, must be considered in determining the profits attributed to the permanent establishment under former Article 7(2). Intra-entity transfers of intangible property cannot be recognized under the former Article 7 and 2008 Commentary, but they are recognized under new Article 7. Nevertheless, applying the authorized OECD approach to transfers of intangible assets involving permanent establishments is likely to be challenging. This requires determining if a transfer of an intangible asset has taken place and what the terms of the notional transfer are as the intangible property may either be subject to a notional sale transaction or a notional licence transaction. These notional transactions involve determining who the economic owner of the transactions is both before and after the notional transaction. In addition, determining the price for notional transfers of intangible property is challenging as comparative transactions are usually unavailable. Intangible property is often a core asset of an international enterprise and these assets are not often sold to independent buyers.

The authorized OECD requires that the transfer pricing methods in the Transfer Pricing Guidelines be applied to a permanent establishment's recognized dealings. Current transfer pricing rules are based on the arm's length principle that requires that transfer prices should reflect prices used in identical or similar uncontrolled transactions. There are difficulties, however, in applying the arm's length principle in practice. The Transfer Pricing Guidelines set out the internationally accepted transfer pricing methods that may be used and state that the most appropriate method must be adopted. In many cases, comparable uncontrolled transactions may be unavailable and the TNMM will often be the best method. As transfer pricing is not an exact science, transfer pricing cases often present

---

[104] BIAC, 'Response to OECD's Invitation to Comment on Transactional Profit Methods' (2006), p. 17.

some uncertainty and attendant challenges for national tax authorities and international enterprises alike.

In recognition of the extensive use of the transactional profit methods, particularly the TNMM, the OECD resolved this gap between the Transfer Pricing Guidelines and practice by giving the transactional profit methods equal status in 2010. The extensive use of the transactional profit methods is due to the lack of comparable transactions required for the application of the traditional transaction methods. This problem was apparent when the Transfer Pricing Guidelines were issued in 1995, and it is surprising that this reform was not implemented until 2010. The TNMM will continue to be a widely used transfer pricing method, as it is a one-sided analysis that does not require close comparables and can be based on published financial statements on net profit indicators. The challenge is to develop and maintain an international transfer pricing system that is appropriate for the current globalized international economy and to minimize the risk of double taxation and under-taxation.

10

New Article 7 of the OECD Model and Commentary

1 Introduction

In 2008, the OECD published the 2008 Report which established the authorized OECD approach for determining the profits that are attributable to permanent establishments under Article 7 in light of modern multinationals. The 2008 Report is based on the principle of applying by analogy the guidance in the Transfer Pricing Guidelines for the purposes of attributing profits to permanent establishments. Moreover, the 2008 Report claimed that there is broad consensus within OECD countries that the principles in the 2008 Report are better than the approach for attributing profits to permanent establishments expressed in the pre-2008 Commentary on former Article 7. The approach developed by the OECD in the 2008 Report was not restricted by the original intent of former Article 7, or by any historical practice and interpretation of former Article 7, as the OECD acknowledged that prior to the publication of the 2008 Report there was no consensus interpretation of former Article 7 in OECD countries.

The OECD claimed in the 2008 Report that the best way to provide tax authorities and taxpayers with certainty on attributing profits to permanent establishments is to replace former Article 7 with a new version of Article 7 which reflects the principles in the 2008 Report.[1] The new version of Article 7 was adopted in 2010 and at the same time the OECD adopted and published a revised version of the 2008 Report, the 2010 Report, 'to ensure that the conclusions of that report could be read harmoniously with the new wording and modified numbering'[2] of the new Article 7. The conclusions in the 2010 Report are identical to those in the 2008 Report, but the 2010 Report reflects the drafting of new Article 7.[3] New Article 7 reflects the principles adopted in the 2010 Report and 'must be interpreted in light of the guidance contained in it'.[4]

---

[1] 2008 Report, p. 8, para. 8.   [2] 2010 OECD Model, pp. 130–1, para. 8.
[3] Ibid.   [4] Ibid., p. 132, para. 9.

The aim of the OECD is to prevent the past interpretations of former Article 7 from being applied to the new provision.

The key challenge for the OECD with new Article 7 is that it may be adopted only by a handful of countries. Although it is expected that it will be used by the US and the UK, the need for a new Article 7 has been questioned.[5] One OECD country, New Zealand, has rejected both new Article 7 and the 2008 Commentary on former Article 7.[6] Other OECD countries, Chile, Greece, Mexico and Turkey, have reserved the right to use the previous version of Article 7. Under new Article 7 a permanent establishment's notional intra-entity transactions, called dealings, are subject to the adapted Transfer Pricing Guidelines. But new Article 7 is very difficult to apply in practice because of this theoretical economic basis and is likely to involve high compliance costs for taxpayers and to result in disputes with tax authorities. An international accounting firm has claimed that tax authorities may be reluctant to devote the significant resources necessary to auditing a taxpayer's economic analysis as required under new Article 7.[7] Consequently, the practical uncertainty arising from this flawed theoretical basis is likely to result in disputes between tax authorities and international enterprises.

The uncertainty is also likely to result in disputes on the profits attributable to a permanent establishment between the tax authority in the permanent establishment's host country and the tax authority in the country in which an international enterprise is resident. Permanent establishments are not separate legal enterprises in law or business practice – they are a seamless part of integrated international enterprises with a common management and a common profit aim. Prior to globalization, permanent establishments may have operated as separate enterprises because of poor international communications systems. But today it would be exceptional for a permanent establishment to operate in practice as a separate enterprise in its dealings with the head office and other permanent establishments of the international enterprise. New Article 7 is based on arm's length economic theory and the legal fiction of treating a branch as a separate enterprise for the purposes of Article 7 but not other treaty provisions.

---

[5] P. Baker QC questioned the need for a new Article 7 at the OECD's 2009 conference 'Treaties and Transfer Pricing in a Changing World', reported in Sheppard, 'Any Takers for the New OECD Model Business Profits Article?' (2009), at p. 1089.

[6] 2010 OECD Model, p. 153, para. 96.

[7] Zolo and Cope, *The OECD's Proposed Article 7: A Work in Progress with an Uncertain Future* (2009).

This chapter begins with an outline of the background leading to the implementation of new Article 7. It focuses on the role of OECD Working Party No. 6 and the challenges the OECD confronted in finalizing a consensus approach in the 2008 Report. Next the chapter considers the terms of new Article 7. Article 7(1) contains the key principle for allocating taxing rights over business profits between a host country and a residence country. The principle is that the residence country has exclusive taxing rights over business profits unless the international enterprise has a permanent establishment in the host country. If there is a permanent establishment, the host country may tax the profits which are attributed to the permanent establishment. The chapter then considers the principles for attributing profits to a permanent establishment under new Article 7(2). Under this provision, a permanent establishment is considered to be a separate enterprise transacting with other parts of the enterprise on arm's length terms. This involves treating these notional transactions as dealings under the separate enterprise legal fiction. The chapter then considers new Article 7(3), which deals with providing relief from double taxation, and Article 7(4) on the interaction between Article 7 and the other treaty Articles. Finally, the chapter considers the provisions of the former Article 7 that were not included in new Article 7. In particular, former Article 7(3) of the 2008 OECD Model was excluded as there was controversy over the role of the provision.

2 Background

The work of the OECD's Committee on Fiscal Affairs is carried out by groups of experts from OECD countries and non-OECD countries.[8] Working Party No. 1 covers tax treaty issues and its members are usually treaty negotiators. Working Party No. 6 covers the taxation of multinational enterprises. The focus of Working Party No. 6 is transfer pricing and its members are usually economists from OECD countries who work on transfer pricing. Both Working Party No. 1 and Working Party No. 6 report directly to the Committee on Fiscal Affairs. Working Party No. 6 is responsible for Transfer Pricing Guidelines. The Transfer Pricing Guidelines were initially intended to apply to both associated enterprises and permanent establishments.[9] But Working Party No. 6

---

[8] OECD, *OECD's Current Tax Agenda*, June 2010 (2010), p. 6.
[9] OECD, *Transfer Pricing Guidelines for Multinational Enterprises and Tax Administrations, Discussion Draft of Part I* (1994), p. 16, para. 16.

was forced to postpone the inclusion of permanent establishments when the Transfer Pricing Guidelines were finalized in 1995.

The work on new Article 7 appears to have its origins in the announcement by the OECD in 1994 that the proposed Transfer Pricing Guidelines would revise the *Transfer Pricing and Multinationals*[10] (1979 Report) and amalgamate it with the *Transfer Pricing and Multinationals (Three Taxation Issues)*[11] (1984 Report).[12] It was expected that the work on permanent establishments would be included in subsequent additions to the Transfer Pricing Guidelines.[13] The 1984 Report deals with three broad issues; the only permanent establishment issue is the taxation of branches of international banks. The 1984 Report contained the principles for a bank branch's entitlement to claim deductions for intra-bank interest expenses. In 2001, the OECD published the 2001 *Discussion Draft on the Attribution of Profits to Permanent Establishments* (2001 Discussion Draft).[14] The 2001 Discussion Draft consisted of general principles on the attribution of profits to permanent establishments and special considerations for applying the proposed principles to permanent establishments on international banks. In publishing the 2008 Report and 2010 Report, the OECD abandoned its initial intention of including the principles on the attributing profits to permanent establishments in the Transfer Pricing Guidelines.

The 2001 Discussion Draft acknowledges the history of Article 7:

> The permanent establishment (PE) concept has a history as long as the history of double taxation conventions. Currently, the international tax principles for attributing profits to a PE are provided in Article 7 of the OECD Model Tax Convention on Income and on Capital, which forms the basis of the extensive network of bilateral income tax treaties between OECD Member countries and between many OECD Member and non-member countries.[15]

But it uses the lack of a consensus interpretation as the rationale for abandoning the history of Article 7, if necessary:

---

[10] OECD, *Transfer Pricing and Multinational Enterprises* (1979).
[11] OECD, *Transfer Pricing and Multinational Enterprises (Three Taxation Issues)* (1984).
[12] OECD, *Transfer Pricing Guidelines for Multinational Enterprises and Tax Administrations, Discussion Draft of Part I* (1994), p. 5.
[13] *Ibid.*, p. 16, para. 16 and 1995 Transfer Pricing Guidelines, p. P-3, para. 11.
[14] OECD, *Discussion Draft on the Attribution of Profits to Permanent Establishments* (2001).
[15] *Ibid.*, p. 4, para. 1.

2 BACKGROUND

There is considerable variation in the domestic laws of OECD Member countries regarding the taxation of PEs. In addition, there is no consensus amongst the OECD Member countries as to the correct interpretation of Article 7. This lack of a common interpretation and consistent application of Article 7 can lead to double, or less than single taxation. The development of global trading of financial products and electronic commerce has helped to focus attention on the need to establish a consensus position regarding the interpretation and practical application of Article 7.

As a first step in establishing a consensus position, a working hypothesis (WH) has been developed as to the preferred approach for attributing profits to a PE under Article 7. This approach builds upon developments since the last revision of the Model Commentary on Article 7 in March 1994, especially the fundamental review of the arm's length principle, the results of which were reflected in the 1995 OECD Transfer Pricing Guidelines (the Guidelines). The Guidelines address the application of the arm's length principle to transactions between associated enterprises under Article 9. The basis for the development of the WH is to examine how far the approach of treating a PE as a hypothetical distinct and separate enterprise can be taken and how the guidance in the Guidelines could be applied, by analogy, to attribute profits to a PE in accordance with the arm's length principle of Article 7. The ongoing development of the WH will not be constrained by either the original intent or by the historical practice and interpretation of Article 7. Rather the intention is to formulate the preferred approach to attributing profits to a PE under Article 7 given modern-day multinational operations and trade.[16]

The OECD's finding that there was no consensus interpretation of Article 7 in OECD countries and the potential for double taxation or double non-taxation was the rationale for the sweeping reform of former Article 7. This conclusion may have been in part based on the National Westminster Bank PLC[17] litigation in the US, which involved a dispute between the taxpayer and the US tax authority on the interest deduction which the US branch of National Westminster Bank, a UK resident, was entitled to claim under Article 7 of the US–UK 1980 tax treaty.

---

[16] *Ibid.*, paras. 2 and 3.
[17] *National Westminster Bank PLC v. United States* (NatWest I) 44 Fed. Cl. 120 (1999); 1999 U.S. Claims LEXIS 154; 99-2 Tax Cas. (CCH) P50 p. 654; 84 A.F.T.R.2d (RIA) 5086; *National Westminster Bank PLC v. US* (2008) (NatWest II) 58 Fed. Cl. 491 (2003); 2003 U.S. Claims LEXIS 332; 2004-1 U.S. Tax Cas. (CCH) P50, 150; 92 A.F.T.R.2d (RIA) 7013; *National Westminster Bank PLC v. United States* (NatWest III) 69 Fed. Cl. 128; 2005 U.S. Claims LEXIS 386; 2006-1 U.S. Tax Cas. (CCH) P50, 107; 97 A.F.T.R.2d (RIA) 369; *National Westminster Bank PLC v. US* (2008) 512 F.3d 1347 (2008), pp. 1349, 1362. These cases are considered in Chs. 6 and 7.

The taxpayer succeeded in claiming that its interest deduction under the treaty was unaffected by US domestic legislation limiting the US branch's interest deduction. The litigation reflected a dispute between the US tax authority and the UK tax authority on this issue and led to the US and UK seeking reform of Article 7 for banks in the OECD.[18] This led to the argument that principles that were designed for bank permanent establishments were incorporated into the authorized OECD approach in the 2006 Report for all permanent establishments, the 2008 Report and the 2010 Report and ultimately resulting in new Article 7. Working Party No. 6 was given the authority to develop principles for the attribution of profits to permanent establishments irrespective of the history of the provision and administrative practices of tax authorities. The 2010 Report states that:

> Despite that work, the practices of OECD and non-OECD countries regarding the attribution of profits to permanent establishments and these countries' interpretation of Article 7 continued to vary considerably. The Committee acknowledged the need to provide more certainty to taxpayers: in its report – Transfer Pricing Guidelines for Multinational Enterprises and Tax Administrations (the Guidelines), adopted in 1995, it indicated that further work would address the application of the arm's length principle to permanent establishments. That work resulted, in 2008, in a report entitled – Attribution of Profits to Permanent Establishments (the 2008 Report). The approach developed in the 2008 Report was not constrained by either the original intent or by the historical practice and interpretation of Article 7. Instead, the focus was on formulating the most preferable approach to attributing profits to a permanent establishment under Article 7 given modern-day multinational operations and trade.[19]

The 2010 Report was initially published as the 2006 Report and then republished in the 2008 Report, which resulted in Working Party No. 6 expanding its influence from Article 9, the associated enterprises Article, to Article 7, which had a separate history.

New Article 7 has been rejected by the UN in 2009:

> The new OECD article 7 was therefore seen as having the potential to change the balance between source and resident taxation, contrary to the interests of many developing countries. It was also explicitly contrary to

---
[18] Sheppard, 'Any Takers for the New OECD Model Business Profits Article?' (2009), p. 1089.
[19] 2010 Report, p. 8, para. 4.

paragraph 3 of the article of the United Nations Model Convention, which did not allow deductions for such notional payments (although banks were treated as a special case in the case of notional interest).[20]

The differences between the business profits Article of the OECD and UN Model are likely to cause problems. The UN Model Article 7 is based on the pre-2008 OECD Model version of Article 7, some of the provisions of Article 7 of the UN Model are 'either unchanged or substantially amended, and some new provisions'.[21] Moreover, the UN Commentary is based on the pre-2008 OECD Commentary and the 2008 Commentary is not being adopted by the UN.[22] This is likely to result in some non-OECD countries continuing to use this provision which is based on the pre-2008 Commentary on former Article 7.

3 New Article 7

New Article 7 of the OECD Model Tax Convention:

1. Profits of an enterprise of a Contracting State shall be taxable only in that State unless the enterprise carries on business in the other Contracting State through a permanent establishment situated therein. If the enterprise carries on business as aforesaid, the profits that are attributable to the permanent establishment in accordance with the provisions of paragraph 2 may be taxed in that other State.
2. For the purposes of this Article and Article [23 A] [23 B], the profits that are attributable in each Contracting State to the permanent establishment referred to in paragraph 1 are the profits it might be expected to make, in particular in its dealings with other parts of the enterprise, if it were a separate and independent enterprise engaged in the same or similar activities under the same or similar conditions, taking into account the functions performed, assets used and risks assumed by the enterprise through the permanent establishment and through the other parts of the enterprise.
3. Where, in accordance with paragraph 2, a Contracting State adjusts the profits that are attributable to a permanent establishment of an enterprise of one of the Contracting States and taxes accordingly profits of the enterprise that have been charged to tax in the other State, the other State shall, to the extent necessary to eliminate double

---

[20] United Nations, *Report of Experts on International Tax Cooperation in Tax Matters* (2009), p. 9, para. 31.
[21] United Nations, *United Nations Model Tax Convention Between Developed and Developing Countries* (2001), p. 96.
[22] United Nations, *Report of Experts on International Tax Cooperation in Tax Matters* (2009), p. 9, para. 34.

taxation on these profits, make an appropriate adjustment to the amount of the tax charged on those profits. In determining such adjustment, the competent authorities of the Contracting States shall if necessary consult each other.

4. Where profits include items of income which are dealt with separately in other Articles of this Convention, then the provisions of those Articles shall not be affected by the provisions of this Article.[23]

Article 7(1) contains the principle for allocating taxing rights, under tax treaties, over business profits derived in a host country by a resident of the other contracting country. The principle is that a host country cannot tax business profits from a source within its borders, derived by a resident of the other country, unless the resident carries on business through a permanent establishment in the host country. The first principle is that business profits derived by a resident with a source in a host country can only be taxed in the residence country.[24] In this situation, the host country has agreed under a tax treaty to forgo its source country taxing rights. This principle has a long history and reflects the international tax treaty consensus view that until an enterprise has a permanent establishment in a host country, it is not regarded as participating in the economic life of the host country.[25] Accordingly, if the foreign enterprise is not participating in the economic life of the host country, then that country does not have the right to tax the business profits of the foreign enterprise.

The second principle, reflected in the second sentence of Article 7(1), is that if a resident carries on business in a host country and derives business profits in the host country, and the profits are attributable to the permanent establishment, the host country has an unlimited right to tax the profits attributable to the permanent establishment. The principles on attributing business profits to a permanent establishment are contained in Article 7(2). Article 7(4) limits the application of Article 7(1)–(3) by prescribing that Article 7 does not affect the application of the other Articles of the OECD Model which provide special rules for certain categories of profits, or certain categories of income that may also be business profits.[26] An example of income which is subject to special rules is the profit from the operation of ships and aircraft under Article 8.

As stated above, under Article 7 the taxing rights of the host country are limited to profits that are attributable to permanent establishments.

---

[23] 2010 OECD Model, pp. 26–7. [24] Ibid., p. 132, para. 10.
[25] Ibid., p. 132, para. 11. [26] Ibid., p. 132, para. 10.

Conversely, if a foreign enterprise with a permanent establishment derives business profits from the host country that are not attributable to its permanent establishment, those profits may not be taxed by the host country. Some countries have attempted to claim a general force of attraction principle, under which business profits, dividends, interest and royalties, which are not attributable to a permanent establishment, are treated as having been derived by it, if the beneficiary has a permanent establishment in the host country. After notionally attributing these items of income to a permanent establishment, the host country then claims the right to tax this income. The OECD notes that some tax treaties have an anti-avoidance measure with a limited force of attraction rule, which only applies to business profits derived by an enterprise from activities that are similar to those carried through by its permanent establishment.[27] Nevertheless, the OECD asserts that the general force of attraction principle has been rejected in international tax treaty practice.[28] Under this approach, the OECD asserts that if a foreign enterprise resident in a treaty country is deriving business profits from a host country, it should examine the separate sources of income that the enterprise derives within the country and then apply to each the permanent establishment threshold test. In support of this approach, the OECD claims that this approach is simpler for both tax authorities and international enterprises, and reflects the way in which international enterprises operate.

As there are numerous international enterprises, some with complex business structures, there is a wide range of ways in which they operate. If an international enterprise carries on business in a host country through a permanent establishment, it may also carry on other business activities in that country that are unconnected with its permanent establishment. The Commentary provides an example of an international enterprise carrying on a manufacturing business through a permanent establishment in a host country. This enterprise may, for legitimate business reasons, sell its goods in that country through an independent agent which is unconnected with its permanent establishment. The enterprise may be carrying on business in the host country in this manner for genuine business purposes, such as commercial convenience, or it is the historical way in which the enterprise's business has been carried on in the host country. If the host country sought to attribute the profits that an enterprise derives through its independent

---

[27] *Ibid.*, pp. 132–3, para. 12.   [28] *Ibid.*

agents, to the enterprise's permanent establishment, in order to aggregate these profits with those of the permanent establishment, this would hinder ordinary business activities. This application of the force of attraction principle would be contrary to the aims of the tax treaty to facilitate international trade and investment and may result in double taxation.[29]

In summary, Article 7(1) of the OECD Model only grants taxing rights to a host country to tax business profits derived by a foreign enterprise if that enterprise has a permanent establishment in the host country and the business profits are attributable to the permanent establishment.[30] This principle prevents a host country from taxing business profits derived by a foreign enterprise which are not attributable to its permanent establishment in the host country subject to the other provisions of the OECD Model. The Commentary claims that the purpose of Article 7(1) 'is to limit the right of one Contracting State to tax the business profits of enterprises of the other Contracting State'.[31] The Commentary notes that this provision does not prevent a country from taxing its own residents under a controlled foreign company regime in its domestic law, despite the tax being based on the profits derived by a controlled foreign company that is resident in the other contracting country.[32] The Commentary confirms that tax levied on residents' accrued profits under a controlled foreign company (CFC) tax regime does not affect the profits derived by the CFC in the other contracting country. When tax is imposed on residents under a CFC regime, the tax cannot be claimed to be levied notionally on the CFC itself. The Commentary also refers to the comments on this issue in paragraph 23 of the Commentary on Article 1 and paragraphs 37 to 39 of the Commentary on Article 10.

4 Article 7(2)

Article 7(2) contains the principles for attributing profits to a permanent establishment. Under the arm's length principle, the profits attributable to a permanent establishment are the profits it would expect to make if it were a separate and independent enterprise engaged in the same or similar activities. This provision also provides principles on notional intra-entity transactions between a permanent establishment and other parts of the international enterprise, i.e. notional transactions between a

---

[29] Ibid. [30] Ibid., p. 133, para. 13. [31] Ibid., pp. 133–4, para. 14. [32] Ibid.

permanent establishment and either the head office or another permanent establishment which are called dealings. Consequently, this provision relies on the legal fiction of treating a permanent establishment as a separate and independent enterprise. A permanent establishment is also treated as being independent of any enterprises that are associated with the permanent establishment's international enterprise. This aspect of the legal fiction applies the arm's length principle, on which Article 9 is based, for the purpose of adjusting the profits of associated enterprises if their transfer prices fail to conform to the arm's length principle.

The authorized OECD approach in the 2010 Report is that a permanent establishment is treated as a functional separate entity for the purposes of Article 7:[33]

> The authorised OECD approach does not dictate the specifics or mechanics of domestic law, but only sets a limit on the amount of attributable profit that may be taxed in the host country of the PE. Accordingly, the profits to be attributed to a PE are the profits that the PE would have earned at arm's length, in particular in its dealings with other parts of the enterprise, if it were a separate and independent enterprise engaged in the same or similar activities under the same or similar conditions, taking into account the functions performed, assets used and risks assumed by the enterprise through the permanent establishment and through the other parts of the enterprise, determined by applying the Guidelines by analogy. This is in line with one of the fundamental rationales behind the PE concept, which is to allow, within certain limits, the taxation of non-resident enterprises in respect of their activities (having regards to assets used and risks assumed) in the source jurisdiction. In addition, the authorised OECD approach is not designed to prevent the application of any domestic legislation aimed at preventing abuse of tax losses or tax credits by shifting the location of assets or risks. Finally, where their domestic law does not recognise loss transactions in certain circumstances between associated enterprises, countries may consider that the authorised OECD approach would not require the recognition of a loss on an analogous dealing in determining the profits of a PE.[34]

But the legal fiction of treating a permanent establishment as a separate enterprise does not extend to other provisions under the 2010 OECD Model:

> The hypothesis by which a PE is treated as a functionally separate and independent enterprise is a mere fiction necessary for purposes of

---

[33] The functional separate entity and the relevant business activity approach are considered in Ch. 6.
[34] 2010 Report, p. 13, para. 9.

determining the business profits of this part of the enterprise under Article 7. The authorised OECD approach should not be viewed as implying that the PE must be treated as a separate enterprise entering into dealings with the rest of the enterprise of which it is a part for purposes of any other provisions of the Convention.[35]

The Commentary on Article 7(2) expressly states that the provision only seeks to attribute the profits of an international enterprise to its permanent establishments on the basis of treating them as separate and independent enterprises.[36] But the provision does not allocate all the profits of an international enterprise.[37] Under this approach, profits may be attributed to a permanent establishment even if the international enterprise as a whole has only made losses. On the other hand, profits may not be attributed to a permanent establishment even though the international enterprise as a whole has made profits.[38]

The Commentary affirms that the principles of Article 7(2) apply to both the residence country and the source country.[39] The residence country has an interest in the provision being properly and consistently applied as it affects their taxing rights over business profits. First, a host country's taxing right under Article 7(1) is not an exclusive taxing right – it is a taxing right that is shared by both countries. The residence country may tax the profits attributable to a permanent establishment, but it must provide a credit for tax paid by the permanent establishment. As Article 7 applies to both the residence country and host country, the residence country is required under Articles 23 A or 23 B to eliminate any double taxation on profits attributable to a permanent establishment. Alternatively, the residence country may exempt the profits attributable to a permanent establishment from taxation. Second, if Article 7(1) is not properly applied by the host country it may result in double taxation, or it may result in under-taxation, if the residence country exempts profits that are attributable to a permanent establishment. If a host country taxes profits under Article 7(1) that are not attributable to a permanent establishment, double taxation will occur as the residence country has an exclusive taxing right over profits that are not attributable to a permanent establishment.

Article 7 reflects the principles set out in the 2010 Report, which deals with applying the separate and independent enterprise fiction in Article 7(2). The Commentary establishes that the 2010 Report provides

---

[35] Ibid., p. 13, para. 11.
[36] 2010 OECD Model, p. 134, para. 16.
[37] Ibid., p. 134, para. 17.
[38] Ibid., p. 134, para. 15.
[39] Ibid., p. 134, para. 18.

the principles for attributing profits to permanent establishments under Article 7(2).[40] Consequently, the 2010 Report has been incorporated into the Commentary on new Article 7(2). Therefore, the Commentary on Article 7 and the 2010 Report should be read together when interpreting Article 7(2). The profits attributed to a permanent establishment under Article 7(2) will follow from the calculation of profits or losses from a permanent establishment's transactions with other parties, including transactions with independent persons, transactions with associated enterprises and intra-entity dealings.[41] The attribution of the profits to a permanent establishment involves a two-step method.

The Commentary contains the following guidance on applying the first step.

> Under the first step, a functional and factual analysis is undertaken which will lead to:
>
> - the attribution to the permanent establishment, as appropriate, of the rights and obligations arising out of transactions between the enterprise of which the permanent establishment is a part and separate enterprises;
> - the identification of significant people functions relevant to the attribution of economic ownership of assets, and the attribution of economic ownership of assets to the permanent establishment;
> - the identification of significant people functions relevant to the assumption of risks, and the attribution of risks to the permanent establishment;
> - the identification of other functions of the permanent establishment;
> - the recognition and determination of the nature of those dealings between the permanent establishment and other parts of the same enterprise that can appropriately be recognised, having passed the threshold test referred to in paragraph 26; and
> - the attribution of capital based on the assets and risks attributed to the permanent establishment.[42]

Under the second step, the transfer prices for transactions with associated enterprises and intra-entity dealings which are attributed to a permanent establishment must comply with the principles in the Transfer Pricing Guidelines.[43] The Transfer Pricing Guidelines are applied by analogy to a permanent establishment's intra-entity

---

[40] *Ibid.*, pp. 134–5, para. 19.   [41] *Ibid.*, p. 135, para. 20.   [42] *Ibid.*, p. 135, para. 21.
[43] 2010 Transfer Pricing Guidelines.

dealings.[44] This step uses transfer prices for intra-entity transactions which comply with the arm's length principle through:

- the determination of comparability between the dealings and uncontrolled transactions, established by applying the Guidelines' comparability factors directly (characteristics of property or services, economic circumstances and business strategies) or by analogy (functional analysis, contractual terms) in light of the particular factual circumstances of the permanent establishment; and
- the application by analogy of one of the Guidelines' methods to arrive at an arm's length compensation for the dealings between the permanent establishment and the other parts of the enterprise, taking into account the functions performed by and the assets and risks attributed to the permanent establishment and the other parts of the enterprise.[45]

The Commentary notes that these two steps are considered in detail in the 2010 Report, which underscores the incorporation of the 2010 Report into the Commentary on Article 7(2).[46] In the 2010 Report, the principles for attributing profits to bank branches are dealt with in Part II, Part III deals with permanent establishments engaged in global trading, and Part IV considers permanent establishments carrying on an insurance business.

The Commentary on Article 7(2) expressly refers to dealings between a permanent establishment and other parts of the enterprise to emphasize that these notional transactions are to be treated as transactions between separate and independent entities in attributing profits to the permanent establishment under the separate and independent enterprise fiction.[47] Article 7(2) also applies to transactions between a permanent establishment and an associated enterprise, as these transactions will affect the attribution of business profits to the permanent establishment. In this case, Article 7(2) requires that in attributing profits to the permanent establishment from the transactions, the conditions of the transactions may be adjusted to reflect the conditions of comparable transactions between independent enterprises.

The Commentary provides the following example on applying the notional separate enterprise principle.[48] Assume that a permanent establishment is located in Country S, and that the international

---

[44] 2010 OECD Model, pp. 135–6, para. 22. [45] *Ibid.* [46] *Ibid.*, p. 136, para. 23.
[47] *Ibid.*, p. 136, para. 24. [48] *Ibid.*

enterprise of which it is part is resident in Country R. Assume further that the permanent establishment buys goods from an associated enterprise which is resident in Country T. Assume that there is a treaty between Country S and Country R, and that there is a treaty between Country R and Country T. If the transfer prices for the permanent establishment's transactions exceed the prices that independent enterprises buying the goods would have paid in similar circumstances, the transactions would breach Article 7(2) of the treaty between Country S and Country R. This breach entitles Country S to adjust the profits attributable to the permanent establishment under Article 7(2) to reflect the lower prices that a separate and independent buyer would have paid. In this case, Country R has the power under Article 9(1) of the treaty between Country R and Country T to make an initial adjustment to the profits of the international enterprise resident in Country R, to reflect the prices which independent buyers would have paid in similar circumstances. This will require Country T to provide a corresponding adjustment under Article 9(2).

The Commentary notes that as intra-entity transactions are not legally binding agreements, because only one entity is involved, there is a need for more scrutiny of these notional transactions than for transactions between associated enterprises, which are legally binding agreements.[49] The Commentary indicates that intra-entity transactions must have documentation to support purported intra-entity dealings.[50] The Commentary acknowledges that the documentation requirements for intra-entity transactions reflect the documentation requirements for transactions between associated enterprises.[51] The documentation requirements in the Transfer Pricing Guidelines should not be overzealously applied by tax authorities, to prevent excessive costs and burdens being imposed on taxpayers which are disproportionate to the circumstances. But the Commentary points out that treating an intra-entity dealing as a real transaction is unique and that tax authorities will expect international enterprises to prove that intra-entity transactions should be recognized as dealings under Article 7. The starting point for recognizing a dealing is an international enterprise's accounting records and contemporaneous documents which establish a transfer of economically significant risks, responsibilities and benefits.[52] It is suggested by the Commentary that if an international enterprise retains contemporaneous documents proving a dealing, the potential for disputes is reduced.

[49] *Ibid.*, pp. 136–7, para. 25. [50] *Ibid.* [51] *Ibid.*, p. 137, para. 26. [52] *Ibid.*

Tax authorities will recognize dealings, even though they are not recognized as transactions under general law, to the extent that:

- the documentation is consistent with the economic substance of the activities taking place within the enterprise as revealed by the functional and factual analysis;
- the arrangements documented in relation to the dealing, viewed in their entirety, do not differ from those which would have been adopted by comparable independent enterprises behaving in a commercially rational manner, or, if they do, the structure as presented in the taxpayer's documentation does not practically impede the tax administration from determining an appropriate transfer price; and
- the dealing presented in the taxpayer's documentation does not violate the principles of the approach put forward in the Report by, for example, purporting to transfer risks in a way that segregates them from functions.[53]

Both associated enterprises and international enterprises must create documentation to support their dealings and prevent the risk of transfer pricing disputes from occurring with tax authorities. Associated enterprises will, at times, seek to avoid the cost of preparing documentation if tax authorities are not conducting transfer pricing examinations. Since the 2008 financial and economic crisis which resulted in reduced national tax revenues in most countries, tax authorities in many countries are scrutinizing transfer pricing documentation of associated enterprises to limit the risk of transfer pricing manipulation. One of the main concerns of taxpayers and their advisers is that the documentation requirements for new Article 7 may, in practice, be more onerous than the documentation requirements for associated enterprises.

The Commentary points out that the phrase 'in each Contracting State' in Article 7(2) means that the provision applies to both the host country and the residence country.[54] First, it applies to the host country to determine the business profits that are attributable to a permanent establishment located in that country, in accordance with the last sentence of Article 7(1). Second, it applies to the residence country for the purposes of Articles 23 A and 23 B to prevent double taxation by either exempting the profits that are attributable to a permanent establishment (Article 23 A) or providing a tax credit for taxes levied by the host country on the profits attributed to the permanent establishment

---

[53] Ibid.   [54] Ibid., p. 137, para. 27.

(Article 23 B). Under either Article 23 A or Article 23 B, the residence country is required to determine the profits that are attributable to the permanent establishment to be able to provide relief from double taxation as required by Article 7(2).

One of the challenges of using legal fictions is setting their limits to prevent misunderstandings. The legal fiction of treating a permanent establishment as a separate and independent enterprise in Article 7(2) applies only for the purpose of determining the profits that are attributable to the permanent establishment. The Commentary emphasizes that the separate enterprise legal fiction applies exclusively for the purposes of Article 7 and does not extend to other treaty provisions.[55] Despite this clear limitation on treating permanent establishments as separate entities there is no single OECD consensus view on this issue, as some OECD countries take a contrary view. There appears to be a majority and minority view on this issue, with the majority view being considered first in the Commentary. Under the majority view, a host country is prevented from claiming that the separate enterprise fiction creates notional income for a non-resident international enterprise that is taxed under the host country's domestic law on the basis that another Article of the treaty applies. Nor can the host country claim that its taxing right is supported by Article 7(4), which provides that other treaty provisions prevail over Article 7(1) in certain circumstances. But under the majority view, the separate entity fiction does extend to capital gains on intra-entity transfers of assets. If there is a transfer of assets between a permanent establishment and other parts of the enterprise that are treated as dealings for the purposes of Article 7(2), the host country is entitled to tax any profits or capital gains from such a dealing under Article 13 of the treaty 'as long as such taxation is in accordance with Article 7'.[56] This issue is also considered in the Commentary on Article 13 (paragraphs 4, 8 and 10 of the Commentary). Examples of the limits on the separate enterprise legal fiction under the majority view are set out in the Commentary and are based on examples in the 2010 Report.[57]

The Commentary provides two examples on restricting the separate enterprise legal fiction to Article 7(2). The first example assumes that an international enterprise has a permanent establishment that operates from premises owned by the international enterprise. Assume further that after a factual and functional analysis, economic ownership of the

---

[55] Ibid., p. 138, para. 28. [56] Ibid. [57] Ibid.

premises is allocated to the head office. In this situation, the permanent establishment is treated as leasing the premises and it is entitled to claim a deduction for notional rent paid to its head office in attributing profits to the permanent establishment. But the separate enterprise fiction cannot be extended by the host country to claim that it has a right to tax the notional rent attributed to the head office as income from immovable property under Article 6 of the treaty. The legal fiction prescribed in Article 7(2) does not affect the income derived by an international enterprise with a permanent establishment in the host country under a tax treaty. The provision only applies to attribute profits to the permanent establishment for the purposes of Articles 7(2), 23 A and 23 B.

The second example deals with providing deductions to a permanent establishment for notional intra-entity interest for the purpose of attributing profits to the permanent establishment under Article 7(2). The Commentary claims that allowing a deduction to a permanent establishment for notional interest under Article 7(2) of a treaty does not mean that the part of the enterprise that has provided the notional loan can be treated as deriving interest income for the purposes of Articles 11(1) and (2) of the treaty.[58] The separate enterprise legal fiction in Article 7(2) does not extend to Article 11, which means that the head office and other permanent establishments of an international enterprise cannot be subject to tax on notional interest under Article 11 in the host country. If an international enterprise pays interest on funds borrowed from an independent lender and the borrowed funds are used by the permanent establishment in carrying on business and the interest is borne by the permanent establishment, the interest may be taxed under Article 11(2) by the host country in which the permanent establishment is located. This requires tracing of the original loan being provided by an independent party via the head office to the permanent establishment. In addition, the permanent establishment must pay the interest on the loan. In some circumstances, this degree of tracing would be relatively easy to establish, particularly if large sums of money were involved. However, if a large international enterprise is constantly raising debt finance it may be difficult or impossible to trace the flow of borrowed funds to a permanent establishment as money is fungible. This would make it difficult for a host country to be able to assert its taxing rights over interest paid to the independent non-resident lender under Article 11(2).

[58] *Ibid.*

The minority view is that as a matter of policy, a permanent establishment under the separate entity fiction should be treated in the same way as subsidiaries, as far as possible, for the purposes of the treaty.[59] Under this view, the separate and independent enterprise legal fiction in Article 7(2) extends to interpreting and applying other Articles of the treaty. The minority seeks to achieve tax symmetry by claiming that if a permanent establishment is entitled to a deduction for a notional intra-entity transaction, the notional recipient of the funds should be assessed by the host country, to the extent possible, on the notional receipt. Consequently, under the minority view the separate entity fiction in Article 7(2) extends to Article 6 for notional income from immovable property and Article 11(2) for notional interest.

The Commentary suggests that the minority OECD countries should include in their treaties provisions expressly providing that charges for notional intra-entity income are recognized under Articles 6 and 11 of their treaties.[60] The Commentary notes these Articles deal only with allocating tax rights between two treaty countries and therefore these countries can only levy tax under Articles 6 and 11 to the extent possible under the country's domestic law.[61] This highlights the principle that treaties do not create jurisdiction to tax; in most countries they allocate taxing rights between the treaty countries on the basis of their respective jurisdiction to tax under their domestic law. The Commentary includes, as an alternative approach, that countries using the minority approach may:

> wish to provide that no internal dealings will be recognised in circumstances where an equivalent transaction between two separate enterprises would give rise to income covered by Article 6 or 11 (in that case, however, it will be important to ensure that an appropriate share of the expenses related to what would otherwise have been recognised as a dealing be attributed to the relevant part of the enterprise).[62]

The Commentary notes that countries considering:

> these alternatives should, however, take account of the fact that, due to special considerations applicable to internal interest charges between different parts of a financial enterprise (e.g. a bank), dealings resulting in such charges have long been recognised, even before the adoption of the present version of the Article.[63]

The role of Article 7(2) is to attribute profits to a permanent establishment for the purposes of Article 7(1), which allocates taxing rights over

---

[59] Ibid., pp. 138–9, para. 29.   [60] Ibid.   [61] Ibid.   [62] Ibid.   [63] Ibid.

business profits.[64] Once profits are attributed to a permanent establishment under Article 7(2), whether such income is taxable and the extent to which it is taxable is then determined under the host country's domestic law, provided there is conformity between Article 7(2) and the other provisions of the treaty. The Commentary expressly states that Article 7(2) does not deal with the issue of whether a permanent establishment's expenses are deductible in determining the taxable income of the international enterprise in either the host country or residence country. A permanent establishment's deductible expenses are determined under the host country's domestic law, subject to treaty provisions, such as Article 24(3) on non-discrimination.

A host country's domestic law will conflict with Article 7(2) if it does not recognize dealings that are recognized under Article 7(2) or prevents a permanent establishment from deducting expenses that are not exclusively incurred for the purposes of the permanent establishment. On the other hand, if a country's domestic law prevents certain types of expenses from being deductible, such as entertainment expenses, such a rule is unaffected by Article 7(2).[65] Similarly, a country's domestic law will not be in conflict with Article 7(2) if it contains rules about when certain expenses may be deducted. Difficulties may arise, according to the Commentary, if a country's domestic law is based on when an expense is actually paid, as notional intra-entity transactions will not involve a payment of funds by a permanent establishment to other parts of the international enterprise. In this situation, a country's domestic law should treat a permanent establishment as having paid these notional expenses to ensure consistency between the domestic law and Article 7(2).[66]

Differences between the domestic law of two treaty countries may result in differences between the taxable income of a permanent establishment in the host country and residence country, even though the profits attributable to the permanent establishment have been calculated under Article 7(2). The Commentary notes that these domestic law differences may result from depreciation rates, timing rules on recognizing income and prohibiting particular deductions.[67] This issue is also considered in the Commentary on Articles 23 A and 23 B (paragraphs 39–43 of the Commentary). As a result, despite Article 7(2) applying equally to both the host country, in which a permanent establishment is located for the purposes of Article 7(1), and the residence country for

[64] Ibid., p. 139, para. 30.   [65] Ibid., p. 139, para. 31.
[66] Ibid.   [67] Ibid. pp. 139–40, para. 32.

the purposes of Articles 23 A or 23 B, an international enterprise's taxable income in the host country will usually be different to the taxable income on which the residence country will provide relief from double taxation under Articles 23 A or 23 B.[68] If a host country prohibits certain expenses, such as entertainment expenses, from being deducted, the difference between an international enterprise's taxable income in the host country and residence country will be permanent. On the other hand, if the differences are due to timing differences on when expenses or income are recognized, the differences between the taxable income in the host country and residence country will be temporary.[69]

According to the Commentary, a host country, in taxing the profits that are attributable to a permanent establishment located in that country, must consider the non-discrimination Article, Article 24(3).[70] This provision requires that expenses must be deductible under the same conditions, whether they are incurred for the purposes of a permanent establishment in the host country or for the purposes of an enterprise of that country. The Commentary on Article 24 notes that:

> Permanent establishments must be accorded the same right as resident enterprises to deduct the trading expenses that are, in general, authorised by the taxation law to be deducted from taxable profits. Such deductions should be allowed without any restrictions other than those also imposed on resident enterprises.[71]

The principle in Article 24(3) applies to all expenses incurred by an international enterprise for the benefit of a permanent establishment irrespective of whether the expenses are taken into account under Article 7(2).[72] In some situations, a dealing between a permanent establishment and other parts of the enterprise may not be recognized. 'In such cases, expenses incurred by an enterprise for the purpose of the activities performed by the permanent establishment will be *directly deducted* in determining the profits of the permanent establishment'[73] (emphasis added). Under Article 24(3) all expenses incurred directly or indirectly by an international enterprise for the benefit of a permanent establishment must not, for tax purposes, be treated less favourably than a similar expense incurred by an enterprise that is resident in that country. The threshold to qualify for a deduction under Article 24(3) is whether a resident enterprise would have qualified for a deduction in

---

[68] *Ibid.* [69] *Ibid.* [70] *Ibid.*, p. 140, para. 33.
[71] *Ibid.*, Commentary on Article 24, p. 341, para. 40.
[72] *Ibid.*, para. 34, p. 140. [73] *Ibid.*

the same circumstances. This principle applies to a permanent establishment if, for the purposes of Article 7(2), an expense is directly attributed to the permanent establishment, or is indirectly attributed to the permanent establishment through a notional charge to the permanent establishment. If a dealing is not recognized under Article 7(2), the costs of expenses incurred by the enterprise for the benefit of a permanent establishment are deductible expenses for the permanent establishment, but a profit margin may not be imposed on the costs.

An example of a direct expense is where the threshold requirements for a dealing to be recognized under Article 7(2) have not been satisfied. In this situation, the expenses of the international enterprise that are directly attributed to a permanent establishment may be claimed as deductible expenses by the enterprise in calculating its profits. For example, in the case of a construction site that qualifies as a permanent establishment of an international enterprise, the salary of a local construction worker, hired and paid in the host country to work exclusively on the construction site, is an expense that is directly attributable to the permanent establishment.[74] Expenses indirectly attributed to a permanent establishment occur when an international enterprise incurs expenses which are attributed to functions performed by other parts of the enterprise, either wholly or partly, for the benefit of a permanent establishment. In this situation, a charge is imposed on the permanent establishment in determining the profits attributable to it. For example, if the head office of an international enterprise provides services to a permanent establishment, the overhead expenses that are connected with the provision of these services may be charged to the permanent establishment.[75] But if the provision of services does not satisfy the requirements for a dealing, the head office is prohibited from charging a profit margin on the overhead costs – only the overhead costs incurred by the head office may be attributed to the permanent establishment.

The OECD (in paragraphs 31–33 of the Commentary) interprets Article 7(2) as having a non-discrimination role which prevails over a host country's domestic law denying permanent establishments deductions for expenses incurred for the purposes of deriving taxable income attributable to the permanent establishment.[76] The Commentary states:

---

[74] *Ibid.*   [75] *Ibid.*
[76] Vann, 'Do We Need 7(3)? History and Purpose of the Business Profits Deduction Rule in Tax Treaties' (2010).

Thus, for example, whilst domestic law rules that would ignore the recognition of dealings that should be recognised for the purposes of determining the profits attributable to a permanent establishment under paragraph 2 or that would deny the deduction of expenses not incurred exclusively for the benefit of the permanent establishment would clearly be in violation of paragraph 2, rules that prevent the deduction of certain categories of expenses (e.g. entertainment expenses) or that provide when a particular expense should be deducted are not affected by paragraph 2. In making that distinction, however, some difficult questions may arise as in the case of domestic law restrictions based on when an expense or element of income is actually paid. Since, for instance, an internal dealing will not involve an actual transfer or payment between two different persons, the application of such domestic law restrictions should generally take into account the nature of the dealing and, therefore, treat the relevant transfer or payment as if it had been made between two different persons.[77]

Vann claims that although Article 7(2) may be interpreted in this way, it is at odds with the language of the provision and its history because the provision is not drafted as a non-discrimination provision and Article 24(3) expressly deals with non-discrimination of permanent establishments.[78] According to Vann, new Article 7 does not prevail over a domestic law provision that prevents deductions for expenses of non-resident enterprises and resident enterprises, if the expenses are paid overseas. This interpretation also applies to Article 7 of the 2008 Model. Vann argues that Article 7(3) of the 2008 OECD Model should not have been retained in new Article 7, but that it should have been included in the 2010 Commentary as an option for some countries.[79] This suggested use of Article 7(3) of the 2008 Model should include a specific statement that it deals with a specific non-discrimination problem that is not dealt with by Article 24 – to provide a deduction for expenses incurred overseas if such expenses are proscribed by a country's domestic law for both resident and non-resident companies.[80] This suggestion creates a reciprocal deduction for permanent establishments in treaty countries for foreign expenses incurred by a permanent establishment.

---

[77] 2010 OECD Model, p. 139, para. 31.
[78] Vann, 'Do We Need 7(3)? History and Purpose of the Business Profits Deduction Rule in Tax Treaties' (2010).
[79] Article 7(3) of the 2008 OECD Model is considered below in section 7.
[80] Vann, 'Do We Need 7(3)? History and Purpose of the Business Profits Deduction Rule in Tax Treaties' (2010).

4.1 Building site permanent establishments

The Commentary expressly deals with building site, construction or installation project permanent establishments, as problems have occurred in attributing profits to these permanent establishments under Article 7(2) of the 2008 OECD Model. Under Article 5(3) a non-resident enterprise will satisfy the permanent establishment threshold if it has a fixed place of business that is a building site, a construction or an installation project in the host country for more than 12 months. According to the Commentary, problems occur when goods are provided, or when services are performed by another part of the enterprise or an associated party, in connection with the building site, construction or installation project.[81] The Commentary notes that while these types of problems can occur with any permanent establishment, they are prevalent for building sites and construction or installation projects. For these permanent establishments, it is necessary to ensure that income is only attributed to them when there is a nexus between the income and the activities of the international enterprise carried out through the permanent establishments. Profits can only be attributed to a permanent establishment if the activities are carried on by the permanent establishment itself.

To illustrate this point, the Commentary has examples on goods and services provided to a permanent establishment by other parts of an international enterprise that are located outside the permanent establishment's host country.[82] The first example is that if goods are supplied to a permanent establishment by other parts of an international enterprise, the profits arising from providing goods to the permanent establishment are not attributable to it. In this situation, the profits arising from the supply of the goods are connected with the business operations of the other parts of the international enterprise. If services, such as planning, designing and providing technical advice, are provided to a building site permanent establishment by other parts of an international enterprise, the profits arising from the services cannot be attributed to the permanent establishment.

---

[81] 2010 OECD Model, p. 141, paras. 35–6.   [82] Ibid., p. 141, para. 37.

5 Article 7(3) mechanisms to relieve double taxation

5.1 Background

The effect of Article 7 and Articles 23 A and 23 B (double tax relief in the country of residence) is intended to prevent the double taxation of profits that are attributable to a permanent establishment in accordance with Article 7. Nevertheless, two treaty countries may be required to resolve double taxation caused by different interpretations of Article 7(2). Consequently, the OECD considered it important, given the different views held by OECD countries, that Article 7(3) provide a method to eliminate any double taxation that may occur as a result of interpretational differences.[83]

The OECD Fiscal Affairs Committee published the 2010 Report with detailed guidance on the meaning of Article 7(2) with the aim of ensuring that two treaty countries reach a common interpretation of the provision to prevent the risk of double taxation.[84] The guidance provided in the 2010 Report is based on the principles in the Transfer Pricing Guidelines. The Commentary acknowledges that there is a risk of double taxation occurring when an international enterprise with a permanent establishment in the host country attributes profits to the permanent establishment in accordance with Article 7(2), as interpreted in the 2010 Report, and the reporting is consistent in both countries.[85] In this situation, the combined operation of Articles 7 and either 23 A or 23 B should ideally prevent double taxation. If each country agrees that the international enterprise has interpreted and applied Article 7(2) in accordance with the 2010 Report, they should not adjust the profits attributable to the permanent establishment to create a different result under Article 7(2).[86] As transfer pricing is an inexact science, differences may arise on how a transfer pricing method is to be applied or which is the best transfer pricing method to be used in particular circumstances. But treaty countries should refrain from making adjustments to transfer prices established by an international enterprise on the basis that a different transfer price should have been used by the international enterprise, provided the international enterprise has complied with Article 7(2).

This point is illustrated in the Commentary by the following example.[87] An international enterprise has a manufacturing plant in

---

[83] Ibid., p. 143, para. 44. [84] Ibid., p. 143, para. 45.
[85] Ibid., p. 143, para. 46. [86] Ibid. [87] Ibid., pp. 143–4, para. 47.

Country R and goods are transferred from the manufacturing plant to the enterprise's permanent establishment in Country S. The notional intra-entity transaction is recognized as a dealing under Article 7(2) as interpreted in the 2010 Report and a notional arm's length price must be set for the dealing. The international enterprise has documentation that is consistent with the functional and factual analysis used by the enterprise to determine the profits that are attributable to its permanent establishment, and the taxable income in each country. Under the dealing, the plant in Country R has sold goods to the permanent establishment in Country S and the transfer price of 100 has been used to determine the profits attributable to the permanent establishment. Both countries agree that the dealing should be recognized for the purposes of Article 7(2) and that the transfer price used by the enterprise complies with the 2010 Report and the Transfer Pricing Guidelines. In this situation, both countries should not adjust the profits attributable to the permanent establishment on the basis that a different transfer price should be used. If the countries agree that the international enterprise has complied with the requirements of Article 7(2) they should desist from claiming that a different transfer price should be used. The Commentary claims that in this situation the tax authorities of the two countries should accept the international enterprise's judgment on the appropriate arm's length conditions as it has complied with Article 7(2).[88] Consequently, in this example, as an arm's length price has been used in both countries, if they respect that transfer price and use it for the purposes of the tax treaty, any double taxation will be eliminated under either Article 23 A or 23 B.

The 2010 Report was unable to establish a single consensus interpretation on several issues, such as determining the equity capital of permanent establishments for the purpose of calculating its deductible interest expense. On this particular issue, the 2010 Report sets out a range of acceptable interpretations, which may result in double taxation if two treaty countries use different methods for determining the equity capital of a permanent establishment.[89] The Fiscal Affairs Committee was concerned that these differing interpretations may create problems for financial institutions.[90] In this situation, the Committee concluded that any double taxation must be relieved if it results from two treaty

---

[88] *Ibid.*   [89] 2010 Report, pp. 18–19, paras. 28–31 and pp. 34–46, paras. 105–71.
[90] 2010 OECD Model, p. 144, para. 49.

countries interpreting Article 7(2) differently where both interpretations are in accordance with Article 7(2), as reflected in the Commentary and 2010 Report.

5.2 New Article 7(3)

The OECD is concerned that relief will be provided for double taxation resulting from treaty countries using differing interpretations in the 2010 Report and Transfer Pricing Guidelines. The Commentary claims that new Article 7(3), which reflects Article 9(2) for associated enterprises, provides double taxation relief arising from a host country and residence country using different interpretations of Article 7(2).[91] But the Commentary claims that recourse to Article 7(3) is expected to be limited.[92] First, if an international enterprise has attributed profits to its permanent establishment in the same manner in the host country and the residence country, and both countries agree that the enterprise has satisfied Article 7(2) as interpreted in the 2010 Report, neither country should adjust the profits attributed to the permanent establishment under Article 7(2).[93] Second, the Commentary directs that Article 7(3) supplements rather than alters the remedies available in the OECD Model to ensure that the treaty countries comply with their obligations under Articles 7 and 23 A or 23 B. If a host country adjusts the profits attributed to a permanent establishment and the adjustment conflicts with Article 7(2), the international enterprise may seek relief from any resulting double taxation because the enterprise is being taxed in a way that is not in accordance with the treaty. The relief mechanisms available to the international enterprise are the remedies in the domestic law of the host country, and the mutual agreement procedure under Article 25 of the treaty.[94]

On the other hand, if an international enterprise, in attributing profits to a permanent establishment, fails to comply with the requirements of Article 7(2), either the host country or the residence country may make an adjustment to ensure that the requirements of this provision are satisfied.[95] If the host country in which the permanent establishment is located makes an adjustment to the profits attributed to a permanent establishment in accordance with Article 7(2), this provision gives the

---

[91] *Ibid.*, p. 144, paras. 49–50. [92] *Ibid.*, p. 144, para. 50.
[93] *Ibid.*, p. 144, para. 51, repeating the comments made at p. 143, para. 46.
[94] *Ibid.*, pp. 144–5, para. 52.   [95] *Ibid.*, p. 145, para. 53.

residence country of the international enterprise the power under Article 7(2) and Article 23 A or 23 B to make a corresponding adjustment to relieve any double taxation. Nevertheless, in some cases a host country's domestic law may prevent it from making an adjustment or that country may decide against making an adjustment if the adjustment reduces the permanent establishment's taxable profits in the host country.[96] Another possibility is that two treaty countries may take differing interpretations of Article 7(2) and both interpretations conform with the provision because on some issues in the 2010 Report there is no single OECD interpretation.[97]

Article 7(3) may be of limited effect in practice. If a country being asked to make a corresponding adjustment agrees that the initial adjustment accords with Article 7(2), it will make the adjustment regardless of the express requirement in Article 7(3) obliging it to make the adjustment. As a matter of efficient administration and maintaining its relationship with treaty partner countries, a country will usually make a corresponding adjustment with or without an express requirement, if it considers that the initial adjustment correctly applies Article 7(2). Article 7(3) therefore only has an effect if two countries have differing interpretations of Article 7(2), but the country being asked to make a corresponding adjustment is obliged to do so if it agrees that the initial adjustment complies with Article 7(2). However, Article 7(3) is easily avoided by a country refusing to make a corresponding adjustment on the basis that it considers the initial adjustment to conflict with Article 7(2). As the principles in Article 7(2) are difficult to apply in practice, and there is significant controversy on applying these principles, a country could easily claim in good faith that it disagrees that an initial adjustment complies with Article 7(2). Consequently, Article 7(3) may be of limited effect in practice as the obligation to make a corresponding adjustment turns on the adjusting country agreeing that the initial adjustment complies with Article 7(2). This point was emphasized in several submissions to the OECD on Article 7 reflecting the role of Article 9(2) for associated enterprises.

A detailed example is included in the Commentary to illustrate the application of Article 7(3).[98] Assume that an international enterprise is a resident of Country R and has a plant in Country R which has sent goods for sale to its permanent establishment in Country S. Under Article 7(2) if the notional intra-entity transaction is recognized as a dealing, a notional arm's length price must then be established. Assume, further, that the enterprise has

---

[96] Ibid. [97] Ibid. [98] Ibid., p. 145, para. 55.

documentation to support its claim for a dealing, and the dealing is consistent with the functional and factual analysis used by the enterprise to determine the profits attributable to the permanent establishment. The dealing is a sale of goods to the permanent establishment with a notional transfer price of 90 used to determine the profits attributable to the permanent establishment. While Country S accepts the notional transfer price used by the international enterprise, Country R decides that the notional transfer price conflicts with both its domestic transfer pricing provisions and Article 7(2) of the treaty. Country R decides that the appropriate notional transfer price should be altered to 110 and it adjusts the tax payable in that country, after reducing the international enterprise's exempt income under Article 23 A or foreign tax credit which the enterprise may claim under Article 23 B, on the enterprise's profits which are attributed to the permanent establishment. In this example, the international enterprise's profits of 20 may be subject to double taxation as Country S is using a transfer price of 90 and Country R is using a transfer price of 110. In this situation, if Country R's adjustment conforms to Article 7(2), Article 7(3) requires Country S to make a corresponding adjustment to the tax payable in Country S on the permanent establishment's profits which are taxed in both countries.

If Country S disagrees that Country R's initial adjustment complies with the requirements of Article 7(2), it may refuse to make a corresponding adjustment.[99] If the country being asked to make an adjustment refuses to do so, the international enterprise may use the mutual agreement procedure in Article 25(1) to attempt to resolve the dispute. Moreover, if necessary, the arbitration procedure in Article 25(5) may be used, as the double taxation involves the issue of whether the actions of one or both treaty countries has resulted, or will result, in taxation of the international enterprise that conflicts with the treaty. The mutual agreement procedure allows the competent authorities of the treaty countries to decide whether the adjustment by Country R was justified under Article 7(2). If the adjustment is justified, then the competent authorities can decide whether Country S should make a corresponding adjustment. Under the mutual agreement procedure the two treaty countries should attempt to agree on the same arm's length price. The arm's length price in this situation is often negotiated to a price that is acceptable to the two treaty countries. In this example, Country R may

---

[99] *Ibid.*, pp. 145–6, para. 56.

decide to alter its transfer price to 100 and Country S may agree to provide a deduction for this transfer price to relieve the double taxation.

The above example illustrates the role of Article 7(3) to provide relief against double taxation that arises from the treaty countries using differing interpretations of Article 7(2) which are authorized in the Commentary and the 2010 Report. In this situation, although a country is complying with the treaty, the resulting double taxation conflicts with one of the key aims of tax treaties. The objective of Article 7(3) is to provide relief from double taxation in this situation.[100] Article 7(3) reflects the features of Article 9(2) and, like that provision, Article 7(3) may be easily avoided by the country being asked to make a corresponding adjustment claiming that it disagrees with the initial adjustment.

If an adjustment is made by one country to the profits attributable to a permanent establishment, it applies reciprocally to the other country.[101] An initial adjustment may be made by the host country in which a permanent establishment is located, or it may be made in the country in which the international enterprise is a resident. Article 7(3) does not apply unless an adjustment is made by either the host country or residence country. But a treaty country is not required to automatically make a corresponding adjustment to a permanent establishment's transfer prices if an adjustment has been made by the other treaty country.[102] A country is only required to make a corresponding adjustment if it considers that the initial adjustment complies with Article 7(2), reflecting the profits a permanent establishment would have made if its dealings were transactions with arm's length transfer prices. According to the Commentary, Article 7(3) may not be used if an initial adjustment attributes profits to a permanent establishment that are different to the profits that would have been attributed in accordance with the principles in Article 7(2).[103] The Commentary prescribes that a country is only required to make a corresponding adjustment if it considers that the initial adjustment complies with the principles in Article 7(2) and that the transfer prices used are appropriate.[104] Nevertheless, if Article 7(3) is inapplicable, an international enterprise may invoke the mutual agreement procedure under Article 25 of the OECD Model to relieve any double taxation.

Article 7(3) is silent on the methods to be used for making corresponding adjustments.[105] If the host country in which a permanent

---

[100] Ibid., p. 146, para. 57. [101] Ibid., p. 146, para. 58. [102] Ibid., p. 146, para. 59.
[103] Ibid. [104] Ibid. [105] Ibid., p. 146, para. 60.

establishment is located makes the initial adjustment, the corresponding adjustment may be made in the residence country, either by adjusting the income exempted under Article 23 A, or by adjusting the credit which may be claimed under Article 23 B. If the initial adjustment is made by the residence country, the host country may make the corresponding adjustment by reducing the taxable income of the permanent establishment to reflect the initial adjustment.

The Commentary notes that under Article 7(3) the issue of secondary adjustments, considered in paragraph 8 of the Commentary on Article 9(2), does not arise.[106] As stated in paragraph 26 of the Commentary, the determination of profits attributable to a permanent establishment is restricted to Articles 7, 23 A and 23 B, and does not affect the other Articles of the OECD Model.

Article 7(3) does not have prescribed time limits, which reflects Article 9(2).[107] The provision leaves open the issue of whether a time limit should be set for the making of corresponding adjustments after an initial adjustment is made. The OECD countries use a variety of methods on this issue. Some countries consider that corresponding adjustments should be unlimited. If the country making the initial adjustment has gone back several years, the international enterprise should be entitled to claim corresponding adjustments in the other country. Other OECD countries consider that a limit should be placed on the period for making corresponding adjustments as a matter of administration. As Articles 7(3) and 9(2) do not have time limits, treaty countries are free to include time limits in their treaties on the period of time that a country is required to make a corresponding adjustment.[108] This issue is also considered in paragraphs 39, 40 and 41 of the Commentary on Article 25 on the mutual agreement procedure.

An initial adjustment made by one treaty country will not result in an immediate corresponding adjustment to the tax imposed on taxable income in the other treaty country if the international enterprise has reported a loss in that country. In this situation the initial adjustment affects the loss attributable to an international enterprise in the other country. The Commentary notes that under Article 7(3) the competent authorities of the treaty countries may decide on the future effect of the initial adjustment on the international enterprise's tax liability in the other country before the tax is levied.[109] Moreover, as a matter of

---

[106] Ibid., p. 147, para. 61.   [107] Ibid., p. 147, para. 62.
[108] Ibid.   [109] Ibid., p. 147, para. 63.

prudent tax administration, the competent authorities may use the mutual agreement procedure at an early stage to determine the extent to which a corresponding adjustment may be required in the future.[110] This provides certainty for the taxpayer and prevents the claim that the time limit for making a corresponding adjustment has expired.

If there is disagreement between treaty countries on the amount and character of a corresponding adjustment, the Commentary asserts that the mutual agreement procedure in Article 25 should be used.[111] The Commentary expressly notes that if a treaty country makes an adjustment to the profits attributable to a permanent establishment, with the other treaty country failing to provide a corresponding adjustment to avoid double taxation, the international enterprise may invoke the mutual agreement procedure in Article 25(1). In addition, it may use arbitration under Article 25(5), which requires the competent authorities to agree that either the initial adjustment by one country or the other country refusing to make a corresponding adjustment, conflicts with the provisions of the treaty.

The Commentary claims that Article 7(3) only applies to the extent necessary to eliminate the double taxation that arises from an adjustment by a treaty country of the profits attributable to a permanent establishment.[112] The provision applies to treaty countries using different interpretations of Article 7(2) which result in profits being attributed to a permanent establishment and with the same profits also being attributed to another part of the international enterprise in accordance with Article 7.[113] It is limited to a situation in which two treaty countries use different interpretations of the appropriate arm's length transfer prices for a dealing. The following example is provided in the Commentary to illustrate this point.[114] Assume that a host country, in which a permanent establishment is located, adjusts its profits because the transfer prices for a dealing between the permanent establishment and another part of the international enterprise failed to comply with the arm's length principle. Assume, further, that the residence country agreed that the transfer prices breached the arm's length requirement. The residence country in this situation is required under Articles 7(2) and 23 A or 23 B to attribute to the permanent establishment the adjusted arm's length transfer prices to relieve double taxation. Article 7(3) applies

---

[110] Ibid. [111] Ibid., pp. 147–8, para. 64. [112] Ibid., p. 148, para. 65.
[113] Ibid., p. 148, para. 66. [114] Ibid., p. 145, para. 55.

in this situation to the extent that the two treaty countries use different views of the transfer prices for the intra-entity dealing.

The key role of Article 7 is to allocate taxing rights over a permanent establishment between the host country and the residence country. Article 7 focuses on attributing profits to a permanent establishment for the purpose of allocating taxing rights between the two treaty countries; it does not deal with determining the taxable income of a permanent establishment.[115] Article 7(2) does not deal with the revenue and expenses that will be used in determining a permanent establishment's taxable income in the host country as these issues are determined under that country's domestic law provided it complies with Article 7(2). If a treaty provision conflicts with a host country's domestic law, the treaty will prevail over domestic law to the extent of any inconsistency to provide reciprocal treaty treatment in the treaty countries. Nevertheless, even though the profits attributed to a permanent establishment may be the same in the host country and residence country, the resulting taxable income in each country may be different because of the differences in the domestic law of the treaty countries. For example, the domestic law of the treaty countries may have different timing rules for recognizing income and deductions, but such differences do not result in double taxation for the purposes of Article 7(3) as they are not permanent differences.

Article 7(3) does not affect the calculation of an exemption under Article 23 A or a tax credit under Article 23 B.[116] Article 7(3) only applies to provide relief against double taxation for tax paid to the host country in which a permanent establishment is located on the profits attributed to the permanent establishment in accordance with Article 7(2). Article 7(3) cannot apply if such profits have been fully exempted in the residence country, or if the tax on these profits has been fully credited against the residence country's tax under that country's domestic law. The proviso is that the exemption in the residence country must comply with Article 23 A and the crediting must comply with Article 23 B.

5.3 Alternative version of new Article 7(3)

Some OECD countries prefer a broader version of Article 7(3) that provides them with the capacity to negotiate with the adjusting country on the most appropriate transfer pricing method or transfer prices

---

[115] *Ibid.*, p. 148, para. 66.   [116] *Ibid.*, p. 148, para. 67.

for notional intra-entity transactions. Under this approach if a treaty country fails to make a corresponding adjustment that results in double taxation, it should be resolved under the mutual agreement procedure instead of the procedure in Article 7(3).[117] The mutual agreement procedure applies without considering the adjusting country's preferred transfer pricing methods or transfer prices. Moreover, if the mutual agreement procedure fails to resolve the double taxation, the arbitration measure in Article 25(5) will apply. An alternative version of Article 7(3) (alternative Article 7(3)) is included in the Commentary. The alternative version of Article 7(3) is:

> Where, in accordance with paragraph 2, a Contracting State adjusts the profits that are attributable to a permanent establishment of an enterprise of one of the Contracting States and taxes accordingly profits of the enterprise that have been charged to tax in the other State, the other Contracting State shall, to the extent necessary to eliminate double taxation, make an appropriate adjustment if it agrees with the adjustment made by the first-mentioned State; if the other Contracting State does not so agree, the Contracting States shall eliminate any double taxation resulting therefrom by mutual agreement.[118]

The aim of the alternative Article 7(3) is to provide the country being asked to make a corresponding adjustment with the ability to require that this be done through the mutual agreement procedure.[119] The main difference between the main version and alternative version is that under the main version the country being asked to make a corresponding adjustment is not under a legal obligation to make a corresponding adjustment, even if it considers that the initial adjustment is in accordance with Article 7(2). The alternative Article 7(3) requires the country being asked to make a corresponding adjustment to negotiate with the other country over the transfer pricing method or transfer prices under the arm's length principle. If a country does not unilaterally make a corresponding adjustment, the alternative Article 7(3) provides the international enterprise with the right to the use of the mutual agreement procedure to have the double taxation relieved. Although the mutual agreement procedure, in this situation, imposes a legal obligation on the treaty countries to resolve the double taxation through negotiation, 'it does not provide a substantive standard to govern which State has the obligation to compromise its position to achieve that mutual agreement'.[120] If the countries fail to agree on eliminating the double

[117] Ibid., pp. 148–9, para. 68.   [118] Ibid.   [119] Ibid., p. 149, para. 69.   [120] Ibid.

taxation, both countries will breach the treaty requirement to resolve the double taxation. The Commentary claims that under the alternative Article 7(3) treaty countries are required to eliminate double taxation, and this obligation exceeds the mutual agreement procedure under Article 25(2), which merely requires the competent authorities to attempt to resolve a dispute by mutual agreement. Under the alternative Article 7(3) the Commentary claims that the comments made in paragraphs 66 and 67 on the main Article 7(3) also apply to the alternative Article 7(3). These comments address the role of Article 7 in allocating taxing rights between two countries.

The main disadvantage of the alternative Article 7(3) is that it is likely to increase the number of cases being decided through mutual agreement, and, in turn, increase the workload of competent authorities in treaty countries. This increase in workload may result in significant delays in resolving double taxation and result in uncertainty for international enterprises waiting for decisions on matters that have been referred to the mutual agreement mechanism. In some jurisdictions, financial accounting legislation may require entities to make provision for tax disputes, which would include unresolved disputes on the attribution of profits to permanent establishments. For example, in the US the Financial Accounting Standards Board issued interpretation No. 48, 'Accounting for Uncertainty in Income Taxes' (FIN48) in 2006. Under this measure taxpayers are required to measure all tax positions and determine whether the taxpayer's position will be sustained after the position is investigated by the US Internal Revenue Service (IRS). Taxpayers are then required to make provision for tax positions that are more likely than not to be sustained following examination by the IRS.

The practical differences between the main Article 7(3) and the alternative 7(3) are unlikely to be significant. It is likely that, under the main Article 7(3), the country being asked to make a corresponding adjustment would conclude that the initial adjustment conflicts with the arm's length principle. In this situation, the double taxation is outside the scope of Article 7(3) for the purposes of obtaining relief. Consequently, an international enterprise would have to invoke the mutual agreement procedure under Article 25 to resolve the double taxation. As transfer pricing is an art and not a science, there is significant scope for disagreement on whether a primary adjustment is consistent with the requirements of Article 7(2). It would probably be rare for a country required to make a corresponding adjustment to conclude that the initial adjustment was consistent with Article 7(2) and that the international enterprise had not complied with Article 7(2). Consequently, main Article 7(3) is unlikely to be successful in providing streamlined relief from double taxation. In summary, double taxation arising from differing interpretations of appropriate transfer prices and transfer pricing methods between treaty countries is likely to be resolved through the mutual agreement procedure under Article 25, which is a costly and time-consuming mechanism.

6 Article 7(4)

The Commentary claims that as the term 'profits' is undefined in the OECD Model, the term has a broad meaning under Article 7 and includes all income from carrying on an enterprise.[121] Profits are also broadly interpreted in other provisions of the OECD Model. As the term profits has a broad meaning under Article 7 there may be situations where this provision and other provisions of the OECD Model apply concurrently. Article 7(4) deals with the interaction between Article 7 and other provisions of the OECD Model by giving priority to treaty Articles dealing with specific types of income under the OECD Model over Article 7.[122] Article 7 applies to business profits which are not within the scope of specific categories of income under the OECD Model. The Commentary notes that the application of Article 7 and a specific Article may result in the same tax treatment, and no practical difference results from the application of either Article.[123] For example, if a permanent establishment in a host country derives rent from immovable property in the host country, Article 7(4) would give priority to Article 6. As both Articles 6 and 7 give the host country an unlimited right to tax the rent, the taxation of the rent in the host country may be the same under either Article. As specific treaty provisions and Article 7 may concurrently apply to business profits, the specific provisions may either retain priority or give priority to Article 7. The following provisions retain priority over Article 7. Article 6, which deals with income from immovable property, provides that Article 6(1) and (3) applies to the income from immovable property of an enterprise. Article 17(1) and (2) dealing with the income derived by artistes and sportsmen prevails over Article 7.

Article 10(4) gives priority over Article 7 to dividends paid by a company resident in a source country and derived by an enterprise

[121] *Ibid.*, p. 149, para. 71.   [122] *Ibid.*, p. 150, para. 72.   [123] *Ibid.*, p. 150, para. 73.

resident in the other country, if the enterprise has a permanent establishment in the source country and the dividends are beneficially owned by the permanent establishment. The permanent establishment must be the economic owner of the shares which is regarded as the:

> equivalent of ownership for income tax purposes by a separate enterprise, with attendant benefits and burdens (*e.g.* the right to the dividends attributable to the ownership of the holdings and the potential exposes to gains or losses from the appreciation or depreciation of the holding).[124]

In effect, Article 10(4) overrides Article 7(4), thereby giving Article 7 priority to tax dividends derived by a permanent establishment which are paid by a company resident in the host country. Other provisions which give priority to Article 7 are: Article 11(4) for interest derived by a permanent establishment; Article 12(3) for royalties derived by a permanent establishment; and Article 21(2) for other income not dealt with in foregoing Articles of the OECD Model if the recipient of the income is a permanent establishment of an enterprise and the income is derived from a right or property which is effectively connected with the permanent establishment.

The rule in Article 7(4) does not affect the classification of business profits for domestic purposes. If a treaty country has a taxing right over income under a treaty, that country may for its domestic tax purposes characterize the income as business profits or a specific category of income, provided the taxation of the income complies with the provisions of the treaty.[125]

The Commentary notes that treaty countries may define the term 'profits' or have explanations of the meaning of the term for a treaty, to clarify the differences between profits and other items of income which are within the scope of provisions, other than Article 7.[126] A situation in which the Commentary notes this may occur is when the treaty negotiations result in definitions of dividends, interest and royalties which are different to the definitions of these terms used in the OECD Model.

The Commentary sets out the history of certain royalties and income from professional services, as these items of income are currently within the scope of Article 7, but under earlier versions of the OECD Model they were covered by specific provisions.[127] First, the term 'royalties' was defined in Article 12(3) of the 1963 OECD Model and 1977 Model to

---

[124] *Ibid.*, p. 193, para. 32.1.   [125] *Ibid.*, p. 150, para. 74.
[126] *Ibid.*, p. 150, para. 75.   [127] *Ibid.*, pp. 150–1, paras. 76–7.

include 'payments for the right to use industrial, commercial or scientific equipment'. The references to these types of income were subsequently deleted from the definition of royalties in Article 12(3) to bring this income from leasing industrial, commercial or scientific equipment, and income from leasing containers, within the scope of Article 7, or Article 8 (shipping, inland waterways transport and air transport), instead of Article 12.[128] This amendment was made in the 1992 OECD Model as the Committee on Fiscal Affairs determined this amendment to be appropriate given the nature of this income.

Second, before 2000, income from professional services and other activities of an independent character were dealt with by former Article 14, a specific provision on this type of income. Former Article 14 was repealed in the 2000 OECD Model. There were significant similarities between former Article 14 and Article 7. One difference was that former Article 14 used the notion of a fixed base rather than a permanent establishment. At times there had been uncertainty over whether certain activities were within the scope of Article 7 or former Article 14. The Commentary claims that the repeal of Article 14 in the 2000 OECD Model reflected that there was no difference between former Article 14 and Article 7.[129] Since former Article 14 was repealed, income from professional services and other activities is within the scope of Article 7. Moreover, the term 'business' was defined in Article 3(1)(h) of the 2000 OECD Model and subsequent OECD Models to include professional services or other activities of an independent character.

7 Provisions deleted from Article 7

Four paragraphs of Article 7 of the 2008 OECD Model were deleted from Article 7. Former Article 7(3) was not included in new Article 7 because of the controversy over the meaning of the provision. The terms of Article 7(3) of the 2008 OECD Model were:

> In determining the profits of a permanent establishment, there shall be allowed as deductions expenses which are incurred for the purposes of the permanent establishment, including executive and general administrative expenses so incurred, whether in the State in which the permanent establishment is situated or elsewhere.[130]

---

[128] Ibid., p. 150, para. 76.   [129] Ibid., p. 151, para. 77.
[130] 2008 OECD Model, pp. 26–7.

The interpretation of this provision under the pre-2008 Commentary was controversial as it could be interpreted as supporting the separate entity approach or the single entity approach. Under the separate entity approach, which is the preferred OECD interpretation, if goods or services are provided to a permanent establishment by other parts of an international enterprise, an arm's length profit margin should be included in the transfer prices. Under the single entity approach, the transfer price was only the actual cost of the goods or services, without an arm's length profit margin.

The Commentary claims that Article 7(3) of the 2008 Model was originally intended to ensure that when profits are attributed to a permanent establishment under Article 7(2), the expenses incurred either directly or indirectly by an international enterprise for the business activities of a permanent establishment are taken into account.[131] These expenses could be incurred either in the host jurisdiction of the permanent establishment or outside the host jurisdiction. It is noted in the Commentary that Article 7(3) has been interpreted, at times, as limiting deductions which indirectly benefited a permanent establishment, to the actual amount of the expenses incurred by the other parts of the international enterprise for the permanent establishment. This construction of Article 7(3) was applied to general and administrative expenses, as these expenses are expressly mentioned in the provision. Under Article 7(2) of the 2008 Model, as interpreted in the 2008 Commentary and preceding Commentaries, this interpretation of Article 7(3) did not create difficulties as general and administrative expenses of an international enterprise were usually only allocated to a permanent establishment at cost, without an arm's length profit margin.[132]

New Article 7(2) requires that intra-entity transactions that are recognized as dealings have arm's length transfer prices, and include an appropriate profit margin. If an international enterprise performs activities for the benefit of a permanent establishment, such as management services, the transfer prices for the dealing must be arm's length prices. A permanent establishment is entitled to claim these arm's length transfer prices as deductions. Article 7(3) of the 2008 Model was deleted from Article 7 to prevent claims that the provision limits deductions for intra-entity transactions to their actual cost. Article 7(2) does not alter the

---

[131] 2010 OECD Model, p. 141, para. 38. See also Vann, 'Do We Need 7(3)? History and Purpose of the Business Profits Deduction Rule in Tax Treaties' (2010).
[132] 2010 OECD Model, p. 141, para. 39.

requirement that in determining the profits that are attributable to a permanent establishment, the expenses incurred by an international enterprise for the benefit of the permanent establishment are deductible, regardless of whether they were incurred directly or indirectly. Consequently, there must be a deduction for expenses incurred by another part of an international enterprise outside the host country for the benefit of a permanent establishment or an arm's length charge for a dealing.

Article 7(4) of the 2008 OECD Model[133] was deleted from the revised Article 7. This provision provided that the attribution of profits to a permanent establishment could be done on the basis of an apportionment of the total profits of an international enterprise to its head office and permanent establishments. The conditions for the use of this method were that the application of this method was customary in a treaty country and that the result complied with the principles of Article 7. The Fiscal Committee concluded that methods other than apportionment of total profits can always be used.[134] The Committee decided to delete this provision because it was rarely used and it was difficult to ensure that the result would comply with the arm's length principle.[135]

Article 7(6) of the 2008 OECD Model[136] was deleted from the revised Article 7. Article 7(6) provided that the profits to be attributed to a permanent establishment are to be determined under the 'same method each year unless there was a good and sufficient reason to the contrary'.[137] This provision was intended to require a consistent treatment provided it was accepted that the profits attributed to a permanent establishment could be determined by direct methods, indirect methods or an apportionment of the total profits of international enterprise to its constituent parts. The Fiscal Committee concluded that the 2010 version of Article 7 does not allow for these methods to be used and, consequently, Article 7(5) of the 2008 OECD Model was superfluous.[138]

A final provision that was deleted from Article 7 was Article 7(5)[139] of the 2008 OECD Model. This provision provided that profits will not be attributed to a permanent establishment if a permanent establishment purchased goods or merchandise for the international enterprise. Under Article 5(4)(d) of the OECD Model, if an enterprise of a contracting state maintains in the other state a fixed place of business used exclusively for purchasing goods for the enterprise, this activity will not satisfy

---

[133] 2008 OECD Model, p. 27. [134] 2010 OECD Model, p. 142, para. 41.
[135] Ibid. [136] 2008 OECD Model, p. 27. [137] Ibid.
[138] 2010 OECD Model, p. 142, para. 42. [139] 2008 OECD Model, p. 27.

the permanent establishment threshold. But this provision has an exclusivity requirement which is breached if an enterprise carries out other activities through its fixed place of business. In this situation, if the permanent establishment threshold test is satisfied then the profits attributable to the permanent establishment are taxed in the host country. Former Article 7(5) provided a tax exemption for the purchasing activities conducted by a permanent establishment for the head office or other permanent establishments of the international enterprise. The Fiscal Committee decided to delete this provision because it was inconsistent with the arm's length principle.[140] Under the arm's length principle, if purchasing activities were performed by an arm's length enterprise, the purchaser would be paid arm's length fees for the purchasing services. Consequently, former Article 7(5) was considered to conflict with the arm's length principle.

8 Conclusion

The 2010 Report is based on arm's length economic theory that treats a permanent establishment as if it were a notional separate enterprise and applying an adapted version of the Transfer Pricing Guidelines to permanent establishments. This theory is in stark contrast to the practical reality that permanent establishments of modern international enterprises are merely a seamless part of international business with a common profit motive and common management. New Article 7 is likely to create uncertainty because of its theoretical base that conflicts with business practice and law. The implementation of new Article 7 is based on creating a legal fiction of treating a permanent establishment as a separate enterprise for the purposes of Article 7 only but not for all treaty purposes.

New Article 7 fully implements the principles in the 2010 Report on attributing profits to permanent establishments and is unlikely to provide certainty for taxpayers and tax authorities. And the measures provided are likely to involve high compliance costs for taxpayers and high administrative costs for tax authorities because of the legal fiction of treating a permanent establishment as a separate and independent enterprise. While some countries may use new Article 7 in treaties that they negotiate or renegotiate, other countries may continue to use the existing Article 7, as updated by the 2008 Commentary. And some,

---

[140] 2010 OECD Model, pp. 142–3, para. 43.

such as New Zealand, may continue to use existing Article 7 with pre-2008 Commentary. As new Article 7 or the 2008 OECD Commentary on Article 7 are not being adopted by the UN, this difference between the models is also likely to limit the number of non-OECD countries willing to use new Article 7. If there is only a partial acceptance of new Article 7, this reform will only add to the total compliance costs of international enterprises. The main advantage of the new provision is alternative Article 7(3), which is not the main provision, on resolving double taxation. The key aspect of this reform is the requirement that the treaty countries themselves are obliged to resolve the double taxation.

11

Unitary taxation

1 Introduction

Developments in communications and information technology have provided international enterprises with the capacity to operate internationally, through either subsidiaries or branches, as highly integrated businesses. Allocating the profits of these international enterprises to the jurisdictions in which they operate for tax purposes is a complex issue. The reason this task is so challenging is that the profits of an integrated international enterprise have no geographic source. The OECD Model and its Commentary use the arm's length principle to allocate profits between associated enterprises operating internationally or within international enterprises operating abroad through branches. Globalization has created an integrated international economy, and the implications of this development for the international tax rules are profound.

An alternative method of allocating profits from international transactions to jurisdictions is unitary formulary apportionment, which treats an international enterprise operating through branches or a group of companies as a unitary business. Unitary formulary apportionment avoids the problems of assuming the economic independence of each part of an international enterprise and the problems of transfer pricing which are inherent in the current tax treaty system. While unitary formulary apportionment overcomes some of the problems associated with the arm's length principle, it also has a number of shortcomings. Moreover, unitary formulary apportionment has not been tested at an international level. The European Union (EU) has recognized the flaws in the bilateral tax treaty system and in transfer pricing, and the European Commission is considering comprehensive reform measures, such as implementing a multilateral tax treaty using formulary apportionment. This is an exciting and promising prospect for international tax reform.

This chapter examines the case for implementing a multilateral tax treaty using unitary formulary apportionment to overcome the shortcomings of the present bilateral tax treaty system. Unitary formulary apportionment has important policy advantages over the arm's length principle because it reflects the economic reality that an international enterprise is a unitary business with a common profit motive. The European Commission's proposals constitute a significant development at the regional level for multilateral taxation of international enterprises using formulary apportionment. This chapter considers the European Commission's proposals and the effectiveness of unitary formulary apportionment. Since international enterprises operating abroad through branches are highly integrated international businesses, this chapter suggests that the European Commission's proposals provide an alternative method of attributing profits to branches of an international enterprise.

The chapter first outlines the problems of the current tax treaty system and the arm's length principle in allocating the profits of international enterprises. The chapter then considers the advantages of a multilateral tax treaty over the current tax treaty system. A multilateral tax treaty is an essential framework for implementing an allocation system based on unitary formulary apportionment. The chapter next makes the case for using unitary formulary apportionment to allocate business profits to permanent establishments under a multilateral tax treaty, focusing on the European Commission's proposals. The chapter concludes with a study of the issues that arise from implementing a unitary formulary apportionment system.

2 The need for international tax reform

The bilateral tax treaty system for allocating the profits of international enterprises is being challenged in a globalized international economy. The problems with the arm's length principle are increasing, making the need for reform a pressing matter. The United Nations has noted that:

> Transfer pricing is a worldwide problem. All countries have experienced difficulties in finding comparable transactions and comparable companies under the arm's length rule . . . Although the arm's length approach is supposed to result in realistic prices, it often falls short in reality.[1]

---

[1] United Nations Economic and Social Council, Report of the Secretary General, *Eleventh Meeting of the Ad Hoc Group of Experts on International Cooperation in Tax Matters* (2004), pp. 9–10.

As it is estimated that a significant amount of world trade takes places within multinational enterprises,[2] the search for comparables is difficult and costly, and finding comparable prices for intangible property is virtually impossible. Another problem is the complexity of the transfer pricing rules of some developed countries.[3]

International enterprises have the capacity to manipulate the current tax treaty system through sophisticated tax planning and, in many cases, they are the only source of information on their operations in a particular jurisdiction.[4] In a globalized economy international businesses are able to use high speed and high quality communication and information technologies to organize their international operations along business lines rather than geographic lines. This increasing international integration erodes the very premise of the arm's length principle for allocating the profits of an international business. The objective remains to establish treaty rules that allocate the profits of an international enterprise in an efficient and equitable manner.[5]

An alternative method for taxing international enterprises would be a multilateral tax treaty using unitary formulary apportionment.[6] As the shortcomings of the arm's length principle in a globalized economy are becoming more obvious, allocation methods using formulary apportionment are becoming more viable alternatives.[7] Commentators are increasingly advocating the need for new international tax rules.[8] Unitary formulary apportionment is a simple profit-allocation method, in which the profits of an international enterprise are treated as being

---

[2] Owens, 'Should the Arm's Length Principle Retire?' (2005), p. 99.
[3] Hellerstein, 'The Case for Formulary Apportionment' (2005), p. 108; Clausing and Avi-Yonah, *Reforming Corporate Taxation in a Global Economy* (2007), p. 10.
[4] Bird and Brean, 'The Interjurisdictional Allocation of Income and the Unitary Taxation Debate' (1986), p. 1388.
[5] *Ibid.*, p. 1382.
[6] The meaning of unitary formulary apportionment is discussed in section 4.
[7] Tanzi, *Taxation in an Integrating World* (1995), p. 139; Spengel and Wendt, 'A Common Consolidated Corporate Tax Base for Multinational Companies in the European Union' (2007), pp. 15–18.
[8] Qureshi, *Public International Law of Taxation* (1994), p. 8; Tanzi, *Taxation in an Integrating World* (1995), p. 139; McLure, 'Globalization, Tax Rules and National Sovereignty' (2001), pp. 340–1; Warren, 'Income Tax Discrimination Against International Commerce' (2001), pp. 168–9; Vann, 'A Model Tax Treaty for the Asian-Pacific Region? (Part I)' (1991), p. 105; Bird, 'The Interjurisdictional Allocation of Income' (1986), p. 354; Avi-Yonah, 'The Structure of International Taxation' (1996), p. 1304; Bravenec, 'Connecting the Dots in US International Taxation' (2002), p. 848; Clausing and Avi-Yonah, *Reforming Corporate Taxation in a Global Economy: A Proposal to Adopt Formulary Apportionment*; Weiner, 'Redirecting the Debate on Formulary Apportionment' (2007).

derived from its branches and associated enterprises. Formulary apportionment allocates the worldwide profits of an international enterprise to the jurisdictions in which it operates on the basis of a formula. By allocating an enterprise's global profits, formulary apportionment overcomes the transfer pricing problems of the current tax treaty system.[9] Richard Musgrave and Peggy Musgrave asserted long ago that international formulary apportionment is superior to the present rules:

> The permanent establishment approach is hardly satisfactory. Implementation of a bona fide separate accounting approach is exceedingly difficult and the dividing line between what does and what does not constitute a separate establishment is arbitrary . . . Ultimately, the only satisfactory solution . . . would be the taxation of such income on an international basis with subsequent allocation of proceeds on an apportionment basis among the participating countries, making allowance for distributional considerations. This is especially called for in view of the rapid growth of the multinational corporation.[10]

The compelling rationale for formulary apportionment is that it reflects economic reality. Bird and Brean illustrated the flaw in the current system of treating branches or subsidiaries as separate entities for allocation purposes under the arm's length principle:

> The underlying rationale of this approach is that the affiliated entities constitute a 'unitary' business, the profits of which arise from the operations of the business as a whole. It is therefore misleading to characterize the income of such a business as being derived from a set of geographically distinct sources . . . As already noted, the unitary approach has in its favour the fact that it recognizes income as the fungible product of a set of integrated income-producing factors under common control, regardless of location. The apportionment of the tax base, once it has been determined, is founded in some fashion on the geographical distribution of property and activities that are presumed to contribute to the integrated income-producing process.[11]

The development of international enterprises, such as international banks, operating around the world through branches demonstrates the strain on the existing treaty system resulting from globalization. The central feature of international enterprises is that they can achieve a

---

[9] Easson, 'A New International Tax Order' (1991), p. 466.
[10] R. A. Musgrave and P. B. Musgrave, 'Inter-Nation Equity' in Bird and Head (eds.), *Modern Fiscal Issues* (1972) 63–85, p. 85.
[11] Bird and Brean, 'The Interjurisdictional Allocation of Income and the Unitary Taxation Debate' (1986), p. 1392.

higher net return by operating abroad through branches or subsidiaries, rather than through independent enterprises.[12] International enterprises are able to internalize and reduce the costs of operating around the world; otherwise, it would be less expensive for them to use independent entities when operating in other countries. International enterprises outsource functions to independent enterprises if they cannot perform these functions more cheaply than independent enterprises. International enterprises internalize the functions in which they have a comparative advantage over independent enterprises. The allocation of profits within an international enterprise is arbitrary because it operates on a unitary basis. Its profits are the result of the operation of integrated income-producing factors under common control, irrespective of differing geographic locations.

The formulary apportionment methods of allocating the profits of international enterprises correspond more closely with economic reality than an allocation method based on the arm's length principle. A multilateral tax treaty using formulary apportionment for allocating profits to permanent establishments would be a transparent and effective method for allocating the profits of an integrated international enterprise. As there is no single economic formula for allocating the profits of an integrated international enterprise,[13] a formula would have to be developed through negotiations between countries. Economic modelling could provide the results of using a particular formula in an industry such as international banking. But the relative weight placed on each factor in a formula alters the allocation of profits, and the formula would have to be settled by negotiation between the participating countries.

3 Multilateral tax treaty

A key element of a move to unitary formulary apportionment is a multilateral tax treaty in which the participating countries agree to divide the profits of an international enterprise on the basis of an agreed formula. A multilateral tax treaty would complement the multilateral trade agreements that have progressively been concluded throughout the world, but the critical issue is obtaining the commitment of countries to

---

[12] See Bird, *The Taxation of International Income Flows* (1987), pp. 38–9.
[13] Bird and Brean, 'The Interjurisdictional Allocation of Income and the Unitary Taxation Debate' (1986), pp. 333–4; Bird, *The Taxation of International Income Flows* (1987), p. 38.

join a multilateral tax treaty. Such a treaty would have significant advantages over the existing bilateral tax treaty system.[14] In the 1920s, the League of Nations recognized the advantages of a multilateral tax treaty, but did not recommend such a treaty because it was unlikely to be accepted by the member countries at that time. Nevertheless, the League of Nations' preferred approach was for a multilateral tax treaty to be developed. The Organisation for European Economic Co-operation (which became the OECD in 1961) and the OECD both preferred a multilateral tax treaty as a long-term solution. In 1980, the UN noted the benefits of a multilateral tax treaty:

> The creation of a network of bilateral tax treaties based on a common model will be an important step on the way leading to the eventual conclusion of a world-wide multilateral tax convention for the avoidance of double taxation. In the meantime, as an intermediate step, groups of countries might consider the possibility of negotiating regional or subregional multilateral tax conventions based on the United Nations Model Convention but adjusted to their requirements and the characteristics of their region or subregion.
>
> The conclusion of regional or subregional conventions for the avoidance of double taxation would not only increase the number of countries which are parties to a double taxation convention but would also promote the co-ordination of tax policies and practices at the international level. The conclusion of such conventions would accelerate the harmonization of tax rules and practices concerning basic definitions, procedures for identifying the source of taxable items, methods for the elimination of double taxation and so on.[15]

This statement was modified in the 2001 UN Model Convention to maintain the emphasis on regional treaties, but without an express reference to a multilateral tax treaty:

> It is hoped that the United Nations Model Convention will contribute to the conclusion of an increasing number of bilateral tax treaties, not only between developed and developing countries but also between developing countries. It is also hoped that the Model Convention will contribute to the standardization of the provisions of such treaties. The creation of a network of bilateral tax treaties based on a common model will be an

---

[14] Thuronyi, 'International Tax Cooperation and a Multilateral Treaty' (2001), p. 1644; Loukota, 'Multilateral Tax Treaty Versus Bilateral Treaty Network' in *Multilateral Tax Treaties* (1998) 83–103, pp. 88–94.
[15] United Nations, *United Nations Model Double Taxation Convention between Developed and Developing Countries* (1980), p. 12.

important step on the way leading to the eventual conclusion of regional or subregional conventions for the avoidance of double taxation.[16]

This modification may be interpreted as a change in emphasis, with the development of regional tax treaties being viewed pragmatically as a precondition to a worldwide multilateral tax treaty. The UN has noted that the bilateral tax treaty system needs to progress from a network of tax treaties to regional multilateral tax treaties.

In 2001, the European Commission noted the flaws in the bilateral tax treaty system within the EU and claimed that major reforms were required to overcome them.[17] Article 293 of the European Community (EC) Treaty requires the Member States to enter into negotiations with each other in order to prevent double taxation. The aim of Article 293 is to ensure that cross-border activities within the EU are not disadvantaged as compared with domestic intra-state activities. Moreover, the European Commission stated that tax discrimination or double taxation arising from activities within the EU cannot be tolerated, and it concluded that the existing tax treaty network in the EU goes some way towards removing distortions, but does not meet the requirements of the internal market.[18] The European Commission noted:

> Finally, bilateral tax treaties based on the OECD Model Double Taxation Convention often do not resolve many of the instances of double taxation which have been described in other sections of this Part of the study. They do not normally provide a solution to the problem of cross-border loss compensation or a definitive solution to the costs and risks of double taxation due to transfer pricing disputes . . . The analysis has shown that there are a significant number of issues of double taxation which are not currently being properly addressed by the bilateral tax treaties in place between Member States or by domestic tax provisions. This is because they do not cover all bilateral relations between Member States, they do not achieve complete abolition of either discrimination or double taxation and, in particular, they never provide any uniform solution for triangular and multilateral relations between Member States. The number and extent of the complexities and difficulties in this area will increase when the European Union expands.[19]

---

[16] United Nations, *United Nations Model Tax Convention Between Developed and Developing Countries* (2001), p. xxiv.
[17] Commission of the European Communities, *Company Taxation in the Internal Market* (2001), p. 284.
[18] *Ibid.*   [19] *Ibid.*, p. 289.

3.1 Advantages of a multilateral tax treaty

The main advantage of a multilateral tax treaty is that it can be holistically reformed in response to international developments and problems as they arise. In particular, a multilateral tax treaty could be readily amended to reflect developments in international trade and to counter tax avoidance arrangements used by international enterprises. Amendments would need to be made only to the multilateral tax treaty, and they could apply to the treaty partner countries prospectively. It is generally accepted that it is difficult to amend the OECD Model and that the OECD therefore seeks to implement some changes by amending the Commentary. The prospect of truly reforming the extensive bilateral tax treaty network within a short period of time is remote because each treaty would have to be renegotiated and the changes implemented. Reforms might be implemented quickly in some countries through changes to the Commentary if the countries use it on an ambulatory basis. In addition, the courts in some countries use the Commentary on an ambulatory basis to interpret the provisions of the country's tax treaties.

A multilateral tax treaty would be easier to interpret because it would be a single instrument bringing uniformity to the participating countries.[20] Interpreting tax treaties under the current bilateral treaty system is complex because each treaty is negotiated independently and is a separate legal instrument. A flaw in the current tax treaty system is that there is significant uncertainty about the meaning of certain treaty provisions and it is difficult for taxpayers to know if they will be uniformly interpreted in the countries in which the taxpayers operate. As a result, taxpayers and tax authorities spend considerable resources on interpreting treaty provisions. If the main provisions of tax treaties are included in a multilateral tax treaty, interpretation would be likely to be more certain because the treaty partner countries would need to develop consensus interpretations of the treaty. The treaty partner countries would be responsible for amending the multilateral tax treaty and preparing a commentary on interpreting it. The commentary would be binding, and this would provide considerable certainty to the tax authorities, taxpayers and tax advisers. If an ambiguity arose as to the meaning of a provision, amendments to the multilateral tax treaty or commentary could be made to remedy the ambiguity.

---

[20] Thuronyi, 'International Tax Cooperation and a Multilateral Treaty' (2001), pp. 1656–9.

Under a multilateral tax treaty, the allocation of profits to the countries in which an international enterprise operates is considered at a holistic level. The current bilateral treaty system operates effectively to allocate all of an international enterprise's profits if the enterprise operated only in the two treaty partner countries. But in a globalized economy, international enterprises operate in several countries. Under the current bilateral treaty network, international enterprises must cope with many tax treaties, which increases the risks of double taxation for the enterprises and the risks of under-taxation for the tax authorities. For example, under the current system, a triangular tax case may result in double taxation even if there are bilateral tax treaties between the countries involved. A multilateral tax treaty minimizes the potential for tax distortions within the treaty partner countries, and an ideal multilateral tax treaty would allocate all of an international enterprise's income equitably and efficiently to the treaty partner countries in which it operates.

3.2 The process for concluding a multilateral tax treaty

A multilateral tax treaty cannot be concluded without widespread acceptance by countries of the multilateral approach, and the negotiating process would take considerable time and effort. Countries will have to be persuaded that the benefits to them of a multilateral tax treaty would exceed those of the existing treaty system. The best potential areas for the conclusion of a multilateral tax treaty are within existing nation groupings such as the OECD, EU, NAFTA[21] and the Asia-Pacific region.[22] At the moment, the best qualified body to oversee the negotiation and conclusion of a worldwide multilateral tax treaty is the OECD because it represents both OECD countries and an extensive group of non-OECD countries.[23] The OECD Model has set the stage for a multilateral tax treaty because the OECD countries and non-OECD countries negotiate treaties which conform to the OECD Model. As the main political problem for countries becoming party to a multilateral tax treaty is the perceived loss of sovereignty, a measured approach would extract certain parts of bilateral tax treaties and include them in a multilateral tax treaty.[24] Such a process is used in international legal

---

[21] McDaniel, 'Colloquium on NAFTA and Tradition: Formulary Taxation in the North American Free Trade Zone' (1994).
[22] Vann, 'A Model Tax Treaty for the Asian-Pacific Region (Part II)' (1991).
[23] Avery Jones, 'The David R. Tillinghast Lecture' (1999), p. 11.
[24] Williams, *Trends in International Taxation* (1991), p. 176, para. 739.

diplomacy. The non-controversial provisions could be made part of the multilateral tax treaty as a starting point for the subsequent negotiation of a more comprehensive treaty. Importantly, the countries that are party to the multilateral tax treaty will nevertheless retain some tax autonomy as each country will choose the tax rate applicable to the profits allocated to them under the treaty.

A two-step process for implementing a worldwide multilateral tax treaty has been suggested.[25] In the first step, countries should agree to negotiate treaties on the basis of a multilateral model tax treaty and to amend their existing tax treaties over a period of time to conform to the model. Amendments to the model and commentary would apply to the countries participating in the process on an ambulatory basis. A multilateral model tax treaty would operate in much the same way as the OECD Model, but with more certainty in interpretation because the amendments to the model and commentary would apply on an ambulatory basis to all the tax treaties with common provisions.[26] The aim of this process would be to establish a treaty network conforming to the multilateral model tax treaty which would pave the way for a worldwide multilateral tax treaty.

In the second step, the multilateral tax treaty would replace the existing bilateral tax treaties.[27] The process for implementing a multinational tax treaty should reflect the process for developing the General Agreement on Tariffs and Trade (GATT). The provisions of the multilateral tax treaty would be negotiated by the participating countries, and its provisions would not differ significantly from those of a bilateral tax treaty. Both types of treaty need to define a range of terms and allocate taxing rights among the participating countries. An essential goal for each type of treaty is the elimination of double taxation. Consequently, most of the provisions of a bilateral tax treaty would be incorporated into the multilateral tax treaty, but the latter would also have to include additional provisions. Special provisions are required for dispute resolution because the precedents set by a dispute with one country will affect the application of the treaty to the other participating countries.

In summary, the ideal international tax treaty system in a globalized economy would be a worldwide multilateral tax treaty. Such a treaty would complement multilateral trade agreements and enhance international trade. Under a multilateral tax treaty, international enterprises

---

[25] Thuronyi, 'International Tax Cooperation and a Multilateral Treaty' (2001), pp. 1670–1.
[26] *Ibid.*, p. 1645.   [27] *Ibid.*, pp. 1670–1.

would be taxed on a consolidated basis, and their profits would be allocated among the participating countries on the basis of unitary formulary apportionment. Realistically, this proposal is idealistic, and support for this approach is unlikely to be readily achieved. Nevertheless, the conclusion of regional multilateral tax treaties is an important forerunner to a worldwide multilateral tax treaty in the future.

4 Unitary formulary apportionment

A multilateral tax treaty using formulary apportionment to allocate business profits to permanent establishments is the most effective allocation method in a globalized world economy.[28] There are two types of formulary apportionment. One refers to using a formula to attribute the profits of a company to different jurisdictions, which may be countries or states in a federation.[29] The other type involves treating a functionally integrated group of companies as one entity for apportionment purposes. The challenge of using unitary formulary apportionment for a group of companies is defining a unitary business.[30] Unitary taxation is used to determine which related companies are a taxable entity for tax purposes. Under unitary formulary apportionment, an international enterprise operating abroad through branches is treated as one entity for tax purposes. In this situation, the taxable entity is consistent with the legal form of an international enterprise. Currently, the arm's length principle creates a legal fiction that branches of an integrated international enterprise, such as an international bank, are separate enterprises dealing with each other at arm's length.

Formulary apportionment may be applied on either the water's edge or worldwide basis. Under the water's edge approach, a jurisdiction cannot look beyond the water's edge in determining the income of a company or corporate group. For a state in a federation, the water's edge consists of its national borders. Associated companies and offshore

---

[28] In 1981 the US General Accounting Office found that the arm's length principle had considerable shortcomings and recommended that the US Treasury study the alternative apportionment methods such as formulary apportionment: US General Accounting Office, *IRS Could Better Protect US Tax Interests in Determining the Income of Multinational Corporations* (1981), pp. viii and 27–8.

[29] See Weiner, *Using the Experience in the US States to Evaluate Issues in Implementing Formula Apportionment at the International Level* (1999), p. 8.

[30] See McLure, Jr, 'Defining a Unitary Business: An Economist's View' in McLure, Jr (ed.) *The State Corporate Income Tax, Issues in Worldwide Unitary Combination* (1984), 89–124.

branches operating exclusively outside the national borders are treated as unrelated separate entities. For this reason, the water's edge approach uses the arm's length principle for such associated companies and offshore branches.[31] The water's edge approach is used in the US for subnational corporate taxation. Under worldwide formulary apportionment, the income of a unitary business from all sources determines its unitary worldwide income. The portion of the unitary business's income that is attributable to a jurisdiction, such as a state in a federation, is determined by the ratios of in-state values of the apportionment factors to their worldwide values. The corporate income attributable to a jurisdiction is usually higher under worldwide formulary apportionment.[32]

Formulary apportionment is more consistent with economic theory because an integrated international enterprise, such as an international bank, operates as a unitary business. Formulary apportionment focuses on an international enterprise's net profits and seeks to allocate them on a fair and agreed basis. It avoids most of the problems caused by the arm's length principle in taxing integrated international enterprises.[33] The main advantages of formulary apportionment over the arm's length principle are that it does not require an examination of the numerous transactions of an international enterprise, it simplifies the profit allocation between countries and it provides greater certainty for taxpayers.[34] In 1983, the United States Supreme Court in *Container Corporation* v. *Franchise Tax Board* recognized the shortcomings of the arm's length principle when applied to integrated businesses:

> ... the profit figures relied on by the appellant are based on precisely the sort of formal geographical accounting whose basic theoretical weaknesses justify resort to formula apportionment in the first place. Indeed, we considered and rejected a very similar argument in *Mobil*, pointing out that whenever a unitary business exists, 'separate [geographical] accounting, while it purports to isolate portions of income received in various States, may fail to account for contributions to income resulting from functional integration, centralization of management, and economies of scale. Because these factors of profitability arise from the operation of the business as a whole, it becomes misleading to characterize the income of the business as having a single identifiable "source".'

---

[31] Carlson and Galper, 'Water's Edge Versus Worldwide Unitary Combination', in C. E. McLure, Jr (ed.) *The State Corporate Income Tax, Issues in Worldwide Unitary Combination* (1984), p. 2.
[32] *Ibid.*
[33] Mintz and Weiner, 'Exploring Formula Allocation for the European Union' (2001), p. 5.
[34] US General Accounting Office, *International Taxation* (1992), p. 69.

Although separate geographical accounting may be useful for internal auditing, for purposes of state taxation it is not constitutionally required. 445 US, at 438 (citation omitted)[35]

Formulary apportionment also reduces the compliance costs for international enterprises and the administrative costs for tax authorities[36] as it precludes the costly reviews of notional and real transactions to determine if they were at arm's length prices.[37]

The allocation of profits under formulary apportionment usually differs from the result under the arm's length principle.[38] Under formulary apportionment, if an international enterprise has a net profit, the profit is distributed, on the agreed basis, between the branches and head office. No part of the enterprise suffers a loss because formulary apportionment treats profitability as being uniform within an enterprise.[39] If an international enterprise has a net loss for an income year, all parts of the enterprise are treated as operating at a loss. The loss is allocated to the branches in the participating countries on the basis of the formula. On the other hand, under the arm's length principle a branch performing a distribution function would be treated as deriving income even if the entire enterprise has suffered a net loss for the income period.

Under formulary apportionment, each jurisdiction taxes the profit that is allocated to it under a formula at the appropriate tax rate. Formulary apportionment does not require an allowance to be made for foreign tax credits because formulary apportionment is territorial.[40] Moreover, it does not require each jurisdiction to have complicated rules, including transfer pricing rules, for determining the taxable income of a permanent establishment of an international enterprise. Formulary apportionment has the potential to achieve tax neutrality; tax planning issues will not be significant because international enterprises will be taxed on a unitary basis.[41]

---

[35] *Container Corporation of America* v. *Franchise Tax Board* 463 U.S. 159 p. 181; 103 S. Ct. 2933 p. 2948, 77 L. Ed. 2d 545 p. 563; 1983 U.S. LEXIS 89. Justice Brennan delivered the opinion of the court.
[36] Bravenec, 'Connecting the Dots in US International Taxation' (2002), p. 849; Mintz, 'Globalization of the Corporate Income Tax' (1999), p. 418.
[37] US General Accounting Office, *International Taxation* (1992), pp. 7 and 69.
[38] Surrey, 'Reflections on the Allocation of Income and Expenses Among National Tax Jurisdictions' (1978), p. 415.
[39] Cnossen, *Tax Policy in the European Union: A Review of Issues and Options* (2002), pp. 72–3.
[40] Bravenec, 'Connecting the Dots in US International Taxation' (2002), p. 849.
[41] *Ibid.*, p. 850.

The literature contains extensive debate on the relative merits of the arm's length principle and formulary apportionment. Some commentators have argued that, while the arm's length principle has serious defects, formulary apportionment would not be an improvement over the current system.[42] Others have argued that the arm's length principle is conceptually superior to formulary apportionment if it can be applied, but the practical application of the arm's length principle is usually problematic.[43] The Transfer Pricing Guidelines, after considering the nature of formulary apportionment and comparing it with the arm's length principle, expressly reject the use of formulary apportionment.[44] Rosenbloom has claimed that formulary apportionment 'must have something compelling in its favor', given the lengths to which the OECD goes in criticizing it.[45] Other commentators contend that formulary apportionment is superior to the arm's length principle in both theory and practice.[46] It has further been contended that formulary apportionment reflects each jurisdiction's economic interest in the profits of an international enterprise and that it is consistent with the analysis by the Committee of Experts of the League of Nations (1921–23).[47]

4.1 Formulary apportionment in the US and Canada

Formulary apportionment is not currently used as a method to allocate the profits of international enterprises among countries, but it is not an untested apportionment method. It is used at the subnational level in the US and Canada. These subnational systems provide models for implementing formulary apportionment at the regional and international

---

[42] Coffill and Willson, 'Federal Formulary Apportionment as an Alternative to Arm's Length Pricing' (1993), pp. 1116–17.
[43] McLure and Weiner, 'Deciding Whether the European Union Should Adopt Formula Apportionment of Company Income' in Cnossen (ed.), *Taxing Capital Income in the European Union* (2000) 243–92, p. 258.
[44] 2009 Transfer Pricing Guidelines, pp. 84–8, paras. 3.58–3.74; 2010 Transfer Pricing Guidelines, pp. 37–41, paras. 1.16–1.32.
[45] Rosenbloom, 'Angels on a Pin: Arm's Length in the World' (2005), p. 524.
[46] R. S. McIntyre and M. J. McIntyre, 'Opinion: Using NAFTA to Introduce Formulary Apportionment' (1993), p. 855; Oldman and Brooks, 'The Unitary Method and the Less Developed Countries: Preliminary Thoughts' (1987), p. 46; M. J. McIntyre, 'The Use of Combined Reporting by Nation-States', in Arnold, Sasseville and Zolt (eds.), *The Taxation of Business Profits under Tax Treaties* (2003) 245–98, p. 246; M. J. McIntyre, 'The Use of Combined Reporting by Nation States' (2004), p. 918; Clausing and Avi-Yonah, *Reforming Corporate Taxation in a Global Economy*, p. 27.
[47] Kaufman, 'Fairness and the Taxation of International Income' (1998), pp. 200–1.

levels. It has been observed that the tax authorities in most OECD countries use formulary apportionment methods in practice, but maintain support for the arm's length principle.[48]

In the US, 45 states and the District of Columbia impose their corporate income tax using formulary apportionment to allocate a corporation's income between the participating states. The apportionment is made using a formula applying objective factors, such as a company's payroll, assets and sales in each state. The aim is to allocate corporate income on the basis of its share of economic activity in each jurisdiction.[49] The states administer their own corporate income tax, but a company's income for state taxation is derived from its income for purposes of the federal corporate tax. Some states use unitary taxation, in which the activities of a group of associated companies are treated as belonging to a unitary business. The determination of whether a corporate group is a unitary business turns on the degree of integration between the companies. A corporate group that is treated as a unitary business under state law lodges a consolidated tax return for the group, and a formula is used to apportion the group's total income to the states involved.[50]

The US system has been criticized as having both theoretical and practical flaws,[51] but others have regarded it as a model that can be adapted at the international level.[52] The main problem with the US system is that a common formula is not used to allocate corporate income between the states. The formulas first used by the states were not uniform. To achieve uniformity, the National Tax Association recommended in 1933 that the states use the 'Massachusetts formula' which placed equal weight on payroll, property and sales.[53] The Massachusetts formula was not regarded as being conceptually superior but

---

[48] Avi-Yonah, 'The Rise and Fall of Arm's Length' (1995), p. 157.
[49] US General Accounting Office, *International Taxation* (1992), p. 68.
[50] C. E. McLure, 'US Federal Use of Formula Apportionment to Tax Income from Intangibles' (1997), p. 862.
[51] Agundez-Garcia, European Commission Taxation Papers, *The Delineation of Apportionment of an EU Consolidated Tax Base for Multi-Jurisdictional Corporate Income Taxation* (2006), p. 44.
[52] M. J. McIntyre, 'The Use of Combined Reporting by Nation States' (2004); Oldman and Brooks, 'The Unitary Method and the Less Developed Countries: Preliminary Thoughts' (1987).
[53] National Tax Association, 'Report of Committee on the Apportionment Between States of Taxes on Mercantile and Manufacturing Business', *Proceedings of the National Tax Association* (1922), 198–212 cited in Hellerstein and C. E. McLure, 'The European Commission's Report on Company Income Taxation' (2004), p. 208.

was justified on the basis that 'uniformity is preferable to scientific accuracy'.[54] Prior to 1957, the definitions of formulary apportionment were not consistent. A major development was the drafting in 1957 of the Uniform Division of Income for Tax Purposes Act (UDITPA) containing a common formula and definitions of the factors used by the state legislatures.[55] Despite this draft, the state corporate income tax laws were not harmonized. In 1967, the states established the Multistate Compact and the Multistate Commission to assist in the development of consistent state corporate income tax laws.[56] The Compact contains the apportionment rules in the UDITPA.

By 1978, most states had moved to the Massachusetts formula. Since the 1980s, the states have increased the weight on the gross receipts factor and decreased the weight on the payroll and property factors.[57] In 2004, 23 states used a formula that placed a weight of 50 per cent on gross receipts and a weight of 25 per cent each on payroll and property. The change in weighting was designed to improve the position of the destination state by shifting from the apportionment factors that are origin factors (payroll and property) to sales, a destination factor.[58] The US states also use industry-specific formulas for sectors such as financial institutions.

Canada also provides an important model for formulary apportionment because a single formula is used, that is simple and uniform. The Canadian provinces impose a company income tax which is administered at the federal level for most of the provinces. Canada's company tax system is uniform because the provincial definition of 'company income' is based on the federal definition of that term. A uniform system was established during World War II when the provinces suspended their company and personal income taxes, allowing the federal government to take over income taxation in exchange for federal transfers, called tax rentals.[59] After the war, the tax rental system continued until 1962.

---

[54] Ibid.
[55] Weiner, *Using the Experience in the US States to Evaluate Issues in Implementing Formula Apportionment at the International Level* (1999), p. 10.
[56] Ibid., p. 11.
[57] Weiner, *Formulary Apportionment and Group Taxation in the European Union* (2005), p. 12. See pp. 13–14 for a table with US state formulas for apportioning corporate income at 1 January 2004.
[58] Hellerstein and McLure, 'The European Commission's Report on Company Income Taxation' (2004), p. 208.
[59] Commission of the European Communities, *Report of the Committee of Independent Experts on Company Taxation* (1992), p. 394.

4 UNITARY FORMULARY APPORTIONMENT

In 1962, the federal and provincial governments negotiated a system of abatement and a series of Federal Collection Agreements. The abatement was an agreement by the federal government to reduce the federal company tax to allow the provinces to again impose company taxes. Under the Federal Collection Agreements, the federal government agreed to collect the provincial company taxes on the condition that a province's company tax law met certain requirements in the definition of the tax base and the allocation rules. Canada has one of the most decentralized company tax systems in the world that is also a uniform system.

Under the Federal Collection Agreements, the provinces agreed to use a two-factor formula that gives equal weight to payroll and sales in apportioning a company's income between the provinces.[60] Under the formula, each participating province taxes a portion of the national income of a company equal to the average of the sales and payroll arising in the province as a percentage of the totals for the whole country. The provinces of Ontario, Alberta and Quebec[61] are not currently part of the Federal Collection Agreements, but they use the same allocation formula as the provinces that are in the Federal Collection Agreements.[62] The Federal Collection Agreements contain a common formula for apportionment and the common tax base which results in eliminating the double taxation or under-taxation of company income, and removes the incentive for tax arbitrage in the participating provinces. Canada also uses specific formulas for certain industries. The factors for allocating the income of banks in Canada are salaries, loans and deposits, with the deposit and loan factors being given double weight.[63] Canada's system does not use unitary taxation; the company tax is imposed on each company. Canada's system is also supplemented by equalization payments to the provinces that participate in the Federal Collection Agreements.[64] This measure discourages tax competition between the provinces. If a province's company tax base increases as a result of a decrease in the company tax rate, the province's payments under the equalization system will be reduced.

---

[60] Section 402(3) of the Income Tax Regulations (Canada).
[61] Quebec has always remained outside the Federal Collection Agreements.
[62] Weiner, *Formulary Apportionment and Group Taxation in the European Union* (2005), p. 15.
[63] Section 404 of the Income Tax Regulations (Canada).
[64] Mintz and Weiner, 'Exploring Formula Allocation for the European Union' (2001), p. 8.

4.2 The European Commission proposals

There have been numerous proposals for developing formulary apportionment at the international level. Suggestions have been made to use formulary apportionment in regional trading blocs. The European Commission's sweeping reform proposal for a common consolidated corporate tax base provides the best potential for implementing a regional multilateral tax treaty using formulary apportionment. As a result of the economic integration of the EU, the European Commission has made considerable progress in replacing the arm's length principle for allocating the profits of subsidiaries and branches with formulary apportionment of the common consolidated corporate tax base. Under this proposal, the EU Member States will apply their own tax rates to their share of the tax base and thereby maintain their tax sovereignty. The proposal that European companies use one set of corporate tax rules for their EU operations is supported by industry.[65]

4.2.1 Background

The EU has an internal market, and it has established economic and monetary union for most of the Member States. This economic integration has placed strains on the arm's length principle for allocating business profits in the EU. This consequence was not unexpected as some pressure was predicted by a 1992 study of the company tax system in the EU, *Report of the Committee of Independent Experts on Company Taxation* – the Ruding Committee:

> While transfer-pricing is a necessary business practice in integrated groups of firms, it can sometimes be very difficult to ascertain the correct range of 'arm's-length' prices, because there may be no comparable market prices for the transactions in question. Hence, in some cases, the determination of such prices may be extremely subjective and, therefore, controversial. A similar problem arises with respect to the correct allocation of common overhead costs among the related parts of a multinational firm. Consequently, the use of separate accounting methods for determining taxable profits may present firms with the opportunity to shift profits from high- to relatively low-tax countries by adjusting transfer prices, and by allocating overhead costs and interest payments to subsidiaries or branches in relatively high-tax countries, thus reducing the firm's overall tax burden. The problem of profits being shifted to comparatively low-tax jurisdictions through what is sometimes euphemistically referred to as 'creative' accounting practices will be

---

[65] *Ibid.*, p. 1.

4 UNITARY FORMULARY APPORTIONMENT   411

compounded by the increased cross-border integration of business activities within the Community. In the longer term, this trend will tend to make it increasingly difficult to determine taxable profits separately for each part of a multinational enterprise in every Member State on the basis of separate accounting methods.[66]

In 2000, the Lisbon European Council announced the following mandate:

> The Union has today set itself a new strategic goal for the next decade, to become the most competitive and dynamic knowledge-based economy in the world, capable of sustainable economic growth with more and better jobs and greater social cohesion.[67]

Under this mandate EU company taxation should contribute to greater economic growth in the EU. The Lisbon Strategy was simplified and relaunched in 2005. The elimination of high compliance costs for intra-EU transactions and transfer pricing problems can contribute to this goal of company taxation.[68] In 2001, the European Commission issued for public discussion its measures for comprehensive reform of company taxation.[69] The reasons for the European Commission's reform measures include: the complexity for EU enterprises in dealing with the different company tax systems in the EU; the allocation of profits and losses within international enterprises or corporate groups on the basis of transfer pricing; the unsatisfactory treatment of cross-border losses; and the tax consequences of group restructuring.[70] The European Commission made the following case for consolidated EU company taxation in a 2001 supplementary report titled *Towards an Internal Market without Tax Obstacles*:

> Only providing multinational companies with a consolidated corporate tax base for their EU-wide activities will really, through a single framework of company taxation, systematically tackle the majority of tax

---

[66] Commission of the European Communities, *Report of the Committee of Independent Experts on Company Taxation* (1992), p. 40.
[67] Presidency Conclusions, Lisbon European Council, 23–24 March 2000 (DOC/00/8 of 24/03/2000).
[68] Commission of the European Communities, Communication from the Commission to the Council, the European Parliament and the European Economic and Social Committee, *Implementing the Community Lisbon Programme: Progress to date and next steps towards a Common Consolidated Corporate Tax Base*, Brussels, 5.4.2006, COM(2006) 157 final, p. 3.
[69] Commission of the European Communities, *Company Taxation in the Internal Market* (2001).
[70] Ibid., p. 371.

obstacles to cross-border economic activity in the Single Market. Companies with cross-border and international activities within the EU should in the future be allowed to

- compute the income of the entire group according to one set of rules and
- establish consolidated accounts for tax purposes (thus eliminating the potential tax effects of purely internal transactions within the group.) . . .

A consolidated corporate tax base for the EU-wide activities of companies would contribute to greater efficiency, effectiveness, and simplicity and transparency in company tax systems and remove the hiatuses between national systems which provide fertile ground for avoidance and abuse. It would reduce compliance costs, allow the EU to reap the full benefits of the Internal Market, thus increase the competitiveness of EU business . . .

The Commission therefore believes it is only logical to steer its company taxation policy towards achieving a comprehensive solution to the existing cross-border tax obstacles in the Internal Market. Future work should be directed towards how to achieve the objective of a consolidated corporate tax base with cross-border relief, and how to design and agree on the necessary allocation mechanism.[71]

The report contains two main reform proposals: one for a 'common consolidated corporate tax base' (CCCTB), and another for 'home state taxation' (HST). Both proposals determine company income on an EU-wide basis and allocate the income to the Member States on the basis of a formula. In April 2002 at the EU Company Tax Conference, the European Commission, following public consultation on these two proposals, committed to a CCCTB for the EU business profits of EU companies.[72] The European Commission proposal to use HST as a five-year pilot scheme for small and medium enterprises was unsuccessful.[73]

4.2.2 Common consolidated corporate tax base

Under the CCCTB proposal, international enterprises would consolidate their accounts for their EU operations, and their taxable profits would be calculated under a common EU-wide tax law.[74] This proposal involves

---

[71] Commission of the European Communities, *Towards an Internal Market without Tax Obstacles* (2001), pp. 15–16.
[72] Weiner, 'EU Commission, Member States Commit to EU-Wide Company Taxation, Formulary Apportionment' (2002), p. 515.
[73] European Commission, 'Commission Proposes "Home State Taxation" for SMEs' (2006).
[74] See Commission of the European Communities, *Company Taxation in the Internal Market* (2001), pp. 375–6.

all the Member States agreeing on a common set of rules for determining the tax base of certain enterprises operating within the EU. Corporate enterprises resident in a Member State would be able to opt to use a common EU tax base for all their operations in the EU carried out through either permanent establishments or subsidiaries. The new EU company tax rules would be administered by the Member State in which a company has its headquarters for all its EU-wide operations. In the case of a group of companies, the group would have to calculate only one tax base and would deal only with the tax administration of the Member State in which the group has its headquarters. Under this proposal, the location of the headquarters of a company or group of companies is not regarded as significant as it affects only the Member State in which the EU company tax rules are administered. Under the CCCTB, the tax rules applicable to a company or group of companies are the same, irrespective of where its headquarters is located.

Under the CCCTB, the taxable profits of an EU company would be allocated to the Member States in which the company operates using the EU formula which is considered below at section 4.2.6. The taxable profits would then be taxed in the Member States to which they are allocated at that Member State's tax rate. International enterprises which opt not to be part of the CCCTB would continue to be taxed under the tax laws of the various Member States. For enterprises using the CCCTB, their profits would be taxed under a single set of tax rules. The major advantage of the CCCTB is that the Member States opting to participate in it could do so without amending their domestic company tax laws. The European Commission expects that over time the domestic company tax laws of the Member States will evolve towards a common code to simplify the domestic administration of the company tax laws. The CCCTB would have to be implemented through an EU multilateral tax treaty. The CCCTB would provide significant simplification and compliance benefits to the EU companies operating in several Member States, compared to the current EU tax treaty system: 'Most importantly because it is a single common base rather than a series of separate bases difficulties stemming from transfer pricing within the EU would be eliminated and enterprises would automatically benefit from consolidation.'[75]

---

[75] *Ibid.*, p. 376.

4.2.3 Home state taxation

An alternative tax reform for the EU is home state taxation (HST).[76] Under HST, the Member States accept that certain EU enterprises operating within the EU will calculate their income under the domestic law of a single Member State, the enterprise's home state.[77] Companies operating within the EU with their headquarters in a Member State would have the option of using the domestic company tax law of their base Member State for all their activities in the EU. The aggregate taxable income, as determined by the home state jurisdiction, would be apportioned using a formula among the Member States in which a group of companies operates. Each Member State would then apply its own tax rate to the taxable income allocated to it.

Under the HST proposal, the profits of a group of companies or a company operating through branches would be determined under the tax laws of the home state.[78] The proposal would be implemented by voluntary bilateral or multilateral cooperation between the Member States.[79] The participating Member States would share the tax base through a formula, with tax being paid at the tax rate of each Member State.[80] The suggested formula was based on value added.[81] As an alternative, the participating Member States would share the tax; i.e. the home state's tax rate would be applied to the enterprise's profits, and the tax revenue would be allocated among the Member States.[82]

HST would be a significant improvement over the current company tax system in the EU. HST would ensure that enterprises have to comply only with the company tax laws of their home state and have to deal only with one tax administration. One contentious issue with HST is how to define an enterprise's home state. In the majority of cases, the home state of a corporate entity would be indisputable, but in some cases, it may be more difficult to determine the home state.

4.2.4 Comparison of the common consolidated corporate tax base and home state taxation

Although the CCCTB and HST proposals raise similar problems that will need to be resolved before they are implemented, there are

---

[76] Lodin and Gammie, *Home State Taxation* (2001).
[77] Commission of the European Communities, *Company Taxation in the Internal Market*, Report No. SEC(2001)1681 (2001), pp. 373–5.
[78] Lodin and Gammie, *Home State Taxation* (2001), pp. 10–11.   [79] *Ibid.*, p. 10.
[80] Mintz and Weiner, 'Exploring Formula Allocation for the European Union' (2001), p. 11.
[81] Lodin and Gammie, *Home State Taxation* (2001), pp. 18 and 47.   [82] *Ibid.*, pp. 50–1.

4 UNITARY FORMULARY APPORTIONMENT 415

significant differences between them. Under the CCCTB, a single set of company tax rules would apply throughout the EU, irrespective of the residence state of an international enterprise.[83] Further, all participating EU companies would be taxed under a common company tax law, regardless of where they operate within the EU. In comparison, under HST the tax base would depend on the residence state of an international enterprise.[84] The HST option has the advantage of immediate introduction because it does not seek to implement a common EU company tax code: 'It is essentially a pragmatic response to the question of how to introduce a common "EU" approach to the taxation of an EU enterprise, without creating a new "EU" tax code.'[85] The HST option is regarded as a compromise which also avoids the problem of the Member States perceiving that they have given up their tax sovereignty.[86]

At the same time, this feature is a disadvantage of HST in that each Member State would continue to operate its own company tax system, which is unlikely to lead to company tax harmonization in the EU. If the HST option is used, the EU would have up to 27 different tax bases subject to apportionment. On the other hand, if the CCCTB option is implemented, there would be a maximum of only two tax bases, the common base and the domestic base, which would provide significant savings in compliance costs for taxpayers.[87] The disadvantage of the CCCTB is that it will take much longer to implement because of the negotiations required. The European Commission regards the CCCTB as the preferable option because it can be drafted to address particular difficulties that arise.[88]

The key issue for implementing either the CCCTB or HST proposal was agreeing on an allocation formula. In 2011, the European Commission announced a CCCTB formula. There are also administrative issues that need to be resolved if the EU moves away from the arm's length principle for allocating the profits of international enterprise among the jurisdictions in which they operate. The business representatives consulted by the European Commission emphasized that the critical issue for them is the creation of a single company tax code for EU companies operating within the EU.[89] They noted that the method

---

[83] Mintz and Weiner, 'Exploring Formula Allocation for the European Union' (2001), p. 17.
[84] Commission of the European Communities, *Company Taxation in the Internal Market* (2001), p. 376.
[85] *Ibid.*, pp. 378–9.   [86] *Ibid.*, p. 379.
[87] Mintz and Weiner, 'Exploring Formula Allocation for the European Union' (2001), p. 17.
[88] Commission of the European Communities, *Company Taxation in the Internal Market* (2001), p. 379.
[89] *Ibid.*, p. 378.

of achieving this goal was less important, making both the CCCTB and HST options acceptable to the business sector.

The European Commission noted that both the CCCTB and HST options would overcome the current transfer pricing problems in the EU resulting from applying the arm's length principle to integrated enterprises. The European Commission observed:

> Transfer pricing issues arising from separate accounting should be eliminated or practically disappear for transactions between connected parties participating in any of the comprehensive approaches where tax consolidation is available since they assume the use of a formula for apportioning income between Member States. The current complexities of interpretation and application of the OECD Guidelines on Transfer Pricing as explained above would therefore cease to exist for activities within the EU. However for transactions with third countries they would remain . . . and therefore EU enterprises would continue to apply the Guidelines for any transactions with enterprises outside the EU. Given the increased level of co-operation between Member States required for implementation of any comprehensive approach it would be reasonable to assume that this would improve the establishment of common interpretations and application.[90]

4.2.5 European accounting standards

In 2002, the EU adopted a regulation requiring listed companies, including banks, to prepare their accounts on a consolidated basis using the International Accounting Standards (IAS) and International Financial Reporting Standards (IFRS).[91] The aim of this regulation is to eliminate the barriers to cross-border trading in securities by ensuring that company accounts throughout the EU are reliable, transparent and comparable. The regulation has the force of law and does not require adoption into domestic legislation. At the April 2002 EU Company Tax Conference, the European Commission considered the need for common accounting rules if the proposals for a common tax base are to be implemented.[92] The coincidence of the regulation requiring the use of the IAS in 2002 and the European Commission's conclusion that EU companies should have a consolidated tax base for their EU operations led to the study of an IAS/IFRS common tax base.[93] In 2005, the

---

[90] *Ibid.*, p. 388.
[91] The IAS and IFRS are accounting standards issued by the International Accounting Standards Board.
[92] European Commission, *Consultation Document* (2003), p. 8.   [93] *Ibid.*

European Commission concluded: 'Therefore, although the common tax base rules may make use of IAS/IFRS terminology and principles the common tax base will not be directly linked to the constantly changing accounting standards (IAS/IFRS).'[94]

As from 2005, about 7,000 listed companies in the EU have been required to prepare annual consolidated financial statements complying with the IFRS. In February 2003, the European Commission asserted:

> In this context it is worth recalling the three key elements essential to the concept of a consolidated tax base:
>
> - It is 'consolidated', which means that the traditional concept of separate accounting by subsidiary or by branch, or by different Member State is no longer necessarily relevant for tax purposes; and cross border mergers or asset transfers may no longer necessarily involve 'exit' or capital gain charges.
> - As some activities may have losses and some profits there will inevitably be an offset of profits and losses between activities in different Member States, i.e. cross border loss consolidation.
> - Since tax rates are determined by, and revenues accrue to, individual Member States a consolidated tax base will have to be divided between Member States according to an agreed mechanism.[95]

The 2002 EU Company Tax Conference supported the CCCTB.[96] The business sector maintained its support for the European Commission's comprehensive reforms, based on either the CCCTB or HST. The significance of the European Commission's proposals is that the Member States and the business community strongly support a move away from the current bilateral tax treaties which rely on the arm's length principle to allocate profits. The sustained economic integration of the EU has highlighted the flaws in the current bilateral treaty system and advanced the imperative for comprehensive reforms. Formulary apportionment with group taxation in the EU has been advocated as the best tax system to reflect the increasing economic integration.[97]

---

[94] European Commission, Common Consolidated Corporate Tax Base Working Group, *Progress to Date and Future Plans for the CCCTB*, 15 November 2005 (CCCTB\wb\020\doc\en), p. 4.
[95] European Commission, *Consultation Document* (2003), p. 5.
[96] Weiner, 'EU Commission, Member States Commit to EU-Wide Company Taxation, Formulary Apportionment' (2002), p. 520.
[97] Weiner, *Formulary Apportionment and Group Taxation in the European Union* (2005), p. 56.

4.2.6 Adoption of the common consolidated corporate tax base

The Member States approved the proposed CCCTB measures at their 2004 Ecofin Council meeting.[98] There, 20 Member States gave broad support for the Commission's proposal to establish a working group to develop a common EU tax base.[99] Although 5 Member States did not support this measure, unanimous support is not necessary for the Commission to develop reform proposals. Tax rate harmonization is not part of the CCCTB measures, and the European Parliament underscored that, under the CCCTB, the Member States would retain the right to set their own tax rates.[100] The European Commission established the Common Consolidated Corporate Tax Base Working Group in 2005 to study the principles that must be developed to implement the CCCTB. In December 2005, the European Parliament adopted a resolution on: 'The taxation of undertakings in the European Union: a common consolidated corporate tax base.'[101] The CCCTB measures will have to deal with the issues of foreign income derived by EU resident entities and income derived within the EU by non-EU entities. In 2005, the European Commission issued a working paper on the international tax issues that need to be covered by the CCCTB.[102] Some of the topics identified by the working paper are: liability to tax of tax resident companies (worldwide/territoriality); definition of tax resident company; double tax relief; taxation of non-resident companies; and coordination and possible extension of existing common practices.[103] The current transfer pricing and double tax issues will remain for cross-border transactions between EU entities subject to the CCCTB and their non-EU branches

---

[98] European Commission, *A Common Consolidated EU Corporate Tax Base*, Commission Non-Paper to informal Ecofin Council, 10 and 11 September 2004. In the paper the European Commission sought 'an indication of how many Member States are broadly supportive in principle of the Commission extending its work in the area of a corporate EU tax base', p. 6.

[99] Martens-Weiner, 'A New Way of Thinking About Company Tax Reform in the European Union', Institute of European Affairs, 7 February 2006, p. 1.

[100] European Parliament, *Report on Taxation of Undertakings in the European Union: A Common Consolidated Corporate Tax Base* (2005), para. 9.

[101] European Parliament resolution (2005/2120(INI)) 13 December 2005.

[102] European Commission, *Consultation Document* (2003).   [103] *Ibid.*, pp. 3–4.

or associated enterprises. The CCCTB measures are supported by the businesses operating within the EU.[104]

In February 2006, the European Economic and Social Committee issued an opinion on the 'creation of a common consolidated corporate tax base'.[105] The opinion and the European Parliament's resolution supported the work of the European Commission on a common consolidated corporate tax base. In conclusion, the European Commission has taken a significant step by considering sweeping EU tax reforms.

In 2011, the European Commission proposed using the CCCTB for calculating the tax base for EU companies as an optional measure which provides them with the ability to consolidate their EU profits and losses.[106] The European Commission estimated that the CCCTB will save EU companies €700 million in reduced compliance costs, and €1.3 billion through consolidation. Under the CCCTB, EU companies will file a single EU tax return and the tax base would be shared by the EU countries in which they operate. Member States will tax their share of the tax base at the country's company tax rate. The CCCTB formula is a three-factor formula consisting of assets, labour and sales, with each factor having equal weight:

- Assets: All fixed tangible assets, including buildings, airplanes and machinery will be covered. The costs incurred for R&D, marketing and advertising in the 6 years prior to a company entering the CCCTB will also be included as a proxy for intangible assets for 5 years.
- Labour: Two factors will be taken into account under the heading of labour: 50% payroll costs and 50% the number of employees.
- Sales: This will be calculated on the basis of where the goods are dispatched to/destined for. For services, this will be where the service is physically carried out.[107]

4.3 Issues in the application of formulary apportionment

A multilateral shift from the arm's length principle to formulary apportionment first requires countries to agree on several issues for which uniformity is mandatory:

---

[104] Martens-Weiner, 'A New Way of Thinking About Company Tax Reform in the European Union, Institute of European Affairs', Institute of European Affairs, 7 February 2006, p.1.
[105] Opinion of the European Economic and Social Committee on the Creation of a Common Consolidated Corporate Tax Base in the EU (Explanatory Opinion) ECO/165, 14 February 2006.
[106] EU Press Release, 'European Corporate Tax Base: Making Business Easier and Cheaper', 16 March 2011 (IP/11/319).
[107] EU Press Release, 'Questions and Answers on the CCCTB', 16 March 2011 (MEMO/11/171).

- one rule on jurisdiction to tax, such as the existence of a permanent establishment;
- the formula;
- the method of measuring the factors in the formula; and
- the definition of a unitary business.[108]

The participating countries must agree on a range of issues because uniform application of the method is a central precondition to unitary formulary apportionment. If there is no uniformity, the potential for double taxation or under-taxation arises.

4.3.1 Unitary taxation

It is necessary to determine to which taxpayers formulary apportionment should apply. In theory, it should apply only to integrated businesses that operate on a unitary basis because their profits cannot be allocated with economic precision to the individual parts of the business.[109] There are problems in defining a unitary business where operations are conducted through subsidiaries, but the problems do not arise with regard to international enterprises operating abroad through branches because the unitary business corresponds with the legal structure of international enterprises. Formulary apportionment may be applied to international enterprises operating through branches, such as international banks, because they are highly integrated businesses. Commentators have suggested that highly integrated international enterprises may prefer to be taxed on a unitary basis because such an enterprise is unable to identify the geographic source of its profits.[110] Consequently, taxing integrated enterprises on a unitary basis reflects the manner in which they operate; thus, if an international enterprise such as an international bank makes its profits on a unitary basis, from a policy perspective it should be taxed on a unitary basis.

4.3.2 The formula

The key element of formulary apportionment is determining the formula. In negotiating the formula for formulary apportionment, countries will seek to establish a formula that suits their own interests; consequently, agreeing on the formula will be a major hurdle that must be overcome

---

[108] C. E. McLure, 'US Federal Use of Formula Apportionment to Tax Income from Intangibles' (1997), at 860–1.

[109] T. A. Adams, 'Interstate and International Double Taxation' in Magill (ed.) *Lectures on Taxation* (1932) 101–28, p. 122.

[110] Weiner, *Using the Experience in the US States to Evaluate Issues in Implementing Formula Apportionment at the International Level* (1999), p. 42.

4 UNITARY FORMULARY APPORTIONMENT

before formulary apportionment can be implemented. It is vital that all the participating jurisdictions use a uniform formula, which involves making compromises. Implementing formulary apportionment at the international or regional level by the US[111] or the EU would encourage other jurisdictions to do the same. As a formula has been negotiated within the EU, there is a significant prospect that other countries will consider agreeing to new rules for allocating profits.

Economics cannot provide a single scientific or economic formula for allocating the profits of international enterprises between jurisdictions because of the integrated operations of most international enterprises. Economics can identify particular factors that generate income within an international enterprise, but economists do not advocate a single formula.[112] It is impossible within an integrated international enterprise to determine with economic precision which factors generate profits and the relative weight to be given to each factor. Any formula will be arbitrary to some extent, and the relative political forces will shape a common formula. One difficulty with formulary apportionment is that using a formula in which all the factors of production are assigned the same rate of return in all the participating countries may distort the allocation of income between them.[113] In addition, if the same formula is used for all industries, distortions may arise, which in turn may create tension between the participating jurisdictions if they take the view that the formula does not reflect the economic activity in them.[114] In settling on a formula, there is the usual trade-off between simplicity and accuracy; the use of a sophisticated formula to achieve greater accuracy will lead to complexity[115] and to increased compliance costs for taxpayers and administrative costs for the tax authorities.

The better approach is to use a simple formula such as the EU formula for the CCCTB, rather than a complex formula on the basis of purported precision. The only 'correct' formula is the one which the participating jurisdictions agree to use, provided it is uniformly applied by them.[116]

---

[111] Bravenec, 'Connecting the Dots in US International Taxation' (2002), p. 850.
[112] McLure and Weiner, 'Deciding Whether the European Union Should Adopt Formula Apportionment of Company Income' in Cnossen (ed.), *Taxing Capital Income in the European Union* (2000) 243–92, pp. 267–8.
[113] Mintz and Weiner, 'Exploring Formula Allocation for the European Union' (2001), p. 5.
[114] *Ibid.*
[115] Weiner, *Using the Experience in the US States to Evaluate Issues in Implementing Formula Apportionment at the International Level* (1999), p. 21.
[116] Agundez-Garcia, European Commission Taxation Papers, *The Delineation of Apportionment of an EU Consolidated Tax Base for Multi-Jurisdictional Corporate Income Taxation* (2006), p. 46.

The main factors in formulary apportionment are payroll, property and sales; the history of formulary apportionment in the US and Canada reveals that there are difficulties in defining these factors.[117] Another issue that needs to be considered is the mobility of the factors used in the formula. As to the three factors, payroll and sales based on destination are regarded as less mobile, whereas property creates distortions as capital is considered the most mobile factor.[118]

It is generally suggested that different factors be used for different businesses,[119] consequently a separate formula should be used for the banking business. In Canada, there are nine separate allocation formulas, and banking is one of the specialized categories.[120] As international banks must meet prudential standards in their home countries, there is a high degree of uniformity in the business practices of the international banking industry. The prudential standards may provide the basis for developing a simple formula for allocating the profits of international banks to their branches. Any formula that is proposed for international banks will have to be negotiated between the participating countries, subject to the limitation that any formula is somewhat arbitrary in nature.

4.3.3 Accounting and compliance requirements

If common accounting standards are established, jurisdictions would be able to agree on a broadly accepted definition of income and the factors to use in formulary apportionment.[121] A vital aspect of the EU proposals is the common corporate reporting requirement for public companies. In the absence of common accounting standards, international enterprises have to report their profits using a range of standards. The International Financial Reporting Standards Foundation sets globally accepted international financial reporting standards through its standard-setting body, the International Accounting Standards Board.[122] In 1998, the G7 Finance Ministers and Central Bank Governors decided

---

[117] Ibid., p. 47. For a discussion of the advantages and disadvantages of using the factors of payroll, property and sales in designing an apportionment formula, and the problems of defining the factors, see pp. 47–59.
[118] Ibid., pp. 51–2.
[119] Weiner, *Using the Experience in the US States to Evaluate Issues in Implementing Formula Apportionment at the International Level* (1999), p. 21.
[120] Weiner, *Formulary Apportionment and Group Taxation in the European Union* (2005), p. 26.
[121] Weiner, *Using the Experience in the US States to Evaluate Issues in Implementing Formula Apportionment at the International Level* (1999), p. 42.
[122] www.ifrs.org/The+organisation/IASCF+and+IASB.htm.

that the private-sector institutions in their countries should comply with internationally agreed principles, standards and codes of best practice.[123] The G7 countries suggested that all the countries that participate in the global capital markets should also comply with these internationally agreed standards and codes.

Some commentators have contended that formulary apportionment would impose significant compliance costs on international enterprises,[124] and that an international enterprise that prepares consolidated accounts would encounter significant difficulties.[125] On the other hand, Hellerstein has argued that the critics of formulary apportionment have no evidence that it will increase the compliance costs of taxpayers and the administrative costs of the tax authorities.[126] But the experience with transfer pricing between associated enterprises in the US is that it involves significant costs for both taxpayers and the tax authorities.[127] A taxpayer's functional analysis for US transfer pricing purposes requires the use of economic specialists and industry experts to analyse the taxpayer's industry. The high cost for taxpayers of complying with the US transfer pricing rules is illustrated by the fact that the large US accounting firms have transfer pricing groups which include accountants, lawyers and economists to provide advice on the application of the rules.

One of the purported requirements for formulary apportionment is that an international enterprise's financial accounts would have to be used for tax purposes. But this comment is illusory because, under the current bilateral tax treaties, international enterprises are required to use financial accounts for tax purposes. Moreover, consolidation mechanisms for corporate groups are being implemented in many countries. The other purported difficulties arising from formulary apportionment are: reconciling inventories; reconciling depreciation methods; conversion of foreign currencies; and reconciling the elections that are available in various jurisdictions.[128] These purported difficulties arise from the lack

---

[123] Chancellor's Statement, *Strengthening International Financial Systems*, Press Release No. 179/98, 30 October 1998, HM Treasury, United Kingdom.
[124] Coffill and Willson, 'Federal Formulary Apportionment as an Alternative to Arm's Length Pricing' (1993), p. 1112; Easson, 'A New International Tax Order' (1991), p. 466.
[125] Coffill and Willson, 'Federal Formulary Apportionment as an Alternative to Arm's Length Pricing' (1993), p. 1112.
[126] Hellerstein, 'Federal Income Taxation of Multinationals' (1993), pp. 1142–3.
[127] US General Accounting Office, *International Taxation: Problems Persist in Determining Tax Effects of Intercompany Prices* (1992), pp. 60–1.
[128] Coffill and Willson, 'Federal Formulary Apportionment as an Alternative to Arm's Length Pricing' (1993), p. 1112.

of uniformity in the company tax laws of the treaty partner countries. The threshold requirements for implementing formulary apportionment are not unique to unitary formulary apportionment; they are also requirements under the current treaty system. But the failure to achieve uniformity is an accepted compromise. McLure argued that the current rules require a high degree of uniformity if they are to operate effectively:

> In a logically consistent system of taxation based on SA/ALP [separate accounting/arm's length principle], all key elements of the system would be uniform across countries. That is, there would be uniform distinctions between the types of income (e.g. royalties and business profits), uniform rules for determining the geographic source of various types of income, a single standard for determining jurisdiction to tax, a single measure of business profits ...[129]

The problems stem from the lack of uniformity in the domestic company tax laws of treaty partner countries. In fact, the present lack of uniformity provides significant scope for tax arbitrage within the existing treaty networks of countries. Thus, the threshold accounting requirements for formulary apportionment should not be overstated; nor should the associated compliance and administrative costs be exaggerated. The current bilateral treaty system involves compromises, as will any move to formulary apportionment. Nevertheless, the compliance and administrative costs of formulary apportionment are likely to be significantly lower than the costs of complying with the current rules. A persuasive factor in adopting formulary apportionment is the argument of the EU business community that a significant reason for supporting the move to formulary apportionment is the high cost of complying with the current rules.

4.3.4 Problems with water's edge formulary apportionment

While formulary apportionment overcomes the problems of the arm's length principle, formulary apportionment gives rise to other problems. First, it does not attempt to determine the economic source of income, and it treats an enterprise's profits as being uniform across all parts of the enterprise and across all jurisdictions in which the enterprise operates.[130] Consequently, threshold rules are required to determine whether a taxpayer has a sufficient connection with a country to fall within its tax

---

[129] C. E. McLure, Jr, 'Replacing Separate Entity Accounting and the Arm's Length Principle with Formulary Apportionment' (2002), p. 597.

[130] McLure and Weiner, 'Deciding Whether the European Union Should Adopt Formula Apportionment of Company Income' in Cnossen (ed.), *Taxing Capital Income in the European Union* (2000) 243–92, p. 258.

jurisdiction.[131] The existing concept of permanent establishment could be used to determine a country's jurisdiction to tax the business profits of an international enterprise under a tax treaty. This is a requirement under the existing treaty system. Second, if the same formula under formulary apportionment is applied to all industries, distortions may arise. For example, in the banking industry, payrolls are not likely to be as significant a factor as they are in other international enterprises. Consequently, separate formulas should be used for different industries.

Third, if formulary apportionment is used in an economic grouping such as the EU, relations with other countries not using formulary apportionment are likely to be strained.[132] In the case of the EU, this situation is likely to cause problems in the OECD because the EU Member States have not dissented from the OECD's rejection of formulary apportionment in the Transfer Pricing Guidelines. For example, if the EU uses formulary apportionment and other countries continue to use the arm's length principle, international enterprises will have to use formulary apportionment in the EU Member States and the arm's length system for allocating profits to the other countries in which they operate. This will impose compliance burdens on international enterprises, but it may also create an incentive for other countries to move towards formulary apportionment.

Finally, there must be uniformity between the participating countries in order for formulary apportionment to work effectively. In Canada and the US, the formulary apportionment methods operate within their respective economic bases that are nationally uniform. Different jurisdictions are likely to have dissimilar domestic laws, making the application of formulary apportionment across national boundaries more difficult. A precondition for formulary apportionment and a multilateral tax treaty is a uniform accounting system. The implementation of a uniform accounting system is assisted by the globalization of industries, such as the banking industry; the international character of accounting firms that provide services to international enterprises; and the computerized nature of financial management used by international enterprises.[133]

---

[131] For what follows in this paragraph see: Mintz and Weiner, 'Exploring Formula Allocation for the European Union' (2001), p. 6.
[132] McLure and Weiner, 'Deciding Whether the European Union Should Adopt Formula Apportionment of Company Income' in Cnossen (ed.), *Taxing Capital Income in the European Union* (2000) 243–92, p. 258.
[133] Hellerstein, 'Federal Income Taxation of Multinationals' (1993), p. 1142.

4.3.5 Tax avoidance

Unfortunately, tax avoidance would not be eliminated by a worldwide multilateral tax treaty using formulary apportionment to allocate income to the jurisdictions in which international enterprises operate. But one of the advantages of formulary apportionment is that it will eliminate opportunities for some forms of avoidance such as transfer pricing manipulation. Under such a multilateral tax treaty, international enterprises would still be able to shift profits to low-tax jurisdictions, but they would have to engage in an active business in tax havens. Under formulary apportionment, a company is taxed on its combined income, and this prevents it from shifting profits between locations through transfer pricing. Transfer pricing manipulation to shift profits to tax havens would be pointless under formulary apportionment because the profits would still be the profits of a unitary business and subject to tax.[134] But with formulary apportionment, profits might be allocated to low-tax countries by manipulating the formula, which would be achieved by locating the factors in the formula in low-tax countries. In the case of international banks, they would be required to engage in an active business in a tax haven if they sought to book loans through that tax haven. The payroll factor in a formula requires business activities to be conducted by individuals. While an international bank may be willing to book loans through a tax haven, the bank is unlikely to set up significant operations in tax havens. The United States General Accounting Office concluded that the empirical evidence was insufficient to determine whether formulary apportionment would distort business decisions on the international location of operations.[135]

4.3.6 Income from intangible property

The difficulty of allocating income from intangibles has been described as the Achilles heel of formulary apportionment.[136] But the arm's length principle also fails to deal adequately with the apportionment of income from intangible property.[137] Under the arm's length principle, there are usually no comparable prices for intangible property, particularly

---

[134] C. E. McLure, 'US Federal Use of Formula Apportionment to Tax Income from Intangibles' (1997), p. 864.
[135] US General Accounting Office, *International Taxation* (1992), p. 70.
[136] C. E. McLure, 'US Federal Use of Formula Apportionment to Tax Income from Intangibles' (1997), pp. 864 and 867; M. J. McIntyre, 'Design of a National Formulary Apportionment Tax System' (1992), p. 6.
[137] McDaniel, 'Colloquium on NAFTA and Tradition' (1994), p. 722.

unique intangible assets. The allocation of income from intangible property between jurisdictions is a significant international tax problem, as most of the capital of an international enterprise is intangible property which has no geographic location.[138]

The difficulties encountered under formulary apportionment are, first, valuing intangibles and income from them, and second, allocating a location to intangible assets.[139] Adapting a simple formula based on sales, payroll and assets, such as the formula used in the US, would be inappropriate at the international level because of the difficulties of allocating income from intangible property.[140] Thus, formulary apportionment encounters problems in dealing with intangible property which are different from the problems encountered under the current treaty system.

Ideally, the method for valuing intangible assets should be the same as the method for valuing tangible assets: the present value of the income stream created by the property. The problem with valuing intangible property is that, at times, intangible property does not generate royalties that may be used to determine its present value. There is also the potential for intra-entity or intra-group royalties to be manipulated for tax avoidance purposes by shifting royalties to low-tax jurisdictions. The European Commission noted that dealing with intangible property in the design of an apportionment formula is a significant challenge:

> Intangibles are a clear tool for strategic corporate tax planning when used for apportionment. Thus, if intangibles were included in the property factor, intra-group royalty payments should be subject to arm's length valuation, with the corresponding search for comparables, etc. That implies that the FA [formulary apportionment] system would still face some of the transfer pricing complexities currently existing under the SA [separate accounting] methodology.[141]

The two alternative methods for dealing with intangible property under formulary apportionment are to exclude it or to base its value on the cost of creating an intangible asset. Excluding intangible property from the property formula only results in ignoring the issue of allocating income from intangible property. But excluding intangibles has the

---

[138] M. J. McIntyre, 'The Use of Combined Reporting by Nation States' (2004), p. 929.
[139] C. E. McLure, 'US Federal Use of Formula Apportionment to Tax Income from Intangibles' (1997), p. 870.
[140] M. J. McIntyre, 'Design of a National Formulary Apportionment Tax System' (1992), p. 6.
[141] Agundez-Garcia, European Commission Taxation Papers, *The Delineation of Apportionment of an EU Consolidated Tax Base for Multi-Jurisdictional Corporate Income Taxation*, p. 50.

advantages of simplicity and minimizing the compliance and administrative costs. Ignoring this income, however, is inappropriate because of the high value of many intangible assets and the overwhelming importance of intangibles.[142] Canada avoids the problem of intangible property by excluding property from its formula. In the US states, which have a property factor in the formulas they use, intangible property is omitted from the formula. The alternative method for dealing with intangible property is to base the value of an intangible asset on the cost of creating it. But this method is inappropriate because there is no direct correlation between the cost of an intangible asset and its value.[143] Moreover, in most cases, the market value of intangible assets exceeds its costs by a significant margin.[144] Neither of these approaches is acceptable; thus, a major remaining problem with formulary apportionment is dealing with intangible property. Attributing geographic location to intangible property is likewise a complex issue, and it is difficult to develop an objective method for doing so. A European Commission working paper suggested that, rather than excluding intangible assets from the property factor, research should be undertaken to find practical solutions for valuing and locating intangible assets.[145] Nevertheless, the EU adopted the compromise of valuing intangible property at cost on entry into the CCCTB. In summary, formulary apportionment cannot deal effectively with income from intangible property, but this failure does not constitute sufficient grounds for rejecting formulary apportionment since the current transfer pricing rules do not effectively deal with intangible property.

5 Conclusion

Globalization has exposed the flaws in the current bilateral tax treaty system based on the arm's length principle. International enterprises operating around the world through branches function as integrated enterprises with a common motive of maximizing profits, but not as independent arm's length profit centres. They have achieved high levels of integration through high speed and high quality communications and

---

[142] C. E. McLure, 'US Federal Use of Formula Apportionment to Tax Income from Intangibles' (1997), p. 865.
[143] Ibid., p. 866.
[144] Agundez-Garcia, European Commission Taxation Papers, *The Delineation of Apportionment of an EU Consolidated Tax Base for Multi-Jurisdictional Corporate Income Taxation*, p. 50.
[145] Ibid., p. 51.

5 CONCLUSION

information technology. This chapter argues that a multilateral tax treaty using unitary formulary apportionment is superior to the bilateral tax treaty system for allocating the profits of international enterprises. The main advantage of unitary formulary apportionment is that it reflects economic reality as opposed to the arm's length principle, which is fictional and impractical. Regional multilateral tax treaties are the most likely vehicles through which unitary formulary apportionment could be implemented at the international level.

The European Commission has recognized the need for an EU-wide tax treaty and the serious shortcomings of the arm's length principle for allocating the profits of international enterprises. The European Commission's sweeping CCCTB proposal has the support of EU Member States and EU businesses alike. Significantly, the parties are willing to incur the costs of shifting to unitary formulary apportionment. The extent of the proposed EU measure underscores the problems of the current arm's length principle. If the EU formulary apportionment measure is implemented, other regions may consider implementing a similar measure. The proposed EU formulary apportionment measure will become a valid alternative to the current treaty rules. This alternative will not solve all the problems of the current rules, but it will result in a more effective method for allocating the profits of EU enterprises to the Member States in which they operate.

Taxing highly integrated international enterprises, operating in the EU through branches, on a unitary basis is appropriate because these businesses operate in the EU on a unitary basis. Moreover, formulary apportionment overcomes the need for the tax authorities in the EU to scrutinize transactions of international enterprises to determine if their transfer prices comply with the arm's length principle. A significant step towards this was the European Commission's announcement in 2011 of the proposed CCCTB for calculating the tax base of enterprises operating in the EU and settling a formula for allocating profits under the CCCTB. The incentives for EU-based enterprises to opt for this measure are the advantages of tax compliance and to avoid the arbitrary results and disputes inherent in the arm's length principle.

12

Conclusion

International enterprises operating through permanent establishments around the world are difficult to tax at a national level because they operate as unitary worldwide businesses. Any mechanism that seeks to attribute the profits of an international enterprise to a country in which it operates through a permanent establishment will be arbitrary because profits and expenses of an international enterprise do not have geographic indicia, they are merely the profits and costs of the enterprise. Not surprisingly, international enterprises seek to maximize their profits and minimize their tax obligations. International enterprises are able to engage in tax arbitrage by exploiting the differences between tax systems in the countries in which they operate. Tax authorities operate at a national level and cannot realistically rely on the goodwill of international enterprises to comply with tax laws. The present tax treaty system – using bilateral tax treaties and the arm's length principle to allocate business profits to permanent establishments of international enterprises – is fundamentally flawed in theory and practice, and reform has become a pressing issue in the globalized international economy. These flaws have become magnified in the past forty years with the globalization and the rapid global expansion of international enterprises, such as international banks. The flaws in the current tax treaty system have been recognized and debated for some years, the system being described as the flawed miracle. The system is a miracle, in that the tax treaties reflect the OECD Model and it has broad support. But it is flawed, because the system was designed in the early part of the twentieth century and has been eroded by progressive globalization.

This book asserted that the arm's length principle, on which former Article 7 and new Article 7 of the OECD Model are based, is an inappropriate principle for attributing profits to permanent establishments of international enterprises. International enterprises, such as international banks, operate through branches as highly integrated businesses with a common profit motive. Conversely, the relationship between independent enterprises is based on the contracts between them. The assumption that permanent establishments and the other parts of an international enterprise can be treated as separate enterprises operating at arm's length conflicts with the economic theory of the firm and business reality. Thus, the arm's length principle is the wrong norm to use in attributing profits to permanent establishments of international enterprises, such as branches of international banks, because they operate as unitary businesses.

This book examined the alternative of a multilateral tax treaty using formulary apportionment to allocate the business profits of international enterprises to their permanent establishments in participating countries. It was suggested that regional multilateral tax treaties would be a valuable first step in the process of creating a broad multilateral tax treaty. The proposals currently being considered by the European Commission are a promising and exciting development down this path.

Chapter 2 established that the current tax treaty system was developed at the beginning of the twentieth century and that it is an inappropriate system to use for allocating profits of highly integrated international enterprises in the twenty-first century. Globalization is strongly challenging the foundations of the tax treaty system. The tax treaty system was designed to allocate profits to permanent establishments from intra-firm purchases and sales of tangible items for which comparable prices may have been available. The world of international trade has changed significantly with globalization involving high speed and high quality communication systems and information systems. Chapter 2 also established that reforms in the tax treaty system have not reflected the significant developments in the international trade system.

Chapter 3 illustrated some of the problems of the tax treaty system. The differences between the tax laws of treaty countries provide international enterprises operating abroad through permanent establishments with the incentive to allocate their profits to permanent establishments in lower-tax countries to reduce their tax liabilities. The bilateral tax treaty system suffers from numerous problems, including treaty shopping, inadequate information exchange between tax authorities and inconsistent treaty interpretation. Chapter 3 also examined the problems of the Transfer Pricing Guidelines for determining transfer prices for transactions between associated enterprises. The transfer pricing difficulties encountered by the EU countries and EU companies led to the EU proposal to implement formulary apportionment for companies operating within the EU.

Chapter 4 surveyed the work of the League of Nations in developing the permanent establishment concept and the use of a bilateral tax treaty model as a compromise measure. The League of Nations preference was for a multilateral tax treaty but it was unable to obtain support for a multilateral tax treaty as member countries were concerned about losing part of their tax sovereignty.

Chapter 5 examined the OECD Model and Commentary and their importance in the tax treaty system. But the chapter claimed that the OECD Commentary should only be applied to assist in interpreting tax treaties concluded before a Commentary was adopted by the OECD. In particular, where material changes are made to the Commentary, such as the 2008 Commentary on former Article 7, that Commentary cannot be used to interpret tax treaties concluded after the Commentary was adopted by the OECD. The claims in the 2008 Commentary that it only incorporated the parts of the authorized OECD approach in the 2008 Report that were consistent with the pre-2008 Commentary are immaterial. The significant changes in the 2008 Commentary on the interpretation of former Article 7 were finalized only after several years of discussions, both within the OECD and with external parties, such as the business sector. Moreover, prior to the publication of the 2008 Commentary there was no consensus interpretation of former Article 7 in OECD countries.

The proposition that the arm's length principle, which is used for allocating business profits under former Article 7 of the OECD Model, is inappropriate was argued in Chapters 6, 7, 8 and 9. The first problem of the arm's length approach is that it does not reflect business reality. The arm's length principle treats an international enterprise operating through permanent establishments as the sum of its parts. But the value of the whole of an international enterprise is greater than the sum of its head office and permanent establishments because of internalization of costs and economies of scale. The second problem with the arm's length principle is its focus on transactions. This transactional focus of the arm's length principle imposes significant compliance costs on taxpayers and high administrative costs on tax authorities. Former Article 7 and new Article 7 treat transfers of assets and funds within an international enterprise as notional transactions, and this approach reflects neither domestic laws nor business practice. The third problem is that for most transactions comparable transactions are often unavailable. Even when comparable transactions are available, an arm's length price is not an exact price but rather a range of prices. Not surprisingly, this range of prices provides some scope for tax planning, or avoidance.

Chapters 6 and 7 considered the lack of a consensus interpretation of former Article 7 of the OECD Model in the pre-2008 Commentary and that double taxation or under-taxation of bank branches is likely to occur. But the lack of a consensus interpretation of former Article 7 reflects the flaws of the arm's length principle. The 2008 Report adapts the Transfer Pricing Guidelines, developed for associated enterprises under Article 9, to permanent establishments under former Article 7 and new Article 7. It is ironic that as the validity of the arm's length principle is being increasingly questioned, the OECD has based its 2008 Commentary on former Article 7 and new Article 7 for permanent establishments on an even more strident application of the arm's length principle. The European Commission has indicated that the flaws in the bilateral tax treaty system and the arm's length principle have created the need for comprehensive rather than piecemeal reforms for the EU.

Chapter 9 examined the challenges in applying the authorized OECD approach in the 2008 Report to business restructuring involving permanent establishments. The 2008 Commentary requires profits made from the intra-entity transfer of assets, apart from intangible property, from a permanent establishment to be recognized for tax purposes. Intangible property is excluded on the ground that the Commentary on former Article 7(3) prevents the recognition of intra-entity transfers of intangible property. Transfers of intangible property from a permanent establishment are recognized under new Article 7.

Chapter 9 also considered the OECD transfer pricing methods in the Transfer Pricing Guidelines and the difficulties in applying the traditional transactional methods to transactions between associated enterprises. It asserted that while the transactional profit methods were to be used as a last resort until 2010, the transactional net margin method is the most commonly used method. In most cases there are inadequate comparables required to use the traditional transactional methods. The OECD did not reflect this important development in transfer pricing practice in the Transfer Pricing Guidelines until 2010. The OECD reform giving the transactional profit methods equal status with the traditional transactional methods was overdue.

Chapter 10 considered the new Article 7 and Commentary which implements the authorized OECD approach in the 2008 Report. The OECD expects that OECD countries and non-OECD countries will include new Article 7 in their tax treaties, but there is the risk that some countries may not use the new provision in their treaties. The advantage of using new Article 7 and Commentary is that the OECD authorized approach may be applied consistently. Nevertheless, new Article 7 relies on the arm's length principle and requires international enterprises to identify recognized intra-entity dealings and to allocate transfer prices to them, which is an abstract and artificial method for highly integrated international enterprises. A key development in new Article 7 was the alternative process for dispute resolution which requires the two treaty countries to find a resolution to disputes arising under Article 7.

Chapter 11 examined the claims that a multilateral tax treaty using formulary apportionment provides a more effective approach for allocating the profits of international enterprises. Formulary apportionment relies on a formula to allocate the profits of international enterprises operating in several countries. The formula has a series of factors that are used to allocate profits, and must be settled by negotiation, because whichever formula is used there will be countries which are winners or losers. It is recognized that any formula is to some extent arbitrary. Nevertheless, the main benefits of formulary apportionment are that it reflects business reality and provides certainty.

While it is asserted that formulary apportionment is a superior method to the arm's length principle for allocating the profits of international enterprises, there will be significant obstacles in achieving acceptance of a multilateral tax treaty using formulary apportionment by developed and developing countries. Formulary apportionment solves the problems of the arm's length approach by ignoring intra-entity transactions. If a formula, settled by negotiation with participating jurisdictions, is applied uniformly it would yield a consistent attribution of business profits to permanent establishments of international enterprises. This would minimize the risks of double taxation or under-taxation of permanent establishments. But formulary apportionment is not a perfect system and it raises other problems. Formulary apportionment will not produce ideal results in all circumstances because economic theory cannot produce a single formula for allocating profits for all enterprises. There is no single perfect economic formula for allocating the profits of international banks; any formula is to some extent arbitrary because international enterprises operate as unitary businesses. Rather, formulary apportionment methods seek to make a reasonable and objective allocation of business profits.

The European Commission's proposals on formulary apportionment provide an important step toward gaining international acceptance of formulary apportionment. Under the common consolidated corporate tax base proposal, EU companies operating in the EU would be taxed under one system and the profits allocated to participating EU countries on the basis of a formula. Thus, the taxable profits of an EU company would be calculated under a common EU-wide tax law. If the EU adopts the proposals on formulary apportionment, the experience derived from such a robust multilateral testing ground would be compelling evidence for future directions in tax treaty development.

In terms of the current tax treaty system, it was developed in the 1920s and the world has significantly changed since then. The tax treaty system has not been able to evolve to adapt successfully to the globalization of international business. One vital aspect of modern business is the globalization of international enterprises. The improvements in communication and information technologies, and the globalization of markets, have fuelled the rise of large integrated international enterprises, such as international banks. The phenomenal expansion of international enterprises has led to intra-firm trade becoming a significant and expanding proportion of world trade. This book has argued that the current tax treaty system must reflect the globalization of international trade and that significant reforms are required. The developments in international tax law have lagged well behind those in international trade law. What is needed now is a new tax treaty system for the current globalized world.

BIBLIOGRAPHY

Abeele, M. V., 'The Coordination of Tax Policy: The EU Experience' in *2000 World Tax Conference* (Tampa Bay, Florida: Canadian Tax Foundation, 2000) **1**:1–9

Adams, T. A., 'Interstate and International Double Taxation' in Magill, R. (ed.) *Lectures on Taxation* (New York: CCH, 1932) 101–28

Adams, T. S., 'International and Interstate Aspects of Double Taxation' (1929) **22** *National Tax Association Proceedings* 193

Agundez-Garcia, A., *The Delineation of Apportionment of an EU Consolidated Tax Base for Multi-Jurisdictional Corporate Income Taxation: A Review of Issues and Options* (European Commission Taxation Papers, Working Paper No. 9/2006)

American Law Institute, *Federal Income Tax Project, International Aspects of United States Income Taxation II, Proposals on United States Income Tax Treaties* (Philadelphia: The American Law Institute, 1992)

Arnold, B. J., 'Future Directions in International Tax Reform' (1988) **5** *Australian Tax Forum* 451

Tax Discrimination Against Aliens, Non-Residents, and Foreign Activities: Canada, Australia, New Zealand, the United Kingdom and the United States (Toronto: Canadian Tax Foundation, 1991)

'The Canadian General Anti-Avoidance Rule' in Cooper, G. S. (ed.), *Tax Avoidance and the Rule of Law* (Amsterdam: IBFD, 1997) 221–45

Arnold, B. J. and Darmo, M., 'Summary of Proceedings of an Invitational Seminar on the Attribution of Profits to Permanent Establishments' (2001) **49** *Canadian Tax Journal* 525

Arnold, B. J. and McDonnell, T. E., 'The Allocation of Income and Expenses Among Countries: Report on the Invitational Conference on Transfer Pricing' (1993) **10** *Australian Tax Forum* 545

Arnold, B. J., Sasseville, J. and Zolt, E. M., 'Summary of the Proceedings of an Invitational Seminar on Tax Treaties in the 21st Century' (2002) **50** *Canadian Tax Journal* 65

'Summary of Proceedings of an Invitational Seminar on the Taxation of Business Profits Under Tax Treaties' (2003) **57** *Bulletin for International Fiscal Documentation* 187

Ault, H. J., *Comparative Income Taxation: A Structural Analysis* (The Hague: Kluwer, 1997)
  'Corporate Integration, Tax Treaties and the Division of the International Tax Base: Principles and Practice' (1992) **47** *Tax Law Review* 565
  'The Role of the OECD Commentaries in the Interpretation of Tax Treaties' in Alpert, H. H. and van Raad, K. (eds.), *Essays on International Taxation* (Deventer: Kluwer, 1993) 61–8
Ault, H. J. and Bradford, D. F., 'Taxing International Income: An Analysis of the US System and its Economic Premises' in Razin, A. and Slemrod, J. (eds.), *Taxation in the Global Economy* (Chicago: University of Chicago Press, 1990) 11–46
Avery Jones, J. F., 'The David R. Tillinghast Lecture: Are Tax Treaties Necessary?' (1999) **53** *Tax Law Review* 1
Avi-Yonah, R. S., 'Globalization, Tax Competition, and the Fiscal Crisis of the Welfare State' (2000) **113** *Harvard Law Review* 1573
  'International Tax as International Law' (2004) **57** *Tax Law Review* 483
  'The Rise and Fall of Arm's Length: A Study in the Evolution of US International Taxation' (1995) **15** *Virginia Tax Review* 89
  'The Structure of International Taxation: A Proposal for Simplification' (1996) **74** *Texas Law Review* 1301
Baker, P. and Collier, R. S., 'General Report' in *Cahiers de droit fiscal international* (Rotterdam: IFA, 2006)
Balkin, R., 'International Law and Domestic Law' in Blay, S., Piotrowicz, R. and Tsamenyi, B. M. (eds.), *Public International Law* (Melbourne: Oxford, 1997) 119–145
Bank of International Settlements, *A New Capital Adequacy Framework, Consultative Paper Issued by the Basel Committee on Banking Supervision* (Bank of International Settlements, Basel, Basel Committee Publications Report No. 50, 1999)
  'Basel III rules text and results of the quantitative impact study issued by the Basel Committee', Press Release, 16 December 2010
  'History of the Basel Committee and its Membership' (April 2009), www.bis.org/bcbs/history.pdf
Basel Committee on Banking Supervision, *Consultative Document: Strengthening the Resilience of the Banking Sector* (Basel: Bank for International Settlements, 2009)
  'Initiatives in response to the crisis by the Basel Committee', Press Release, 30 March 2009
  'Instruments eligible for inclusion in Tier 1 capital' (October 1998)
  International Convergence of Capital Measurement and Capital Standards: A Revised Framework, Comprehensive Version (Basel: Bank for International Settlements, 2006)

Bebchuck, L. A. and Spamann, H., *Regulating Bankers' Pay*, Harvard Law School (Cambridge, Massachusetts), Discussion Paper No. 641 (2009)

Beveridge, F. C., *The Treatment and Taxation of Foreign Investment under International Law* (Manchester University Press, 2000)

BIAC, *BIAC Comments on OECD Revised Commentary on Article 7 of the OECD Model Tax Convention*, Business and Industry Advisory Committee of the OECD (2007)

  Comments on the OECD Public Discussion Draft: Draft Comments of the 2008 Update to the OECD Model Convention (31 May 2008)

  Comments on the 2001 Discussion Draft (2001)

  'Response to OECD's Invitation to Comment on Transactional Profit Methods' (2006)

Bird, R. M., 'International Aspects of Integration' (1975) **28** *National Tax Journal* 302

  'Shaping a New International Tax Order' (1988) **42** *Bulletin for International Fiscal Documentation* 292

  'The Interjurisdictional Allocation of Income' (1986) **3** *Australian Tax Forum* 333

  The Taxation of International Income Flows: Issues and Approaches (Wellington: Victoria University Press, 1987)

  'Why Tax Corporations?' (2002) *Bulletin for International Fiscal Documentation* 194

Bird, R. M. and Brean, D. J., 'The Interjurisdictional Allocation of Income and the Unitary Taxation Debate' (1986) **34** *Canadian Tax Journal* 1377

Bird, R. M. and Mintz, J. M., 'Introduction' in Bird, R. M. and Mintz, J. M. (eds.), *Taxation to 2000 and Beyond* (Toronto: Canadian Tax Foundation, 1992) 1–28

Bird, R. M. and Wilkie, J. S., 'Source- vs. Residence-Based Taxation in the European Union: The Wrong Question?' in Cnossen, S. (ed.) *Taxing Capital Income in the European Union* (Oxford: Oxford University Press, 2000) 78–109

Blumenthal, M. and Slemrod, J. B., 'The Compliance Cost of Taxing Foreign-Source Income: Its Magnitude, Determinants, and Policy Implications' (1995) **2** *International Tax and Public Finance* 37

Board of Governors of the Federal Reserve System, *Using Subordinated Debt as an Instrument of Market Discipline*, Report No. Staff Study 172 (1999)

Braithwaite, J. and Drahos, P., *Global Business Regulation* (Cambridge: Cambridge University Press, 2000)

Bravenec, L. L., 'Connecting the Dots in US International Taxation' (2002) **27** *Tax Notes International* 845

Brean, D. S., 'Here or There? The Source and Residence Principles of International Taxation' in Bird, R. M. and Mintz, J. M. (eds.), *Taxation to 2000 and Beyond* (Toronto: Canadian Tax Foundation, 1992) 303–33

Brennan, G. and Buchanan, J. M., *The Power to Tax* (Cambridge: Cambridge University Press, 1980)

British Bankers' Association, London Investment Banking Association and the Foreign Banks and Securities Houses Association, 'Public Comments Received on the Discussion Draft of the Attribution of Profits to Permanent Establishments – Part II (Special Considerations for Applying the Working Hypothesis to Permanent Establishments of Bank)' (2001)

Burgers, I., *Taxation and Supervision of Bank Branches* (Amsterdam: IBFD Publications BV, 1992)

(ed.) *The Taxation of Permanent Establishments* (Amsterdam: IBFD Publications BV, 1994)

Burns, J. D., 'How the IRS Applies the Intercompany Pricing Rules of Section 482: A Comparative Survey' (1980) **454** *Journal of Taxation* 308

Carlson, G. N. and Galper, H., 'Water's Edge Versus Worldwide Unitary Combination', in McLure, Jr, C. E. (ed.), *The State Corporate Income Tax, Issues in Worldwide Unitary Combination* (Stanford: Hoover Institution Press, 1984)

Carroll, M. B., *Taxation of Foreign and National Enterprises*, League of Nations (Geneva), Report No. C.452(b).M.217(b).1933.II.A. (1933)

Clausing, K. A., 'The Impact of Transfer Pricing on Intrafirm Trade' in Hines, J. R. (ed.) *International Taxation and Multinational Activity* (Chicago: University of Chicago Press, 2001) 173–94

Clausing, K. A. and Avi-Yonah, R. S., *Reforming Corporate Taxation in a Global Economy: A Proposal to Adopt Formulary Apportionment*, The Hamilton Project, Discussion Paper 2007–08 (Washington: The Brookings Institution, 2007)

Cnossen, S., *Tax Policy in the European Union: A Review of Issues and Options* (CESifo Working Paper No. 758, 2002)

Coase, R. H., *The Firm, the Market and the Law* (Chicago: University of Chicago Press, 1988)

'The Nature of the Firm (1937)' in Williamson, O. E. and Winter, S. G. (eds.), *The Nature of the Firm* (New York: Oxford University Press, 1991) 18–33

'The Nature of the Firm: Influence' in Williamson, O. E. and Winter, S. G. (eds.), *The Nature of the Firm* (New York: Oxford University Press, 1991) 61–74

'The Problem of Social Cost' (1960) **3** *Journal of Law and Economics* 1

Coffill, E. J. and Willson, P., 'Federal Formulary Apportionment as an Alternative to Arm's Length Pricing: From the Frying Pan to the Fire?' (1993) **59** *Tax Notes* 1103

Commission of the European Communities, Communication from the Commission to the Council, the European Parliament and the European Economic and Social Committee, *Implementing the Community Lisbon Programme: Progress to date and next steps towards a Common Consolidated Corporate Tax Base*, Brussels, 5.4.2006, COM(2006) 157 final

Company Taxation in the Internal Market, European Union (Brussels), Report No. SEC(2001)1681 (2001)

Report of the Committee of Independent Experts on Company Taxation, Commission of the European Communities (Brussels), Report No. (SEC(92) 1118) (1992)

Towards an Internal Market without Tax Obstacles: A Strategy for Providing Companies with a Consolidated Corporate Tax Base for their EU-Wide Activities, Commission to the Council, the European Parliament and the Social Committee (Brussels), Report No. COM(2001) 582 final (2001)

Culbertson, R. E., 'A Rose by Any Other Name: Smelling the Flowers at the OECD's (Last) Resort' (1995) **10** *Tax Notes International* 370

Dash, E., Morgenson, G. and Story, L., 'US Approves Plan to Let Citigroup Weather Losses', *The New York Times*, 24 November 2008

Davies, D. R., *Principles of International Double Tax Relief* (London: Sweet & Maxwell, 1985)

Demirguc-Kunt, A. and Huizinga, H., 'The Taxation of Domestic and Foreign Banking' (2001) **79** *Journal of Public Economics* 429

Doernberg, R. and Hinnekins, L., *Electronic Commerce and International Taxation* (The Hague: Kluwer, 1999)

Dunning, J. H. and Lundan, S. M., *Multinational Enterprises and the Global Economy* (2nd edn, Cheltenham: Edward Elgar, 2008)

Easson, A. J., 'A New International Tax Order – Responding to the Challenge' (1991) **45** *Bulletin for International Fiscal Documentation* 465

'Do We Still Need Tax Treaties?' (2000) **54** *Bulletin for International Fiscal Documentation* 619

Economic and Financial Commission, *Report on Double Taxation Submitted to the Financial Committee by Professors Bruins, Einaudi, Seligman and Sir Josiah Stamp*, League of Nations (Geneva), Report No. E.F.S. 73.F. 19. (1923)

Eden, L., 'Taxes, Transfer Pricing, and the Multinational Enterprise' in Rugman, A. and Brewer, T. (eds.), *Oxford Handbook of International Business* (Oxford: Oxford University Press, 2009) 591–619

Taxing Multinationals: Transfer Pricing and Corporate Income Taxation in North America (Toronto: University of Toronto Press, 1998)

Edgar, T., 'Designing and Implementing a Target-Effective General Anti-Avoidance Rule' in Duff, D. G. and Erlichman, H. (eds.), *Tax Avoidance in Canada After Canada Trustco and Mathew* (Toronto: Irwin Law, 2007) 221–56

Edgar, T. and Holland, D., 'Source Taxation and the OECD Project on the Attribution of Profits to Permanent Establishments' (2005) **37** *Tax Notes International* 525

Ernst & Young, 'Global Transfer Pricing Update' (2006) **44** *Tax Notes International* 939

Precision under Pressure, Global Transfer Pricing Survey 2007–2008 (2007) www.ey.com/Publication/vwLUAssets/Precision_under_pressure/$FILE/Precision_under_pressure.pdf

'Tax Administration Goes Global: Complexity, Risks and Opportunities' (2007) **45** *Tax Notes International Magazine* 813

'Transfer Pricing 1999 Global Survey: Practices, Perceptions, and Trends for 2000 and Beyond' (1999) **19** *Tax Notes International* 1907

2009 Global Transfer Pricing Survey. Tax Authority Insights: Perspectives, Interpretations and Regulatory Changes (2009) http://ey.mobi/Publication/vwLUAssets/2009_EY_Global_transfer_pricing_survey/$FILE/Ernst%20&%20Young%202009%20Global%20transfer%20pricing%20survey.pdf

European Commission, *A Common Consolidated EU Corporate Tax Base*, Commission Non-Paper to informal Ecofin Council, 10 and 11 September 2004

Consultation Document: The Application of International Accounting Standards (IAS) in 2005 and the Implications for the Introduction of a Consolidated Tax Base for Companies' EU-Wide Activities, European Commission (2003)

'Commission Proposes "Home State Taxation" for SMEs' Press Release, 10 January 2006, IP/06/11: Company taxation

Common Consolidated Corporate Tax Base Working Group, *Progress to Date and Future Plans for the CCCTB*, 15 November 2005 (CCCTB\wb\020\doc\en)

European Parliament, *Report on Taxation of Undertakings in the European Union: A Common Consolidated Corporate Tax Base* (2005) A6-0386/2005 (2005/2120 (INI))

Fiscal Committee, *London and Mexico Model Tax Conventions: Commentary and Text*, League of Nations (Geneva), Report No. C.88.M.88.1946.II.A. (1946)

Report to the Council on the Work of the First Session of the Committee, League of Nations (Geneva), Report No. C.516.M.175.1929.II. (1929)

Report to the Council on the Work of the Second Session of the Committee, League of Nations (Geneva), Report No. C.340.M.140.1930.II. (1930)

Report to the Council on the Work of the Third Session of the Committee, League of Nations (Geneva), Report No. C.415.M.171.1931.II.A. (1931)

Report to the Council on the Fourth Session of the Committee, League of Nations (Geneva), Report No. C.399.M.204.1933.II.A. (1933)

Report to the Council on the Fifth Session of the Committee, League of Nations (Geneva), Report No. C.252.M.124.1935.II.A. (1935)

Report to the Council on the Seventh Session of the Committee, League of Nations (Geneva), Report No. C.490.M.331.1937.II.A. (1937)

Report to the Council on the Work of the Eighth Session of the Committee, League of Nations (Geneva), Report No. C.384.M.229.1938.II.A. (1938)

Report to the Council on the Work of the Ninth Session of the Committee, League of Nations (Geneva), Report No. C.181.M.110.1939.II.A. (1939)

Report on the Work of the Tenth Session of the Committee, League of Nations (Geneva), Report No. C.37.M.37.1946.II.A. (1946)

Frenkel, J. A., Razin, A. and Sadka, E. (eds.), *International Taxation in an Integrated World* (Cambridge, Massachusetts: MIT Press, 1991)

G20, Communiqué, 'Meeting of Finance Ministers and Central Bank Governors', Busan, Republic of Korea (5 June 2010).

'Declaration on Strengthening the Financial System', London (2 April 2009).

'Declaration Summit on Financial Markets and the World Economy' (15 November 2008), para. 3.

Gajaria, H. and Kale, W., 'Transfer Pricing in Emerging Markets – An Indian Perspective', (2006) **28** *International Tax Review* 13

Ginsberg, A., *International Tax Planning* (Deventer: Kluwer, 1994)

GlaxoSmithKline (US), 'GSK settles transfer pricing dispute with IRS', Press Release, 11 September 2006

Graetz, M. J., 'The David R. Tillinghast Lecture: Taxing International Income: Inadequate Principles, Outdated Concepts, and Unsatisfactory Policies' (2001) **54** *Tax Law Review* 261

Graetz, M. J. and O'Hear, M. M., 'The "Original Intent" of US International Taxation' (1997) **46** *Duke Law Journal* 1021

Graetz, M. J. and Oosterhuis, P. W., 'Structuring an Exemption System for Foreign Income of US Corporations' (2001) **54** *National Tax Journal* 771

Green, R. A., 'The Future of Source-Based Taxation of the Income of Multinational Enterprises' (1993) **79** *Cornell Law Review* 18

Griffith, R., Hines, J. and Sorensen, P. B., 'International Capital Taxation' (2008) Chapter prepared for *Reforming the Tax System for the 21st Century: The Mirrlees Review* (The Institute for Fiscal Studies) www.ifs.org.uk/mirrleesreview/press_docs/international.pdf

Guttentag, J. H., 'Key Issues and Options in International Taxation: Taxation in an Interdependent World' (2001) **55** *Bulletin for International Fiscal Documentation* 546

Haldane, A. G., 'Rethinking the Financial Network' (Paper presented at the Financial Student Association, Amsterdam, 2009)

Hamaekers, H., 'Arm's Length – How Long?' in Kirchhof, P. et al. (eds.), *International and Comparative Taxation: Essays in Honour of Klaus Vogel* (The Hague: Kluwer Law, 2002) 29–52

Harris, P. and Oliver, D., *International Commercial Tax* (Cambridge: Cambridge University Press, 2010)

Harris, P. A., *Corporate/Shareholder Income Taxation and Allocating Taxing Rights between Countries* (Amsterdam: IBFD, 1996)

Hejazi, J., 'Should Depreciation Be Marked Up in a Transactional Net Margin Method Context for Service Providers?' (2008) **15** *International Transfer Pricing Journal* 26, 27

Hellerstein, J. R., 'Federal Income Taxation of Multinationals: Replacement of Separate Accounting with Formulary Apportionment' (1993) **60** *Tax Notes* 1131

Hellerstein, W., 'The Case for Formulary Apportionment' (2005) **3** *International Transfer Pricing Journal* 103

Hellerstein, W. and McLure, C. E., 'The European Commission's Report on Company Income Taxation: What the EU Can Learn from the Experience of the US States' (2004) **11** *International Tax and Public Finance* 199

Hill, G., 'The Interpretation of Double Taxation Agreements – The Australian Experience' (2003) **57** *Bulletin for International Fiscal Documentation* 320

Hines, J. R. (ed.) *International Taxation and Multinational Activity* (Chicago: University of Chicago Press, 2001)

Hoffman, L., 'Tax Avoidance' (2005) *British Tax Review* 197

Hoover's Handbook of World Business (Austin: Hoover Business Press, 2009)

Hoover's Handbook of World Business (Austin: Hoover Business Press, 2010)

Horst, T., 'The Comparable Profits Method' (1993) **6** *Tax Notes International* 1443

Hu, H., 'Misunderstood Derivatives: The Causes of Informational Failure and the Promise of Regulatory Incrementalism' (1993) **102** *Yale Law Journal* 1457

Hufbauer, G. C., *US Taxation of International Income* (Washington: Institute for International Economics, 1992)

Institute of International Bankers, 'Comments on the OECD Discussion Draft on the Attribution of Profits to Permanent Establishments' (2001) **23** *Tax Notes International* 477

Internal Revenue Service, 'IRS Accepts Settlement Offer in Largest Transfer Pricing Dispute', Press Release No. IR-2006-142, 11 September 2006

International Fiscal Association (ed.), *The Attribution of Profits to Permanent Establishments* (Rotterdam: Cahiers de droit fiscal international, 2006)

Jackson, J. H. and Davey, W. J., *Legal Problems of International Economic Relations* (2nd edn, St Paul, Minnesota: West Publishing Company, 1986)

Jeffery, R. J., *The Impact of State Sovereignty on Global Trade and International Taxation* (The Hague: Kluwer Law, 1999)

Joint Committee on Taxation, *Report of Investigations of Enron Corporation and Related Entities Regarding Federal Tax and Compensation Issues, and Policy Recommendations*, US Congress (Washington), Report No. JCS-3-03 (2003)

Kandev, M. N. and Wiener, B., 'Some Thoughts on the Use of Later OECD Commentaries After Prevost Car' (2009) **54** *Tax Notes International* 667

Kaufman, N. H., 'Fairness and the Taxation of International Income' (1998) **29** *Law and Policy in International Business* 145

Kingston, C. I., 'The David Tillinghast Lecture: Taxing the Future' (1998) **51** *Tax Law Review* 641

Knechtle, A. A., *Basic Problems in International Fiscal Law* (London: HFL, 1979)

Kobetsky, M., 'Attribution of Profits to Branches of International Banks: The OECD Discussion Drafts' (2005) **20** *Banking and Finance Law Review* 319

'The Aftermath of the *Lamesa* Case: Australia's Tax Treaty Override' (2005) **59** *Bulletin for International Fiscal Documentation* 236

'The Tax Treaty Implications of the Foreign Bank Tax Measures' (2002) **17** *Banking and Finance Law Review* 181

KPMG, *OECD Discussion Draft on the Attribution of Profits to Permanent Establishments, Representations of KPMG's Worldwide Banking Tax Practice* (KPMG, 2001) www.oecd.org/dataoecd/48/16/2673215.pdf

Krugman, P. R. and Obstfeld, M., *International Economics: Theory and Policy* (8th edn, Boston: Pearson Addison-Wesley, 2009)

Lang, M. and Brugger, F., 'The Role of the OECD Commentary in Tax Treaty Interpretation' (2008) **23** *Australian Tax Forum* 95

Langbein, S. I., 'A Modified Fractional Apportionment Proposal for Transfer Pricing' (1992) **54** *Tax Notes* 719

'The Unitary Method and the Myth of Arm's Length' (1986) **30** *Tax Notes* 625

Lebowitz, B. E., 'Transfer Pricing and the End of International Taxation' (1999) **19** *Tax Notes International* 1201

Li, J., 'Global Profit Split: An Evolutionary Approach to International Income Allocation' (2002) **50** *Canadian Tax Journal* 823

'Slicing the Digital Pie with a Traditional Knife – Effectiveness of the Arm's Length Principle in the Age of E-Commerce' (2001) **24** *Tax Notes International* 775

Li, J. and Sandler, D., 'The Relationship between Domestic Anti-Avoidance Legislation and Tax Treaties' (1997) **45** *Canadian Tax Journal* 891

Lodin, S. O., 'International Tax Issues in a Rapidly Changing World' (2001) **55** *Bulletin for International Fiscal Documentation* 2

Lodin, S. O. and Gammie, M., *Home State Taxation* (Amsterdam: IBFD, 2001)

Lokken, L., 'Territorial Taxation: Why Some US Multinationals May Be Less than Enthusiastic About the Idea (and Some Ideas They Really Dislike)' (2006) **59** *Southern Methodist Law Review* 751

Loukota, H., 'Multilateral Tax Treaty Versus Bilateral Treaty Network' in *Multilateral Tax Treaties* (London: Kluwer Law International, 1998) 83–103

Martens-Weiner, J., 'A New Way of Thinking About Company Tax Reform in the European Union', Paper presented to the Institute of European Affairs, 7 February 2006

Meenan, P., Dawid, R. and Hulshorst, J., 'Is Europe One Market? A Transfer Pricing Economic Analysis of Pan-European Comparables Sets', Deloitte White Paper (2004), p. 1: reproduced in European Commission, *EU Joint Transfer Pricing Forum* (Brussels: 2004, Taxud/C1/LDH/WB)

Mercader, A. and Peña, H., 'Transfer Pricing and Latin American Integration' in Tanzi, V., Barreix, A. and Villela, L. (eds.) *Taxation and Latin American Integration* (Washington: Inter-American Development Bank and the David Rockefeller Center for Latin American Studies, Harvard University, 2008)

McDaniel, P. R., 'Colloquium on NAFTA and Tradition: Formulary Taxation in the North American Free Trade Zone' (1994) **49** *New York University Tax Review* 691

'Territorial vs Worldwide Taxation: Which Is Better for the US?' (2007) **8** *Florida Tax Review* 283

'Trade and Taxation' (2001) **26** *Brooklyn Journal of International Law* 1621

McIntyre, M. J., 'Design of a National Formulary Apportionment Tax System' (Paper presented at the National Tax Association–Tax Institute of America, Proceedings of the 84th Annual Conference, Williamsburg, Virginia, 1992)

'Guidelines for Taxing International Capital Flows: The Legal Perspective' (1993) *National Tax Journal* 315

'The Design of Tax Rules for the North American Free Trade Alliance' (1994) **49** *Tax Law Review* 769

'The Use of Combined Reporting by Nation States', in Arnold, B. J., Sasseville, J. and Zolt, E. M. (eds.), *The Taxation of Business Profits under Tax Treaties* (Toronto: CTF, 2003)

'The Use of Combined Reporting by Nation States' (2004) **35** *Tax Notes International* 917

McIntyre, R. S. and McIntyre, M. J., 'Opinion: Using NAFTA to Introduce Formulary Apportionment' (1993) **6** *Tax Notes International* 851

McLure, C. E., 'Globalization, Tax Rules and National Sovereignty' (2001) **55** *Bulletin for International Fiscal Documentation* 328

'International Aspects of Tax Policy for the 21st Century' (1990) **8** *The American Journal of Tax Policy* 167

(ed.) *State Income Taxation of Multistate Corporations in the United States of America. The Impact of Multinational Corporations on Development and on International Relations, Technical Papers: Taxation* (New York: United Nations, 1974, Sales No. E.74.II.A.6)

'Tax Assignment and Subnational Fiscal Autonomy' (2000) **54** *Bulletin for International Fiscal Documentation* 626

'US Federal Use of Formula Apportionment to Tax Income from Intangibles' (1997) **14** *Tax Notes International* 859

McLure, Jr, C. E., 'Defining a Unitary Business: An Economist's View' in McLure, Jr, C. E. (ed.), *The State Corporate Income Tax, Issues in Worldwide Unitary Combination* (Stanford: Hoover Institution Press, 1984)

'Replacing Separate Entity Accounting and the Arm's Length Principle with Formulary Apportionment' (2002) **56** *Bulletin for International Fiscal Documentation* 586

McLure, C. E. and Weiner, J. M., 'Deciding Whether the European Union Should Adopt Formula Apportionment of Company Income' in Cnossen, S (ed.) *Taxing Capital Income in the European Union* (Oxford: Oxford University Press, 2000) 243–92

Mintz, J. and Weiner, J. M., 'Exploring Formula Allocation for the European Union' (Paper presented at the Tax Policy in the European Union, The Hague, 2001)

Mintz, J. M., 'Globalization of the Corporate Income Tax: The Role of Allocation' (1999) **56** *Finanzarchiv* S.389

Mintz, J. M. and Chen, D., 'Will Corporate Income Tax Wither?' in *2000 World Tax Conference Report* (Toronto: Canadian Tax Foundation, 2000)

Mullins, P., *Moving to Territoriality? Implications for the United States and the Rest of the World*, International Monetary Fund Report No. WP/06/161 (2006)

Murray, B. and Wilkie, S., 'GlaxoSmithKline Settles US Transfer Pricing Dispute for $3.4 Billion: What Lessons Can Be Learned?' *Lexpert/American Lawyer Guide to the Leading 500 Lawyers in Canada* (2007)

Musgrave, P. B., 'Sovereignty, Entitlement, and Cooperation in International Taxation' (2001) **26** *Brooklyn Journal of International Law* 1335

  United States Taxation of Foreign Investment Income: Issues and Arguments (Cambridge, Massachusetts: The Law School of Harvard University, 1969)

Musgrave, R. A. and Musgrave, P. B., 'Inter-Nation Equity' in Bird, R. M. and Head, J. G. (eds.), *Modern Fiscal Issues* (Toronto: University of Toronto Press, 1972) 63–85

  Public Finance in Theory and Practice (5th edn, New York: McGraw-Hill, 1989)

Newlon, T. S., 'Transfer Pricing and Income Shifting in Integrated Economies' in Cnossen, S. (ed.) *Taxing Capital Income in the European Union* (Oxford: Oxford University Press, 2000) 214–42

Noren, D. G., 'The US National Interest in International Tax Policy' (2001) **54** *New York University Tax Review* 337

Nye, J. S., *The Paradox of American Power* (Oxford: Oxford University Press, 2002)

OECD, *OECD's Current Tax Agenda*, June 2010 (Paris: OECD, 2010)

  Discussion Draft on the Attribution of Profits to Permanent Establishments (Paris: OECD, 2001)

  Discussion Draft on the Attribution of Profits to Permanent Establishments: Part I General Considerations (Paris: OECD, 2004)

  Discussion Draft on the Attribution of Profits to Permanent Establishments: Part II (Banks) (Paris: OECD, 2003)

  Discussion Draft on the Attribution of Profits to Permanent Establishments: Part III (Global Trading of Financial Instruments) (Paris: OECD, 2005)

  Discussion Draft on the Attribution of Profits to Permanent Establishments: Part IV (Insurance) (Paris: OECD, 2005)

  Double Taxation Conventions and the Use of Conduit Companies (Paris: OECD, 1986)

  Draft Double Taxation Convention on Income and Capital (Paris: OECD, 1963), Report No. C(63)87

'Fifth Meeting of the OECD Forum on Tax Administration', FTA Communiqué, Paris, 28–29 May 2009, p. 2

Harmful Tax Competition, An Emerging Global Issue (Paris: OECD, 1998)

Improving Access to Bank Information for Tax Purposes (Paris: OECD, 2000)

International Tax Avoidance and Evasion (Paris: OECD, 1987)

Measuring Globalisation: OECD Economic Globalisation Indicators (Paris: OECD, 2005)

Model Tax Convention: Attribution of Income to Permanent Establishments (Paris: OECD, 1994)

Model Tax Convention on Income and on Capital (Paris: OECD, 1992)

Model Tax Convention on Income and on Capital (Paris: OECD, 2005)

Model Tax Convention on Income and on Capital (Paris: OECD, 2008)

Model Tax Convention on Income and on Capital (Paris: OECD, 2010)

OECD Economic Outlook (Paris: OECD, 2002), Report No. 71

OECD Reference Guide on Sources of Information from Abroad (Paris: OECD, 2006)

Proposed Revision of Chapters I–III of the Transfer Pricing Guidelines (Paris: OECD, 2009)

Report on the Attribution of Profits to Permanent Establishments (Paris: OECD, 2006)

Report on the Attribution of Profits to Permanent Establishments (Paris: OECD, 2008)

Report on the Attribution of Profits to Permanent Establishments (Paris: OECD, 2010)

Restricting the Entitlement to Treaty Benefits (Paris: OECD, 2002)

Revenue Statistics 1965–2009 (Paris: OECD, 2010)

Revised Discussion Draft of a New Article 7 of the OECD Model Tax Convention (Paris: OECD, 2009)

Tax Aspects of Transfer Pricing Within Multinational Enterprises: The United States Proposed Regulations: A Report by the Committee on Fiscal Affairs on the Proposed Regulations under Section 482 IRC (Paris: OECD, 1993)

Tax Treaty Overrides (Paris: OECD, 1989)

Taxing Profits in a Global Economy, Domestic and International Issues (Paris: OECD, 1991)

Transactional Profit Methods: Discussion Draft for Public Comment (Paris: OECD, 2008)

Transfer Pricing and Multinational Enterprises (Paris: OECD, 1979)

Transfer Pricing and Multinational Enterprises (Three Taxation Issues) (Paris: OECD, 1984)

Transfer Pricing Aspects of Business Restructurings: Discussion Draft for Public Comment (Paris: OECD, 2009)

Transfer Pricing Guidelines for Multinational Enterprises and Tax Administrations, Discussion Draft of Part I (Paris: OECD, 1994)

Transfer Pricing Guidelines for Multinational Enterprises and Tax Administrations (loose-leaf) (Paris: OECD, 1995)

Transfer Pricing Guidelines for Multinational Enterprises and Tax Administrations (Paris: OECD, 2009)

Transfer Pricing Guidelines for Multinational Enterprises and Tax Administrations (Paris: OECD, 2010)

OEEC, *The Elimination of Double Taxation* (Paris: Organisation for European Economic Co-operation, 1958)

The Elimination of Double Taxation, Second Report of the Fiscal Committee (Paris: Organisation for European Economic Co-operation, 1959), Report No. C(59) 147

The Elimination of Double Taxation, Third Report of the Fiscal Committee (Paris: Organisation for European Economic Co-operation, 1960), Report No. C(60)157

The Elimination of Double Taxation, Fourth Report of the Fiscal Committee (Paris: Organisation for European Co-operation, 1967), Report No. C(61)97

O'Haver, R., 'Transfer Pricing: A Critical Issue for Multinational Companies' (2006) **42** *Tax Notes International* 407

Oldman, O. and Brooks, J. S., 'The Unitary Method and the Less Developed Countries: Preliminary Thoughts' (1987) *International Business Law Journal* 45

Olson, P. F., 'Globalization and the US International Tax Rules' (Paper presented at the IRS/George Washington University 15th Annual Institute on Current Issues in International Taxation, Washington, 12 December 2002), reproduced in (2002) *Worldwide Tax Daily* 240–17

Owens, J., 'Emerging Issues in Tax Reform: The Perspective of an International Bureaucrat' (1997) **15** *Tax Notes International* 2035

'Should the Arm's Length Principle Retire?' (2005) **3** *International Transfer Pricing Journal* 99

Parks, E. T. and Parks, L. F. (eds.), *Memorable Quotations of Franklin D. Roosevelt* (New York: Thomas Y. Crowell Co, 1965)

Przysuski, M. and Lalapet, S., 'A Comprehensive Look at the Berry Ratio in Transfer Pricing' (2005) **40** *Tax Notes International* 759

Przysuski, M., Lalapet, S. and Swaneveld, H., 'Transfer Pricing Method Selection in the United States and Canada' (2004) **5** *Corporate Business Taxation Monthly* 7

Qureshi, A. H., 'The Freedom of a State to Legislate in Fiscal Matters under General International Law' (1987) **41** *Bulletin for International Fiscal Documentation* 14

Public International Law of Taxation (London: Graham & Trotman, 1994)

Raad, K. van, 'Deemed Expenses of a Permanent Establishment under Article 7 of the OECD Model' in Lindencrona, G., Lodin, S.-O. and Wiman, B. (eds.),

International Studies in Taxation: Law and Economics (London: Kluwer, 1999) 285–95

Radaelli, C. M., *The Politics of Corporate Taxation in the European Union* (London: Routledge, 1997)

Redmiles, M. and Wenrich, J., 'A History of Controlled Foreign Corporations and the Foreign Tax Credit' (2007) **27** *Statistics of Income Bulletin (US Internal Revenue Service)* 129

Report and Resolutions submitted by the Technical Experts to the Financial Committee, *Double Taxation and Tax Evasion* (Geneva: League of Nations, 1925)

Report Presented by the Committee of Technical Experts on Double Taxation and Tax Evasion, *Double Taxation and Tax Evasion* (Geneva: League of Nations, 1927), Report No. C.216.M.85.1927.II.

Report Presented by the General Meeting of Government Experts on Double Taxation and Tax Evasion, *Double Taxation and Tax Evasion* (Geneva: League of Nations, 1928), Report No. C.562.M.178.1928.II.

Reyneveld, J., Gommers, E. and Lund, H., 'Pan-European Comparables Searches – Analysing the Search Criteria', (2007) **14** *International Transfer Pricing Journal* 79

Richman [Musgrave], P. B., *Taxation of Foreign Investment Income* (Baltimore: Johns Hopkins Press, 1963)

Rigby, M., 'A Critique of Double Tax Treaties as a Jurisdictional Coordination Mechanism' (1991) **8** *Australian Tax Forum* 301

Rosenbloom, H. D., 'Angels on a Pin: Arm's Length in the World' (2005) **38** *Tax Notes International* 523

'The David R. Tillinghast Lecture: International Tax Arbitrage and the "International Tax System"' (2000) **53** *Tax Law Review* 137

'What's Trade Got to Do with It?' (1994) **49** *Tax Law Review* 593

Rosenbloom, H. D. and Langbein, S. L., 'United States Tax Treaty Policy: An Overview' (1981) **19** *Columbia Journal of Transnational Law* 359

Ross, S. G., 'International Tax Law: The Need for Constructive Change' in Stein, H. (ed.) *Tax Policy in the Twenty-First Century* (New York: Wiley, 1988) 87–100

Sasseville, J., 'The Future of the Treaty Rules for Taxing Business Profits' in *2000 World Tax Conference Report* (Toronto: Canadian Tax Foundation, 2000) **5**:1–14

Sato, M. and Bird, R. M., 'International Aspects of the Taxation of Corporations and Shareholders' (1975) **22** *International Monetary Fund Staff Working Papers* 384

Seligman, E. R., *Double Taxation and International Fiscal Cooperation* (New York: Macmillan, 1928)

Essays in Taxation (10th edn, New York: Macmillan, 1931)

Shaviro, D., 'Why Worldwide Welfare as a Normative Standard in US Tax Policy?' (2007) **60** *Tax Law Review* 155

Shay, S. E., Fleming, J. C. and Peroni, R. J., 'The David R. Tillinghast Lecture: What's Source Got to Do with It? Source Rules and US International Taxation' (2002) **56** *Tax Law Review* 81

Sheppard, L. A., 'Any Takers for the New OECD Model Business Profits Article?' (2009) *Tax Notes International* 1089

'NatWest Revisited in the New British Treaty' (2001) **23** *Tax Notes International* 1503

Shipwright, A. (ed.), *Tax Avoidance and the Law* (London: Key Haven, 1997)

Shoup, C. (ed.) *Taxation of Multinational Corporations. The Impact of Multinational Corporations on Development and on International Relations* (New York: United Nations, 1974)

Skaar, A. A., *Permanent Establishment: Erosion of a Tax Treaty Principle* (Deventer: Kluwer, 1991)

Slemrod, J., 'Introduction' in Slemrod, J. (ed.) *Tax Progressivity and Income Inequality* (Cambridge: Cambridge University Press, 1994) 1–8

Spence, I., 'Globalization of Transnational Business: The Challenge for International Tax Policy' (1997) **25** *International Tax Review* 143

Spengel, C. and Wendt, C., 'A Common Consolidated Corporate Tax Base for Multinational Companies in the European Union: Some Issues and Options' (2007) Oxford University Centre for Business Taxation, Working Paper 07/17

Stamp, J., *The Fundamental Principles of Taxation* (London: Macmillan, 1936)

Stein, H. (ed.) *Tax Policy in the Twenty-First Century* (New York: Wiley, 1988)

Surrey, S. S., 'Current Issues in the Taxation of Corporate Foreign Investment' (1956) **56** *Columbia Law Review* 815

'Reflections on the Allocation of Income and Expenses Among National Tax Jurisdictions' (1978) **10** *Law and Policy in International Business* 409

'United Nations Group of Experts and the Guidelines for Tax Treaties Between Developed and Developing Countries' (1978) **19** *Harvard International Law Journal* 1

Tanzi, V., 'Forces that Shape Tax Policy' in Stein, H. (ed.) *Tax Policy in the Twenty-First Century* (New York: Wiley, 1988) 266–77

'Globalization, Tax Competition and the Future of Tax Systems' (1996) *Working Paper of the International Monetary Fund* 1

Taxation in an Integrating World (Washington: The Brookings Institute, 1995)

Tanzi, V., 'The Impact of Economic Globalisation on Taxation' (1998) 52 *Bulletin for International Fiscal Documentation* 338

'The Nature and Effects of Globalization on International Tax Policy, Technological Developments, and the Work of Fiscal Termites' (2001) **26** *Brooklyn Journal of International Law* 1261

Thomas, C., 'Customary International Law and State Taxation of Corporate Income: The Case for the Separate Accounting Method' (1996) **14** *Berkeley Journal of International Law* 99

Thuronyi, V., 'International Tax Cooperation and a Multilateral Treaty' (2001) **26** *Brooklyn Journal of International Law* 1641

Tiley, J., *Revenue Law* (6th edn, Oxford: Hart Publishing, 2008)

Trebilcock, M. J. and Howse, R., *The Regulation of International Trade* (3rd edn, London: Routledge, 2005)

UK Inland Revenue, Budget 2002, REV BN 25, 'Taxation of UK Branches of Foreign Companies', 17 April 2002

UNCTAD, *World Investment Report: Transnational Corporations, Agricultural Production and Development* (New York and Geneva: UN, 2009)

UNCTAD, *World Investment Report: Transnational Corporations, and the Infrastructure Challenge* (New York and Geneva: UN, 2008)

United Nations, *Draft Manual for the Negotiation of Bilateral Tax Treaties between Developed and Developing Countries* (New York: UN, 2001), Report No. ST/ESA

International Co-operation in Tax Matters, Guidelines for International Co-operation Against the Evasion and Avoidance of Taxes (with Special Reference to Taxes on Income, Profits, Capital and Capital Gains) (New York: UN, 1984), Report No. ST/ESA/142

Report of Experts on International Tax Cooperation in Tax Matters (New York: UN, 2009)

Transfer Pricing (Geneva: UN, 2001), Report No. ST/SG/AC.8/2001/CRP.6

United Nations Conference on the Law of Treaties, First and Second Sessions, Official Records (New York: UN, 1971)

United Nations Model Double Taxation Convention between Developed and Developing Countries (New York: UN, 1980), Report No. ST/ESA/02

United Nations Model Tax Convention Between Developed and Developing Countries (New York: UN, 2001)

World Investment Report 1993: Transnational Corporations and Integrated Production (New York: UN, 1993), Report No. E93.II.A.14

United Nations Economic and Social Council, Report of the Secretary General, *Eleventh Meeting of the Ad Hoc Group of Experts on International Cooperation in Tax Matters*, Report No. E/2004/51 (2004)

US Department of the Treasury, *Corporate Inversion Transactions: Tax Policy Implications* (Washington: Department of Treasury, 2002)

'Corporate Inversion Transactions: Tax Policy Implications' reproduced in (2002) *Worldwide Tax Daily* 103–38

Report to Congress on Earning Stripping, Transfer Pricing and US Income Tax Treaties (Washington: US Department of the Treasury, 2007)

US Department of the Treasury (Office of Tax Analysis), *Income Shifting from Transfer Pricing: Further Evidence from Tax Return Data* (Washington: US Department of the Treasury, 2008)

US Department of the Treasury (Office of Tax Policy), *Selected Tax Policy Implications of Global Electronic Commerce* (Washington: US Department of Treasury, 1996)

The Deferral of Income Earned Through US Controlled Foreign Corporations: A Policy Study (Washington: Office of Tax Policy, Department of the Treasury, 2000)

US General Accounting Office, *International Taxation: Problems Persist in Determining Tax Effects of Intercompany Prices* (Washington: United States General Accounting Office, 1992), Report No. GAO/GGD-92-89

IRS Could Better Protect US Tax Interests in Determining the Income of Multinational Corporations (Washington: General Accounting Office, 1981), Report No. GGD-81-81

US Government Accountability Office, *US Multinational Corporations: Effective Tax Rates Are Correlated with Where Income Is Reported*, Report No. GAO-08-950 (2008)

US Internal Revenue Service, 'Everson Chairs International Tax Form, Emphasizes Enforcement', IR-2206-120 (1 August 2006)

'IRS Accepts Settlement Offer in Largest Transfer Pricing Dispute', IR-2006-142 (11 September 2006)

US President's Advisory Panel on Federal Tax Reform, *Simple, Fair, and Pro-Growth: Proposals to Fix America's Tax System* (Washington: President's Advisory Panel on Federal Tax Reform, 2005)

US Treasury Department and Internal Revenue Service, White Paper, *A Study of Intercompany Pricing*, Discussion Draft (Washington: 1988) (Notice 88-123, 1988-2 C.B. 458)

Vanistendael, F., 'Legal Framework for Taxation' in Thuronyi, V. (ed.) *Tax Law Design and Drafting* (Washington: International Monetary Fund, 1996) 15–70

Vann, R. J., 'A Model Tax Treaty for the Asian-Pacific Region? (Part I)' (1991) **45** *Bulletin for International Fiscal Documentation* 99

'A Model Tax Treaty for the Asian-Pacific Region (Part II)' (1991) **45** *Bulletin for International Fiscal Documentation* 151

'Do We Need 7(3)? History and Purpose of the Business Profits Deduction Rule in Tax Treaties' (Paper presented at the Tax History Conference, Cambridge 2010)

'International Aspects of Income Tax' in Thuronyi, V. (ed.) *Tax Law Design and Drafting* (Washington: International Monetary Fund, 1998) 718–810

'Reflections on Business Profits and the Arm's Length Principle' in Arnold, B. J., Sasseville, J. and Zolt, E. M. (eds.), *The Taxation of Business Profits Under Tax Treaties* (Toronto: Canadian Tax Foundation, 2003) 133–69

Vogel, K., 'Double Tax Treaties and their Interpretation' (1986) **4** *International Tax and Business Lawyer* 4

Klaus Vogel on Double Tax Conventions (3rd edn, London: Kluwer, 1997)
'The Influence of the OECD Commentaries on Treaty Interpretation' (2000) **54** *Bulletin for International Fiscal Documentation* 612
'Worldwide vs. Source Taxation of Income – A Review and Re-evaluation of Arguments (Part I)' (1988) **16** *Intertax* 216
'Worldwide vs. Source Taxation of Income – A Review and Re-evaluation of Arguments (Part III)' (1988) **16** *Intertax* 310
Ward, D. A., 'Attribution of Income to Permanent Establishments' (2000) **48** *Canadian Tax Journal* 559
Warren, A. C., 'Income Tax Discrimination Against International Commerce' (2001) **54** *Tax Law Review* 131
Wattel, P. J. and Marres, O., 'The Legal Status of the OECD Commentary and Static or Ambulatory Interpretation of Tax Treaties' (2003) **57** *Bulletin for International Fiscal Documentation* 222
Weeghel, S. van, *The Improper Use of Tax Treaties* (London: Kluwer, 1998)
Weiner, J. M., *Formulary Apportionment and Group Taxation in the European Union: Insights from the United States and Canada* (European Commission Taxation Papers Working Paper No. 8/2005)
'EU Commission, Member States Commit to EU-Wide Company Taxation, Formulary Apportionment' (2002) **26** *Tax Notes International* 515
'Redirecting the Debate on Formulary Apportionment' (2007) **46** *Tax Notes International* 1213
Using the Experience in the US States to Evaluate Issues in Implementing Formula Apportionment at the International Level, US Department of Treasury (Washington), Report No. OTA Paper 83 (1999)
Weissman, G. H., 'Unitary Taxation: Its History and Recent Supreme Court Treatment' (1983) **48** *Albany Law Review* 48
Wickham, D. W. and Kerester, C. J., 'Tax Policy Forum – New Directions Needed for Solution of the Transfer Pricing Puzzle' (1992) **5** *Tax Notes International* 399
Williams, D. W., *Trends in International Taxation* (Amsterdam: IFA, 1991)
Wood, D., *Governing Global Banking, The Basel Committee and the Politics of Financial Globalisation* (Aldershot, Hampshire: Ashgate Publishing, 2005)
World Trade Organization, *Understanding the WTO* (5th edn, Geneva: World Trade Organization, 2010) www.wto.org/english/thewto_e/whatis_e/tif_e/understanding_e.pdf
Zolo, T. M. and Cope, C., *The OECD's Proposed Article 7: A Work in Progress with an Uncertain Future* (KPMG, Washington National Office, 12 October 2009)

INDEX

ability to pay principle, 25, 26, 30, 115
Adams, T. *see* tax treaties, multilateral
anti-avoidance measures, 40–2, 144, 359
  general, 40–2
  multilateral agreement, 140–1
  specific, 40–2, 65, 72, 97–8
arm's length principle
  advantages, 73–5
  disadvantages, 75–6
  economic reality, 79–80
  rate of interest, 248–52
associated enterprises
  level of world trade, 71–2
  OECD Model
    Article 9(1), 70
attribution of profits, 240–3
authorized OECD approach, 179–80, 207–8
  first step, 222, 287–96
  functional analysis, 289–91
    assets, 291–4
    risks, 294–6
  key entrepreneurial risk-taking functions, 290, 299–300
  royalty, 328
  second step, 222
  significant people functions, 288, 291, 295–6, 299–300, 329, 363

Basel Accord. *see* international banking
benefit principle, 25–6
best method rule, 343–6
bilateral tax treaties. *see* tax treaties, bilateral
branches. *see* permanent establishments

Brennan, W. J., 14
business profits Article. *see* OECD model, Article 7
business restructuring, 219, 433

capital export neutrality, 19–22
capital import neutrality, 22–3
Carroll Report, 134–6
Committee of Experts. *see* League of Nations: 1923 Report
Committee of Fiscal Experts. *see* League of Nations: 1927 Report
Committee of Technical Experts. *see* League of Nations: 1925 Report
common consolidated corporate tax base, 412–13, 414–16
  adoption, 418–19
comparable uncontrolled price method, 91, 344
comparative uncontrolled price method, 332–3
contract manufacturing, 335–7
controlled foreign company, 36–7, 40, 360
corporate groups, 51, 403, 407, 411, 423
cost contribution arrangements, 330–2
cost plus method, 334–7
  contract manufacturing, 335–7
  toll manufacturing, 335–7

dividend withholding tax, 18, 312
domestic tax law, 43
double tax treaty. *see* tax treaties, bilateral
double taxation, 44–7

454

economic, 44–7
history, 108–10
inter-nation equity, 17–18
international juridical, 107–8
juridical, 44–7
national neutrality, 19
neutrality
 capital export, 19–22
 capital import, 22–3
relief, 43, 46, 50, 95, 108, 134, 208, 235, 353, 367, 371, 377, 380, 383, 385–6, 418
 classification, 113
 division method, 113
 exemption, 43, 46, 113
 foreign tax credits, 43, 46, 113
residence jurisdiction.
 see jurisdiction to tax
residence taxation. *see* jurisdiction to tax
source jurisdiction. *see* jurisdiction to tax
source taxation. *see* jurisdiction to tax
dualist doctrine, 47–9

economic allegiance, 26, 111–16
economic double taxation, 44–7
Enron, 42, 293
equity capital, 265–74, 296–312
European Commission
 accounting standards, 416–17
 proposals, 410–19
  common consolidated corporate tax base, 412–13, 414–16, 419
  home state taxation, 414–16
exchange of information measures, 59–60
experts (League of Nations). *see* League of Nations: 1923 Report

firm, theory of, 80–4
Fiscal Committee (League of Nations). *see* League of Nations: Fiscal Committee
Fiscal Experts. *see* League of Nations: 1927 Report

force of attraction principle, 198, 208, 286, 358–60
foreign tax credits system, 43, 46, 113
foreign tax exemption. *see* double taxation: exemption
foreign tax relief. *see* double taxation: relief
formulary apportionment, 3, 93–4, 403–28
 European Commission proposals, 410–19
 issues, 419–28
  accounting and compliance, 422–4
  formula, 420–2
  intangible assets income, 426–8
  tax avoidance, 426
  unitary taxation, 420
 US and Canada, 406–10
functional analysis, 289–91
 assets, 291–4
 risks, 294–6
functional separate entity approach, 202–4

General Agreement on Tariffs and Trade, 53
General Meeting of Government Experts, 142
General Meeting of Government Experts on Double Taxation and Tax Evasion (1928), 123–7
globalization, 52–62
 business, markets and regulation, 54–6
 effect on international tax policy, 56–62
 emergence, 52–4

Holmes, O. W., 15
home state taxation, 412, 414–16

interest withholding tax, 43, 141, 312
inter-nation equity, 17–18
international banking
 equity capital, 265–74, 296–312
  allotted, branches with, 266–70
  allotted, branches without, 270–4

international banking (cont.)
  Basel Accord, 302–3
  OECD approach, 303–9
  simplified method, 309–12
international tax avoidance. *see* tax avoidance
international tax system, 12, 13, 57
international taxation
  avoidance. *see* tax avoidance
  domestic tax law, 43
  effectiveness, 62–4
  inter-nation equity, 17–18
  juridical double taxation, 107–8
  neutrality, 18–23
    capital export, 19–22
    capital import, 22–3
  outline, 42–3
  policy, 14–15
  raising revenue and protecting the tax base, 15
  trade and investment policy, 15–17
interpretation of tax treaties. *see* tax treaties: treaty interpretation
intra-bank loans
  deductions, 243–5
  tracing, 258–62
intra-entity dealings, 225–8
  goods, 225–6
  intangible property, 225–6
  services, 226–8
intra-entity loans, 228–31

juridical double taxation, 44–7
jurisdiction to tax, 12–13, 23–38
  residence jurisdiction, 27–9
  residence taxation, 34–8
  source jurisdiction, 29–34
  source taxation, 34–8

key entrepreneurial risk-taking functions, 290, 299–300

Langbein, S. I., 94, 125
League of Nations, 111–43
  1923 Report, 112–17
    context, 114–17
  1925 Report, 117–20
  1927 Report, 120–3
  1928 Report, 123–7
  Carroll Report, 134–6
  Fiscal Committee
    1st meeting (1929), 128–30
    2nd meeting (1930), 130–2
    3rd meeting (1931), 132–3
    4th meeting (1933), 136–7
    5th meeting (1935), 137–8
    6th meeting (1936), 138–40
    7th meeting (1937), 140–1
    8th meeting (1938), 141–2
    9th meeting (1939), 142
    10th meeting (1945), 142–3
  London Model Treaty, 142–9

Mexico Model Treaty, 142–9
model conventions
  London, 142–9
  Mexico, 142–9
  OECD, 1–6, 50–2
  UN, 50–2
monist doctrine, 47–9
multilateral tax treaties, 127–8
mutual agreement procedure, 47, 377–86

national neutrality, 19
National Westminster Bank case, 253–8
neutrality principle, 18–23
non-discrimination, 17–18, 270, 370–3

OECD draft double tax convention, 156–7
OECD model, 1–6, 50–2
  Article 7 (2010), 357–91
    7(2), 360–75
    7(3), 375–83
    7(3) alternate, 383–6
    7(4), 386–8
    Commentary, 193–4
    Provisions deleted from, 388–91
  Article 7 (former)
    2008 Commentary, 191–3
    7(1), 196–8
    7(1) 2008 Commentary, 207–8
    7(1) 2008 Report, 205–7

INDEX

7(2) 2008 Commentary, 221–2, 233–6
7(2) separate entity approach, 208–15
7(3) single entity approach, 222–5
functional separate entity approach, 202–4
inconsistent interpretations, 186–9
intra-entity dealings, 225–8
intra-entity loans, 228–31
meaning of, 184–6
pre-2008 Commentary, 219–21, 231–3
relevant business activity approach, 198–202
reliance on an international enterprise's accounts, 218–19
separate and single entity approach, 194–6
symmetrical accounts, 215–18
attribution of profits to permanent establishments
2008 Report, 190–1
discussion drafts, 189–90
Commentary, 162–8
influence on Australia, 175–7
influence on Canada, 170–5
influence on USA, 168–70
history, 154
influence of, 159–60
role, 153–4
since 1977, 159
Working Party No. 1, 5, 354, 356
Working Party No. 6, 5, 354, 356
OEEC Fiscal Committee, 154–6

permanent establishment
authorized OECD approach, 287–96
concept, emergence of, 110–11
definition of, 182–4
functional separate enterprise, 285–7
OECD approach, 312–14
OECD transfer pricing
cost contribution arrangements, 330–2
OECD transfer pricing methods, 318–32

comparability analysis, 324
intangible assets, 326–32
intra-entity transactions, 321–4
tangible assets, 324–6
primary adjustment, 385
protecting the tax base, 15

quasi-thin capitalization, 300

reciprocity, 17–18
relevant business activity approach, 198–202
resale price method, 333–4
residence jurisdiction, 27–9
residence taxation, 34–8
restructuring. *see* business restructuring
Roosevelt, F. D., 15

Schanz, G. V., 112–15
secondary adjustment, 381
Seligman, E. R., 109–11
separate currency pool method, 262–5
separate entity approach, 208–15, 245–8
significant people functions, 288, 291, 295–6, 299–300, 329, 363
single entity approach, 222–5, 252–3
source jurisdiction, 29–34
source taxation, 34–8
symmetrical accounts, 215–18

tax avoidance, 38–42, 65–70, 137, 151, 219
anti-avoidance measures, 40–2
international banks, 69
revenue consequences, 69–70
tax competition, 35, 38, 67, 69, 70, 409
tax evasion, 38–42, 66–70
international banks, 69
revenue consequences, 69–70
tax neutrality, 18–23
tax planning, 38–42
tax policy
economic basis, 25–6
ability to pay principle, 26
benefit principle, 25–6
economic allegiance, 26

tax policy (cont.)
  jurisdiction to tax, 12–13, 23–38
    residence jurisdiction, 27–9
    residence taxation, 34–8
    source jurisdiction, 29–34
    source taxation, 34–8
tax treaties, 44
  auditing, 102–4
  benefits, 49–50
  bilateral, 1
    emergence, 111
    problems, 94–5
  exchange of information measures, 59–60
  history, 149–50
  implementation
    dualist doctrine, 47–9
    monist doctrine, 47–9
  international reform, 104–5
  London Model, 142–9
  Mexico Model, 142–9
  multilateral, 127–8
    draft, 134
  mutual agreement procedure, 47, 377–86
  network, 101–2
  non-discrimination, 17–18, 270, 370–3
  OECD model. see OECD model
  outline, 1–6
  reciprocity, 17–18
  relationship with domestic laws, 47–9
  system, 64, 105
  treaty interpretation, 101
  treaty network, 98–101
  treaty override, 98–101
  treaty shopping, 39, 95–8
  UN Model, 50–2
taxpayer compliance issues, 87–9
Technical Experts. see League of Nations: 1925 Report
territorial (source) taxation. see jurisdiction to tax
theory of firm, 80–4
thin capitalization, 271–2, 300
  quasi, 300
toll manufacturing, 335–7

transactional net margin method, 9, 89, 317, 337, 340–3
transactional profit method, 337–8
transactional profit split method, 338–40
transfer pricing, 70–3, 332–49
  administrative burden, 77
  authorized OECD approach
    functional analysis, 289–91
    functional analysis assets, 291–4
  authorized OECD approach
    functional analysis of risks, 296
  best method rule, 343–6
  comparative uncontrolled price method, 332–3
  cost contribution arrangements, 330–2
  erosion of traditional methods, 346–9
  formulary apportionment. see formulary apportionment
  guidelines, 284–5
  history, 281–2
  intangible assets, 77–8
  manipulation, 65–75
  mutual agreement procedure, 47, 377–86
  OECD approach, 278–80
  OECD methods
    evolution, 89–93
  OECD Report 1979, 284
  permanent establishments, 280–1
  primary adjustment, 385
  problems, 84–7
    1981 Report, 84–6
    1992 Report, 86–7
  secondary adjustment, 381
  taxpayer compliance issues, 87–9
  uncertainty, 79
Transfer Pricing Guidelines, 284–5
transfer pricing manipulation, 65–75
Transfer pricing methods
  arm's length principle
    advantages, 73–5

disadvantages, 75–6
economic reality, 79–80
rate of interest, 248–52
comparable uncontrolled price, 91, 344
cost plus, 334–7
contract manufacturing, 335–7
toll manufacturing, 335–7
resale price, 333–4
transactional net margin, 340–3
transactional profit, 337–8
transactional profit split, 338–40
treaty override, 98–101
treaty shopping, 39, 95–8

UN Model, 50–2
unitary taxation
formulary apportionment, 3, 93–4, 403–28
multilateral treaty, 397–403
reform, 394–7

Vann, R. J., 232–3, 373
Vienna Convention, 160–2

Working Party No. 1, 4
Working Party No. 6, 4, 356
worldwide (residence) taxation. *see* jurisdiction to tax

For EU product safety concerns, contact us at Calle de José Abascal, 56–1°,
28003 Madrid, Spain or eugpsr@cambridge.org.

www.ingramcontent.com/pod-product-compliance
Ingram Content Group UK Ltd.
Pitfield, Milton Keynes, MK11 3LW, UK
UKHW020349060825
461487UK00008B/590